Clinical Neuropsychology and the Psychological Care of Persons with Brain Disorders

CLINICAL NEUROPSYCHOLOGY AND THE PSYCHOLOGICAL CARE OF PERSONS WITH BRAIN DISORDERS

George P. Prigatano, PhD

EMERITUS CHAIRMAN OF CLINICAL NEUROPSYCHOLOGY
AND NEWSOME CHAIR OF NEUROPSYCHOLOGY

BARROW NEUROLOGICAL INSTITUTE

ST. JOSEPH'S HOSPITAL AND MEDICAL CENTER

PHOENIX, ARIZONA

OXFORD
UNIVERSITY PRESS

OXFORD
UNIVERSITY PRESS

Oxford University Press is a department of the University of Oxford. It furthers the University's objective of excellence in research, scholarship, and education by publishing worldwide. Oxford is a registered trade mark of Oxford University Press in the UK and certain other countries.

Published in the United States of America by Oxford University Press
198 Madison Avenue, New York, NY 10016, United States of America.

© Oxford University Press 2020

All rights reserved. No part of this publication may be reproduced, stored in a retrieval system, or transmitted, in any form or by any means, without the prior permission in writing of Oxford University Press, or as expressly permitted by law, by license, or under terms agreed with the appropriate reproduction rights organization. Inquiries concerning reproduction outside the scope of the above should be sent to the Rights Department, Oxford University Press, at the address above.

You must not circulate this work in any other form
and you must impose this same condition on any acquirer.

Library of Congress Cataloging-in-Publication Data
Names: Prigatano, George P., author.
Title: Clinical neuropsychology and the psychological care of persons with brain disorders / George P. Prigatano, Ph.D., Emeritus Chairman of Clinical Neuropsychology and Newsome Chair of Neuropsychology, Barrow Neurological Institute, St. Joseph's Hospital and Medical Center, Phoenix, Arizona.
Description: New York, NY : Oxford University Press, [2020] | Includes bibliographical references.
Identifiers: LCCN 2019012606 | ISBN 9780190645939 (hardback) | ISBN 9780190645946 (updf) | ISBN 9780190645953 (epub)
Subjects: LCSH: Brain damage—Diagnosis. | Clinical neuropsychology.
Classification: LCC RC387.5 .P748 2019 | DDC 616.8—dc23
LC record available at https://lccn.loc.gov/2019012606

1 3 5 7 9 8 6 4 2

Printed by Sheridan Books, Inc., United States of America

This book is dedicated to the memory of Lou and Evelyn Grubb, who made this book become a reality given their philanthropic support.

CONTENTS

Preface ix

1. Introduction 1

PART I: BRIEF DESCRIPTION OF NORMAL NEUROPSYCHOLOGICAL FUNCTIONING OVER THE LIFE SPAN

2. Human Nature in Light of the Natural Plan of the Central Nervous System 19

3. The Evolution of Normal Brain–Behavior Relationships 31

4. Neuropsychological and Psychosocial Competencies Throughout the Human Life Span 48

5. Conscious and Unconscious Manifestations of Higher Integrative Brain Functions 70

PART II: BRIEF DESCRIPTION OF ABNORMAL NEUROPSYCHOLOGICAL FUNCTIONING OVER THE LIFE SPAN

6. The Problem of Not Developing Normally After a Brain Disorder During Childhood and Adolescence 95

7. The Problem of Lost Normality After a Brain Disorder During Adulthood 117

8. The Problem of Unexpected and Accelerated Loss of Competency After a Brain Disorder During Aging 135

9. Disturbances of Self-Awareness Related to Brain Dysfunction Versus Psychological Distress: A Phenomenological Approach   148

PART III: ASSESSMENT, EDUCATION, AND TREATMENTS: CORE ACTIVITIES IN THE PSYCHOLOGICAL CARE OF PERSONS WITH A BRAIN DISORDER

10. A Medically Necessary and Personally Relevant Neuropsychological Consultation and Examination   171

11. Neuropsychological Consultation Before and After Neurosurgery   191

12. The Multifaceted Nature of Psychological Treatments   207

PART IV: CLINICAL APPLICATIONS

13. Psychological Care of Persons with Cerebral Anoxia Secondary to Cardiac Arrest   231

14. Psychological Care of Persons with Parkinson's Disease   254

15. Psychological Care of Persons with Multiple Sclerosis   282

16. Psychological Care of Persons with a Primary Malignant Brain Tumor   302

17. Psychological Care of Persons with a History of Aneurysmal Subarachnoid Hemorrhage   323

18. Psychological Care of Persons with Aphasia Secondary to a Cerebral Vascular Accident or Traumatic Brain Injury   342

19. Psychological Care of Persons with Hemiplegia/Hemiparesis Secondary to a Cerebral Vascular Accident or Traumatic Brain Injury   366

20. Psychological Care of Persons with Progressive Cognitive Decline and Early Stage Dementia   384

21. Psychological Care of Persons with Cognitive and Behavioral Disorders Secondary to Traumatic Brain Injury   413

22. Psychological Care of Children with Known or Suspected Acquired Brain Disorders   436

23. Psychological Care of Persons with Both Epileptic and Nonepileptic (Psychogenic) Seizures   451

24. Psychological Care of Persons with Psychiatric-Based Cognitive Complaints   467

PART V: POSTSCRIPT

25. Synthesis and Postscript   487

Author Index   495
subject index   515

PREFACE

EVERY BOOK has a story behind it. The story behind this book consciously originates from experiences during my predoctoral clinical psychology internship at the University of Oklahoma Health Sciences Center (1971–1972). At that time, I discovered a new field of study called neuropsychology. Oscar Parsons, PhD, was the Vice Chair of the Department of Psychiatry and Behavioral Sciences and became my first mentor in the field. The idea that psychological tests could reveal important information regarding the state of brain function fascinated me. Could such information be used in patient diagnosis and perhaps treatment and rehabilitation? Initially trained as a clinical psychologist, I wanted to integrate neuropsychology with clinical psychology.

During my internship year, I had supervision from exceptional psychotherapists, some of whom were psychoanalysts. They included Marshall D. Schechter, MD; Paul Toussieng, MD; C. V. Ramana (lay analyst); and Robert Wienecke, MD. I was interested in combining all three fields of study into my practice (i.e., clinical psychology, neuropsychology, and psychotherapy). I also wanted to integrate them into my teaching and research efforts. Many of my earlier teachers encouraged me to choose one field of study but not try to combine these three disciplines. I elected not to take their advice and was encouraged by the insights of C. G. Jung that emphasized the need of the person to be true to one's own inclinations and not be easily swayed by others' opinions.

I furthermore had the good fortune to come in contact with Dr. Barton Carl, neurosurgeon. Dr. Carl allowed me to examine his patients before the final neurological diagnosis was made (this was at the same time that computed tomography scans of the brain became a reality).

I attended neurosurgery, examined patients before and after surgery, and sometimes was with patients as they came out of anesthesia after surgery. These were extraordinary experiences and greatly influenced my enduring respect for neurosurgeons and my personal belief that talking to patients about what they subjectively or personally experience after the onset of a brain disorder is a valuable source of information for the practice and science of clinical neuropsychology.

After leaving the Department of Psychiatry and Behavioral Sciences at the University of Oklahoma Health Sciences Center, I also had the good fortune to study with Karl Pribram, MD, at Stanford University. He challenged my thinking capacity as no one else ever has. Although he influenced my thinking in many ways, one of his comments remains exceptionally clear to me to this day. He would often comment that in science we often just collect facts, but true knowledge comes when we resolve paradoxes via the scientific method or other systematic means of observation.

In 1985, I was recruited to the Barrow Neurological Institute (BNI) at St. Joseph's Hospital and Medical Center in Phoenix, Arizona, by the first Chairman of Neurology, Dr. Joseph White. I was asked to develop a rehabilitation day treatment program similar to the one I developed in Oklahoma City with the support and help of Dr. Barton Carl and Mr. Harry Neer, President of Presbyterian Hospital at that time (between 1979 and 1985). I accepted the invitation, and it proved to be a very important decision. In addition to starting that rehabilitation program, I requested that a Department of Clinical Neuropsychology also be established. It was established, and I was fortunate to serve as Chair of that department for nearly 30 years.

My experiences at the BNI have always been invigorating. Many different types of patients with a wide range of neurological and neurosurgical disorders were evaluated and treated medically and surgically. All of these patients had excellent neuroimaging studies of their brains. This not only aided in their care but also provided extremely important information for the clinical neuropsychologists attempting to correlate abnormal neuropsychological functioning with brain imaging data. A significant number of these patients also underwent neuropsychological examinations, and some later received rehabilitation services that were, in part, guided by concepts derived from neuropsychology, clinical psychology, and psychiatry. A smaller number of patients were also treated from a psychotherapeutic viewpoint, often after formal rehabilitation activities ended.

The physicians and psychologists in that setting were dedicated to expanding our knowledge to aid in the care of these patients. The development of a holistic, neuropsychological day treatment program provided many rich and intensive experiences to observe how various forms of brain dysfunction influenced a person's thinking, feelings, and behavior in both structured and unstructured situations. It also provided experiences that allowed for a better understanding of what families go through when living with a person who has significant cognitive and behavioral deficits. Although such programs are extremely valuable, not all patients can afford to undergo such care. This should be an embarrassment to our health care system, but unfortunately, it is not.

These realities led me to write the book, *Principles of Neuropsychological Rehabilitation*. I hoped it would help clinicians work with patients and their families even if they were not involved in a holistic, neuropsychological-oriented day treatment program. I also wanted to extend that work to children. Through the support of Mr. and Mrs. Louis Grubb, an extraordinarily generous gift was made. They provided philanthropic funds to develop a Children's Neuropsychological Rehabilitation Program. When that program did not develop for economic and political reasons, the remaining Grubb donation was used to provide funding to prepare this book. The efforts of their son, Mr. Dan Grubb, and of Ms. Jacky Alling, Chief Philanthropic Services Officer of the Arizona Community Foundation, made this a reality for which I am very grateful. I have worked on this project during the past 3 years, and it truly has been a "labor of love."

The book is intended as a resource mainly for clinical neuropsychologists and clinical psychologists. However, I hope it is also useful for psychiatrists, physiatrists, neurologists, nurses, and social workers. It attempts to review salient neuropsychological facts associated with different brain disorders that have relevance to psychological care. It also attempts to integrate those observations with a basic understanding of human nature and the psychological approaches found in the literature relevant to helping patients positively cope with the immediate and long-term effects of a brain disorder throughout the life span.

My collaborative work with many individuals throughout the years has helped develop and form the ideas presented in this text. I have already mentioned the profound influence Karl Pribram has had on my thinking. However, in retrospect, two other experiences in my professional life deserve special mention.

While serving as a predoctoral intern at the University of Oklahoma Health Sciences Center, I was asked to present a case to Bruno Bettelheim, PhD, who was a Visiting Professor for one our seminars. When I apologized for presenting Rorschach data because of the test's known problems with reliability and validity, Bettelheim appropriately chastised me for not recognizing that the patient's responses to the Rorschach cards were valid in the sense that they revealed what the patient was experiencing. I later thought of this as a form of phenomenological validity. The second experience came from hearing a lecture by Ralph Reitan, PhD, at an American Psychological Association convention in Montreal, Canada, in 1973. He reminded those of us in the audience that as clinical neuropsychologists, we often did not have a good clinical sense of what constituted normal neuropsychological functioning. Relying on normative data was helpful, but it did not adequately solve the problem. Years of clinical experience are necessary because there is a great deal of variability in the level of neuropsychological skills in different domains of functioning and for different individuals with different educational backgrounds and in different age ranges. This reality has repeatedly proven true to me over many years of practice.

As the reader will also find, I am equally indebted to the insightful writings and observations of many "giants" in the fields of clinical psychology, neuropsychology, psychology, psychiatry, psychotherapy, psychoanalysis, neurology, and biology. They include (but are not limited to) John Hughlings Jackson, Charles Darwin, Roger Sperry, Sigmund Freud, C. G. Jung, Alfred Adler, Shephard Ivory Franz, Kurt Goldstein, Karl S. Lashley, D. O. Hebb, Eric Erikson, A. R. Luria, Carl Rogers, B. F. Skinner, and Ward Halstead. I especially acknowledge Leonard Diller and Yehuda Ben-Yishay for allowing me to learn from them as I began to work in the field of neuropsychological rehabilitation. Dr. Diller's advice to spend more time in professional writing as I became the Emeritus Chairman of Clinical Neuropsychology at the BNI was especially helpful to me during a time of professional transition in my work-related activities. Dr. Diller's and Dr. Ben-Yishay's friendship and guidance throughout the years have meant a lot to me.

It is also important to recognize the work of Angela Abbott in helping me technically prepare the manuscript and Nicole Galvin and Molly Harrington for accessing hundreds of articles that were reviewed in preparing this book. Philip R. Beard was also especially helpful in copyediting several of the chapters of this book. His efforts helped me prepare the manuscript in a timely manner. I also acknowledge Ronald Ruff, PhD, Joseph R. Ricker, PhD, Rudi Coetzer, PhD, Christian E. Salas, PhD, and Ritva Laaksonen, PhD, for reviewing earlier versions of the manuscript and providing very helpful suggestions for improving it. Finally, I recognize Dr. Robert F. Spetzler for appointing me as the Newsome Chair and Ms. Judith Beresford of the Dignity Health International & Barrow

Foundation UK for the economic support associated with the Newsome Chair. Part of those funds also allowed me additional time to prepare this book and make additional changes that I hope have improved the clarity of the ideas presented.

My hope is that this book will demonstrate that it is clinically useful to combine knowledge from many sources when attempting to provide psychological care for persons with various brain disorders. These individuals deserve an approach that combines and understands their basic human nature, their personal history (which includes their psychodynamic struggles and stage of psychosocial development), and the effects of a brain disorder on their complex neuropsychological functioning. This integrated approach provides a depth of understanding and a broader perspective that ultimately can improve their psychological care by reducing their psychological suffering and allowing them to engage life as lively as they can.

George P. Prigatano, PhD
October 15, 2018

1

INTRODUCTION

A MIDDLE-AGED man suffered a ruptured aneurysm stemming from the right posterior communicating artery. At the request of his neurosurgeon, he was seen for a neuropsychological consultation approximately 1 month after the ruptured aneurysm was successfully clipped. The patient was quiet and somewhat subdued, but he cautiously revealed two things that were disturbing him. He was convinced that there were two Barrow Neurological Institutes, one in Phoenix and one in Scottsdale, Arizona. Even though he had lived in the greater Phoenix area for many years and recognized the seemingly illogical nature of his conviction, nevertheless that is what he experienced, and he was secretly concerned about his mental status. He was afraid to tell his wife and his neurosurgeon about this experience for fear of what they would think of him. He revealed this information only after he felt comfortable talking with a clinical neuropsychologist who was interested in his experiences after surgery and took time to listen to him. When the clinical neuropsychologist explained to this patient that reduplicative paramnesia is a well-known phenomenon (Young, 1996) that is observed in some individuals with focal lesions typically involving the right side of the brain (Hakim, Verma, & Greiffenstein, 1988), he was immediately relieved. The patient then felt secure enough to reveal his second, secret concern.

He was having a very disturbing and reoccurring dream about hell and the devil. When asked to describe the dream, he noted many features that were reminiscent of a painting replicated in C. G. Jung's (1964) book, *Man and His Symbols*. The picture was shown to the patient, and he was asked if it was similar to what he had been experiencing in his dreams. His mouth fell open. The image was very similar to what he had seen in his dream, and he "no longer felt crazy." He was very grateful to have someone to talk with him privately about these experiences, which were both frightening and confusing to him. He no longer was alone with what scared him, and he went on to make a good neuropsychological recovery.

No psychometric tests were administered to him during this time of heightened vulnerability. He felt emotionally supported by the clinical neuropsychologist, who was knowledgeable about syndromes of brain–behavior disturbances as well as recurring psychodynamic concerns of people. He remained very grateful for the neuropsychological consultation for many years, and later in life he returned for two other consultations when faced with recurring health problems.

This brief scenario provides an introduction to the topic of psychological care of a person with a brain disorder within the context of the practice of clinical neuropsychology. It highlights some of its essential features. The consulting clinical neuropsychologist must have a scientific understanding of known brain–behavior relationships and how those relationships can be disturbed after specific brain lesions. Second, the consulting clinical neuropsychologist must have the interest and sufficient time to listen to patients' subjective experiences to be maximally helpful to them. Third, the consulting clinical neuropsychologist must be conversant with many sources of knowledge about human beings in order to help patients understand the probable basis of their subjective experiences. At a minimum, this knowledge includes an informed understanding of human nature, an appreciation of psychodynamic insights about people's motivations and internal conflicts, and an appreciation of the predictable psychological concerns of people at different times in life. It also includes an appreciation of how cultural, religious, and environmental factors influence what patients may be experiencing and how they tend to understand their behavior and feeling states. Fourth, it requires the treating clinician, whether a clinical neuropsychologist or not, to provide psychotherapeutic or behavioral interventions that help reduce the psychological distress or suffering of the individual. If successful, these interventions build a therapeutic bond between the patient and the treating clinician that often leads the patient to return for continued help when psychological adjustment issues occur later in the individual's life.

It is natural for most clinical neuropsychologists to want to examine and "test" their patients. This provides objective assessment of a patient's neuropsychological status that can be very helpful in his or her medical care. However, if patients are simply tested and not talked to in a manner that encourages them to describe their subjective experiences, the full benefit of a clinical neuropsychological consultation is often not realized. The primary goal of this text is to demonstrate to clinical neuropsychologists that they have much more to offer patients than psychometric assessment and interpretation of their neuropsychological status. They can actively participate in the psychological care of these patients if they expand their scope of practice.

In this text, summaries of different sources of information about human beings relevant to the psychological care of brain dysfunctional individuals are presented. The information is offered in a manner that can help treating clinicians understand their patients' subjective experiences and behavior irrespective of clinicians' professional background and professional identity (e.g., clinical neuropsychologists, clinical psychologists, psychiatrists, psychiatric nurse practitioners, social workers, and vocational rehabilitation counselors). However, the specific neuropsychological and psychiatric features of various brain disorders are summarized in a manner that is most familiar to clinical neuropsychologists. Examples of common behavioral or psychotherapeutic approaches to address these problems are also included.

When the psychological care of specific patients with different brain disorders is discussed, case examples and case vignettes help illustrate how integrating different levels of information can guide psychological care. Clinical features of the dialogue between the patient and the treating clinical neuropsychologist are also summarized to help readers draw their own conclusions as to what features are most important in a patient's psychological treatment.

It is argued that collection of "group data" based on scientific observations is a necessary first step in the psychological care of patients with different brain disorders. It is often, however, not the last step in their care. Those scientifically based observations are helpful only if the treating clinician can utilize them to facilitate a positive adjustment process that is helpful to individual patients given their pre-injury characteristics and their neuropsychological and psychiatric status after the onset of the brain disorder.

FOUNDATIONS OF PSYCHOLOGICAL CARE

The psychological care of children and adults who suffer a brain disorder must be based, first of all, on an informed understanding of human nature. Human nature, however, is not always easy to define. It requires studying the development of the brain over time and the neuropsychological capabilities of humans as their brains change due to natural developmental alterations over the life span. Knowledge of what "makes us human" also derives from many other sources, including the study of history and the humanities (e.g., the study of art, music, and literature).

The psychological care of persons with a brain disorder also requires the practitioner to have an understanding of how brain disorders, at different time periods in the life cycle, produce similar and yet different neuropsychological disturbances with inevitable psychosocial adjustment difficulties. This knowledge is necessary to understand what problems a given patient is experiencing and what personal struggles the patient must address in order to avoid further adjustment issues.

The third source of knowledge needed to provide psychological care is an understanding of what actions can be taken to reduce human suffering and substantially help persons meaningfully cope with their life problems in light of their human nature and their neuropsychological strengths and limitations. This must be done with an appreciation of each person's psychosocial stage or state of development and the cultural milieu in which the individual functions. Knowledge emanating from diverse studies on psychotherapy can be very useful in this regard. Yet this knowledge also needs to be supplemented with knowledge of what actions or activities are known to more broadly foster physical and psychological well-being beyond formal psychotherapeutic efforts.

The task of providing psychological care for children and adults can be challenging, with inevitable disappointments. However, it can also be extremely rewarding for the clinical neuropsychological practitioner. Humans are constantly experiencing a mixture of satisfying and dissatisfying experiences. Although they can have moments of psychological well-being, those moments can quickly shift to moments of distress and unhappiness. As Charlie Chaplin (1992) wrote in his autobiography, "I did not have to read books to know that the theme of life is conflict and pain" (p. 210). This is true with or without a brain disorder. Psychological caregivers for persons with a brain disorder must accept the fact that the care they provide will at times appear inadequate and at other times appear extremely effective in helping the person.

Learning how to talk to and interact with a person with a brain disorder that seamlessly combines an integrated knowledge of neuropsychology, psychotherapy, and human nature is a crucial skill for an effective psychological care provider. It is a skill that constantly needs to be developed and "refreshed." It requires having good teachers and mentors, an opportunity to work with a wide variety of patients, and a constant thirst for improving one's understanding of each of the dimensions of knowledge outlined previously.

A DEFINITION OF PSYCHOLOGICAL CARE

A more complete and detailed description of the various activities that can be justifiably referred to as psychological care will be expanded upon throughout this text, but a beginning or "working definition" of this term is now considered. The term *psychological* is, of course, an adjective that refers to the mental and emotional state of a person. The term *care* refers to providing activities/experiences that are necessary to foster health and well-being. Thus, when using the term *psychological care*, one is referring to a potentially large number of activities or experiences that help maintain and protect the psychological health and well-being of another person.

Although various forms of psychotherapy (including cognitive–behavioral therapy) often have as their goal the specific improvements in personal adjustment to some underlying psychiatric, interpersonal, and/or behavioral disturbance, the term psychological care is used to go beyond specific adjustment issues (e.g., getting a person back to work after a brain disorder) and the relief of "symptoms" (e.g., reducing angry outbursts or suicidal ideation). Psychological care, as discussed later, borrows heavily from the knowledge bases seen in various forms of psychotherapy and health management activities that foster "resilience" in the patient's capacity to repetitively deal with life's problems. This often requires helping the patient obtain a "broader view" of human nature and a consideration of the various activities that not only foster a positive psychological adjustment to life's problems but also help the person experience that "the nature of life is struggle." Helping patients engage in activities that maintain a sense of "philosophical patience" when dealing with their personal struggles becomes important for helping them with their immediate and long-term psychological needs (Prigatano, 1999b). This requires helping patients to have a better understanding of themselves and what they must do to effectively deal with the inevitable problems of life that they may be experiencing now and may experience in the future.

Because individuals with a brain disorder often have reduced problem-solving capacities with associated memory impairments, the need to guide them becomes important. Yet this has to be done within the confines of ethical principles and a good understanding of their neuropsychological (and at times psychodynamic) status. Equally important is having a patient's family members or significant others understand the complexity of the patient's situation. The psychological care interventions may be brief (e.g., a 5-minute phone call) or extend into weekly, hour-long, long-term psychotherapy sessions. In some cases, prolonged day treatment/rehabilitation programs are necessary to foster long-term psychological well-being.

This may seem naive to some, and it may be economically impossible for others. Our present health care systems demand shorter (less expensive) psychological interventions for patients and their families. Moreover, "evidence-based" therapies will be the only ones funded, and the (erroneous) assumption is that there is only one major source of evidence—randomized clinical control studies (Benson & Hartz, 2000; Concato, Shah, & Horwitz, 2000; Erikson, 1964; Prigatano, 1999a, 2003). Although these pressures can be substantial, psychological care providers have to remember why they are doing the work they are doing. It is to reduce human suffering and improve the patient's psychological status in order to avoid psychiatric complications (which can be a medical necessity). The patient's needs come first and the needs of economic institutions second.

In light of the previous introductory observations, a relatively brief historical perspective is presented to help clarify how clinical neuropsychology has developed in the United States and why there has been an apparent lack of sustained interest in addressing the psychological care issues of patients with brain disorders by clinical neuropsychologists.

CLINICAL NEUROPSYCHOLOGY AND ITS EARLY BEGINNINGS

Neuropsychology is typically defined as the scientific study of brain–behavior relationships. It attempts to systematically relate disturbances in cognitive, affective, and behavioral functioning to underlying brain dysfunction of various types. At its core, it attempts to address the demanding question: How does the brain (in conjunction with other organ systems of the body) produce "mind"? The practice of clinical neuropsychology in the United States has greatly expanded from its early beginnings in the mid-1950s and early 1960s. The request for neuropsychological services has dramatically grown as physicians have recognized the potential clinical and research value of having objective and quantifiable measures of disturbances in higher integrative brain (i.e., neuropsychological) functions (HIBFs). Physicians routinely pose a number of important questions that they ask neuropsychologists to help answer. For example, is there objective evidence that the patient has a memory disorder? If so, what are the likely causes? Does a patient with a known traumatic brain injury (TBI) demonstrate neurocognitive and behavioral disturbances compatible with his or her medical history? If yes, what sort of rehabilitation is needed? Is a patient with multiple sclerosis demonstrating a decline in cognitive function that would warrant medical disability? Does a patient with sleep disturbance and hallucinations present with neuropsychological findings suggestive of Lewy body dementia? Is there evidence of a decline in cognitive functioning in a person suspected of dementia? Does the level of decline warrant residential care and possible power of attorney? Is there evidence of cognitive impairment in a patient with long-standing communicating hydrocephalus? The answer to this last question may help a neurosurgeon decide whether a shunt revision is necessary. Many other questions are asked that have relevance to the medical and possible surgical care of patients.

The growing clinical demand has resulted in a very "test-oriented" and psychometric approach to professional activities. The psychometric tradition, upon which much of American clinical neuropsychology has depended, is strongly rooted in the history of psychology and its clinical applications. Early interest in classifying levels of cognitive impairment in children with subnormal intelligence was found helpful, especially when considering school placement issues (Anastasi, 1976). Psychometric tests, particularly tests of intelligence, were helpful in demonstrating that children classified as having a learning disability may well have normal intellectual abilities (Waber, 2010). Their specific inability to learn to read or spell, for example, was not necessarily an indication of subnormal cognitive abilities.

Psychometrically oriented approaches were also applied to personality assessments that were considered "objective" (e.g., the Minnesota Multiphasic Personality Inventory) and were used in conjunction with, or independent of, projective measures of personality that were found useful in some psychiatric settings (Rapaport, Schafer, Gill, & Holt, 1974). The psychometric tradition also spilled over into such areas as the selection of military personnel who could successfully cope with the stresses of war, including intensive interrogation and torture if captured (US Office of Strategic Services, 1948). As clinical psychologists were asked to assess for "organic brain damage" (Baker, 1956), the need for psychometrically sound measures of cognitive and affective functioning became progressively obvious (Halstead, 1947; Wechsler, 1939).

As useful as this approach has been, many clinical neuropsychologists recognize that their patients (and the patients' family members) often want more than an objective psychometric assessment of their neuropsychological status. They have many practical questions and psychological needs surrounding the findings from the neuropsychological examination. They frequently ask the following: Do the results support a certain diagnosis? What are my treatment options? Will the person get better or worse with time? How rapidly will change occur? What can be done to help the person cope with the residual cognitive (behavioral and emotional/motivational) disturbances? What can be done to help a family member cope with a loved one's impaired neuropsychological status? Should the person seek medical disability, drive a car, be allowed to handle personal finances, and be allowed to be left alone at home during the day and/or night? Will the person ever be able to return to work? What kinds of rehabilitation does the person need now and possibly in the future? A spouse might ask, "How do I learn to live with my partner, who has now become so dependent on me [and at times childlike in manner]?"

For children with brain disorders, several other questions are asked: Do they need a special form of schooling? Will they "grow out" of their cognitive/behavioral problems that seem to be negatively affecting school performance? How does one help a child with brain dysfunction succeed in school? How does that child learn to make friends? How does one help the teachers better understand the needs of the child? How does one help the child understand his or her neuropsychological strengths and limitations without needlessly discouraging the child (and the parents)? Parents will ultimately also express their concern about the long-term effects of their child's brain injury and whether their child will be able to be gainfully employed, marry, and have a family.

These practical questions often give way to more personal and existential (philosophical) questions, such as the following: Why did this happen to me? Is life worth living with my brain disorder? Why did the neurosurgeons save me if they knew I would be so impaired? How do I deal with my loneliness, anxiety, anger, and depression for the rest of my life? Can I ever live a meaningful life again?

These and other pressing questions deserve to be addressed and, when possible, answered by the clinical neuropsychologist interested in the psychological care of the patient. Although clinical neuropsychologists often refer these patients and family members to other health care providers interested in "doing therapy," the first central tenet of this book is that the "test-oriented" and psychometrically based practice of clinical neuropsychology should be extended to include services aimed at improving the psychological care of an individual with a brain disorder as well as the person's family members.

OBSERVATIONS FROM DONALD HEBB

Donald Hebb has been recognized as one of the early and premier neuropsychologists in North America (Meier, 1992). In his 1949 book, *The Organization of Behavior*, he proposed the concept of cell assembly to help explain the neural basis of learning. His ideas influenced the fields of both neurophysiology and psychology (Fuster, 2003). The basic idea was that neurons that repeatedly "fire" in temporal relation to one another facilitate synaptic transmission between each other. This helps form neuronal circuits underlying both complex and simple behavioral responses. Today, we speak of neuronal networks, but the ideas are closely related and help explain various aspects of learning and motor control, as well as some aspects of brain organization. In fact, Hebb is often recognized by scientists outside the field of psychology as an early major contributor to modern neuroscience. Against this background, it is worthwhile to reflect on how he approached the broad field of psychology.

Hebb (1974), in a seminal article titled "What Psychology Is About," made the following observations. Psychology is the scientific study of the mind. Crediting Karl Lashley, who was his mentor (Meier, 1992), he then defined mind as follows: "Mind . . . is the capacity for thought, and thought is the integrative activity of the brain" (p. 75). As a science, psychology must impose limits on its methods of study and topics of investigation. It can make progress only by focusing on "answerable" questions given the testable hypotheses, methodology, and technology available. Second, Hebb stated that scientific psychology is limited in helping people "live wisely and well" (p. 74). He noted that classical literature and the arts appear to do a better job of guiding people in this regard. Although he did not advocate trying to make psychological science a literary venture, his article implies that both sets of knowledge may be useful in helping real people deal with real problems, especially those seen in neurological clinics. This is the second tenet of this book: Combining neuropsychological knowledge with some basic understanding of the psychological characteristics of humans (taken from multiple sources) may lead us to improve the psychological care of persons with brain disorders.

In an article on the role of neuroscience within psychology, Schwartz, Lilienfeld, Meca, and Sauvigné (2016) reviewed the dangers of "fervent monism." Schwartz and colleagues effectively argued that trying to explain complex psychological functions purely with neuroimaging or neurological correlates can be quite misleading. The major point of their article, however, is that relying too heavily on a single explanation of any phenomenon is dangerous in science. I add that it is dangerous in clinical care as well. Providing psychological help to persons with brain disorders requires a wide clinical perspective with different explanations and methods of intervention carefully considered before implementation is attempted.

A BRIEF HISTORICAL REVIEW RELEVANT TO PRESENT-DAY APPROACHES IN CLINICAL NEUROPSYCHOLOGY AND PSYCHOLOGICAL CARE

The clinicopathological approach in medicine formed the foundation of modern neuropsychology. The early observations of Paul Broca in 1861 and Karl Wernicke in 1865 (for a description of these observations, see Catani & ffytche, 2005; Hécaen & Albert, 1978) demonstrated that the location of brain lesions and specific abnormalities of language could be associated. Although that body of knowledge has substantially changed throughout the years (e.g., compare the first edition of the edited volume of *Clinical Neuropsychology* in 1979 by Heilman and Valenstein to their fifth edition in 2010), neurologists and neuropsychologists continue to rely on this methodological approach; however, the descriptions of the underlying brain lesions have greatly expanded with modern neuroimaging techniques (Siegel et al., 2016).

Building on the initial observation of John Hughlings Jackson that localization of a deficit is not the same as localization of functional capacity, A. R. Luria (1966) later proposed that the higher cortical or integrative brain functions are reliant on overlapping brain systems and subsystems. Differences in how a focal lesion influenced the organization of the underlying brain systems would determine specific neuropsychological deficits. Knowledge of the dysfunction in the systems (and associated subsystems) would lead to more effective clinical diagnosis and rehabilitation (Luria, 1948/1963; Luria, Naydin, Tsvetkova, & Vinarskaya, 1969; Luria, Pribram, & Homskaya, 1964). Although in principle this is a very appealing idea, it has been difficult to demonstrate in both clinical practice and scientific investigations. Yet Luria's insights have essentially been reaffirmed by modern functional imaging studies of the brain when individuals are engaged in the performance of various psychological tasks (Christensen, Goldberg, & Bougakov, 2009).

In everyday clinical practice, however, many persons with brain disorders have a combination of focal and nonfocal brain abnormalities. For some individuals, the lesions may have occurred abruptly (e.g., following severe TBI), whereas for others, gradual processes seem to underlie the emergence of the brain lesions and associated symptoms (e.g., multiple sclerosis). Understanding the similarities and differences of these patients from a neuropsychological standpoint becomes an important focus for clinical neuropsychologists involved in patient care, even at the purely diagnostic level.

Thus, the need for objective neuropsychological methods for diagnosing the presence (and, in some cases, the absence) of underlying brain pathology was the first step. There can be little doubt that the work of Ward Halstead (1947) and his student Ralph Reitan (1955) was of monumental significance to this venture in the United States. For the first time, there was scientific evidence that measurable responses on psychologically based instruments (i.e., tests) could identify whether a brain disorder was present and what side of the brain seemed most affected. In an attempt to reduce clinicians' biases when examining patients, Reitan trained technicians to administer and score tests thought to reveal important information about brain function. Reitan and his numerous students (including James and Homer Reed, Charles Matthews, Hallgrim Klove, Harry Klonoff, Igor Grant, Robert Heaton, Sureyya Dikmen, and Carl Dodrill) produced several influential research articles attesting to the validity of the Halstead–Reitan Neuropsychological Test Battery and its clinical utility (as one example, see Grant & Adams, 2009). This battery of tests with supplementary measures, however, could take several hours to administer. This was neither cost-effective nor necessary in some clinical settings.

Soon after the standardization and cross-validation of the Halstead–Reitan Neuropsychological Test Battery (Vega & Parsons, 1967), other developments were taking place in brain–behavior research studies that would also have profound influence on how clinical neuropsychologists would conceptualize neuropsychological functions and examine patients. The work of Gazzaniga and Sperry (1967) brought clear attention to the scientific community that the two cerebral hemispheres carried out different, but complementary, neuropsychological functions. The left cerebral hemisphere was actively involved in various forms of verbal problem-solving and capable of enabling persons to verbally report information that was perceived by the left hemisphere. In contrast, the right cerebral hemisphere appeared especially suited to performing visual spatial tasks and could be shown to enable persons to perceive/recognize information that could not be verbally reported if the corpus callosum connecting the two cerebral hemispheres was surgically resected. Sperry (1974) summarized these findings, and the scientific world (which included the world of the clinical neuropsychologists) began studying in detail how the two cerebral hemispheres are involved in complex psychological functions (for a review, see Volz & Gazzaniga, 2017).

Another important advance in brain–behavior research that influenced neuropsychology was the observations of Brenda Milner. She reported that patients undergoing bilateral hippocampal lesions had profound memory loss (Scoville & Milner, 1957). Her research, coupled with the observations of Sperry, introduced a new wave of research that explored the specific functions of the right and left hemispheres (Milner & Taylor, 1972; for a summary of Milner's monumental contributions to how neuropsychologists examine patients with known brain lesions, see Watkins & Klein, 2018).

These observations led a number of experimental and clinical neuropsychologists to recognize the importance of studying how specific brain disorders or neurological conditions differentially affect different neuropsychological functions. Now the goal was not only to identify whether a brain disorder was present but also to investigate how a specific brain disorder adversely affected certain psychological functions or HIBFs. Barr (2018) has provided a scholarly and insightful review of these historical trends that have shaped modern approaches to neuropsychological assessment.

The development of briefer and "more flexible" approaches to neuropsychological assessment therefore became popular (Grant & Adams, 2009; Morgan & Ricker, 2018). Although this was clearly in the tradition of Luria's work (Luria, 1966; see also Christensen, 1974), the goal for many neuropsychologists was to objectively study specific features of neuropsychological test performance that revealed important information for differential diagnosis, patient management, and the expansion of the scientific database underlying clinical practice. Barr (2008) noted that Edith Kaplan's "process approach" (which reflects this tradition in the United States and was influenced by the work of Heinz Werner, Martin Scheerer, Norman Geschwind, and Luria and Vygotsky) "calls for developing standardized methods for observing, scoring, and analyzing qualitative features of behavior in addition to interpreting traditional test scores" (p. 13).

The neuropsychological work of Harold Goodglass, Edith Kaplan, and Nelson Butters in Boston (Milberg, Hebben, & Kaplan, 2009) and Arthur Benton in Iowa (Tranel, 2009) championed this flexible battery approach to neuropsychological testing and interpretation in the 1970s and 1980s. The even earlier work of Lauretta Bender (1938) with children in New York City helped clarify the potential value of this approach and also influenced many psychologists to explore how quantitative and qualitative test findings could be used in clinical neuropsychological assessments. As the insights of these observant clinician/researchers began to be disseminated to many students of psychology interested in neuropsychology, the methodological approach popularized by Halstead and Reitan became more obvious. Patients with independently identifiable brain lesions were administered psychological tests and compared to different control groups, with important demographic variables held constant.

Test scores and qualitative features of test performance (Prigatano & Borgaro, 2003) were now utilized by practicing clinical neuropsychologists to greatly advance the profession of clinical neuropsychology in medical environments (Lezak, Howieson, Bigler, & Tranel, 2010). Yet, as important as these advances were, many clinical neuropsychologists were not vested in studying the impact of these ideas on the rehabilitation of brain dysfunctional individuals.

The professional "roots" of modern clinical neuropsychology were to focus exclusively on brain–behavior relationships (for an academic review of the beginnings of clinical neuropsychology in the United States and Europe, see Meier, 1992).

Thus, clinical neuropsychologists were not trained to attend to the psychological care of their patients, preferring to refer them to psychiatrists, clinical psychologists, or medical social workers for this purpose. In fact, there was a not-so-subtle bias that "respectable" clinical neuropsychologists limited their work to assessment and diagnosis. Clinical neuropsychologists were also interested in adding to the scientific basis of neuropsychology. Rehabilitation questions were not addressed because so many variables seem to influence positive outcomes if and when they occur.

In the 1970s, the brain injury rehabilitation work of Leonard Diller and Yehuda Ben-Yishay began to demonstrate to the rehabilitation world that meaningful outcomes could be achieved with post-acute young adults who suffered severe brain injuries (Ben-Yishay & Diller, 2011; Prigatano, 1999b). Although the term "neuropsychological rehabilitation" began to appear in the literature (Meier, Benton, & Diller, 1987; Prigatano, 1986), the demonstration of how specific knowledge of a person's underlying brain disorder and associated neuropsychological deficits guided his or her rehabilitation activities was often not clearly specified. All patients might receive, for example, cognitive retraining to improve processing speed or memory compensation training to deal with a memory impairment. Most patients had difficulties with social interaction and required practice at developing social skills in group settings. Thus, "holistic" approaches to neuropsychological rehabilitation became popular. Was it true, however, that "one size [i.e., one approach] fits all"? The Diller and Ben-Yishay approach, which emphasized the holistic model, strongly suggested that although underlying neuropsychological deficits may be only modestly remediated, the patient could learn to adapt to the neuropsychological and neurological deficits in a manner that increased social integration and reduced social isolation and socially inappropriate behaviors. Diller and Ben-Yishay's approach borrowed heavily from the insights of Kurt Goldstein (1942, 1952) that emphasized the importance of the therapeutic milieu in treatment outcomes. Early research work supported this model (Klonoff, Lamb, & Henderson, 2001; Prigatano, 1995; Prigatano et al., 1984, 1994). More recent evidence-based reviews have also suggested that it is indeed the treatment of choice in many instances (Cicerone et al., 2008, 2011).

However, the treatment effect sizes, measured using traditional statistical models, were considered generally mild and in some cases moderate (Rohling, Faust, Beverly, & Demakis, 2009). The field lacked—and continues to lack—long-term, well-designed follow-up studies to show that patients who have undergone such treatment in fact demonstrate better long-term psychosocial outcomes with less economic burden on the health care system (Diller & Ben-Yishay, 2003). Thus, reimbursement for such rehabilitation activities is difficult to obtain, and patients and their families often seek out less expensive and less intensive forms of care.

ATTENDING TO THE PSYCHOLOGICAL NEEDS OF PATIENTS IN THE PRACTICE OF CLINICAL NEUROPSYCHOLOGY

A common determining factor that is repetitively associated with good neuropsychological rehabilitation outcome is reflected in Goldstein's (1954) important observation that patients do best when they can accept limitations (imposed by their brain injury) without resentment. This task, however, is not easy to accomplish, as this book will demonstrate. Technical knowledge about the brain disorder and associated neuropsychological deficits is helpful to this process. It helps clinicians, family members, and the patient better understand "what is wrong" with the person, but this in and of itself does not determine the patient's outcome. Focusing on the emotional disturbances of patients involved in brain rehabilitation has become progressively recognized as a crucial component for successful outcome, even by those neuropsychologists who at one time emphasized the predominant role of cognitive retraining in neuropsychological rehabilitation (Mateer & Sira, 2008; Sohlberg & Mateer, 1989). During the past several years, a number of chapters and books have thus been published on the role of psychotherapy for persons with brain disorders to specifically address their emotional distress and successful adaptation after a brain disorder (Klonoff, 2010; Laaksonen & Ranta, 2013; Prigatano, 1986, 1999b, 2008, 2011; Ruff & Chester, 2014).

Although these advances are important, they often do not articulate how other variables need to be attended to when addressing the psychological needs of patients. Thus, the third tenet of this book is that in addition to cognitively oriented rehabilitation therapies and psychotherapeutic interventions with patients and their family members, clinical neuropsychologists can improve the psychological care of persons with brain disorders by developing a long-term professional relationship with the patients (and, at times, the family) to guide them at different time periods when they are making important choices relevant to their clinical condition. A firm appreciation of the patient's culture, religious beliefs, sleep patterns, eating habits, physical mobility, exercise habits, methods of interpersonal interactions, personal aspirations, and psychodynamics is crucial for this work, as is the ability to understand the patient's neuropsychological strengths and limitations.

It requires clinical neuropsychologists to expand their view of the scope of their practice (Prigatano & Morrone-Strupinsky, 2010). At times, it requires them to function as a neuropsychologist, a clinical psychologist, and, to some degree, a health psychologist within an evolving health care system that emphasizes brief but integrated and timely interventions for patients treated by different types of physicians. This shift is difficult to achieve. Years ago, a very influential neuropsychologist was emphatic over a dinner conversation that studying brain–behavior relationships is a specialty of its own. Clinical neuropsychologists should not try to practice as clinical psychologists. According to that psychologist, it weakens both professions. I disagree, but I understand the basis of the position.

Many clinical neuropsychologists have made substantial contributions to scientific knowledge and patient care by focusing their professional efforts on understanding and systematically measuring disturbances in neuropsychological functioning and relating those findings to important medical outcomes. For example, Christina A. Meyers' neuropsychological work demonstrated that severity of impairment of certain neurocognitive functions is related to length of survival in patients with malignant brain tumors (Johnson, Sawyer, Meyers, O'Neill, & Wefel, 2012; Meyers & Cantor, 2003). This type of information is very important to patients, family members, and physicians when making treatment decisions. However, there is value in extending the scope of activities without weakening the practice of clinical neuropsychology.

For example, several years ago, I was impressed that patients with severe TBI often underreported their cognitive and behavioral difficulties (Prigatano & Altman, 1990; Prigatano, Altman, & O'Brien, 1990). Those initial clinical observations led to studying whether this underreporting was due to "psychological denial" or reflected some form of unawareness directly related to brain lesion location and size (Prigatano & Schacter, 1991). Perhaps more important, it led other clinicians and researchers to recognize that some form of unawareness may exist in quite divergent patient groups (Buunk et al., 2017; Jacus, 2017; Meier, 1992; Prigatano, Hendin, & Heiserman, 2014). These and other findings had clear implications for the study of anosognosia (Prigatano, 2010). They also helped clarify the important role of disturbances of self-awareness in brain injury rehabilitation (Sherer & Sander, 2014). The scope of my work at that time included neuropsychological assessments as well as cognitive retraining and psychotherapy. It was the combination of these professional activities that led to those observations and resultant clinical and research efforts.

I realize that my opinion on and proposed expansion of the professional scope of practice will not occur by simple didactics (in verbal or written form). It will only occur if it can be demonstrated to many clinical neuropsychologists that such an approach not only helps their patients but also substantially improves the quality and satisfaction level of their professional work.

Box 1.1 reiterates the three tenets on which this book is based. In light of these tenets, Chapter 2 attempts to demonstrate that understanding the "natural plan of the central nervous system" gives us a natural starting point for understanding the nature of human beings. The more we understand about human nature, the more reasonable and practical we become when attempting to provide psychological care after a brain disorder. This discussion is followed by a summary of brain changes that naturally occur over an individual's life span that have relevance to understanding the evolution and natural decline of neuropsychological abilities. Both phylogenetic and ontological perspectives are considered (Chapter 3). Clinical neuropsychologists also need a working understanding of how specific neuropsychological functions may underlie "real-world functioning" at different stages of psychosocial development. This information is crucial in planning for the psychological care of individuals after the occurrence of their brain disorder (Chapter 4).

Although the HIBFs are often thought to be primarily conscious in nature, a growing literature suggests that unconscious processes can also influence behavioral choices (Bargh & Morsella,

> **Box 1.1. The Three Tenets on Which This Book Is Based**
>
> 1. The "test-oriented" and psychometrically based practice of clinical neuropsychology should be extended to include services aimed at improving the psychological care of an individual with a brain disorder.
> 2. Combining neuropsychological knowledge with basic understanding of the psychological characteristics of humans (taken from multiple sources) and methods for improving psychological adjustments to losses helps clinical neuropsychologists improve their skills when providing psychological care of persons with brain disorders.
> 3. Clinical neuropsychologists can improve the psychological care of persons with brain disorders by developing a long-term consultant relationship that provides guidance concerning important choices relevant to their clinical condition.

2008). This becomes a very important topic when one goal of psychological care is to help patients make choices that foster their well-being over time. Chapter 5 is devoted to this often neglected (and controversial) topic. It illustrates conscious and unconscious manifestations of HIBFs in our behavior, thought processes, and emotional/motivational reactions. This understanding provides a more interesting template for approaching/perceiving the subjective world of the patient. Thus, Part I of this book is a brief summary of normal neuropsychological functioning over the life span.

Part II briefly describes selected features of abnormal neuropsychological functioning observed in clinical practice. Chapters 6–8 summarize selected studies that describe clinically relevant observations concerning how brain lesions affect the HIBFs during childhood and adolescence, during the adult years, and in elderly individuals. Chapter 9 summarizes information relevant to understanding disturbances of self-awareness commonly observed after a brain disorder. Because disturbances in self-awareness can also be observed in psychiatric disorders, it is important to reapproach the topic of "organically" based disturbances in self-awareness versus those disturbances that appear to reflect psychological methods of coping with overwhelming feelings of emotional distress. Some guidelines can be offered in this regard.

This background information sets the stage for a discussion of what constitutes a medically necessary and personally relevant neuropsychological examination and consultation. In Part III, Chapter 10 discusses questions that the neuropsychological examination attempts to answer and how the information obtained from the examination will be discussed with the patient and family members in a manner that is accurate as well as understandable to them. If this is done in a clinically competent and sensitive manner, the patient and/or family members often inquire about what further assistance might be offered to help the patient improve functioning or adjustment to the neuropsychological impairments that are now better understood following the examination.

Chapter 11 briefly considers how the insights gleaned from the study of neuropsychology (and the neurosciences) can be used when providing neuropsychological consultations before and after brain surgery. The importance of neuropsychological consultation, especially before surgery, is a neglected topic in the psychological care of persons and needs to be thoroughly discussed.

Chapter 12 describes in more detail several important observations relevant to providing psychological care, including understanding the likely causes of "placebo effects" and factors that help people cope with adversity. The observations also include some traditional insights from various approaches to psychotherapy.

In Part IV, Chapters 13–24 describe in more detail how the application of this background information can have relevance in providing psychological care for patients with different brain disorders. Individual case examples and case vignettes provide a realistic description of when the psychological care interventions were successful and when they were not. Not all clinical conditions encountered by clinical neuropsychologists are considered. The patient groups described are ones I have personally worked with from a psychological care perspective. Several of these individuals have been followed for more than 10 years and some for more than 30 years.

In Part V, Chapter 25 concludes the book with a few personal and professional reflections. If I have been successful in my efforts, then the potential impact of this approach to the psychological care of persons with brain disorders will be clarified.

REFERENCES

Anastasi, A. (1976). *Psychological testing*. New York, NY: Macmillan.

Baker, G. (1956). Diagnosis of organic brain damage in the adult. In B. Klopfer (Ed.), *Developments in the Rorschach technique* (Vol. 2, pp. 318–375). New York, NY: World Book.

Bargh, J. A., & Morsella, E. (2008). The unconscious mind. *Perspectives on Psychological Science, 3*(1), 73–79.

Barr, W. B. (2008). Historical development of the neuropsychological test battery. In J. Morgan & J. Ricker (Eds.), *Textbook of clinical neuropsychology* (pp. 3–17). New York, NY: Taylor & Francis.

Barr, W. B. (2018). Historical trends in neuropsychological assessment. In J. Morgan & J. Ricker (Eds.), *Textbook of clinical neuropsychology* (2nd ed., pp. 3–13). New York, NY: Taylor & Francis.

Bender, L. (1938). *A visual motor gestalt test and its clinical use*. New York, NY: American Orthopsychiatric Association.

Benson, K., & Hartz, A. J. (2000). A comparison of observational studies and randomized, controlled trials. *New England Journal of Medicine, 342*(25), 1878–1886.

Ben-Yishay, Y., & Diller, L. (2011). *Handbook of holistic neuropsychological rehabilitation: Outpatient rehabilitation of traumatic brain injury*. New York, NY: Oxford University Press.

Buunk, A. M., Spikman, J. M., Veenstra, W. S., van Laar, P. J., Metzemaekers, J. D., van Dijk, J. M. C., . . . Groen, R. J. (2017). Social cognition impairments after aneurysmal subarachnoid haemorrhage: Associations with deficits in interpersonal behaviour, apathy, and impaired self-awareness. *Neuropsychologia, 103*, 131–139.

Catani, M., & ffytche, D. H. (2005). The rises and falls of disconnection syndromes. *Brain, 128*(10), 2224–2239.

Chaplin, C. (1992). *My autobiography*. New York, NY: Melville House.

Christensen, A.-L. (1974). *Luria's neuropsychological investigation: Text* (2nd ed.). Vojens, Denmark: Schmidts Bogtrykkeri.

Christensen, A.-L., Goldberg, E., & Bougakov, D. (Eds.). (2009). *Luria's legacy in the 21st century*. New York, NY: Oxford University Press.

Cicerone, K. D., Langenbahn, D. M., Braden, C., Malec, J. F., Kalmar, K., Fraas, M., . . . Bergquist, T. (2011). Evidence-based cognitive rehabilitation: Updated review of the literature from 2003 through 2008. *Archives of Physical Medicine and Rehabilitation, 92*(4), 519–530.

Cicerone, K. D., Mott, T., Azulay, J., Sharlow-Galella, M. A., Ellmo, W. J., Paradise, S., & Friel, J. C. (2008). A randomized controlled trial of holistic neuropsychologic rehabilitation after traumatic brain injury. *Archives of Physical Medicine and Rehabilitation, 89*(12), 2239–2249.

Concato, J., Shah, N., & Horwitz, R. I. (2000). Randomized, controlled trials, observational studies, and the hierarchy of research designs. *New England Journal of Medicine, 342*(25), 1887–1892.

Diller, L., & Ben-Yishay, Y. (2003). The clinical utility and cost-effectiveness of comprehensive (holistic) brain injury day-treatment programs. In G. P. Prigatano & N. H. Pliskin (Eds.), *Clinical neuropsychology and cost outcome research: A beginning* (pp. 293–328). New York, NY: Psychology Press.

Erikson, E. H. (1964). *Insight and responsibility*. New York, NY: Norton.

Fuster, J. M. (2003). *Cortex and mind: Unifying cognition*. New York, NY: Oxford University Press.

Gazzaniga, M. S., & Sperry, R. W. (1967). Language after section of the cerebral commissures. *Brain*, *90*(1), 131–148.

Goldstein, K. (1942). *Aftereffects of brain injuries in war: Their evaluation and treatment. The application of psychologic methods in the clinic*. New York, NY: Grune & Stratton.

Goldstein, K. (1952). The effect of brain damage on the personality. *Psychiatry*, *15*(3), 245–260.

Goldstein, K. (1954). The concept of transference in treatment of organic and functional nervous disease. *Psychotherapy and Psychosomatics*, *2*(3–4), 334–353.

Grant, I., & Adams, K. M. (2009). *Neuropsychological assessment of neuropsychiatric and neuromedical disorders* (3rd ed.). New York, NY: Oxford University Press.

Hakim, H., Verma, N. P., & Greiffenstein, M. F. (1988). Pathogenesis of reduplicative paramnesia. *Journal of Neurology, Neurosurgery, and Psychiatry*, *51*(6), 839–841.

Halstead, W. C. (1947). *Brain and intelligence: A quantitative study of the frontal lobes*. Chicago, IL: University of Chicago Press.

Hebb, D. O. (1949). *The organization of behavior: A neuropsychological approach*. New York, NY: Wiley.

Hebb, D. O. (1974). What psychology is about. *The American Psychologist*, *29*(2), 71–79.

Hécaen, H., & Albert, M. L. (1978). *Human neuropsychology*. New York, NY: Wiley.

Heilman, K. M., & Valenstein, E. (Eds.). (1979). *Clinical neuropsychology*. New York, NY: Oxford University Press.

Heilman, K. M., & Valenstein, E. (Eds.). (2010). *Clinical neuropsychology* (5th ed.). New York, NY: Oxford University Press.

Jacus, J. P. (2017). Awareness, apathy, and depression in Alzheimer's disease and mild cognitive impairment. *Brain and Behavior*, *7*(4), e00661.

Johnson, D. R., Sawyer, A. M., Meyers, C. A., O'Neill, B. P., & Wefel, J. S. (2012). Early measures of cognitive function predict survival in patients with newly diagnosed glioblastoma. *Neuro-oncology*, *14*(6), 808–816.

Jung, C. G. (1964). *Man and his symbols*. London, UK: Aldus.

Klonoff, P. S. (2010). *Psychotherapy after brain injury: Principles and techniques*. New York, NY: Guilford.

Klonoff, P. S., Lamb, D. G., & Henderson, S. W. (2001). Outcomes from milieu-based neurorehabilitation at up to 11 years post-discharge. *Brain Injury*, *15*(5), 413–428.

Laaksonen, R., & Ranta, M. (2013). *Introduction to neuropsychotherapy: Guidelines for rehabilitation of neurological and neuropsychiatric patients throughout the lifespan*. New York, NY: Psychology Press.

Lezak, M. D., Howieson, D. B., Bigler, E. D., & Tranel, D. (2010). *Neuropsychological assessment* (5th ed.). New York, NY: Oxford University Press.

Luria, A. R. (1963). *Restoration of function after brain injury*. London, UK: Pergamon. (Original work published 1948)

Luria, A. R. (1966). *Higher cortical functions in man*. New York, NY: Basic Books.

Luria, A. R., Naydin, V., Tsvetkova, L., & Vinarskaya, E. (1969). Restoration of higher cortical function following local brain damage. In P. Vinken & B. Bruyn (Eds.), *Handbook of clinical neurology: Disorders of higher nervous activity* (Vol. 3, pp. 368–433). Amsterdam, the Netherlands: North-Holland.

Luria, A. R., Pribram, K., & Homskaya, E. (1964). An experimental analysis of the behavioral disturbance produced by a left frontal arachnoidal endothelioma (meningioma). *Neuropsychologia*, *2*(4), 257–280.

Mateer, C., & Sira, C. (2008). Practical rehabilitation strategies in the context of clinical neuropsychology feedback. In J. Morgan & J. Ricker (Eds.), *Textbook of clinical neuropsychology* (pp. 996–1007). New York, NY: Taylor & Francis.

Meier, M. J. (1992). Modern clinical neuropsychology in historical perspective. *The American Psychologist*, *47*(4), 550.

Meier, M. J., Benton, A. L., & Diller, L. E. (Eds.). (1987). *Neuropsychological rehabilitation*. London, UK: Churchill Livingstone.

Meyers, C., & Cantor, S. (Eds.). (2003). *Neuropsychological assessment and treatment of patients with malignant brain tumors*. New York, NY: Psychology Press.

Milberg, W. P., Hebben, N., & Kaplan, E. (2009). The Boston process approach to neuropsychological assessment. In I. Grant & K. Adams (Eds.), *Neuropsychological assessment of neuropsychiatric and neuromedical disorders* (3rd ed., pp. 42–65). New York, NY: Oxford University Press.

Milner, B., & Taylor, L. (1972). Right-hemisphere superiority in tactile pattern-recognition after cerebral commissurotomy: Evidence for nonverbal memory. *Neuropsychologia*, *10*(1), 1–15.

Morgan, J. E., & Ricker, J. H. (Eds.). (2018). *Textbook of clinical neuropsychology* (2nd ed.). New York, NY: Taylor & Francis.

Prigatano, G. P. (Ed.). (1986). *Neuropsychological rehabilitation after brain injury*. Baltimore, MD: Johns Hopkins University Press.

Prigatano, G. P. (1995). Preparing patients for possible neuropsychological consequences after brain surgery. *BNI Quarterly, 11*(4), 4–8.

Prigatano, G. P. (1999a). Commentary: Beyond statistics and research design. *Journal of Head Trauma Rehabilitation, 14*(3), 308–311.

Prigatano, G. P. (1999b). *Principles of neuropsychological rehabilitation*. New York, NY: Oxford University Press.

Prigatano, G. P. (2003). Challenging dogma in neuropsychology and related disciplines. *Archives of Clinical Neuropsychology, 18*(8), 811–825.

Prigatano, G. P. (2008). Neuropsychological rehabilitation and psychodynamic psychotherapy. In J. E. Morgan & J. H. Ricker (Eds.), *Textbook of clinical neuropsychology* (pp. 985–995). New York, NY: Taylor & Francis.

Prigatano, G. P. (2010). *The study of anosognosia*. New York, NY: Oxford University Press.

Prigatano, G. P. (2011). Psychotherapy. In J. M. Silver, T. W. McAllister, & S. C. Yudofsky (Eds.), *Textbook of traumatic brain injury* (2nd ed., pp. 571–577). Washington, DC: American Psychiatric Publishing.

Prigatano, G. P., & Altman, I. (1990). Impaired awareness of behavioral limitations after traumatic brain injury. *Archives of Physical Medicine and Rehabilitation, 71*(13), 1058–1064.

Prigatano, G. P., Altman, I. M., & O'Brien, K. P. (1990). Behavioral limitations that traumatic-brain-injured patients tend to underestimate. *The Clinical Neuropsychologist, 4*(2), 163–176.

Prigatano, G. P., & Borgaro, S. R. (2003). Qualitative features of finger movement during the Halstead finger oscillation test following traumatic brain injury. *Journal of the International Neuropsychological Society, 9*(1), 128–133.

Prigatano, G. P., Fordyce, D. J., Zeiner, H. K., Roueche, J. R., Pepping, M., & Wood, B. C. (1984). Neuropsychological rehabilitation after closed head injury in young adults. *Journal of Neurology, Neurosurgery, and Psychiatry, 47*(5), 505–513.

Prigatano, G. P., Hendin, B. A., & Heiserman, J. E. (2014). Denial or unawareness of cognitive deficit associated with multiple sclerosis? A case report. *Journal of Clinical and Experimental Neuropsychology, 36*(4), 335–341.

Prigatano, G. P., Klonoff, P. S., O'Brien, K. P., Altman, I. M., Amin, K., Chiapello, D., . . . Mora, M. (1994). Productivity after neuropsychologically oriented milieu rehabilitation. *Journal of Head Trauma Rehabilitation, 9*(1), 91–102.

Prigatano, G. P., & Morrone-Strupinsky, J. (2010). Advancing the profession of clinical neuropsychology with appropriate outcome studies and demonstrated clinical skills. *The Clinical Neuropsychologist, 24*(3), 468–480.

Prigatano, G. P., & Schacter, D. L. (Eds.). (1991). *Awareness of deficit after brain injury*. New York, NY: Oxford University Press.

Rapaport, D., Schafer, R., Gill, M. M., & Holt, R. R. (1974). *Diagnostic psychological testing*. New York, NY: International Universities Press.

Rohling, M. L., Faust, M. E., Beverly, B., & Demakis, G. (2009). Effectiveness of cognitive rehabilitation following acquired brain injury: A meta-analytic re-examination of Cicerone et al.'s (2000, 2005) systematic reviews. *Neuropsychology, 23*(1), 20–39.

Ruff, R. M., & Chester, S. K. (2014). *Effective psychotherapy for individuals with brain injury*. New York, NY: Guilford.

Schwartz, S. J., Lilienfeld, S. O., Meca, A., & Sauvigné, K. C. (2016). The role of neuroscience within psychology: A call for inclusiveness over exclusiveness. *The American Psychologist, 71*(1), 52–70.

Scoville, W. B., & Milner, B. (1957). Loss of recent memory after bilateral hippocampal lesions. *Journal of Neurology, Neurosurgery, and Psychiatry, 20*(1), 11.

Sherer, M., & Sander, A. M. (Eds.). (2014). *Handbook on the neuropsychology of traumatic brain injury*. New York, NY: Springer.

Siegel, J. S., Ramsey, L. E., Snyder, A. Z., Metcalf, N. V., Chacko, R. V., Weinberger, K., . . . Corbetta, M. (2016). Disruptions of network connectivity predict impairment in multiple behavioral domains after stroke. *Proceedings of the National Academy of Sciences of the USA, 113*(30), E4367–E4376.

Sohlberg, M. M., & Mateer, C. A. (1989). *Introduction to cognitive rehabilitation: Theory and practice*. New York, NY: Guilford.

Sperry, R. W. (1974). Lateral specialization in the surgically separated hemispheres. In F. O. Schmitt & F. G. Worden (Eds.), *The neurosciences third study program* (pp. 5–19). Cambridge, MA: MIT Press.

Tranel, D. (2009). The Iowa–Benton school of neuropsychological assessment. In I. Grant & K. Adams (Eds.), *Neuropsychological assessment of neuropsychiatric and neuromedical disorders* (pp. 66–83). New York, NY: Oxford University Press.

US Office of Strategic Services. (1948). *Assessment of men*. New York, NY: Rinehart.

Vega, A., Jr., & Parsons, O. A. (1967). Cross-validation of the Halstead–Reitan tests for brain damage. *Journal of Consulting Psychology, 31*(6), 619–625.

Volz, L. J., & Gazzaniga, M. S. (2017). Interaction in isolation: 50 years of insights from split-brain research. *Brain, 140*(7), 2051–2060.

Waber, D. P. (2010). *Rethinking learning disabilities: Understanding children who struggle in school.* New York, NY: Guilford.

Watkins, K. E., & Klein, D. (2018). Brenda Milner on her 100th birthday: A lifetime of "good ideas." *Brain, 141*(1), 2527–2532.

Wechsler, D. (1939). *The measurement of adult intelligence.* Baltimore, MD: Williams & Wilkins.

Young, A. W. (1996). Reduplication. In J. Graham Beaumont, P. M. Kenealy, & M. J. C. Rogers (Eds.), *The Blackwell dictionary of neuropsychology.* Cambridge, UK: Blackwell.

PART I

BRIEF DESCRIPTION OF NORMAL NEUROPSYCHOLOGICAL FUNCTIONING OVER THE LIFE SPAN

PART I provides a context for understanding core features of human beings in light of the "natural plan of the central nervous system" and how that plan normally unfolds in humans throughout their life. It attempts to describe changes in normal neuropsychological functioning associated with the development and decline of certain psychosocial competencies from early childhood to the later years of life. It concludes with a discussion of how both conscious and unconscious features of higher integrative brain functions influence behavioral choices. Understanding what is normal neuropsychological functioning provides a basis for then evaluating possible abnormal neuropsychological functioning following various brain lesions. This latter information has implications for conducting a clinical neuropsychological interview and later examination of patients. It also has implications for the psychological care of persons with brain disorders.

2

HUMAN NATURE IN LIGHT OF THE NATURAL PLAN OF THE CENTRAL NERVOUS SYSTEM

INTRODUCTION

In order to provide reasonable and potentially helpful psychological care for persons with a brain disorder, it is necessary to have an informed understanding of human nature. Human nature is not always easy to define, and there are certainly different perspectives on this topic. It is an area of study that has attracted considerable attention from psychologists, psychiatrists, anthropologists, neuroscientists, philosophers, literary artists, theologians, and historians. It is not the intention of this chapter to review the diverse sources of information and perspectives pertinent to the topic of human nature. Rather, a more practical point of view is followed.

Human nature is descriptively defined as the universal characteristics of people observed across recorded times and cultures. It is proposed that human nature "in general" is best revealed by understanding the "natural plan" of the human central nervous system (which of course includes the brain, brain stem, and spinal cord) and how that plan undergoes alterations with time. Studying the individual variations of this general plan is also crucial for understanding the personality of specific individuals (McAdams & Pals, 2006) before and after a brain disorder. Moreover, the development of certain cognitive and motivational features that appear unique to humans may help explain how cultures develop and in turn influence people's cognitions and behavior (Tomasello, Carpenter, Call, Behne, & Moll, 2005). Some have even suggested that such an evolutionary point of view is necessary for understanding how our moral values develop and divide us (Haidt, 2012).

THE NATURAL PLAN OF THE CENTRAL NERVOUS SYSTEM FOR HUMANS

A. R. Luria (see Cole & Cole, 1979) credits Lev Vygotsky for suggesting a strategy for scientifically studying human "higher psychological processes" that gives us a useful approach for understanding human nature. The first goal, according to Luria and Vygotsky, was to clarify the natural plan of the central nervous system (CNS) by studying the biological processes that preceded the development of complicated psychological functions. The second goal was to "study the dissolution of higher psychological functions as the result of some kind of insult to the organism" (Cole & Cole, 1979, p. 56). More precisely, how do focal and diffuse injuries to the brain at different stages of development "alter the plan of the CNS"? What are the neuropsychological disturbances observed, and how do they impact our human nature? This neuropsychological perspective is also seen in the writings of Kurt Goldstein (1939), the "father" of modern-day neuropsychological rehabilitation (Newcombe, 2002), as well as in Luria's earlier work on human conflicts (Luria, 1932).

Luria also emphasized another important aspect of his work. In addition to understanding the negative effects of a brain insult on "higher psychological functions," he was interested in understanding what changes in brain mechanisms that control those functions might occur to explain partial or complete restoration of those higher psychological functions. This capacity to reorganize or partially regain lost (impaired) neuropsychological functions adds further knowledge regarding human nature. Figure 2.1 presents a drawing of Vygotsky and a picture of Luria.

In light of these questions, what does the CNS do? At the most rudimentary level, the CNS allows for successful operation of essential bodily organs that sustain life (heart, lungs, kidneys, etc.). The brain structures at the level of the brain stem carry these functions out "automatically" (Blumenfeld, 2010). The brain stem and the spinal cord also allow us to move in space. This capacity to move is crucial not only to find food, shelter, a mate, and avoid danger but also to provide stimulus input into the

Lev Vygotsky (1896–1934)   A. R. Luria (1902–1977)

FIGURE 2.1 (Left) A drawing of Lev Semenovich Vygotsky. (Right) A picture of Alexander Romanovich Luria.

Source: Courtesy of Dr. Janna Glozman, a student of A. R. Luria.

various organ systems that are needed to sustain those systems that in turn sustain life (e.g., forcing the lungs to breathe in oxygen and expel carbon dioxide). Without these feedback loops, various organs (e.g., the lungs) become dysfunctional, and disease and death can easily follow.

Luria (see Cole & Cole, 1979) also notes that Vygotsky emphasized that "from the moment of birth, children are in constant interaction with adults who actively seek to incorporate them into their culture and its historically accumulated store of meanings and ways of doing things" (p. 45). Thus, for Vygotsky,

> the origins of higher forms of conscious behavior were to be found in the individual's social relations with the external world. But man is not only a product of his environment; he is also an active agent in creating that environment. (p. 43)

Herein lies perhaps the most useful way to begin the discussion of human nature. Men and women have CNSs that help sustain basic functions of living and in so doing are able to move. They are in constant contact with other humans in order to learn certain skills necessary to function within that environment. Moving, learning, and doing are the natural building blocks of human nature. The edifice that those building blocks construct is the capacity not only to survive, procreate the species, and function within an existing environment but also to act on and change that environment. Language, as a symbolic representation system that conveys and defines experiences (Sapir, 1949), creates via words imagined, but not yet realized, experiences. This becomes a crucial endeavor for humans. It is an essential feature of human nature.

AN EVOLUTIONARY PERSPECTIVE ON BRAIN AND BEHAVIOR CHANGES IN HUMANS

Paxinos and Mai (2004) provide a detailed analysis of the evolution and development of the brain, brain stem, and spinal cord. Striedter (2004) focuses on the "evolution of uniquely human brains." He states that

> most strikingly, human brains contain 15–24% more neocortical gray matter (and 22% more neocortical white matter) than would be expected for nonhuman primate brains of equal size. . . . Interestingly, this phylogenetic size increase affects some neocortical regions more than others. (pp. 14–15)

He also notes that the prefrontal cortex is significantly more developed, followed by specific regions involving portions of the parietal and temporal lobes. Certain subcortical regions (e.g., the dorsal thalamic nuclei) and the cerebellar hemispheres and their numerous connections to the cerebral hemispheres "are unexpectedly large in humans" (p. 15). Striedter goes on to note that in the human brain, there are important changes in neuronal connectivity not seen in the nonhuman, primate brain.

Catani and ffytche (2005) highlight this same observation when discussing the phenomena of cross-modality associations in the human brain. Figure 2.2, reproduced from their article, illustrates a very important observation relevant to our basic understanding of human nature: "In the monkey, primary sensory cortex connects only to their association cortices with intermodality connections mediated by the limbic cortex. In man, the majority of intermodality connections are mediated by higher-order association cortex in the parietal lobe" (p. 2229). Direct "limbic" input is not necessary when responding to a stimulus for humans. For humans, the inferior parietal lobe plays a very important role integrating visual, tactical, and auditory information necessary for written language—another uniquely human function. Thus, it is the structural and connectivity changes within the human brain that give us our first view of what it means to be human.

Although Striedter (2004) appropriately points out that it is difficult to relate different

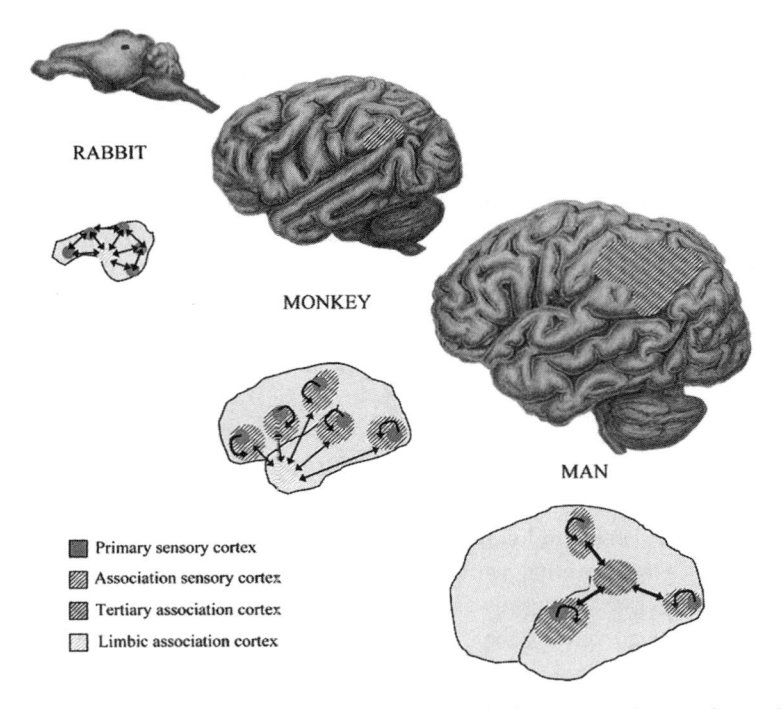

FIGURE 2.2 The top diagonal sequence shows the expansion of inferior parietal cortex from rabbit through monkey to man. The bottom diagonal sequence shows the differences in brain circuitry between the species. In man, the majority of intermodality connections are mediated by higher order association cortex in the parietal lobe (See color plates).

Source: Reprinted from Catani and ffytche (2005), *Brain, 128*(10), p. 2230 with permission from Oxford University Press.

behavioral and cognitive competencies in a systematic way to differences in the human versus monkey brain, he makes the following important observation: "It is likely, for example, that the fine digital dexterity and power grip of humans are due to specific phylogenetic changes in the human corticospinal tract (Heffner & Masterton, 1983). Similarly, the phylogenetic co-option of the prefrontal cortex into the vocal control system probably facilitated the emergence of symbolic language during hominid evolution (Deacon, 1998). More generally, it seems reasonable to speculate that the phylogenetic enlargement of the prefrontal cortex in modern humans has enhanced their ability to inhibit automatic responses, form symbolic representations of external objects, monitor the contents of working memory, and plan courses of action (see Deacon, 1998; Owen, Doyon, Petrides, & Evans, 1996; Owen et al., 1999)"

(Strieder, 2004, pp. 15–16). These impressive developments, however, are built upon brain structures that function to meet the basic biological needs of the organism. These structures include the spinal cord, brain stem, cerebellum, basal ganglia, hypothalamus, thalamus, fornix, mammillary bodies, amygdala, hippocampus, and septal nuclei.

MacLean (1990) describes the human brain as a "triune brain" (i.e., consisting of three layers of evolutionary development). He describes these layers as "reptilian," paleomammalian (limbic system), and neomammalian. The reptilian brain allows for sustaining of "autonomic functions" but influences behavior in a stereotypical manner. This is seen in various subroutines of behavior that are used for defending territory, courtship, and fighting behaviors. As one goes up the phylogenetic ladder, more complex behaviors are observed in pre-primates and "early" primates (the paleomammalian brain). They include such activities as "grooming," "hoarding," "breeding," and collective actions involved in flocking and migratory behaviors. Emotional reactions seem to influence several primary cooperative behaviors related to social interactions to sustain survival. As we progress into the neomammalian stage of development, the behaviors become more complex and include harassing others, developing routines that can become "rituals," re-enacting certain events (by repetitive behaviors such as dances, drawings, and storytelling), and using deceit to get one's personally perceived needs/desires met.

The development of language (spoken and written), the capacity to inhibit a behavior as the social situation demands, and the ability to plan actions without immediate "limbic" input clearly reflect important developments of the human brain that define our "humanness." Yet, all of this is done in connection with other human beings. Thus, the early emotional/motivational experiences that allow for human bonding (Bowlby, 1969, 1973, 1980) and the "separation cry" of primates when deprived of their mother (MacLean, 1985) lay a universal "imprint" on how we act, feel, and think. Tomasello et al. (2005) also suggest another important feature of human behavior: We develop in a manner that allows us to understand the intentions of others and to form shared intentional activities. They also suggest that we are psychologically motivated to do so, but it takes time to develop these human characteristics.

Beginning with early childhood and then developing over the life span, human beings across all cultures want to eventually know who they are (identity issue), where they came from (their biological and cultural beginnings), and how they can best survive and sustain life while creating human life (the basic struggles of daily living). They also want to know why they behave in certain ways (the process of self-reflection, particularly when personal and interpersonal problems emerge) and what is the meaning of their life (spiritual and religious strivings). These universal questions of the human mind have been recorded throughout history and seem to become relevant in a human being's life when the experience of consciousness of the self and the others emerges. This forms the basis by which humans begin to reflect on themselves and their social situations.

THE IMPORTANCE OF CONSCIOUSNESS AND SELF-REFLECTION FOR HUMAN NATURE

Individuals often reflect back on their first memories in life. These early memories often have important personal meaning to the individual. Not uncommonly, these partially remembered experiences seem to influence behavior later in life, as both psychoanalytic (Freud, 1900) and behavioral theorists (Watson & Rayner, 1920) have demonstrated. In some instances, emotionally charged experiences in childhood may continue to influence patterns of adult behavior not immediately recognized by the individual. For example, psychoanalytic (Bettelheim, 1989) and Jungian therapists (Dieckmann & Matthews, 1986) have clinically demonstrated how certain fairy tales that greatly appealed to children when read to them correlated with later adult behavioral patterns that were not immediately obvious to the person but became so during psychotherapy.

Awareness of the self and others, memories of emotionally important personal experiences, and the struggle to understand the meaning of those events or experiences play an important role in human behavior. The development of language helps the child reconstruct what he or she remembered and emotionally experienced and also "make sense out of" that experience. Remember that the language used was taught by the parents (or their representatives). Thus, the parents' view of the world (reflected in what they said and did with the child) often becomes, or at least greatly influences, the child's view of the world. As the child begins to think for him- or herself, the child may challenge the parental view of the world, but the influence remains in some format.

It is important to note that it is natural for human beings to understand their life in terms of the relationship they had with their parents and the social–cultural environment that they and their parents inhabited. There can be no psychological care of another human being without understanding this relationship "in general" and how it applies to a given person "in particular."

The brain circuitry underlying human consciousness and our capacity for self-reflection or awareness is not well understood (Prigatano, 2010). Yet it appears to include our ability to retrieve "old memories" and compare them "online" (or in working memory) with present perceptions of our self. It is a constant comparison system in which the "old" with the "now" representations enter conscious experience and "produce" what we refer to as self-awareness. As such, this self-awareness or consciousness appears to be an "emergent brain function" (Sperry, 1969). It is important to note that this comparison system is not static. If fluctuates in its mental images and associated affective valences while still maintaining a unitary "sense of self" in humans. Language can change those mental images and alter the affective valences, at least momentarily and sometimes over a long period of time. This is a very important aspect of our human nature and psychological care.

People often experience some "normal" emotional ambivalence regarding themselves, their beliefs, and their relationships to others. Humans are in a state of "psychological flux" that can easily shift thought patterns and emotional reactions. Thus, our sense of personal satisfaction and "happiness" can rapidly change and often does without us fully understanding why. More than one observer of human behavior has further noted that humans may consciously "seek happiness," but at the same time their behavior appears to foster "unhappiness" in their life (Watzlawick, 1993). This is an important behavioral paradox observed in humans that must be reckoned with when providing psychological care for another human being.

This reality forces us to recognize another important component to our human nature and mental processes. Our behavior, thought processes, and emotional/motivational reactions may not always be under "conscious control" (Haidt, 2012; Rees, Kreiman, & Koch, 2002). This has been difficult for the rational mind to accept, but it is a reality seen every day in psychological clinics and in human interaction. We often get a "glimpse" of this reality as we interact with various individuals over time and start to recognize (if we are lucky) recurring patterns of behaving and reacting that have no logical (i.e., conscious) explanation. Since the turn of the 20th century, the writings of Sigmund Freud, Alfred Adler, and C. J. Jung have helped us make sense of this characteristic of human beings. More is said about this reality in later chapters, but here it is important to mention it as part of the list of universal characteristics that constitute human nature.

THE SOCIAL "HEIGHTS" AND DESTRUCTIVE ASPECTS OF HUMAN NATURE

Although the biological analysis of what constitutes the CNS and how early life experiences may be of great help in understanding human beings, Luria (as cited in Cole & Cole, 1979) in his last book wrote, "I finally concluded that it was an error to assume that one can deduce human behavior from the biological 'depths' of mind, excluding its social 'heights'" (p. 24).

As people function in groups (small and large), their behavior can and often does change in response to environmental contingencies (Haidt, 2012). Although individual biological and psychological needs may initially predominate, the interpersonal interactions with others can result in people not focusing on their own needs but, rather, focusing on the needs of others. In fact, for many, the personal sense of "meaning in life" may come from this interaction. During these times, it is common for people to try to protect and care for others. There is frequently a personal sense of satisfaction with the self and life in general when one's behavior is perceived as substantially improving the quality of life of another. This can be seen in how parents care for their children, how children care for their aging parents, and how husband and wife care for each other. Social organizations that attempt to meet the needs of "the many" also represent the "social heights" to which Luria was referring. Various political organizations and types of governmental societies often view themselves as the leaders of this humane approach to human existence. Religious leaders who encourage others to help the poor and be merciful toward those who offend or hurt them are other examples of this important part of human nature.

There is, of course, the opposite polarity observed in human beings when they enter groups. As kind and humane as people can be, they can be equally destructive. In the name of God and one's religion, any human atrocity can be performed on another human being or large numbers of human beings, as history of the human race has repeatedly demonstrated and continues to demonstrate to this day. In the name of national pride and revenge, any destructive act is viewed not only as excusable but also as needed. This existential struggle to understand the opposing constructive versus destructive forces/motives/needs of human beings has been the focus of many, but it is perhaps best expressed in the work of artists. Paul Gauguin, the French post-Impressionist artist, reportedly struggled with the apparent contradictory forces of opposites experienced by people in their everyday lives that seem to produce so much human misery. This defining feature of human behavior is also found in the writings of Dostoyevsky (particularly *The Brothers Karamazov* [1880]), which provide powerful descriptions of destructive aspects of human nature.

HUMAN NATURE IN LIGHT OF ANIMAL COGNITION

More than one insightful scientist has argued that to understand human nature, one must integrate insights from animal behavior (Lorenz, 1937; Striedter, 2004). Premack (2007) provided a systematic analysis comparing the similarities and differences of various cognitive functions observed in humans compared to other animals. Premack noted that although certain animals are observed to "teach" their young how to stalk and eat other animals, the steps taken are aimed at behavior modification to achieve a specific goal. In humans, teaching of their young consists of three more complex related functions: observing, making judgments regarding observed behaviors, and taking steps to modify behaviors. These activities require practice and repetition. The goal is not just to make an immediate change in a specific behavior but also to influence different classes of behavior to achieve multiple and even different goals at the same time.

For example, teaching basic self-hygiene not only circumvents certain illnesses or diseases but also makes one more physically attractive to others. In turn, it increases self-esteem and fosters a desire to be attentive to other self-care needs. It also results in praise from parents, who reinforce a sense of group membership and security. The proposed algorithm suggested previously can be easily applied to more complicated behaviors. Premack's (2007) major point is that practice and teaching go together for humans. According to Premack, this is not observed in chimpanzees.

Most important for the current discussion, however, is Premack's (2007) argument that human beings are able to develop complex social interactions because they have a well-developed "theory of mind" capacity not seen in other animals. Moreover, the use of language expands this capacity. We, as humans, observe others' behavior and draw conclusions about what they are experiencing and what they may do in the future. We use language to test our hypotheses and to persuade others before they act.

We also use language to describe quantity and are able to develop mathematical models that help us predict events in the future as well as reveal relationships found in nature that are not easily observed in the "here and now" (Tononi, 2008). Some have suggested that human beings are really *Homo negotiates* because as a species we are "keen to count and compare" (Rochat, 2005, p. 714). Finally, via language and an expanded theory of mind capacity, we develop empathy for others' suffering. This may be the basis of our sense of morality, which is crucial for peaceful human coexistence.

HUMAN NATURE: A BRIEF SUMMARY

Although human beings share many biological and psychological characteristics with other animals, particularly primates, some important differences are noted. The human brain has evolved neurocircuits that allow for problem-solving with less input from deeper, limbic structures. The parietal area, particularly the inferior parietal lobe, is an important structure for integrating visual, auditory, and tactile information. The beginnings of written language seem dependent on this shift in brain evolution.

The prefrontal cortex has further developed to allow for the inhibition of automatic responses that may aid survival and further develop the capacity for problem-solving. Various courses of action can be thought about or written down before action is taken. Likewise, humans can anticipate the thoughts and actions of others, which has obvious survival value. Humans can achieve shared intentionality with others.

The parietal–frontal regions of the brain appear to play an important role in self-reflection, monitoring of one's thoughts, feelings, and actions (Prigatano, 2014). They are important for learning motor skills necessary for operating complex tools and instruments (Greene, 2005). Thus, it has been suggested that integration of parietal and frontal lobe development may constitute the essential substrate for what has been labeled "biological intelligence" (Halstead, 1947; Jung & Haier, 2007).

It is the development and use of language within a given cultural setting, however, that seem to alter brain functional capacities and particularly influence social interactions. Language depends on multiple brain circuits that interconnect frontal, parietal, temporal, and occipital regions of the brain. Recent work in the cognitive neurosciences suggests that the white matter fibers that connect frontal–parietal regions (i.e., the arcuate fasciculus) may play an important role in the phonological aspects of language (i.e., correctly repeating what we hear). Another fiber tract connecting frontotemporal and occipital regions (i.e., the left inferior fronto-occipital fasciculus) may play an important role in understanding what one hears (i.e., the semantic meaning of detected verbalizations; Almairac, Herbet, Moritz-Gasser, de Champfleur, & Duffau, 2015).

These highly defined neural networks, however, appear to serve the more primitive brain structures/functions necessary to sustain life in a changing external environment. They help human beings deal with basic needs of finding food, water, and shelter. They play a key role in managing aggressive and sexual impulses at different stages of development within the context of specific civilizations and cultures. They play an important role in recording history through writings, dance, and storytelling to help sustain a sense of identify based on one's ancestral past.

Ultimately, these brain structures are capable of developing symbols that form a type of language, but they may go beyond the conscious use of a language (Jung, 1964). These symbols have reoccurred throughout the ages and reflect on many recurring human experiences that demand external representation. These symbols can guide human behavior for the better or the worse (Prigatano, 1999). For example, people can save the life of another based on their religious beliefs or take that life, irrespective of that other person's actual behavior toward them. In fact, one of the most interesting and disturbing aspects of human nature is that human beings appear to function in a more irrational (i.e., not logical and conscious) manner compared to the "lower animals," whose behavior is much more predictable (Hebb, 1974). Thus, human beings, with their advanced cognitive processes, live in a state of psychological flux, in which constructive and destructive impulses emerge quickly and without obvious conscious control. Freud recognized that this makes the prediction of an individual's behavior in different circumstances quite difficult (Pribram & Gill, 1976).

Box 2.1 summarizes 10 features of human nature in light of the information and observations reviewed in this chapter. It is proposed that these 10 features are relevant to the psychological care of people.

Box 2.1. Ten Features of Human Nature That Have Relevance for the Psychological Care of Individuals Before and After a Brain Disorder

1. Humans universally need to move and manipulate objects (for food, shelter, avoiding danger, and finding and engaging in mating behaviors).
2. Humans universally need to communicate with others (via verbal and/or written language) to allow for group activities necessary for biological and social survival of the individual and the group.
3. Humans universally need to use the language and bonding experiences with their primary caregivers (typically mother and/or father) to construct their first sense of reality.
4. Humans universally need to develop their cognitive capacities in order to produce and exchange symbolic expressions of what they experience or imagine (e.g., mathematic equations, storytelling, drawings, sculptures, music, and rituals) to enhance problem-solving and to solidify group membership. These symbols can reflect both conscious and unconscious strivings of individuals.
5. Humans universally need to develop conscious awareness of others and of the self that allows for advanced problem-solving (in the present as well as in the future).
6. Humans universally struggle with answering "key" questions concerning their existence. Where did I come from (biological and cultural identity)? Who am I now (personal identity)? What must I do to best "ensure" my own survival and sustain human life of others (i.e., meet the basic struggles of daily living)? Why do I behave the way I do (the process of self-reflection particularly when faced with conflict or personal losses)? What is the meaning of my life (spiritual or religious strivings)?
7. Humans universally experience a consciousness that is in a state of constant psychological flux while paradoxically experiencing a "unified" sense of self (i.e., there is one "me" but paradoxical and opposing "sides" to me that I directly and indirectly observe).
8. Humans universally demonstrate that their behavior is not always under "conscious control." Consciously, they may seek one goal, but their behavior may paradoxically result in achieving an opposing or a different goal.
9. Humans universally can be empathetic to the needs of others and be equally destructive toward others.
10. Humans universally have had experiences in life in which the need for meaning in life may become more important than the need to sustain their own life.

PSYCHOLOGICAL CARE OF HUMANS IN LIGHT OF THEIR NATURE

The psychological care of an individual must directly or indirectly incorporate or address each of the 10 common features of human beings listed in Box 2.1. In many ways, these essential features determine the degree to which psychological care is possible. People's life history, the stage of life in which they are in, and whether or not they have suffered specific types of brain disorders will determine which of the 10 universal human experiences are most important to focus on and in what order of priority. At this point, however, it is important to emphasize that effective psychological care helps the individual pursue the natural "goals of the central nervous system" to the degree to which it appears practical and possible.

Human nature is such that efforts at psychological care are not always welcomed. There is both a "rational" and an "irrational" side to human thought and emotional/motivational reactions. There are also both conscious and unconscious influences on human behavior. The person can consciously seek "help" and yet behave in a way that undermines actually obtaining it. The same can be true of the caregivers of that person.

Human nature is such that efforts at psychological care must address the consciously and not consciously represented perceptions of the individual and their relationships to others. If the psychological intervention (or effort at care) is experienced as reducing the frustrations of the person and helping them obtain their personal goals, a bond can be built. That bond, however, will reflect both the positive and the negative bonding experiences that occurred much earlier in life for that individual (Prigatano, 2008).

Human nature is such that efforts at psychological care must help the person develop motor and language skills necessary for successful group membership and problem-solving. Related cognitive abilities (e.g., working memory) and impulse control need to be developed and sustained. Psychological care must reduce social isolation and foster physical and psychological independence, again to the degree to which it appears practical and possible.

Human nature is such that efforts at psychological care must foster a "learning attitude" within the individual for maintaining and protecting their psychological well-being over time. It fosters the process of decision-making by comparing options and different strategies when faced with a variety of problems. As such, it helps develop "advanced" problem-solving skills. Again, this is done to the degree to which it is practical and possible for a given individual considering their life's circumstances.

Human nature is such that efforts at psychological care must accommodate the natural "psychological flux" observed in human consciousness and, at times, paradoxical reactions. Humans will independently fluctuate in their mood state and ways of perceiving life's events. No form of psychological care will produce a "perfect sense" of well-being that is maintained forever. This is a part of the "human condition" and must be accepted as an existential reality of life.

Human nature is such that efforts at psychological care must face both constructive and destructive forces that exist in each human being. The process of improving self-awareness should help people understand their capacity to be loving and empathetic and their equal capacity to be angry and destructive. True knowledge of one's self can lead to decisions that greatly aid positive adjustment to life's problems even in the presence of "destructive" tendencies.

Finally, human nature is such that efforts at psychological care must address the "big questions" of life: Who am I? Where did I come from? What is the purpose of my existence? It is not always necessary to answer these questions for the person. Rather, the questions should be seriously considered by the person and their psychological caregiver. In some instances, the psychotherapeutic process can help individuals answer some of these questions for themselves and thereby aid the process of determining one's self-identity and purpose in life.

REFERENCES

Almairac, F., Herbet, G., Moritz-Gasser, S., de Champfleur, N. M., & Duffau, H. (2015). The left inferior fronto-occipital fasciculus subserves language semantics: A multilevel lesion study. *Brain Structure & Function, 220*(4), 1983–1989.

Bettelheim, B. (1989). *The uses of enchantment: The meaning and importance of fairy tales.* New York, NY: Vintage.

Blumenfeld, H. (2010). *Neuroanatomy through clinical cases.* Sunderland, MA: Sinauer.

Bowlby, J. (1969). *Attachment and loss, Volume I: Attachment.* New York, NY: Basic Books.

Bowlby, J. (1973). *Attachment and loss, Volume II: Separation.* New York, NY: Basic Books.

Bowlby, J. (1980). *Attachment and loss, Volume III: Loss.* New York, NY: Basic Books.

Catani, M., & ffytche, D. H. (2005). The rises and falls of disconnection syndromes. *Brain, 128*(10), 2224–2239.

Cole, M., & Cole, S. (Eds.). (1979). *A. R. Luria: The making of mind. A personal account of Soviet psychology.* Cambridge, MA: Harvard University Press.

Deacon, T. (1998). *The symbolic species: The coevolution of language and the human brain.* New York, NY: Norton.

Dieckmann, H., & Matthews, B. (1986). *Twice-told tales: The psychological use of fairy tales.* Wilmette, IL: Chiron.

Dostoyevsky, F. (1880). *The Brothers Karamazov* (D. McDuff, Trans.). London, UK: Penguin.

Freud, S. (1900). *The interpretation of dreams.* London, UK: Hogarth.

Goldstein, K. (1939). *The organism: A holistic approach to biology derived from pathological data in man.* New York, NY: American Book Company.

Greene, J. (2005). Apraxia, agnosias, and higher visual function abnormalities. *Journal of Neurology, Neurosurgery, and Psychiatry, 76*(Suppl. 5), v25–v34.

Haidt, J. (2012). *The righteous mind: Why good people are divided by politics and religion.* New York, NY: Vintage.

Halstead, W. C. (1947). *Brain and intelligence: A quantitative study of the frontal lobes.* Chicago, IL: University of Chicago Press.

Hebb, D. O. (1974). What psychology is about. *The American Psychologist, 29*(2), 71–79.

Heffner, R. S., & Masterton, R. B. (1983). The role of the corticospinal tract in the evolution of human digital dexterity. *Brain, Behavior and Evolution, 23*(3–4), 165–183.

Jung, C. G. (1964). *Man and his symbols.* London, UK: Aldus.

Jung, R. E., & Haier, R. J. (2007). The parieto-frontal integration theory (P-FIT) of intelligence: Converging neuroimaging evidence. *Behavioral and Brain Sciences, 30*(2), 135–154.

Lorenz, K. (1937). On the formation of the concept of instinct. *Natural Sciences, 25*(19), 289–300.

Luria, A. R. (1932). *The nature of human conflicts or emotion, conflict and will* (W. H. Gantt, Trans.). New York, NY: Liveright.

MacLean, P. D. (1985). Brain evolution relating to family, play, and the separation call. *Archives of General Psychiatry, 42*(4), 405–417.

MacLean, P. D. (1990). *The triune brain in evolution: Role in paleocerebral functions.* New York, NY: Springer.

McAdams, D. P., & Pals, J. L. (2006). A new Big Five: Fundamental principles for an integrative science of personality. *The American Psychologist, 61*(3), 204–217.

Newcombe, F. (2002). An overview of neuropsychological rehabilitation: A forgotten past and a challenging future. In W. Brouwer, E. van Zomeren, I. Berg, A. Bouma, & E. de Haan (Eds.), *Cognitive rehabilitation: A clinical neuropsychological approach* (pp. 23–51). Amsterdam, the Netherlands: Boom.

Owen, A. M., Doyon, J., Petrides, M., & Evans, A. C. (1996). Planning and spatial working memory: A positron emission tomography study in humans. *European Journal of Neuroscience, 8*(2), 353–364.

Owen, A. M., Herrod, N. J., Menon, D. K., Clark, J. C., Downey, S. P., Carpenter, T. A., . . . Robbins, T. W. (1999). Redefining the functional organization of working memory processes within human lateral prefrontal cortex. *European Journal of Neuroscience, 11*(2), 567–574.

Paxinos, G., & Mai, J. K. (Eds.). (2004). *The human nervous system* (2nd ed.). San Diego, CA: Academic Press.

Premack, D. (2007). Human and animal cognition: Continuity and discontinuity. *Proceedings of the National Academy of Sciences of the USA, 104*(35), 13861–13867.

Pribram, K. H., & Gill, M. M. (1976). *Freud's "Project" re-assessed: Preface to contemporary cognitive theory and neuropsychology.* New York, NY: Basic Books.

Prigatano, G. P. (1999). *Principles of neuropsychological rehabilitation.* New York, NY: Oxford University Press.

Prigatano, G. P. (2008). The problem of not developing normally and pediatric neuropsychological rehabilitation: The Mitchell Rosenthal Lecture. *Journal of Head Trauma Rehabilitation, 23*(6), 414–422.

Prigatano, G. P. (2010). *The study of anosognosia.* New York, NY: Oxford University Press.

Prigatano, G. P. (2014). Anosognosia and patterns of impaired self-awareness observed in clinical practice. *Cortex, 61,* 81–92.

Rees, G., Kreiman, G., & Koch, C. (2002). Neural correlates of consciousness in humans. *Nature Reviews Neuroscience, 3*(4), 261–270.

Rochat, P. (2005). Humans evolved to become *Homo negotiatus* . . . the rest followed. [Commentary]. *Behavioral and Brain Sciences, 28*(5), 714–715.

Sapir, E. (1949). *Selected writings of Edward Sapir in language, culture and personality.* Berkeley, CA: University of California Press.

Sperry, R. W. (1969). A modified concept of consciousness. *Psychological Review, 76*(6), 532–536.

Striedter, G. F. (2004). Brain evolution. In G. Paxinos & J. K. Mai (Eds.), *The human nervous system* (2nd ed., pp. 3–21). San Diego, CA: Academic Press.

Tomasello, M., Carpenter, M., Call, J., Behne, T., & Moll, H. (2005). Understanding and sharing intentions: The origins of cultural cognition. *Behavioral and Brain Sciences, 28*(5), 675–691.

Tononi, G. (2008). Consciousness as integrated information: A provisional manifesto. *Biological Bulletin, 215*(3), 216–242.

Watson, J. B., & Rayner, R. (1920). Conditioned emotional reactions. *Journal of Experimental Psychology, 3*(1), 1–14.

Watzlawick, P. (1993). *The situation is hopeless, but not serious: The pursuit of unhappiness.* New York, NY: Norton.

3

THE EVOLUTION OF NORMAL BRAIN–BEHAVIOR RELATIONSHIPS

INTRODUCTION

In Chapter 2, several features of human nature were summarized in light of the "natural plan of the central nervous system." Ten features of human nature were identified that have relevance for the psychological care of individuals before and after a brain disorder. In this chapter, the evolution of brain–behavior relationships is further considered from both phylogenetic and ontological perspectives. This is a complex topic, but selected observations of several investigators are summarized to provide a context in which to understand how changes in brain–behavior relationships may have evolved and ultimately underlie some of the important psychosocial competencies during the human life span. The psychological care of a person with a brain disorder is in part dictated by their age and associated psychosocial skills when efforts at psychological care are attempted.

THE EVOLUTION OF HIGHER INTEGRATIVE BRAIN FUNCTIONS

Merlin Donald (1991) made the insightful observation that cognitive scientists have not been concerned with questions pertaining to the origins of cognition in humans. Yet the study of origins is often a mainstream interest in other areas of science, as witnessed by our preoccupation with understanding the origins of the universe (Hawking, 1996). Understanding the origins of cognitive development may provide insights into understanding how the human "mind" is structured, how it is altered by the environment, and how, in turn, it may alter the environment. The natural starting point for this discussion is the writings of Charles Darwin (1859) because his perspective has continued to dominate our current scientific paradigm for understanding the origins of human life.

Donald (1991) notes that Darwin was captivated with the natural "continuity" of life forms and their modifications by means of a process he referred to as "natural selection." Darwin believed that intellectual abilities developed very gradually and that humans tend to underestimate the cognitive abilities of other animals. Dogs in particular were known to demonstrate many complex emotional reactions with associated learned behaviors that appear to reflect important, underlying cognitive processes. Affection and, at times, shame could readily be seen in their actions/responses. Their protective qualities and dedication to their masters can be quite impressive, as dog owners have repeatedly reported throughout the years. Darwin also observed that monkeys were capable of deceit and at times demonstrated clear signs of intellectual curiosity. The capacity for focused attention was another cognitive capacity observed in both humans and animals. Yet, Darwin argued that the capacity to maintain a "long train of thought" seemed improbable without the development of language. Finally, Darwin was intrigued with how vocal sounds, including changes in tone and volume, reflected the emotional and motivational states of animals. Rudimentary bird songs were especially interesting and believed to possibly represent the earliest precursors of language.

Donald (1991) goes on to note that Darwin believed that the range of emotional expressions on humans' faces far exceeds those of animals. Their vocal sounds associated with different emotional/motivational states also seem to exceed those of other animals. Humans may have first produced those sounds via imitation, but later they appeared to produce and modify these sounds via intended, voluntary actions. This was an important modification achieved during the evolutionary process and represents a key feature of "higher" brain function. These and other observations led Darwin to speculate about how language might have emerged over the course of evolution.

According to Donald (1991), "Darwin knew that animal communication—for instance, bird song—is not always fixed; the particular notes of a bird song must be learned, just as the specifics of any human language must be learned" (p. 32). But how did this learning process begin? Donald presents some intriguing ideas. He suggests that the intention to communicate must have evolved first, before refinements in the vocalization capacity and apparatus of early humans would allow for speech to evolve (i.e., the use of meaningful sounds for purposes of communications in different contexts). He argues that song predated speech because it reflected the emotional state of the animal. Song expressed emotions and in so doing often involved limb movements that later developed into dance and possibly rituals. These may have been the early precursors of later cultural activities necessary for group identity and survival.

When the vocal apparatus developed to allow for rudimentary sequences of sound in song, early hominids had more control over communication efforts. Vocalizations could now not only convey emotions and intended actions associated with emotional and motivational states but also be used to convey information for a variety of purposes. For example, different vocalizations could signal the presence of danger, the location of food, the presence of a potentially receptive mate, and group membership.

In summary, from this perspective, emotions and associated movements came first in the evolution of the higher integrative brain functions. Feelings reflecting biological urges necessary to sustain and produce life led to a series of simple and then progressively more complex actions involving the entire body. For primates and later for humans, this culminated in bipedalism and the highly developed use of the hands for tool making and then perhaps drawing and later writing. It also contributed to the development of motor systems involved in vocalization that allowed for the construction of complex sounds. Those sounds could then be used to initiate and signal actions of a nonvocal nature. This was the emergence of spoken language.

Donald (1991) makes the fascinating comment that Darwin "presents us with an evolutionary dilemma: Language is supposed to depend upon rudimentary cognitive abilities that were useful before humans possessed speech and that nevertheless depend upon speech for their full expression" (p. 42). The important question or paradox then becomes the following: What is the nature of this intellectual or cognitive ability that makes language possible but yet cannot adequately develop until language develops?

The answer, in part, may relate to the phylogenetic enlargement of the prefrontal cortex in modern humans, as suggested by Striedter (2004; see also Chapter 2, this volume). Fuster (1997) extensively summarized (and studied) the anatomy, physiology, and neuropsychology of the frontal lobes. He noted that the prefrontal cortex plays a complicated role in attention, working memory, and what he refers to as "motor set and control." The primary, overarching functional activity of the prefrontal cortex, however, is described as the "temporal organization of behavior" (p. 4). That is, it is devoted to action and the inhibition of action to aid learning and survival. It does this by performing actions or inhibiting actions in some organized and sequential manner that is time efficient and time sensitive to environmental pressures.

Such a system would clearly be important for informed, quick, and efficient sequences of motor movements involved in vocalization and other forms of problem-solving. The system would be crucial for developing plans of action (which in some cases would include delayed action necessary for observational learning and avoidance of danger). Such skills would be vital to surviving in groups. When these skills are severely compromised, social isolation would be expected, and this in fact has been reported in both monkeys with surgically induced brain lesions (Franzen & Myers, 1973) and humans who suffer severe traumatic brain injury (Prigatano, 1999).

In his later work, Fuster (2003) suggested that the emergence of cortical networks in humans has evolved for complex associations that are at the core of memory and problem-solving (including abstract reasoning). This early form of learning is referred to today as operant conditioning. In short form, operant conditioning works on a simple paradigm: "If this, then that." If a certain behavior is performed or spontaneously occurs, a certain consequence may follow in close time proximity. The consequence helps determine if the behavior will occur in the future. If the associations become more complex, the chain of associations can be expanded: "If this, then that; if that, then this" (J. Fuster's observations in a lecture given at Barrow Neurological Institute in November 2004). Now a string of contingencies may occur, and if vocalizations (including inner speech) allow these contingencies to be maintained in working memory, one can easily understand how language helps develop the prefrontal cortex-mediated activities and, in turn, the mediated activities of the prefrontal cortex may well be necessary for language to develop. This line of reasoning helps resolve the paradox Darwin presented and Donald (1991) and others (e.g., Fuster, 2003) have helped answer.

Box 3.1 lists a series of proposed evolutionary (i.e., phylogenetic) changes underlying the development of higher integrative brain functions (HIBFs) in humans. Brief references to the brain structures that appear to play a pivotal role in their execution or development are also included. The HIBFs are, of course, not static and change with time in humans. The changes have been repeatedly linked to the age of the individual. The correlation between phylogenetic developments in brain anatomy and function with ontogenetic brain development in humans has been noted by others (Paxinos & Mai, 2004). Selected ontological findings regarding brain anatomy and functions in humans are thus briefly reviewed.

Box 3.1. Proposed Evolutionary Perspective on the Development of Higher Integrative Brain Functions in Humans

1. In the beginning, it was not "the word" but, rather, the feeling and the movements. Deep (phylogenetic old) brain structures involving the limbic system (e.g., the thalamus, cingulate gyrus, and insular cortex) signaled via feeling states the homeostatic condition and needs of the organism. When the homeostatic status of the organism has to be adjusted for survival reasons, subjectively experienced feeling states lead to movements to restore homeostatic balance.
2. Self-initiated movements, reflecting feeling states, often had consequences that aided or impeded personal and social learning. The striatum of the brain has been linked to this very rudimentary form of learning (Baez-Mendoza & Schultz, 2013; Squire & Dede, 2015). It consists of a very simple paradigm: "If this, then that." This type of learning is called operant conditioning.
3. There are also movements (i.e., responses) that are a result of environmental changes (e.g., eye blinks when air hits the eye). These movements (responses) can be paired with either pleasant or unpleasant experiences, which also alter the action/movement sequence. This type of learning has been called "classical conditioning" and appears primarily dependent on "cerebellum and associated brain stem circuitry" (Squire & Dede, 2015, p. 8).
4. Movements became progressively more complex, with hand and finger dexterity showing notable changes in humans. The use of the index finger and the thumb appears to have special significance in human development and often reflects a growing association of frontal, parietal, and basal ganglia structures.
5. Sequences of movements that push air in and out of the airways through the mouth can result in rhythmic sounds, further reflecting the "need states" of the organism. Although initially "automatic," they became modified by their consequences (i.e., the gradual development of the ability to learn to make certain sounds and control those sounds). Changes in volume and pitch appeared to reflect the emotional/motivational state of the animal and were later referred to as "songs."
6. Auditory perception and understanding the meanings of these rhythmical sounds became very important for survival. The temporal regions of the brain may play an especially important role in the recognition of these sound patterns.
7. These sound patterns also became associated with limb movements. They are thought to have evolved into dance, which is a semi-automatic limb/motor response when listening to certain sounds (or songs).
8. Sounds (songs) and dance stimulated group cohesion and bonding. They formed the basis of evolving rituals on which cultures develop (Darwin, 1859; Donald, 1991). Again, the striatum, which includes ventral medial prefrontal cortex, appears to play an especially important role in this type of behavior, which is necessary for social learning (Baez-Mendoza & Schultz, 2013).
9. Rudimentary song appeared to be the precursor of speech and, later, language. As control over the vocalizations occurred via learning (i.e., articulated sounds), the observations and intentions of the animal could be signaled vocally as well as through nonvocal means (gesturing and posturing).

10. The capacity for expressing intentions or controlling those expressions until the appropriate time and place becomes a key feature of human behavior necessary for sustaining social networks. The development of the prefrontal cortex has been implicated in this capacity of the human brain (Fuster, 2003).
11. The execution of movements to achieve certain goals of the organisms required enhanced attentional skills, working memory capacity, inhibitory control, associative learning, and efficient processing speeds of performance. Multiple memory systems (Squire & Dede, 2015) and attentional systems (Peterson & Posner, 2012) are involved in these coordinated activities.
12. The ability to produce a variety of speech sounds that had different meanings became the hallmark of a well-developed language system. Spoken language served two purposes: It conveyed to others what the person wanted to express, and it allowed the person to "hear" what they were saying (i.e., experiencing). This latter capacity, as discussed in Chapter 10, is crucial to the psychological care of the person before and after a brain disorder.
13. The recording of spoken language allowed for a reconstruction of what was once said or experienced and became the foundation of "laws" and "agreements." Some have suggested that the recording of spoken language enhanced "working memory" in everyday life, which in turn increased our problem-solving capacities (Donald, 2001).
14. Although much of human learning initially required intentional observing and doing, once certain actions reliably resulted in achieving certain goals, "automatic" response sequences occurred to solve a problem or deal with an environmental demand (Squire & Dede, 2015).
15. The automatic, nonconscious aspect of human behavior involved both vocal and nonvocal responses and reflected previously experienced associated emotional/motivational states. Social psychologists have termed this capacity (unconscious) behavioral guidance systems (Bargh & Morsella, 2008).
16. These automatic, nonconscious aspects of human behavior became templates for behavioral choices. The reactions could have positive and negative effects from apparently simple activities, such as eating certain foods, to more complex activities associated with emotional bonding, establishing group memberships, and choice of work activities. The striatum of the brain appears especially important for this type of "habit learning" (Squire & Dede, 2015).
17. Symbols developed to reflect the conscious, thoughtful responses/reactions of individuals. The neocortex and especially the medial temporal lobe may play an important role in this type of "declarative" memory (Squire & Dede, 2015). With time, however, symbols can also reflect the unconscious emotional relevance of an event or object for a given person that initially involved amygdala input as well (Squire & Dede, 2015).
18. Ultimately, humans began to self-reflect, given their language and symbolic skills, and thereby asked basic existential questions regarding their existence. This is perhaps the most complex and uniquely human form of higher integrative brain activity and requires integration of multiple brain systems.

ONTOLOGICAL DEVELOPMENT OF THE HUMAN BRAIN: EMBRYONIC CONSIDERATIONS

The development of the central nervous system in humans is a complicated but rapid process (Müller & O'Rahilly, 2004). At approximately 2 weeks post fertilization, the "neural plate" can be identified. By 4 weeks post fertilization, the neural tube begins to form. Embryonic brain development is initially identified as a three-vesicle stage (at 4 weeks), followed by a five-vesicle stage (at 6 weeks) during which regions of the telencephalon, diencephalon, metencephalon, myelencephalon, and spinal cord are observed. The outward development of brain structures during this time frame is relatively easy to visualize. The inner development of cellular formation and the growth and differentiation of neurons and their synaptic connections are clearly more complicated and challenging to understand.

A complex pattern of genetic influences determines the formation of various cells and their synaptic arrangements that make up different brain regions with different patterns of cytoarchitectural formations (Zilles, 2004). Neuronal migration also develops early and is thought to largely be complete by 26–29 weeks after fertilization (Tau & Peterson, 2010). Adding to this dynamic complexity is the "remarkable intersubject variability of the human cerebral cortex" as it relates to both the gross morphology and the microstructure of the brain (Roland et al., 1997, p. 222).

An important analogy is that although humans normally develop to have two eyes, one nose, and one mouth, these are clearly unique (individual) features across people's faces. The basic underlying structures responsible for these organs are essentially the same, but great variability in phenotypic characteristics can be readily observed. The same is true with regard to the development and formation of all humans brains and associated neuropsychological functions. Thus, when discussing normal brain changes and related neuropsychological changes, individual differences have to be constantly considered. This is especially important when measuring neuropsychological functions and interpreting what is "normal" during the various stages of development.

ONTOLOGICAL DEVELOPMENT: POSTNATAL BRAIN AND BEHAVIOR CHANGES OBSERVED IN INFANTS, SCHOOL-AGE CHILDREN, AND ADOLESCENTS

Gogtay et al. (2004) note that phylogenetically older brain areas mature earlier in the human brain than in the newer structures. Specifically, the higher order association areas of the cortex mature only after the "lower order" somatosensory and visual cortices show enhanced stages of development. Some have suggested that primary visual cortical networks may develop more rapidly than primary motor networks in humans (Angulo-Barroso & Tiernan, 2008; Gervan, Berencsi, & Kovacs, 2011; Iliescu & Dannemiller, 2008).

Casey, Galvan, and Hare (2005) summarize many important observations related to human brain development and behavior. Figure 3.1 illustrates some of these changes.

Initial proliferation and migration of cells occur mostly during fetal development, as noted previously. Nature gives the human brain a very large number of neurons, typically estimated to be at least 100 billion (Herculano-Houzel, 2009), which are used to form various neural circuits necessary for survival and learning (Tau & Peterson, 2010). As this occurs, some available neurons die (approximately 20–80%, depending on the brain region studied) while new and densely organized synaptic connections are formed. Kolb and Fantie (2009) outline four distinct phases of development: "(1) the birth of neurons (neurogenesis), (2) the migration of neurons to their correct location, (3) the differentiation of neurons into different types and their subsequent maturation of connections and (4) the pruning back of connections and cells themselves"

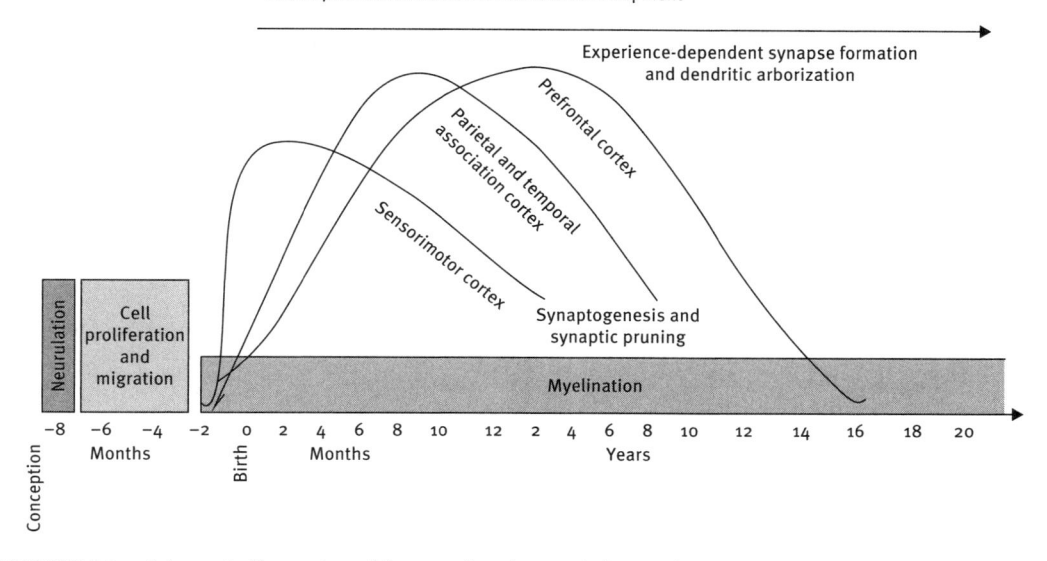

FIGURE 3.1 Schematic illustration of the complex changes in human brain anatomy occurring over time as summarized by Casey, Tottenham, et al. (2005) (See color plates).

Source: Reprinted from *Trends in Cognitive Sciences*, 9(3), Casey, B., Tottenham, N., Liston, C., & Durston, S., Imaging the developing brain: What have we learned about cognitive development?, p. 104–110, Copyright (2005), with permission from Elsevier.

(p. 21). Edelman (1987) refers to this as neural Darwinism or the theory of neuronal group selection. This complicated process appears, in part, to be under genetic control as well as being experience dependent. That is, the nature of the stimulus inputs that the human brain encounters early in life influences this process of neuronal connectivity/neurocircuitry.

As Figure 3.1 illustrates, the sensorimotor cortex shows major synaptogenesis and synaptic pruning during the first few months of life. By 12 months, the human infant often can walk a few steps unaided. During this time, the first few words are normally spoken. Vocal, rhythmic sounds precede the first spoken words, which later have meaning attached to them (i.e., the development of language per se). Movement of the legs and arms, the ability to produce sounds, and the apparent use of emotions/ motivations to guide those activities are seen in human development as they are seen in phylogenetic stages of development.

The temporal cortex is intimately involved in recording new experiences (e.g., memory) and hearing and detecting speech sounds. It is also rapidly changing during the first few months of life, but generally more time is required to reach maximum synaptogenesis and synaptic pruning.

This process can be seen in everyday life by observing infants and young children learning to walk, speak (or make sounds that have meaning), and develop a language. Parent often first speak to children with "baby talk" while holding or moving them to get their attention. The spoken words of the parent are typically made in a rhythmic manner to further evoke interest and positive feelings. This often occurs very early in life and before the infant or child can reciprocate with any clearly perceived imitative sound sequence. However, at some point the child emits sounds for which the parent typically imitates and adds modifications. The child often then imitates or repeats the sounds he or she hears the parent say. The process continues until an identifiable word is recognized by the parent and the child. Joy or some form of satisfaction is then expressed by both parties. The

Evolution of Normal Brain–Behavior Relationships • 37

child then begins to repeat the familiar sounds that reflect the beginnings of spoken language.

Posner and Rothbart (2007) summarize some of the research in this important area of study. They note that "sounds to which the infant is exposed tend to solidify and form a unit around prototypical phonemes in the language, whereas the ability to discriminate unfamiliar sound units from familiar ones begins to disappear" (pp. 211–212). They further make the important observation that "infants raised in English-speaking homes can maintain their ability to discriminate phonemes in a foreign language, such as Mandarin Chinese, if exposed to a speaker of those sounds" (pp. 211–212). This only occurs, however, when exposed to an actual person versus a video recording. The nature of the human, interpersonal interaction clearly influences how the brain develops and in so doing processes and acts on stimulus inputs that convert a disorganized sensory experience into a meaningful one that aids adaptation and survivability (as Vygotsky, Luria, Freud, and many others have noted throughout the years).

Casey, Galvan, et al. (2005) also note that the parietal and temporal association cortices have a prolonged time frame of synaptogenesis and synaptic pruning, extending to 4–8 years of life. It is during this time frame that children are introduced to schooling and begin to learn the basics of writing letters and numbers, reading, and, later, grammar and sentence structure. The concept of number quantity and the potential relationships between numbers (as revealed in the multiplication tables) are also introduced and expanded upon during this time.

As noted in Chapter 2, the development of the inferior parietal cortex is especially important for language development and the capacity for semantic meaning. Things, ideas, and words are now interconnected into a matrix of knowledge that can be added to as the child learns more about his or her cultural world and the ideas it attempts to convey.

Prefrontal cortex synaptogenesis and synaptic pruning are also occurring in parallel with these changes but take longer to develop. Children have to learn to "pay attention" and to inhibit responses that interfere with their observations/learning as well as the observations/learning of other children around them. Self-talk or "inner speech" seems to allow for greater control of behavior necessary for the development of impulse control, social judgment, and complex problem-solving when confronted with new information. Behaviorally, the HIBFs mediated via the prefrontal cortex are noted "to develop gradually in the course of ontogeny" (Fuster, 1997, p. 97).

Gogtay et al. (2004) note that "human brain development is structurally and functionally a nonlinear process" (p. 8174). They measured gray matter density changes in 13 healthy children between the ages of 4 and 21 years in a prospective, longitudinal manner. As noted by Casey, Tottenham, Liston, and Durston (2005), synaptic pruning resulted in the loss of neurons that occurs during the maturational process. Moreover, considerable gray matter volume loss begins to occur at approximately puberty. The process "begins first in dorsal parietal cortices, particularly the primary sensorimotor areas near the interhemispheric margin, and then spreads rostrally over the frontal cortex and caudally and laterally over the parietal, occipital, and finally the temporal cortex" (Casey, Tottenham, et al., 2005, p. 8175). Frontal and occipital poles lose gray matter early, whereas the dorsolateral prefrontal cortex does not show maximum loss until the end of adolescence. Casey, Tottenham, et al. note that the oldest of the cortical regions (from a phylogenetic perspective) show a loss of gray matter sooner than do other regions of the brain. During this time of gray matter loss, white matter increases, and it continues to do so for at least the first four decades of life. Because white matter or myelinated sheets have been related to speed of neuronal transmission, this may account for the increase in speed of information processing that is observed during childhood and adolescence (Kail, 1991).

Nagy, Westerberg, and Klingberg (2004) note that the myelination of axons is one of the most important events underlying brain development. This process is not uniform, and different rates of myelination have been reported for different regions of the brain, as first suggested by Flechsig in 1920 (cited in Nagy et al., 2004). Nagy and colleagues also report that the early work of Yakovlev and Lecours (1967) essentially confirmed Flechsig's observations and suggested that the normal development cycles of myelination may continue "even after 20 years of age" (p. 237).

Giedd et al. (2012) summarize a large number of observations concerning gray and white matter changes occurring in the brains of children and adolescents. They note differences between males and females and volume changes occurring in different regions of the brain. Although the total brain volume is at 95% of its peak value by age 6 years, the total cerebral volume is smaller in females and peaks earlier than in males. The authors note, however, "a striking feature of brain size measures is the high variability across individuals" (p. 17) with no obvious connection to functional abilities. Again, the total gray matter volume peaks at different time periods for boys and girls. These changes correlate with average earlier age of puberty in females compared to males, and thus the authors suggest that hormones may influence the various trajectories observed in brain development.

Hofman (2014) provides a useful review of primate brain evolution and notes specific morphological changes associated with the development of the human cortex. The phenomena of cortical folding, which is responsible for the formation of sulci and gyri, is viewed as necessary for increased connectivity between brain structures, allowing for faster processing speeds. This becomes an important characteristic of human brain development and later decline, as described later. He also notes that the cortical surface allocated to "higher order association cortex" compared to primary sensory and motor cortex is greatly expanded in humans. The increase in the complexity of cortical circuits appears to allow for more specialized hierarchical organization that is characteristic of the human brain.

Durston et al. (2006) suggest that there is a shift from diffuse to focal cortical activity that occurs throughout child development and culminates in the adult human brain. This dynamic process may account for many of the "classical" neuropsychological syndromes and associated findings observed in adults with focal brain injuries (Heilman & Valenstein, 2003). As the brain "ages," however, some important changes occur that parallel changes in neuropsychological functioning.

ONTOLOGICAL DEVELOPMENT: BRAIN AND BEHAVIOR CHANGES IN ADULTHOOD

It has been suggested that the human brain structural changes do not reach full maturity until the mid-20s (see the MIT Young Adult Development Project website at http://hr.mit.edu/static/worklife/youngadult). What is occurring in the brain during this time remains only partially understood. However, the same brain changes observed in adolescents seem to continue to occur in young adulthood, including increased myelination and continued adding and pruning of neuronal connections. Interconnections between prefrontal cortex and other regions of the brain appear to be enhanced as efficiency in problem-solving skills and greater emotional control become more common. The MIT Young Adult Development Project's website states,

> As a number of researchers have put it, "the rental car companies have it right." The brain isn't fully mature at 16, when we are allowed to drive, or at 18, when we are allowed to vote, or at 21, when we are allowed to drink, but closer to 25, when we are allowed to rent a car.

Numerous psychometric studies have noted that speed of information processing, including the speed of learning new information, rapidly improves in childhood and adolescence (Kail, 1991). Speed of fine motor movement involving the fingers and hand, as measured by such tasks as the Halstead Finger Tapping Test, also reaches its peak during this time frame, with slower speeds occurring throughout the aging process (for normative data, see Heaton, Grant, & Matthews, 1991). "Raw score" test performance on several subtests of the Wechsler Adult Intelligence Test IV (Wechsler, Coalson, & Raiford, 2008) that specifically require time-efficient problem-solving shows a similar pattern. Peak performance is often observed in the 20s to late 30s and declines thereafter. What may underlie these changes?

Westlye et al. (2009) studied white matter (WM) changes in the human brain, including fractional anisotropy (FA; indexing directional coherence of water displacement along WM tracts), over the life span (i.e., from age 8 to age 85 years). In their cross-sectional study, a sharp developmental increase in FA was observed between ages 8 and 28 years. The pattern appeared relatively stable into the late 40s. They further noted that WM volume peaks at approximately 50 years of age. FA starts to decline in the early 60s, with steady decline observed up to 75 years or older (Figure 3.2).

Given that FA measures consistently relate to speed and efficiency of information processing and learning (Burgmans et al., 2011; Turken et al., 2008), these findings "map on nicely" with the behavioral data noted previously. They may help explain a well-recognized deterioration of these functional capacities as the person ages.

Bishop, Lu, and Yankner (2010) explore the molecular mechanisms that may underlie the aging process in the human brain. They note, as have others before them (e.g., Morrison & Hof, 1997), that "neuronal loss is minimal in most cortical regions of the normal aging brain" (p. 530). One factor that may be responsible for the decline in certain cognitive functions is a degrading of large neuronal networks underlying certain cognitive abilities.

Andrews-Hanna et al. (2007) compared functional magnetic resonance imaging activation patterns in what has been described as the default mode network (DMN) in young (average age, 22.4 years) versus old (average age, 76.5 years) healthy individuals. This network "activates" during times of "internally directed mental states including remembering, planning and related cognitive functions" (p. 924). It involves increased blood flow occurring in close time sequence between the medial prefrontal cortex, posterior cingulate/retrosplenial cortex, lateral parietal cortex, and medial temporal regions of the brain. Functional connectivity for this network was higher for the younger group compared to the older group. In the older group, the correlations were less robust. Moreover, cognitive performance on standardized neuropsychological tests correlated with the degree to which the DMN components (i.e., shifts in blood flow) showed strong connectivity. Older individuals, who performed most poorly on these neuropsychological measures, showed smaller to nonexistent correlation patterns of activation between the various brain structures involved in the DMN. The authors suggest that the cognitive decline observed in normal aging may reflect subtle and progressive disconnection between large-scale brain interacting systems involving the DMN.

Cabeza (2002) made another interesting observation relevant to declining cognitive abilities during the aging process. Cerebral hemispheric asymmetrical activation patterns seen in younger adults when performing certain cognitive tasks begin to give way to more bilateral activation patterns when older adults perform the same tasks. Bishop et al. (2010) suggest that these findings signal a potential reduction of localized mediated higher cerebral functions in the aging population. A return to a more "diffuse" or at least less localized (and efficient) pattern of cerebral activation when performing various cognitive tasks may underlie some of the "normal" cognitive decline observed in one's 70s, 80s, and 90s. Interestingly, this appears to be the opposite

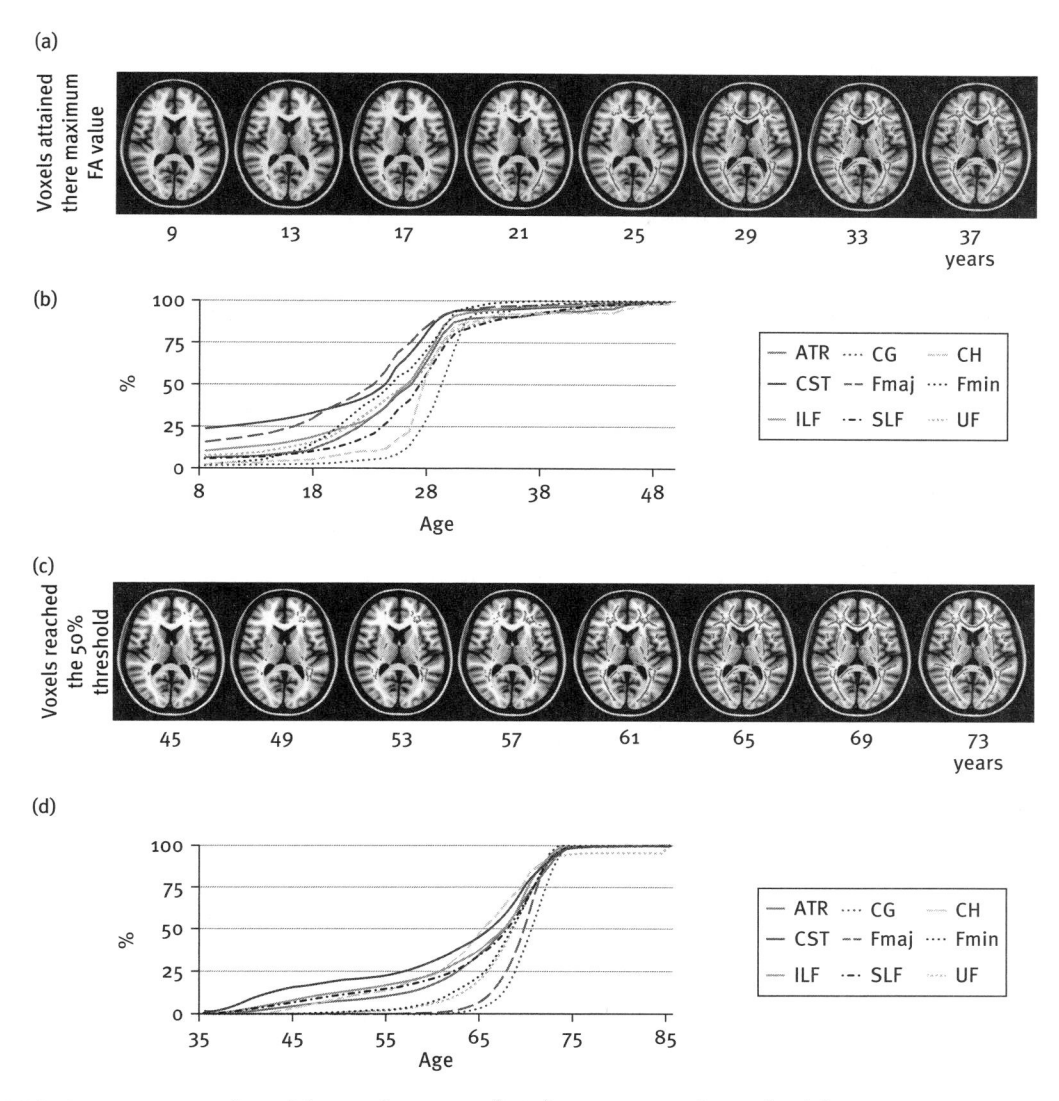

FIGURE 3.2 Regional variability in white matter (WM) maturation and age-related deterioration. (A) Skeleton voxels (red) having attained maximum fractional anisotropy (FA) value at different stages of chronological development in years (as estimated by regression locally estimated scatterplot smoothing). The skeleton voxels are superimposed on a transversal section of a T_1-weighted Montreal Neurological Institute template ($z = 83$). Only voxels showing a significant inverse U pattern across the life span were included in the peak estimations. Relatively early maturation (<21 years) is seen in occipital and frontal areas. (B) Percentage of voxels per tract having reached maximum FA value as a function of age (8–49 years). (C and D) Estimated age-related deterioration as indexed by age when FA fell below the value equal to 50% of the difference between maximum FA and FA at maximum age. Parts of the SLF reached the threshold at approximately 30 years of age, followed by areas encompassing F_{min} in the late 40s and posterior areas, including the occipital lobes, in the early 60s. As indicated by the cumulative curves (D), the vast majority of voxels reached the threshold in the 60s (See color plates).

Source: Reprinted from Westlye, L. T., Walhovd, K. B., Dale, A. M., Bjørnerud, A., Due-Tønnessen, P., Engvig, A., . . . Fjell, A. M., Life-span changes of the human brain white matter: Diffusion tensor imaging (DTI) and volumetry, *Cerebral Cortex, 20*(9), 2009, p. 2055–2068, by permission of Oxford University Press.

pattern observed in the development of cognitive processes during childhood and into adolescence, as noted previously (Durston et al., 2006).

Although age certainly correlates with level of psychometric test performance in very interesting ways, so does the educational background of individuals. The level of one's educational achievements often reflects the degree to which both language-based functions and non-language-based functions are developed, as illustrated next.

THE IMPORTANT INTERACTION OF AGE AND EDUCATION IN INFLUENCING NEUROPSYCHOLOGICAL FUNCTIONING THROUGHOUT THE LIFE SPAN

As noted previously, brain changes (e.g., synaptogenesis and synaptic pruning) throughout the life span appear to be under genetic control but are also "environmentally" dependent. That is, the learning experiences of the person influence the development of the person's higher cerebral functions. One major learning experience is the type and length of "formal" education. In children aged 6–14 years studied in the United States, there is a strong positive correlation between their biological age and the number of years of formal education (in the study reported next, $r = .978$). It is not surprising, therefore, that their performance on various neuropsychological measures is correlated equally on both of these variables.

For purposes of illustration, a description of findings obtained on a screening test of higher cerebral functions used by the author over several years and in a variety of studies will highlight observations relevant to this discussion. The Barrow Neurological Institute Screen for Higher Cerebral Functions (BNIS; Prigatano, Amin, & Rosenstein, 1995) was developed to provide a brief but reliable and valid assessment of cognitive and affective functions that could help detect underlying brain dysfunction in adults. Later, a school-age children's version of this test was developed (Prigatano & Gagliardi, 2005) so that similar observations (i.e., similar behavioral tasks) could be presented and studied in individuals throughout the life span.

When studying children's test performance on the BNI Screen for Higher Cerebral Functions for School-Age Children (BNIS-C), the correlation between BNIS-C total score and grade level at time of testing was $r = .712$ ($n = 232$, $p < .001$). The correlation between BNIS-C total score and age of the child at time of testing was $r = .671$ ($n = 232, p < .001$).

The relationship of age and education to neuropsychological test performance, however, was observed to change in adults. On the BNIS, which was standardized mainly on adults (age range, 15–84 years), the correlation between BNIS total score and age was $r = -.55$ ($n = 200$, $p < .001$). The relationship, therefore, was now a negative one (i.e., older patients perform at lower levels on this test). Years of formal education, however, continued to reflect a positive relationship, but the magnitude of the relationship lessened somewhat ($r = .31$; $n = 197$, $p < .001$). These findings have been replicated in two western European cross-validation studies (Denvall et al., 2002; Prigatano et al., 2013). For example, in France, the correlation of BNIS total score and age was $r = -.622$ ($n = 167$, $p < .001$). For education, the correlation was $r = .539$ ($n = 167, p < .001$).

Interestingly, in countries with a high rate of illiteracy and quite variable educational experiences, the relationships between age and education to BNIS total score appear to change again. In a standardization study of the BNIS with a Brazilian population (Prigatano, Souza, & Braga, 2017), for which the illiteracy rate is high (average of 9% but can be >20% of the population in some areas) and the quality of education is quite variable, age correlated $r = -.36$ with BNIS total score, but education correlated $r = .68$. Moreover, education level correlated with test performance on almost every dimension studied, whereas age did not. Figures 3.3

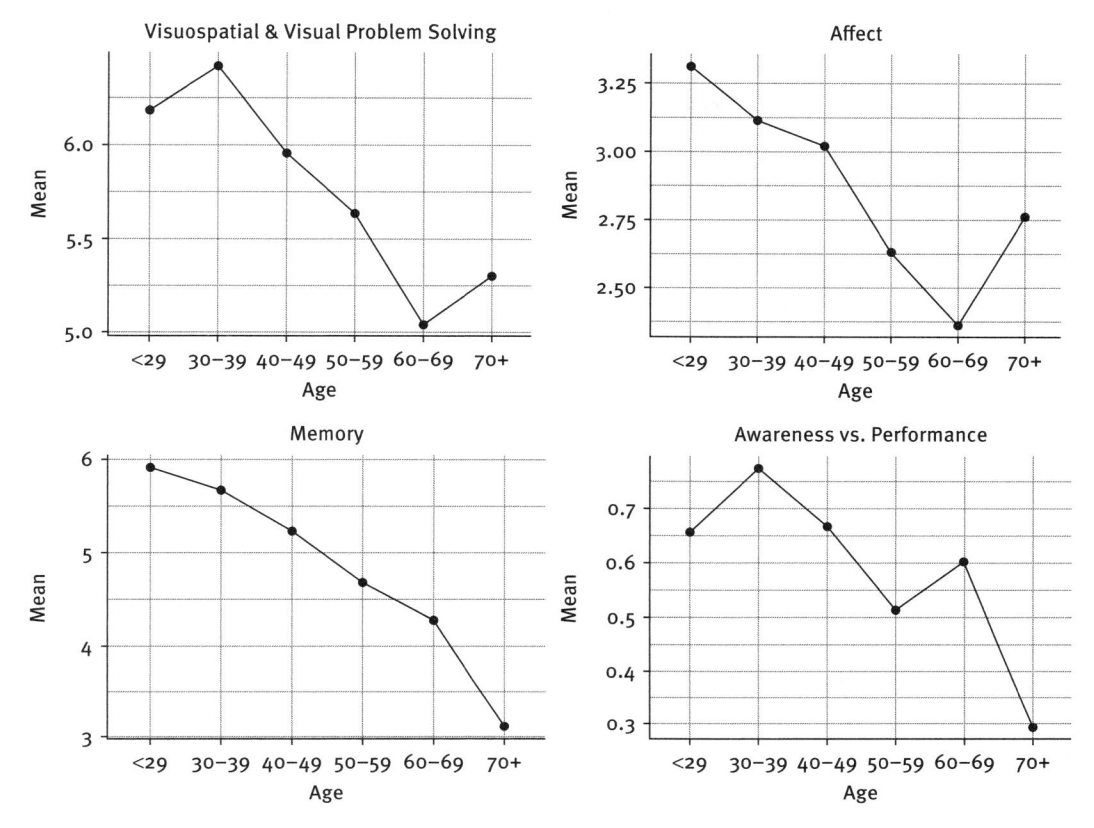

FIGURE 3.3 Graphic visualization of the BNIS subscales and age associations that had statistically significant differences.

Source: Reprinted from Prigatano, G., Souza, L., & Braga, L. W., Performance of a Brazilian sample on the Portuguese translation of the BNI Screen for Higher Cerebral Functions. *Journal of Clinical and Experimental Neuropsychology, 40*(2), 2018, p. 172–182, by permission of Taylor & Francis Ltd.

and 3.4 graphically illustrate how age and education related to the various subtests of the BNIS. Note that education level does not just correlate with measures of language function but also correlates with several other dimensions, including visuospatial abilities, memory, and affect expression and perception.

These findings (and many similar findings reported in the scientific literature) bring attention to the fact that neuropsychological functions not only develop in close connection with the age of the individual but also appear to be greatly influenced by the educational (and cultural) experiences of the individual as the person ages. This is exactly what Vygotsky proposed (see Chapter 2, this volume).

In this regard, it is important to note that education level clearly correlates with one's vocabulary level (e.g., Schroeder and Salthouse [2004] reported $r = .515$). Knowing what words mean is crucial for further learning in school. Education level also correlates with IQ estimates at a similar magnitude (Deary & Johnson, 2010). The more educated a person is, the greater likelihood that they can approach problems from different perspectives. This can be broadly described as "cognitive flexibility." This capacity is important to the adaptation process and is considered a key feature of "resiliency," as described later in this book. Resiliency can play a very important role

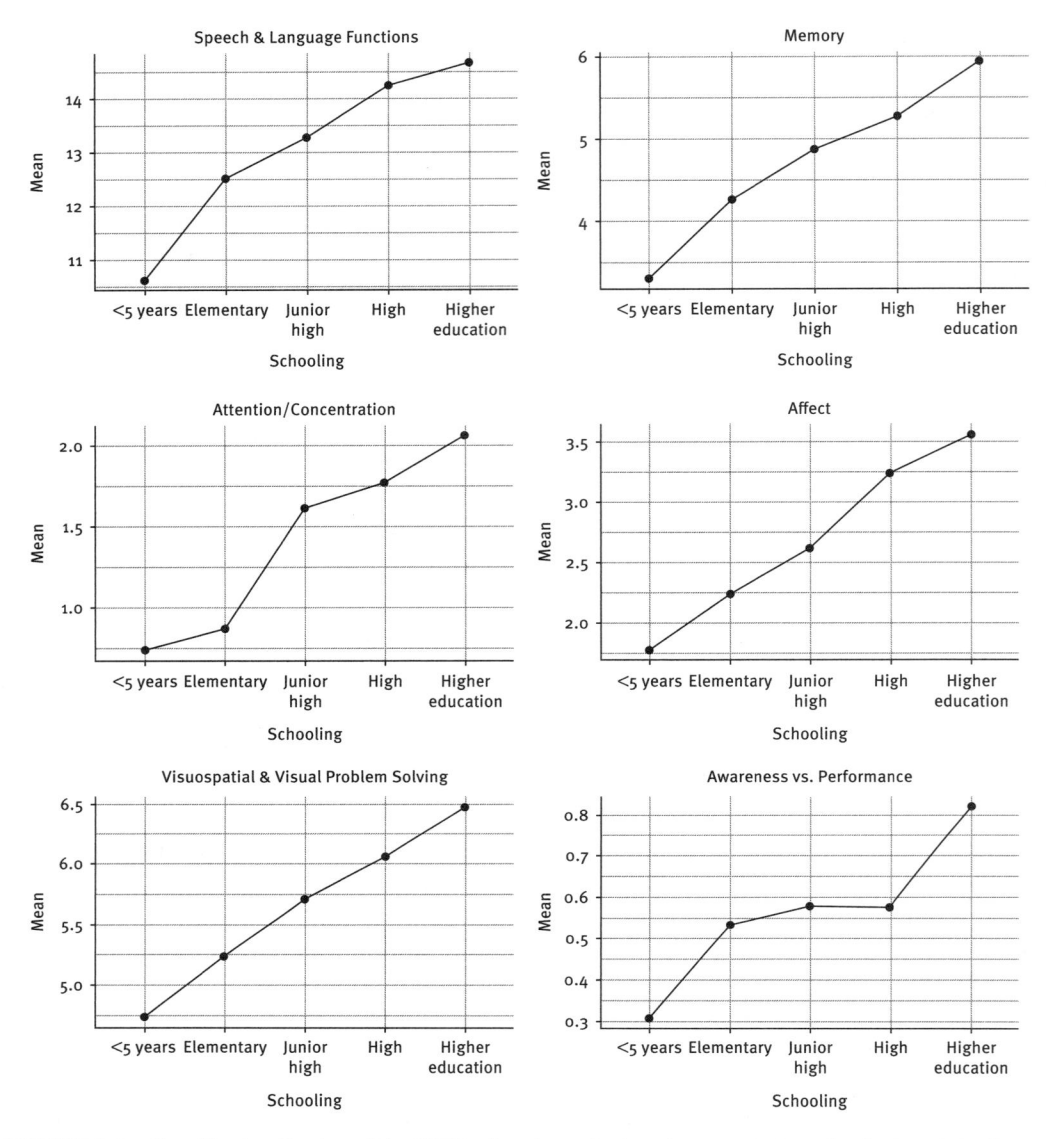

FIGURE 3.4 Graphic visualization of the BNIS subscales and education associations that had statistically significant differences.

Source: Reprinted from Prigatano, G., Souza, L., & Braga, L. W., Performance of a Brazilian sample on the Portuguese translation of the BNI Screen for Higher Cerebral Functions. *Journal of Clinical and Experimental Neuropsychology*, 40(2), 2018, p. 172–182, by permission of Taylor & Francis Ltd.

in the psychological adjustment to losses imposed by brain damage of various types.

CONCLUDING OBSERVATIONS AND IMPLICATIONS

From a brain evolutionary standpoint, HIBFs were developed to meet the biological needs of the organism. Feelings, movements, and sounds appeared to direct a series of behaviors that had "learned" consequences necessary for environmental adaptation and therefore survival. The development of limb motor movements (especially the hands and fingers) and associated control of the vocal muscular structures necessary to imitate and later inititate meaningful sounds appeared especially important for human brain development. The reciprocal development of forming increasingly complex intentions of action (driven by emotional states of the organism) and the shift from meaningful vocal sounds to the complex functions of language may underlie the development of cognition in humans.

The formation of focal and extensive "neuronal networks" necessary for these processes to develop required a "pruning" of neurons with enhanced interconnections between surviving neurons via white matter (i.e., axonal) tracts within the brain. As these networks of brain activity develop, so do cognitive or, more broadly stated, neuropsychological functions. As these networks' structural and functional features decline, so do cognitive (i.e., neuropsychological) functions. These changes occur naturally over the life cycle of humans.

The educational (including broader cultural) experiences of humans seem to greatly influence how these neuronal networks are developed and perhaps maintained over the life span.

Thus, close attention to the feeling state of individuals, how they are able to move, and the quality of their vocalizations (which include language functions) reveal important information concerning the state of development or decline of their HIBFs. Their formal and informal educational (including cultural and interpersonal) backgrounds will further influence these functions and their expressions. These realities have to be considered in the neuropsychological examination of individuals with brain disorders and in efforts to provide psychological care.

The stage is now set for a more detailed discussion of the different phases of human nature development and the neuropsychological functions associated with these development changes.

REFERENCES

Andrews-Hanna, J. R., Snyder, A. Z., Vincent, J. L., Lustig, C., Head, D., Raichle, M. E., & Buckner, R. L. (2007). Disruption of large-scale brain systems in advanced aging. *Neuron, 56*(5), 924–935.

Angulo-Barroso, R. M., & Tiernan, C. W. (2008). Motor systems development. In C. A. Nelson & M. Luciana (Eds.), *Handbook of developmental cognitive neuroscience* (2nd ed., pp. 147–160). Cambridge, MA: MIT Press.

Baez-Mendoza, R., & Schultz, W. (2013). The role of the striatum in social behavior. *Frontiers in Neuroscience, 7*(233). doi:10.3389/fnins.1203.00233

Bargh, J. A., & Morsella, E. (2008). The unconscious mind. *Perspectives on Psychological Science, 3*(1), 73–79.

Bishop, N. A., Lu, T., & Yankner, B. A. (2010). Neural mechanisms of ageing and cognitive decline. *Nature, 464*(7288), 529–535.

Burgmans, S., Gronenschild, E. H., Fandakova, Y., Shing, Y. L., Van Boxtel, M. P., Vuurman, E. F., . . . Raz, N. (2011). Age differences in speed of processing are partially mediated by differences in axonal integrity. *Neuroimage, 55*(3), 1287–1297.

Cabeza, R. (2002). Hemispheric asymmetry reduction in older adults: The HAROLD model. *Psychology and Aging, 17*(1), 85–100.

Casey, B., Galvan, A., & Hare, T. A. (2005). Changes in cerebral functional organization during cognitive development. *Current Opinions in Neurobiology, 15*(2), 239–244.

Casey, B., Tottenham, N., Liston, C., & Durston, S. (2005). Imaging the developing brain: What have we learned about cognitive development? *Trends in Cognitive Sciences, 9*(3), 104–110.

Darwin, C. (1859). *The origin of species by means of natural selection.* London, UK: Murray.

Deary, I. J., & Johnson, W. (2010). Intelligence and education: Causal perceptions drive analytic processes and therefore conclusions. *International Journal of Epidemiology, 39*(5), 1362–1369.

Denvall, V., Elmstahl, S., & Prigatano, G. P. (2002). Replication and construct validation of the Barrow Neurological Institute Screen for Higher Cerebral Functions with a Swedish population. *Journal of Rehabiliation Medicine, 34*(3), 153–157.

Donald, M. (1991). *Origins of the modern mind: Three stages in the evolution of culture and cognition.* Cambridge, MA: Harvard University Press.

Donald, M. (2001). *A Mind So Rare: The evolution of human consciousness.* W.W. Norton & Company, New York.

Durston, S., Davidson, M. C., Tottenham, N., Galvan, A., Spicer, J., Fossella, J. A., & Casey, B. (2006). A shift from diffuse to focal cortical activity with development. *Developmental Science, 9*(1), 1–8.

Edelman, G. M. (1987). *Neural Darwinism: The theory of neuronal group selection*. New York, NY: Basic Books.

Flechsig, P. E. (1920). *Anatomie des menschlichen Gehirns und Rückenmarks auf myelogenetischer Grundlage*. Leipzig, Germany: Thieme.

Franzen, E., & Myers, R. (1973). Neural control of social behavior: Prefrontal and anterior temporal cortex. *Neuropsychologia, 11*(2), 141–157.

Fuster, J. M. (1997). *The prefrontal cortex: Anatomy, physiology, and neuropsychology of the frontal lobe* (3rd ed.). Philadelphia, PA: Lippincott–Raven.

Fuster, J. M. (2003). *Cortex and mind: Unifying cognition*. New York, NY: Oxford University Press.

Gervan, P., Berencsi, A., & Kovacs, I. (2011). Vision first? The development of primary visual cortical networks is more rapid than the development of primary motor networks in humans. *PLoS One, 6*(9), e25572.

Giedd, J. N., Stockman, M., Weddle, C., Liverpool, M., Wallace, G. L., Lee, N. R., . . . Lenroot, R. K. (2012). Anatomic magnetic resonance imaging of the developing child and adolescent brain and effects of genetic variation. In V. F. Reyna, S. B. Chapman, M. R. Dougherty, & J. Confrey (Eds.), *The adolescent brain: Learning, reasoning, and decision making* (pp. 15–35). Washington, DC: American Psychological Association.

Gogtay, N., Giedd, J. N., Lusk, L., Hayashi, K. M., Greenstein, D., Vaituzis, A. C., . . . Toga, A. W. (2004). Dynamic mapping of human cortical development during childhood through early adulthood. *Proceedings of the National Academy of Sciences of the USA, 101*(21), 8174–8179.

Hawking, S. (1996). *A brief history of time*. New York, NY: Bantam Dell.

Heaton, R. K., Grant, I., & Matthews, C. G. (1991). *Comprehensive norms for an expanded Halstead–Reitan battery: Demographic corrections, research findings, and clinical applications; With a supplement for the Wechsler Adult Intelligence Scale–Revised (WAIS-R)*. Lutz, FL: Psychological Assessment Resources.

Heilman, K. M., & Valenstein, E. (2003). *Clinical neuropsychology* (4th ed.). New York, NY: Oxford University Press.

Herculano-Houzel, S. (2009). The human brain in numbers: A linearly scaled-up primate brain. *Frontiers in Human Neuroscience, 3*, 31.

Hofman, M. A. (2014). Evolution of the human brain: When bigger is better. *Frontiers in Neuroanatomy, 8*, 15.

Iliescu, B. F., & Dannemiller, J. L. (2008). Brain–behavior relationships in. In C. A. Nelson & M. Luciana (Eds.), *Handbook of developmental cognitive neuroscience* (2nd ed., pp. 127–146). Cambridge, MA: MIT Press.

Kail, R. (1991). Developmental change in speed of processing during childhood and adolescence. *Psychological Bulletin, 109*(3), 490.

Kolb, B., & Fantie, B. D. (2009). Development of the child's brain and behavior. In C. R. Reynolds & E. Fletcher-Janzen (Eds.), *Handbook of clinical child neuropsychology* (pp. 19–46). New York, NY: Springer.

Morrison, J. H., & Hof, P. R. (1997). Life and death of neurons in the aging brain. *Science, 278*(5337), 412–419.

Müller, F., & O'Rahilly, R. (2004). Embryonic development of the central nervous system. In G. Paxinos & J. K. Mai (Eds.), *The human nervous system* (pp. 22–48). New York, NY: Elsevier.

Nagy, Z., Westerberg, H., & Klingberg, T. (2004). Maturation of white matter is associated with the development of cognitive functions during childhood. *Journal of Cognitive Neuroscience, 16*(7), 1227–1233.

Paxinos, G., & Mai, J. K. (Eds.). (2004). *The human nervous system* (2nd ed.). San Diego, CA: Academic Press.

Peterson, S. E., & Posner, M. I. (2012). The attention system of the human brain: 20 years after. *Annual Review of Neuroscience, 35*, 73–89.

Posner, M. I., & Rothbart, M. K. (2007). *Educating the human brain*. New York, NY: American Psychological Association.

Prigatano, G. P. (1999). *Principles of neuropsychological rehabilitation*. New York, NY: Oxford University Press.

Prigatano, G. P., Amin, K., & Rosenstein, L. (1995). *Administration and scoring manual for the BNI Screen for Higher Cerebral Functions*. Phoenix, AZ: Barrow Neurological Institute.

Prigatano, G. P., & Gagliardi, C. (2005). *The BNI Screen for Higher Cerebral Functions in School-Age Children: A manual for administration and scoring*. Phoenix, AZ: Barrow Neurological Institute.

Prigatano, G. P., Tonini, A., Truelle, J. L., & Montreuil, M. (2013). Performance of a French sample on the French translation of the BNI Screen for Higher Cerebral Functions. *Brain Injury, 27*(12), 1435–1440.

Prigatano, G. P., Souza, L., & Braga, L. W. (2017). Performance of a Brazilian sample on the Portuguese translation of the BNI Screen for Higher Cerebral Functions. *Journal of Clinical and Experimental Neuropsychology, 40*(2), 173–182.

Roland, P., Geyer, S., Amunts, K., Schormann, T., Schleicher, A., Malikovic, A., & Zilles, K. (1997). Cytoarchitectural maps of the human brain in

Schroeder, D. H., & Salthouse, T. A. (2004). Age-related effects on cognition between 20 and 50 years of age. *Personality and Individual Differences, 36*(2), 393–404.

Squire, L. R., & Dede, A. J. (2015). Conscious and unconscious memory systems. *Cold Spring harbor Perspectives in Biology, 7*(3), a021667.

Striedter, G. F. (2004). Brain evolution. In G. Paxinos & J. K. Mai (Eds.), *The human nervous system* (2nd ed., pp. 3–21). San Diego, CA: Academic Press.

Tau, G. Z., & Peterson, B. S. (2010). Normal development of brain circuits. *Neuropsychopharmacology, 35*(1), 147–168.

Turken, U., Whitfield-Gabrieli, S., Bammer, R., Baldo, J. V., Dronkers, N. F., & Gabrieli, J. D. (2008). Cognitive processing speed and the structure of white matter pathways: Convergent evidence from normal variation and lesion studies. *Neuroimage, 42*(2), 1032–1044.

Wechsler, D., Coalson, D. L., & Raiford, S. E. (2008). *WAIS-IV: Wechsler Adult Intelligence Scale*. San Antonio, TX: Pearson.

Westlye, L. T., Walhovd, K. B., Dale, A. M., Bjørnerud, A., Due-Tønnessen, P., Engvig, A., . . . Fjell, A. M. (2009). Life-span changes of the human brain white matter: Diffusion tensor imaging (DTI) and volumetry. *Cerebral Cortex, 20*(9), 2055–2068.

Yakovlev, P., & Lecours, A. (1967). The myelogenetic cycles of regional maturation of the brain. In A. Minkowski (Ed.), *Regional development of the brain in early life* (pp. 3–65). Oxford, UK: Blackwell.

Zilles, K. (2004). Architecture of the human cerebral cortex: Regional and laminar organization. In G. Paxinos & J. K. Mai (Eds.), *The human nervous system* (Vol. 2, pp. 997–1055). New York, NY: Elsevier.

4

NEUROPSYCHOLOGICAL AND PSYCHOSOCIAL COMPETENCIES THROUGHOUT THE HUMAN LIFE SPAN

INTRODUCTION

Brain injuries of various types occur at different time periods during the human life span. Therefore, providing psychological care for a person with a brain disorder requires an understanding of what neuropsychological functions are developing or declining at the time of the brain disorder. Those neuropsychological functions are constantly interacting with (and perhaps being modified by) the psychosocial situation of the individual. Understanding the psychosocial and interpersonal influences on cognition and personality development is therefore crucial to meaningfully examine and provide psychological care for a person with a brain disorder. Although different cultural perspectives are needed, the theoretical work and clinical insights of Eric Homburger Erikson (1902–1994) provide a useful framework for clinical neuropsychologists vested in the psychological care of patients over the life span.

A PSYCHOSOCIAL THEORY OF HUMAN DEVELOPMENT

The scientific study of neuropsychology and related neurosciences provides many interesting facts concerning brain function and anatomy and their relationship to human and animal behavior, as the preceding chapters have in part demonstrated. Yet, these facts often seem disconnected from a broader, more clinically relevant understanding of people in general and of specific patients in particular. Erik Erikson's ideas and writings often provide the opposite experience. Although there is an absence of "scientifically oriented data," his clinical observations about people and their inner or psychological states at different times in the life cycle often appear penetrating and clinically relevant. The goal of this chapter is to integrate some of Erikson's ideas with selected observations emanating mainly from neuropsychology.

In introducing Erikson's work, Hall and Lindzey (1978) described the essential features of a psychosocial theory of human development. They stated, "It means specifically that the stages of a person's life from birth to death are formed by social influences interacting with a physically and psychologically maturing organism" (p. 88). Thus, a psychosocial theory of development takes into consideration three major variables: the biological development of the person, the associated psychological developmental characteristics, and the social milieu in which other individuals impart to the person what is expected of them to successfully function within that social environment. It emphasizes the important interactional influences that people have on each other's behavior, language characteristics, and possibly thought processes at different stages of neuropsychological development. It links these changes to the entire life span within a given culture.

"Stage theory" models suggest that there are distinct levels of functioning that exist at different time periods of a person's life. The person has to achieve certain "developmental milestones" and master certain cognitive–behavioral–social skills before they can adequately move on to the next state or stage of development. Developmental psychologists, however, have pointed to the reality that these models of human behavior tend to oversimplify how different children and adults actually function at different time periods in their life (Mitchell & Ziegler, 2007).

There are, however, two assumptions about human behavior that make stage theories (or a version of them) of interest to clinical neuropsychologists. The first assumption is that cognitive processes and approaches to problem-solving that a child develops greatly influence later cognitive and behavioral competencies as an adult. Piaget and Vygotsky emphasized this point. Wood, Bruner, and Ross (1976) used the metaphor of scaffolding to provide a mental image of how new knowledge and problem-solving are built on older methods of thinking/doing. Thus, some rudimentary skills must be developed that form the basis of more complicated skill learning. This may occur in "stages," as Piaget emphasized in the young child (Wadsworth, 1996).

The second assumption, which is perhaps most important for neuropsychologists, is the proposition that the higher integrative brain functions only adequately develop by means of appropriate social interactions (i.e., social observations/learning). If one accepts this later Vygotskian proposition, understanding the social influences on human development from birth to death is very relevant for a theory of human neuropsychology and the practice of clinical neuropsychology. Therefore, approaching Erikson's model from a neuropsychological perspective is warranted. This is a challenging task, however, and the following discussion is only an "introduction" to this complex area of study.

Vaillant and Milofsky (1980) attempted to empirically study some of Erikson's clinical propositions. In doing so, they make an important point. They suggest that when describing complex adult development, the word "stage" as used by Erikson should be taken in a metaphorical manner. What Erikson was referring to were actually different developmental tasks that were faced by the person at different times in their life. How the person did or did not achieve successful mastering of those tasks influenced their personality development and their manner of interpersonal interactions.

Erikson initially proposed that there are eight stages of psychosocial development. Later in life, he and his wife described a ninth stage corresponding to "very old age" (Erikson & Erikson, 1998). To properly understand Erikson's thinking, it is important to begin with his clinical observations in light of his psychoanalytic work.

Erikson (1964) notes that "a seeming paradox of human life is man's collective power to create his own environment, although each individual is born with a naked vulnerability extending into a prolonged infantile dependence" (p. 113). He also notes, however, that the very feature of this highly dependent, new human life stimulates in caregivers a desire to provide care. He states that the "healthy infant" experiences a very rudimentary form of hope and trust that his or her needs will be properly met by attentive and loving caregivers. He notes that it is

> hard to specify the criteria for this state, and harder to measure it: yet he who has seen a hopeless child, knows what is *not* there. Hope is both the earliest and the most indispensable virtue inherent in the state of being alive. (p. 115)

He goes on to make a very insightful statement relevant to the theme of this book—namely that "if life is to be sustained hope must remain, even where confidence is wounded, trust impaired" (p. 115).

Erikson (1964) considers that the first state or stage of life presents the infant with experiences that foster a sense of trust (which provides the basis of developing the virtue of hope that one's needs will be met) or, conversely, lead to an internal sense of mistrust (and the experience of a loss of hope). He uses the term *virtue* not with a moralistic intent but, rather, to describe an "adaptive strength" that emerges when the psychological tensions over different life experiences reach a *crisis*. He uses the term "crisis" in the traditional medical sense of the word. It is meant to convey a "turning point for better or for worse, a crucial period in which a decisive turn *one way or another* is unavoidable" (p. 139).

Understanding how Erikson uses these terms and the phenomena they refer to is necessary to understand his stages or states of psychosocial development. Figure 4.1, taken from his last book (Erikson & Erikson, 1998), charts stages of life (from infancy to old age) and the psychosocial crises typically faced during each of the initial eight stages of development. Erikson makes the important point that

> the chart also makes clear in its verticals that each step (even wisdom) is grounded in all the previous ones: which in each horizontal, the developmental maturation (and psychosocial crisis) of one of these virtues gives new connotations to all the "lower" and already developed stages as well as to the higher and still developing ones. This can never be said often enough. (p. 59)

Thus, as a person changes and develops or conversely does not adequately change or develop, previous adaptive strengths can be modified in a positive and negative manner over the life span. This is a relevant observation from both a neuropsychological and a psychotherapeutic perspective. Let's now consider in some detail Erikson's initial eight stages of psychosocial development.

The first four stages of life, as described by Erikson, occur during infancy and childhood. The fifth stage occurs during adolescence and the last three stages during the adult years (Hall & Lindzey, 1978, p. 91).

In Erikson's model of psychosocial development, the first 18 months of life provide infants with a variety of experiences that give them their first sense of reality. Infants are often focused on food and eating. They have top priority. Infants visually scan the environment, point to what interests them (especially when watching parents eat), and cry (make sounds of distress) when their bodily needs are not apparently met.

Erikson suggests that if the parent–child interactions provide the infant with experiences that convey that the infant's needs will be met and life is secure despite times of frustrations, a trusting bond emerges. It is assumed and supported in part by Bowlby's work (R. Bowlby & King, 2004) that this trusting bond is very

PSYCHOSOCIAL STAGES OF LIFE

	I	II	III	IV	V	VI	VII	VIII
Old Age VIII MATURITY								*Ego* Integrity vs. Despair. WISDOM
Adulthood VII							Generativity vs. *Stagnation* Self-Absorption. CARE	
Young Adulthood VI						Intimacy vs. Isolation. LOVE		
Adolescence V PUBERTY AND ADOLESCENCE					Identity vs. Confusion. FIDELITY			
School Age IV LATENCY				Industry vs. Inferiority. COMPETENCE				
Play Age III LOCOMOTOR-GENITAL			Initiative vs. Guilt. PURPOSE					
Early Childhood II MUSCULAR-ANAL		Autonomy vs. Shame, Doubt. WILL						
Infancy I ORAL-SENSORY	Basic Trust vs. Basic Mistrust. HOPE							

FIGURE 4.1 Schematic diagram of the "stages" of psychosocial development.

Source: Reprinted from Kivnick, H. Q., & Wells, C. K., Untapped richness in Erik H. Erikson's rootstock, *The Gerontologist*, 54(1), 1994, p. 40–50, by permission of Oxford University Press, and from Erikson, E. H., Erikson, J. M., & Kivnick, H. Q., *Vital involvement in old age*, 1994, by permission of W. W. Norton & Company.

important for the child's cognitive, emotional, and behavioral growth. Early impulse control can be facilitated by soothing sounds, words, gestures, and touch initiated by the caregiver that reassure that gratifications of the infant's needs are "on their way." Infants' smiles and early behavioral choices of who they wish to hold them reflect the infants' earliest social–emotional responses to parents and caregivers.

If infants do not develop this trusting bond, their behavior often reveals the opposite pattern. Uncontrolled crying and/or nonresponsiveness to efforts at comforting them are often present. Later problems with impulse control and interpersonal bonding are common, with potential delays in cognitive and motor development (discussed later). The adaptive strength of *hope* is or is not learned at this very early stage of development, according to Erikson.

During the next stage or phase of development (i.e., early childhood, which ranges between ages 2 and 3 years), the child becomes more mobile and communicative. Crawling gives way to walking as the child improves balance when sitting and standing. The child can combine words and can express observations as well as wants and desires. The child begins to express (via their behavior) their first sense of autonomy. It is typically during this time period that the child is asked to learn to control their bowels and bladder for the benefit of all. The latter activity can be a struggle, as parents can easily describe. Erikson notes that toilet training is a social requirement that is typically associated with excessive praise if the child does it properly. This becomes an early source of pride for the child.

The sense of personal autonomy becomes further strengthened as the child is praised and rewarded for developments in other competencies associated with new learning. However, toilet training has special significance, according to Erikson. Reactions of disgust and displeasure are often intense when the child does not learn to control their bowels and bladder. This can produce a sense of shame for the young child and doubt in their capacities to please others. Erikson notes that if the child is repeatedly scolded for failure to achieve this important social goal of bowel and bladder control, shame and self-doubt tend to flourish. The adaptive strength or virtue of *will* is formed during this early time of development.

As the child learns to walk safely, talk sensibly, and control bodily functions, they are ready for expanded social interactions that go beyond the family unit. The "preschool" years or "play age" (from ages 3 to 5 years) has arrived. The desire to "explore" the world, the tendency to make spontaneous verbal comments about their surroundings and ask questions about the nature of the world and "why" things happen, is in bloom. Depending on the reactions the child receives regarding their exploratory behaviors, they can experience a wide range of emotions. If their explorations are associated with parental (and teacher) reactions that are positive, a sense of personal initiative is reinforced, according to Erikson. During this time, considerable learning about the outside world becomes possible. If, however, their numerous questions are a source of irritation to important caregivers, the child is prone to feel "bad" or guilty about their inquisitive behaviors. In reality, this is not an "either/or" situation. The child most likely develops both senses simultaneously, but it is a matter of degree over which feeling predominates during this time period given the degree of task achievements of the child. Erikson suggests that it is during this time that the adaptive strength of having *purpose* to one's actions is or is not established.

When the child enters first grade (typically ages 6 and 7 years), they are now considered capable of knowing "right from wrong" because language skills have substantially developed. They are expected to begin learning what their society deems necessary for their personal and social adjustment/adaptation. Now they must learn to identify letters and numbers, write, and draw. As they progress to the second grade (ages 7 and 8 years) and third grade (ages 8 and 9 years) and beyond, language and mathematic skills are further developed. Reading and spelling skills should become solidified so that learning other subjects, such as social studies, history, and biology, is possible. The beginning signs of a "learning disability" may now be identifiable in some children. It is during these early school years (which according to Erikson range from ages 6 to 11 years) that children either feel good about themselves and are eager to do schoolwork and develop a sense of industry—meaning hard work pays off—or they sense they are not as "good as others" in accomplishing academic goals and develop a sense of "inferiority." The adaptive strength of *competence* weighs in the balance.

These preadolescent years set in place a "template" for how the child views themselves and their relationship to others. It is also during these years that the child's identification with certain "heroes" or persons they wish to emulate begins to emerge. Psychological care can be greatly enhanced by understanding why certain heroes had special appeal to a person during childhood (Bettelheim, 1989). Modern attempts to develop a scientific understanding of human personality have rediscovered the importance of these narratives for individual psychological (i.e., personality) development (McAdams & Pals, 2006).

It is the onset of puberty that ushers in the next stage of psychosocial development (ages 12–18 years). Adolescents have developed sexual maturity but not the intellectual and behavioral maturity necessary for adult life and responsibilities. The earlier sense of who one is and who one wants to become is now a major focus of life. Handling sexual and aggressive impulses becomes of central importance to human beings and further defines their human nature during this time frame. Erikson (1964) states that it is during this time that there is a major struggle over establishing a firm sense of identity. The adolescent is notorious for trying different experiences, including a propensity for risk-taking behaviors. Some experiences are confusing to adolescents, whereas others help them make important life decisions. It can be a time of "considerable psychological flux" regarding emotions and decision-making. Parental guidance is crucial during this time period. Social relationships, however, also help individuals know "who they are" and what they want to become. How they are able to handle this psychological crisis determines their ability to develop the adaptive strength of *fidelity*. It allows for commitments to be made and honored in the face of conflict and disagreements. This virtue, like others, however, may not be entirely settled during the adolescent years and may take several more years to develop.

As individuals develop various academic and/or non-academic skills necessary for work, the experience of young adulthood (the next stage of psychosocial development) begins, which is generally between the ages of 18 and 25 years. This phase, however, according to Erikson, can be and is often expanded into one's 30s and even the early 40s (Arnett, 2000). It is during this time period that the individual struggles with achieving intimacy with others or remaining psychologically isolated even when having physically and sexually intimate contact with others. It provides the groundwork for establishing the adaptive strength of *love*. It is a powerful time during human development that allows for adult work and love relationships to be realistically established in life. Without it, interpersonal isolation is common, and emotional estrangement with others is readily observed. The nature of interpersonal relationships during this time period often becomes a template for interacting with others for the remainder of one's life.

If successful, the stability of committed and mutually satisfying interpersonal relationships at "home and work" allows for the next stage of development to occur. Erikson described a "middle" stage of adult development. Individuals are not only capable of sustained relationships but also capable of creative work. They can more effectively tolerate disappointments and make important life decisions based on an expanded series of previous social experiences. They more completely understand the responsibilities of parenting and fostering the development of others. It is a time of "generativity" of ideas, wealth, and relationships versus "stagnation" and a failure to thrive in life's creative and interpersonal efforts. The age range that Erikson gave for this stage was rather large, from roughly 40 to 65 years, which was the traditional age of retirement in the United States. It is the time that the adaptive strength of *care* is typically established.

After the formal work years were complete, Erikson initially envisioned a final stage of development that he referred to as "maturity." It roughly coincided with the time of retirement to death. It was a time to reflect on one's life, to make sense of one's existence, and to give to others so they could further build on what the person achieved in their life. It was a time of closeness to those whom one loved and at times fought with earlier in life. Erikson described the major challenge of this stage of life as developing a sense of "ego integrity." That is, the person had to develop a sense that who they are now and what they were in the past were interconnected and had some meaning (or least some understanding) to them. Their "individuality" (to use a Jungian term) was better understood and accepted. They had a greater sense of completion in life's journey. If this did not occur, then depression and despair were common. Suffering with physical ailments and life's disappointments was the focus of their attention, and death became the final, necessary disappointment. The adaptive strength of *wisdom* was considered to either develop or not develop at this time, depending on how the psychosocial crisis was met.

Toward the end of his life, Erikson proposed that a ninth stage of life (very old age—beginning in the 80s and extending into the 90s or longer) be considered. At this time in his life, Erikson described wisdom as "informed and detached concern with life itself in the face of death itself" (Erikson & Erikson, 1998, p. 61). Returning to his chart (see Figure 4.1), he noted that it emerges only when a sense of personal integrity overrides a sense of personal despair about life. In looking for a word that would capture the final adaptive strength (virtue) that occurs in very old age, Erikson stated that "the word faith suggests itself" (p. 62). Faith, he noted, is ultimately based on hope, and hope is the ultimate bridge from the beginning of life to the end of life. It is "the most basic quality of 'I'-ness, without which life could not begin or meaningfully end" (p. 62).

Erikson suggests that in the end, "the life cycle turns back on the beginnings" (Erikson & Erikson, 1998, p. 62) and that the hope is that what one has done well in life will truly be helpful for generations to come. It allows one to die with a deepened sense of wisdom that is embodied in the adaptive strength of *faith*. It is faith in the meaning of one's life and the lives of others—those past, present, as well as those in the future. The oldest of the old wise person returns to a childlike state of wonder and enjoyment of the numerous sensations of life. As Joan Erikson writes with her husband, true wisdom "opens your ears and eyes" (Erikson & Erikson, 1998, p. 116). A reconnection to the senses—to what we see, hear, and touch—becomes the last major enjoyment of life with inevitable declining health and ultimately death. Later chapters in this book return to the penetrating wisdom of Erikson and Erikson's observations when discussing practical steps for providing psychological care for persons with different brain disorders at different stages of life.

EMPIRICAL AND CLINICAL OBSERVATIONS REGARDING ERIKSON'S INSIGHTS

In an attempt to scientifically test some of Erikson's ideas, Vaillant and Milofsky (1980) conducted two large-scale prospective studies on men during a 40-year time period. They provide psychometric evidence in support of some of Erikson's propositions. They note that the features of middle-life behaviors are in fact correlated with measures of trust, autonomy, and initiative. They further suggest that the "stage" theory model should be modified and viewed more as a spiral. They subdivide stage 6 into "intimacy" and "career consolidation." Stage 7, "generativity," is also subdivided into a stage 7a, referring to "keepers of the meaning." Their approach not only allows for a psychometric assessment of a complex set of ideas but also helps clarify important subcomponents of psychosocial functioning that brain dysfunctional patients may face.

Clinically, the psychosocial "tasks" of development that Erikson envisioned provide an aerial view of potentially key states of psychological development that people experience in society. Knowing that these psychological states exist and that they may be more prominent at different age ranges can be helpful to clinical neuropsychologists involved in the psychological care of their patients. For example, when examining a school-age child with a history of "moderate" traumatic brain injury who has a limited vocabulary, it is important to recognize that their limited vocabulary not only compromises their academic performance but also contributes to the child's sense of inferiority, which is heightened during this time period. Helping the child "build their vocabulary" not only improves school performance but also strengthens the child's overall sense of competence and reduces feelings of inferiority. These overlapping experiences (better school performance and less feeling of inferiority) foster the development of a therapeutic or working alliance between the child, the parent, and the clinical neuropsychologist. The child and parent experience the clinical neuropsychologist as having a good understanding of how specific neuropsychological limitations are important to the child's daily functioning and personal sense of well-being. This experience often encourages the child and/or parent to obtain further consultation when other neuropsychological-based adjustment issues are encountered later in life.

Selected neuropsychological and neuroscience observations that are relevant for understanding some of the emerging and dissolving brain–behavior relationships that appear related to psychosocial competencies (i.e., task completions) over the life span are considered next. This is, of course, also a very complicated area of study. Extensive review of the literature is not attempted. Rather, the selected observations are of special relevance to psychological care issues after a brain disorder.

NEUROPSYCHOLOGICAL AND PSYCHOSOCIAL COMPETENCIES DURING INFANCY

The first 18 months of life are marked by substantial changes in synaptogenesis and synaptic pruning that are experience dependent, as noted in Chapter 3. Visual recognition of familiar faces associated with different voices appears especially important during this period of time (Posner & Rothbart, 2007). Certainly, the occipital cortex undergoes considerable development, with important changes occurring at different layers of the visual cortex during infancy (Huttenlocher, 1990). Also during this time period, somatosensory functions begin to dramatically change. Povinelli and Davis (1994) note, for example, that pointing with the index finger is observed in some infants as early as 18 days of life. The pointing appears to reflect intentional pursuits of the infant that in turn help direct the visual attention of the infant and caregiver regarding wants and desires. They also note that various manual pointing gestures develop during 12–14 months of life and become crucial for meaningfully interacting with caregivers. These two rudimentary, but integrative, brain functions of visual object recognition and pointing to objects may foster the development of working memory skills.

Diamond (2002) eloquently demonstrated a progressive expansion of working memory capacity in infants as they were asked to perform the famous A-not-B task introduced by Piaget (1936/1954). In this task, the infant is visually shown some desirable object in location A. This object is then hidden from the infant's sight for variable time periods, and then the infant is confronted with two possible locations where the object might be (A and B sites). The infant is asked to find the desired object. During 7–12 months of life, children are quite variable in how long they can keep the mental representation of the location of the object. On average, a 12-month-old infant can correctly find or point to the location of the desired object after a 10-second delay, whereas a 7½-month-old infant can do so only after a (nearly) 2-second delay. Diamond related these behavioral achievements to the development of the dorsolateral prefrontal cortex, in line with observations made by Donald (1991) and Fuster (1997) described in Chapter 3.

Diamond (2002) also reviewed a series of studies of other investigators that highlight additional important features of infant neuropsychological functioning. Citing the work of Koslowski and Bruner (1972), she notes that the ability to inhibit a natural motor tendency in order to obtain a desired object develops in a progressive manner from 12 to 24 months of age. This capacity, however, becomes more functional in preschool years, as reviewed later.

As motor and working memory skills develop, important co-developments in language are occurring during these early stages of life. For example, the ability to independently sit between 3 and 5 months of life has been found to correlate with vocabulary level at 10–14 months of age (Libertus & Violi, 2016). Age of walking has been related to language development, as noted in Chapter 3 (also see Walle & Campos, 2014). Vocabulary level improves as verbal short-term memory (or working memory) expands (Gupta & MacWhinney, 1997).

During the first 24 months of life, a predictable sequence occurs regarding the development of the four main components of language. Phonology (auditory perception and accurate vocal production of vowel/consonant sounds) proceeds first, followed by semantics (using words in a certain way to convey a specific meaning). Next, grammar develops, which requires both syntax (how words are arranged in sentences to make them understandable) and morphology (how words are used to express the complexities of events in time and, later, passive and active voice). This is followed by the development of pragmatics (saying something in a way that gets one's needs met in different social settings). The question now becomes why is it so important for language to develop during these very early stages of life? The answer appears to be related to the importance of developing a system of communication that allows for simultaneous effective interaction with one's caregivers and the ability to deal with "external" as well as "internal, subjective" reality. As noted previously, the development of language is never a purely cognitive task. It is a task that simultaneously involves sounds, feelings, movement, and touch.

As noted in Chapter 3, during the infancy period of development, limbic structures are reportedly well established (Gogtay et al., 2004). J. Bowlby (1980) provides powerful clinical examples of how emotional deprivations of various types during infancy have profound effects on attachment styles well into adulthood. Neuropsychologists, however, have not found a way to easily measure how the emotional states of infants interact with their cognitive and possibly motor development. An intriguing paper by Als et al. (2004) suggests, however, that there is indeed an important connection.

In a randomized clinical trial, Als et al. (2004) investigated the effects of early life experiences on brain function and structure in medically healthy preterm infants. They compared the behavioral and neuroimaging findings of premature infants who received intensive early interventions to reduce their level of distress (e.g., assuring restfulness, calm breathing, calm digestive tract, and restful postures) during the first few weeks of life with those of infants who received good, standard clinical care. The treatment group, however, received interventions that were individualized to the specific infant's clinical state, 24 hours a day, 7 days a week. At 9 months of age, the treated infants showed greater motor development compared to the control group. In addition, they showed greater emotional regulation. For some of the children receiving the individualized intensive care, there was greater anisotropy of white matter tracts in the posterior limbs of the internal capsule. These findings are in line with a long list of psychiatric clinicians' observations that emotional experiences in infancy indeed impact the psychological and related neuropsychological development in children in substantial ways.

NEUROPSYCHOLOGICAL AND PSYCHOSOCIAL COMPETENCIES DURING EARLY CHILDHOOD

Between 2 and 3 years of life, considerable changes in brain function occur. During this time, myelination of Wernicke's area is almost complete (Bergen & Woodin, 2011). Spoken (and auditorily perceived) words can be linked to visual pictures as well as to the objects themselves. The child can now point to a picture of the "moo cow" when the parent says the words and asks the child to find the "moo cow." Language begins to control behavior. Bowel training is often accomplished during this time. Vestibular functions, as reflected in balance and walking skills, notably improve. These functions not only make the child more "mobile" but also may become quite important for sustaining visual gaze necessary for the later development of reading skills (Wiener-Vacher, Hamilton, & Wiener, 2013).

It is also during this time that the child is eagerly exploring the environment and can insistently ask "Why?" when requested to do a variety of tasks. It has been noted that during the 18- to 24-month period, there is a rapid development of the child's vocabulary level. Infant vocabulary level is a predictor of later language skills in children (Duff, Reen, Plunkett, & Nation, 2015; Reilly et al., 2010). However, the amount of later variance for which it accounts is often less than 20% (Duff et al., 2015). A history of family illiteracy or language difficulties is reported to account for an additional 10% of the variance (Duff et al., 2015).

Temper tantrums are also quite common during this time. The relationship between language skills of infants and their ability to control emotional reactions is less understood. As Diamond (2002) notes, very little is known about prefrontal lobe development during this time frame. However, by age 3½ years, impulse control becomes more prominent.

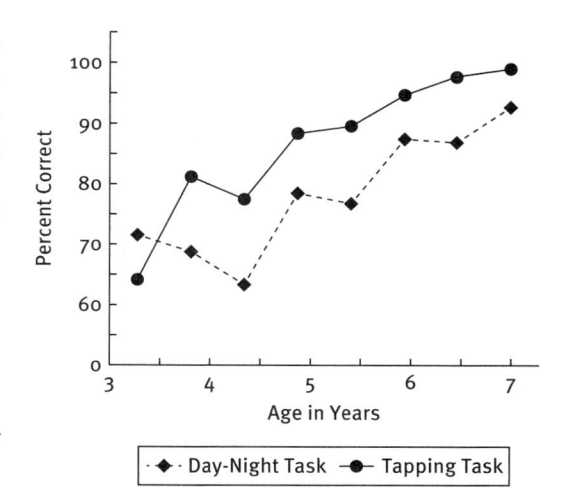

FIGURE 4.2 Illustration of the developmental progression of children on the day–night and tapping tasks.

Source: Reprinted from Diamond, A., Normal development of prefrontal cortex from birth to young adulthood: Cognitive functions, anatomy, and biochemistry, in D. Stuss & R. T. Knight (Eds.), *Principles of frontal lobe function*, p. 466–503, Copyright (2002), by permission of Oxford University Press.

NEUROPSYCHOLOGICAL AND PSYCHOSOCIAL COMPETENCIES OF PRESCHOOL CHILDREN

At approximately ages 4 and 5 years, there is notable development of working memory, and the ability to inhibit motor tendencies improves. Basic language and associated cognitive skills dramatically improve. Case (1985) emphasizes that age 5 years is associated with revolutionary changes in intellectual functioning, with great variability observed in children in this age range.

Figure 4.2 illustrates the accuracy of performance of children aged 3–7 years when asked to carry out tasks that required keeping rules in mind while inhibiting natural response tendencies. In the first task, the child must say the word "night" when shown a white card with a picture of the sun and "day" when presented a black card with a picture of the moon and stars. In the second "tapping" task, the child must tap once when the examiner taps twice and twice when the examiner taps once. By age 5 years, the percentage of correct responses greatly improves over earlier years.

A major task that preschoolers face is developing the ability to delay gratification of a specific need for a greater long-term goal. This can be viewed as a more advanced version of inhibiting response tendencies. Mischel, Shoda, and Rodriguez (1989) reported that 4-year-old children who could do this performed better on the SAT as late adolescents compared to children who were less able to delay gratification. In a 40-year follow-up study, which included neuroimaging findings (Casey et al., 2011), it was found that the ability to delay gratification during preschool years was associated with greater self-control, as measured by performance on a "go" versus "no-go" task as adults. This was the case, however, only for tasks that had a strong positive emotional appeal.

Second, patterns of brain activation varied somewhat depending on the social/emotional context in which the individual had to inhibit a response. Under non-emotional situations (Casey et al. [2011] term this "cool" stimulus conditions), right inferior frontal gyrus significantly activated when a response needed to be inhibited (i.e., the no-go situation). When the task was to inhibit a response (during a no-go situation) that had strong positive emotional appeal for the person, individuals who had greater difficulties with delayed gratification showed increased activation of the ventral striatum.

Casey et al. (2011) interpret these findings as suggesting that there are two "neurocognitive systems" involved in delayed gratification. One is the cortical (perhaps more cognitive) control of the behavioral response (or inhibiting of the response); the other is the "deep brain" systems that process "desires and rewards" (p. 15001). These findings emphasize two important points for clinical neuropsychologists involved in providing psychological care to patients with brain disorders. First, at least some of the neuropsychological (and related psychological) characteristics of a person during early childhood may persist into adulthood (Friedman et al., 1993). Second, decision-making during childhood and adulthood is not always under cortical (or cognitive) control. What is emotionally appealing to the individual can clearly influence performance on a neuropsychological decision-making task (as well as making decisions in the real world). Although this is obvious to clinical psychologists and psychiatrists trained in psychodynamic approaches, it is often not fully appreciated by clinical neuropsychologists, who study primarily the effects of brain lesions on cognitive functioning.

The development of language during the preschool years is also of considerable importance. In contrast to the 70-word vocabulary observed in many children at 12 months of age, it has been estimated that the average 4-year-old expands their vocabulary to approximately 2,000 words (Hauser-Lindstrom & Steinfelt, 1998). The question of "why" that is often asked in approximately the second year of life is expanded to "what" and "how" in the fourth year of life. As language develops, greater control of behavior is observed. Children can "negotiate" with each other, which appears to contribute to their ability to play with one another. It is suggested that during the fourth year of life, children improve in their ability to take turns when playing with other children, and this should be the natural way of interaction (Hauser-Lindstrom & Steinfelt, 1998).

During the fifth year of life, language skills as well as various problem-solving abilities develop rapidly in some children. The potential role of educational experiences in influencing this development becomes more apparent. Noble, Norman, and Farah (2005) compared cognitive performance in kindergarten children (mean age, 5 years 10 months) from middle socioeconomic status (SES) families to that of children from low SES families. Not surprisingly, the children with higher SES background performed significantly better on tests that assessed language and "executive" functions. There was no difference between the two groups of children on tests of memory performance. Other research has shown that the quality of educational experience can clearly influence such skills as verbal fluency (Prigatano, Gray, & Lomay, 2008). Basic memory skills, which are perhaps more dependent on "deep brain" structures, may be less influenced by the educational experiences of the young child.

Summary

It appears that after visual object recognition develops, the pointing response emerges to aid attention and indicate intention. Spoken language then evolves to the point of expressing feelings and perceptions as well as (imperfectly) controlling behavior and aiding working memory. However, it is the ability to inhibit a natural motor or response tendency that marks a substantial shift in the development of higher integrative brain functions. The development of language may be crucial for this skill to be firmly established. These are the skills necessary for not only exploring the environment but also learning from those explorations. The basic capacity for "rote" learning and memory appears to be dependent on more "primitive" brain structures (e.g., the hippocampus and other structures comprising the limbic system), which in turn must be in place in order for the higher cognitive functions to properly develop. Decision-making, as reflected by response inhibition capacity and the use of language to control behavior, can be effectively used by the child to evaluate consequences and the emotional valence of the stimulus for them.

The development of these skills seems to occur in a progressive and overlapping manner, and in and of themselves, they do not strongly support a "stage" theory of neuropsychological development. However, if visual (and then auditory and tactile) object recognition, pointing and gesturing, and working memory do not adequately develop in an age-appropriate manner, it is probable that other neuropsychological skills that are partially dependent on them will develop "imperfectly." Thus, the scaffolding model of cognitive, behavioral, and emotional development appears more probable. However they develop, these skills reflect the crucial neuropsychological functions that underlie the psychosocial competencies needed by the infant, the toddler, and the preschool child.

NEUROPSYCHOLOGICAL AND PSYCHOSOCIAL COMPETENCIES OF SCHOOL-AGE CHILDREN

During the early school-age years, the child must learn to develop the cognitive, motor, language, and behavioral skills necessary for extended social interaction and the acquisition of information necessary for successful competition within a given cultural environment. Motor skills for holding a pencil, drawing, making symbols (including letters of the alphabet and numbers), and engaging in competitive group (play) activities become important.

In her discussion of the intimate connection between broadly defined cognitive development and motor development, Diamond (2002) notes that the cerebellum and the prefrontal cortex show a close time-linked coactivation when performing a variety of tasks. Lesions of the prefrontal cortex are often associated with hypometabolic changes in the contralateral cerebellum. Conversely, lesions of the cerebellum have been shown to produce frontal hypometabolism. She further notes that some developmental disorders in children may represent a disturbance of the normal cognitive control of motor movements that require proper timing and coordination. Other investigators have provided findings that are, in part, compatible with this hypothesis. Studying children aged 4–11 years, Davis, Pitchford, and Limback (2011) reported a positive correlation ($r = .515$) between a composite measure of overall cognitive functioning and an overall motor score in a sample of 248 children.

Appropriate social interactions require the development of language necessary for learning the information that a given culture requires of its children. Gleason and Ratner (2013) summarize many important features associated with the development of language skills before and during school-age years. The child must be able to produce words with adequate fluency and in an intelligible manner (i.e., the absence of dysarthria or immature speech production—"baby talk"). The child must be able to repeat what is said to them. Auditory comprehension must be extended from simple words or phrases to complex instructions. Finally, language must be developed to solve problems and persuade others. A key skill at age 6 years is the beginning ability to learn to read. Failure to do so often raises concerns about the presence of a learning disability (Waber, 2010). During the 6- to 8-year-old range, children's knowledge of numbers also expands. Addition, subtraction, multiplication, division, and concepts involving quantity are introduced and made possible with verbal and nonverbal instructions.

Play behavior also begins to change. Typically, girls do not want to play with boys and vice versa. Most children can now identify a "best friend," and the capacity to make and keep friends becomes quite important for developing a sense of group membership, demonstration that one's behavior is acceptable to the group, and ultimately one's personal sense of how one fits into the group.

Erikson notes that during this time frame, the child either enjoys the academic challenges of school and develops a sense of "industry" (i.e., "Hard work pays off; I receive the admiration of parents, teachers, and some of my peers") or develops a deep sense of inferiority (i.e., "I am not as good as others. I am stupid").

From a neuropsychological perspective, problem-solving abilities slowly but progressively improve between the ages of 6 and 11 years. Korkman, Kemp, and Kirk (2001) noted, however, that "age effects" were most pronounced between 6 and 8 years. Between 9 and 11 years, neuropsychological performance of children was often quite similar.

Waber et al. (2007) reported on the neuropsychological performance of healthy children (aged 6–18 years) in a National Institutes of Health-funded magnetic resonance imaging (MRI) project concerning normal brain development. Some of the findings are reproduced in Figures 4.3; they support Korkman et al.'s (2001) observations.

Vocabulary skills seem to improve most rapidly up to approximately age 10 years, with continued steady improvement into adolescence. The same is observed on visual spatial problem-solving tasks, as reflected by performance on the Block Design subtest of the Wechsler Abbreviated Scale of Intelligence. However, other functions, such as speed of information processing as measured by the Coding subtest of the Wechsler Intelligence Scale for Children, show a somewhat different pattern. Here, a slow, progressive, and nearly linear relationship appears to exist between age and level of performance. Although processing speed has been related to the integrity of white matter pathways in the brain (Rabinowitz, Hart, Whyte, & Kim, 2018; Turken et al., 2008), Rypma et al. (2006) presented evidence that fast and accurate processing speed when performing a version of the Coding subtest actually depends on the degree to which frontal and parietal brain regions communicate efficiently when the person engages in this task. The "automatization" of certain cognitive functions becomes an important feature of a normally developing brain. In Chapter 5, this important observation is discussed in more detail.

Finally, note that performance levels on standard tests of intelligence in school-age children are not strongly associated with measures of cortical thickness (Karama et al., 2011). Although statistically significant correlations were found given a large group sample (the correlation coefficients ranged from .15 to .32), only a very small portion of the variance is accounted for by cortical thickness at various sites on the cerebral mantle.

Genetic factors appear to have greater value for predicting performance on measures of intelligence in large groups of children (Deary, Spinath, & Bates, 2006; Sternberg, 2012). Here, the correlation coefficients range from .4 to .8 (Sternberg, 2012). This is primarily true for measures of general intellectual abilities (or the g factor), when using such measures as the Wechsler Intelligence Scale. Interestingly, the heritability of intellectual performance appears greater in families of higher SES than in lower SES families (Sternberg, 2012).

Kagan (2013) also commented on the importance of non-brain variables (e.g., family, class, and ethnicity) as sources of influence on cognitive development in children. He made the following important observation that should be heeded by clinical neuropsychologists evaluating and treating children (and adults):

> Every human allele is a part of a genome; every genome is part of a brain–body; every brain–body is in agent; every agent is in a family; every family is in a community; every community is in a society; and every society is in a historical era. Hence, it will prove impossible to predict a behavior or mood from the alleles or brain state. (p. 353)

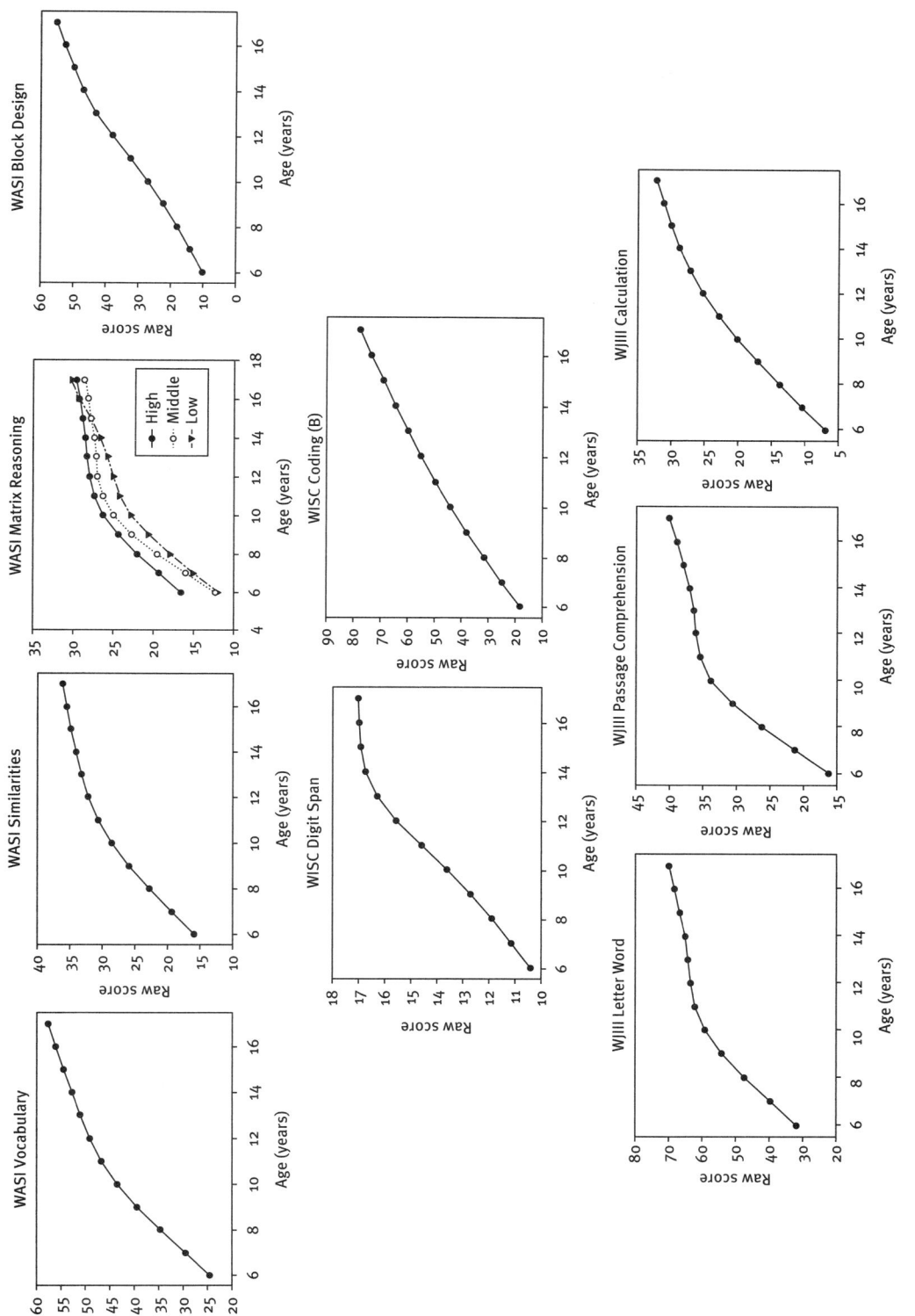

FIGURE 4.3 Graph of raw scores of subtests of the Wechsler Abbreviated Scale of Intelligence (WASI), the Wechsler Intelligence Scale for Children (WISC), and the Woodcock–Johnson III (WJIII) as a function of age.

Source: Reprinted from Waber, D. P., De Moor, C., Forbes, P. W., Almli, C. R., Botteron, K. N, Leonard, G., . . . Rumsey, J., The NIH MRI study of normal brain development: Performance of a population based sample of healthy children aged 6 to 18 years on a neuropsychological battery, *Journal of the International Neuropsychological Society, 13*(5), 2007, p. 729–746, by permission of Cambridge University Press.

It is the interaction of these and yet thought of variables that contributes to the neuropsychological substrates for social competencies in school-age children.

NEUROPSYCHOLOGICAL AND PSYCHOSOCIAL COMPETENCIES DURING ADOLESCENCE

There has been a growing interest in understanding the neural correlates of adolescent behavior (Reyna, Chapman, Dougherty, & Confrey, 2012). It has long been recognized that the period of adolescence is associated with greater risk-taking behaviors and a propensity for challenging parental authority as well as the "rules of society." Moffitt (1993) noted that the prevalence and incidence of criminal offenses appeared highest during adolescence.

The adolescent period (which is classically between ages 12 and 18 years) corresponds to "the physical and psychological dimensions of puberty" (Blos, 1962, p. 1). As Erikson notes, this is a time in which social relationships become of paramount importance to the person. Adolescents become acutely aware of others' opinions about themselves and other individuals in a group. Self-consciousness and concerns about others' opinions of them can greatly influence their behavior. Thus, whereas abstract reasoning skills develop with associated improvements in divided attention, working memory, and language functions, the importance of response inhibition to peer influence appears to be a crucial neuropsychological skill to develop during this time frame. Cascio et al. (2014) conducted a functional MRI (fMRI) study in which adolescents engaged in a driving simulation task in the presence of "risky" versus "cautious" peers. Increased activation of a "response inhibition network" (which included the right inferior frontal gyrus) in the presence of a cautious peer (but not the risky peer) was related to safer driving performance 1 week after the fMRI study was completed. This was observed independently of the self-reported susceptibility to peer pressures.

Another important neuropsychological feature of adolescence is the ability to understand the "other's perspective" when disagreements occur. Choudhury, Blakemore, and Charman (2006) reviewed a series of studies that attempt to correlate this behavioral skill with fMRI findings. As is true with adults, the circuitry of the prefrontal cortex, the inferior parietal lobule, and the superior temporal cortex is activated when adolescents are involved in tasks that require self and other perspectives. This circuitry has been repeatedly linked to not only self-awareness but also awareness of the other's mental state (i.e., theory of mind research). This is not a new function during adolescence, but it appears to become a progressively developed functional capacity during this time frame. Recall from Chapter 2 that Premack (2007) considers this to be one of the defining features of human nature. Tomasello, Carpenter, Call, Behne, and Moll (2005) consider this to be a very important feature of human development. It allows for "shared intentions" between humans that make it feasible to develop "cultural cognitions" necessary for human development.

Managing pleasurable experiences during adolescent is also an important challenge. This includes managing sexual pleasures as well as the pleasures involved in eating (and weight control). It has been suggested that during adolescence there is a period of "dopaminergic reward sensitivity." Telzer (2016) reviewed several studies that assessed the behavioral correlates of dopaminergic reactivity in adolescence. She concludes that both positive and negative consequences have been reported with this "reward sensitivity." For example, under conditions in which adolescents are involved in an activity that supports family members and consequently makes them feel "happier," there is an associated increase in ventral striatum activation. It has also been reported that peaks in ventral striatum activation during adolescence are associated with risk-taking behaviors. The point of Telzer's analysis, however, is that the heightened sense of pleasure associated with various "rewards" can have both positive and negative social outcomes. Much depends on the social context in which surges of dopaminergic activity appear. This increase in dopaminergic reward sensitivity may also relate to the idealism experienced in adolescence in which everything seems possible, and great pleasure is experienced in finding and identifying with one's hero in life and life's purpose.

NEUROPSYCHOLOGICAL AND PSYCHOSOCIAL COMPETENCIES DURING YOUNG ADULTHOOD

Late adolescence ushers in "young adulthood." This time period, according to Erikson, ranges between 19 and 40 years. With the use of Web-based data collection procedures, some interesting observations have recently been collected regarding when different cognitive functions "peak" during the young adult years. Hartshorne and Germine (2015), for example, note that processing speed of information (as measured by the Digit Symbol Coding subtest of the Wechsler Intelligence Scale) peaks at approximately age 19 or 20 years. As discussed previously (Waber, 2010), performance on this task steadily improves, almost in a linear manner, from age 6 to 18 years. Yet, verbal/auditory working memory skills as measured by the Digit Span subtest peak in the early 30s. Quite interestingly, vocabulary level peaks much later in life (as described later). The point of these observations is that neurocognitive functioning is not "static" during young adulthood. Rather, dynamic changes seem to be occurring. This is of considerable importance because the "psychosocial competencies" expected of a 20-year-old person are clearly different from those expected of a 40-year-old person.

Rypma et al. (2006) found that poor (i.e., slow) performance on the Digit Symbol task was related to less efficient communication between prefrontal and parietal regions of the brain when carrying out this task, as noted previously. The frontal–parietal circuitry of the brain has been thought to be especially related to the emergence of working memory skills, which are important in the development of abstract reasoning or problem-solving abilities (R. Jung & Haier, 2007). Peak performance of processing speed may help provide the basis for more efficient working memory capacity during young adulthood. In this regard, it is also interesting to note that verbal/auditory working memory skills appear to reach "peak performance" (as measured by the Digit Span subtest) at approximately 30 years of age (Hartshorne & Germine, 2015). Equally important, performance on this test seems fairly stable throughout the 30s, 40s, 50s, and even the 60s, with only gradual decline in the late 60s and early 70s.

NEUROPSYCHOLOGICAL AND PSYCHOSOCIAL COMPETENCIES DURING MIDDLE ADULTHOOD

This stage is also rather broad; Erikson places it roughly between ages 40 and 65 years. Interestingly, it is a period of time in which language function (at least as measured by knowledge of what words mean; i.e., vocabulary level) continues to improve and tends to reach maximum capacity.

Many "high-level" jobs require advanced language and analytic abilities. Middle-age adults are often involved in managing large numbers of people, handling medical emergencies, as well as leading nations. For example, the average age to begin practicing as a neurosurgeon in the United States is between 40 and 42 years. The average age at becoming president of the United States is 54 years and 11 months. The median age of S&P 500 CEOs is 55 years. Something about this "middle adulthood" range reflects the "peaks" of professional achievements. Neuropsychological abilities appear relatively stable, with only mild and very subtle decline in cognitive functioning (Hartshorne & Germine, 2015). There are, however, important psychological and social characteristics of adults during this time period.

By the time one reaches middle adulthood, several efforts at problem-solving have been explored and utilized. They are broadly referred to as "years of experience." It is not just a period of cognitive problem-solving per se but also cumulative experiences involving successes and failures that foster the development of judgment. The motivational and emotional consequences of certain behavioral choices become more evident. This may help the middle-age adult make "wiser" decisions.

It is also the time for the famous "midlife crisis" observed in some individuals. The second half of life is now keenly experienced by the individual. The personal value of extensive efforts put into work and obtaining various resources is re-evaluated. Conflicts within the marriage and work appear more important to understand and confront. Continued management of sexual and aggressive drives occurs, but thoughts regarding the "meaning in life" predominate during the second half of life. Recognizing that not all behaviors (including one's personal behavior and choices) are under conscious control may become more apparent to some during this time period. The appreciation of unconscious motivations and mental processes becomes clearer when facing earlier losses in life and one's emotional reactions to those losses. This appears to be the beginning phase of maturity that holds the opportunity for wisdom.

NEUROPSYCHOLOGICAL AND PSYCHOSOCIAL COMPETENCIES DURING MATURITY

Glisky (2007) summarizes many of the cognitive changes that have been studied in human aging after age 65 years (the maturity phase described by Erikson). It is well known that during this time, there are important declines in perceptual (vision, hearing, and tactile senses) and motor skills that may relate to decline in certain cognitive domains. Glisky notes that "visual impairments can limit mobility and interact with attentional deficits to make driving a particularly hazardous activity" during this time (p. 9). Whereas attention, memory, and working memory show predictable declines after 65 years, speech and language skills (especially vocabulary) seem to be "largely intact in older adults under normal conditions" (p. 9). More recent data, with large sample sizes, suggest that vocabulary level may continue to develop with advancing age (Hartshorne & Germine, 2015). Glisky also notes that the higher level problem-solving skills that have traditionally been related to prefrontal regions of the brain may show the greatest and most rapid decline during this time period. This includes formulating new strategies when problem-solving, inhibiting distracting stimuli when problem-solving, and the capacity to efficiently adjust to changing and unpredictable environmental demands (e.g., learning to effectively use a computer).

To add to these changes, there generally is a decline in health, with an associated decline in sexual functioning. Cardiovascular disease, cancer, and chronic respiratory illnesses are the leading causes of death after age 65 years. Although the average life expectancy in the United States is currently 76 years for males and 81 years for women, these figures can be deceiving. For example, social security data suggest that if a male lives to age 65 years, he has an average life expectancy of 84.3 years. For women who reach age 65 years, the average life expectancy is 85 years. During this time frame, however, a variety of health problems accrue and have to be managed.

In light of these changes, how is "wisdom" possible during "maturity"? How does "ego integrity" actually occur? For some, the retirement years represent the "great reward" (as one patient stated), whereas for others they represent a time of boredom, frustration, and pain before death.

Effectively dealing with normal decline of the central nervous system has been associated with a return to religious and community activities, taking joy in caring for one's grandchildren or animals, and enjoying nature. These activities provide for considerable tactile, visual, and auditory stimulation. They may help restore a childlike sense of wonder and hope. These feeling are often further reflected in symbolic expressions important to a person's life. Symbolism involves an integration of feelings and thoughts, some of which are not clearly consciously expressed but seem to have some "unconscious" appeal (C. Jung, 1964). The role of symbolism, connection with others, and reflection on life gives a perspective on life that at times can be realistically referred to as "wisdom." Wisdom means knowing what matters at different stages of life rather than simply responding to the pressures of society. Wisdom means making choices that are later shown to be more valuable or practical than was originally thought of by others. It means having a realistic sense of the world without being too discouraged or negative about the nature of human beings.

More than one academic neuropsychologist has written "their last book" with a clear desire to talk about what is relevant, what was and is still meaningful to them in light of their professional experiences, and what got them into neuropsychology in the first place (e.g., Luria's book, *The Making of Mind*, and Weiskrantz's book, *Consciousness Lost and Found*). Therefore, the maximum use of language-related skills may be especially important during the last psychosocial phase of life.

SUMMARY AND REFLECTIONS/IMPRESSIONS

In fulfilling the natural plan of the central nervous system, the human organism undergoes constant change and modification in brain–behavior relationships. Although there is no strict timetable for cognitive and emotional/motivational development or decline in humans, important age-related trends have been documented by both clinicians and researchers. Both have emphasized the great individual variability in cognitive (and related neuropsychological) functional changes that occur at different times in life.

Early in life, the sensory functions develop in such a way as to provide for recognized and "remembered" perceptual patterns. In this regard, the visual modality seems most important for the very young infant. Vision helps identify meaningful objects in the environment. These objects are approached, and finger movements identify where they are and what is wanted. Vocalizations also develop during these early times in such a way as to provide for recognized and remembered sound patterns. These sound patterns are copied or imitated by the infant and caregiver. Language becomes possible (although it is still not understood exactly how).

The development of working memory allows for these functions to further develop and be expanded. It also seems relevant to the development of retaining memories/experiences over time. The bond between memory and emotion/motivations becomes obvious. This can be demonstrated for both positive and negative emotional experiences. As described in Chapter 5, certain negative emotional experiences may influence how a person behaves and what choices they make without being "aware" of what guides or motivates those choices. "Irrational" behavior, based on emotional conflicts, is first observed during these early childhood days.

Learning contingencies ultimately form the earliest basis for problem-solving: "If this, then that; if that, then this." Expanding contingencies between relationships of objects (e.g., striking a stone to produce a spark that results in fire) is the first form of learning that allows humans to survive in their external environments. Expanding contingencies between words that represent objects as well as concepts results in a second order of problem-solving. For example, this can be reflected in simple mathematic operations, such as $2 \times 4 = 8$, and complex contingencies observed in theoretical physics, such as $E = mc^2$. Expanding contingencies between symbols forms the basis of creative thought and reflects conscious and nonconscious problem-solving activities. These latter activities may play an especially important role in personal psychological development that helps the individual understand their own feelings and behavioral choices.

In the context of all these activities, learning to delay gratification and control impulsive responding seems crucial for intentional and observation learning. Incidental learning becomes important for later problem-solving and creativity. It may be most readily affected by any brain disorder (for a discussion of the importance of the Location score on the Tactual Performance Test as a measure of "biological intelligence," see Reitan, 1955).

Box 4.1. Neuropsychological Functional Capacities Relevant to Psychosocial Competencies over the Life Span

1. Emotional engagement of others to facilitate their support for purposes of social adaptation and survival.
2. Hand and finger movements that explore the environment in a time efficient manner that aid survival.
3. Visual scanning/tracking and auditory perception to locate emotional and motivationally relevant stimuli.
4. Conscious representation of the immediate past and present when problem-solving (i.e., working memory).
5. Learning from doing (1) basic associative learning—"if this, then that; if that, then this"—and (2) development of "abstract" concepts as a result of the associative learning process.
6. Inhibitory control of impulsive responding in order to facilitate observation learning and functioning within a group setting.
7. Accurate perception and expression of emotions.
8. Attention to detail (which implies selective and divided attention) during problem-solving.
9. Memory for past information necessary for immediate and future problem-solving.
10. Sustained "mental energy" during problem-solving.
11. Processing information at a speed necessary for efficient problem-solving.
12. Comprehension and production of language (and related skills such as mathematics), for expanding learning possibilities and aiding adaptation to the environment.
13. Recognizing relationships between objects (including people) and events that are practical (judgment) and theoretical (abstract reasoning) that can be used for immediate and later problem-solving.
14. Planning ahead or anticipating how to solve a problem with evidence of "foresight" and impulse control.
15. Empathetic responding to the needs of others once language skills develop. This implies the evolution of a subjective or phenomenological state of one's own existence (i.e., self-awareness) that allows for the awareness of the other's phenomenological state (i.e., theory of mind).
16. Self-perceptions that appear realistic and aid adaptive choices that, in turn, enhance creativity and satisfaction with life at different stages of psychosocial development.
17. Exploration and seeking new opportunities/environments compatible with one's psychosocial stage of development.

From this analysis, the higher integrative brain functions clearly develop to meet the biological needs of the organism. Freud made the same basic point when he emphasized that development of ego functions was in the service of the id. However, much more occurs in evolution than cognitive and related functions. In the context of human interaction, as well as human–other animal interaction, emotional development takes place as various emotions are progressively, consciously, and then automatically learned to become "controlled." It is also a time in which the phenomenon of empathy occurs. A variety of theorists have suggested that empathy appears to be the foundation of morality and the central value for guiding an ethical life. Thus, from the ego emerges the superego—again to use a Freudian analogy/terminology. These changes in "mental apparatus" seem to undergo stages of development that are in part reflected in Erikson's first eight stages of psychosocial development.

Progressively, humans develop an enhanced sense of self-reflection that appears to guide decision-making (Donald, 1991). Yet some consciously guided decisions appear "irrational," and this has led to the exploration of the possibility of unconscious thought processes and emotions as having important influences on human behavior. This forms the topic of Chapter 5. For now, Box 4.1 proposes a series of neuropsychological functions that appear related to psychosocial competencies over the life span and that require psychological and neuropsychological evaluation when attempting to provide psychological care.

REFERENCES

Als, H., Duffy, F. H., McAnulty, G. B., Rivkin, M. J., Vajapeyam, S., Mulkern, R. V., . . . Conneman, N. (2004). Early experience alters brain function and structure. *Pediatrics, 113*(4), 846–857.

Arnett, J. J. (2000). Emerging adulthood: A theory of development from the late teens through the twenties. *The American Psychologist, 55*(5), 469–480.

Bergen, D., & Woodin, M. (2011). Neuropsychological development of newborns, infants, and toddlers (0 to 3 years old). In A. S. Davis (Ed.), *Handbook of pediatric neuropsychology* (pp. 15–30). New York, NY: Springer.

Bettelheim, B. (1989). *The uses of enchantment: The meaning and importance of fairy tales*. New York, NY: Vintage.

Blos, P. (1962). *On adolescence: A psychoanalytic interpretation*. New York: The Free Press of Glencoe, Inc.

Bowlby, J. (1980). *Attachment and loss, Volume III: Loss*. New York, NY: Basic Books.

Bowlby, R., & King, P. (2004). *Fifty years of attachment theory*. London, UK: Karnac.

Cascio, C. N., Carp, J., O'Donnell, M. B., Tinney, F. J., Jr., Bingham, C. R., Shope, J. T., . . . Falk, E. B. (2014). Buffering social influence: Neural correlates of response inhibition predict driving safety in the presence of a peer. *Journal of Cognitive Neuroscience, 27*(1), 83–95.

Case, R. (1985). *Intellectual development: Birth to adulthood*. New York, NY: Academic Press.

Casey, B., Somerville, L. H., Gotlib, I. H., Ayduk, O., Franklin, N. T., Askren, M. K., . . . Teslovich, T. (2011). Behavioral and neural correlates of delay of gratification 40 years later. *Proceedings of the National Academy of Sciences of the USA, 108*(36), 14998–15003.

Choudhury, S., Blakemore, S.-J., & Charman, T. (2006). Social cognitive development during adolescence. *Social Cognitive and Affective Neuroscience, 1*(3), 165–174.

Cole, M., & Cole, S. (Eds). (1979). *A. R. Luria: The making of mind. A personal account of Soviet Psychology*. Cambridge, MA: Harvard University Press.

Davis, E. E., Pitchford, N. J., & Limback, E. (2011). The interrelation between cognitive and motor development in typically developing children aged 4–11 years is underpinned by visual processing and fine manual control. *British Journal of Psychology, 102*(3), 569–584.

Deary, I. J., Spinath, F. M., & Bates, T. C. (2006). Genetics of intelligence. *European Journal of Human Genetics, 14*(6), 690–700.

Diamond, A. (2002). Normal development of prefrontal cortex from birth to young adulthood: Cognitive functions, anatomy, and biochemistry. In D. Stuss & R. T. Knight (Eds.), *Principles of frontal lobe function* (pp. 466–503). Oxford, UK: Oxford University Press.

Donald, M. (1991). *Origins of the modern mind: Three stages in the evolution of culture and cognition*. Cambridge, MA: Harvard University Press.

Duff, F. J., Reen, G., Plunkett, K., & Nation, K. (2015). Do infant vocabulary skills predict school-age language and literacy outcomes? *Journal of Child Psychology and Psychiatry, 56*(8), 848–856.

Erikson, E. H. (1964). *Insight and responsibility*. New York, NY: Norton.

Erikson, E. H., & Erikson, J. M. (1998). *The life cycle completed (extended version)*. New York, NY: Norton.

Friedman, H. S., Tucker, J. S., Tomlinson-Keasey, C., Schwartz, J. E., Wingard, D. L., & Criqui, M. H. (1993). Does childhood personality predict longevity? *Journal of Personality and Social Psychology, 65*(1), 176–185.

Fuster, J. M. (1997). *The prefrontal cortex: Anatomy, physiology, and neuropsychology of the frontal lobe* (3rd ed.). Philadelphia, PA: Lippincott–Raven.

Gleason, J. B., & Ratner, N. B. (2013). *The development of language* (8th ed.). New York, NY: Pearson.

Glisky, E. L. (2007). Changes in cognitive function in human aging. In D. R. Riddle (Ed.), *Brain aging: Models, methods, and mechanisms* (pp. 3–20). Boca Raton, FL: CRC Press.

Gogtay, N., Giedd, J. N., Lusk, L., Hayashi, K. M., Greenstein, D., Vaituzis, A. C., . . . Toga, A. W. (2004). Dynamic mapping of human cortical development during childhood through early adulthood. *Proceedings of the National Academy of Sciences of the USA, 101*(21), 8174–8179.

Gupta, P., & MacWhinney, B. (1997). Vocabulary acquisition and verbal short-term memory: Computational and neural bases. *Brain and Language, 59*(2), 267–333.

Hall, C. S., & Lindzey, G. (1978). *Theories of personality* (3rd ed.). New York, NY: Wiley.

Hartshorne, J. K., & Germine, L. T. (2015). When does cognitive functioning peak? The asynchronous rise and fall of different cognitive abilities across the life span. *Psychological Science, 26*(4), 433–443.

Hauser-Lindstrom, D., & Steinfelt, V. (1998). *Ages and stages: 4 to 8 year olds*. Retrieved from http://ag.arizona.edu/pubs/family/az1036.html

Huttenlocher, P. R. (1990). Morphometric study of human cerebral cortex development. *Neuropsychologia, 28*(6), 517–527.

Jung, C. G. (1964). *Man and his symbols*. London, UK: Aldus.

Jung, R. E., & Haier, R. J. (2007). The parieto-frontal integration theory (P-FIT) of intelligence: Converging neuroimaging evidence. *Behavioral and Brain Sciences, 30*(2), 135–154.

Kagan, J. (2013). Equal time for psychological and biological contributions to human variation. *Review of General Psychology, 17*(4), 351–357.

Karama, S., Colom, R., Johnson, W., Deary, I. J., Haier, R., Waber, D. P., . . . Evans, A. C. (2011). Cortical thickness correlates of specific cognitive performance accounted for by the general factor of intelligence in healthy children aged 6 to 18. *Neuroimage, 55*(4), 1443–1453.

Korkman, M., Kemp, S. L., & Kirk, U. (2001). Effects of age on neurocognitive measures of children ages 5 to 12: A cross-sectional study on 800 children from the United States. *Developmental Neuropsychology, 20*(1), 331–354.

Koslowski, B., & Bruner, J. S. (1972). Learning to use a lever. *Child Development, 43*(3), 790–799.

Libertus, K., & Violi, D. A. (2016). Sit to talk: Relation between motor skills and language development in infancy. *Frontiers in Psychology, 7*, 475.

McAdams, D. P., & Pals, J. L. (2006). A new Big Five: Fundamental principles for an integrative science of personality. *The American Psychologist, 61*(3), 204–217.

Mischel, W., Shoda, Y., & Rodriguez, M. L. (1989). Delay of gratification in children. *Science, 244*(4907), 933.

Mitchell, P., & Ziegler, F. (2007). *Fundamentals of development: The psychology of childhood*. New York, NY: Psychology Press.

Moffitt, T. E. (1993). Adolescence-limited and life-course-persistent antisocial behavior: A developmental taxonomy. *Psychological Review, 100*(4), 674–701.

Noble, K. G., Norman, M. F., & Farah, M. J. (2005). Neurocognitive correlates of socioeconomic status in kindergarten children. *Developmental Science, 8*(1), 74–87.

Piaget, J. (1954). *The construction of reality in the child* (M. Cook, Trans.). New York, NY: Basic Books. (Original work published 1936)

Posner, M. I., & Rothbart, M. K. (2007). *Educating the human brain*. New York, NY: American Psychological Association.

Povinelli, D. J., & Davis, D. R. (1994). Differences between chimpanzees (*Pan troglodytes*) and humans (*Homo sapiens*) in the resting state of the index finger: Implications for pointing. *Journal of Comparative Psychology, 108*(2), 134–139.

Premack, D. (2007). Human and animal cognition: Continuity and discontinuity. *Proceedings of the National Academy of Sciences of the USA, 104*(35), 13861–13867.

Prigatano, G. P., Gray, J. A., & Lomay, V. T. (2008). Verbal (animal) fluency scores in age/grade appropriate minority children from low socioeconomic backgrounds. *Journal of the International Neuropsychological Society, 14*(1), 143–147.

Rabinowitz, A. R., Hart, T., Whyte, J., & Kim, J. (2018). Neuropsychological recovery trajectories in moderate to severe traumatic brain injury: Influence of patient characteristics and diffuse axonal injury. *Journal of the International Neuropsychological Society, 24*(3), 237–224.

Reilly, S., Wake, M., Ukoumunne, O. C., Bavin, E., Prior, M., Cini, E., . . . Bretherton, L. (2010). Predicting language outcomes at 4 years of age: Findings from Early Language in Victoria Study. *Pediatrics, 126*(6), e1530–e1537.

Reitan, R. (1955). An investigation of the validity of Halstead's measures of biological intelligence. *Archives of Neurology and Psychiatry, 73,* 28–35.

Reyna, V. F., Chapman, S. B., Dougherty, M. R., & Confrey, J. E. (2012). *The adolescent brain: Learning, reasoning, and decision making*. Washington, DC: American Psychological Association.

Rypma, B., Berger, J. S., Prabhakaran, V., Bly, B. M., Kimberg, D. Y., Biswal, B. B., & D'Esposito, M. (2006). Neural correlates of cognitive efficiency. *Neuroimage, 33*(3), 969–979.

Sternberg, R. J. (2012). Intelligence. *Dialogues in Clinical Neuroscience, 14*(1), 19–27.

Telzer, E. H. (2016). Dopaminergic reward sensitivity can promote adolescent health: A new perspective on the mechanism of ventral striatum activation. *Developmental Cognitive Neuroscience, 17,* 57–67.

Tomasello, M., Carpenter, M., Call, J., Behne, T., & Moll, H. (2005). Understanding and sharing intentions: The origins of cultural cognition. *Behavioral and Brain Sciences, 28*(5), 675–691.

Turken, U., Whitfield-Gabrieli, S., Bammer, R., Baldo, J. V., Dronkers, N. F., & Gabrieli, J. D. (2008). Cognitive processing speed and the structure of white matter pathways: Convergent evidence from normal variation and lesion studies. *Neuroimage, 42*(2), 1032–1044.

Vaillant, E., & Milofsky, E. (1980). Natural history of male psychological health: IX. Empirical evidence for Erikson's model of the life cycle. *American Journal of Psychiatry, 137*(11), 1348–1359.

Waber, D. P. (2010). *Rethinking learning disabilities: Understanding children who struggle in school.* New York, NY: Guilford.

Waber, D. P., De Moor, C., Forbes, P. W., Almli, C. R., Botteron, K. N., Leonard, G., . . . Rumsey, J. (2007). The NIH MRI study of normal brain development: Performance of a population based sample of healthy children aged 6 to 18 years on a neuropsychological battery. *Journal of the International Neuropsychological Society, 13*(5), 729–746.

Wadsworth, B. J. (1996). *Piaget's theory of cognitive and affective development: Foundations of constructivism.* New York, NY: Longman.

Walle, E. A., & Campos, J. J. (2014). Infant language development is related to the acquisition of walking. *Developmental Psychology, 50*(2), 336.

Weiskrantz, L. (1997). *Consciousness Lost and Found: A Neuropsychological Exploration.* Oxford England, Oxford University Press.

Wiener-Vacher, S. R., Hamilton, D. A., & Wiener, S. I. (2013). Vestibular activity and cognitive development in children: Perspectives. *Frontiers in Integrative Neuroscience, 7,* 92.

Wood, D., Bruner, J. S., & Ross, G. (1976). The role of tutoring in problem solving. *Journal of Child Psychology and Psychiatry, 17*(2), 89–100.

5

CONSCIOUS AND UNCONSCIOUS MANIFESTATIONS OF HIGHER INTEGRATIVE BRAIN FUNCTIONS

INTRODUCTION

In Chapter 2, it was proposed that human nature is such that our behavior is not always under "conscious control." In Chapter 3, it was noted that the higher integrative brain functions (HIBFs) evolve as feelings influence movements and movements have consequences. An early learning paradigm becomes "if this, then that." This paradigm becomes extended into "if this, then that; if that, then this." This progressively expanded contingency may be consciously perceived when it first happens but later (often with repetition) may become "automatic" with no conscious control. It was also suggested that some behavioral choices or reactions are unconsciously mediated. If this can be demonstrated, it has considerable significance to what must be attended to when providing psychological care.

Scientifically trained psychologists effectively argue that one needs empirical evidence to propose that there are unconscious manifestations of the HIBFs and unconscious manifestations are relevant to understanding human behavior and have clinical significance. In this regard, an important question to ask is: What constitutes empirical evidence? By definition, the word *empirical* means observable findings by multiple people that are consistently and reliably reported. To meet this criterion of evidence, one must demonstrate that the observable phenomenon can be produced under predicable circumstances. This criterion is the standard criterion used in all science. For example, the laws of chemistry are based on this principle. Water can be demonstrated to have two molecules of hydrogen for every one molecule of oxygen irrespective of whether it is in a liquid or a gas form. Moreover, the structure of hydrogen remains the same in either gas or hydride storage (Crabtree, Dresselhaus, & Buchanan, 2004). Is this level of evidence needed in psychology?

The answer is a difficult one because some features of human mental functioning are only subjectively experienced and therefore the criterion of publicly observed phenomena cannot be met. Also, different subjective experiences may trigger different publicly observable behaviors across individuals. Explaining the different reactions *after* the event rather than predicting the reaction *before* the event also fails to meet the typical standards of scientific proof.

This rigorous form of thinking or logic, however, gives way under certain personal and clinical experiences. For example, a man may be aware that he is very frustrated with his wife's reactions. Yet he may have difficulty directly and effectively expressing his frustrations and associated anger. He may find himself suddenly getting very angry at a clerk in a store for having to wait a little longer than is typically the case. Upon experiencing his angry outburst, this person may recognize that the intensity of his reaction was driven by factors not immediately consciously experienced. This is a common experience of many people and the phenomenon has been named *displacement* (American Psychiatric Association, 2000). Can this phenomenon be reliably and predictably produced? The answer is no. Some people may never express the intensity of their anger in an outward form and others may kick their dog when they come home. Yet the phenomenon of displacement has been subjectively experienced by many people over time and therefore it is accepted as a "fact of life" or a "fact of human behavior" that does not meet the traditional scientific definition of what constitutes a fact. In this chapter, both scientific and clinical evidence of the importance of unconscious manifestations of the HIBFs are presented after considering two historical views that underlie the importance of consciousness in the HIBFs.

TWO HISTORICAL VIEWS ON THE NATURE OF HIGHER INTEGRATIVE BRAIN FUNCTIONS

Traditionally, the higher psychological functions of humans were described as the "higher cortical functions" (Luria, 1966). This view has progressively changed in light of the overwhelming evidence that both cortical and subcortical functions are intimately connected and form the basis of what is more properly referred to as the HIBFs, as Chapman, Thetford, Berlin, Guthrie, and Wolff (1958) suggested many years ago. Two of the most influential theories regarding these functions were proposed by Ward Halstead (1947) and A. R. Luria (1966).

Halstead (1947) made a distinction between *psychometric intelligence* and *biological intelligence*. The former term reflected accumulated knowledge and problem-solving skills based on experience, including educational experiences. The latter term, in Halstead's model, referred to the human brain's biological capacity for successful problem-solving (another term for the HIBFs). He attempted a statistical analysis of key features of biological intelligence. He was aware that his analysis was limited (p. 96), but he argued that it did provide a scientifically based approach to understanding the nature of the higher brain functions.

Halstead (1947) proposed that biological intelligence was composed of four major factors: the central integrative field factor, abstraction, the power factor, and the directional (i.e., modality) factor. The power factor was important for arousal and the emotional state of mental functions that influenced problem-solving. According to Halstead, the power factor "operates as a kind of mordant for experience which helps bind together the saliencies of our central integrative field factor C" (p. 69). Halstead was also especially alert to the "motor concomitants of affect and brain localization" (p. 68) and noted that the memory component of the Tactual Performance Test tended to load on the power factor.

Central to Halstead's (1947) thinking about the nature of the higher brain functions was the central integrative field factor, C. This factor is not clearly defined, but it refers to the human brain's capacity to combine common and diverse sources of information into some meaningful mosaic necessary for problem-solving. Halstead noted that many of his neuropsychological test scores load on this factor. They included scores from the Category Test (which also loaded highly on the abstraction factor), as well as scores from the Halstead Finger Oscillation (or Tapping) Test. He also noted,

> Of the four it is the writer's guess, set forth here only in the interest of urging basic neurophysiological and psychological research on the problem, that consciousness is a scalable entity which is closely related to our central integrative field factor C. (p. 96)

Thus, for Halstead, consciousness was a key feature of the higher brain functions because it helped combine and contrast different sources of information about the world, which was necessary for problem-solving.

Halstead (1947) also appreciated the special role of sensory–motor and perceptual skills as reflecting key components of biological intelligence (the directional factor, D). Although Halstead was concerned about the lack of statistical evidence in support of this factor, his final tests of biological intelligence clearly reflected the importance of this factor in his model. The Seashore Rhythm Test measured the ability to match different tonal patterns found in music. The Speech Perception Test measured the ability to detect vowel/consonant sounds of speech. The speed of performance on the Tactual Performance Test was considered a very sensitive measure of brain dysfunction. As reviewed in Chapters 3 and 4, these measures make good biological sense because they clearly reflect important features found in the evolution of human brain–behavior development.

Halstead (1947), as well as others of his generation (e.g., Goldstein, 1939), was also impressed with the human brain's capacity for abstraction, which he labeled the A factor. Humans have a capacity to think beyond the obvious. They can see relationships between objects and events that may not be immediately observed but that are clearly important for successful adaptation and for creative problem-solving (Heilman, 2005). This capacity for abstraction has something to do with the symbols mankind has created. Perhaps the most obvious symbolic system was the development of language, a key dimension of the HIBFs emphasized by Luria.

Luria (1966) provided one of the most specific definitions of what he referred to as the higher cortical functions in man. His famous definition is as follows: "From the point of view of modern psychology, the higher human mental functions are complex reflex processes, social in origin, mediate in structure, and conscious and voluntary in mode of functioning" (p. 32). Although there is no doubt that consciousness was a key feature of the higher brain functions from Luria's perspective, speech and language facilitated the social influences on the development of human mental functioning and allowed for a constant reorganization of its "mediate in structure" feature. Language is not only a "signal" system (i.e., alerts the child and adult as to what needs to be done) but also crucial in the control of individual behavior. Moreover, language "codes" information in interesting and complex ways. How something is said can be as important as "what is being said." Language also aids learning and continually modifies the underlying structure of human mental functioning. When describing the "mediate in structure" component of higher brain functions, Luria noted that humans have various tools or strategies for combining and manipulating information (a concept similar to Halstead's C factor). Something "stands for something else." This can serve as a trigger for memory and related problem-solving. The example Luria gave was that a person may want to remember something by taking a handkerchief and tying a knot with it. The handkerchief can then be put into the person's pocket, and when the person returns home and retrieves the handkerchief from the pocket, the observed knot triggers a memory of what needs to be done. Note that there is no inherent information in the knot, but the knot stimulates (or, broadly speaking, mediates) a cognitive process we refer to as a conscious memory. It is in this way that language is crucial for the development and maintenance of the HIBFs, according to Luria and Vygotsky, as described in Chapter 2.

Luria (1966) specifically stated that consciousness and intentionality are considered the "modes of functions" for human mental activity. In other words, we have the capacity to be aware of what we want to do and then we do it when we want to do it. This is a defining feature of the higher brain functions, according to Luria.

CONTEMPORARY UNDERSTANDING OF THE NATURE OF HIGHER INTEGRATIVE BRAIN FUNCTIONS

One of Luria's (1966) most substantial contributions to understanding the higher brain functions was to emphasize that there are various "systems" and "subsystems" that underlie complex psychological functioning. If modern neuroimaging studies have done anything, they have provided overwhelming support for this basic proposition (Sporns, 2013). These studies highlight important structural and functional connectivity patterns throughout the human brain necessary for neuropsychological functioning. Different neural networks become more or less activated when different tasks are presented to the human brain to solve. For example, the conscious intentional initiation of speech is correlated with increased blood flow in the cerebellum and left frontal and temporal regions of the brain (Ackermann, Wildgruber, Daum, & Grodd, 1998; Petersen, Fox, Posner, Mintun, & Raichle, 1988). The conscious intentional initiation of motor grip (or squeezing a dynamometer) is related to contralateral activation of the sensory–motor strip and ipsilateral cerebellar activation (Ward, Brown, Thompson, & Frackowiak, 2003). The conscious intentional effort to bring a memory to mind as well as to suppress memories is related to hippocampal activation or reduction in activation, respectively. The dorsolateral region of the frontal lobes also seems to play an important role in these processes (Anderson et al., 2004).

We no longer think of the higher cortical functions as purely reflex processes; rather, we view the brain as a high-demand energy system (Raichle & Gusnard, 2002) that is an "inference machine" (Carhart-Harris & Friston, 2010). The brain has almost always been thought about in terms of its ability to solve problems. As an inference machine, it must constantly reduce prediction error (i.e., what happens in light of what was expected). This process includes many functions that are poorly defined by such vague terms as *perception, attention, intention, memory, emotion, motivation, reasoning, abstraction,* and *consciousness*. Languages, the symbolic systems that evolved with human brain development, seem to play an extremely important role in guiding these systems. However, a growing body of knowledge suggests that human brain function relies on both conscious and unconscious processes to successfully navigate in the world and therefore the defining features of the HIBFs need to be modified.

NEUROPHYSIOLOGICAL EVIDENCE OF UNCONSCIOUS PROCESSES

In 1985, Benjamin Libet and colleagues reported a simple but far-reaching empirical finding (summarized in Haggard & Libet, 2001). When a person was asked to carry out a motor response whenever he or she felt the conscious urge to do so, it was noted that a physiological response, known as a readiness potential (RP), predated the urge that came to awareness. This neurophysiological finding provided empirical evidence that some mental or underlying brain processes outside of conscious awareness existed prior to a consciously experienced "feeling" or "urge" to act. The finding has been replicated by others (see Haggard & Libet, 2001) and has stimulated considerable discussion about whether "free will" is a fact or a fantasy. Libet suggests that unconscious processes may well underlie and predate a conscious thought or tendency for action (see Haggard & Libet, 2001). However, the person can "veto" or stop or suppress that thought or action once it reaches consciousness. Having a thought or feeling does not mean we act on it.

Although Freudian terminology is not used, this neurophysiological finding and the later interpretation by Libet are quite similar to the traditional concepts of "ego" and "superego." Ego functions imply an integrated problem-solving system that automatically weaves together thought processes and affective experiences (Erikson, 1964, p. 147). This system is not totally conscious in nature, but it serves the purposes of the individual once a conscious thought, feeling, or urge is experienced. Our "mental apparatus" (Salas & Yuen, 2016) also includes the capacity to potentially modify what we perceive, think, and feel (i.e., the veto power of the superego; see Prigatano, 2016). Whether or not one wishes to use this terminology is irrelevant. The important point is to understand that there is neurophysiological evidence that the human brain is involved in some form of physiological activity necessary for task performance before it is consciously aware of wanting to perform that task. Also note that the RP recorded by Libet (1985) was from the supplementary motor area. Other researchers, using functional magnetic resonance imaging (fMRI) and somewhat different research designs (Soon, Brass, Heinze, & Haynes, 2008), have suggested that the frontopolar cortex (Brodmann area 10) and the parietal cortex may be associated with unconscious motor preparedness during different problem-solving situations.

NEUROPSYCHOLOGICAL EVIDENCE OF CONSCIOUS AND UNCONSCIOUS MEMORY PROCESSES

Squire and Dede (2015) summarize the evidence that there are both conscious and unconscious memory systems that have been documented in the mammalian brain. Figure 5.1 summarizes an organizational structure of mammalian long-term memory systems. Memory is conceptualized as involving several different types of activities. In general, however, two major features of memory function have been described in the scientific literature: declarative knowledge/memory and nondeclarative memory. Squire and Dede note that declarative knowledge or memory represents information that can be accessed via conscious recollection. It can include several sources of information obtained over a lifetime, including memories of childhood, the names of family members or co-workers, the physical appearance of one's mother and father, the location of a person during the time of an emotionally significant event, and the mental image of an old girlfriend when the odor of a certain perfume is detected. These features of declarative memory are referred to as *episodic memory* because they concern specific time and place events.

There is also a body of knowledge that can be retrieved via conscious effort that references "facts about the world." This type of memory might include recalling events that led up to the Civil War, the chemical composition of water, and the formula for calculating the length of the hypotenuse of a triangle. It can also include what specific words mean and how numbers are added or subtracted. This has been referred to as *semantic memory*. Brain lesions of different types can differentially affect episodic and semantic features of declarative memories. However, in the normally functioning

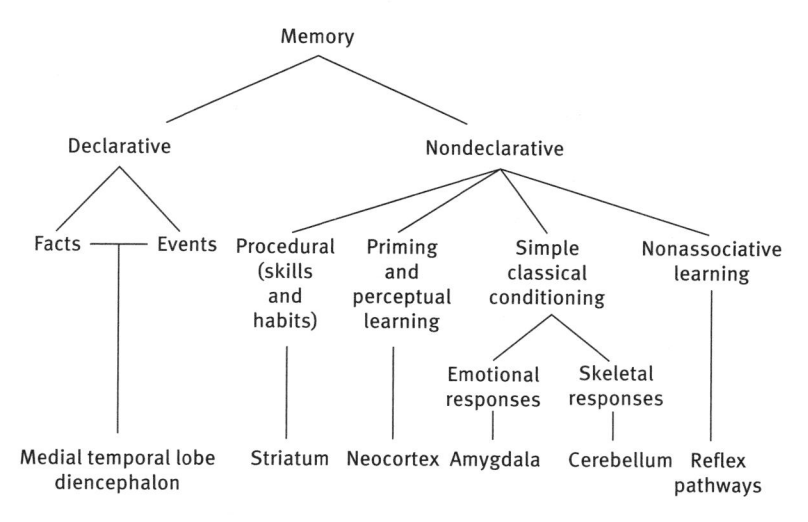

FIGURE 5.1 Organization of mammalian long-term memory systems. Brain structures thought to be especially important for each form of memory are shown. In addition to its central role in emotional learning, the amygdala is able to modulate the strength of both declarative and nondeclarative memory.

Source: Reprinted from Squire, L. R., & Dede, A. J., Conscious and unconscious memory systems, *Cold Spring Harbor Perspectives in Biology*, 7(3), 2015, by permission of Cold Spring Harbor Laboratory Press.

individual, there is support for the proposition that this type of memory is mediated by medial temporal lobes and the diencephalon.

Unlike declarative memories, there are also memories that are not accessed via conscious recollection but nevertheless represent an imprint from past learning experiences that can influence cognitive, affective, and behavioral reactions of the individual. Squire and Dede (2015) describe these as nondeclarative memories. They note that this type of memory is "dispositional and expressed through performance rather than recollection" (p. 3). They state:

> Nondeclarative memory provides for myriad unconscious ways of responding to the world. The unconscious status of nondeclarative memory creates some of the mystery of human experience. Here arise the habits and preferences that are inaccessible to conscious recollection, but they nevertheless are shaped by past events, they influence our current behavior and mental life, and they are a fundamental part of who we are. (p. 3)

As depicted in Figure 5.1, these types of memories appear to be dependent on numerous brain structures, including the entire neocortex, the striatum, the amygdala, and the cerebellum.

The influence of nondeclarative memory functions can be observed while carrying out cognitive tasks as well as when responding emotionally to a given situation. Citing the work of Tulving and Schacter (1990) and Schacter and Buckner (1998), Squire and Dede (2015) summarize some of the research on "priming effects" during memory experiments. Simply being exposed to a specific or related item several times without being aware of it can improve later conscious recall of that type of information. An unpleasant event with a vicious dog may or may not be consciously recalled, but fear of large dogs may exist without an independent recollection of the unpleasant event.

The amygdala has attracted considerable attention with regard to "emotional learning" because it has been thought to play an important role in determining a child's temperament (Kagan & Snidman, 2009). Feinstein, Adolphs, and Tranel (2016) described the developmental and adult behavior of a patient who suffered bilateral amygdala damage very early in life. Despite performing "normally" on various neuropsychological tests, this person failed to develop the subjective experience of fear associated with external threats. Her adult behavior was marked by significant errors in judgment that put her at constant risk of being either injured or exploited. Her emotional learning was severely affected, and she never learned the "habit" of being cautious. This "automatic" or "unconscious" mode of processing important information in everyday life did not develop.

The research summarized by Squire and Dede (2015) also highlights the fact that the capacity of the human brain to form memories can be observed at multiple levels, which includes conscious verbal and nonverbal recall, performance of various skills and habits, affective reactions, and skeletal responses. This higher integrative brain activity called "memory" exerts an influence at all levels of brain functioning.

In addition to the empirical studies reviewed by Squire and Dede (2015), there are clinical phenomena that reveal that disturbing emotional experiences can influence behavior in a manner that may remain out of consciousness. Several years ago, I was asked to see the wife of a patient who had suffered a severe traumatic brain injury (TBI). This woman was constantly critical of the rehabilitation staff's activities as they related to her husband's care. It had gotten to the point that the rehabilitation staff were thinking of discharging the patient because of the wife's behavior. Because the patient was receiving workers' compensation health benefits, the insurance company was vested in stopping this behavior, which was disruptive to the rehabilitation process. Interestingly, this same pattern of behavior was observed in at least three other prior rehabilitation settings in which the patient was treated. It was costing the insurance company a significant amount of money to have to constantly find a rehabilitation setting that was satisfactory to the patient's wife.

When I initially saw her, she explicitly stated that I should not attempt to change her attitude because her husband needed the best possible care and she would not tolerate any staff incompetence. Note that these "incompetencies" included the nursing staff getting the patient up 5–10 minutes late in the morning and taking longer than the scheduled time to brush his teeth. This occasionally would have the adverse effect of causing a speech and language therapy session to start late and run long by a few minutes, which in turn limited his occupational therapy time. These are common occurrences on busy inpatient neurorehabilitation units, where unpredictable events with different patients can influence a given patient's daily schedule. There are other examples as well, but the point is that being even a few minutes off an initial schedule agreement put this patient's wife into a "rage" in which she would aggressively verbally attack the nursing and rehabilitation staff as being incompetent. She could not stand "the injustice" of the situation.

After several months of conversation with the wife on a weekly basis regarding her husband, his behavior after his severe TBI, and her relationship to him before and after his brain injuries, she suddenly (i.e., after a therapeutic relationship had been established) had an old memory come to mind that was highly emotional for her. This occurred during a relatively "calm session." She remembered being raped as an adolescent girl. Although her mother knew of the event, her mother did not take action to ensure that the boys who raped her were punished, and therefore "justice was not served."

In the course of psychotherapy, the patient's wife could experience (this was not interpreted to her) that any perceived injustice (to her husband), no matter how slight, seemed to trigger a series of behavioral responses in her that would be appropriate for an earlier personal life experience of injustice but did not seem appropriate (i.e., rational) in the current situation. As she now consciously evaluated her behavioral reactions (i.e., reflected about the past event and its connection to her current behavior), she knew that emotions outside of her awareness were indeed triggering her behavioral reactions. What seemed to be "irrational behavior" on the part of this woman actually was rational for her, but at an unconscious level (for further discussion of this important point, see Turnbull & Solms, 2007). It is this type of clinical experience that has convinced many psychotherapists that unconscious mental activity can indeed influence thoughts and behaviors in substantial ways despite the absence of traditional scientific proof.

The phenomenon of intentionally not wanting to think of something painful has been experienced by most people in their everyday life. Anderson et al. (2004) conducted an experimental analysis of this type of consciously driven desire to forget or at least inhibit a memory from coming to consciousness. They instructed their subjects to attempt not to recall a memory. The experiment demonstrated (inferred via fMRI) that in this process, the subjects experienced a series of predictable shifts in blood flow. The researchers also noted a decrease in activation of the subjects' hippocampal region (which is often activated during the desire to consciously recall information) as well as an increase in activation of the dorsal lateral frontal region. Although other changes in related brain structures were also reported, the point is that this universal human activity was clearly related to phasic brain activation patterns. One could not observe the intended act of forgetting, but one could observe one marker of the neural correlates of such actions.

In this context, another important clinical feature must be noted. In addition to the conscious, intentional act of trying to forget something, clinicians often observe that during times of severe anxiety there may be a nonintentional "forgetting" or "denial" response. This was observed in a 70-year-old woman who lost her vision secondary to a large pituitary tumor. She initially stated that she could see without difficulty. When it was demonstrated that she had a loss of vision, she dismissed the evidence but seemed uneasy in her response. As time went on, however, she became visibly anxious and stated that the "doctors are now scaring me" that her vision might not return. She actively avoided any conversation about the possible permanence of her visual loss. This is a different type of subjective response than is observed in anosognosia for cortical blindness (Anton's syndrome), as described in Chapter 9.

Another type of clinical phenomenon involving memory and repression is the experience of a person being ill at ease in carrying out what seemingly is a rather routine responsibility. For example, a woman reported to her psychiatrist that she had a daily resistance to placing a new puppy into a cage when she had to leave the house. When describing the situation, she believed it could potentially be harmful to the dog—but she did not know why. Via her dialogue with the psychiatrist, who was also working as a psychotherapist, she had a memory of a dog being taken away from her as a child, which was very disturbing. When free associating to the disturbing feeling, she had a "brief" or "quick" memory of being left alone as a child, which was also disturbing to her. Eventually, it came to light that during some of those times of being left alone, she had been sexually molested by a mentally retarded uncle. This chain of events describes what clinical evidence means. As the woman was able to relate apparently separate events to a common feeling, an explanation about her uneasiness in placing the dog in a cage became obvious to her and her psychotherapist. It is another clinical example of how past memories/emotions influence behavior in the present. This is true for people with and without a brain disorder.

BEHAVIORAL EVIDENCE OF UNCONSCIOUS GUIDANCE SYSTEMS

In the field of social psychology, Bargh and Morsella (2008) reviewed an impressive body of evidence that demonstrates the existence of "several independent unconscious behavioral guidance systems" that influence decision-making and alter behavioral reactions (p. 73). They make a very important distinction when using the term *unconscious* in social psychology experiments. They (2008) state,

> If one shifts the operational definition of the unconscious from the processing of stimuli of which one is not aware to the influences of effects of stimulus processing of which one is not aware, suddenly the true power and scope of the unconscious in daily life becomes apparent. (p. 74)

That is, we automatically and reflexively *respond* to certain stimuli in a nonaware manner that can greatly influence a sequence of behaviors. One interesting example of this reality is found in studies on eating behavior and food choices. It has been reliably shown that when people are choosing food in a buffet line, they tend to take most of their food (two-thirds of it) from the first three food items presented to them (i.e., a triggering stimuli). This occurs irrespective of the taste or nutritional value of those food items compared to other foods that are available to them (Pollan, 2015). They are often totally unaware of this behavioral response pattern.

Another example cited by Bargh and Morsella (2008) involves reaction times and motor movements. When people are asked to move objects off a video screen as fast as possible, the reaction times are faster both when the movement is toward themselves for objects they like and when the movement is away from themselves for objects they dislike (Chen & Bargh, 1999). Reportedly, this occurred when the individuals were asked to simply move all objects off the screen as quickly as possible. The "emotional" valence of the object (i.e., the triggering stimulus) differentially influenced the speed of their movements in different directions.

Bargh and Morsella (2008) suggest that cognitive psychology has had a "conscious-centric" bias given the evidence that behavioral responses are initiated by stimuli outside of one's awareness. They argue that often "action precedes reflection." In support of this view, they reviewed the neuroimaging data reported by Soon et al. (2008), who asked subjects to press a button with the right or left index finger "as they felt the need to do so" (p. 543) and to remember what letter was presented when they made the finger-pressing movements. Soon et al. monitored shifts in cerebral blood flow using fMRI during these times. Although they report several interesting findings, of special relevance is their observation that increased blood flow was recorded in the frontopolar cortex (Brodmann area 10) 7–10 seconds before the person consciously felt the urge to press the lever. Activation was also recorded in parietal cortex, extending from the precuneus to the posterior cingulate cortex. Soon et al. suggest that "a network of high level control areas . . . begin to prepare an upcoming decision long before it enters awareness" (p. 543). Recent research with primates suggests that an essential function of Brodmann area 10 of the brain is the rapid learning of alternative choices and their relative values (i.e., emotional/motivation valence) to the primate (Boschin, Piekema, & Buckley, 2015).

These observations support the general model that action (in the brain and linked to behavior) not only can precede conscious awareness but also is intimately connected to the choices available before those choices reach consciousness. In the previously cited work by Anderson et al. (2004), decreased activation involved in the suppression of memories was associated with various regions of the frontal cortex, including the dorsolateral cortex, the ventrolateral prefrontal cortex, and the bilateral frontopolar cortex. The implication is that several regions of the frontal lobe appear to be involved in influencing the conscious representation of urges and memories. The potentially important role of the lateral prefrontal cortex for the integration of emotion and cognition also has been suggested by Gray, Braver, and Raichle (2002).

THE "COGNITIVE UNCONSCIOUS" AND PRELIMINARY EVIDENCE FOR UNCONSCIOUS INFLUENCES ON NEUROPSYCHOLOGICAL TEST PERFORMANCE

In 1987, Kihlstrom introduced the term *cognitive unconscious*. He provided initial evidence that complex higher mental processes could proceed without conscious awareness. Glaser and Kihlstrom (2005) further reviewed the evidence from cognitive psychology, which suggests that "much of human mental life operates without awareness or intent" (p. 171). These findings have not appeared to influence the practice of clinical neuropsychology. Yet Hassin and colleagues continue to make the point that the findings are relevant to clinical neuropsychology.

Hassin (2013) reviewed a series of studies demonstrating that "high-level cognition" (e.g., working memory) can be influenced by unconscious (i.e., not subjectively or consciously perceived) priming effects. Although his review of the literature has been criticized as "overly idealized" (Hesselmann & Moors, 2015, p. 584), subliminal priming effects have repeatedly been shown to influence working memory and various forms of problem-solving in some individuals. In a recent investigation on executive functions in older adults, Cohen-Zimerman and Hassin (2018) conducted two studies that demonstrated that increasing motivation to perform the Wisconsin Card Sorting Test can result in improved performance on this test. What is interesting about their studies is that the participants were unaware that their motivation was being manipulated. Older subjects were first asked to perform a word search task. In one condition, the words they were searching for were designed to unconsciously stimulate the desire for "achievement (ambitious, aspiration, competition, excellence, first, race and win). In the control conditions, these words were replaced by motivational neutral ones (carpet, diamond, farm, hat, table, topaz, and window)" (Cohen-Zimerman & Hassin, 2018, p. 270). The investigators then asked study participants to perform the Wisconsin Card Sorting Test. They reported that older individuals who previously had performed the motivational primary task made less perseverative errors and achieved more categories. If these findings can be replicated and then applied to clinical populations, it would help demonstrate to clinical neuropsychologists how unconscious motivations may well influence neuropsychological test performance and further support the notion that there are both conscious and unconscious manifestations of the HIBFs. To further enhance this discussion, it may be of value to consider how the conscious and unconscious aspects of mental functioning are revealed during a typical day–night cycle.

DISCERNIBLE STATES OF INTEGRATIVE BRAIN FUNCTIONING

Neurophysiological studies of normally functioning individuals during a 24-hour period, using electroencephalographic recordings, suggest three basic states of brain activity: the "awake state," sleeping, and dreaming (or paradoxical sleep; Jouvet, 1999).

If one were to record a person's thoughts, feelings, and actions (or behaviors) during these three neurophysiologically distinct periods, four different neuropsychological states seem to exist. State 1 corresponds to the "awake state," in which individuals verbally report having conscious experiences of what they think, feel, and do. During this state, individuals have a subjective sense of who they are, what actions they intend to perform and whether or not they performed those actions.

State 2 corresponds to the nonawake state known as sleep, in which individuals have no conscious representation of the self or the world. When they awaken from sleep, they say they were in "a dead sleep," and some openly wonder if that is what death may be like. This state is typically associated with slow-wave sleep, which is described in more detail later.

State 3 corresponds to the "state of dreaming." Persons are not awake but have mental experiences similar to, but not the same as, those in the awake conscious state. Persons subjectively experience thoughts, feelings, and actions even though they are not always logical. In normal conditions, however, individuals are paralyzed from making any intentional movements during this time (Carskadon & Dement, 2010).

State 4 corresponds to what can best be described as the awake state in which thoughts and feelings occur (or exist) that influence decision-making and behavior, but persons are not aware of their influence. This state refers to what psychiatrists and psychologists traditionally have described as the "unconscious" component in psychological functioning in the awake individual.

Although initially considered to reflect mainly emotional and motivation experiences that the individual wishes would not reach consciousness (i.e., the affective or psychodynamic unconscious; Freud, 1900), the term *unconscious* has been expanded to include certain types of motor and emotional memories as described by Squire and Dede (2015) and discussed in Chapters 2 and 3. This state also includes the phenomenon of awake individuals engaging in a variety of behaviors or thought patterns without being aware of why they are doing what they are doing. This corresponds to the initiation of various "behavioral guidance systems" described by Bargh and Morsella (2008).

THE CONSCIOUS AWAKE STATE

Posner, Saper, Schiff, and Plum (2007) define consciousness as "the state of full awareness of the self and one's relationship to the environment" (p. 5). They state that consciousness has two essential components: arousal and content. The arousal component is mediated by deep brain structures, namely the ascending arousal system. This system includes the thalamus and upper brain stem. This system allows for sleep–wake cycles to occur during the 24-hour day period. Once adequate arousal is established, the person is "awake." The content of the person's consciousness, during the awake state, is mediated at the cerebral cortical level, according to Posner et al. (2007). They note that specific brain lesions to different cortical areas can produce alterations in the content of consciousness. For example, the person may have a lack of awareness of hemiplegia (i.e., anosognosia for hemiplegia) while at the same time being aware of who he or she is. The person also may experience "some memory problems."

Roger Sperry (1969), the Nobel laureate, partially defines consciousness as "a dynamic emergent property of cerebral excitation" (p. 533). He suggests that as an emergent property of brain function, it cannot be simply explained on the basis of chemistry, physiology, or anatomy as we now understand these fields of study. He describes it as transcending "the properties of nerve impulse traffic in the cerebral networks" (p. 533) and notes that it exerts a causal effect on brain function. It does so by influencing the activation patterns of large neural networks. Sperry also states, "Obviously, it also works the other way around, that is, the conscious properties of cerebral patterns are directly dependent on the action of the component neural elements" (p. 534). Neuropsychologists and neurologists are well acquainted with this phenomenon because lesions of the brain can produce a wide range of disturbances in consciousness, ranging from coma to anosognosia, as noted previously.

Sperry (1969) notes,

> To determine precisely how the more elemental physiological aspects of brain activity are used to build the emergent qualities of awareness becomes the central challenge for the future. At present, even the general principles by which cerebral circuits produce conscious

effects remain obscure. Very possibly, these will become understandable, not in terms of circuit principles, but only in terms of advances in cerebral design superimposed on the background of an already elaborately evolved central nervous system. There is reason to think that the critical organizational features of the neural circuitry for generating conscious awareness are mainly genetic or inherent and are activated through the brain-stem arousal system, and once activated, become exquisitely responsive to changing sensory as well as centrally generated input. (p. 535)

In other words, subjective awareness or human consciousness is an important property of brain function that directly influences other related brain functions and, in turn, is affected by them, according to Sperry.

During the conscious, awake state, individuals need to act and make decisions that ensure physical and social survival. Cognitive psychologists have been especially interested in the conscious, cognitive processes underlying these abilities. Daniel Kahneman (2003), also a Nobel laureate, reviewed his and Amos Tversky's (1937–1996) work on "the psychology of bounded rationality." He notes that the topic was actually introduced by Herbert A. Simon (1955, 1979), another Nobel laureate. Kahneman (2003) suggests that "intuitive judgments occupy a position—perhaps corresponding to evolutionary history—between the automatic operations of perception and the deliberate operations of reasoning" (p. 697). Intuitive responses can be described as "fast, automatic, effortless, associative, and implicit (not available to introspection), and often emotionally charged" (p. 698). Occasionally, this type of response leads to errors in problem-solving, and in other instances it can be remarkably accurate, especially if made by experienced and well-trained individuals during times of emergency. The point, as it relates to this discussion, is that an intuitive response is often associative in nature and influenced by both emotion and reason during important decision times. In the hands of an experienced person, these judgments may be very accurate under certain pressured circumstances.

The second type of thinking that Kahneman (2003) describes conforms more to classical views of what reasoning is all about during the conscious, awake state. Here, the decision-making process tends to be "slower, serial, effortful, more likely to be consciously monitored and deliberately controlled" (p. 698). This type of thinking is more rule governed; can be evoked and modified via language; and often involves explicit conscious representations of past, present, and future events. This type of "thinking" often does not come easily and involves effort. In general, it involves judgments that are not rushed. It involves dealing with uncertainty and doubt. It reportedly is less influenced by emotions. Important economic decisions, for example, are often thought to be of this nature.

Kahneman (2003) also notes, however, that the way economic choices are framed (i.e., the context presented) can greatly influence "rational" choices. Unexpected changes in circumstances can trigger emotion, and emotions can and do influence the most "rational" of choices depending on the context (how the problem is presented or framed). This analysis not only describes "faster" versus "slower" judgments and decision-making but also emphasizes the important role of emotion in decision-making and behavior during the conscious, awake state from another perspective. The important point is that the impact of emotion on the thought process and decision-making tendencies is often not consciously recognized or at least is overlooked.

As described in preceding chapters, however, the evolution and development of the HIBFs are in large part based on feelings that "drive" mental activity and observable behavioral responses (see Chapter 3, this volume). These feelings form the covert and overt manifestations of "intentions," which further drive (verbal and nonverbal) communications, culminating in "speech and language." Speech and language influence the expression of drive choices, intentions, and actions. This results in reactions from the social (i.e., interpersonal) environment, which determines learning and enhances problem-solving at both cognitive and feeling levels. Ultimately, various symbolic systems are devised to aid the recording and expansion of knowledge, which is the base of what later can be called "cultural knowledge or wisdom." This conscious, awake state absorbs a considerable amount of brain energy (Raichle & Gusnard, 2002), and by the end of the waking day, the person is tired and wants to sleep. The scientific study of sleep has revealed its importance for problem-solving and memory consolidation during the awake state.

THE NONAWAKE, SLEEP STATE

A natural shift from conscious to unconscious brain functioning occurs every night when people fall asleep. The study of sleep encompasses a vast amount of information, which has been summarized by Kryger, Roth, Eloni, and Dement (2011). It has ushered in the relatively new field of "sleep medicine." Before attempting to integrate insights from sleep research into a more complete understanding of the HIBFs, I review some rudimentary characteristics of sleep.

Carskadon and Dement (2010) provide a simple behavioral definition of sleep: "a reversible behavioral state of perceptual disengagement from and unresponsiveness to the environment" (p. 15). Physiologically, sleep has been characterized as reflecting two separate states. One form of sleep is characterized as having non-rapid eye movement (NREM); the other state is characterized by rapid eye movement (REM). The electroencephalogram (EEG) patterns are different during these two separate states. According to Carskadon and Dement,

> The EEG pattern in NREM sleep is commonly described as synchronous, with such characteristic waveforms as sleep spindles, K-complexes, and higher voltage slow waves. . . . The four NREM stages (stages 1, 2, 3, and 4) roughly parallel a depth of sleep continuum, with arousal thresholds generally lowest in stage 1 and highest in stage 4 sleep. (p. 15)

NREM sleep is often the time in which persons experience "deep" sleep and are difficult to arouse, as noted previously.

In contrast, REM sleep is associated with EEG activation of fast, asynchronous activity. It is also linked to muscle atonia. It has reliably been shown that REM sleep is associated with dreaming. Jouvet (1999) has described dreaming as "paradoxical sleep" because the EEG patterns during this type of sleep are similar to those of the awake state of the brain.

A predictable progression of sleep stages is observed in young healthy adults, as depicted in Figure 5.2. These predictable patterns, however, are somewhat altered during childhood and during older years of life.

Typically, when one "falls asleep," he or she enters stage 1 sleep, which persists for a short time (1–7 minutes in the young adult; Carskadon & Dement, 2010). During this stage, a person can be awakened with a light touch or by calling out his or her name. This stage periodically disappears and then reoccurs throughout the night and appears to occur at different stages of sleep transition.

In stage 2 sleep, sleep spindles or K-complexes are observed, and the person needs more intense stimulation to wake up. As stage 2 progresses, there is a gradual increase in slow-wave activity. This is followed by briefer periods of stage 3 sleep, which quickly transitions into stage 4 sleep. In normal, "healthy" sleep, stage 4 NREM slow-wave sleep (SWS) typically accounts for approximately 50% of sleep time during the night. Generally, it occurs in "spurts" lasting between 20 and 40 minutes. Sleep researchers typically consider a combination of stages 3 and 4 to consist of SWS (Carskadon & Dement, 2010).

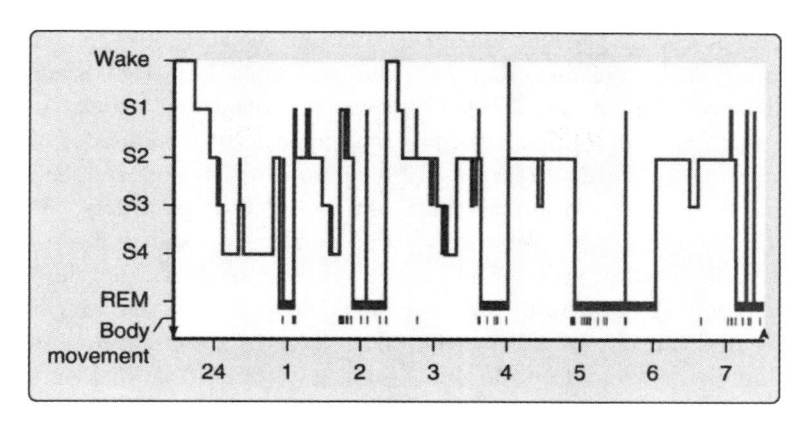

FIGURE 5.2   The progression of sleep stages across a single night in a normal young adult volunteer is illustrated in this sleep histogram. The text describes the "ideal" or "average" pattern. This histogram was drawn on the basis of a continuous overnight recording of electroencephalogram, electro-oculogram, and electromyogram in a normal 19-year-old man. The record was assessed in 30-second epochs for the various sleep stages. REM, rapid eye movement (See color plates).

Source: Reprinted from Normal human sleep: An overview, Carskadon & Dement, in M. H. Kryger, T. Roth, & W. C. Dement (Eds.), *Principles and Practice of Sleep Medicine* (5 ed.), p. 16–26, Copyright (2010), with permission from Elsevier.

REM sleep then periodically occurs after episodes of SWS through the night, with the shortest duration typically occurring during the first cycle of REM. It has been further noted that in the young healthy individual, REM sleep predominates in the last third of the night and is related to circadian rhythms (Carskadon & Dement, 2010, p. 20). It is noteworthy that there is a decrease in the amount of SWS in the healthy elderly (Bliwise, 2000). It remains debatable whether there is any decline in the proportion of REM sleep during the later years of life (Bliwise, 2000).

What is the function of sleep and particularly of NREM versus REM sleep? Although sleep in general appears to help maintain normal circadian rhythms necessary for regulating functions such as body temperature, metabolism, and breathing patterns, it has been suggested that SWS has a very important role to play in what has been termed *synaptic homeostasis* of the brain. Tononi and Cirelli (2006) suggest that

> under normal conditions, total synaptic strength increases during wakefulness and reaches a maximum just before going to sleep. Then, as soon as sleep ensues, total synaptic strength begins to decrease, and reaches a baseline level by the time sleep ends. (p. 50)

It is suggested that it is precisely during SWS that "synaptic downscaling" occurs, and this process allows the individual to efficiently learn new information the next day (after sleep). A major corollary to this hypothesis is that disruption of SWS would cause some form of cognitive (and affective) dysfunction. Atherton et al. (2016) note that the amount of SWS is positively related to memory performance in healthy young adults. However, the effect is less robust in persons with epilepsy. Thus, in the "healthy brain," the advantages of SWS on memory are clear. When the brain is in a dysfunctional state, however, the same degree of advantage may not exist.

THE NONAWAKE STATE OF DREAMING

Because dreaming occurs primarily during REM sleep, the obvious question is, What role does REM sleep play in maintaining life and influencing neuropsychological functioning? Jouvet (1999) suggests that dreaming is necessary for preserving our individuality. It allows us to rehearse important life (awake) events necessary for important individual (emotionally driven) decision-making and to maintain a sense of continuity of the "self." A corollary to this hypothesis is that disruption of REM sleep would cause a breakdown in the "sense of self," and the individuality of the person would be compromised. Without our dreams, we cannot be the person we are. As discussed next, increases in limbic activation are common during the dream states, but interestingly, important deactivation of frontal and parietal regions occurs as well.

Maquet et al. (2005) carried out a meta-analysis of positron emission tomography (PET) scans acquired on healthy young males during wakefulness, SWS, and REM sleep. Their goal was to more precisely describe changes in frontal and parietal cortices during the dreaming state of brain function. They begin by noting that

> decreased firing in brainstem structures causes a hyperpolarization of thalamic neurons and triggers a cascade of processes responsible for the generation of various non-REM sleep rhythms (spindles, theta, and slow rhythm). During REM sleep, as compared to wakefulness, significant activations were found in the pontine tegmentum, thalami nuclei and limbic and paralimbic areas (e.g., amygdaloid complexes, hippocampal formation and anterior cingulate cortex). Posterior cortices in temporo-occipital areas are also activated and their functional interactions are different in REM sleep than in wakefulness.... In contrast, the dorso-lateral prefrontal cortex, parietal cortex as well as the posterior cingulate cortex and the precuneus are the least active brain regions. (pp. 219–220)

Maquet et al. (2005) go on to note that during REM sleep (or dreaming), specific areas of frontal and parietal regions appear most hypoactive: the inferior frontal gyrus, the temporoparietal region, and the inferior lobule of the parietal cortex. During SWS, the medial prefrontal cortex shows the most significant decreases in cerebral blood flow. In the awake brain, these regions show increases in blood flow, especially during important problem-solving activities. Reviewing a number of studies in cognitive neuropsychology, Maquet et al. note that these regions play an important role in sustained attention, decision-making, planning, and inhibitory control. These are the key activities necessary for the expression and formation of conscious intentions. During dreaming, the normal inhibitory control of various conscious intentions appears to lessen. Perhaps it is at this time that intentions that are not consciously mediated (but represent unconscious intentions) are given a free expression.

A personal example may help clarify this point. Several years ago, a neighbor of mine called me on the phone and informed me that there was a major waterline break in front of a home I own in a beach community. I have great affection for this home for a variety of reasons. Upon hearing the notice, I calmly thanked him and immediately contacted the water company in that community. I calmly and rationally gave them the details as they were conveyed to me and asked the water company to fix the problem immediately. I knew the project would be costly, but I had the financial resources to handle the situation. After I completed the phone call and put into action a rational plan for solving the problem, I went back to my normal daily activities with no conscious worries. That night I had the following dream: I was walking up my driveway (which is on a slight hill) and was avoiding waves of water coming over the sidewalk. I became obviously concerned, and upon entering the front door of my beach house, I saw that the downstairs areas were flooded. I was in a panic and tried to get the water out as fast as I could but made little progress. I woke up disturbed by the dream as well as grateful for it.

This dream demonstrated to me in a very personal way that my awake, conscious, logical, and "in control" self that calmly and rationally handled the worry of the day was in fact different from what my more basic, nonconscious feeling reactions were when hearing the news regarding the water leak in front of my beach home. The analytic frontal–parietal circuits had "gone to sleep," and the underlying limbic and paralimbic circuits were given "free rein" to expresses themselves.

Not all dreams follow this simple pattern, but this example highlights two important features. First, we do have feelings and cognitive reactions that we may not consciously experience during the waking state. Second, dream activity may reflect those cognitive and feeling states when the "inhibitory" controls of logic (perhaps in part mediated by frontal–parietal circuits) are relaxed during sleep, specifically during REM sleep.

The study of sleep provides some interesting hypotheses regarding the relationship between awake and nonawake states of the brain and the HIBFs. At a minimum, the hypotheses that should be seriously considered are that (1) SWS may be necessary for synaptic downloading, which is necessary for efficient new learning the next day; (2) REM sleep (i.e., dreaming) may allow for the re-evaluation of problematic situations an individual faces when normally inhibitory controls of thoughts and feelings can be relaxed in a "safe or protected environment"; and (3) a person is not able to move (or act) when dreaming (if the brain is "healthy"). "Being true to ourselves" involves the ongoing process of understanding both our conscious and unconscious thoughts and feelings and acting on those thoughts and feelings in a manner that reflects our evolving individuality. This is a key component to psychological care, as discussed in later chapters. Figure 5.3 summarizes and pictorially represents some of the observations made by Maquet et al. (2005) as well as earlier observations made by Schwartz and Maquet (2002).

THE AWAKE, NONAWARE STATE

When we awaken from sleep and dreaming, we can feel rested, tired, or disturbed. Sleep with

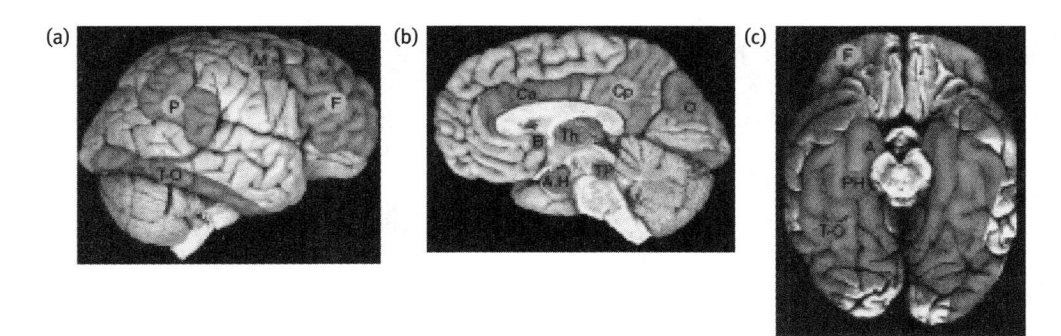

FIGURE 5.3 Schematic representation of the relative increases and decreases in neural activity associated with rapid eye movement (REM) sleep. Regions colored in red are those in which regional cerebral blood flow (rCBF) increases during REM sleep; those in blue correspond to rCBF decreases. (a) Lateral view, (b) medial view, and (c) ventral view. A, amygdala; B, basal forebrain; Ca, anterior cingulate gyrus; Cp, posterior cingulate gyrus and precuneus; F, prefrontal cortex; H, hypothalamus; M, motor cortex; P, parietal supramarginal cortex; PH, parahippocampal gyrus; O, occipital–lateral cortex; Th, thalamus; T-O, temporo-occipital extrastriate cortex; TP, pontine tegmentum (See color plates).

Source: Reprinted from Schwartz, S., & Maquet, P., Sleep imaging and the neuro-psychological assessment of dreams, *Trends in Cognitive Sciences*, 6(1), p. 23–30, Copyright (2002), with permission from Elsevier.

"pleasant dreams" often reflects a greater calmness in our awake lives. In contrast, "disturbing dreams" often reflect issues or problems that are distressing to us during the awake, conscious state—even though the connection may or may not be obvious (Freud, 1900). It is for this reason that historically dreams were often thought to relate to unconscious, emotional experiences the individual had in an earlier awake state. As described in later chapters, dream images of patients with brain disorders can provide very useful information about what they are experiencing even if they cannot verbally describe those experiences. Previously, a clinical case vignette highlighted one example of how unconscious emotional experiences and memories influence ongoing behaviors. Here, another example is provided to highlight this important phenomenon in the awake, nonaware state.

Several years ago, I was involved in attending to patients presenting at the emergency room of a university hospital who were in some sort of psychiatric crisis. One woman I saw had been admitted to the emergency room on a Friday night after having been badly beaten by her alcoholic husband. I was intent on helping her as an eager (and somewhat naive) clinical psychologist at that time. When she arrived in my office on Monday morning, I began outlining some logical steps she could take to get away from her abusive husband. In the context of that discussion, she revealed two important facts. This was her third husband, but the two previous ones were also men with alcoholism who also beat her. Second, she did not know why, but she seemed to be attracted to alcoholic men. She described herself as having "bad luck" with men and observed this recurring pattern of behavior of choosing alcoholic men who would beat her, but she had no understanding of why this pattern occurred. This type of phenomenon is frequently seen and has been described as reflecting "core conflictual relationships" (Book, 1998). When properly treated, the individual can slowly begin to modify the self-punitive behavior over time. However, this frequently requires understanding and management of the "triggers" for maladaptive response patterns (Book, 1998). In light of these observations, some concluding remarks about the nature of the HIBFs are presented next.

THE HIGHER INTEGRATIVE BRAIN FUNCTIONS: HISTORICAL AND CONTEMPORARY OBSERVATIONS

The HIBFs do not appear to be purely conscious in nature, nor are they purely rational or "fixed" in their organizational integrity. Instead, the HIBFs are emergent properties of cerebral excitation (Sperry, 1969) most likely "genetic in nature" and "activated through the brainstem arousal system" (p. 535). They are intimately connected with the phenomenon of subjective consciousness or personal awareness of the self and the environment. These emergent properties appear to be at first diffusely organized in the brain (Durston et al., 2006), but during early childhood they start to become more regionalized and then more modular in nature. In the adult (nondeclining) brain, large neural networks further develop according to principles of cerebral design that we do not yet understand (Sperry, 1969) but about which progress has been made (Tononi, 2008). They involve both cortical and subcortical structures that appear to allow for efficient, coordinated neural activity that requires less conscious effort. Avena-Koenigsberger, Misic, and Sporns (2018) note that contemporary neuroimaging studies suggest there are topographic networks within the brain that appear to underlie the HIBFs, including the default-mode network (DMN), the dorsal attentional network, the ventral attentional network, the salience network, the temporal network, the somatomotor network, and the visual network.

As noted in previous chapters, the DMN includes the medial prefrontal cortex, the posterior cingulate cortex, the inferior parietal lobule, the lateral and inferior temporal cortex, and the medial temporal lobes. In contrast, the large-scale neural networks associated with attention include the superior parietal lobe, the intraparietal sulcus, the motion-sensitive middle temporal area, the frontal eye fields, the dorsal anterior cingulate, the dorsolateral prefrontal cortex, the ventral prefrontal cortex, and the frontal operculum. Petersen and Posner (2012) emphasize that different components of this "attention" network are involved in "alerting" and "orienting" versus sustaining focal attention for purposes of regulating cognition and emotion. In this latter regard, Telzer (2016) suggests that the ventral prefrontal cortex may play a special role in attending to emotionally salient or significant events occurring in the environment.

These systems roughly allow us to reflect on ourselves but to rapidly attend to the world as the situation demands and flexibly return to a "self-reflective" mode, again as the situation (or social environment) demands. These large-scale intrinsic networks serve to reduce ambiguity in the "inner" and "outer" worlds of the person's subjective experience. As such, the brain does appear to function as "an inference machine" (Carhart-Harris & Friston, 2010, p. 1267).

As the brain declines in its HIBF capacities, the integrity of these large neural networks declines. As noted in Chapter 3, a reduction of close coupling of the brain structures involved in the DMN, for example, has been associated with a decline in performance on many cognitive tests in the elderly population (Andrews-Hanna et al., 2007).

These neural networks appear to be organized around "hierarchical brain systems" much as Luria (l966) originally proposed and others have recently suggested (Barrett, 2012). However, it is now appreciated that "higher-level association cortices not only receive feedforward signals from sensory regions but also anticipate and reciprocate these inputs with backward connections conferring context-specificity and higher-level constraints (i.e., predictions)" (Carhart-Harris & Friston, 2010, p. 1270). Thus, the HIBFs, by their nature, have feedback and feedforward features that aid effective problem-solving (Prigatano, 1999, p. 43).

A key feature of the HIBFs is the ability to record and act upon (even in a nonconscious manner) context-specific information necessary for adaptation and survival. If a context-dependent learning experience is associated with emotionally charged constraints (e.g., "If I do this, I get this extremely negative or positive reaction"), the emotional valence of that learning experience is imbedded in the feedback loops that help the brain reduce ambiguity and aid accurate predictions necessary for decision-making.

From this analysis, the HIBFs by their nature include conscious and unconscious mental activities that have symbolic (e.g., "This stands for that, and that stands for this") and emotionally relevant associations experienced when interacting with others (i.e., the social environment) as well as objects and ideas. Feelings and thoughts become inseparable as these emergent neural networks allow for extracting meaning (seeing previously unseen convergent connections) and establishing predictable relationships of people and events (i.e., judgments). Under time pressures, these judgments may be "fast, automatic, effortless, associative and implicit in nature" (Kahneman, 2003, p. 698), with a strong emotional valence. In other instances, the judgments can be slow, serial, effortful, and consciously monitored (p. 698) as the situation presents itself. This reveals the truly adaptive nature of the HIBFs.

Luria (1966) noted that "speech plays a decisive role in the mediation of mental processes" (p. 33). This is seen from early childhood through all stages of learning. After a brain disorder, speech and other symbolic expressions become vital to the clarification and communication of what is meaningful to the individual as the person attempts to cope with life's challenges. Speech and various symbolic expressions aid the constant restructuring and modification of the contents of the neural networks that allow humans to re-evaluate thoughts and feelings, as well as present and

> **Box 5.1. Proposed Unconscious Manifestations of Higher Integrative Brain Functions That Have Clinical Relevance**
>
> 1. Electrophysiological recordings suggest that brain activation or response patterns (i.e., the readiness potential) may predate a conscious "urge" or "feeling" to act when involved in a problem-solving task.
> 2. Recurring behavioral patterns or choices (some of which may be harmful to the individual) can be put in motion (or triggered) by stimuli outside of the person's awareness.
> 3. Habits and preferences that are inaccessible to conscious recollection may be shaped by past learned events.
> 4. Forgotten episodic memories can influence ongoing behavioral responses that influence social adaptation.
> 5. There may be a "natural" evolutionary tendency to consciously negate intensely painful experiences, but people often later attempt to consciously understand and manage those painful experiences in the waking state.
> 6. Artistic expressions of various types appear to reflect unconscious as well as conscious thoughts and feelings.

past modes of behavior. It becomes the "lifeline" to problem-solving in the "real world" and affords us an understanding of the inner, subjective world of another person. This becomes crucial for providing psychological care and neuropsychological assessment.

Box 5.1 summarizes six propositions regarding unconscious manifestations of higher integrative brain functions that have clinical relevance.

THE POLITICS OF LANGUAGE WHEN DESCRIBING CONSCIOUS AND UNCONSCIOUS INFLUENCES ON BEHAVIOR

In this chapter, different sources of "evidence" were reviewed to demonstrate that human behavior is, in fact, guided or influenced by both conscious and unconscious intentions. There has always been a reluctance to use the term *unconscious mental activities* when discussing human behavior because of the negative reaction the scientific community has to Freudian and Jungian theories of human mental functioning. When faced with the evidence that unconscious mental activities do in fact exist, there is often the preference to use other words or phrases, such as procedural learning, implicit memory, responding before reflection, or behavioral guidance systems.

This preference is due to the fact that language is used not only to describe and define experiences but also to influence and control other individuals' behaviors. One is more likely to get research funding, for example, for a neuropsychological research project if the accepted scientific terminology is used in describing the goals of the project. This approach, however, can stifle clinical practice and alter the way we approach patients in our diagnostic and therapeutic work (Prigatano, 2003). Full recognition of conscious and unconscious influences on the behavior and "mental state" of the person is crucial for a personally relevant clinical neuropsychological examination and openness to the various forms of psychological care that may help the individual.

Challenging "dogma" in both clinical practice (Prigatano, 2003) and scientific research always comes with a price—but in many instances it is often a price well worth paying.

William Dement (2000), a well-recognized and pioneering researcher on sleep, eloquently described what happened to him when his research on the nature of sleep revealed EEG patterns of activation during REM sleep that did not fit in with the "dogma" of the times. He stated,

> It is very difficult today (circa 1990) to understand and appreciate the exceedingly controversial nature of these findings. I wrote them up, but the paper was nearly impossible to publish because it was completely contradictory to the totally dominant neurophysiological theory of the time. The assertion by me that an activated EEG could be associated with unambiguous sleep was considered absurd. As it turned out, previous investigators had observed an activated EEG during sleep in cats, but simply could not believe it and ascribed it to arousing influences during sleep. A colleague who was assisting me was sufficiently skeptical that he preferred I publish the paper as sole author. After four or five rejections, to my everlasting gratitude, Editor-in-Chief Herbert Jasper accepted the paper without revision for publication in *Electroencephalography and Clinical Neurophysiology*. (p. 7)

The need to describe what we observe in clinical and research work is vital irrespective of the existing scientific models that guide research and clinical observation.

SUMMARY

Part I of this volume has offered a brief description of human nature and normal neuropsychological functioning over the life span. In Part II, a brief description of common neuropsychological consequences of focal and multifocal brain lesions observed during childhood and adolescence, adulthood, and the declining or "aging years" is presented. Collectively, these descriptions provide background information relevant to conducting a medically necessary and personally relevant clinical neuropsychological examination, as well as guiding different forms of psychological care of persons with different brain disorders at different times in the life span.

REFERENCES

Ackermann, H., Wildgruber, D., Daum, I., & Grodd, W. (1998). Does the cerebellum contribute to cognitive aspects of speech production? A functional magnetic resonance imaging (fMRI) study in humans. *Neuroscience Letters, 247*(2), 187–190.

American Psychiatric Association. (2000). *Diagnostic and statistical manual of mental disorders* (4th ed., text rev.). Washington, DC: Author.

Anderson, M. C., Ochsner, K. N., Kuhl, B., Cooper, J., Robertson, E., Gabrieli, S. W., . . . Gabrieli, J. D. (2004). Neural systems underlying the suppression of unwanted memories. *Science, 303*(5655), 232–235.

Andrews-Hanna, J. R., Snyder, A. Z., Vincent, J. L., Lustig, C., Head, D., Raichle, M. E., & Buckner, R. L. (2007). Disruption of large-scale brain systems in advanced aging. *Neuron, 56*(5), 924–935.

Atherton, K. E., Nobre, A. C., Lazar, A. S., Wulff, K., Whittaker, R. G., Dhawan, V., . . . Butler, C. R. (2016). Slow wave sleep and accelerated forgetting. *Cortex, 84,* 80–89.

Avena-Koenigsberger, A., Misic, B., & Sporns, O. (2018). Communication dynamics in complex brain networks. *Nature Reviews Neuroscience, 19*(1), 17–33.

Bargh, J. A., & Morsella, E. (2008). The unconscious mind. *Perspectives on Psychological Science, 3*(1), 73–79.

Barrett, H. C. (2012). A hierarchical model of the evolution of human brain specializations. *Proceedings of the National Academy of Sciences of the USA, 109*(Suppl. 1), 10733–10740.

Bliwise, D. L. (2000). Normal aging. In M. H. Kryger, T. Roth, & W. C. Dement (Eds.), *Principles and practice of sleep medicine* (3rd ed., pp. 26–42). Philadelphia, PA: Saunders.

Book, H. E. (1998). *How to practice brief psychodynamic psychotherapy*. Washington, DC: American Psychological Association.

Boschin, E. A., Piekema, C., & Buckley, M. J. (2015). Essential functions of primate frontopolar cortex in cognition. *Proceedings of the National Academy of Sciences of the USA, 112*(9), E1020–E1027.

Carhart-Harris, R. L., & Friston, K. J. (2010). The default-mode, ego-functions and free-energy: A neurobiological account of Freudian ideas. *Brain, 133*(4), 1265–1283.

Carskadon, M. A., & Dement, W. C. (2010). Normal human sleep: An overview. In M. H. Kryger, T. Roth, & W. C. Dement (Eds.), *Principles and practice of sleep medicine* (5th ed., pp. 16–26). Philadelphia, PA: Saunders.

Chapman, L., Thetford, W., Berlin, L., Guthrie, T., & Wolff, H. (1958). Highest integrative functions in man during stress. *Research Publications— Association for Research in Nervous and Mental Disease, 36*, 491–534.

Chen, M., & Bargh, J. A. (1999). Consequences of automatic evaluation: Immediate behavioral predispositions to approach or avoid the stimulus. *Personality and Social Psychology Bulletin, 25*(2), 215–224.

Cohen-Zimerman, S., & Hassin, R. R. (2018). Implicit motivation improves executive functions of older adults. *Consciousness and Cognition, 63*(1), 267–279.

Crabtree, G. W., Dresselhaus, M. S., & Buchanan, M. V. (2004). The hydrogen economy. *Physics Today, 57*(12), 39–44.

Dement, W. C. (2000). History of sleep physiology and medicine. In M. H. Kryger, T. Roth, & W. C. Dement (Eds.), *Principles and practice of sleep medicine* (3rd ed., pp. 1–14). Philadelphia, PA: Saunders.

Durston, S., Davidson, M. C., Tottenham, N., Galvan, A., Spicer, J., Fossella, J. A., & Casey, B. (2006). A shift from diffuse to focal cortical activity with development. *Developmental Science, 9*(1), 1–8.

Erikson, E. H. (1964). *Insight and responsibility.* New York, NY: Norton.

Feinstein, J. S., Adolphs, R., & Tranel, D. (2016). A tale of survival from the world of Patient SM. In D. G. Amaral & R. Adolphs (Eds.), *Living without an amygdala* (pp. 1–38). New York, NY: Guilford.

Freud, S. (1900). *The interpretation of dreams.* London, UK: Hogarth.

Glaser, J., & Kihlstrom, J. F. (2005). Compensatory automaticity: Unconscious volition is not an oxymoron. In R. R. Hassin, J. S. Uleman, & J. A. Bargh (Eds.), *The new unconscious* (pp. 171–195). New York, NY: Oxford University Press.

Goldstein, K. (1939). *The organism: A holistic approach to biology derived from pathological data in man.* New York, NY: American Book Company.

Gray, J. R., Braver, T. S., & Raichle, M. E. (2002). Integration of emotion and cognition in the lateral prefrontal cortex. *Proceedings of the National Academy of Sciences of the USA, 99*(6), 4115–4120.

Haggard, P., & Libet, B. (2001). Conscious intention and brain activity. *Journal of Consciousness Studies, 8*(11), 47–64.

Halstead, W. C. (1947). *Brain and intelligence: A quantitative study of the frontal lobes.* Chicago, IL: University of Chicago Press.

Hassin, R. R. (2013). Yes it can: On the functional abilities of the human unconscious. *Perspectives on Psychological Science, 8*(2), 195–207.

Heilman, K. M. (2005). *Creativity and the brain.* New York, NY: Psychology Press.

Hesselmann, G., & Moors, P. (2015). Definitely maybe: Can unconscious processes perform the same functions as conscious processes? *Frontiers in Psychology, 6*, 584.

Jouvet, M. (1999). *The paradox of sleep: The story of dreaming.* Cambridge, MA: MIT Press.

Kagan, J., & Snidman, N. (2009). *The long shadow of temperament.* Cambridge, MA: Harvard University Press.

Kahneman, D. (2003). A perspective on judgment and choice: Mapping bounded rationality. *The American Psychologist, 58*(9), 697.

Kihlstrom, J. F. (1987). The cognitive unconscious. *Science, 237*(4821), 1445–1452.

Kryger, M., Roth, G., Eloni, D., & Dement, W. (2011). *Principles and practice of sleep medicine* (5th ed.). New York, NY: Elsevier.

Libet, B. (1985). Theory and evidence relating cerebral processes to conscious will. *Behavioral and Brain Sciences, 8*(4), 558–566.

Luria, A. (1966). *Higher cortical functions in man.* New York, NY: Basic Books.

Maquet, P., Ruby, P., Maudoux, A., Albouy, G., Sterpenich, V., Dang-Vu, T., . . . Peigneux, P. (2005). Human cognition during REM sleep and the activity profile within frontal and parietal cortices: A reappraisal of functional neuroimaging data. *Progress in Brain Research, 150*, 219–227.

Petersen, S. E., Fox, P. T., Posner, M. I., Mintun, M., & Raichle, M. E. (1988). Positron emission tomographic studies of the cortical anatomy of single-word processing. *Nature, 331*(6157), 585–589.

Petersen, S. E., & Posner, M. I. (2012). The attention system of the human brain: 20 years after. *Annual Review of Neuroscience, 35*, 73–89.

Pollan, M. (2015). *In defense of food: An eater's manifesto* [Documentary]. Menlo Park, CA: Kikim Media.

Posner, J. B., Saper, C. B., Schiff, N. D., & Plum, F. (2007). *Plum and Posner's diagnosis of stupor* and coma (4th ed.). Oxford, UK: Oxford University Press.

Prigatano, G. P. (1999). *Principles of neuropsychological rehabilitation*. New York, NY: Oxford University Press.

Prigatano, G. P. (2003). Challenging dogma in neuropsychology and related disciplines. *Archives of Clinical Neuropsychology, 18*(8), 811–825.

Prigatano, G. P. (2016). Positive and negative turning points after neuropsychological rehabilitation ended. In Y. Ben-Yishay & L. Diller (Eds.), *Turning points* (pp. 56–63). Youngsville, NC: Lash & Associates.

Raichle, M. E., & Gusnard, D. A. (2002). Appraising the brain's energy budget. *Proceedings of the National Academy of Sciences of the USA, 99*(16), 10237–10239.

Salas, C. E., & Yuen, K. S. (2016). Revisiting the left convexity hypothesis: Changes in the mental apparatus after left dorso-medial prefrontal damage. *Neuropsychoanalysis, 18*(2), 85–100.

Schacter, D. L., & Buckner, R. L. (1998). Priming and the brain. *Neuron, 20*(2), 185–195.

Schwartz, S., & Maquet, P. (2002). Sleep imaging and the neuro-psychological assessment of dreams. *Trends in Cognitive Sciences, 6*(1), 23–30.

Simon, H. A. (1955). A behavioral model of rational choice. *Quarterly Journal of Economics, 69*, 99–118.

Simon, H. A. (1979). Rational decision making in business organizations. *American Economic Review, 69*(4), 493–513.

Soon, C. S., Brass, M., Heinze, H.-J., & Haynes, J.-D. (2008). Unconscious determinants of free decisions in the human brain. *Nature Neuroscience, 11*(5), 543–545.

Sperry, R. W. (1969). A modified concept of consciousness. *Psychological Review, 76*(6), 532–536.

Sporns, O. (2013). Structure and function of complex brain networks. *Dialogues in Clinical Neuroscience, 15*(3), 247–262.

Squire, L. R., & Dede, A. J. (2015). Conscious and unconscious memory systems. *Cold Spring Harbor Perspectives in Biology, 7*(3), a021667.

Telzer, E. H. (2016). Dopaminergic reward sensitivity can promote adolescent health: A new perspective on the mechanism of ventral striatum activation. *Developmental Cognitive Neuroscience, 17*, 57–67.

Tononi, G. (2008). Consciousness as integrated information: A provisional manifesto. *Biological Bulletin, 215*(3), 216–242.

Tononi, G., & Cirelli, C. (2006). Sleep function and synaptic homeostasis. *Sleep Medicine Reviews, 10*(1), 49–62.

Tulving, E., & Schacter, D. L. (1990). Priming and human memory systems. *Science, 247*(4940), 301–306.

Turnbull, O. H., & Solms, M. (2007). Awareness, desire, and false beliefs: Freud in the light of modern neuropsychology. *Cortex, 43*(8), 1083–1090.

Ward, N., Brown, M., Thompson, A., & Frackowiak, R. (2003). Neural correlates of motor recovery after stroke: A longitudinal fMRI study. *Brain, 126*(11), 2476–2496.

PART II

BRIEF DESCRIPTION OF ABNORMAL NEUROPSYCHOLOGICAL FUNCTIONING OVER THE LIFE SPAN

PART II addresses the second question that Luria and Vygotsky (cited in Cole & Cole, 1979) raised: How do disruptions of brain function "affect the plan of the central nervous system?" The answer to this complicated question has significant implications for the study of disturbed higher integrative brain functions. Clinical neuropsychologists rely on information obtained from addressing this question to interpret the neuropsychological meaning of psychometric findings obtained from children and adults. It also provides the second major source of information needed to plan psychological care interventions at different times in the life cycle or life span of the individual. In this regard, it is important to also note that Luria and Vygotsky stressed the point that studying deficits was only part of the task of neuropsychology. Studying "restoration of high psychological functions as the result of some kind of insult to the organism" was the second, complementary task (Cole & Cole, 1979, p. 56). Thus, a review of deficits and patterns of partial recovery is the focus of Part II.

Like Part I, however, Part II is only a summary of some of the important facts. It proposes that neuropsychological disturbances occurring at different stages of life interact in a complicated manner with the developmental state of the brain at the time of the injury. Equally important, the psychosocial adjustment challenges the individual faces also differ in light of the person's age. Underlying neuropsychological disturbances often negatively affect the ability of the child or adult to successfully cope with the major tasks that are faced at different stages of life. This reality has to be understood when providing meaningful psychological care interventions.

Part II also considers the special problem of impaired self-awareness observed in many patients with brain disorders. Because disturbances in self-awareness have also been described in various psychiatric conditions, an attempt is made to compare and contrast disturbances in self-awareness that appear related to brain dysfunction versus psychological distress.

REFERENCE

Cole, M., & Cole, S. (Eds.). (1979). *A. R. Luria: The making of mind. A personal account of Soviet psychology*. Cambridge, MA: Harvard University Press.

6

THE PROBLEM OF NOT DEVELOPING NORMALLY AFTER A BRAIN DISORDER DURING CHILDHOOD AND ADOLESCENCE

INTRODUCTION

Given the predictable developmental changes in brain–behavior relationships over the life span, how do lesions of the brain during childhood and adolescence typically affect neuropsychological functioning? Also, what are the immediate and long-term psychosocial consequences of these early brain injuries? These are important questions. The initial focus of this chapter is to address the first question. Later in the chapter, the second question is addressed.

Although it is a relatively straightforward question to ask how lesions of the brain during childhood and adolescence affect neuropsychological functioning, the answer is complicated. This is because several variables have been shown to influence neuropsychological functioning during these time frames, including the following: lesion location/lateralization (Max, 2004; B. Woods, 1980), multiple versus single lesions (Westmacott, Askalan, MacGregor, Anderson, & Deveber, 2010), size of lesion (Banich, Levine, Kim, & Huttenlocher, 1990; Prigatano, 2007), age at time of lesion onset (S. Anderson, Damasio, Tranel, & Damasio, 2000; Levin et al., 1988; Mosch, Max, & Tranel, 2005), age at time the child is examined (S. Anderson et al., 2000), nature of the underlying neuropathology (Gerrard-Morris et al., 2010; O'Keeffe et al., 2014), gender of the child (C. Anderson & Arciniegas, 2010; Kolk & Talvik, 2000), genetic characteristics of the child (Sheese, Voelker, Rothbart, & Posner, 2007), genetic abnormalities of the child (Dunn et al., 2017), and psychosocial setting/family environment of the child (Gerrard-Morris et al., 2010; Yeates et al., 1997).

All of these variables have the potential to influence neuropsychological functioning. Teasing apart the potential interactions of these variables is a monumental task. However, the interacting effects of some of these variables on certain neuropsychological functions have been described in the literature. Two types of brain disorders commonly encountered throughout the life span are cerebral vascular accidents (CVAs) or strokes and traumatic brain injury (TBI). In both conditions, injury to the brain occurs rather abruptly. During childhood and adolescence, TBI often occurs in relatively healthy or "normally developing" individuals, but not uncommonly it occurs in families with lower socioeconomic means (Hawley, 2003). CVAs in children are often associated with underlying congenital heart disease or sickle cell anemia, but in more than one-third of cases the cause is unknown (Lynch, Hirtz, DeVeber, & Nelson, 2002).

CVAs and TBIs were historically thought to provide useful information on how primarily focal versus multifocal lesions to the brain might affect the developing neuropsychological status of the child and adolescent. In the case of unilateral stroke, the lesion, as measured by computed tomography or magnetic resonance imaging (MRI) scans of the brain, appeared confined to a specific region of the brain (often on one side of the brain). In the case of moderate to severe TBI secondary to high-speed motor vehicle accidents, lesions were often in multiple locations. They typically included damage to neurons and axonal fibers on both sides of the brain. Therefore, they were considered "diffuse" or "multifocal" in nature.

This simple dichotomy, however, was ultimately shown to have significant limitations. First, "single" focal lesions of the brain are not necessarily "small" lesions to the brain (Corbetta, 2017). The larger the lesion, the more likely it will negatively impact various distributed networks in the brain. Consequently, some focal lesions can indeed have "bilateral effects" or diffuse effects within a given cerebral hemisphere (Corbetta, 2017; Siegel et al., 2016). Second, the underlying pathologies of CVA and TBI are not identical (Mohr, Choi, Grotta, & Wolf, 2004; Smith, 2011). This finding further complicated comparisons. Third, the regions of the brain injured by these two types of neurological conditions often differ. For example, it is common to observe bilateral frontal and temporal lobe contusions after severe TBI in older children and adolescents (Smith, 2011). In contrast, middle cerebral artery (MCA) strokes secondary to ischemic injury are most common in children (Andrade et al., 2016). Because of the distribution of this cerebral artery, the brain insults appear lateralized but negatively affect diverse areas of unimodal and heteromodal cortex (typically involving frontal, parietal, and temporal cortex). If different areas of the brain are affected by these two conditions, comparison between the two groups becomes especially challenging. Both types of brain injuries can produce similar neuropsychological disturbances, but differences do exist, as reviewed later. First, however, the classification systems reported in the literature when studying the effects of CVAs and TBIs on neuropsychological functioning require a brief introduction.

CLASSIFICATION OF CEREBRAL VASCULAR ACCIDENTS AND TRAUMATIC BRAIN INJURIES

The brain, of course, needs a constant supply of blood to maintain normal neuropsychological functioning. It is estimated that the human brain requires approximately 50 ml of blood per 100 g of brain tissue per minute to maintain its functional integrity (Ganong, 1981). A CVA, by definition, interrupts normal blood flow (or perfusion) to the brain, which ultimately can result in cell death. There are two main types of stroke: ischemic and hemorrhagic. Ischemic strokes interrupt the blood supply to the brain. Hemorrhagic strokes are, by definition, a bleeding into the brain secondary to a tear or rupture of a blood vessel. In this case, there is a loss of blood supply and damage to surrounding brain issue. Achieving the optimal balance between blood supply and demand is crucial for maintaining life and the integrity of brain function.

Sacco, Toni, Brainin, and Mohr (2004) report that infarctions caused by ischemia are at least three times more common than hemorrhages. Hemorrhages can be in the brain (i.e., intracerebral) or outside of the brain (e.g., subarachnoid hemorrhages, but still within the skull). The causes of a large number of infarctions are often not known and are referred to by the term *cryptogenic stroke*. Recent research suggests, however, that atrial fibrillations may be an important contributing factor to cryptogenic stroke (Sanna et al., 2014).

Ischemic strokes are commonly caused by a thrombosis (i.e., obstruction of a blood vessel by a blood clot formed locally) or an embolism (i.e., obstruction due to an embolus from elsewhere in the body, most often the heart). Other common causes of ischemic stroke include a general decrease in blood supply to the brain (hypoperfusion), atherosclerosis, and cerebral venous sinus thrombosis. However, Ay (2011) has brought attention to the fact that more than 100 pathological conditions can contribute to causing an ischemic stroke. Thus, the classification of stroke subtypes remains somewhat challenging. In another review of the incidence of various strokes, Howard and Howard (2011) noted that more than 50% of all strokes studied could not simply be classified as due to hemorrhage or infarction.

Different terms are used to describe strokes during infancy and early childhood. According to a consensus conference of the National Institute of Neurological Disorders (Lynch et al., 2002), a focal-appearing vascular injury that occurs between 28 weeks of gestation and 28 days after birth is referred to as a *perinatal stroke*. Strokes that occur between 30 days after birth and 18 years of life are considered a *childhood stroke*. It has been challenging for clinicians and researchers in the field of childhood stroke to arrive at a consensus concerning the classification of perinatal and childhood strokes (Lynch et al., 2002).

Two other vascular conditions can produce a "stroke" at any age but are most commonly observed in young and middle adult years. The first is a ruptured arteriovenous malformation (AVM). It is defined as "an abnormal collection of blood vessels wherein arterial blood flows directly into draining veins without the normal interposed capillary beds" (Greenberg, 2010, p. 1098). These are congenital malformations, with a prevalence rate "probably slightly higher than the usual quoted 0.14%" (p. 1098). The average age of a ruptured cerebral AVM is approximately 33 years. The second vascular condition is a cerebral aneurysm. An aneurysm is defined as an abnormal extension of a cerebral artery that often forms at the branch point of an artery "where the arterial pulsation stress is maximal" (Lawton & Vates, 2017, p. 258). It is estimated that 1% or 2% of the population has a cerebral aneurysm. There are multiple potential causes of cerebral aneurysms (Greenberg, 2010; Lawton & Vates, 2017), but they are considered congenital in nature for many individuals. Although it has been estimated that 2% of ruptured cerebral aneurysms occur during childhood (Greenberg, 2010), ruptured cerebral aneurysms most commonly occur among people in their 50s (Lawton & Vates, 2017).

The classification of TBI is constantly undergoing revision as neuroimaging and neuropathological findings further clarify the nature of the regions of the brain that are compromised and the associated neuropathology secondary to various external trauma to the head (Bigler, 2011; Orman, Kraus, Zaloshnja, & Miller, 2011; Smith, 2011). Biomechanical forces to the brain can produce various forms of neuropathology, from hemorrhagic and ischemic injuries to direct neuronal and axonal injury.

In its simplest form, TBI is often subdivided into an "open" (i.e., penetration of the skull and entering the brain) or "closed" (i.e., nonpenetration of the skull but with damage

Table 6.1 Severity of Brain Injury Stratification

CRITERIA	MILD	MODERATE	SEVERE
Structural imaging	Normal	Normal or abnormal	Normal or abnormal
Loss of consciousness	<30 minutes	30 minutes to 24 hours	>24 hours
Alteration of consciousness/mental state	A moment to 24 hours	>24 hours	>24 hours
Post-traumatic amnesia	0–1 days	>1 and <7 days	>7 days
Glasgow Coma Scale (best available score in 24 hours)	13–15	9–12	3–8
Abbreviated Injury Severity Scale	1–2	3	4–6

Source. Adapted from US Department of Veterans Affairs/US Department of Defense. (2009). *VA/DoD clinical practice guideline: Management of concussion/mild traumatic brain injury* (Version 1.0). Washington, DC: Author. Retrieved May 18, 2017, from https://www.healthquality.va.gov/guidelines/Rehab/mtbi/concussion_mtbi_full_1_0.pdf

occurring in the brain) injury. Length of disturbed consciousness or period of post-traumatic amnesia has been used to describe the severity level of closed TBI (Russell, 1971). Also, the Glasgow Coma Scale (GCS) is commonly used to classify severity of TBI and has proven to be helpful in neurosurgical settings (Jennett & Teasdale, 1981). Scores at the time of the injury are as follows: 13–15 (mild TBI), 9–12 (moderate TBI), and 3–8 (severe TBI). The presence of space-occupying lesions (e.g., hematomas) in the brain can further contribute to the classification of the type and the severity of TBI. In cases of closed TBI secondary to high-speed motor vehicle accidents, bilateral cerebral damage often occurs. Table 6.1 summarizes one recent classification system (Orman et al., 2011).

NEUROPSYCHOLOGICAL CONSEQUENCES OF AN EARLY DISRUPTION OF THE CENTRAL NERVOUS SYSTEM

Recall that phylogenetically older brain structures mature earlier than the newer brain structures. During the first few months of life, synaptic arrangements of somatosensory and visual cortical networks develop at a rapid pace (see Chapter 2, this volume). The child's visual skills and hand–eye coordination allow for exploration of the environment and new learning (especially for face and object recognition). A major and tragic cause of TBI in very young children is non-accidental trauma (NAT). One common form of NAT has been referred to as *shaken baby syndrome*. This syndrome has three cardinal features: subdural hematoma, retinal hemorrhage, and encephalopathy (Paul & Adamo, 2014). Duhaime, Christian, Moss, and Seidl (1996) followed 100 children who were injured before the age of 2 years and presented with this syndrome. Persistent and severe cognitive deficits were reported in 50% of the patients. Lind et al. (2016) described the functional capacities of children several years after the onset of NAT (median length of follow-up was 8 years). In their sample of 47 children, only 15% had a "good outcome" using the Glasgow Outcome Scale. Motor (45%) and visual deficits (45%) were reported in nearly half of the children. Attentional deficits (79%) and behavioral disorders (53%) were also common.

Many children with NAT suffer from hypoxic ischemia (Duhaime, Christian, Rorke, & Zimmerman, 1998). Hoyt (2007) notes that perinatal hypoxic ischemia is the leading cause of visual impairments in young children. This can result in damage to the primary visual cortex, visual associative cortices, optic radiations, optic nerves, and visual attention pathways. Hoyt also notes, however, that some of these children have poorly defined visual difficulties without obvious injury to the optic radiations or primary visual cortex.

Children with NAT often have been shown to have substantial difficulties sustaining attention, and they can be highly impulsive (Lind et al., 2016). Such was the case of a female child who suffered hypoxic ischemia secondary to NAT at age 2 years, 10 months and was later seen for a clinical neuropsychological examination at age 3 years, 2 months (i.e., 4 months after the trauma). She was then followed over a 10-year period. Noteworthy was the great variability of subtest scores on different versions of the Wechsler Scale of Intelligence for Children given to her throughout the years. Her vocabulary level was consistently within the average to low average range. However, visual–spatial disturbances were commonly observed on subtests such as the Block Design and the Symbol Search. Although she improved with time, she had persistent visual difficulties that required constant accommodation within the school setting. She also demonstrated impulsive behaviors with associated problems sustaining attention. Hand–eye control and coordination difficulties were also observed. These difficulties negatively affected her ability to learn to copy letters, draw simple objects (i.e., graphomotor disturbance), and perform visual matching tasks. Note that these difficulties were observed in a child who showed no obvious auditory or verbally expressed language difficulties. However, on several occasions, her adoptive parents, teachers, and examining neuropsychologists described her as being "immature" for her age and as having a tendency for uncooperative behavior even several years after the injury. These characteristics were present despite average verbal comprehension skills and adoptive parents who provided a stable home environment and arranged for ongoing rehabilitation therapies.

Studying the effects of early unilateral vascular lesions to the brain on the ability to draw the Rey–Osterrieth Complex Figure Test (Knight & Kaplan, 2003), Akshoomoff, Feroleto, Doyle, and Stiles (2002) reported similar findings reported in children with NAT. Interestingly, they noted that at very young ages, the ability to draw this figure was severely compromised in children with either left or right hemispheric CVAs. Moreover, as these children aged, their drawing performance improved regardless of the site of injury. Despite improvement in the accuracy of the children's drawings, these investigators continued to describe the drawings of the children as "immature" in nature. That is, the drawings appeared to continue to reflect early disruption of visual–perceptual/motor skills despite developmental improvements in hand–eye motor control (e.g., drawing). In a review of cognitive outcomes in children with a history of perinatal stroke, Murias, Brooks, Kirton, and Iaria (2014) concluded that visual–spatial skills may be more profoundly affected than basic language skills in children with early ischemic damage to the brain.

As infants are able to develop the fine and gross motor skills necessary for taking a few steps and exploring objects with their hands, they begin to talk (see Chapter 3, this volume). Is there a connection or an association of impaired visual–spatial and visual–motor skills with the development of language skills in children with a known or suspected brain disorder? Akshoomoff, Stiles, and Wulfeck (2006) asked school-age children with "specific language impairment" (LI) of unknown etiology to draw the Rey–Osterrieth figure. They noted that these children performed significantly worse on the drawing task compared to typically developing children who had no LI. The findings are consistent with the hypothesis that early disruption of developing brain neuro-networks (in this case, those most likely involving visual association cortex and visual attention pathways) can be associated with and perhaps influence other developing neuropsychological skills undergoing important changes during the same time periods. Although some form of compensation or "plasticity" or "developmental restoration" may be occurring in the young brain after a brain insult, the brain remains rather "unforgiving," and the consequences of an early brain injury can often be observed throughout the life span.

Although early brain lesions disrupt the plan of the central nervous system (CNS), the human CNS is so constructed that the "plan continues," but less perfectly. For example, basic language skills may develop in a relatively normal manner following an early brain insult (Bates et al., 2001; Murias et al., 2014), but more complex language skills may not. Murias et al. reviewed, for example, findings from several investigators that suggested that children with early vascular lesions to the brain often have difficulty with complex syntax and with providing details during storytelling compared to age-matched peers. This can occur irrespective of the laterality of the CVA during childhood. The same phenomenon has been reported in children with severe TBI. Chapman (1995), for example, reported that children who suffered a severe TBI before age 4 years had more difficulty performing language tasks compared to children injured later in life.

Repeated neuropsychological examination findings obtained from a 9-year-old boy who suffered a CVA at 6 months of age were compatible with the important observations mentioned previously. Five years after his CVA, an MRI of the brain revealed an atrophic right hippocampal formation as well as chronic-appearing lacunar infarcts in the right posterior thalamus. Earlier medical records reported, however, a stroke in the right temporal–occipital region of the brain of unknown cause.

The patient's mother noted that immediately after his stroke, he presented with a left hemiparesis. It resolved with time and physical therapy. Why was the same not true for his cognitive impairments? Table 6.2 lists several of his neuropsychological test findings obtained during a 6-year period. His speed of finger tapping in the left hand was slightly below average when he was tested at age 7 years, 4 months, but it steadily improved and was within the normal range by the time he was 9 years old. Also, his vocabulary level and verbal reasoning seemed to improve by age 9 years. Other areas of cognitive functioning did not improve, including some measures of working memory (e.g., low Digit Span scale score) and verbal learning and recall. Irrespective of his neuropsychological findings, his mother repeatedly described him as "childlike" in his manner. His mother also reported that he behaved in an "immature" manner relative to his age-matched peers.

The patient was brought for a neuropsychological examination because of frequent "meltdowns." When he could not perform certain tasks (this behavioral pattern is also reported by Lind et al., 2016), he would quickly become upset, throw objects, yell, and scream. His mother thought the behaviors might be manipulative in nature (i.e., to get his way) when, in fact, they appeared to represent what Goldstein (1948) described as the "catastrophic reaction" seen in many individuals with brain dysfunction. When he was unable to solve an apparently simple task for his age, he quickly became overwhelmed with feelings of anxiety and anger. With this insight, the boy's mother, his teachers, and the clinical neuropsychologist carefully chose the tasks presented to him at home and school in light of his cognitive skills. As a result, his "meltdowns" were much less frequent. During the years that he was followed, his mother further commented about his difficulties in communication despite his improved vocabulary. The mother described her son's verbal responses to questions as disjointed and tangential, which reflected an apparent breakdown in his thought process. This was present without evidence of a frank aphasic condition and normal Verbal Comprehension Index scores (see Table 6.2). In comparing the relative effects of unilateral vascular lesions on neuropsychological functions in adults versus

Table 6.2 Serial Neuropsychological Test Findings in a Male Child Who Suffered a Cerebral Vascular Accident at Age 6 Months

AGE AT TESTING	7 YEARS, 4 MONTHS	9 YEARS, 11 MONTHS	11 YEARS, 5 MONTHS	13 YEARS, 11 MONTHS
BNI-Screen Children	23/50, $T < 20$	42/50, $T = 42$	43/50, $T = 44$	46/50, $T = 50$
Peabody Picture Vocabulary Test	6 years, 11 months	9 years, 11 months		
WISC-IV				
Verbal Comprehension Index	67 (1st %ile)	106 (66th %ile)		99 (47th %ile)
Similarities	ss = 3	ss = 7		ss = 10
Vocabulary	ss = 6	ss = 9	ss = 7	ss = 9
Information	ss = 4	ss = 11	ss = 7	
Comprehension				ss = 11
Perceptual Reasoning Index	86 (18th %ile)	92 (30th %ile)		102 (55th %ile)
Block Design	ss = 10	ss = 12	ss = 8	ss = 13
Matrix Reasoning	ss = 8	ss = 7		ss = 9
Picture Concepts	ss = 5	ss = 7		ss = 9
Picture Completion	ss = 5	ss = 8		
Working Memory Index	77 (6th %ile)	91 (27th %ile)		83 (13th %ile)
Digit Span	ss = 6	ss = 8	ss = 6	ss = 6
Arithmetic	ss = 6	ss = 6		
Letter–Number Sequencing		ss = 9		ss = 8
Processing Speed Index	80 (9th %ile)	78 (7th %ile)		85 (15th %ile)
Symbol Search	ss = 4	ss = 6	ss = 7	ss = 9
Coding	ss = 9	ss = 6	ss = 5	ss = 6
Full Scale IQ	72 (3rd %ile)	91 (27th %ile)		92 (31th %ile)
RAVLT				
Learning trials		4, 6, 6, 9, 9	5, 6, 7, 8, 7	7, 7, 7, 11, 9
Total words		34, $T = 26$	33, $T = 22$	42, $T = 37$

(continued)

Table 6.2 Continued

AGE AT TESTING	7 YEARS, 4 MONTHS	9 YEARS, 11 MONTHS	11 YEARS, 5 MONTHS	13 YEARS, 11 MONTHS
Immediate delay (words)		2/15, $T = 21$	7/15, $T = 35$	8/15, $T = 26$
20-Minute delay (words)		3/15, $T = 20$	6/15, $T = 24$	7/15, $T = 29$
Children's Memory Scale				
Immediate Recall		ss = 6		ss = 12
Delayed Recall		ss = 8		ss = 11
Recognition Memory		ss = 14		ss = 11
BVMT-R				
Learning trials			Trial 1: $T = 53$	Trial 1: $T = 48$
			Trial 2: $T = 47$	Trial 2: $T = 47$
			Trial 3: $T = 50$	Trial 3: $T = 49$
25-Minute delay			10/12, $T = 50$	10/12, $T = 54$
NEPSY-II Phonemic (i.e. Letter) Fluency			ss = 2	ss = 4
NEPSY-II Semantic (i.e. Category) Fluency			ss = 5	ss = 7
Trail Making A	$T = 55$	$T = 51$	$T = 32$	$T = 36$
Time, errors	31 seconds, 0 errors	24 seconds, 0 errors	30 seconds, 0 errors	24 seconds, 0 errors
Trail Making B	$T = 60$	$T = 54$	$T = 44$	$T < 20$
Time, errors	52 seconds, 1 error	46 seconds, 0 errors	51 seconds, 0 errors	97 seconds, 1 error
Finger Tapping Test				
Dominant right hand	32.2, $T = 42$	36.1, $T = 55$	48.2, $T = 67$	45.6, $T = 52$
Nondominant left hand	25.2, $T = 36$	35.2, $T = 65$	41.4, $T = 60$	40.2, $T = 51$

BNI, Barrow Neurological Institute; BVMT-R, Brief Visuospatial Memory Test–Revised; NEPSY-II, Neuropsychological Assessment–Second Edition; RAVLT, Rey Auditory Verbal Learning Test; ss, scaled score; WISC-IV, Wechsler Intelligence Scale for Children–Fourth Edition; %ile, percentile rank.

children, Mosch et al. (2005) noted that children with a history of early CVA often had difficult-to-detect cognitive impairments as they aged, and there was frequently some disturbance in language functions and later in the ability to acquire academic skills. These children frequently had difficulty interacting in a socially appropriate manner. This certainly was the case for this child and for other children reported in the literature.

In partial summary, children with very early brain insults secondary to TBIs or CVAs tend to be impulsive, quick to anger, inattentive, and "more immature" in their social interactions, and they often have visual perceptual and motor difficulties. With time, they often demonstrate greater difficulty developing higher order, pragmatic language skills even when an aphasic condition or severe reduction in verbal comprehension skills is not present. The processing of new information is often slow, and these children appear to have difficulty with complex problem-solving tasks even when their IQ scores are in the average range compared to normal age-matched peers.

The clinical picture is somewhat different for children who have substantially below average intelligence secondary to severe TBI early in life (Gerrard-Morris et al., 2010) or large cortical lesions secondary to a CVA (Murias et al., 2014). These children often have profound difficulties with new learning, behavioral control, motor skills, and the ability to develop even superficially normal language skills. Interestingly, "children with perinatal strokes often do not display hemispheric or location-specific deficits commonly seen with lesions at later ages" (Murias et al., 2014, p. 138). That is, when tested several years after their perinatal stroke, these children do not show greater Verbal IQ impairments if their lesion was on the left side of the brain, nor do they show relatively greater nonverbal or Performance IQ impairments if their lesion was on the right side of the brain. There is often a general suppression of cognitive development in multiple domains. Many, if not all, of these children remain severely compromised throughout their developmental years and depend on parents into adulthood. Some individuals ultimately require residential living arrangements secondary to their severely limited cognitive skills.

If the immature brain is in a state of transition from diffuse to regional and then focal neuro-network development in order to allow for specific cognitive skills development (as suggested by Durston et al., 2006), large lesions that affect multiple brain sites may cause this normally occurring transition not to occur. One would therefore expect abnormal patterns of cerebral activation in these children when they perform certain cognitive tasks. In fact, Murias et al.'s (2014) discussion of neuroimaging studies supports this proposition. They noted that when these children performed cognitive tasks (many of which involve language), the patterns of activation showed "atypical localization" (p. 144). Alternative ipsilateral and contralateral activation patterns were frequently observed.

Murias et al. (2014) also brought attention to a potentially important observation by Mineyko, Brooks, Carlson, Bello-Espinosa, and Kirton (2012), who reported that in perinatal arterial ischemic stroke (AIS), children who had clearly abnormal neuropsychological findings showed abnormal electroencephalogram (EEG) discharges during slow-wave sleep (SWS). In contrast, children with a history of perinatal AIS without abnormal EEG patterns during SWS had less severe neuropsychological disturbances. If replicated, these findings continue to highlight the interdependency of cognitive functioning with SWS (Atherton et al., 2016; see also Chapter 5, this volume).

Clearly, the long-term consequences of very early focal injuries to the brain have not been adequately studied. However, S. Anderson et al. (2000) provide further insightful observations regarding two children with focal prefrontal cortex damage that occurred before 16 months of age. As these children were followed throughout childhood and into adolescence and young adulthood, profound difficulties in "decision making, behavioral dyscontrol, social defects, and abnormal emotion" were documented (p. 281). When they were tested later in life using traditional neuropsychological tests, many aspects of their test performance were within the average range. This highlights the limits of many existing neuropsychological measures for detecting disturbances in brain–behavior relationships occurring "in the real world" and not just in the neuropsychology testing laboratory. Interestingly, however, both of these patients had relative difficulties on the Coding or Digit Symbol subtest of the Wechsler Adult Intelligence Scale–Revised (WAIS-R; age-adjusted scale scores of 8). This measure has been related to efficiency of frontal–parietal functioning by some investigators (Rypma et al., 2006; see also Chapter 4, this volume). This may be an important indicator of subtle cognitive impairments that can be sampled over the life span, as later chapters demonstrate.

NEUROPSYCHOLOGICAL CONSEQUENCES OF DISRUPTING THE CENTRAL NERVOUS SYSTEM OBSERVED DURING THE SCHOOL-AGE YEARS

As noted in Chapter 2, the parietal and temporal association cortex has a prolonged time frame of synaptogenesis and synaptic pruning that extends to 4–8 years of age (Casey, Galvan, & Hare, 2005). These regions of the brain are important for visual and verbal memory skills. Kail (1991) notes that visual recognition memory of pictures often improves rapidly from age 4 or 5 years to age 10 years. Verbal memory, however, may take longer to develop. In an early study of school-age children with TBI, Levin et al. (1988) demonstrated that visual memory seems to be equally affected after severe TBI in children who suffered those injuries during three age ranges (6–8, 9–12, and 13–15 years). In contrast, some aspects of verbal learning and memory were relatively more compromised during the adolescent years (ages 13–15 years). It was argued that those skills not fully developed may show the greatest relative effects from severe trauma to the brain when studied.

O'Keeffe et al. (2014) studied the neuropsychological and behavioral characteristics of childhood AIS. They noted that most ischemic strokes involved the basal ganglia and the distribution of the MCA, with relative sparing of the frontal lobe. Forty-nine children between the ages of 6 and 18 years were studied. The average age at the time of their stroke was 5 years, and the average age at the time of testing was 11 years. However, some children had AIS as early as 4 months of life. Twenty-one of the 49 children had their stroke at age 5 years or older. As reported by other investigators (Max, 2004), children with right versus left unilateral strokes did not differ in terms of their Verbal IQ or Performance IQ scores using the Wechsler Abbreviated Scale of Intelligence (WASI). However, children with right-sided stroke performed significantly better than children with left-sided stroke on the Matrix Reasoning subtest of the WASI even though this subtest is used to calculate the Performance IQ. Age at injury (for this sample of children) was also not related to IQ scores. As a group, however, these children had substantial difficulties on tasks of divided attention (e.g., Delis–Kaplan Executive Function System Trail Making Task and Letter–Number Sequencing) and speed of new learning. The average age-adjusted Coding subtest score on the Wechsler Intelligence Scale for Children/WAIS was 7.81. The investigators also noted that problems with response inhibition and dual attention were especially compromised in these children. Overall IQ scores were average to low average despite the children's behavioral and neurocognitive impairments.

Because the parietal areas are especially important for sustained and divided attention (Petersen & Posner, 2012) and undergo significant developmental changes during childhood, the finding of large size effects on dual-attention difficulties is noteworthy. The temporal lobes also undergo significant developmental changes during this time and are known to be important for memory. Unfortunately, O'Keeffe et al. (2014) did not include measures of memory functioning. However, Max (2004) included two measures of memory functioning in his study on the effects of unilateral childhood stroke and found no difference between children with either right or left hemisphere strokes on the California Verbal Learning Test–Children's form (a measure of rote verbal learning and recall) and the Rey–Osterrieth figure delayed recall. However, Max noted that for both groups of children, the level of performance on the verbal learning and delayed recall was considered "low average," whereas the nonverbal, visual–spatial recall was described as "mildly to moderately impaired." Memory impairments, however, are often substantial in school-age children who suffer severe TBI. Jaffe, Polissar, Fay, and Liao (1995) longitudinally studied various neuropsychological functions in school-age children who suffered a TBI between 6 and 15 years of age. For children with severe TBI, memory skills (as measured by a test of rote verbal learning) remained significantly below average during a 2- or 3-year follow-up period. Likewise, speed and accuracy of motor performance (using a combination of measures) remained significantly below average for these children during this same follow-up period. Early researchers studying children similar in age also emphasized that those with severe injuries resulting from TBI were especially prone to perform slowly on tests that had high-speed demands. That is, faster scores resulted in "higher levels of performance" (Bawden, Knights, & Winogron, 1985). These findings suggest that although unilateral CVAs in school-age children can have profound negative effects on their neuropsychological status and occasionally "equal those" of children with severe TBI, children with severe TBI often demonstrate more obvious difficulties in memory, simple and complex motor activities, and speed of performance.

Gorman et al. (2016) reported that speed of performance, as measured by the Coding subtest of the Wechsler Scale of Intelligence, was significantly impaired in school-age children with severe TBI. Although this was not a new finding (Jaffe et al., 1995; Rutter, 1981), Gorman et al. demonstrated that "working memory" problems commonly observed in these children could, in part, be explained by their slow processing speeds.

School-age children with a history of moderate to severe TBI often have difficulties meeting academic requirements (as reported by several investigators, including Jaffe et al., 1995) and demonstrate a combination of memory difficulties, slow processing speeds, and below-average working memory. Consequently, they do not understand either the content of classroom-presented academic material or homework instructions. Not uncommonly, they may simply be quiet and look "confused" when given instructions. They are, however, prone to distractibility because they cannot follow what is being taught to them in school and frequently fail to turn in their homework.

What are the long-term neuropsychological consequences of TBI in children? Jonsson, Catroppa, Godfrey, Smedler, and Anderson (2013) studied a group of 118 children with TBI during a 10-year period and reported different patterns of recovery or lack of recovery on different subtests of the Wechsler Scales of Intelligence. In their sample, children who initially demonstrated problems with processing speed appeared to go on to show greater cognitive improvements when tested 10 years after the trauma. However, children who had lower verbal comprehension scores tended not to show as much recovery. These observations are potentially clinically significant. If school-age children with focal or multifocal lesions do not understand what words mean at a level comparable to that of their age-matched peers, this puts them at risk not only for poor school performance but also for a tendency to withdraw from social activities. Clinically, many of these children prefer to finish high school at home, using online courses, rather than be continually insulted by their age-matched peers within the traditional school environment. This topic is revisited in a later chapter.

One final observation needs to be considered that is relevant to understanding how focal versus diffuse injuries to the brain in school-age children may affect the natural plan of the CNS. The architecture of the default mode network (DMN) described in Chapters 3 and 5 is underdeveloped in school-age children compared to adults. Fair et al. (2008) note that the connections between the posterior cingulate and the lateral parietal regions are underdeveloped in early school-age children (ages 7–9 years), as depicted in Figure 6.1. They also note that normally developing children can learn and retain new information at the time the DMN is not fully developed. However, the amount of information children are able to learn does improve as they become older. Also, their ability to reflect on the relevance of certain facts in relation to other facts they have learned becomes progressively important as they age. This increased learning capacity may relate to the development of alternative problem-solving strategies that are observed in school-age children. The progressive development of the DMN may facilitate this process. If this is the case, large lesions to the brain or multiple lesions to the brain that negatively alter important neuro-connectivity patterns of the DMN may well affect children's awareness of their functional capacities and their level of "overall intelligence." Further studies

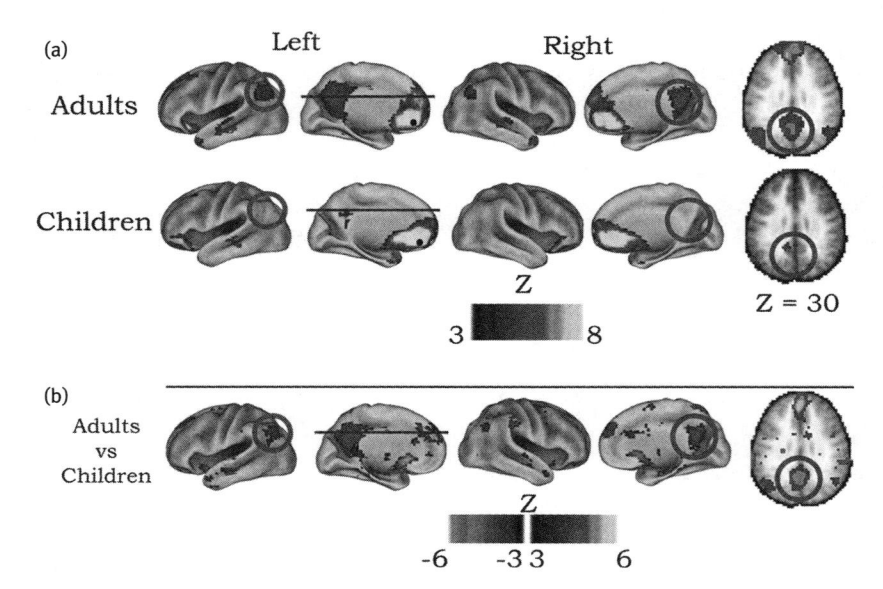

FIGURE 6.1 Voxelwise resting-state functional connectivity maps for a seed region (black circle) in the medial prefrontal cortex (mPFC; ventral: -3, 39, -2). (A) Qualitatively, the resting state functional connectivity MRI map for the mPFC (ventral) seed region reveals the commonly observed adult connectivity pattern of the default network (9, 18, 19). The connectivity map in children, however, significantly deviates from that of adults. Functional connections with regions in the posterior cingulate and lateral parietal regions (blue circles) are present in the adults but absent in children. (B) These qualitative differences between children and adults are confirmed by the direct comparison (random effects) between adults and children. mPFC (ventral) functional connections with the posterior cingulate and lateral parietal regions are significantly stronger in adults than in children (See color plates).

Source: Reprinted from Fair, D. A., Cohen, A. L., Dosenbach, N. U., Church, J. A., Miezin, F. M., Barch, D. M., . . . Schlaggar, B. L., The maturing architecture of the brain's default network. *Proceedings of the National Academy of Sciences of the USA, 105*(10), p. 4028–4032, with permission. Copyright (2008) National Academy of Sciences, U.S.A.

are needed to explore this possibility. However, clinical observations suggest that school-age children with major CVAs affecting the cortex and children with severe TBIs often demonstrate a reduction in their overall intelligence and may well have difficulty being aware of the extent of their neurocognitive impairments (Jacobs, 1993).

NEUROPSYCHOLOGICAL CONSEQUENCES OF DISRUPTION OF THE CENTRAL NERVOUS SYSTEM DURING THE ADOLESCENT YEARS

As children mature and grow into adolescence, their pattern of performance begins to resemble that observed in young adulthood. For example, it is well known that in adults, left frontal lesions often result in greater word fluency difficulties compared to nonfrontal injuries. This is often not seen in the early school-age years but becomes progressively more common as the child matures and approaches adolescent years. Figure 6.2 highlights this finding (Levin, Song, Ewing-Cobbs, Chapman, & Mendelsohn, 2001). At age 7 years, children with left frontal injuries secondary to TBI show no difference in the words they can generate on a verbal fluency task compared to children who have nonfrontal injuries to the brain. However, in older children and early adolescent children, verbal fluency scores are lower for the group with frontal injuries.

It is during adolescence that frontal cortex undergoes considerable experience-dependent synapse formation and dendritic arborization (see Chapter 3, this volume). However, prefrontal cortical development has a protracted developmental course. Consequently, lesions to this brain region can negatively alter developing functions necessary for the transition from childhood to adolescence and from adolescence to young adulthood (Case, 1985). Reyna, Chapman, Dougherty, and Confrey (2012) emphasize the importance of "learning, reasoning, and decision making" during adolescence. Acquiring academic knowledge via the effective use of language skills can be especially compromised during this time, particularly after severe TBI.

Chapman, Gamino, and Mudar (2012) summarize some of their observations in this area. They note that adolescents with a history of severe TBI have difficulty summarizing complex textual information presented to them in verbal and written form. They often have difficulties identifying the main theme or underlying "gist" of what is being conveyed. This can exist even if underlying rote verbal learning skills appear relatively intact and IQ scores are in the average range. Chapman et al. state that these difficulties can be even more pronounced during the adolescent years if a child's TBI occurred during earlier stages of development.

Other researchers have noted that mathematical reasoning skills often undergo substantial development during the adolescent years (Knuth, Kalish, Ellis, Williams, & Felton, 2011). Clinically, parents of adolescents with a history of severe TBI often emphasize their child's difficulties in learning math concepts. Although this can clearly occur earlier in childhood as a

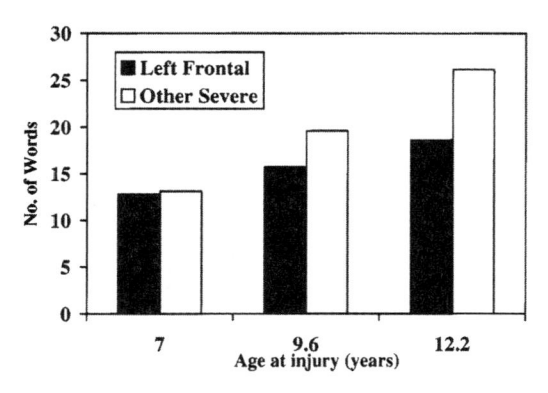

FIGURE 6.2 Histogram showing left frontal effect on mean total number of words recalled in longitudinal study, reflecting a greater lesion effect on word fluency in older children than in younger children.

Source: Reprinted from Levin, H. S., Song, J., Ewing-Cobbs, L., Chapman, S. B., & Mendelsohn, D., Word fluency in relation to severity of closed head injury, associated frontal brain lesions, and age at injury in children, *Neuropsychologia, 39*(2), p. 122–131, Copyright (2001), with permission from Elsevier.

result of focal or multifocal injuries, during the adolescent years, the math concepts to which the child is exposed are more challenging. A 16-year-old girl who suffered a moderate to severe TBI (admitting GCS score of 10, but who had a right hemispheric cerebral contusion) was able to graduate from high school because her teachers excused her from completing certain math requirements. However, she had to drop out of her first year of community college because even with tutorial help, she repeatedly failed an algebra class. It had a devastating effect on her self-concept because she then felt "stupid" and searched for recognition via sexually inappropriate behavior with boys and later with men. This latter problem is seen in various forms, but it basically relates to an underlying difficulty with impulse control, which is common after moderate to severe TBI that occurs in the adolescent years.

Galván (2012) notes that adolescents are more inclined to engage in risk-taking behavior. She relates this behavior to potential changes in the adolescent brain's responsiveness to pleasurable experiences. She suggests: "While the adolescent may experience greater neural activation following rewards, which subsequently biases him or her to engage in further reward-seeking and risky behavior, the prefrontal cortex is not yet ready to regulate this reward-driven behavior" (p. 268). Damage to the prefrontal cortex during adolescence may influence this dynamic balance in different ways. One 15-year-old boy, with bilateral prefrontal contusions secondary to a severe TBI, seemed apathetic and was no longer interested in riding his motor bike at high rates of speed. His parents commented that he was a "lot nicer now" and was less likely to go out with friends and drink alcohol as he did prior to his brain injury. He was now content to be at home. In contrast, the 16-year-old girl described previously was more likely to engage in risky sexual behaviors, which was atypical of her before her TBI. Another 14-year-old girl, with a history of moderate to severe TBI at age 5 years, took verbal teasing literally from a boy her age. She quickly became angry with him and did not realize that as an adolescent boy, his teasing reflected an interest in her.

Difficulties developing socially appropriate initiation and inhibition are often seen in adolescents with a significant TBI. They are more likely to make "inappropriate comments" when speaking in social gatherings and look perplexed when others convey the inappropriateness of what they just said. The converse, however, is also true. Occasionally, they will not begin conversations or will avoid interactions with their peers because they do not know what to say or how to keep a conversation "going" and make it interesting. These features are certainly reminiscent of the potential effects of prefrontal injuries to the brain because they are involved in planning and flexibility in responding to internal and external demands (Fuster, 1997; see also Chapter 3, this volume).

Another typical feature of adolescents is a heightened social sensitivity to what others think about them. Being a part of the "in crowd" becomes very important as it relates to one's social status with peers. During this time, adolescents are progressively developing a sense of "who they are" and "what they might become." The development of one's self-concept and self-awareness begins to take form, and focal and nonfocal or multifocal injuries to the brain can and do influence these interrelated psychological functions or features. These do so, however, in complicated ways. For example, an adolescent girl suffered a bleed (or hemorrhage) of a right frontoparietal AVM. As a result, she had weakness of the left arm and leg and could not wear high heels, which were very important for her sense of developing womanhood. She felt less feminine and could not continue to go to dances with friends. She experienced periodic bouts of anger and depression over her clinical condition and avoided social gatherings.

An 18-year-old adolescent male suffered bilateral frontal contusions. He subjectively reported no cognitive limitations after his brain injury. He (and his neurosurgeon at the time) minimized any cognitive or behavioral problems, and he attempted college following his graduation from high school. To his and other people's surprise, he had trouble passing his college classes. He eventually dropped out of school and sought help through neuropsychological rehabilitation. One day he was observed trying to make social contact with a young woman while waiting in line at a cafeteria. His comments were inane, and he was not picking up the social cues that the young woman was not interested in his advances. When this was brought to his attention, he was honestly perplexed with the feedback. He had no (self) awareness of his socially insensitive behavior. He felt her rejection but did not know why. This problem of impaired self-awareness is often seen after severe TBI in adolescence and early adulthood (Prigatano, 2010), and it ushers in another problem that is discussed in more detail in later chapters.

LONGITUDINAL CHANGES IN CORTICAL THICKNESS AND "FRONTAL LOBE DYSFUNCTION" IN CHILDREN AFTER TRAUMATIC BRAIN INJURY

Although the neuropsychological and behavioral difficulties of school-age children with TBI are well known and extend into adolescence and young adulthood (Babikian, Merkley, Savage, Giza, & Levin, 2015), the relationship of these difficulties to measurable changes in brain anatomy has remained very challenging. Wilde et al. (2012), however, studied cortical thickness changes over time in children with moderate to severe TBI and orthopedic controls and related their findings to behavioral regulation and emotional control. Although they report several findings, one unexpected finding is most interesting. They report that there was a failure to undergo expected developmental cortical thinning in the right medial frontal and right anterior cingulate gyrus. This neuroanatomical finding was positively correlated with worse behavioral and emotional control as reported by parents.

These regions, as discussed in further detail in Chapter 9, are also correlated with behavioral features of "frontal lobe dysfunction" in which "unawareness" of cognitive limitations may be present in an adult.

PSYCHOSOCIAL CONSEQUENCES OF NEUROPSYCHOLOGICAL IMPAIRMENTS IN CHILDREN AND ADOLESCENTS

The psychosocial consequences of neuropsychological impairments of children and adolescents are many and have been documented in several articles and chapters (Beauchamp, Dooley, & Anderson, 2010; Max, 2005; Meadows et al., 2017; Prigatano, 2008; Prigatano & Gray, 2007; Prigatano & Gupta, 2006; Yeates et al., 2012). At a minimum, they often involve reduced or poor academic performance; "immature" responding to others; emotional dyscontrol; poor social decision-making; inattentive, disruptive remarks; impulsive reactions; a loss of friendships; and a tendency to either withdraw from social interaction or respond aggressively when frustrated in social situations. Many of these children have difficulty learning from life experiences, which can greatly interfere with the ability to later obtain and maintain work as well as friendships (Beauchamp et al., 2010). Thus, by and large, many of these children do not develop normally (Prigatano, 2008), which causes considerable distress for them and their parents. Many go on to develop secondary psychiatric disturbances associated with depression and anxiety.

Box 6.1 summarizes some of the common neuropsychological and psychosocial difficulties of these children. In closing this section, it is important to note that the neuropsychological consequences of a very early brain injury may not be obvious on standardized neuropsychological tests when individuals are examined in adolescence or adulthood. Subtle difficulties in visual–spatial abilities, motor skills, higher order language skills, and social judgment may be more meaningful for determining the focus of psychological care of these children, particularly as they grow into adolescence and adulthood.

GENERAL OBSERVATIONS REGARDING THE PSYCHOLOGICAL CARE OF CHILDREN AND ADOLESCENTS WITH BRAIN DISORDERS

As noted previously, very young children who have "acquired brain injuries" often present with visual–spatial/motor disturbances, attentional problems, and difficulty with impulse control or with delaying gratification when asked to perform different tasks. A key component of their psychological care has been to guide them to sustain their attention and mirror or copy what caring family members (often parents) do as it relates to simple and then more complex visual–motor activities. Braga and Campos da Paz (2006) outline how this can be done using a "context-sensitive, family-based approach" to development. When parents are either absent or unable/unwilling to provide such family-based (and reinforced) teaching, a skilled clinical neuropsychologist can take on this role. Psychodynamic issues often quickly come to light under such circumstances. For example, a 5-year-old child with moderate memory and intellectual impairments secondary to cerebral vascular lesions of unknown origin was described as frequently yelling and hitting his mother. He also was described as very impulsive and had major difficulties focusing and maintaining his attention in his kindergarten class. His father was absent and left the mother during her pregnancy with this child. When a male neuropsychologist began working with him on attentional tasks that were "fun" for him, his impulsive responding decreased. As the neuropsychologist, who was also a musician, taught him to play simple tunes on a guitar, the child's behavior continued to improve. He was much less likely to impulsively respond when developing a skill he enjoyed.

Later, the mother confided that she told her son that the father had left because he could not handle the boy's medical problems. The boy appeared to become angry with his mother after she told him. It appeared to make him feel bad and unworthy. Thus, he physically struck out at her on several occasions. The mother was then told to convey a different message—the truth of what happened. She then told the child that she wanted his father to stay, but they (the parents) had problems they could not work out together. It was not the boy's fault that the father had left. The male clinical neuropsychologist was teaching the child skills that a father might do. With time, the boy became considerably calmer. The mother was astounded by how much her son's behavior improved as a result of these interventions.

In addition to the child with a brain injury being distressed, D. Woods, Catroppa, and Anderson (2012) make the important point that behavioral problems of these children can produce great distress in very caring family members. They also note how these children can become more anxious, depressed, and socially isolated if their behavioral problems are not under control. Teaching parents how to manage their child's behavior at home, using a variety of behavioral techniques, can therefore be especially helpful. Both the parents and the child benefit from the systematic use of behavioral or functional analysis techniques. Woods et al. describe a "flexible family-centered socio-behavioral intervention" program that can be applied to children with acquired brain injuries.

Woods et al.'s (2012) insightful presentation and review of the literature makes two very important points when considering this form of psychological care for these children. First, children with severe brain disorders, as is often seen following severe TBI, may have a reduced capacity to benefit from behavioral reinforcements because of the underlying nature of their cognitive–behavioral impairments. Second, when such treatments are shown to be empirically effective, they are conducted under very well-controlled circumstances. The data resulting from such research suggest

> **Box 6.1. Common Neuropsychological and Psychosocial Difficulties Observed in Children and Adolescents Who Suffer a Brain Disorder**
>
> **Neuropsychological Disturbances**
> 1. Disturbances in visual–motor coordination and speed
> 2. Disturbances in the initiation and inhibition of responses as the situation demands (reflected in behaviors at multiple levels of functioning, including impulsive responding, reduced effortful control on attentional tasks, and planning ahead in order to achieve a successful performance)
> 3. Disturbances in attention (focused and divided)
> 4. Disturbances in behavioral control
> 5. Disturbances in higher order language skills, including understanding the essential features or "gist" of complicated information as well as the pragmatics of speech
> 6. Disturbances in new learning memory
> 7. Disturbances in speed of information processing
> 8. Disturbances in working memory
> 9. Disturbances in concept formation when learning new material, especially in mathematics
> 10. Disturbances in self-monitoring (and self-awareness)
> 11. Disturbances in the perception, expression, and regulation of affect
>
> **Psychosocial Consequences**
> 1. Poor academic performance
> 2. Immature responding to frustrations compared to age-matched peers
> 3. Emotional dyscontrol
> 4. Difficulties verbally expressing themselves in a clear and concise manner
> 5. Inattentive, disruptive verbal remarks in social interactions
> 6. Poor social decision-making
> 7. Fine motor control difficulties that limit athletic interactions necessary to build friendships
> 8. Limited (or lost) friendships
> 9. Reduced interpersonal sensitivity
> 10. Uncooperative behaviors
> 11. Social withdrawal and isolation
> 12. Impaired self-awareness
> 13. Increased depression, anxiety, and, occasionally, angry outbursts or "meltdowns"

the feasibility and efficacy of such treatments (p. 362). The question remains: How effective are these behavioral strategies when conducted in the typical clinical setting? There is no doubt that improved behavioral control is important for these children, especially in light of the consistent finding that poor impulse control is a major behavioral characteristic of some children with acquired brain injuries. Appealing to the children's "inner reality" might become very important, however, as they begin to develop better language skills and can express a variety of emotions associated with their clinical condition.

In this regard, it is interesting to note that Mark Ylvisaker, who was an early proponent of functional behavioral analysis to help control children's disruptive behavior after a brain disorder, recognized later in his career the use of "metaphors" to help adolescents and adults. The use of metaphors could help develop a sense of personal identity that assisted children and adolescents to choose appropriate goals, which would in turn sustain their efforts in rehabilitation (Ylvisaker, McPherson, Kayes, & Pellett, 2008). Although not citing the work of psychoanalytic theorists or therapists in this regard (e.g., Bettelheim, 1989), Ylvisaker et al.'s conclusions were similar. Appealing to children's fantasies and identifying "heroes in their life" could serve as a major means of helping them. It solidified an approach that helped with a common psychosocial crisis experienced in adolescence, namely finding role models that help establish a firm sense of identity. This is often achieved in both conscious and unconscious strivings of human beings as they relate to their favorite heroes in life, who are often depicted in stories and fairy tales.

A clinical vignette highlights this point. A 12-year-old girl underwent a craniotomy for a right frontal brain tumor (i.e., meningioma). Her cognitive recovery was excellent, but her mother reported that her daughter was depressed and uninterested in life, including that she did not want to make new friends. In the course of her serial neuropsychological examinations, she saw a book on a shelf that held her interest. It was a book of fairy tales. As she paged through the book, she came across the story of "The Ugly Duckling." She was immediately drawn to the story and the picture of the ugly duckling. She spontaneously stated that this is how she felt at times—ugly! In reality, she was not ugly but, rather, an attractive young adolescent girl. As she and the clinical neuropsychologist talked, it came to light that she felt ugly because she was so tall for her age. She was given examples of how some tall women are attractive and have accomplished much in life. She appeared somewhat relieved. In a way, it fulfilled the promise of the ugly duckling story. She clearly felt happy with this discussion and wanted to share the story with her mother.

When she showed her mother the picture and story of "The Ugly Duckling," her mother spontaneously stated that she also felt ugly because she was taller than the average woman. As the mother and daughter reflected on the message of this metaphoric story, both smiled again and appeared emotionally relieved. They often wanted to return and talk with the clinical neuropsychologists because they both were helped by the consultation. A long-term relationship was established, and the psychological care of the child continues to this day. She continues to seek guidance when faced with important decisions in her life. Her mother also looks forward to such consultations. When psychotherapeutic efforts with an adolescent do not go so well, long-term adjustment problems are frequently encountered in young adulthood and during the later adult years, as later chapters illustrate.

SUMMARY

Focal and multifocal injuries to the brain during various phases of brain development have predictable neuropsychological and psychosocial consequences. Children with such injuries and their parents are faced with the long-term problem of not developing normally. Although focal and relatively small brain lesions can have serious consequences for neuropsychological functioning, large and bilateral lesions seem to have more severe cognitive consequences with resultant greater psychosocial difficulties.

It is clear from the study of children with a history of CVA or TBI that the natural plan of the CNS continues despite its disruption. So development continues, but it does not continue "normally." This reality has to be addressed with the parents as well as the child. Normal developmental changes may appear to override the effects of certain brain lesions (e.g., failure to develop basic drawing skills), but always in an "imperfect" way. In cases of severe and bilateral lesions, other functions clearly do not improve with time (e.g., the overall level of intelligence when measured relative to one's age-matched peers). Laterality effects seen in adults are often not seen in young children with brain disorders or are observed to a lesser extent. The specific neuropsychological vulnerabilities observed when children have cerebral vascular or traumatically induced brain injuries at different times in their development are only partially understood, but the psychosocial consequences are well known and are relatively common to both conditions.

Providing psychological care to children and youth is an extremely important venture for clinical neuropsychologists. Attending to their behavioral problems within the context of family-centered interventions is an ideal starting point. These families and children, however, often require ongoing psychological care interventions provided by a clinical neuropsychologist who understands the complexity of children's difficulties and subjective experiences. Such interventions often lead to a long-standing working alliance between the child, the parents, and the treating psychological clinician who has an understanding of human nature, neuropsychological disturbances, and the psychosocial challenges these children or adolescents face.

REFERENCES

Akshoomoff, N., Stiles, J., & Wulfeck, B. (2006). Perceptual organization and visual immediate memory in children with specific language impairment. *Journal of the International Neuropsychological Society, 12*(4), 465–474.

Akshoomoff, N. A., Feroleto, C. C., Doyle, R. E., & Stiles, J. (2002). The impact of early unilateral brain injury on perceptual organization and visual memory. *Neuropsychologia, 40*(5), 539–561.

Anderson, C. A., & Arciniegas, D. B. (2010). Cognitive sequelae of hypoxic–ischemic brain injury: A review. *NeuroRehabilitation, 26*(1), 47–63.

Anderson, S. W., Damasio, H., Tranel, D., & Damasio, A. R. (2000). Long-term sequelae of prefrontal cortex damage acquired in early childhood. *Developmental Neuropsychology, 18*(3), 281–296.

Andrade, A., Bigi, S., Laughlin, S., Parthasarathy, S., Sinclair, A., Dirks, P., . . . MacGregor, D. (2016). Association between prolonged seizures and malignant middle cerebral artery infarction in children with acute ischemic stroke. *Pediatric Neurology, 64*, 44–51.

Atherton, K. E., Nobre, A. C., Lazar, A. S., Wulff, K., Whittaker, R. G., Dhawan, V., . . . Butler, C. R. (2016). Slow wave sleep and accelerated forgetting. *Cortex, 84*, 80–89.

Ay, H. (2011). Classification of ischemic stroke. In J. P. Mohr, P. A. Wolf, J. C. Grotta, A. Moskowitz, M. Mayber, & R. von Kummer (Eds.), *Stroke: Pathophysiology, diagnosis, and management* (5th ed., pp. 295–307). Philadelphia, PA: Elsevier.

Babikian, T., Merkley, T., Savage, R. C., Giza, C. C., & Levin, H. (2015). Chronic aspects of pediatric traumatic brain injury: Review of the literature. *Journal of Neurotrauma, 32*(23), 1849–1860.

Banich, M. T., Levine, S. C., Kim, H., & Huttenlocher, P. (1990). The effects of developmental factors on IQ in hemiplegic children. *Neuropsychologia, 28*(1), 35–47.

Bates, E., Reilly, J., Wulfeck, B., Dronkers, N., Opie, M., Fenson, J., . . . Herbst, K. (2001). Differential effects of unilateral lesions on language production in children and adults. *Brain and Language, 79*(2), 223–265.

Bawden, H. N., Knights, R. M., & Winogron, H. W. (1985). Speeded performance following head injury in children. *Journal of Clinical and Experimental Neuropsychology, 7*(1), 39–54.

Beauchamp, M., Dooley, J., & Anderson, V. (2010). Adult outcomes of pediatric traumatic. In J. Donders & S. J. Hunter (Eds.), *Principles and practice of lifespan developmental neuropsychology* (pp. 315–328). New York, NY: Cambridge University Press.

Bettelheim, B. (1989). *The uses of enchantment: The meaning and importance of fairy tales*. New York, NY: Vintage.

Bigler, E. D. (2011). Structural imaging. In J. M. Silver, T. W. McAllister, & S. C. Yudofsky (Eds.), *Textbook of traumatic brain injury* (2nd ed., pp. 73–90). Arlington, VA: American Psychiatric Publishing.

Braga, L. W., & Campos da Paz, A. (2006). *The child with traumatic brain injury or cerebral palsy: A context-sensitive, family-based approach to development*. Boca Raton, FL: Taylor & Francis.

Case, R. (1985). *Intellectual development: Birth to adulthood*. New York, NY: Academic Press.

Casey, B., Galvan, A., & Hare, T. A. (2005). Changes in cerebral functional organization during cognitive development. *Current Opinions in Neurobiology, 15*(2), 239–244.

Chapman, S. B. (1995). Discourse as an outcome measure in pediatric head-injured populations. In S. H. Broman & M. E. Michel (Eds.), *Traumatic head injury in children* (pp. 95–116). New York, NY: Oxford University Press.

Chapman, S. B., Gamino, J. F., & Mudar, R. A. (2012). Higher order strategic gist reasoning in adolescence. In V. F. Reyna, S. B. Chapman, M. R. Dougherty, & J. Confrey (Eds.), *The adolescent brain: Learning, reasoning, and decision making* (pp. 123–151). Washington, DC: American Psychological Association.

Corbetta, M. (2017). *Behavioral clusters and brain network mechanisms of impairment and recovery.* Paper presented at the annual meeting of the International Neuropsychological Society, New Orleans.

Duhaime, A.-C., Christian, C., Moss, E., & Seidl, T. (1996). Long-term outcome in infants with the shaking-impact syndrome. *Pediatric Neurosurgery, 24*(6), 292–298.

Duhaime, A.-C., Christian, C. W., Rorke, L. B., & Zimmerman, R. A. (1998). Nonaccidental head injury in infants—The "shaken-baby syndrome." *New England Journal of Medicine, 338*(25), 1822–1829.

Dunn, P., Prigatano, G., Szelinger, S., Roth, J., Siniard, A., Claasen, A., . . . Moskowitz, A. (2017). A de novo splice site mutation in CASK causes FG syndrome-4 and congenital nystagmus. *American Journal of Medical Genetics Part A, 173*(3), 611–617.

Durston, S., Davidson, M. C., Tottenham, N., Galvan, A., Spicer, J., Fossella, J. A., & Casey, B. (2006). A shift from diffuse to focal cortical activity with development. *Developmental Science, 9*(1), 1–8.

Fair, D. A., Cohen, A. L., Dosenbach, N. U., Church, J. A., Miezin, F. M., Barch, D. M., . . . Schlaggar, B. L. (2008). The maturing architecture of the brain's default network. *Proceedings of the National Academy of Sciences of the USA, 105*(10), 4028–4032.

Fuster, J. M. (1997). *The prefrontal cortex: Anatomy, physiology, and neuropsychology of the frontal lobe* (3rd ed.). Philadelphia, PA: Lippincott–Raven.

Galván, A. (2012). Risky behavior in adolescents: The role of the developing brain. In V. F. Reyna, S. Chapman, M. Dougherty, & J. Confrey (Eds.), *The adolescent brain: Learning, reasoning, and decision making* (pp. 267–289). Washington, DC: American Psychological Association.

Ganong, W. (1981). *Review of medical physiology.* Los Altos, CA: Lange.

Gerrard-Morris, A., Taylor, H. G., Yeates, K. O., Walz, N. C., Stancin, T., Minich, N., & Wade, S. L. (2010). Cognitive development after traumatic brain injury in young children. *Journal of the International Neuropsychological Society, 16*(1), 157–168.

Goldstein, K. (1948). *Language and language disturbances: Aphasic symptom complexes and their significance for medicine and theory of language.* New York, NY: Grune & Stratton.

Gorman, S., Barnes, M. A., Swank, P. R., Prasad, M., Cox, C. S., Jr., & Ewing-Cobbs, L. (2016). Does processing speed mediate the effect of pediatric traumatic brain injury on working memory? *Neuropsychology, 30*(3), 263–273.

Greenberg, M. (2010). *Handbook of neurosurgery.* Tampa, FL: Greenberg Graphics.

Hawley, C. A. (2003). Reported problems and their resolution following mild, moderate and severe traumatic brain injury amongst children and adolescents in the UK. *Brain Injury, 17*(2), 105–129.

Howard, V. J., & Howard, G. (2011). Distribution of stroke: Heterogeneity by age, race, and sex. In J. P. Mohr, P. A. Wolf, J. C. Grotta, A. M. Moskowitz, M. C. Mayberg, & R. von Kummer (Eds.), *Stroke* (5th ed., pp. 189–197). Philadelphia, PA: Elsevier.

Hoyt, C. (2007). Brain injury and the eye. *Eye, 21*(10), 1285–1289.

Jacobs, M. P. (1993). Limited understanding of deficit in children with brain dysfunction. *Neuropsychological Rehabilitation, 3*(4), 341–365.

Jaffe, K. M., Polissar, N. L., Fay, G. C., & Liao, S. (1995). Recovery trends over three years following pediatric traumatic brain injury. *Archives of Physical Medicine and Rehabilitation, 76*(1), 17–26.

Jennett, B., & Teasdale, G. (1981). *Management of head injuries.* Philadelphia, PA: Davis.

Jonsson, C. A., Catroppa, C., Godfrey, C., Smedler, A.-C., & Anderson, V. (2013). Cognitive recovery and development after traumatic brain injury in childhood: A person-oriented, longitudinal study. *Journal of Neurotrauma, 30*(2), 76–83.

Kail, R. (1991). Developmental change in speed of processing during childhood and adolescence. *Psychological Bulletin, 109*(3), 490.

Knight, J. A., & Kaplan, E. (2003). *The handbook of Rey–Osterrieth Complex Figure usage: Clinical and research applications.* Lutz, FL: Psychological Assessment Resources.

Knuth, E., Kalish, C., Ellis, A., Williams, C., & Felton, M. (2011). Adolescent reasoning in mathematical and nonmathematical domains: Exploring the paradox. In V. F. Reyna, S. B. Chapman, M. R. Dougherty, & J. Confrey (Eds.), *The adolescent brain: Learning, reasoning, and decision making.*

Washington, DC: American Psychological Association.

Kolk, A., & Talvik, T. (2000). Cognitive outcome of children with early-onset hemiparesis. *Journal of Child Neurology, 15*(9), 581–587.

Lawton, M. T., & Vates, G. E. (2017). Subarachnoid hemorrhage. *New England Journal of Medicine, 377*(3), 257–266.

Levin, H. S., High, W. M., Jr., Ewing-Cobbs, L., Fletcher, J. M., Eisenberg, H. M., Miner, M. E., & Goldstein, F. C. (1988). Memory functioning during the first year after closed head injury in children and adolescents. *Neurosurgery, 22*(6), 1043–1052.

Levin, H. S., Song, J., Ewing-Cobbs, L., Chapman, S. B., & Mendelsohn, D. (2001). Word fluency in relation to severity of closed head injury, associated frontal brain lesions, and age at injury in children. *Neuropsychologia, 39*(2), 122–131.

Lind, K., Toure, H., Brugel, D., Meyer, P., Laurent-Vannier, A., & Chevignard, M. (2016). Extended follow-up of neurological, cognitive, behavioral and academic outcomes after severe abusive head trauma. *Child Abuse & Neglect, 51,* 358–367.

Lynch, J. K., Hirtz, D. G., DeVeber, G., & Nelson, K. B. (2002). Report of the National Institute of Neurological Disorders and Stroke workshop on perinatal and childhood stroke. *Pediatrics, 109*(1), 116–123.

Max, J. E. (2004). Effect of side of lesion on neuropsychological performance in childhood stroke. *Journal of the International Neuropsychological Society, 10*(5), 698–708.

Max, J. E. (2005). Children and adolescents. In J. M. Silver, T. W. McAllister, & S. C. Yudofsky (Eds.), *Textbook of traumatic brain injury* (pp. 477–494). Washington, DC: American Psychiatric Publishing.

Meadows, E. A., Yeates, K. O., Rubin, K. H., Taylor, H. G., Bigler, E. D., Dennis, M., . . . Hoskinson, K. R. (2017). Rejection Sensitivity as a Moderator of Psychosocial Outcomes Following Pediatric Traumatic Brain Injury. *Journal of the International Neuropsychological Society, 23*(6), 451–459.

Mineyko, A., Brooks, B., Carlson, H., Bello-Espinosa, L., & Kirton, A. (2012). *Electroencephalographic biomarkers of abnormal neuropsychological development following perinatal stroke.* Paper presented at the 3rd Canadian Stroke Congress, Calgary, Canada.

Mohr, J., Choi, D., Grotta, J., & Wolf, P. (2004). *Stroke: Pathophysiology, diagnosis, and management* (4th ed.). Baltimore, MD: Churchill Livingstone.

Mosch, S. C., Max, J. E., & Tranel, D. (2005). A matched lesion analysis of childhood versus adult-onset brain injury due to unilateral stroke: Another perspective on neural plasticity and recovery of social functioning. *Cognitive and Behavioral Neurology, 18*(1), 5–17.

Murias, K., Brooks, B., Kirton, A., & Iaria, G. (2014). A review of cognitive outcomes in children following perinatal stroke. *Developmental Neuropsychology, 39*(2), 131–157.

O'Keeffe, F., Liégeois, F., Eve, M., Ganesan, V., King, J., & Murphy, T. (2014). Neuropsychological and neurobehavioral outcome following childhood arterial ischemic stroke: Attention deficits, emotional dysregulation, and executive dysfunction. *Child Neuropsychology, 20*(5), 557–582.

Orman, J. A. L., Kraus, J. F., Zaloshnja, E., & Miller, T. (2011). Epidemiology. In J. M. Silver, T. W. McAllister, & S. C. Yudofsky (Eds.), *Textbook of traumatic brain injury* (2nd ed., pp. 3–22). Arlington, VA: American Psychiatric Publishing.

Paul, A. R., & Adamo, M. A. (2014). Non-accidental trauma in pediatric patients: A review of epidemiology, pathophysiology, diagnosis and treatment. *Translational Pediatrics, 3*(3), 195–207.

Petersen, S. E., & Posner, M. I. (2012). The attention system of the human brain: 20 years after. *Annual Review of Neuroscience, 35,* 73–89.

Prigatano, G. P. (2007). Cognitive and behavioral dysfunction in children with hypothalamic hamartoma and epilepsy. *Seminars in Pediatric Neurology, 14*(2), 65–72.

Prigatano, G. P. (2008). The problem of not developing normally and pediatric neuropsychological rehabilitation: The Mitchell Rosenthal Lecture. *Journal of Head Trauma Rehabilitation, 23*(6), 414–422.

Prigatano, G. P. (2010). *The study of anosognosia.* New York, NY: Oxford University Press.

Prigatano, G. P., & Gray, J. A. (2007). Parental concerns and distress after paediatric traumatic brain injury: A qualitative study. *Brain Injury, 21*(7), 721–729.

Prigatano, G. P., & Gupta, S. (2006). Friends after traumatic brain injury in children. *Journal of Head Trauma Rehabilitation, 21*(6), 505–513.

Reyna, V. F., Chapman, S. B., Dougherty, M. R., & Confrey, J. E. (2012). *The adolescent brain: Learning, reasoning, and decision making.* Washington, DC: American Psychological Association.

Russell, W. R. (1971). *The traumatic amnesias.* Oxford, UK: Oxford University Press.

Rutter, M. (1981). Psychological sequelae of brain damage in children. *American Journal of Psychiatry, 138,* 1533–1544.

Rypma, B., Berger, J. S., Prabhakaran, V., Bly, B. M., Kimberg, D. Y., Biswal, B. B., & D'Esposito, M. (2006). Neural correlates of cognitive efficiency. *Neuroimage, 33*(3), 969–979.

Sacco, R. L., Toni, D., Brainin, M., & Mohr, J. P. (2004). Classification of ischemic stroke. In J. P. Mohr, D. Choi, J. Grotta, B. Weir, & P. Wolf (Eds.), *Stroke: Pathophysiology, diagnosis, and management* (4th ed., pp. 61–74). Philadelphia, PA: Churchill Livingstone.

Sanna, T., Diener, H.-C., Passman, R. S., Di Lazzaro, V., Bernstein, R. A., Morillo, C. A., . . . Beckers, F. (2014). Cryptogenic stroke and underlying atrial fibrillation. *New England Journal of Medicine, 370*(26), 2478–2486.

Sheese, B. E., Voelker, P. M., Rothbart, M. K., & Posner, M. I. (2007). Parenting quality interacts with genetic variation in dopamine receptor D4 to influence temperament in early childhood. *Development and Psychopathology, 19*(4), 1039–1046.

Siegel, J. S., Ramsey, L. E., Snyder, A. Z., Metcalf, N. V., Chacko, R. V., Weinberger, K., . . . Corbetta, M. (2016). Disruptions of network connectivity predict impairment in multiple behavioral domains after stroke. *Proceedings of the National Academy of Sciences of the USA, 113*(30), E4367–E4376.

Smith, C. (2011). Neuropathology. In J. M. Silver, T. W. McAllister, & S. C. Yudofsky (Eds.), *Textbook of traumatic brain injury* (2nd ed., pp. 23–36). Arlington, VA: American Psychiatric Publishing.

US Department of Veterans Affairs/US Department of Defense. (2009). *VA/DoD clinical practice guideline: Management of concussion/mild traumatic brain injury* (Version 1.0). Washington, DC: Author. Retrieved May 18, 2017 from https://www.healthquality.va.gov/guidelines/Rehab/mtbi/concussion_mtbi_full_1_0.pdf

Westmacott, R., Askalan, R., MacGregor, D., Anderson, P., & Deveber, G. (2010). Cognitive outcome following unilateral arterial ischaemic stroke in childhood: Effects of age at stroke and lesion location. *Developmental Medicine & Child Neurology, 52*(4), 386–393.

Wilde, E. A., Merkley, T. L., Bigler, E. D., Max, J. E., Schmidt, A. T., Ayoub, K. W., . . . Li, X. (2012). Longitudinal changes in cortical thickness in children after traumatic brain injury and their relation to behavioral regulation and emotional control. *International Journal of Developmental Neuroscience, 30*(3), 267–276.

Woods, B. T. (1980). The restricted effects of right-hemisphere lesions after age one: Wechsler test data. *Neuropsychologia, 18*(1), 65–70.

Woods, D., Catroppa, C., & Anderson, V. (2012). Family-centered and parent-based models for treating socio-behavioural problems in children with acquired brain injury. In V. Anderson & M. H. Beauchamp (Eds.), *Developmental social neuroscience and childhood brain insult* (pp. 350–369). New York, NY: Guilford.

Yeates, K. O., Bigler, E. D., Gerhardt, C. A., Rubin, K. H., Stancin, T., Taylor, H. G., & Vannatta, K. (2012). Theoretical approaches to understanding social function in childhood brain insults. In V. Anderson & M. H. Beauchamp (Eds.), *Developmental social neuroscience and childhood brain insult: Theory and practice* (pp. 207–229). New York, NY: Guilford.

Yeates, K. O., Taylor, H. G., Drotar, D., Wade, S. L., Klein, S., Stancin, T., & Schatschneider, C. (1997). Preinjury family environment as a determinant of recovery from traumatic brain injuries in school-age children. *Journal of the International Neuropsychological Society, 3*(6), 617–630.

Ylvisaker, M., McPherson, K., Kayes, N., & Pellett, E. (2008). Metaphoric identity mapping: Facilitating goal setting and engagement in rehabilitation after traumatic brain injury. *Neuropsychological Rehabilitation, 18*(5–6), 713–741.

7

THE PROBLEM OF LOST NORMALITY AFTER A BRAIN DISORDER DURING ADULTHOOD

INTRODUCTION

During the early and middle years of adulthood, neuroanatomical regions of the brain reach optimal development. It is a time in which the "natural plan of the central nervous system" allows for extensive new learning, the forming and maintaining of intimate relationships, the procreation and care of children, and the ability to identify and participate in one's "life's work." Disruption of the central nervous system (CNS) during this time frame can substantially interfere with these major life activities and responsibilities. What was previously normal functioning for the individual is often dramatically changed. Thus, during this time frame, the problem of lost normality is often faced by the young or middle-aged adult who has suffered a brain disorder (Prigatano, 1991).

Specific neuropsychological syndromes, often related to cerebral vascular lesions, have been identified during this age range, They include: amnestic disorders, aphasic syndromes, disorders of visual–spatial perception, neglect syndromes, and apraxias and agnosias of various types (Heilman & Valenstein, 2010). Moderate to severe traumatic brain injury (TBI) during this time also produces predictable patterns of neuropsychological impairments (Roebuck-Spencer & Sherer, 2018). As observed in school-age children, there can be considerable overlap in the neuropsychological disturbances caused by cerebral vascular accidents (CVAs) and TBI during young and middle-age adulthood. However, important differences exist. For example, Roebuck-Spencer and Sherer (2018) note that persistent aphasic syndromes are rare in persons with a history of moderate to severe

TBI, but they are more common following stroke. Although stroke patients often demonstrate problems with "executive functioning," this is more often a hallmark of the effects of severe TBI than many forms of CVAs. Finally, as is the case with children, there are important differences regarding lesion location and the typical age at time of a CVA versus a TBI. For example, focal vascular cerebral insults are more common in middle to late adulthood (Mohr, Choi, Grotta, & Wolf, 2004). In contrast, multifocal and diffuse injuries, caused by severe TBI, are more common in young adult years (Orman, Kraus, Zaloshnja, & Miller, 2011). In this chapter, neuropsychological and psychosocial consequences of CVAs and moderate to severe TBI in adults are summarized because they help clarify the major psychological care issues faced during this time period.

NEUROPSYCHOLOGICAL CONSEQUENCES OF DISRUPTION OF THE CENTRAL NERVOUS SYSTEM DURING YOUNG ADULTHOOD FOLLOWING MODERATE TO SEVERE TRAUMATIC BRAIN INJURY

Epidemiological studies report that TBIs severe enough to warrant emergency room care occur most commonly in people aged 15–34 years (Orman et al., 2011). In an early but highly informative paper, Thomsen (1984) conducted a clinically valuable 10- to 15-year follow-up study of 50 patients who suffered severe TBI. Their mean age at time of injury was 21.5 years (range, 15–44 years). She observed persistent memory impairments in these patients. At 2.5 years post brain injury, 80% demonstrated severe memory impairments. At 10–15 years post brain injury, little change had occurred because 75% of the patients continued to demonstrate severe memory impairments. Also of interest is Thomsen's observation that several of these patients (i.e., 24%) "denied memory impairments" (p. 264). Patients were also described as being very slow in performing a variety of tasks. She further noted that psychosocial adjustment issues were by far the most serious long-term consequences of these patients' brain injuries. Emotional lability, irritability, "restlessness," and a "loss of social contact" were common long-term problems. Interestingly, the person's "sensitivity to distress" and "lack of interests" became more prevalent with time. The picture was sobering and suggested not only the permanency of severe neuropsychological impairments but also a possible decline in psychosocial and emotional functioning over time. These early observations paralleled what other clinicians later reported in subsequent years (Prigatano, 1999; Roebuck-Spencer & Sherer, 2018; Sherer & Sander, 2014).

Approximately 10 years after Thomsen's (1984) follow-up study, Dikmen, Machamer, Winn, and Temkin (1995) summarized their highly influential longitudinal findings on 436 adults with a history of head trauma. Average age of their sample was 28.9 years. They administered a large number of neuropsychological tests and correlated test findings to the time it initially took for patients to follow commands after their TBI. They reported that virtually all of their neuropsychological findings at 1 year were related to severity of TBI. Measures of simple motor speed and psychomotor problem-solving, however, showed the most robust correlations with severity of initial TBI (e.g., speed of finger tapping correlated $r = -.51$ in the dominant hand and $-.47$ in the nondominant hand, respectively; time to complete the Tactual Performance Test correlated $r = .61$). Figure 7.1 plots some of the neuropsychological findings reported by Dikmen et al. Although memory and cognitive impairments of various types were observed, the size effects were greater for speed of simple finger tapping. With severe TBI, slow speeds were clearly observed.

A number of investigators have demonstrated the sensitivity of motor-related dysfunctions following severe TBI even when apparently "good" motor recovery seems to have occurred. Prigatano and Borgaro (2003)

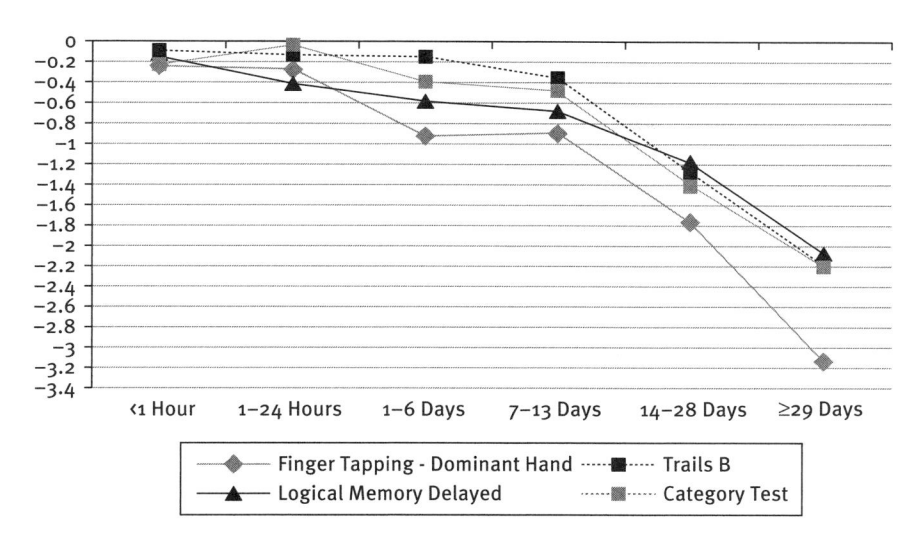

FIGURE 7.1 Visual depiction of the relation between brain injury severity and neurocognitive outcome at 1 year as reported by Dikmen et al. (2015). Time to follow commands was used to sort patients into severity groups. Four test scores were selected to illustrate fine motor speed, processing speed and flexibility, delayed verbal memory, and reasoning. The values represent effect sizes compared to trauma control subjects. By convention, Cohen's effect sizes are interpreted as follows: 0.2 = small, 0.5 = medium, and 0.8 = large.

Source: Graphed by Grant Iverson, PhD, and reproduced with his permission.

demonstrated that young adults with a history of severe TBI were not only slow in carrying out speed of finger movements on the Halstead Finger Tapping Test (HFTT) but also had notable difficulties inhibiting adjacent finger movements when carrying out this task (Figure 7.2). Heaton, Chelune, and Lehman (1978) noted that tapping speed correlated with employment status in a heterogeneous group of brain dysfunctional patients. Also, improved

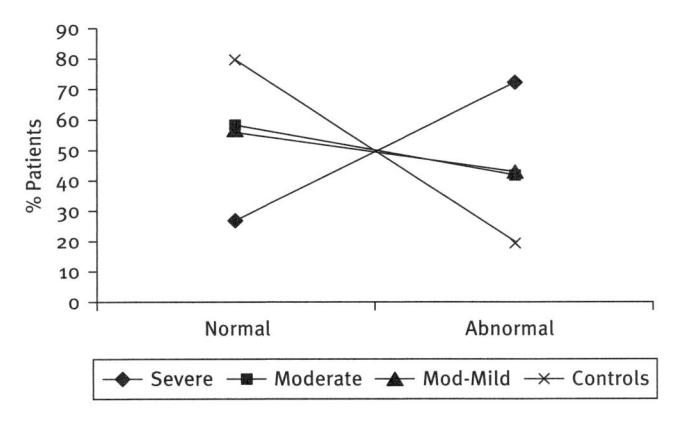

FIGURE 7.2 Percentage of TBI patients and normal controls who showed a pattern of normal versus abnormal qualitative response characteristics when performing the Halstead Finger Oscillation (or Tapping) Test with the dominant hand.

Source: Reprinted from Prigatano, G. P., & Borgaro, S. R., Qualitative features of finger movement during the Halstead Finger Oscillation Test following traumatic brain injury, *Journal of the International Neuropsychological Society, 9*(1), 2003, p. 128–133, by permission of Cambridge University Press.

speed of finger tapping has been consistently related to functional recovery and achievement of inpatient rehabilitation goals (Haaland, Temkin, Randahl, & Dikmen, 1994; Prigatano & Wong, 1997).

Experimental research on finger movements after TBI helps clarify why tapping speeds parallel the severity of TBI in young adults. Di Russo, Incoccia, Formisano, Sabatini, and Zoccolotti (2005) found significantly reduced movement-related cortical potentials when young adults with severe TBI simply performed flexion movements with the index finger (the same finger used when performing the HFTT). Compared to controls, these TBI patients showed abnormal electrophysiological recordings during the motor preparation aspect of the task. Kasahara et al. (2010) studied the functional magnetic resonance imaging (fMRI) correlates of performing a repetitive finger–thumb oppositional task in adults with varying degrees of severity of TBI and compared their results with those of a matched control group. Kasahara et al. noted that TBI patients showed a pattern of neuro-network disconnections suggesting "reduced interhemispheric and perhaps inhibitory control of finger movements in patients" (p. 174). Thus, reduced speed and coordination of simple finger movements appears to reflect important changes in neural connectivity patterns following severe TBI in young adulthood. Alterations of white matter tracts, secondary to diffuse axonal injury, were also considered a possible contributing factor to the findings reported by Kasahara et al.

Johnson, Bigler, Burr, and Blatter (1994) attempted to relate brain atrophy several months post TBI to performance on the Wechsler Adult Intelligence Scale–Revised form in 64 adults. The mean age of their subjects was 29 years. The ventricle-to-brain ratio (a measure of atrophy) was correlated with level of performance on the Digit Symbol or Coding subtest in males only ($r = -.59$). This test measures several functions, including speed of hand–eye movements (e.g., writing) and speed of new learning. The findings were compatible with Dikmen et al.'s (1995) observations and the results of neuropsychological studies of school-age children with severe TBI (see Chapter 6, this volume). Collectively, these findings suggest that slow and inefficient learning and reduced motor processing speeds directly relate to the extent or severity of TBI.

Rabinowitz and Levin (2014) summarized other neurocognitive observations following moderate to severe TBI in young adults. They suggest that for many of these patients, memory problems are common (much like Thomsen [1984] previously reported). The memory difficulties of these patients may be related to inefficient or disorganized encoding and retrieval strategies rather than problems of memory storage per se (which are more common in patients with Alzheimer's disease). In addition to memory disturbances, persons with a history of severe TBI often show notable difficulties in higher order language skills (e.g., expressing their thoughts in a clear and coherent manner), reasoning through different problem-solving situations, and being realistically aware of their changed neuropsychological status. Rabinowitz and Levin note that these patients often present with "behavioral executive" dysfunctional difficulties. For example, they can be very impulsive when problem-solving.

Recent neuroimaging studies have also helped clarify the relationship between specific brain abnormalities and specific neuropsychological disturbances commonly seen after moderate to severe TBI. Recall that the default mode network (DMN) includes several "nodes" or regions of the brain, including "the medial prefrontal cortex, the posterior cingulate cortex, the inferior parietal lobe, the lateral and inferior temporal cortex and the medial temporal lobes" (Carhart-Harris & Friston, 2010, p. 1268). Damage to frontal and temporal regions of the brain is common after severe TBI, as is diffuse axonal injury (Smith, 2011). Sharp et al. (2011) demonstrated that white matter disruption interfered with the normal functional connectivity of the DMN in patients with TBI. This was especially true when the splenium of the corpus callosum was affected (which is a common finding in some children and adults with severe TBI). Sharp et al. further reported that "patients were able to perform task accurately, but showed slow and variable responses. Brain regions activated by the task were similar between the groups (i.e., controls and TBI patients), but patients showed greater deactivation with the default mode network" (p. 2233).

Sharp and colleagues (Bonnelle et al., 2012) went on to show that a disruption of the DMN in TBI patients was also associated with ongoing difficulties with response inhibition or impulse control. Recall that these are also common features seen in children and adolescents with a history of severe TBI. Of special interest in their report, however, was the finding that problems of impulse control were especially correlated with a disruption of white matter tracts involving the right anterior insula, the supplementary motor areas, and dorsal anterior cingulate cortex. They noted that these regions are also a part of the "salience network" of the brain—that is, a specific neuronetwork that appears important for identifying situations that require efficient behavioral change for successful adaptation.

Another important feature of patients with severe TBI is the presence of post-trauma amnesia (PTA), which is one predictor of severity of TBI, as noted in Chapter 6. De Simoni et al. (2016) investigated whether disruptions of the DMN were related to this phenomenon. Nineteen acute TBI patients who were judged to be in a state of PTA were compared to 17 healthy controls with regard to their performance on neuropsychological tests and resting state functional connectivity. They replicated their previous finding that functional connectivity of the DMN was abnormal in the TBI group but not in the healthy control group. Decreased functional connectivity between the posterior cingulate cortex and the parahippocampal gyrus was associated with poorer memory performance. Most interesting, this altered pattern of functional connectivity showed a trend toward returning to normal connectivity as PTA reduced with time.

Disturbances in self-awareness are seen in a subgroup of young adults who have a history of severe TBI (Prigatano, 2014). An earlier report referred to them as "denying" their cognitive limitations (Thomsen, 1984). Ham et al. (2013) asked a heterogeneous sample of TBI adults to perform a monitoring task while undergoing fMRI studies. They were interested in the ability of patients to detect their own errors when performing the task. Ham et al. related performance on this vigilance task with a measure of self-awareness using a discrepancy score of patients' views of how they were functioning compared to relatives' views of their functioning. Patients who were very poor at detecting errors (i.e., low performance monitoring [PM]) were judged, using the discrepancy measure, as generally showing poor self-awareness (or impaired self-awareness [ISA]) on daily tasks thought to reflect frontal lobe functioning. Importantly, all patients who had low PM scores had a history of moderate/severe TBI versus mild TBI (p. 595). Lesion location or "the extent of focal injuries" (p. 593) as well as measures of traumatic axonal injury were *not* related to PM scores. However, TBI patients with low PM scores "showed greater activation than control subjects in both bilateral insulae and parietal operculum in response to errors" (p. 592). These researchers note that the anterior insulae are closely linked to the dorsal anterior cingulate cortex. They conclude that ISA in TBI patients may be related to a disruption of frontal–parietal circuitry. They acknowledge that self-awareness is a highly complex and emergent property of network activity (as Sperry noted in 1969; see Chapter 5, this volume) and, therefore, cannot or at least has not yet been specifically localized to any single region of brain functional activity.

Avena-Koenigsberger, Misic, and Sporns (2018) made an interesting observation regarding the integrative properties of certain components of the DMN. They noted that the "precuneus, posterior cingulate, medial prefrontal cortex and bilateral insulae" of the DMN were brain regions that appeared to spread signals between various other topographic networks within the brain (p. 29). Therefore, damage to these structures or "nodes" may have quite adverse effects on multiple neuroconnectivity patterns in the adult and developing brain. This point is further considered in Chapter 11. It is important to note here, however, that young or middle-aged persons with a history of moderate to severe TBI often demonstrate a complex array of neuropsychological impairments. These impairments may improve somewhat, but they are often permanent in nature. Equally important are changes in personality and behavior observed in these individuals.

PERSONALITY AND BEHAVIORAL CHANGES AFTER TRAUMATIC BRAIN INJURY IN YOUNG ADULTS

Young adults who suffer moderate to severe TBI frequently present with significant personality and behavioral disturbances, some of which qualify for a formal psychiatric diagnosis (Prigatano & Maier, 2009). Not uncommonly, these changes are difficult to measure but are obvious to family members and rehabilitation therapists. Historically, these individuals have been described as irritable or quick to anger (van Zomeren, 1981). Others demonstrate a reduction in emotional or motivational responding and appear apathetic (Prigatano, 1999). Still others have been described as "childlike" because they demonstrate socially inappropriate behaviors (Prigatano & Maier, 2009). A portion of TBI patients, however, go on to become severely anxious and/or depressed several months after their brain injury. This is often observed during the time they show maximum cognitive recovery. For some, these difficulties appear to be in reaction to their growing awareness of how they have been affected. For others, they may be a reaction to years of experiencing a series of failures in life that they do not fully understand (Prigatano, 2011; Silver, McAllister, & Yudofsky, 2011).

It is important to note, however, that some behavioral disturbances exist before the onset of a TBI. They, too, can impact the clinical picture and outcomes from various forms of rehabilitation. Sela-Kaufman, Rassovsky, Agranov, Levi, and Vakil (2013), for example, demonstrated that severity of a person's initial TBI was predictive of employment in young adults. However, premorbid personality characteristics were also predictive of outcome. A pre-existing history of a severe avoidant attachment style negatively influenced return to work irrespective of the initial severity of TBI in young adults. This is an exceptionally important observation in light of the long-term psychosocial consequences of TBI in adulthood.

PSYCHOSOCIAL CONSEQUENCES OF SEVERE TRAUMATIC BRAIN INJURY IN ADULTHOOD

The psychosocial consequences of severe TBI occurring in adulthood are relatively well known. Dikmen et al. (1994) noted that only approximately 25% of these patients return to gainful employment within 1 year of the TBI. Although the percentages increase modestly at 2 years, many of these individuals appear to go back to work prematurely. Some are not realistically aware of their changed neuropsychological status. As a consequence, a common problem for patients with a history of severe TBI in young adulthood is that they are unable to maintain work and often have multiple jobs that do not last long. Although detailed statistics regarding these clinical impressions are not available, it is again of some value to consider Thomsen's (1984) previous observations.

Thomsen (1984) reported that only 15% of the TBI patients she studied were gainfully employed 10–15 years post severe TBI. In a 10-year follow-up study, Ponsford et al. (2014) reported that only 11.8% of TBI patients studied returned to their pre-injury level of employment. When work was possible, it often required the patients to work only part-time and to take on work responsibilities other than what they were previously able to do. Importantly, many of these patients eventually dropped out of the workforce as they became older. This was especially true for individuals with a history of "moderate to very severe TBI" (Ponsford et al., 2014, p. 70).

As individuals are unable to return to their previous level of neuropsychological functioning and maintain gainful employment, other psychosocial problems begin to occur. Marital distress often increases. Ponsford et al. (2014) reported a similar observation indicating that "difficulty in personal relationships and getting on with friends increased over time" (p. 70). These researchers also reported persistent difficulties with irritability, making friends, and social isolation, much like Thomsen (1984) noted. A common contributing factor to these progressive psychosocial difficulties appears to be unresolved problems of ISA after moderate to severe TBI. This impression dates back to the early observations of Adolf Meyer in 1904 and Paul Schilder in 1934 (see Prigatano, 2010). Sherer, Meyers, and Bergloff (1997) demonstrated that ISA was a significant predictor of employment outcome after TBI. A more extensive discussion of ISA and denial phenomena is provided in Chapter 9.

NEUROPSYCHOLOGICAL CONSEQUENCES OF DISRUPTION OF THE CENTRAL NERVOUS SYSTEM DURING MIDDLE ADULTHOOD FOLLOWING A UNILATERAL CEREBRAL VASCULAR ACCIDENT

Corbetta and colleagues (Corbetta et al., 2015; Ramsey et al., 2017; Siegel et al., 2016) have provided the most contemporary and thorough analysis of how focal vascular lesions of the brain—secondary to a single, first-time stroke in adulthood—affect the plan of the CNS. They employed structural and functional brain imaging techniques to study 100 stroke patients and 27 controls. The mean age of the patients studied was 52.8 years (range, 22–77 years). They demonstrated that focal strokes disturbed neuro-networks within the cerebral hemisphere in which the stroke occurred and also interhemispheric functional connectivity (FC). This finding indicates that a single stroke can negatively affect many domains of cognitive functioning. Second, neurological and neuropsychological functions appeared to be differentially affected by the location of the stroke versus the degree of disruption of FC caused by the stroke. Figure 7.3 illustrates some of their observations. Lesion location accounted for more of the variance for visual and motor deficits following a stroke compared to FC measures. In contrast, visual and verbal memory impairments, as well as attention deficits, were more readily accounted for by FC changes than by lesion location. Note that both lesion location and FC measures related to both neurological and neuropsychological disturbances, but the relative contributing factors differed. The exception to this trend is language disturbances. As illustrated in Figure 7.3, language impairments appear similarly affected by both lesion location and FC. In their detailed analyses of language function, they noted that the effects appear to be accounted for by disruption of communication networks within the left hemisphere. This is not the case for other neuropsychological deficits they studied, which are frequently associated with FC disturbances between both cerebral hemispheres. Figure 7.4 illustrates these findings with visual images that further help clarify the relative effects of lesion location and FC changes as related to motor, visual, language, attention, and visual and motor deficits after a stroke.

An important question raised by Corbetta and colleagues regarding psychological care concerns mechanisms of recovery or lack thereof following a focal CVA. They ask the following question: Is recovery better explained by reorganization or normalization of function? (Corbetta, 2017) Their findings suggest

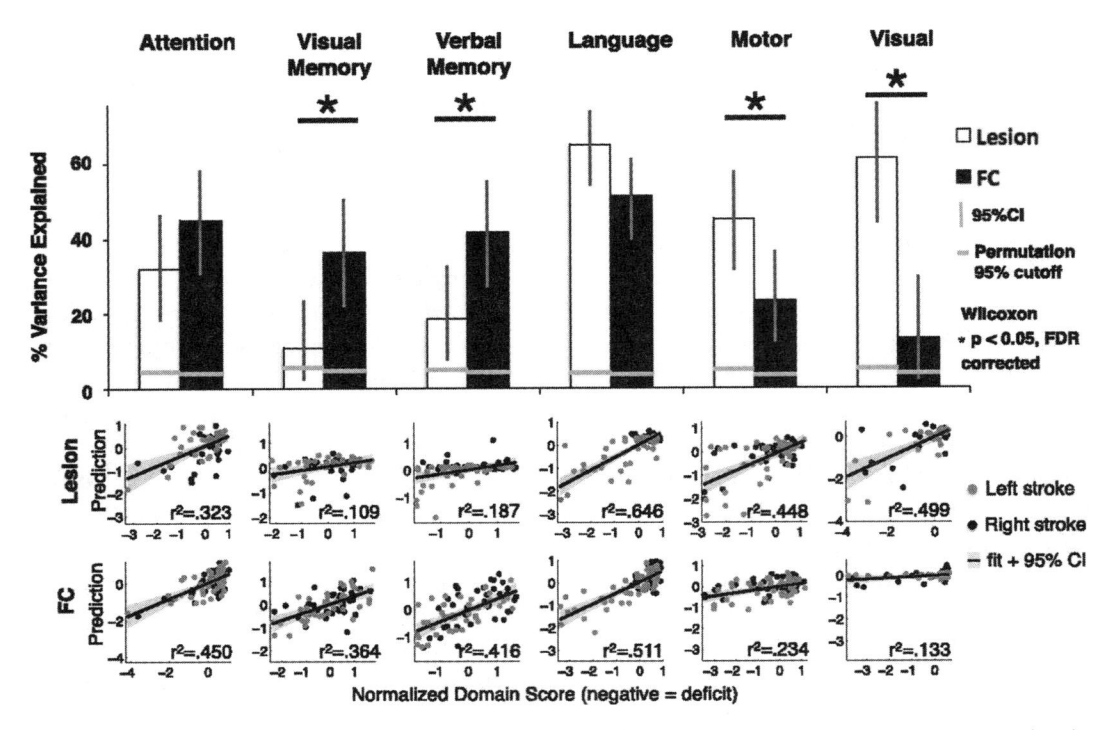

FIGURE 7.3   Lesion-deficit and functional connectivity (FC)-deficit model accuracies vary by domain. (Top) The graph shows percentage of variance explained across the six behavioral domains. White bars are lesion-deficit models, and black bars are FC-deficit models. Lesion location predicts deficit significantly better in motor and visual domains. FC predicts deficit significantly better in visual memory and verbal memory domains. Statistical comparisons between lesion-deficit and FC-deficit models (indicated by asterisks) were performed using a Wilcoxon signed rank test of prediction error and were false discovery rate (FDR) corrected. Horizontal gray lines represent $p = .05$ cutoffs for the null model generated by permuting domain scores 10,000 times for each domain. All models perform significantly better than chance. (Bottom) The scatterplots show the comparison between predicted and measured scores from lesion-deficit models and FC-deficit models. Behavior scores are a composite of multiple tests in each domain and are on a z-normalized (mean = 0, SD = 1) scale. Motor and visual deficits were predicted separately for each hemisphere and the contralateral side but were combined for visualization. CI, confidence interval.

Source: Reprinted from Siegel, J. S., Ramsey, L. E., Snyder, A. Z., Metcalf, N. V., Chacko, R. V., Weinberger, K., . . . Corbetta, M., Disruptions of network connectivity predict impairment in multiple behavioral domains after stroke, *Proceedings of the National Academy of Sciences of the USA*, 113(30), 2016, p. E4367-E4376, by permission of United States National Academy of Sciences.

that it is a return to modularity (not reorganization) that results in better recovery of attention, memory, and language skills. This suggests that restoration of a neuropsychological function, at least in this patient group, may be limited unless the nature of the stroke did not substantially impact the initial neuro-networks crucial for carrying out that function. When ancillary neuro-networks within the brain, both intrahemispherically and interhemispherically, attempt to carry out the function, less observable "recovery" is often observed. During this time, patients may report excessive fatigue when attempting to recruit brain regions to carry out complex neuropsychological functions that they did not initially develop to carry out. This finding is predicted by the early observations of John Hughlings Jackson in 1888 (see Prigatano, 1999) and addresses Luria's important question regarding how recovery or improvement is achieved after a brain disorder.

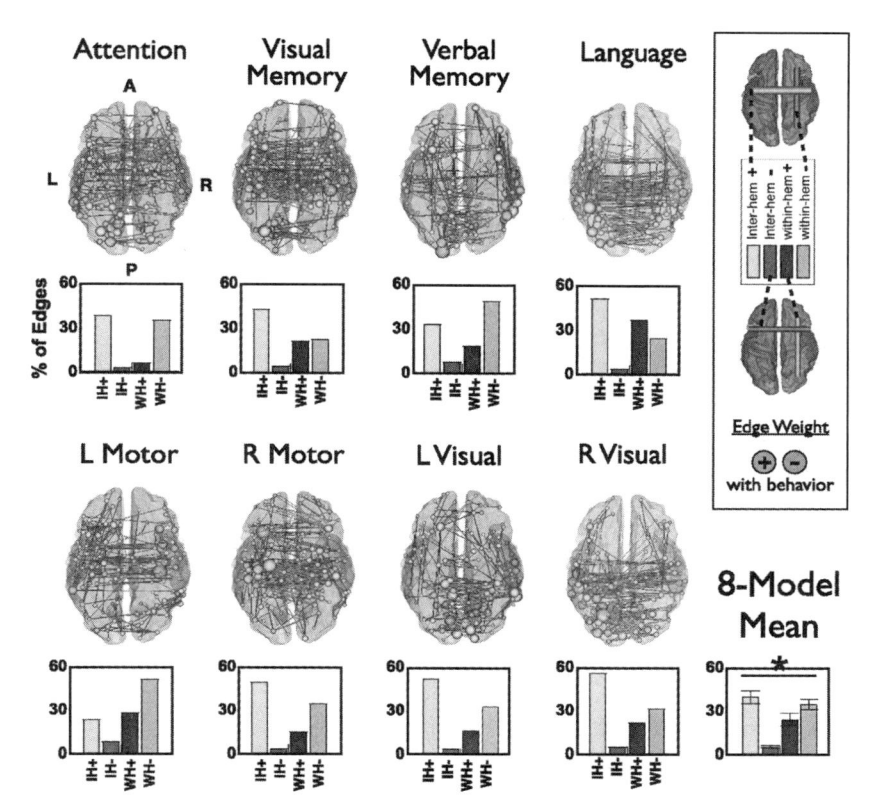

FIGURE 7.4 Most predictive connections and nodes for each functional connectivity (FC)-deficit model. (Top) The top 200 connections driving each FC-behavior model are projected back onto a semitransparent cerebrum (Population-Average, Landmark-, and Surface-based [PALS] atlas). Green connections indicate positive weights (increased FC predicts better performance), and orange connections indicate negative weights (increased FC predicts worse performance). The subset of the 324 parcels included in the top 200 weights are displayed as spheres, sized according to their contribution to the model. (Bottom) Weights from each FC-behavior model are divided into four groups: interhemispheric positive, interhemispheric negative, intrahemispheric positive, and intrahemispheric negative. Bars indicate the average contribution of each of the four groups. The average across models is shown at the bottom right. Analysis of variance (ANOVA) indicates a significant difference in contribution of the four connection types ($p = 1.6 \times 10^{-6}$) (See color plates).

Source: Reprinted from Siegel, J. S., Ramsey, L. E., Snyder, A. Z., Metcalf, N. V., Chacko, R. V., Weinberger, K., ... Corbetta, M., Disruptions of network connectivity predict impairment in multiple behavioral domains after stroke, *Proceedings of the National Academy of Sciences of the USA*, 113(30), 2016, p. E4367–E4376, by permission of United States National Academy of Sciences.

One final observation regarding Corbetta and colleagues' extraordinary work on neuro-network disruptions after a focal stroke is worth mentioning (see Corbetta, 2017). Reduction in interhemispheric FC was partly predicted by lesion load ($r = .46$). Lesion location was less predictive of FC disturbances. This finding is also predicted by Karl Lashley's earlier work (1929) and that of Kurt Goldstein (1942) (see Prigatano, 1999). Lesion location is of importance as it relates to complex neuropsychological disturbances (e.g., learning and memory), but the actual size of the lesion may play a more predominant role. The same basic observation was made when evaluating the factors that contribute to a significant reduction in intellectual functioning in children after a TBI (see Chapter 6, this volume).

PSYCHOSOCIAL AND EMOTIONAL CONSEQUENCES OF A UNILATERAL STROKE IN ADULTHOOD

When focal vascular lesions produce frank aphasic and neglect syndromes, the negative psychosocial consequences are substantial. Tanaka, Toyonaga, and Hashimoto (2014) studied return-to-work outcomes of 351 Japanese stroke patients with a mean age of 55.3 years (standard deviation [SD] = 7.2 years). Only 22.7% of stroke patients with aphasia returned to work. In a literature review, Graham, Pereira, and Teasell (2011) also suggested that less than one-third (i.e., 28.4%) of young adults with aphasia secondary to stroke were able to return to gainful employment.

Robinson and Starkstein (2010) reviewed the prevalence of post-stroke depression and its relationship to lesion location and comorbid or pre-existing psychiatric disturbances. During the acute stages, left frontal lesions are frequently associated with severe depression but often can be relieved via medications. During the post-acute phase, however, persistent and poorly treated depression is often related to a history of pre-stroke depression and other pre-stroke adjustment problems. In addition to the problems of a frank depression, aphasic patients may experience periods in which they are overwhelmed with their language/communication difficulties and periodically experience what Goldstein (1939) referred to as a "catastrophic reaction." During these times, patients are unable to cope with the consequences of their disabilities/impairments and can become highly anxious, angry, belligerent, and significantly depressed. For example, a 57-year-old man with a fluent aphasic condition suddenly became extremely irritable and depressed because he was unable to successfully perform some of his previous job responsibilities. His wife became very concerned that his functional abilities were deteriorating. However, when the clinical neuropsychologist explained a catastrophic reaction to them and how the husband's behaviors seemed to reflect such a reaction, both of them were visibly relieved. The patient could literally not put into words his level of frustration and that he suddenly felt overwhelmed by his language impairments. The neuropsychologist's explanation was of great help to him and his wife in understanding what had happened.

Sinanović (2010) notes that whereas aphasia is a common consequence of left hemisphere stroke, unilateral neglect and anosognosia for hemiplegia (AHP) are common after a right hemisphere stroke. Heilman, Watson, and Valenstein (2003) define neglect as "the failure to report, respond, or orient to novel or meaningful stimuli presented to the side opposite a brain lesion, when this failure cannot be attributed to either sensory or motor defects" (p. 296). They note that sensory neglect is a form of inattention and can manifest itself in several ways. Typically, the person does not attend to information on the side of his or her body contralateral to the brain lesion location. It is most frequently observed after right cerebral hemisphere lesions. Although it can certainly improve with time, persistent problems with attention are frequently observed after significant right hemisphere lesions affecting frontal and parietal regions of the brain (Petersen & Posner, 2012). These patients are prone to having automobile accidents given their persistent problems with inattention on the left side of space.

Tanaka et al. (2014) note that problems with attention and walking safely predict failure to return to work similarly as does aphasia. In their study, only 22.9% of patients with attentional dysfunction returned to work, whereas for aphasic patients, the figure was 22.7%. Unlike patients with aphasia, however, patients with attentional dysfunction are not immediately prone to depression. Rather, they are more likely apathetic, indifferent, or unaware of the extent of their functional limitations, at least during the acute phase following a stroke (Robinson & Starkstein, 2010). These patients may also demonstrate a lack of prosody in their speech, suggesting blunted emotional reactions and possibly experiences.

Of concern to many family members is the development of mania in some of these patients. Robinson and Starkstein (2010) suggest that in patients with mania post right hemisphere stroke, their lesions seem to impact the limbic system of the brain. This system, as noted previously, is important in the experience and expression of emotion. Robinson and colleagues (Paradiso, Anderson, Ponto, Tranel, & Robinson, 2011) have also demonstrated that right middle cerebral artery (MCA) strokes can, in fact, negatively affect emotional responsiveness, particularly for pleasant experiences. This may contribute to reports of apathy particularly in this patient group. It is also important to note that "tonic alertness is heavily lateralized to the right hemisphere" (Petersen & Posner, 2012, p. 74).

Many patients with right cerebral hemisphere strokes often appear hypoaroused and inattentive several months and years post stroke. They can be unrealistic with regard to the extent of their cognitive difficulties and are prone to making significant social judgment errors. For example, a 61-year-old university professor suffered a right MCA stroke. He had minimal motor involvement but considerable difficulties with inattention and reduced organizational skills. After a 6-month intensive neuropsychological rehabilitation program (Prigatano, 1986), he felt confident he could return to his old teaching position. The rehabilitation staff had the opposite opinion. With the help of an experienced occupational therapist, he was given the opportunity to give a lecture at a local community college. The occupational therapist worked closely with the patient to help him organize his notes and practice his lecture. Despite these efforts, the patient was not able to successfully deliver the lecture. When he observed for himself his difficulties, he sadly agreed to retire from work. It must be emphasized that patients with right hemisphere strokes can develop depression, anxiety, and angry reactions when they cannot return to full adult living. Many of these patients have "some awareness" of their functional limitations. The more challenging situation is when the patient has no or minimal awareness of his or her persistent functional limitations.

To appreciate how this story can unfold, it is important to consider the phenomenon of AHP after a large unilateral right hemisphere stroke versus severe ISA of one's cognitive and behavioral disturbances following large bilateral frontal and temporal contusions secondary to severe TBI. These two conditions provide further insight into how the "natural plan" of the CNS is permanently altered, but in different ways, following a focal stroke versus following multifocal and diffuse injuries to the brain resulting from severe TBI.

ANOSOGNOSIA FOR HEMIPLEGIA AFTER A RIGHT CEREBRAL HEMISPHERE STROKE

Anosognosia for hemiplegia occurs immediately after a right MCA stroke in approximately 20–30% of individuals (Bisiach, Vallar, Perani, Papagno, & Berti, 1986; Karnath & Baier, 2010). An interesting and unexplained phenomenon is that it often resolves within the first few weeks after the stroke. Vocat, Staub, Stroppini, and Vuilleumier (2010) performed the first comprehensive and prospective study on the neuroanatomical, neurological, neuropsychological, and psychological correlates of the evolution of AHP in a large group of patients who had focal right hemispheric strokes. During the first 3 days after a stroke, one-third of the patients demonstrated "a clear lack of awareness of their motor deficits" (Vocat et al., 2010, p. 3584). At 1 week post stroke, 18% had impaired awareness of the motor deficits. However, by 6 months, only 1 patient in the sample (or 5%) demonstrated this phenomenon. During the first 3 days, several neurological and neuropsychological deficits were observed to correlate with AHP. As it resolved, however, improvements in proprioception, visuospatial neglect, and spatiotemporal disorientation were noted. Anatomical lesion analysis demonstrated that AHP during the first 3 days was correlated with damage to several brain regions, at both cortical and subcortical levels. Interestingly, the "size of brain damage (as determined by the number of voxels composing the lesion of interest)" was only statistically correlated with AHP after the 3-day period of observation (Vocat et al., 2010, p. 3590). Damage to the insular cortex was noted to be prominent during the very acute phase of AHP. During the subacute phase, other regions of the brain were associated with continued AHP, including the premotor cortex, dorsal cingulate, parietotemporal junction, hippocampus, and amygdala. Vocat et al. did not employ the more recently available neuroimaging technology used by Corbetta and colleagues when studying the neuropsychological effects of large focal vascular lesions. Given recent findings (as briefly described previously), it appears probable that AHP exists when extensive intrahemispheric and interhemispheric FC is disrupted.

AHP in a 51-year-old woman, who also had hemineglect and complete cortical blindness, was associated with bilateral slow speed of finger tapping (Prigatano, Matthes, Hill, Wolf, & Heiserman, 2011). However, as the speed of finger tapping improved in the so-called unaffected hand (i.e., the right hand), resolution of hemineglect occurred. This shortly preceded recovery from AHP. When the person became aware of her hemiplegia, she was able to initiate tapping in the affected hand for the first time. This observation raised two interesting propositions. First, AHP may resolve quickly if the contralateral cerebral hemisphere returns to more normal functioning (as in part reflected by speed of finger movements) within a short period of time. Second, if a person suffers permanent bilateral cerebral dysfunction (particularly involving the DMN), then anosognosia or severe impaired self-awareness of specific cognitive and behavioral problems may not resolve with the passage of time. This appears to be the case after severe TBI.

PROLONGED IMPAIRED SELF-AWARENESS AFTER A SEVERE TRAUMATIC BRAIN INJURY

Although typically not demonstrating AHP after severe TBI, numerous studies have reported that post-acute TBI patients who initially suffered severe TBI (admitting Glasgow Coma Scale of 3–8) demonstrate persistent unawareness of their residual cognitive and behavioral impairments (Prigatano, 2005, 2010). The estimates typically range between 30% and 40% of this patient population. Although virtually any area of the brain can be damaged following severe TBI, prefrontal and anterior temporal lobe contusions are often observed in the presence of diffuse axonal injury, as noted previously (see also Bigler, 2011). A subgroup of these patients typically do not verbally report or subjectively experience significant alterations in memory or problem-solving ability for several weeks, months, or years post injury. They often do not self-perceive or recognize when their behavior in socially inappropriate. They are prone to dismiss or discount any objective information concerning their cognitive and behavior limitations. The neuroanatomical basis of persistent ISA continues to be debated because different methods are commonly used to measure different versions of ISA (Orfei, Caltagirone, & Spalletta, 2010).

Johnson et al. (2002) reported activation of the medial prefrontal cortex and the posterior cingulate cortex in normal individuals performing a self-reflective task. The same task was later performed by individuals with a history of severe TBI (Schmitz, Rowley, Kawahara, & Johnson, 2006). Compared to controls, the TBI patients exhibited a similar pattern of activation but showed greater signal changes in the anterior cingulate, precuneus, and right temporal lobe. Using linear regression analysis, increased activation of the right anterior dorsal prefrontal cortex was related to more accurate self-awareness in the TBI subjects. Note, however, that these TBI patients had the predictable patterns of bilateral contusions involving frontal and temporal regions of the brain. On a number of neuropsychological tests, they showed the predictable difficulties performing memory and speed of information process tasks. Yet, these cognitive difficulties per se did not predict poor self-awareness.

This is an important observation that was noted in the very early studies that attempted to identify neuropsychological correlates of ISA in TBI patients (Prigatano & Altman, 1990). This led to the formulation that ISA associated with TBI is "not a purely cognitive dysfunction" but most likely reflects some basic disruption of the capacity to integrate feelings and thoughts when realistically reflecting on one's abilities (Prigatano, 1991, 1999, 2010, 2014). As such, psychologically working with the problem of ISA associated with various brain disorders requires the clinician to understand that a purely cognitive or a purely "affective" approach to this problem is likely to be ineffective. It requires developing a trusting relationship with patients so they can be professionally guided to make decisions that are in their best interest when they do not experience the problems that others observe in them. Examples of successes and failures in dealing with this problem are described in later chapters of this book.

DISRUPTING THE NATURAL PLAN OF THE CENTRAL NERVOUS SYSTEM IN YOUNG AND MIDDLE YEARS OF ADULTHOOD: IMPLICATIONS FOR PSYCHOLOGICAL CARE

Focal lesions to the brain caused by stroke can disrupt neural networks between the two cerebral hemispheres, but perhaps in less severe ways than those observed following severe TBI. It is possible to appreciate that the psychosocial consequences of these lesions often appear similar but are in some ways different during the young and middle adult years of life.

In both cases, employment opportunities are substantially reduced secondary to residual cognitive impairments. The percentage of individuals returning to work using traditional rehabilitation methods is strikingly similar (i.e., 25–30%) between the two groups. However, following focal lesions, patients often have adequate awareness of why they are unable to work, at least several months post onset of their stroke. In contrast, following multifocal lesions to the brain produced by severe TBI, patients are often perplexed about why they cannot work several months and even years post trauma. The same is true when asked about their personal or intimate relationships. The former group often understands that their cognitive and motor problems result in a loss of intimate partners (Korpelainen, Nieminen, & Myllylä, 1999). The latter group is prone to blame the other person for their loss. Social isolation is perhaps the most common psychosocial consequence after any brain disorder experienced during the adult years. Patients with bilateral cerebral dysfunction (often affecting frontal and temporal regions of the brain) often have unrealistic perceptions of themselves and others that persist. This can and often does lead to suspicious thinking and paranoid observations (Prigatano & Maier, 2009).

The previously described 51-year-old woman who suffered AHP was followed for several years after her stroke. She never recovered the use of her left arm or leg. She was totally dependent on an older sister for care in the home and for taking her to doctor appointments. She could never work again. She understandably became depressed and withdrew from contact with others. She was painfully aware of her limitations. The 57-year-old man with an aphasic condition, also previously described, recognized he could not complete written reports or make a verbal presentation necessary in his work. He recognized he needed to go on disability. He, too, suffered from depression and was keenly aware of how depression adversely affected his relationship with his wife. In contrast, two TBI patients with severe ISA described elsewhere (Prigatano, 2014) developed paranoid ideation and would become quick to anger if their limitations were reviewed with them. They were described as being childlike in their manner, with a loss of understanding of other people's needs. The two stroke patients with focal lesions were not described in this manner.

The previous observations suggest that when the natural plan of the CNS is seriously disrupted during the adult years, the person does not complete significant portions of that plan. This results in social isolation, depression, anxiety, and a loss of work and pre-existing family relationships. What was once normal is now lost; consequently, there is an associated loss of hope regarding one's future. If hope is not restored, this often has devastating effects on the long-term psychological functioning of the individual (note the observations of Erikson & Erikson, 1998).

Throughout the years, however, it has been shown that many of these patients can reduce their social isolation and begin to recapture a productive and meaningful life (Ben-Yishay & Diller, 2011; Prigatano, 1986, 1991). This often requires holistic milieu-oriented neuropsychological rehabilitation approaches to their initial psychological care. Such rehabilitation can provide meaningful ways by which deficits can be compensated for and a renewed sense of competency restored. However, as with children and adolescents, the level of functioning often remains less than that observed in age-matched peers. During the adult years, however, the person can draw on previously developed neuropsychological and psychodynamic strengths to improve their functional adaptation. Often, partially preserved functional capacities can be built upon with the aid of proper psychosocial support systems. This is described in more detail in later chapters. Box 7.1 lists common neuropsychological and psychosocial consequences of focal and multifocal brain lesions imposed by severe TBI or vascular lesions during adulthood.

SUMMARY

Focal and multifocal injuries to the brain during adulthood have predictable neuropsychological and psychosocial outcomes. "More lateralized" neuropsychological syndromes are observed during this time frame as the higher integrative brain functions reach their natural development "potential." However, the importance of intra- and interhemispheric coordination to maintain a variety of integrative brain functions in adulthood has become increasingly clear. Studies that have employed measures of neural connectivity patterns in normal-functioning individuals and those who have suffered from strokes and TBI have helped explain how relatively "focal" lesions of the brain can have often "bilateral" effects (Prigatano, 1999). They have also helped explain the mechanisms by which some indications of recovery appear to be possible.

However, studies continue to demonstrate that the brain is relatively "unforgiving" in its adult and development stages of its existence. Larger brain lesions (unilateral and bilateral in nature) disrupt neuroconnectivity patterns that often negatively affect multiple neural networks (e.g., disturbances of the DMN can alter signaling patterns to the ventral and dorsal attentional networks, the frontoparietal network, the salience network, etc.). Modern neuroimaging studies of the brain have helped explain why patients seldom have neuropsychological deficits in one domain but more commonly have deficits in multiple domains of neuropsychological functioning.

Perhaps most devastating is that the adult brain that has suffered severe injury loses its preexisting capacity to function as it normally did. Sometimes the affected individuals are aware of these changes, and sometimes they are not. The focus of psychological care of these individuals often centers on helping them understand what abilities have been impaired and to what extent. This leads to learning compensatory skills that help build their resilience to cope with the adversities caused by their brain injury. The process is highly individualized and requires a good appreciation of each person's pre-brain injury cognitive and behavioral strengths and limitations. It also requires understanding

> **Box 7.1. Common Neuropsychological and Psychosocial Difficulties Observed in Young and Middle-Aged Adults Who Suffer a Brain Disorder**
>
> **Neuropsychological Disturbances**
> 1. Classical neurobehavioral/neuropsychological syndromes (e.g., amnestic syndromes, aphasic syndromes, neglect syndromes, apraxias, agnosias, and anosognosia)
> 2. Common symptoms that do not present as syndromes per se
>   - Impaired memory (not a classic amnestic syndrome)
>   - Slow information processing and new learning
>   - Slow and uncoordinated motor activities (typically involving the hands)
>   - Reduced working memory skills
>   - Persistent difficulties with sustained and divided attention
>   - Disorganized and inefficient encoding and retrieval when attending to and learning new information
>   - Difficulties with response inhibition (or failures at self-control)
>   - Disturbances in "basic" and "higher order" language skills necessary for social communication and adult interpersonal interaction
>   - Alterations in behavioral control with increased risk-taking behaviors
>   - Impairment of the "abstract attitude" or executive functions
>   - Increased physical and mental fatigue when solving cognitive tasks
>   - Impaired self-awareness of the nature and degree of neuropsychological disturbances after bilateral and multifocal brain lesions
>   - Onset of "childlike behaviors" with a tendency for suspicious ideation and breakdown of "reality testing" skills
>
> **Psychosocial Disturbances**
> 1. Persistent unemployment or reduced levels of employment
> 2. Less physically attractive
> 3. Loss of friends and intimate relationships
> 4. Loss of social status
> 5. Social isolation and withdrawal
> 6. Increased psychiatric comorbidity (severe depression, anxiety, etc.)
> 7. Increased risk for addictive behaviors (use of alcohol, drugs, etc.)
> 8. Premature adult dependence on others, which further disturbs family relationships
> 9. A tendency for a loss of hope in their lives

individuals' subjective experiences in light of their cultural and psychodynamic backgrounds.

REFERENCES

Avena-Koenigsberger, A., Misic, B., & Sporns, O. (2018). Communication dynamics in complex brain networks. *Nature Reviews Neuroscience, 19*(1), 17–33.

Ben-Yishay, Y., & Diller, L. (2011). *Handbook of holistic neuropsychological rehabilitation: Outpatient rehabilitation of traumatic brain injury*. New York, NY: Oxford University Press.

Bigler, E. D. (2011). Structural imaging. In J. M. Silver, T. W. McAllister, & S. C. Yudofsky (Eds.), *Textbook of traumatic brain injury* (2nd ed., 73–90). Washington, DC: American Psychiatric Publishing.

Bisiach, E., Vallar, G., Perani, D., Papagno, C., & Berti, A. (1986). Unawareness of disease following lesions of the right hemisphere: Anosognosia for hemiplegia and anosognosia for hemianopia. *Neuropsychologia, 24*(4), 471–482.

Bonnelle, V., Ham, T. E., Leech, R., Kinnunen, K. M., Mehta, M. A., Greenwood, R. J., & Sharp, D. J. (2012). Salience network integrity predicts default mode network function after traumatic brain injury. *Proceedings of the National Academy of Sciences of the USA, 109*(12), 4690–4695.

Carhart-Harris, R. L., & Friston, K. J. (2010). The default-mode, ego-functions and free-energy: A neurobiological account of Freudian ideas. *Brain, 133*(4), 1265–1283.

Corbetta, M. (2017). *Behavioral clusters and brain network mechanisms of impairment and recovery.* Paper presented at the annual meeting of the International Neuropsychological Society, New Orleans.

Corbetta, M., Ramsey, L., Callejas, A., Baldassarre, A., Hacker, C. D., Siegel, J. S., . . . Lang, C. E. (2015). Common behavioral clusters and subcortical anatomy in stroke. *Neuron, 85*(5), 927–941.

De Simoni, S., Grover, P. J., Jenkins, P. O., Honeyfield, L., Quest, R. A., Ross, E., . . . Waldman, A. D. (2016). Disconnection between the default mode network and medial temporal lobes in post-traumatic amnesia. *Brain, 139*(12), 3137–3150.

Di Russo, F., Incoccia, C., Formisano, R., Sabatini, U., & Zoccolotti, P. (2005). Abnormal motor preparation in severe traumatic brain injury with good recovery. *Journal of Neurotrauma, 22*(2), 297–312.

Dikmen, S. S., Machamer, J. E., Winn, H. R., & Temkin, N. R. (1995). Neuropsychological outcome at 1-year post head injury. *Neuropsychology, 9*(1), 80.

Dikmen, S. S., Temkin, N. R., Machamer, J. E., Holubkov, A. L., Fraser, R. T., & Winn, H. R. (1994). Employment following traumatic head injuries. *Archives of Neurology, 51*(2), 177–186.

Erikson, E. H., & Erikson, J. M. (1998). *The life cycle completed (extended version).* New York, NY: Norton.

Goldstein, K. (1939). *The organism: A holistic approach to biology derived from pathological data in man.* New York, NY: American Book Company.

Goldstein, K. (1942). *Aftereffects of brain injuries in war: Their evaluation and treatment. The application of psychologic methods in the clinic.* New York, NY: Grune & Stratton.

Graham, J. R., Pereira, S., & Teasell, R. (2011). Aphasia and return to work in younger stroke survivors. *Aphasiology, 25*(8), 952–960.

Haaland, K. Y., Temkin, N., Randahl, G., & Dikmen, S. (1994). Recovery of simple motor skills after head injury. *Journal of Clinical and Experimental Neuropsychology, 16*(3), 448–456.

Ham, T. E., Bonnelle, V., Hellyer, P., Jilka, S., Robertson, I. H., Leech, R., & Sharp, D. J. (2013). The neural basis of impaired self-awareness after traumatic brain injury. *Brain, 137*(2), 586–597.

Heaton, R. K., Chelune, G. J., & Lehman, R. A. (1978). Using neuropsychological and personality tests to assess the likelihood of patient employment. *Journal of Nervous and Mental Disease, 166*(6), 408–416.

Heilman, K. M., Watson, R. T., & Valenstein, E. (2003). Neglect and related disorders. In K. M. Heilman & E. Valenstein (Eds.), *Clinical neuropsychology* (4th ed., pp. 296–346). New York, NY: Oxford University Press.

Heilman, M. K. M., & Valenstein, E. (Eds.). (2010). *Clinical neuropsychology* (5th ed.). New York, NY: Oxford University Press.

Johnson, S. C., Baxter, L. C., Wilder, L. S., Pipe, J. G., Heiserman, J. E., & Prigatano, G. P. (2002). Neural correlates of self-reflection. *Brain, 125*(8), 1808–1814.

Johnson, S. C., Bigler, E. D., Burr, R. B., & Blatter, D. D. (1994). White matter atrophy, ventricular dilation, and intellectual functioning following traumatic brain injury. *Neuropsychology, 8*(3), 307.

Karnath, H.-O., & Baier, B. (2010). Anosognosia for hemiparesis and hemiplegia: Disturbed sense of agency and body ownership. In G. Prigatano (Ed.), *The study of anosognosia* (pp. 39–62). New York, NY: Oxford University Press.

Kasahara, M., Menon, D., Salmond, C., Outtrim, J., Tavares, J. T., Carpenter, T., . . . Stamatakis, E. (2010). Altered functional connectivity in the motor network after traumatic brain injury. *Neurology, 75*(2), 168–176.

Korpelainen, J. T., Nieminen, P., & Myllylä, V. V. (1999). Sexual functioning among stroke patients and their spouses. *Stroke, 30*(4), 715–719.

Lashley, K. S. (1929). *Brain mechanisms and intelligence.* Chicago, IL: University of Chicago Press.

Mohr, J., Choi, D., Grotta, J., & Wolf, P. (2004). *Stroke: Pathophysiology, diagnosis, and management* (4th ed.). Baltimore, MD: Churchill Livingstone.

Orfei, M. D., Caltagirone, C., & Spalletta, G. (2010). The behavioral measurement of anosognosia as a multifaceted phenomenon. In G. Prigatano (Ed.), *The study of anosognosia* (pp. 429–452). New York, NY: Oxford University Press.

Orman, J. A. L., Kraus, J. F., Zaloshnja, E., & Miller, T. (2011). Epidemiology. In J. M. Silver, T. W.

McAllister, & S. C. Yudofsky (Eds.), *Textbook of traumatic brain injury* (2nd ed., pp. 3–22). Washington, DC: American Psychiatric Publishing.

Paradiso, S., Anderson, B. M., Ponto, L. L. B., Tranel, D., & Robinson, R. G. (2011). Altered neural activity and emotions following right middle cerebral artery stroke. *Journal of Stroke and Cerebrovascular Diseases, 20*(2), 94–104.

Petersen, S. E., & Posner, M. I. (2012). The attention system of the human brain: 20 years after. *Annual Review of Neuroscience, 35,* 73–89.

Ponsford, J. L., Downing, M. G., Olver, J., Ponsford, M., Acher, R., Carty, M., & Spitz, G. (2014). Longitudinal follow-up of patients with traumatic brain injury: Outcome at two, five, and ten years post-injury. *Journal of Neurotrauma, 31*(1), 64–77.

Prigatano, G. P. (1991). Disturbances of self-awareness of deficit after traumatic brain injury. In G. Prigatano & D. L. Schacter (Eds.), *Awareness of deficit after brain injury: Clinical and theoretical issues* (pp. 111–126). New York, NY: Oxford University Press.

Prigatano, G. P. (1999). *Principles of neuropsychological rehabilitation*. New York, NY: Oxford University Press.

Prigatano, G. P. (2005). Disturbances of self-awareness and rehabilitation of patients with traumatic brain injury: A 20-year perspective. *Journal of Head Trauma Rehabilitation, 20*(1), 19–29.

Prigatano, G. P. (2010). *The study of anosognosia*. New York, NY: Oxford University Press.

Prigatano, G. P. (2011). The importance of the patient's subjective experience in stroke rehabilitation. *Topics in Stroke Rehabilitation, 18*(1), 30–34.

Prigatano, G. P. (2014). Anosognosia and patterns of impaired self-awareness observed in clinical practice. *Cortex, 61,* 81–92.

Prigatano, G. P. (Ed.). (1986). *Neuropsychological rehabilitation after brain injury*. Baltimore, MD: Johns Hopkins University Press.

Prigatano, G. P., & Altman, I. (1990). Impaired awareness of behavioral limitations after traumatic brain injury. *Archives of Physical Medicine and Rehabilitation, 71*(13), 1058–1064.

Prigatano, G. P., & Borgaro, S. R. (2003). Qualitative features of finger movement during the Halstead finger oscillation test following traumatic brain injury. *Journal of the International Neuropsychological Society, 9*(1), 128–133.

Prigatano, G. P., & Maier, F. (2009). Neuropsychiatric, psychiatric, and behavioral disorders associated with traumatic brain injury. In I. Grant & K. M. Adams (Eds.), *Neuropsychological assessment of neuropsychiatric disorders* (3rd ed., 618–631). New York, NY: Oxford University Press.

Prigatano, G. P., Matthes, J., Hill, S. W., Wolf, T. R., & Heiserman, J. E. (2011). Anosognosia for hemiplegia with preserved awareness of complete cortical blindness following intracranial hemorrhage. *Cortex, 47*(10), 1219–1227.

Prigatano, G. P., & Wong, J. L. (1997). Speed of finger tapping and goal attainment after unilateral cerebral vascular accident. *Archives of Physical Medicine and Rehabilitation, 78*(8), 847–852.

Rabinowitz, A. R., & Levin, H. S. (2014). Cognitive sequelae of traumatic brain injury. *Psychiatric Clinics of North America, 37*(1), 1–11.

Ramsey, L., Siegel, J., Lang, C., Strube, M., Shulman, G., & Corbetta, M. (2017). Behavioural clusters and predictors of performance during recovery from stroke. *Nature Human Behaviour, 1*(3), 0038.

Robinson, R. G., & Starkstein, S. E. (2010). Neuropsychiatric aspects of cerebrovascular disorders. In S. C. Yudofsky & R. E. Hales (Eds.), *Essentials of neuropsychiatry and behavioral neurosciences* (2nd ed., pp. 299–322). Washington, DC: American Psychiatric Publishing.

Roebuck-Spencer, T., & Sherer, M. (2018). Moderate and severe traumatic brain injury. In J. Morgan & J. Ricker (Eds.), *Textbook of clinical neuropsychology* (2nd ed., pp. 387–410). New York, NY: Taylor & Francis.

Schmitz, T. W., Rowley, H. A., Kawahara, T. N., & Johnson, S. C. (2006). Neural correlates of self-evaluative accuracy after traumatic brain injury. *Neuropsychologia, 44*(5), 762–773.

Sela-Kaufman, M., Rassovsky, Y., Agranov, E., Levi, Y., & Vakil, E. (2013). Premorbid personality characteristics and attachment style moderate the effect of injury severity on occupational outcome in traumatic brain injury: Another aspect of reserve. *Journal of Clinical and Experimental Neuropsychology, 35*(6), 584–595.

Sharp, D. J., Beckmann, C. F., Greenwood, R., Kinnunen, K. M., Bonnelle, V., De Boissezon, X., . . . Leech, R. (2011). Default mode network functional and structural connectivity after traumatic brain injury. *Brain, 134*(8), 2233–2247.

Sherer, M., Meyers, C. A., & Bergloff, P. (1997). Efficacy of postacute brain injury rehabilitation for patients with primary malignant brain tumors. *Cancer, 80*(2), 250–257.

Sherer, M., & Sander, A. M. (Eds.). (2014). *Handbook on the neuropsychology of traumatic brain injury*. New York, NY: Springer.

Siegel, J. S., Ramsey, L. E., Snyder, A. Z., Metcalf, N. V., Chacko, R. V., Weinberger, K., . . . Corbetta, M. (2016). Disruptions of network connectivity predict impairment in multiple behavioral domains after stroke. *Proceedings of the National Academy of Sciences of the USA, 113*(30), E4367–E4376.

Silver, J. M., McAllister, T. W., & Yudofsky, S. C. (Eds.). (2011). *Textbook of traumatic brain injury.* Washington, DC: American Psychiatric Publishing.

Sinanović, O. (2010). Neuropsychology of acute stroke. *Psychiatria Danubina, 22*(2), 278–281.

Smith, C. (2011). Neuropathology. In J. M. Silver, T. W. McAllister, & S. C. Yudofsky (Eds.), *Textbook of traumatic brain injury* (2nd ed., pp. 23–36). Washington, DC: American Psychiatric Publishing.

Sperry, R. W. (1969). A modified concept of consciousness. *Psychological Review, 76*(6), 532–536.

Tanaka, H., Toyonaga, T., & Hashimoto, H. (2014). Functional and occupational characteristics predictive of a return to work within 18 months after stroke in Japan: Implications for rehabilitation. *International Archives of Occupational and Environmental Health, 87*(4), 445–453.

Thomsen, I. V. (1984). Late outcome of very severe blunt head trauma: A 10–15 year second follow-up. *Journal of Neurology, Neurosurgery, and Psychiatry, 47*(3), 260–268.

van Zomeren, A. H. (1981). *Reaction time and attention after closed head injury.* Lisse, the Netherlands: Swets & Zeitlinger.

Vocat, R., Staub, F., Stroppini, T., & Vuilleumier, P. (2010). Anosognosia for hemiplegia: A clinical–anatomical prospective study. *Brain, 133*(12), 3578–3597.

8

THE PROBLEM OF UNEXPECTED AND ACCELERATED LOSS OF COMPETENCY AFTER A BRAIN DISORDER DURING AGING

INTRODUCTION

During the older years of life, the natural plan of the central nervous system (CNS) is to continue to cope with the struggles of life. However, during this time period, the nature of those struggles begins to naturally change. The struggles are no longer centered on developing functional skills necessary to obtain work and find a mate. The famous goals of "to work and to love" have or have not been achieved by this time. With advancing years, work ends and children are often "grown-up" and no longer need the same degree of assistance to meet their life's responsibilities. Sustaining a meaningful and active life is important to the elderly, but during this time physical and cognitive capabilities begin to decline. For many, the decline is gradual, and the elderly individual begins to explore ways of coping with that decline.

Sleep patterns are frequently altered with a decline in several measures of sleep quality (Ohayon, Carskadon, Guilleminault, & Vitiello, 2004). Sexual drive and sexual performance also decline with an increase in a variety of medical conditions that require attention (Kubin, Wagner, & Fugl-Meyer, 2003). For many, there is now the realization that their cognitive skills are also not the same and seem to be slowly changing (for the worse). One recent review on changes in episodic memory in older individuals emphasized, for example, declines in overall brain volume, white matter integrity, and pre- and post-synaptic dopamine receptors (Wang, Daselaar, & Cabeza, 2017). Collectively, these and many other changes can produce a "crisis" in a person's life as Erik Erikson employed that term (see Chapter 4, this volume).

Do older adults now better understand the nature of their personal life and perhaps "life in general"? Do they now experience their journey as meaningful and want to continue engaging in it? Or are they overwhelmed with how painful certain life experiences have been and continue to be? Do they wish to die? Do they now feel a sense of personal integrity (i.e., "wholeness"), or do they experience hopelessness and discouragement that death is no longer a "distant reality"? These are the challenges of old age, and brain injuries of various types can greatly influence how these challenges are met. The person's earlier ways of coping with adversity clearly influence this process of dealing with expected and unexpected changes following a brain disorder in the older adult. In this chapter, observations regarding "successful aging" are first considered, followed by a review of how cerebral vascular accidents (CVAs) and traumatic brain injury (TBI) produce unexpected and accelerated loss of neuropsychological functions.

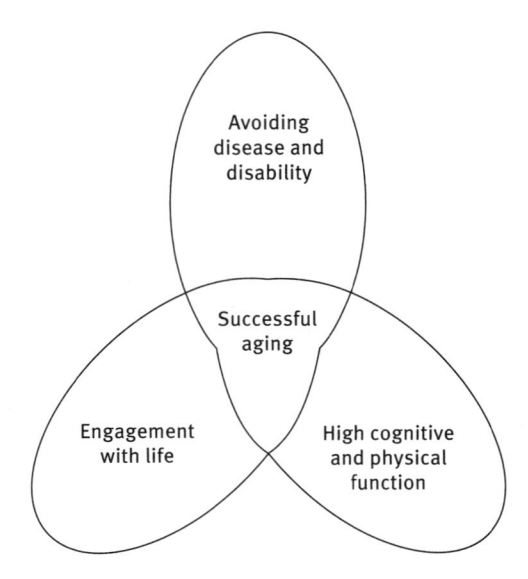

FIGURE 8.1 A model of successful aging.

Source: Reprinted from Rowe, J. W., & Kahn, R. L., Successful aging, *The Gerontologist*, 37(4), 1997, p. 433–440, by permission of Oxford University Press.

SUCCESSFUL AGING OF THE CENTRAL NERVOUS SYSTEM

As noted previously, the natural plan of the CNS is to continue to deal with life's problems with diminishing physical and associated cognitive resources. How does one do this "successfully" as one ages? Rowe and Kahn (1997) summarized key observations regarding what constitutes "successful aging." They suggested that there are three interacting components: "low probability of disease and disease-related disability, high cognitive and physical functional capacity, and active engagement with life" (p. 433). Figure 8.1 illustrates the model they suggested. They also presented a figure that illustrates the probable relationship of advancing age to the experience of disease, disability, and eventually death (Figure 8.2). In their model, by age 75 years, there is a high probability that one will experience some form of chronic disease with associated disabilities. The problems become more likely as one gets older. Published in 1997, their model also suggests that there is a 50/50 chance of death by or around age 80 years. Present-day statistics seem to support some of these predictions.

Anderson and Horvath (2004), as well as many other researchers, have noted that chronic health care problems substantially increase with age. They estimated that 85% of people aged 65 years or older have at least one chronic health problem. More recent reports suggest that the numbers substantially increase after age 75 years, particularly when multiple comorbid health care problems exist. For example, in a report by the National Institute of Aging (Salive, 2013), 59.9% of patients aged 65–74 years, 73.4% of those aged 75–84 years, and 79.5% of those older than age 85 years had multiple chronic health conditions. Although there are many chronic health care conditions, heart failure, atrial fibrillations, diabetes, and chronic kidney diseases are especially common in those older than age 65 years. Note that depression is often a frequent comorbid problem. Dementia is becoming more important as more people are living longer lives, and its incidence steadily increases with age (Querfurth & LaFerla, 2010).

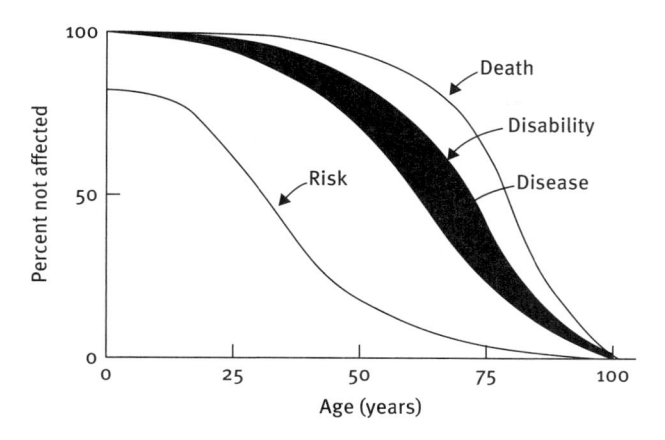

FIGURE 8.2 Relation of risk of disease to the presence of disease, disability, and death in an aging population.

Source: Reprinted from Rowe, J. W., & Kahn, R. L., Successful aging, *The Gerontologist*, 37(4), 1997, p. 433–440, by permission of Oxford University Press.

In addition to declining health, many older individuals face economic challenges. The National Council on Aging (2017) reports that 21% of married social security recipients and 43% of single recipients depend on social security benefits for 90% or more of their income. One-third of senior households report having no money left at the end of the month, and many have increasing debt. The loss of wages results in considerable economic worries for many in this age range.

To add to the losses associated with increased health problems and economic worries related to sustaining a reasonable quality of life, cognitive and physical declines associated with old age can lead some to experience a sense of loss of relevance in life. Even if they have no significant economic worries, their opinions, insights, or judgments may no longer "count" with family members or the people who help care for them, not to mention their professional peers. They have difficulty learning new skills and keeping up with technological advances (e.g., the personal computer) for navigating in the world (Aula, 2004).

Rowe and Kahn (1997) suggested that sustaining self-efficacy (i.e., being able to learn and perform tasks necessary for negotiating in the real world) was crucial for successful aging. They emphasized the importance of diet and lifestyle changes to reduce cholesterol levels and maintain low blood pressure. They also emphasized the importance of exercise to sustain adequate gait and reduce balance problems (thus helping avoid falls) in addition to maintaining peak pulmonary flow rates. Finally, they emphasized the ability to sustain educational activities, which may be a major protective factor against cognitive decline. Remaining socially active and productive (even if not gainfully employed) were also identified as key variables to successful aging. When a brain disorder negatively affects one's capacity for sustaining self-efficacy (physically and mentally), the natural plan of the CNS is unexpectedly compromised in old age. The process of the decline is often accelerated. Although depression and a loss of hope are the immediate reactions for many, human nature is such that the desire to live and fight adversity remains. It is especially strong in those who have lived and continue to live a meaningful life.

NEUROPSYCHOLOGICAL CONSEQUENCES OF CEREBRAL VASCULAR ACCIDENTS IN OLDER ADULTS

The incidence of stroke increases with age. G. Howard and Howard (2004) reported, for example, that the incidence of stroke is, on average, less than 600 per 100,000 in the 55- to 64-year-old age range, whereas it is more than 1,600 per 100,000 in the 75 years or older age range. In a more recent report, V. Howard and Howard (2011) noted the same trend, but they also noted racial differences. Younger than age 55 years, strokes are more common in the African American population compared to Whites. However, after age 75 years, the difference disappears.

Recall from Chapter 3 that the integrity of white matter tracts in the brain begins to rapidly decline in the 70s (Westlye et al., 2009), with an associated decline in the speed of processing new information. Andrews-Hanna et al. (2007) also noted that the default mode network appears to show changes during the aging process that are associated with poorer neuropsychological test performance on several measures. Raz, Rodrigue, and Haacke (2007) further documented regional brain shrinkage in the elderly population, with the prefrontal cortex and hippocampus showing the largest naturally occurring changes. These regions are known to be important for attention, working memory, planning, organizational skills, and memory.

Stephens et al. (2004) evaluated cognitive dysfunction in 381 stroke patients aged 75 years or older. They documented many of the same cognitive difficulties observed in younger stroke patients that were described in Chapter 7. They noted, however, a high incidence of attentional deficits as well as disturbances in "executive" functions in older CVA patients compared to controls. If the prefrontal cortex is undergoing natural decline as we age, the effects of a CVA might exacerbate and/or accelerate that decline.

Meier et al. (2011) studied verbal working memory performance after acute stroke in older and younger patients. Controlling for the estimated volume of infarction, they compared young stroke patients (mean age, 43 years) to older stroke patients (mean age, 61.9 years) on a verbal working memory task. They noted that this type of task often results in left hemisphere activation in younger normal subjects but bilateral activation in older normal subjects, consistent with the Hemispheric Asymmetry Reduction in Older Adults (HAROLD) model suggested by Cabeza (2002). Their findings suggest that injury to either hemisphere impacted performance on this task more negatively in older CVA patients than in a small group of younger adult CVA patients ($n = 6$). They interpreted their findings as being supportive of Cabeza's (2002) view that "older patients need both hemispheres intact in order to successfully perform the verbal WM task" (p. 195).

While studying seizure patients, Grivas et al. (2006) made some interesting observations relevant to this discussion. They reported that although seizure control was reasonably good in older adults and comparable to that in younger patients, the neuropsychological outcomes were not as good in older adults. They demonstrated that older patients had proportionally worse performance on tests of attention and verbal and nonverbal memory before surgery compared to younger patients with similar years of epilepsy prior to surgery. Also, the older patients showed less improvement in neuropsychological functioning post-surgery. For example, 20.6% of older patients showed improvement in verbal memory compared to 50% of younger patients. Perhaps even more relevant to this discussion is the authors' observation that

> in our older sample, we did not detect a significant effect of the side of surgery on the postoperative changes in memory performances. . . . In contrast, a significant impact of left-sided operations on verbal performance was found in the larger younger control group. (p. 1368)

Note that not all studies have reported this finding, and clinicians' opinions vary regarding the neuropsychological consequences of epilepsy surgery in older individuals. However, the findings reported by Grivas et al. are compatible with those of other studies that suggest older individuals may be at risk for having greater neuropsychological impairments associated with their brain disorder when that disorder impacts neuroconnectivity patterns within the brain that are naturally declining with age. If those patterns of neuroconnectivity are becoming less regionalized and "more diffuse" during the elderly years, bilateral stimulation of brain functions may be advantageous for this group of individuals. Interestingly, a recent study reported that *only* bihemispheric transcranial direct current stimulation helped improve verbal learning in older normal adults but was ineffective for younger normal adults (Fiori et al., 2017).

THE IMPORTANT PROBLEM OF FATIGUE FOLLOWING UNILATERAL STROKE IN OLDER ADULTS

In addition to understanding how focal and multifocal brain lesions may differently affect neuropsychological findings in older versus younger individuals, the effect of their brain injuries on fatigue is an important question. Older individuals have a number of health problems that naturally affect their energy level. Unilateral CVAs may further increase this naturally occurring vulnerability.

In a 2-year follow-up study, Glader, Stegmayr, and Asplund (2002) noted "fatigue is frequent and often severe, even late after stroke" (p. 1327). Although the type of stroke did not appear to relate to subjective reports about fatigue severity, age did. Older subjects reported more constant fatigue. Overall health status, feelings of anxiety, and depression were also related to reports of fatigue. Interesting to neuropsychologists was the finding that the act of speaking, in and of itself, was statistically related to fatigue level. This was observed even when frank aphasia was not present. Brodal (1973), a distinguished professor of anatomy, eloquently described how a small infarction in the right internal capsule of the brain was associated with increased fatigue when he attempted to verbally express himself. He also noted that it took a great deal of "mental energy" to move his fingers, write, or follow a line of reasoning when reading scientific papers. He described these difficulties at a time when his IQ estimates remained very high (Wechsler Adult Intelligence Scale Verbal IQ = 142; Performance IQ = 122).

Subsequent research has supported Brodal's (1973) personal observations. Van Zandvoort, Kappelle, Algra, and De Haan (1998) noted, for example, that very small subcortical strokes involving the internal capsule or the corona radiata were associated with patients reporting difficulties performing cognitive tasks that required strenuous effort. This was present even if a patient's overall level of cognitive performance was within the average range.

Ongoing research on fatigue following stroke emphasizes its multifactorial nature (Colle, Bonan, Leman, Bradai, & Yelnik, 2006) but suggests that fatigue may be a consequence of any brain disorder that negatively affects neural networks involved in sustaining an optimal level of alertness or attention (Staub & Bogousslavsky, 2001). Corbetta's work (e.g., Siegel et al., 2016) also raises the possibility that failure of the brain to re-establish old patterns of neuronal activity for carrying out any cognitive function may place an extra burden on cognitive efficiency and, in so doing, may easily "tire" the patient. Early efforts at cognitive retraining of younger patients with a history of TBI noted they were often very tired at the end of their cognitive rehabilitation day. With time and practice, they gained more energy as their cognitive performance on well-rehearsed tasks improved (Prigatano, 1986).

NEUROPSYCHOLOGICAL CONSEQUENCES OF TRAUMATIC BRAIN INJURY IN OLDER ADULTS

Orman, Kraus, Zaloshnja, and Miller (2011) noted that when excluding emergency department visits, TBI-related hospitalization and death rates were highest in older adults aged 75 years or older. The most common cause of TBI in this age range was falls. Hukkelhoven et al. (2003) reported on the morbidity and mortality of severe TBI in a large patient sample. Unfortunately, the two oldest groups they compared were aged 55–64 years ($n = 214$) and 65 years or older ($n = 100$). Forty-five of the 214 patients (21%) in the younger group died compared to 73 of 100 patients (73%) in the 65 years old or older group. The percentage of individuals showing moderate disability did not vary between these two age groups (estimated 14.4% and 15%, respectively). However, specific neuropsychological functions were not assessed in these two age groups. Green et al. (2008) specifically evaluated the effects of age at time of TBI on measures of processing speeds during a 12-month period. They demonstrated worse processing speed scores in TBI patients older than age 66 years. Unlike other age groups, these older patients showed a decline in processing speeds after an initial recovery period post trauma. Their findings are also compatible with the notion that a naturally declining neuropsychological function with age may be accelerated when an acquired brain injury negatively impacts neuroconnectivity patterns subserving that function.

Senathi-Raja, Ponsford, and Schönberger (2010) also documented "disproportionately greater" neurocognitive impairments in older TBI individuals compared to younger TBI patients (p. 339). This was especially noted on measures of processing speed and attention. In a recent study, Rabinowitz, Hart, Whyte, and Kim (2018) measured neuropsychological recovery trajectories in patents with a history of moderate to severe TBI. Although younger age was associated with a more favorable recovery on measures of executive functions and processing speed, one finding was especially relevant. Like Green et al. (2008), they noted a progressive decline in processing speed in TBI patients who were older (Figure 8.3). This decline was not observed on measures of executive functioning or verbal learning/memory.

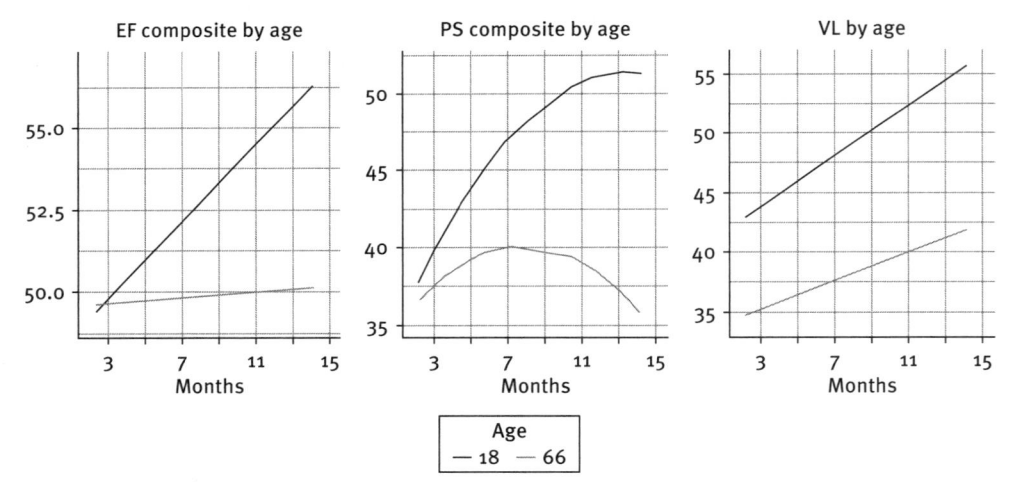

FIGURE 8.3 Cognitive change trajectories by age for each of the three cognitive domains. Cognitive domain scores are in T-score units. Time is depicted as time post-injury in months. EF, executive function; PS, processing speed; VL, verbal learning.

Source: Reprinted from Rabinowitz, A. R., Hart, T., Whyte, J., & Kim, J., Neuropsychological recovery trajectories in moderate to severe traumatic brain injury: Influence of patient characteristics and diffuse axonal injury, *Journal of the International Neuropsychological Society*, 2017, p. 1–10, by permission of Cambridge University Press.

Goldstein et al. (1994) studied neuropsychological consequences of mild and moderate TBI in older adults (aged 50–87 years; mean, 76.8 years). Compared to age-matched healthy individuals, neuropsychological impairments were observed in the areas of language function, attention, memory, and executive functions. Their results paralleled findings often reported for younger adults with a history of moderate TBI. In a later study, Goldstein, Levin, Goldman, Clark, and Altonen (2001) demonstrated that up to 2 months post trauma, older individuals with a history of moderate TBI (mean age, 65.2 years) performed worse on cognitive tests compared to older individuals with a mild TBI (mean age, 62.3 years). These researchers noted the fact that both groups of older TBI individuals reported more depression and anxiety with somatic concerns compared to controls.

ADDITIONAL NEUROPSYCHOLOGICAL COMPARISONS IN OLDER ADULTS WITH BRAIN DISORDERS

Schoenberg et al. (2006) compared performance on the Rey Auditory Verbal Learning Test (RAVLT) in different patient groups, including those with a history of stroke, TBI, and dementia. Unfortunately, the severity of TBI and the lateralization/location of the strokes were not identified in their report. However, a large group ($n = 158$) of patients were described as showing probable dementia of the Alzheimer's type (i.e., Alzheimer's disease [AD]). In both stroke and TBI patients, progressive recall of increasingly more words with repetition was observed at the group level (as similarly reported by Goldstein et al., 2001). This was observed at all age levels, although the groups of older subjects recalled fewer words. In patients with probable AD, much less of a normal "learning curve" was present. On this test, the person is read 15 words five times, and the total number of words recalled on each trial is recorded. In the 66- to 88-year-old age range, patients with probable AD recalled, on average, 2.97 words on Trial 1 and 4.25 and 4.96 words on Trials 2 and 3, respectively. On Trials 4 and 5, the average number of words recalled was 5.22 and 5.75 words, respectively. Rapid forgetting was also noted.

Davis et al. (2003) studied how normally functioning adults performed on the RAVLT at different age ranges. At each age range, a group learning curve was observed. That is, there was a tendency to recall increasingly more words with repetition. This was clearly demonstrated in the younger group of adults (aged 30–45 years), but it was less robust in older, normal individuals (aged 61–75 years). The latter group showed progressive improvement during the first three trials but (as a group) showed no statistically significant improvement in the average number of words recalled from Trial 4 to Trial 5. Davis et al. commented that the age differences were especially noticeable in terms of the number of words recalled on the initial learning trial, with younger adults recalling more words (in a somewhat linear manner) compared to progressively older adults.

A comparison of Davis et al.'s (2003) findings to those of Schoenberg et al. (2006) for individuals aged 75–90 years of age is worth noting. On average, the number of words recalled for the normally functioning older group was approximately six words on Trial 1 and nine words on Trial 5. Also, the normal functioning older group recalled progressively more words during the next two trials. Patients with probable AD did not show this pattern.

Clinically, normally functioning older adults (those older than age 75 years) show improved memory performance with practice. The amount they learn, however, is less than the amount learned by younger individuals. The learning process also seems to require more effort. The point is that sustaining self-efficacy is a challenging but "doable" task in older individuals without a brain disorder, whereas it is often much more difficult following a brain disorder.

THE PSYCHOSOCIAL CONSEQUENCES OF TRAUMATIC BRAIN INJURY AND CEREBRAL VASCULAR ACCIDENTS IN OLDER ADULTS

A number of articles have documented that older individuals make poorer recovery after TBI compared to younger individuals (Juengst et al., 2015; Rothweiler, Temkin, & Dikmen, 1998; Testa, Malec, Moessner, & Brown, 2005). Rothweiler et al. noted that individuals with a history of TBI who were aged 60 years or older required more supervised living arrangements. Also, older individuals who suffered a TBI were less functional in more domains of independent living (Testa et al., 2005). Satisfaction with life after a TBI, however, is not as clearly affected by age. The relationship is moderated by several variables, such as whether the older person continues to work or participates in leisure and religious activities (Juengst et al., 2015). Juengst et al. noted that participation in religious activities tends to increase in the general population as individuals age and is often associated with a positive view of life in older individuals.

Depression, cognitive disability, and physical disability are strong mediators of quality of life in patients with a history of CVA or TBI (as well as other patient groups), as discussed in more detail in later chapters. Reducing depression, ongoing efforts at improving physical functioning, and developing effective cognitive compensations are crucial activities for sustaining self-efficacy. Thus, they are very important for improving psychological adjustment in older individuals who suffer a brain disorder.

How an individual reacts to the neurological and neuropsychological consequences of a stroke is quite varied and often related to the person's personality before the stroke. Literary descriptions of how stroke patients have or have not successfully coped with the effects of their stroke provide insights not easily gleaned from scientific papers. Kirk Douglas' (2002) book, *My Stroke of Luck*, highlights how this positive and successful actor recognized some important personal lessons in life he may not have learned if he did not suffer a stroke. With humor, he describes how the stroke affected him and what he learned about himself and life following his stroke. The lessons he reports learning mirror Erik Erikson's insights regarding successfully coping with old age and a decline in functioning (see Chapter 4, this volume). Douglas was 80 years old at the time of what is believed to be an ischemic stroke involving Broca's area. He was severely depressed after his stroke and struggled to improve his speech. At one point, he even attempted to take his life, but with humor he overcame this impulse. He also found that attending to the needs of others helped him reduce his depression and reconstruct a sense of meaning in his life. He states, "I found the one thing that took me out of myself, out of my sadness, out of my fear, and out of my darkness: helping others. It gave me hope and courage" (p. 35). Another statement he makes is also very congruent with Erikson's notions about successful aging. Douglas states,

> Since my stroke, I have begun to see so many miracles all around me. I look out of the window in my room: verdant grass, silver-tipped oak leaves, tall palm trees gently swaying as they reach to the sky, masses and masses of roses. All colors, so many shapes, exquisite fragrances. (p. 108)

He describes a return to the childhood wonders of experiencing nature in all of its glory and enjoying the sensations immensely. Erikson and Erikson (1998) spoke of how very important this experience is during old age.

Erikson also emphasized how each crisis in life revisits earlier crises and modifies, to some extent, how we psychologically continue to develop (or decline). He speaks of the importance of hope during the first stage of life: Hope is built on the infant's sense of trust obtained from a loving relationship with his or her parents, particularly the mother. Thus, it is very interesting to read what Douglas (2002) has to say about his mother. He reports an especially loving and supportive relationship with his mother when he was a child, which helped him sustain hope as an adult suffering the consequences of a stroke at age 80 years. He reflects on how memories of that relationship nourished him as he struggled with his depression.

Individuals who are deprived of these experiences may well give into suicide after a stroke. In his book *The Creation of Doctor B: A Biography of Bruno Bettelheim*, Richard Pollak (1998) provides a penetrating description of the life of Bruno Bettelheim. Bettelheim was recognized by many for his psychological insights and his extraordinary book, *The Uses of Enchantment* (Bettelheim, 1989). Yet, Bettelheim was a difficult man who often appeared unduly angry and aggressive. Although this was often attributed to the years he spent in a concentration camp, other early life experiences may have contributed to Bettelheim's behavior. Pollak traces out, in considerable detail, events in Bettelheim's life that seemed to influence his character development and manner of interpersonal interaction. He notes that Bettelheim made bitter comments about the lack of mothering he had as a child. Bettelheim experienced his mother in a manner that appears opposite to what Kurt Douglas reported regarding his relationship to his mother. After a series of "small" strokes, he became physically dependent on others and experienced reduced language skills. He often voiced that he wished to die and ultimately took his life. Although lesion location, type of vascular lesion, age at lesion onset, and resultant neurological and neuropsychological effects may contribute to the extent of depression and the choice to end one's life or not, literary descriptions of the types just mentioned make a very strong argument for the importance of early childhood experiences in influencing a person's character. Early life experiences seem to influence whether a person is able to find humor (and hope) in the face of adversity. They may also ultimately contribute to the choice to help others when a person is periodically overwhelmed with considerable losses that occur during the later stages of life.

DEMENTIA IN OLD AGE

Although this and the previous two chapters have focused on the effects of CVA and TBI on the natural plan of the CNS, the problem of dementia in older individuals also needs to be briefly considered. Various forms of dementing conditions affect the natural plan of the CNS in different ways. However, the ability to sustain self-efficacy skills is universally compromised. Although the specific neuropsychological dysfunctions people with dementia may experience appear to depend on the brain regions most directly affected by their underlying neurodegenerative process (Seeley, Crawford, Zhou, Miller, & Greicius, 2009), a central feature of these people's functioning is typically some confusion and perplexity as to what is happening to them. Some are openly frightened about their condition, whereas others appear oblivious to the changes while their family members are quite concerned. Many of these individuals are referred for a neuropsychological examination. How these individuals and family members are interviewed is extremely important. How the patient and family members describe the patient's daily functioning gives very important clues as to how the natural plan of the CNS has been affected and how it may continue to be affected as time goes on. Listening carefully to the patient and family members and providing them practical feedback based on the neuropsychological examination findings can set the stage for meaningfully helping them during the patient's last stages of life. A major focus is now on preserving patients' dignity as declining neuropsychological functions progressively limit their self-efficacy. It should be constantly kept in mind that older adults who are in the early stages of a dementing condition may still possess considerable wisdom about life. Despite memory difficulties or word-finding problems in free speech, their years of experience can provide important perspectives about how to deal with life's problems. When this was noted during a psychotherapy session with a patient and his wife, the patient immediately felt a sense of value and his depression was visibly reduced.

GENERAL IMPLICATIONS FOR PSYCHOLOGICAL CARE FOR OLDER ADULTS

As the CNS naturally declines and abnormal brain changes occur during older years, the natural plan of progressive decline of the CNS is amplified and often accelerated in a manner that is devastating to the patient and caregivers. Because the human brain appears to rely increasingly more on bilateral cerebral activation during the aging process when carrying out specific cognitive tasks, unilateral and bilateral lesions often have profoundly negative effects. The person is not only less efficient in carrying out self-efficacy tasks but also becomes unable to do many of them. The person has to rely on others for external support. The goal is no longer to try to develop normally so that later one can obtain and sustain work and love relationships while maintaining one's individuality. The goal of older adults with a declining CNS, which is further complicated by a brain disorder, is to maintain self-independence as long as possible. They are also biologically and psychological programmed to give to others what they have learned and obtained during their lifetime. The experience of helping others during this time of decline is crucial to the process of psychological care for the older adult, as Kurt Douglas' (2002) descriptions of what he experienced highlight. If this can be done utilizing pre-existing competencies (e.g., the application of superior verbal skills or technical visual–spatial skills) in new and creative ways, a greater sense of personal well-being and dignity may be achieved (Perry, Ruggiano, Shtompel, & Hassevoort, 2015), even in the face of declining functions and resources.

In normal aging, there are constant struggles that have to be dealt with on a daily basis. Douglas (2002) made references to finding "little heroes" in daily life that helped inspire courage in him to face adversity after his stroke. This same point has been made by others who describe the "hero's journey" as a metaphor for successful living (Campbell, 2008). It helps re-establish hope (Prigatano & Salas, 2017), and for the elderly, it especially fosters the notion that future generations will benefit from one's existence and achievements. This is often depicted in movies that have great appeal to the general public because they reflect the hero's journey during the last years of life (e.g., *Star Wars: The Last Jedi*; Johnson, 2017).

The basic themes of sustaining self-efficacy, reducing depression by helping others, and finding experiences that foster a reawakening of the senses during the last stages of life are considered in more detail in later chapters on psychological care after brain disorders. Box 8.1 summarizes some of the common neuropsychological and psychosocial consequences of brain disorders in the older adult years.

REFLECTIONS ON HUMAN NATURE IN LIGHT OF THE NATURAL CHANGE IN THE PLAN OF THE CENTRAL NERVOUS SYSTEM OVER TIME

In light of what has been reviewed in this and previous chapters, a few reflections on human nature are in order. Human nature, at its core, is an animal nature that has evolved to the point at which language has become possible as well as the capacity for self-reflection and the capacity to understand and predict the thoughts and actions of others. In the course of human development, there is first a slow but reliable development of sensory–motor skills necessary for ambulation and object manipulation. The development of focused attention and capacity for working memory occurs during these early years of life and fosters the development of visual–motor perception and the perception of

> **Box 8.1. Common Features of Neuropsychological and Psychosocial Difficulties Observed in Older Adults Who Suffer a Brain Disorder**
>
> **Neuropsychological Disturbances**
> 1. The syndromes and symptoms are similar to those discussed in Chapter 7, with less clear lateralization of earlier predictable brain–behavior disturbances.
> 2. The ability to naturally process information under normal processing speed requirements appears especially compromised in the elderly population.
> 3. Unilateral lesions of brain secondary to CVAs appear to have a greater negative impact on working memory skills in older individuals compared to younger individuals.
> 4. Apparent "natural" decline in attention, organizational skills, memory, and speed of processing of information and performing motor skills adversely interacts with neuropsychological disturbances caused by brain lesions to produce greater levels of neuropsychological impairment than seen in younger populations with similar brain pathology.
> 5. Increased "mental fatigue" when problem-solving seems to occur in older individuals, which can negatively impact their decision to use compensatory aids in everyday life.
>
> **Psychosocial Disturbances**
> 1. Progressive loss of independence in daily activities and need to rely on others
> 2. Enhanced depression and anxiety as scope of independence becomes limited with associated sleep disturbances
> 3. Loss of sense of competency with associated loss of self-esteem and recognition by others
> 4. Potential for a growing sense of despair and loss of hope over one's life circumstances
> 5. Increased social isolation
> 6. Increased disorientation and judgment that puts them at risk for being exploited by others or inadvertently placing themselves in danger

rudimentary speech sounds. These skills evolve into the first interpersonal communication patterns that facilitate human bonding. That bonding is necessary for providing a human environment that makes later physical and psychological development possible. During the young and middle years of adulthood, skills are learned that allow for efficient problem-solving necessary to obtain work and establish a love relationship or at least interpersonal connections necessary for procreation and the continuance of life. In this process, humans not only want to "work and love" but also want to actualize their unique or individual aspirations about life. They want to be "who they are." Once this is achieved, the normal aging process often slowly begins to show a decline in physical and cognitive functional capacities that are paralleled by specific changes in brain function and neural connectivity. Lesions of the brain at different developmental time periods affect the evolution and achievement of the natural plan and goals of the CNS in complicated but somewhat predictable ways, as this chapter and Chapters 6 and 7 have attempted to outline. Psychological care is the process of understanding these dynamic and predictable patterns of change and helping individuals sustain activities that let the plan unfold over their life span. A key barrier to this process, however, can be a disturbance in patients' subjective experience of their altered neuropsychological functioning. This disturbance has been described in different ways, including a lack of judgment, a lack of insight, anosognosia, impaired self-awareness, and denial. In light of this "special problem" for clinical neuropsychology, Chapter 9 focuses on it from a psychological care perspective.

REFERENCES

Anderson, G., & Horvath, J. (2004). The growing burden of chronic disease in America. *Public Health Reports, 119*(3), 263–270.

Andrews-Hanna, J. R., Snyder, A. Z., Vincent, J. L., Lustig, C., Head, D., Raichle, M. E., & Buckner, R. L. (2007). Disruption of large-scale brain systems in advanced aging. *Neuron, 56*(5), 924–935.

Aula, A. (2004). Learning to use computers at a later age. *HCI and the Older Population, 3*, 1–4.

Bettelheim, B. (1989). *The uses of enchantment: The meaning and importance of fairy tales.* New York, NY: Vintage.

Brodal, A. (1973). Self-observations and neuro-anatomical considerations after a stroke. *Brain, 96*(4), 675–694.

Cabeza, R. (2002). Hemispheric asymmetry reduction in older adults: The HAROLD model. *Psychology and Aging, 17*(1), 85–100.

Campbell, J. (2008). *The hero with a thousand faces.* Novato, CA: New World Library.

Colle, F., Bonan, I., Leman, M. G., Bradai, N., & Yelnik, A. (2006). Fatigue after stroke. *Annales de Réadaptation et de Médecine Physique, 49*, 361–364.

Davis, H. P., Small, S. A., Stern, Y., Mayeux, R., Feldstein, S. N., & Keller, F. R. (2003). Acquisition, recall, and forgetting of verbal information in long-term memory by young, middle-aged, and elderly individuals. *Cortex, 39*(4), 1063–1091.

Douglas, K. (2002). *My stroke of luck.* New York, NY: Morrow.

Erikson, E. H., & Erikson, J. M. (1998). *The life cycle completed (extended version).* New York, NY: Norton.

Fiori, V., Nitsche, M., Iasevoli, L., Cucuzza, G., Caltagirone, C., & Marangolo, P. (2017). Differential effects of bihemispheric and unihemispheric transcranial direct current stimulation in young and elderly adults in verbal learning. *Behavioural Brain Research, 321*, 170–175.

Glader, E.-L., Stegmayr, B., & Asplund, K. (2002). Poststroke fatigue. *Stroke, 33*(5), 1327–1333.

Goldstein, F., Levin, H., Presley, R., Searcy, J., Colohan, A., Eisenberg, H., . . . Bertolino-Kusnerik, L. (1994). Neurobehavioural consequences of closed head injury in older adults. *Journal of Neurology, Neurosurgery, and Psychiatry, 57*(8), 961–966.

Goldstein, F. C., Levin, H. S., Goldman, W. P., Clark, A. N., & Altonen, T. K. (2001). Cognitive and neurobehavioral functioning after mild versus moderate traumatic brain injury in older adults. *Journal of the International Neuropsychological Society, 7*(3), 373–383.

Green, R. E., Colella, B., Christensen, B., Johns, K., Frasca, D., Bayley, M., & Monette, G. (2008). Examining moderators of cognitive recovery trajectories after moderate to severe traumatic brain injury. *Archives of Physical Medicine and Rehabilitation, 89*(12), S16–S24.

Grivas, A., Schramm, J., Kral, T., Von Lehe, M., Helmstaedter, C., Elger, C. E., & Clusmann, H. (2006). Surgical treatment for refractory temporal lobe epilepsy in the elderly: Seizure outcome and neuropsychological sequels compared with a younger cohort. *Epilepsia, 47*(8), 1364–1372.

Howard, G., & Howard, V. J. (2004). Distribution of stroke: Heterogeneity of stroke by age, race, and sex. In J. P. Mohr, D. Choi, J. Grotta, B. Weir, & P. Wolf (Eds.), *Stroke: Pathophysiology, diagnosis, and management* (4th ed., pp. 3–12). Philadelphia, PA: Churchill Livingstone.

Howard, V. J., & Howard, G. (2011). Distribution of stroke: Heterogeneity by age, race, and sex. In J. P. Mohr, P. A. Wolf, J. C. Grotta, A. M. Moskowitz, M. C. Mayberg, & R. von Kummer (Eds.), *Stroke* (5th ed., pp. 189–197). Philadelphia, PA: Elsevier.

Hukkelhoven, C. W., Steyerberg, E. W., Rampen, A. J., Farace, E., Habbema, J. D. F., Marshall, L. F., . . . Maas, A. I. (2003). Patient age and outcome following severe traumatic brain injury: An analysis of 5600 patients. *Journal of Neurosurgery, 99*(4), 666–673.

Johnson, R. (Writer). (2017). *Star wars: The last jedi* (J. J. Abrams, Producer). San Francisco, CA: Lucasfilm.

Juengst, S. B., Adams, L. M., Bogner, J. A., Arenth, P. M., O'Neil-Pirozzi, T. M., Dreer, L. E., . . . Dijkers, M. P. (2015). Trajectories of life satisfaction after traumatic brain injury: Influence of life roles, age, cognitive disability, and depressive symptoms. *Rehabilitation Psychology, 60*(4), 353.

Kubin, M., Wagner, G., & Fugl-Meyer, A. R. (2003). Epidemiology of erectile dysfunction. *International Journal of Impotence Research, 15*(1), 63–71.

Meier, T. B., Naing, L., Thomas, L. E., Nair, V. A., Hillis, A. E., & Prabhakaran, V. (2011). Validating age-related functional imaging changes in verbal working memory with acute stroke. *Behavioural Neurology, 24*(3), 187–199.

National Council on Aging. (2017). *Economic security for seniors facts.* Retrieved from https://www.ncoa.org/news/resources-for-reporters/get-the-facts/economic-security-facts

Ohayon, M. M., Carskadon, M. A., Guilleminault, C., & Vitiello, M. V. (2004). Meta-analysis of quantitative sleep parameters from childhood to old age in healthy individuals: Developing normative sleep values across the human lifespan. *Sleep, 27*(7), 1255–1274.

Orman, J. A. L., Kraus, J. F., Zaloshnja, E., & Miller, T. (2011). Epidemiology. In J. M. Silver, T. W. McAllister, & S. C. Yudofsky (Eds.), *Textbook of traumatic brain injury* (2nd ed., pp. 3–22). Washington, DC: American Psychiatric Publishing.

Perry, T. E., Ruggiano, N., Shtompel, N., & Hassevoort, L. (2015). Applying Erikson's wisdom to self-management practices of older adults: Findings from two field studies. *Research on Aging, 37*(3), 253–274.

Pollak, R. (1998). *The creation of Doctor B: A biography of Bruno Bettelheim.* New York, NY: Simon & Schuster.

Prigatano, G. P. (Ed.). (1986). *Neuropsychological rehabilitation after brain injury.* Baltimore, MD: Johns Hopkins University Press.

Prigatano, G. P., & Salas, C. (2017). Psychodynamic psychotherapy after severe traumatic brain injury. In R. Wood, T. McMillan, & A. Worthington (Eds.), *Neurobehavioral disability and social handicap following traumatic brain injury* (pp. 188–201). Philadelphia, PA: Taylor & Francis.

Querfurth, H., & LaFerla, F. (2010). Alzheimer's disease. *New England Journal of Medicine, 362*, 329–344.

Rabinowitz, A. R., Hart, T., Whyte, J., & Kim, J. (2018). Neuropsychological recovery trajectories in moderate to severe traumatic brain injury: Influence of patient characteristics and diffuse axonal injury. *Journal of the International Neuropsychological Society, 24*(3), 237–246.

Raz, N., Rodrigue, K. M., & Haacke, E. (2007). Brain aging and its modifiers. *Annals of the New York Academy of Sciences, 1097*(1), 84–93.

Rothweiler, B., Temkin, N. R., & Dikmen, S. S. (1998). Aging effect on psychosocial outcome in traumatic brain injury. *Archives of Physical Medicine and Rehabilitation, 79*(8), 881–887.

Rowe, J. W., & Kahn, R. L. (1997). Successful aging. *The Gerontologist, 37*(4), 433–440.

Salive, M. E. (2013). Multimorbidity in older adults. *Epidemiologic Reviews, 35*(1), 75–83.

Schoenberg, M. R., Dawson, K. A., Duff, K., Patton, D., Scott, J. G., & Adams, R. L. (2006). Test performance and classification statistics for the Rey Auditory Verbal Learning Test in selected clinical samples. *Archives of Clinical Neuropsychology, 21*(7), 693–703.

Seeley, W. W., Crawford, R. K., Zhou, J., Miller, B. L., & Greicius, M. D. (2009). Neurodegenerative diseases target large-scale human brain networks. *Neuron, 62*(1), 42–52.

Senathi-Raja, D., Ponsford, J., & Schönberger, M. (2010). Impact of age on long-term cognitive function after traumatic brain injury. *Neuropsychology, 24*(3), 336.

Siegel, J. S., Ramsey, L. E., Snyder, A. Z., Metcalf, N. V., Chacko, R. V., Weinberger, K., . . . Corbetta, M. (2016). Disruptions of network connectivity predict impairment in multiple behavioral domains after stroke. *Proceedings of the National Academy of Sciences of the USA, 113*(30), E4367–E4376.

Staub, F., & Bogousslavsky, J. (2001). Fatigue after stroke: A major but neglected issue. *Cerebrovascular Diseases, 12*(2), 75–81.

Stephens, S., Kenny, R., Rowan, E., Allan, L., Kalaria, R., Bradbury, M., & Ballard, C. (2004). Neuropsychological characteristics of mild vascular cognitive impairment and dementia after stroke. *International Journal of Geriatric Psychiatry, 19*(11), 1053–1057.

Testa, J. A., Malec, J. F., Moessner, A. M., & Brown, A. W. (2005). Outcome after traumatic brain injury: Effects of aging on recovery. *Archives of Physical Medicine and Rehabilitation, 86*(9), 1815–1823.

Van Zandvoort, M., Kappelle, L., Algra, A., & De Haan, E. (1998). Decreased capacity for mental effort after single supratentorial lacunar infarct may affect performance in everyday life. *Journal of Neurology, Neurosurgery, and Psychiatry, 65*(5), 697–702.

Wang, W.-C., Daselaar, S. M., & Cabeza, R. (2017). Episodic memory decline and healthy aging. In J. H. Byrne (Ed.), *Learning and memory: A comprehensive reference* (2nd ed., pp. 475–497). New York, NY: Elsevier.

Westlye, L. T., Walhovd, K. B., Dale, A. M., Bjørnerud, A., Due-Tønnessen, P., Engvig, A., . . . Fjell, A. M. (2009). Life-span changes of the human brain white matter: Diffusion tensor imaging (DTI) and volumetry. *Cerebral Cortex, 20*(9), 2055–2068.

9

DISTURBANCES OF SELF-AWARENESS RELATED TO BRAIN DYSFUNCTION VERSUS PSYCHOLOGICAL DISTRESS

A PHENOMENOLOGICAL APPROACH

INTRODUCTION

The higher integrative brain functions (HIBFs) develop and decline throughout the life span in a fairly predictable manner, as previous chapters have illustrated. One of the emergent HIBFs is the development of consciousness. How this actually occurs, however, remains poorly understood (see Chapter 5, this volume). Any injury to the brain that adversely affects the HIBFs has the potential to negatively influence consciousness, including a person's self-awareness of altered neuropsychological and at times neurological functioning. As noted in Chapter 7, impaired self-awareness (ISA) following severe traumatic brain injury (TBI) does not appear to represent a purely cognitive dysfunction. ISA appears to represent a basic disruption in the capacity of the brain to integrate feelings and thoughts about one's functional status (Prigatano, 1991, 1999, 2014). Certainly, neuroimaging studies that attempt to correlate ISA in TBI patients with brain activation patterns have reported findings that implicate cortical and limbic involvement (see Chapter 7, this volume). If this is the case, close attention to patients' subjective experiences may provide important clues for separating disturbances in ISA secondary to a brain disorder from the phenomenon of denial observed in everyday life and in patients experiencing considerable psychological distress. This chapter argues that ISA and denial are indeed separate clinical phenomena. Patients' subjective experiences help distinguish these two conditions. Neuropsychological test findings and neuroimaging data add confidence to the clinical separation of these conditions. Finally, understanding these two complex phenomena can lead to improved patient care.

HOW IS SELF-AWARENESS ASSESSED?

One can only judge if a person's self-awareness of disturbed functional capacities is compromised by (1) talking to the person to obtain some assessment of his or her verbal explicit awareness (or unawareness) of altered HIBFs or (2) asking the person to complete tasks that yield information about his or her implicit nonverbal awareness of any altered functioning (Orfei, Caltagirone, & Spalletta, 2010; Ramachandran, 1994). The point is that we never measure ISA (or denial) in its severe or subtle forms directly. It is always measured indirectly. It is the phenomenological experience of a person.

In clinical practice, it is not uncommon to encounter patients (children and adults) with a brain disorder whose self-reports about their functioning appear at odds with the clinician's observations about their functioning. In children, it is often assumed that a child's powers of self-observation have not adequately developed to provide objective information regarding his or her functioning. Even in adolescents, a common belief is that the person has not developed adequate insight into the self and others to be objective in self-reports about his or her functioning capabilities. Although some children and adolescents appear to demonstrate a disturbance in self-awareness secondary to a brain disorder (Jacobs, 1993), methods for assessing such disturbances have not been adequately developed. In normally functioning adults, one expects fairly objective reporting of one's basic functional capacities.

Several perplexing questions exist, however, when assessing ISA. Do patients' self-reported experiences differ from the reliable reports of others because patients do not know how to answer the questions about their functioning? That is, do they not have sufficient knowledge to answer the questions or, conversely, do they really not understand what is being asked of them? Are divergent statements a reflection of a patient's tendency to be cautious when describing himself or herself? Is it a natural tendency to minimize one's faults when describing any limitations? Or are people just very poor at objectively describing themselves?

Although all of these factors may influence self-reports of one's functional abilities, clinical observations of patients with brain dysfunction suggest that a brain disorder can indeed substantially influence one's subjective judgments about personal functional abilities (Prigatano & Wolf, 2010). However, patients with a psychiatric disorder (Amador & David, 2004) and those experiencing significant psychological distress (e.g., a situationally based reactive depression) may also demonstrate disturbances in their subjective experience of functional limitations. On the other hand, there may be important differences between the alterations of subjective experiences (i.e., self-awareness) in persons who have a brain disorder versus those experiencing psychological distress. Selected case reports can be used to argue this point.

CASE STUDIES ON ALTERATIONS OF SUBJECTIVE EXPERIENCE SECONDARY TO A BRAIN DISORDER

Sandifer (1946) provided a very detailed and informative description of a person who presented with anosognosia for hemiplegia (AHP). Critchley (1953) quoted verbatim an excerpt from that article because it captures many of the salient behavioral and subjective features of AHP. It is as follows:

Ex: Give me your right hand! (Correct.) Now give me your left! (The patient presented the right again. The right hand was held.)
Give me your left! (Patient looked puzzled and did not move.)
Is there anything wrong with your left hand?
Pat: No, doctor.
Ex: Why don't you move it, then? (The left hand was held before her eyes.)

Pat: I don't know.
Ex: Is this your hand?
Pat: Not mine, doctor.
Ex: Whose hand is it, then?
Pat: I suppose it's yours, doctor.
Ex: No, it's not; look at it carefully.
Pat: It is not mine, doctor.
Ex: Look at it—it is your hand.
Pat: Oh, no, doctor.
Ex: Where is your left hand then?
Pat: Somewhere here, I think. (Making groping movements near her left shoulder.) (pp. 245–246)

The patient also denied that her left leg belonged to her or that it was paralyzed. The left arm was examined twice more, each time with similar results. At the third test, the patient was temporarily convinced that her left arm was hers, but when examined a few hours later, she had already forgotten, as evidenced by a similar conversation:

Ex: Is this your hand?
Pat: Not mine, doctor.
Ex: Yes, it is, look at that ring; whose is it?
Pat: That's my ring; you've got my ring, doctor.
Ex: No, I haven't. It's your hand. Look how different it is from mine.
(Patient, bewildered, felt her left shoulder, her left upper arm and followed downward to the wrist.) Then she said, It must be my hand.
Ex: And do you still say there is nothing wrong with it?
Pat: It seems I am wrong. (pp. 245–246)

The dialogue and description of the patient's different reactions are informative. First, the patient appears puzzled or perplexed with the request to present the examiner with her left (paralyzed) hand. Second, the patient explicitly denies that there is anything wrong with her left hand. The patient can become momentarily convinced that the paralyzed hand is hers, but she often seems bewildered when making this verbal acknowledgment. She frequently reverts to her belief that there is nothing wrong with her left hand. She cautiously admits (without much conviction) that maybe her hand has been affected. This is only after being interrogated by the medical examiner. There is no oppositional tone in her responses. In Sandifer's (1946) report, he also notes the patient was compliant with her doctor's request and did not resist treatment. These characteristics are hallmark features described in other patients with AHP (Prigatano, Matthes, Hill, Wolf, & Heiserman, 2011).

William German, an experienced neurosurgeon, describes an alteration in his subjective experiences (i.e., self-awareness) following the onset of a subdural hematoma after riding on a rollercoaster at Disneyland (German, Flanigan, & Davey, 1966). In his report, he begins by noting that while on the ride, there was

a certain hairpin curve in which the angular acceleration reaches a very considerable number of radians per second. About two-thirds of the way through the left curve the patient [referring to himself] felt a dull thud which seemed to be inside the right frontal cranium. An immediate response was the thought "Wouldn't it be silly if I got a subdural hematoma from this?" (p. 344)

In his further written descriptions about himself, German states the following:

As he approached the end of the 5th week (after his rollercoaster ride) there was evident inattention to the right side; leaving a slipper on the right foot when getting into bed; neglecting to bring the right foot into bed; even an impression that the right side of the car took up too much room on the road and needed particular care in steering. (p. 345)

Note that German did not seem to be alarmed by these experiences (even though he was a neurosurgeon) and tended to accept these altered abilities without directly connecting them to his initial conscious concern that he may have suffered a subdural hematoma. His affect was calm; his subjective experiences reflect awareness of changes in functioning, but he did not connect them to a possible brain disorder, even though it is likely that he had observed many patients with such symptoms in the course of his practice. Later, in his self-descriptions, he reports being "surprised" by his inability to find a desired word in conversation secondary to his slowly developing aphasia of which he was not consciously aware. This led him to seek further treatment/consultation for his evolving condition.

In another case report, Bryan Kolb (1990), a well-known experimental neuropsychologist and neuroscientist, reports on his experiences after a right occipital stroke:

> I arose early on the morning of Jan. 8, 1986 in order to prepare a lecture. Upon rising, I walked to the kitchen in the dark and turned the lights on. My first reaction was that the lighting was rather dim and that one of the kitchen lights must have burned out. I proceeded to open a can of cat food, and in doing so, I was startled to discover that I could not see my left hand. My initial assumption was that I must have had a retinal detachment. When I tested my visual fields independently, however, using a kitchen knife that I brought across the visual field from the left, I was shaken to discover that the field defect was binocular, indicating that the disorder was central and involved most of the left visual field. (p. 133)

Again, a perceptual difficulty was recognized, but the initial reaction was to attribute it to an outward physical cause (i.e., the light burned out). Then there was the self-discovery of a visual field deficit and with that discovery a *normal* fear reaction (i.e., "I was shaken to discover"). The fear response was not overwhelming and led this competent man to take further necessary steps to get proper medical attention. Later in his self-report, Kolb eloquently describes the "emotional effects" of his recognizing the potential impact of disturbed neurological functioning several weeks after the stroke. He states,

> Once it became clear that I could not simply return to my previous life I did suffer periods of depression, which were characterized by considerable lability of affect. I could be happy one moment and in tears the next—for no apparent reason. While the affective experiences were clearly related to the stroke, they did not appear to be any different than one normally experiences with other traumatic experiences. On one occasion about 4 weeks after the stroke, I had a "panic attack" as I attempted to go shopping for groceries in a large supermarket. The store was crowded, and I was having a great difficulty in reading the labels on items. I simply bolted from the store, leaving my basket in the aisle. Having never experienced such an event before, I was quite shaken by it. (p. 136)

What Kolb (1990) describes appears to be a normal reactionary depression with features of a catastrophic reaction, as initially described by Goldstein (1942). Note that there is no "defensiveness" over what he experiences, even though external factors are originally invoked to explain his altered subjective experiences (just like William German stated that the car took up too much room on the road).

In each of the three case studies, the patient who had a disturbed sense of self-awareness of functional capacities following a brain disorder was initially unaware that anything was wrong with him or her. When the changes were initially brought to the person's attention, the reaction was perplexed, bewildered, indifferent, or neutral. Upon discovering the impairments, some of these individuals reported anxiety and depression, but not to the point at which they resisted treatment. None refused to "admit to difficulties." The technical psychiatric term *denial* (as a method of warding off or reducing anxiety or some threatening feeling) would not seem to apply to these individuals.

Yet there are patients with unequivocal brain disorders whose clinical picture is more complicated. This is especially true for persons who suffer severe TBI. During their acute and post-acute neurorehabilitation, some of these patients significantly underreport their residual neurocognitive and behavioral difficulties. Some patients appear "indifferent" or "surprised" when given feedback about their abnormal neuropsychological functioning. Others appear more "defensive" and argumentative when given such feedback (Prigatano & Klonoff, 1997). Are these latter reactions a reflection of denial of their clinical condition as a method of psychologically coping with their anxiety and cognitive confusion? The early work of Weinstein and Kahn (1955) and, later, Ramachandran (1994) suggests that this could be the case for some patients.

Given Edwin A. Weinstein's astute clinical observations regarding denial phenomena in persons with and without a brain disorder, it is helpful to consider what he had to say about denial phenomena in neurological patients. The following are lengthy quotations, but they are important for this chapter. Weinstein explains the origin of his observations and opinions about denial syndromes in neurological patients (Prigatano & Weinstein, 1996):

> I became interested in the denial syndromes when I was a resident at The Mount Sinai Hospital in New York. As a medical student I had worked in the laboratory of Professor Stephen W. Ranson on the effects of stimulation and lesions of the hypothalamus and went on to study the mood changes of several patients with pathology in the region of the third ventricle. Like other young American neurologists, I was profoundly influenced by the writings of Hughlings Jackson. I was also trained in psychiatry and was impressed by the views of the interpersonal theorist, Harry Stack Sullivan, and the anthropologist and linguist, Edward Sapir. Sapir's work awakened my interest in language which had previously been confined to aphasia. I was particularly taken with Sapir's idea that language was not only a device for reporting experience but, to a considerable degree, defined experience for its speakers, and that we perceive reality not directly but symbolically. (p. 306)
>
> When Robert Kahn and I began our studies after the war, we were impressed by how many aspects of disability other than left hemiplegia were denied and by the many ways in which denial could be expressed. Also, the degree of denial might vary depending on the way the patient was questioned. Patients denied multiple incapacities: A woman might deny not only her left hemiplegia but her urinary incontinence and the fact that she had undergone a craniotomy. Rarely was denial the only abnormality. It was almost invariably associated with one or more of the following: retrograde amnesia, confabulation, environmental and temporal disorientation, reduplicative delusions and misidentifications, nonaphasic misnaming and other changes in language and mood disorders. Because of my interest in language, we interviewed our patients several times a week and recorded the sessions. We questioned patients systematically as many would not offer a confabulation or a reduplicative delusion or a nonaphasic naming error unless specifically asked. The patients were from acute neurological and neurosurgical services and so had a high incidence of brain tumors, head injuries, acute strokes, and ruptured aneurysms of the circle of Willis. Originally, we tried to divide the patients into denial and

nondenial groups and to compare the anatomical localization of their lesions (without the benefit of computer tomography and magnetic resonance imaging). We found, however, that patients who admitted their impairments verbally might deny or represent them symbolically in other ways—in metaphors, delusions, humor, and dramatic gestures. Patients with comparable lesions might have quite different clinical pictures. Thus, one man with a right frontoparietal lesion might explicitly deny a hemiparesis, another might admit some weakness but assign it a trivial cause, and another might joke about it in a ludic fashion, another might have a delusion, another might ignore questions and lie with head and eyes diverted from the affected side. There was also a great diversity of mood disturbances. Some patients were mildly euphoric, others hypomanic, some depressed, and others emotionally indifferent. Such observations made it difficult for us to accept the hypothesis, based on anosognosia for left hemiplegia, of a disruption of the body image localized in the right parietal lobe. (p. 307)

It became apparent that the term anosognosia in its literal meaning of lack of knowledge of disease was inaccurate. Many patients displayed implicit knowledge in that they might deny a disability in one context of language but not another. A hemiplegic patient might admit that his arm did not move but deny that he was paralyzed. Rather than having lost knowledge, the patient seemed to regard the incapacity as outside of the self as evidenced by his references to it in the third syntactical person as an inanimate object or even as another person. (p. 308)

The manner in which patients adapt to and symbolically represent their disabilities after brain injury is determined by a number of factors: (1) the type, severity, rate of onset, location, and extent of the brain pathology, (2) the nature of the disability, (3) the *meaning* of the incapacity as determined by the patient's premorbid experience and values and (4) the milieu in which the behavior is elicited and observed. (pp. 308–309)

Weinstein goes on to conclude,

Denial is not limited to the classical anosognosias of Anton and Babinski, but is a concept that can be extended to include other incapacities and traumatic events. . . . Denial is distinguished from loss of insight, in terms of its association with confabulation, symbolic disorientation, reduplication, and nonaphasic misnaming, and the presence of implicit knowledge. Denial syndromes are adaptive in the sense that they represent and explain the patient's incapacity and impart a *feeling* of reality. Premorbid personality characteristics are important determinants of the *meaning* of the incapacity, type of adaptation, and the content of delusions and confabulations. (p. 321)

A key element of Weinstein's argument that the patient is denying the disabilities versus being "unaware" of the disabilities/impairments is the phenomenon of implicit awareness of the disability. Recent research has been conducted on implicit awareness in patients who present with frank AHP and has relevance to this discussion. It places Weinstein's observations into a more contemporary perspective.

IMPLICIT AWARENESS IN ANOSOGNOSIA FOR HEMIPLEGIA

Fotopoulou, Pernigo, Maeda, Rudd, and Kopelman (2010) have provided experimental evidence that implicit awareness of a deficit associated with AHP can exist for some patients who explicitly and consciously report no motor limitations. These patients tend to have subcortical lesions affecting the insula, inferior motor areas, basal ganglia, and limbic structures. Patients with explicit unawareness and no evidence of implicit knowledge regarding their AHP tend to have larger cortical lesions, often involving frontal and parietal regions of the brain. Patients with large cortical lesions associated with AHP often self-report minimal anxiety or depression, although there are exceptions, as Fotopoulou et al. report.

Implicit knowledge does not necessarily imply that the patient is using a psychological method of coping with anxiety or dysphoric mood associated with a neurological condition. Turnbull, Fotopoulou, and Solms (2014) also suggest an interesting "twist" regarding "anosognosia as motivated unawareness." They specifically state that anosognosia (for hemiplegia) is not "psychogenic" in nature (i.e., motivated by unconscious conflicts that do not reach conscious awareness and thereby are converted into a somatic–motor symptom). Rather, they suggest the interesting hypothesis that AHP represents a neurological condition in which there is "a dynamic shift in the relations between cognitive constraints and developmentally-early (poorly-regulated) emotional tendencies" (p. 24). AHP is not "a purely cognitive deficit *in itself,* but rather a dynamic, emotional by-product of a cognitive deficit" (p. 24). They go on to state that it is a disturbance in the balance between cognitive control and emotional experience and represents a disorder in emotional regulation, not emotional experience per se. They suggest that the problem of emotional regulation is related to the cognitive disturbance in "*spatial* cognition" (p. 26). They hypothesize,

> Patients with right hemisphere lesions are more likely to perceive things egocentrically, as they *want* them to be, rather than allocentrically, as they really *are*, due to damage to the part of the brain that represents the world as it is. (p. 26)

This approach is certainly consistent with the broad perspective suggested previously in this chapter. Human subjective awareness of functional capacities (which are reliably observed by others) represents an intimate integration of "thinking" and "feeling," which is an emergent brain function (as originally suggested by Sperry, 1969; see Chapter 5, this volume). Consequently, ISA after any brain injury represents a disturbance of this integration. Recovery from ISA requires adequate neuropsychological functioning to allow for a partial reintegration of these interconnected functions. It was proposed that the greater the bilateral cerebral dysfunction with associated frontal lobe systems dysfunction, the less likely that ISA will improve, particularly after TBI (see Chapter 7, this volume).

THE MULTIPLE MANIFESTATIONS OF DENIAL

Goldberger (1983) notes that "denial is, and always has been, a fuzzy and complex concept which has acquired many meanings and connotations, depending upon the context in which it has been invoked as an explanation" (p. 85). From a psychodynamic perspective, denial is a defense mechanism (and a defense mechanism is a hypothetical construct). As a defense mechanism, denial is viewed as an automatic psychological reaction to protect an individual from a perceived threat that is in some ways overwhelming to the person. The components of this reaction have been difficult to define and measure. Ferrario et al. (2017) suggest a three-factor model for assessing denial of physical illness. Denial may be reflected in three behavioral markers: (1) a strong tendency to keep negative emotions out of awareness, (2) resistance to change (when such change would improve the health status of the individual), and (3) conscious avoidance of thinking or talking about the illness. These dimensions are appealing because they are often observed in clinical practice.

As Ferrario et al. (2017) and others note, denial is on a continuum. In some instances, it can have an immediate adaptive value, but in other instances prolonged denial can have maladaptive consequences. For example, upon hearing of the unexpected death of a close friend, a person reflexively responded with the word "No!" The initial news was something so unexpected and so unwanted that, without thinking, the person said no, this can't be true. It is briefly keeping a negative emotion out of awareness. A few minutes later, the reaction changed to sadness and loss as the reality that an old friend was killed could be more realistically processed and adjusted to. Maladaptive manifestations of denial can be seen in persons with and without a brain disorder. For example, a 70-year-old woman with a history of depression and anxiety disorder lost her vision secondary to a large pituitary brain tumor that compressed the optic chiasm. After being told by her doctors that she would most likely not regain her vision, she later told others she would regain it. She went on to say that her vision was improving when it was not and could be clearly demonstrated to her. She persisted in these views and often insisted that further rehabilitation was not necessary because she would completely regain her sight. Neuroimaging studies revealed no impairments involving the occipital cortex or surrounding association cerebral cortex. In fact, no lesions to the brain could be identified in any location other than the one involving the pituitary gland, which severely compressed optic nerves at the level of the optic chiasm. Although the patient had mild memory difficulties, she was fully oriented with no evidence of delirium or severe cognitive impairments. She had no language impairments. She fully understood what was said to her, but she denied her visual loss. Any time the topic was brought up, she avoided discussing it. She stated that she did not want to talk about it. She was visibly anxious and upset when the topic was brought to her attention. She repeatedly stated that she wanted to go home and refused any form of rehabilitation offered to her. She refused any follow-up visits to monitor her clinical state. She tried to keep negative emotions out of conscious awareness. She was resistant to changing her attitudes and behavior to obtain further help. She consciously and actively avoided any discussion of her clinical condition. This case example is, in part, keeping with Weinstein's observations (Prigatano & Weinstein, 1996). Premorbid personality characteristics (which reflect methods of psychological coping) may contribute to the persistent denial of severe functional limitations caused by a medical illness.

Denial of acute medical illness, however, can also be observed in patients without a brain disorder. Not infrequently, these individuals have a history of psychiatric illness. Such was the case of a 24-year-old woman who denied she had suffered any injuries following a car–bicycle accident. When seen at a Level 1 trauma center, she had a T7 burst fracture, a left intra-articular distal humerus fracture, and a retroperitoneal hematoma. She appeared to be in considerable pain but insisted, "There's nothing wrong with me. The only problem is I have to use the bathroom. Help me up" (Andrews, McKnight, Caplan, & Prigatano, Manuscript in preparation). Like the preceding patient, attempts to talk with this patient about her injuries and need for medical/surgical care were met with responses ranging from impatience to openly hostile remarks. She would shout at the consulting psychiatrist to leave the room when he attempted to talk about her injuries and the need to consent for surgical treatment. When looking at the deformity of her left arm, she simply reiterated that the deformity was of no consequence. She repeated that she was "fine." There were no obvious cognitive impairments, but a full mental status examination was not conducted. The patient eventually became less hostile when her injuries were discussed and passively agreed to surgical treatments. During this time, her affect was described as "inappropriately bright." During her rehabilitation therapies, she would often make the comment that "deep down I don't think there's anything wrong with me."

History obtained from a family member of the patient indicated that she was a person who always wanted to avoid problems and "didn't talk about controversial topics." Approximately a year after her daughter was born, she developed manic episodes that reached psychotic proportions. She was eventually stabilized on lithium, but she discontinued taking her medications because she believed she did not need them (a common finding in some psychotic patients; Amador & David, 2004). This patient's behavior is a classic example of the three common features of patients who deny physical illness: a strong (premorbid) tendency to keep negative emotions out of awareness, resistance to change when such change would clearly benefit their health status, and conscious avoidance of thinking or talking about the illness. This conscious avoidance is usually associated with clear signs of anxiety (as illustrated in the 70-year-old patient with a pituitary tumor and loss of vision) or angry, hostile remarks, which have the effect of stopping further questions voiced about the illness (as reflected in this patient's behavior). Clearly, the behavioral manifestations of denial of illness and the subjective experience of patients who are significantly denying medical illnesses appear different from what is observed in frank anosognosia or impaired self-awareness after a brain disorder.

It is also important to note that denial, as an apparent method of psychological coping with a disturbing reality, can exist for a medical disability (or illness) and for an intact neurological or psychological ability. Again, the manifestations can be dramatic or subtle. One example is that of a 21-year-old man who developed progressive and disabling neck and truncal dystonia that impaired his ability to walk. Interestingly, he could run better than he could walk. Medical evaluation concluded that he presented with a psychogenic movement disorder. The condition developed at a time when he had to abandon a church activity that was most important to him and his family. An underlying conflict appeared to trigger this event. Initially, he self-reported only "mild to moderate" anxiety and no depression. He often appeared generally happy and "upbeat." In fact, he was recognized and admired by others for his very positive attitude and concern for helping others. His dreams, and later psychotherapy sessions, revealed another story. In two consecutive sessions during the early phase of his psychotherapy, he described intensely fearful dreams. In both dreams, he was faced with situations in which he was trying to escape and become "invisible." Initially, he saw no connection between the frightening situations in his dreams and his present disability. With time, he recognized the "possibility" of the connection. His disability helped him escape a highly conflictual and anxiety-provoking situation in his life. He was not immediately aware of the connection, but with time and several discussions of his feelings and life circumstances, the connection became more probable for him. During this time, his ability to walk somewhat improved.

Less dramatic manifestations of altered subjective awareness of ability can be seen in other clinical situations. For example, there are individuals who believe their memory functions have substantially declined when in fact they have not. These individuals are often referred for a neuropsychological examination. When asked to make subjective ratings regarding their cognitive and affective functioning, it is not uncommon for these patients to report greater cognitive difficulties in themselves than what their relatives report regarding them (Denney & Prigatano, 2019). Their significant others also commonly describe them as having more anxiety and depression than what they subjectively report or experience (Denney & Prigatano, 2019). Treatment of their anxiety (or depression) often results in reduced reports of memory impairment and improved self-reports of functioning in their everyday life (see Chapter 24, this volume). There is a large literature that demonstrates that patients who consistently underestimate their cognitive abilities (perhaps a form of denial of ability) tend to have high levels of anxiety and depression (Prigatano & Hill, 2018). This can occur in patients with neurological conditions such as multiple sclerosis (Middleton, Denney, Lynch, & Parmenter, 2006) and epilepsy (Fargo et al., 2004), as well as in those with non-neurological conditions such as psychogenic seizures (Prigatano & Kirlin, 2009).

CLINICAL FEATURES ASSOCIATED WITH ALTERATIONS IN SELF-AWARENESS SECONDARY TO A BRAIN DISORDER VERSUS PSYCHOLOGICAL DISTRESS

Identifying clinical features that may separate or distinguish alterations in self-awareness secondary to a brain disorder from alterations secondary to psychological distress begins with a definition of terms. In an attempt to do so, several definitions are suggested. *Anosognosia* is defined as a complete lack of awareness (or subjective experience) of an impaired neurological or neuropsychological function directly attributed to a brain lesion(s), but in a very precise way, as will soon be defined. Classic examples of anosognosia are AHP, anosognosia for complete visual loss secondary to damage of the visual association cortex (Anton's syndrome), and anosognosia for certain forms of language impairments secondary to damage to the left superior temporal lobe (e.g., jargon aphasia). Anton (1898) provided the defining characteristics/features of anosognosia (translation of his paper by Förstl, Owen, & David, 1993).

The brain lesions underlying anosognosia occur in a brain region (i.e., cortical) known to be important for that function that is not perceived to be impaired. In some instances, such as Anton's syndrome, this often involves bilateral lesions of the brain that are "almost symmetrical" (Prigatano & Wolf, 2010, p. 456). Furthermore, when patients are provided with reasonable information about their neurological condition, they discard or discount any objective evidence that they have lost their functional capacity. Finally, they discard or discount this information even though they appear to have adequate cognitive abilities to understand and evaluate the information presented. Although not a part of Anton's (1898) description of the clinical features and neurological correlates of anosognosia, alterations of patients' affect are often present. Clinically, these patients often appear apathetic or indifferent in their responses. They often have "blunted" affect. Later, Babinski specifically brought attention to this phenomenon when describing anosodiaphoria in patients with AHP (see Heilman & Harciarek, 2010). In Babinski's words, these patients seem "to attach no importance" to their paralysis (as cited in Heilman & Harciarek, 2010, p. 104). Behaviorally, they typically follow their physician's advice, albeit in a passive manner. When questioned about their clinical condition, they do not avoid the discussion but are often perplexed by it. There is a lack of anxiety or hostility when talking to others about their situation.

ISA refers to the clinical condition in which patients have limited (but not a complete loss of) awareness (or subjective experience) of either a neurological dysfunction or a neuropsychological dysfunction (Prigatano, 2014). The most well-studied form of ISA is ISA for memory impairments. However, ISA can exist for any altered neuropsychological function. Again, defining characteristics include lesions in brain regions known to be important for the functional impairment and adequate cognitive ability to evaluate the information presented regarding neurological or neuropsychological limitation. Yet, in light of that information, these patients disregard, discount, or are "neutral" in their affective responses to the objective evidence. They often follow the advice of their physicians but do so in a passive manner. They do not avoid a discussion of their clinical condition.

Psychological denial of a disability/medical illness presents in a different manner. Patients report no impairment or restriction in their functional abilities. Yet objective evidence exists to document the disability or/medical illness. Patients have adequate cognitive abilities to evaluate objective information regarding their functional limitations, but they disregard or discount the evidence of their functional limitations. Not uncommonly, they are insistent that the feedback given to them by their treating clinicians is "wrong." They are not perplexed, bewildered, or neutral in their responses. They clearly want to avoid discussing their limitations and present with a "defensiveness" that discourages the examiner or clinician from asking too many questions about their condition. The expression of negative affect by these patients is clear, often involving anxiety or anger. If a brain lesion is present, it is not in a cortical area known to be important for the functional incapacity that the patients are not recognizing. Table 9.1 summarizes the clinical features that may separate patients who present with ISA of a disability or illness as a result of a specific brain lesion(s) versus those who deny a disability or illness not related to a specific brain lesion but that appears to be related to severe psychological distress.

In the context of this discussion, it is also important to recognize that one can observe denial of intact abilities as well as denial of a disability or impairment. However, psychological denial of an intact ability presents in more varied and complex ways. Although patients may report "some anxiety," they often are not aware of the extent of their emotional distress. They often do not perceive any connection between their emotional state and their symptoms. In classic somatoform disorders, in which this phenomenon is readily observed, patients may appear extremely "positive" or "upbeat" in their interactions with others. When properly treated from a psychological perspective, they are surprised with the degree of anxiety and/or anger they experience about important personal events in their life or interactions with others. In depressed individuals who report significant impairments in cognitive functioning, particularly memory, they may again acknowledge "some depression" or "stress at work." Given that they experience significant cognitive difficulties in day-to-day functioning, they cannot believe emotions could produce such functional limitations. Not uncommonly, these individuals have difficulties with concentration that affects incidental learning. Again, when properly treated, these patients are often surprised to notice a return to normal cognitive functioning when their emotional distress is substantially reduced.

NEUROPSYCHOLOGICAL AND BEHAVIORAL CORRELATES OF ALTERATIONS IN SELF-AWARENESS IN PATIENTS WITH A BRAIN DISORDER

Psychometric evaluation of persons with a history of severe TBI who show significant ISA, as measured by instruments such as the Patient Competency Rating Scale (PCRS; Prigatano, 1986), often demonstrate behavioral signs of executive dysfunction (Sherer & Fleming, 2014, p. 235). Some of these patients show greater right cerebral hemisphere dysfunction as measured by their speed of finger tapping in the left nondominant hand (Prigatano & Altman, 1990). A case report of a patient with multiple sclerosis and ISA for her cognitive deficits showed a similar pattern of findings (Prigatano, Hendin, & Heiserman, 2014). Patients with impaired awareness of motor limitations secondary to Parkinson's disease also show behavioral and neuroimaging findings of right cerebral hemisphere dysfunction (Maier et al., 2016). It is important to note that not all patients with ISA show this pattern, but many do. Recent studies of ISA in patients with aneurysmal subarachnoid hemorrhage (Buunk et al., 2017) and dementia of the Alzheimer's type (Jacus, 2017) have reported a positive correlation between severity of ISA and measures of severity of apathy in these patient groups. These findings are compatible with Babinski's observations about anosodiaphoria. Anxiety is often conspicuously absent in persons with ISA secondary to a brain disorder.

Table 9.1 Clinical Features of Persons with Impaired Self-Awareness Due to a Brain Disorder Versus Psychological Distress

ALTERATIONS OF SELF-AWARENESS AS A DIRECT EFFECT OF A BRAIN DISORDER	ALTERATIONS OF SELF-AWARENESS AS A DIRECT EFFECT OF PSYCHOLOGICAL DISTRESS
1. Brain lesions occur in regions known to be important for that function (e.g., occipital lobe for vision and temporal lobe for hearing) (Anton, 1898; Förstl et al., 1993).	1. If a brain lesion is present, it is not in a region known to be important for that function.
2. The patient has adequate cognitive skills to understand the evidence presented to him or her about the existence of an impaired neurological or neuropsychological function (Anton, 1898).	2. The patient has adequate cognitive skills to understand the evidence presented to him or her about the existence of an impaired neurological or neuropsychological function (Anton, 1898).
3. The patient discards or discounts any objective evidence that he or she has lost his or her functional capacity (Anton, 1898).	3. The patient discards or discounts any objective evidence that he or she has lost his or her functional capacity (Anton, 1898).
4. The patient's emotional reaction to feedback regarding his or her clinical condition is "blunted." The patient shows "diminished concern of illness or disability" (Babinski, 1914 as reported by Heilman & Harciarek, 2010). The patient often appears apathetic.	4. The patient's emotional reaction to feedback regarding his or her clinical condition is not "blunted." The patient typically shows signs of anxiety and/or anger when receiving this feedback. The patient is not apathetic.
5. The patient does not avoid answering the questions the examining clinician poses concerning the illness or disability.	5. The patient actively avoids answering the questions the examining clinician poses concerning the illness or disability.
6. The patient does not appear "defensive" in reactions to feedback regarding the clinical condition. The patient does not behave in a manner that discourages further questions from the clinician.	6. The patient appears "defensive" in reactions to feedback regarding the clinical condition. The patient behaves in a manner that discourages further questions from the clinician.
7. The patient does not resist efforts at treatment. The patient often passively accepts treatment recommendations while showing signs of cognitive confusion or perplexity as to why the treatment is necessary.	7. The patient often actively resists efforts at treatment and often emphatically states it is not needed. With time, the patient may accept treatments, but at the same time the patient states that further treatment (or rehabilitation) is not necessary.

Patients with a history of severe TBI who appear primarily denying their disabilities present in a manner different from those judged to be demonstrating ISA. Although they may initially disavow any cognitive or behavioral impairment and subjectively report no anxiety, they show behavioral signs of avoiding talking about "what is wrong." In a study by Kortte, Wegener, and Chwalisz (2003), avoidance behavior correlated with denial in TBI patients. These investigators reported that TBI patients who appeared to demonstrate defensive denial (as measured by the Denial of Disability Scale; Prigatano & Klonoff, 1997) scored the highest on an avoidance measure. Patients who were described as having primarily ISA (as measured by the Impaired Self-Awareness Scale; Prigatano & Klonoff, 1997) did not show this finding. This finding, however, needs to be replicated.

Belchev et al. (2017) attempted to assess denial in TBI patients who underreported their functional limitations (i.e., showed signs of ISA) compared to TBI patients who overreported their functional limitations (denial of ability). The latter group was viewed as having some disturbance in subjective awareness but not of the type frequently described in the ISA literature. This pattern of overreporting limitations has consistently been observed in patients with depression (as noted previously). Belchev et al. asked a sample of 43 patients with varying degrees of severity of TBI to complete the PCRS (Prigatano, 1986). They also asked the patients' relatives and treating therapists to complete the scale. Using this measure, Belchev et al. attempted to classify TBI patients into three categories: those showing good estimation of their abilities (compared to the perception of others regarding them), those demonstrating overestimation of their abilities, and those underestimating their level of ability. The researchers compared these three groups of patients on measures of initial severity of brain injury, time since injury, and level of performance on several neuropsychological measures. They also administered the Beck Depression Inventory (BDI) and the Thematic Apperception Test, a projective test of personality features. Good estimators (i.e., those assumed to have good self-awareness) generally showed less emotional difficulties compared to the other two subgroups of TBI patients. TBI patients who overestimated their abilities had the lowest mean scores on the BDI. TBI patients who underestimated their abilities had the highest BDI scores. This latter finding has also been reported by other investigators (Smeets, Vink, Ponds, Winkens, & van Heugten, 2017) and suggests that this subgroup of TBI patients are more depressed than the other subgroups of TBI patients. However, both TBI overestimators and TBI underestimators were judged to have higher scores on measures of denial using projective testing. The actual meaning of this latter finding is difficult to interpret.

To date, no study has systematically classified TBI patients as showing primarily ISA (i.e., a tendency to significantly overreport their functional competencies correlated with specific underlying brain lesions) versus those who show primarily denial of disability (DD; i.e., who also overreport their functional competencies presumably to minimize their psychological distress) and compared them on several measures of pre-injury and post-injury functioning. Does the latter group show a greater tendency not to think about or talk about negative thoughts, resistance to change behavior, and conscious avoidance of talking about their impairments? Do they differ on objective and projective measures of anxiety and depression? They also need to be compared on measures of TBI severity, location of brain lesions, and level and pattern of neuropsychological functioning. Until studies on this issue are performed, the utility of the concepts of ISA and DD remains in question from a scientific standpoint, but it continues to be useful from a clinical perspective.

Table 9.2 summarizes some of the clinical and behavioral characteristics that I have encountered in patients thought to show ISA

Table 9.2 Clinical Observations of Different Forms of Altered Subjective Awareness of Neuropsychological Functioning

METHOD OF OBSERVATION	"PURE" ISA WITH NO OR MINIMAL DENIAL IN PERSONS WITH A BRAIN DISORDER	DENIAL OF DISABILITY COEXISTING WITH MILD TO MODERATE ISA (PARTICULARLY AFTER SEVERE TBI)	DENIAL OF DISABILITY/ ILLNESS IN PERSONS WITH OR WITHOUT A BRAIN DISORDER	DENIAL OF ABILITY IN DEPRESSED/ANXIOUS PERSONS WITH COGNITIVE COMPLAINTS AND NO BRAIN DISORDER	DENIAL OF ABILITY IN PERSONS WITH "PSYCHOGENIC" MOVEMENT DISORDERS
Subjective experience of cognitive functioning	Patient self-reports minimal, if any, cognitive dysfunction. Relatives and clinicians report significant neuropsychological impairments.	Patient self-reports minimal, if any, cognitive dysfunction. Relatives and clinicians report significant neuropsychological impairments.	Patient self-reports experiencing no impairments or illnesses requiring medical attention.	Patient self-reports high levels of cognitive impairment. Relatives often report fewer cognitive difficulties than reported by the patient.	Patient self-reports no or mild cognitive difficulties (especially in concentration). Relatives often report fewer cognitive difficulties than reported by the patient.
Subjective experience of affect or emotional functioning	Patient self-reports no affective disturbance. Relatives vary in their views, often reporting that the patient is not "bothered" by the condition but they are.	Patient self-reports no affective disturbances. Relatives vary in their views. Patient often believes others are unduly critical.	Patient self-reports no affective disturbances. Relatives vary in their view. The clinician often observes signs of emotional distress.	Patient often self-reports greater affective disturbances (particularly anxiety). Relatives often agree with this view.	Patient self-reports no or mild affective difficulties. Patient is often perceived as positive or "upbeat" when interacting with others.
Performance on neuropsychological examination	Neuropsychological dysfunction clearly documented.	Neuropsychological dysfunction clearly documented.	Neuropsychological functioning is variable.	Normal neuropsychological test performance once the patient feels comfortable with the examining neuropsychologist and neuropsychological tests. If cognitive problems are present, they often are in the areas of attention/working memory versus learning and delay recall.	Neuropsychological functioning is usually normal. If not, problems are mainly in concentration/ attention or working memory.

(continued)

Table 9.2 Continued

METHOD OF OBSERVATION	"PURE" ISA WITH NO OR MINIMAL DENIAL IN PERSONS WITH A BRAIN DISORDER	DENIAL OF DISABILITY COEXISTING WITH MILD TO MODERATE ISA (PARTICULARLY AFTER SEVERE TBI)	DENIAL OF DISABILITY/ILLNESS IN PERSONS WITH OR WITHOUT A BRAIN DISORDER	DENIAL OF ABILITY IN DEPRESSED/ANXIOUS PERSONS WITH COGNITIVE COMPLAINTS AND NO BRAIN DISORDER	DENIAL OF ABILITY IN PERSONS WITH "PSYCHOGENIC" MOVEMENT DISORDERS
Performance on measures of personality or affective functioning	Variable, but a clear "perplexity" in patient's responses to questions about clinical status. There is frequently a "bland" or apathetic quality to patient's emotional reactions.	Variable, but commonly there is some expression of anger or irritation when responding to questions about clinical status.	Variable. History often suggests or documents a psychiatric disorder.	Variable	Abnormal (especially on the MMPI-2).
Dream content	General reduction of dream contents, with the patient reporting less dreaming or inability to remember dreams after the onset of the brain disorder. Little evidence of anxiety if dreams are reported.	General reduction in dream contents, with the patient reporting less dreaming or inability to remember dreams after the onset of the brain disorder. When dream content is reported, anxiety is often present.	Several dreams of anxiety or severe threat, and ineffective efforts at reducing the anxiety and threat in the dreams. This is only revealed if the patient has a trusting relationship with the treating clinician.	Patient often reports disturbed sleep with "nightmares" in the initial clinical interview.	Several dreams of anxiety or severe threat, and ineffective efforts at reducing the anxiety and threat in the dreams. This is often only revealed if the patient has a trusting relationship with the treating clinician.

Avoidance behaviors	Avoidance behaviors are not observed. Patient often will engage in a conversation about the clinical condition, but appear "neutral" in reactions to comments about any impairments.	Agitation and avoidance when empathetically confronted with cognitive and behavioral limitations. History of addictive behaviors or significant interpersonal difficulties prior to the TBI.	Clear avoidance of discussing any impairment or fact associated with an illness. Patient is often openly anxious or hostile when such discussions are attempted.	Avoidance behaviors regarding work are often observed. Work is often viewed as very stressful and threatens the person's sense of competency.	Avoidance of presenting historical information regarding the development of the motor systems until a close working relationship with the treating clinician is established. Often, clearly conflictual feelings are produced that are experienced as producing some "confusion" in the patient's mind when later that confusion is recognized as anxiety.
Functional competency in daily behaviors (discrepancy between patient and reliable relatives' reports)	Patient often self-reports as more functional in everyday life compared to relatives' reports. For example, on PCRS the patient's self-reported total score is often 20 points higher than the relative's report on the PCRS-R total score.	Patient often self-reports as more functionally competent in everyday life compared to relatives' reports. For example, on PCRS the patient's self-reported total score is often 20 points higher than the relative's report on the PCRS-R total score.	Variable reporting.	Patient often self-reports as less functional in everyday life compared to relatives' reports. For example, on PCRS the patient's self-reported total score is often 20 points lower than the relative's report on the PCRS-R total score.	Patient often self-reports as less functional in everyday life compared to relatives' reports. For example, the patient's self-reported PCRS total score is at least 20 points lower than the relatives' ratings of the patient on the PCRS-R total score.

ISA, impaired self-awareness; MMPI-2, Minnesota Multiphasic Personality Inventory-2; PCRS, Patient Competency Rating Scale; PCRS-R, Patient Competency Rating Scale–Relatives; TBI, traumatic brain injury.

secondary to a brain disorder versus patients who show denial of disability and denial of ability. Possible methods for assessing these phenomena are also listed. These methods are presented for purely heuristic purposes and require further empirical investigation before confidence in them can be established.

NEUROIMAGING CORRELATES OF ALTERATIONS IN SELF-AWARENESS IN PATIENTS WITH A BRAIN DISORDER

Neuroimaging studies have revealed several interesting findings about the possible correlations between brain functional activity and altered subjective awareness in patients with known brain disorders as well as psychiatric disorders. Only a few studies that have relevance to this chapter are reviewed. A more extensive review of this information can be found in Prigatano (2010) and a special issue of the journal *Cortex* (Volume 61; also see Prigatano, 2014). In an early functional magnetic resonance imaging study (cited in Chapter 7, this volume), Johnson et al. (2002) asked 11 healthy young adults to make subjective introspective judgments about themselves. The researchers then compared the participants' patterns of activation when they made reflective judgments about objective external information. For each participant, self-reflective judgments were associated with activation of the prefrontal cortex and the posterior cingulate gyrus. Using the same research paradigm, Schmitz, Rowley, Kawahara, and Johnson (2006; also cited in Chapter 7, this volume) studied 20 patients with a history of TBI and compared their performance to that of a healthy control group. Although TBI patients showed greater activation in several areas of the brain when engaged in self-reflective thoughts, the degree of ISA measured by the PCRS (Prigatano, 1986) was negatively correlated with activation in the right superior frontal gyrus. The findings suggested that when this region is dysfunctional, greater ISA for complex personal and social behaviors may be observed in this patient group.

Ham et al. (2013) investigated the ability of TBI patients to be aware of monitoring errors when performing an attention task (as noted in Chapter 7, this volume). TBI patients demonstrated a complex pattern of findings relating to frontoparietal activation, the performance of monitoring attentional processes, and level of awareness in detecting monitoring errors. The authors concluded that "impairments of self-awareness after traumatic brain injury result from breakdown of functional interactions between nodes within the fronto-parietal control network" (p. 586). Again, a repeated finding is that ISA of a given neurological or neuropsychological function is often correlated with objective evidence that regions of the brain important in carrying out that function have been compromised.

Understanding the neural correlates of denial and repression is clearly a more demanding task. In an early study, Vuilleumier et al. (2001) demonstrated that patients with hysterical sensorimotor loss showed decreased cerebral blood flow in the thalamus, caudate, and putamen. When the patients were treated with medications and psychotherapy, their symptoms remitted. During the time of remission, there was improved blood flow in those areas. In a study referred to in Chapter 5, Anderson et al. (2004) demonstrated that intentional suppression of unwanted memories in normally functioning individuals resulted in reduced activation in the hippocampus (an area well known for its role in normal memory). At the same time, there was increased activation in the dorsolateral and ventrolateral prefrontal cortex, as well as the anterior cingulate. It appears that when there is a conscious effort to suppress unwanted memories, dorsolateral frontal activation may be important. A hypothesis that deserves to be further tested is whether cortical suppression of subcortical brain activity is a common correlate of denial and repression as a method of psychological coping.

IMPLICATIONS FOR PSYCHOLOGICAL CARE

For patients with ISA and minimal or no denial, a major goal is to foster improved self-awareness, with the ultimate psychological goal of building resiliency in how they manage their neurological and/or neuropsychological impairments. This is often a slow, arduous process. Patients require daily therapeutic activities that help them recognize the presence and extent of their impairments. When a cognitive retraining task stimulates a patient's awareness of a cognitive impairment he or she did not previously recognize, the dialogue with the patient at such times is very important. If the patient can "see" an unrecognized impairment for the first time, a key educational experience is at hand. During such times, the following analogy may help solidify for the patient what is happening: "If the kidney is hurt, it tells the brain; but when the brain is hurt, who does it tell? When the brain is hurt, it does not always know it is hurt." Rehabilitation can help "open the patient's eyes" as to what is wrong and at the same time do so in a manner that can later foster the experience of hope. In knowing what is wrong, the patient can explore with therapists what might be done to compensate for the previously unrecognized problem. Thus, when trust is established and the working alliance fosters hope, the patient is on the way to accepting and acting upon needed restrictions caused by the brain disorder with no or minimal resentment (Goldstein, 1954). Even with the best efforts, however, many TBI patients with significant ISA do not reduce their ISA with intensive neuropsychological rehabilitation (Smeets et al., 2017). These patients (and often their families) require ongoing guidance in light of this severe neuropsychological impairment. If they can be helped to live independently and work in some capacity, social isolation and the development of comorbid psychiatric problems appear to lessen.

In patients with psychological denial of ability or disability, the course of treatment is also slow but more complicated. Patients are encouraged to talk about all aspects of their life, not just how they may have been injured or hurt. Recording dreams and describing favorite stories, movies, and fairy tales can make the dialogue interesting and lively. Attention to how hero figures coped with threats and sources of anxiety becomes a natural point of departure in the psychological dialogue between the patient and the treating clinician. Ultimately, certain avoidance behaviors are mutually observed and become an important area of inquiry. Patients are guided to understand how their anxiety, anger, and depression may underlie avoidance behaviors. Unspoken sources of anxiety now become spoken about and, in so doing, patients can at times feel relief. With this psychological relief, patients with medical or neurological disabilities can talk about their resentments with more clarity. They can be guided to make decisions that are in their best interest. In so doing, many somatic features of anxiety, such as headache, are clinically observed to be reduced. Patients begin to cope more effectively (but not perfectly) with their impairments and anxieties. This scenario of providing psychological care for a person with memory impairment secondary to cerebral anoxia is more fully described in Chapter 13.

When the defenses of denial and repression are significant features of a patient's premorbid personality, the situation is much more difficult, and the prognosis is often worse. One example of this reality is a 30-year-old woman who suffered a severe TBI. She was initially quite unaware of her altered neurological and neuropsychological status during her extensive period of post-traumatic amnesia. Her neuroimaging at the time revealed frontal lobe contusions and a small right basal ganglia hemorrhage secondary to trauma. As she worked in an intensive day treatment program that fostered a neuropsychological-oriented milieu program (Prigatano, 1995, 1999), she slowly verbally acknowledged her cognitive limitations while readily describing her physical limitations. She worked hard both in cognitive rehabilitation activities and in physical therapy, although she preferred only the physical therapy. She would cautiously admit it was difficult for her to talk about her cognitive limitations. When her history of alcohol use and abuse was discussed in her psychotherapy sessions (which were a part of her neuropsychological rehabilitation program), she consistently downplayed the use of alcohol as a problem at all. She would admit enjoying alcohol but stated that her drinking was a natural pleasure and was done purely for relaxation. She reported that her drinking was totally under her control. She actively avoided any discussion regarding the details of her alcohol use or the need to stop drinking.

Toward the end of her rehabilitation program, this patient described her intense fear, as a child, of her mother. Because of this fear, she would not accept any support from her parents after her formal rehabilitation had ended. She returned to very heavy use of alcohol and several years later died of complications due to alcohol abuse. Her denial of her alcohol use was never adequately treated, and her death could be directly attributed to the failure to deal with this psychological problem, which existed both before and after her brain disorder. This patient had many of the neuropsychological features of frontal dysfunction as measured by psychometric tests. Her pattern of neuropsychological test findings, cognitive appraisal of situations, and behavior suggested a true mixture of ISA and DD. Her psychological denial, however, appeared to be the major barrier to helping her.

SUMMARY

Disturbances in a person's subjective experience of neurological and neuropsychological functioning are commonly encountered in clinical practice. This chapter described features of alterations in subjective experiences or self-awareness following a brain disorder. It contrasted these descriptions with what has been reported when the disturbances in self-awareness appear to be related to psychiatric conditions in which the level of psychological distress appears high. Suggestions for providing psychological care to patients with "pure" ISA versus those with mainly denial were outlined; these are expanded upon in later chapters. Finally, clinical features and methods for measuring correlates of ISA and different features of denial were suggested (see Table 9.2). It was briefly argued that the subjectively reported experiences of the person (i.e., the phenomenological state) have diagnostic value in distinguishing alterations in self-awareness secondary to a brain disorder from psychological distress. Further scientific evaluation of these clinical phenomena is clearly needed. Perhaps the most important point of this chapter, however, is to recognize that disorders of subjective awareness are very common in patients who come to the attention of clinical neuropsychologists. Attempting to understand individuals with these disorders is important when developing reasonable approaches to their psychological care.

REFERENCES

Amador, X. F., & David, A. S. (2004). *Insight and psychosis: Awareness of illness in schizophrenia and related disorders* (2nd ed.). New York, NY: Oxford University Press.

Anderson, M. C., Ochsner, K. N., Kuhl, B., Cooper, J., Robertson, E., Gabrieli, S. W., . . . Gabrieli, J. D. (2004). Neural systems underlying the suppression of unwanted memories. *Science, 303*(5655), 232–235.

Andrews, M., McKnight, C., Caplan J., & Prigatano, G. (in preparation). "No, I'm fine": Denial of acute severe orthopedic injuries.

Anton, G. (1898). Ueber Herderkrankungen des Gehirnes, welche von Patienten selbst nicht wahrgenommen warden. *Wiener Klinische Wochenschrift, 11,* 227–229.

Belchev, Z., Levy, N., Berman, I., Levinzon, H., Hoofien, D., & Gilboa, A. (2017). Psychological traits predict impaired awareness of deficits independently of neuropsychological factors in chronic traumatic brain injury. *British Journal of Clinical Psychology, 56*(3), 213–234.

Buunk, A. M., Spikman, J. M., Veenstra, W. S., van Laar, P. J., Metzemaekers, J. D., van Dijk, J. M. C., . . . Groen, R. J. (2017). Social cognition impairments after aneurysmal subarachnoid haemorrhage: Associations with deficits in interpersonal behaviour, apathy, and impaired self-awareness. *Neuropsychologia, 103,* 131–139.

Critchley, M. (1953). *The parietal lobes.* New York, NY: Hafner.

Denney, D., & Prigatano, G. (2019). Subjective ratings of cognitive and emotional functioning in patients with mild cognitive impairment and patients with subjective memory complaints but normal cognitive functioning. *Journal of Clinical and Experimental Neuroposychology.* Advanced on line publication// doi.org/10.1080/ 13803395.2019.1588229

Fargo, J. D., Schefft, B. K., Szaflarski, J. P., Dulay, M. F., Testa, S. M., Privitera, M. D., & Yeh, H.-S. (2004). Accuracy of self-reported neuropsychological functioning in individuals with epileptic or psychogenic nonepileptic seizures. *Epilepsy & Behavior, 5*(2), 143–150.

Ferrario, S. R., Giorgi, I., Baiardi, P., Giuntoli, L., Balestroni, G., Cerutti, P., . . . Fornara, R. (2017). Illness denial questionnaire for patients and caregivers. *Neuropsychiatric Disease and Treatment, 13,* 909.

Förstl, H., Owen, A. M., & David, A. S. (1993). Gabriel Anton and "Anton's symptom": On focal diseases of the brain which are not perceived by the patient (1898). *Neuropsychiatry, Neuropsychology, & Behavioral Neurology, 6*(1), 1–8.

Fotopoulou, A., Pernigo, S., Maeda, R., Rudd, A., & Kopelman, M. A. (2010). Implicit awareness in anosognosia for hemiplegia: Unconscious interference without conscious re-representation. *Brain, 133*(12), 3564–3577.

German, W. J., Flanigan, S., & Davey, L. (1966). Remarks on subdural hematoma and aphasia. In S. J. John, W. C. Cotter, S. Flanigan, R. Ojemann, & J. Stoll (Eds.), *Clinical neurosurgery: Proceedings of the Congress of Neurological Surgeons* (Vol. 12, pp. 344–350). Baltimore, MD: Williams & Wilkins.

Goldberger, L. (1983). The concept and mechanisms of denial: A selective overview. In S. Breznitz (Ed.), *The denial of stress* (pp. 83–95). New York, NY: International Universities Press.

Goldstein, K. (1942). *Aftereffects of brain injuries in war: Their evaluation and treatment. The application of psychologic methods in the clinic.* New York, NY: Grune & Stratton.

Goldstein, K. (1954). The concept of transference in treatment of organic and functional nervous disease. *Psychotherapy and Psychosomatics, 2*(3–4), 334–353.

Ham, T. E., Bonnelle, V., Hellyer, P., Jilka, S., Robertson, I. H., Leech, R., & Sharp, D. J. (2013). The neural basis of impaired self-awareness after traumatic brain injury. *Brain, 137*(2), 586–-597.

Heilman, K. M., & Harciarek, M. (2010). Anosognosia and anosodiaphoria of weakness. In G. Prigatano (Ed.), *The study of anosognosia* (pp. 89–112). New York, NY: Oxford University Press.

Jacobs, M. P. (1993). Limited understanding of deficit in children with brain dysfunction. *Neuropsychological Rehabilitation, 3*(4), 341–365.

Jacus, J. P. (2017). Awareness, apathy, and depression in Alzheimer's disease and mild cognitive impairment. *Brain and Behavior, 7*(4), e00661.

Johnson, S. C., Baxter, L. C., Wilder, L. S., Pipe, J. G., Heiserman, J. E., & Prigatano, G. P. (2002). Neural correlates of self-reflection. *Brain, 125*(8), 1808–1814.

Kolb, B. (1990). Recovery from occipital stroke: A self-report and an inquiry into visual processes. *Canadian Journal of Psychology, 44*(2), 130–147.

Kortte, K. B., Wegener, S. T., & Chwalisz, K. (2003). Anosognosia and denial: Their relationship to coping and depression in acquired brain injury. *Rehabilitation Psychology, 48*(3), 131–136.

Maier, F., Williamson, K. L., Tahmasian, M., Rochhausen, L., Ellereit, A. L., Prigatano, G. P., . . . Fink, G. R. (2016). Behavioural and neuroimaging correlates of impaired self-awareness of hypo- and hyperkinesia in Parkinson's disease. *Cortex, 82,* 35–47.

Middleton, L. S., Denney, D. R., Lynch, S. G., & Parmenter, B. (2006). The relationship between perceived and objective cognitive functioning in multiple sclerosis. *Archives of Clinical Neuropsychology, 21*(5), 487–494.

Orfei, M. D., Caltagirone, C., & Spalletta, G. (2010). The behavioral measurement of anosognosia as a multifaceted phenomenon. In G. Prigatano (Ed.), *The study of anosognosia* (pp. 429–452). New York, NY: Oxford University Press.

Prigatano, G. P. (Ed.). (1986). *Neuropsychological rehabilitation after brain injury.* Baltimore, MD: Johns Hopkins University Press.

Prigatano, G. P. (1991). Disturbances of self-awareness of deficit after traumatic brain injury. In G. Prigatano & D. L. Schacter (Eds.), *Awareness of deficit after brain injury: Clinical and theoretical issues* (pp. 111–-126). New York, NY: Oxford University Press.

Prigatano, G. P. (1995). Preparing patients for possible neuropsychological consequences after brain surgery. *BNI Quarterly, 11*(4), 4–8.

Prigatano, G. P. (1999). *Principles of neuropsychological rehabilitation.* New York, NY: Oxford University Press.

Prigatano, G. P. (2010). *The study of anosognosia*. New York, NY: Oxford University Press.

Prigatano, G. P. (2014). Anosognosia and patterns of impaired self-awareness observed in clinical practice. *Cortex, 61*, 81–92.

Prigatano, G. P., & Altman, I. (1990). Impaired awareness of behavioral limitations after traumatic brain injury. *Archives of Physical Medicine and Rehabilitation, 71*(13), 1058–1064.

Prigatano, G. P., Hendin, B. A., & Heiserman, J. E. (2014). Denial or unawareness of cognitive deficit associated with multiple sclerosis? A case report. *Journal of Clinical and Experimental Neuropsychology, 36*(4), 335–341.

Prigatano, G. P., & Hill, S. W. (2018). Cognitive complaints, affect disturbances, and neuropsychological functioning in adults with psychogenic nonepileptic seizures. In W. C. LaFrance, Jr., & S. C. Schacter (Eds.), *Gates & Rowan's non-epileptic seizures* (4th ed., pp. 158–164). Cambridge, UK: Cambridge University Press.

Prigatano, G. P., & Kirlin, K. A. (2009). Self-appraisal and objective assessment of cognitive and affective functioning in persons with epileptic and nonepileptic seizures. *Epilepsy & Behavior, 14*(2), 387–392.

Prigatano, G. P., & Klonoff, P. S. (1997). A clinician's rating scale for evaluating impaired: Self-awareness and denial of disability after brain injury. *The Clinical Neuropsychologist, 12*(1), 56–67.

Prigatano, G. P., Matthes, J., Hill, S. W., Wolf, T. R., & Heiserman, J. E. (2011). Anosognosia for hemiplegia with preserved awareness of complete cortical blindness following intracranial hemorrhage. *Cortex, 47*(10), 1219–1227.

Prigatano, G. P., & Weinstein, E. A. (1996). Edwin A. Weinstein's contributions to neuropsychological rehabilitation. *Neuropsychological Rehabilitation, 6*(4), 305–326.

Prigatano, G. P., & Wolf, T. (2010). Anton's syndrome and unawareness of partial or complete blindness. In G. Prigatano (Ed.), *The study of anosognosia* (pp. 455–467). New York, NY: Oxford University Press.

Ramachandran, V. (1994). Phantom limbs, neglect syndromes, repressed memories, and Freudian psychology. *International Review of Neurobiology, 37*, 291–333.

Sandifer, P. (1946). Anosognosia and disorders of body scheme. *Brain, 69*(2), 122–137.

Schmitz, T. W., Rowley, H. A., Kawahara, T. N., & Johnson, S. C. (2006). Neural correlates of self-evaluative accuracy after traumatic brain injury. *Neuropsychologia, 44*(5), 762–773.

Sherer, M., & Fleming, J. (2014). Impaired self-awareness. In M. Sherer & A. M. Sander (Eds.), *Handbook on the neuropsychology of traumatic brain injury* (pp. 233–255). New York, NY: Springer.

Smeets, S. M., Vink, M., Ponds, R. W., Winkens, I., & van Heugten, C. M. (2017). Changes in impaired self-awareness after acquired brain injury in patients following intensive neuropsychological rehabilitation. *Neuropsychological Rehabilitation, 27*(1), 116–132.

Sperry, R. W. (1969). A modified concept of consciousness. *Psychological Review, 76*(6), 532–536.

Turnbull, O. H., Fotopoulou, A., & Solms, M. (2014). Anosognosia as motivated unawareness: The "defence" hypothesis revisited. *Cortex, 61*, 18–29.

Vuilleumier, P., Chicherio, C., Assal, F., Schwartz, S., Slosman, D., & Landis, T. (2001). Functional neuroanatomical correlates of hysterical sensorimotor loss. *Brain, 124*(6), 1077–1090.

Weinstein, E. A., & Kahn, R. L. (1955). *Denial of illness: Symbolic and physiological aspects*. Springfield, IL: Charles C Thomas.

PART III

ASSESSMENT, EDUCATION, AND TREATMENTS

Core Activities in the Psychological Care of Persons with a Brain Disorder

PARTS I and II of this book laid a foundation for discussing three core activities involved in the psychological care of persons with a brain disorder. Given a basic understanding of human nature and the normal patterns and levels of various neuropsychological functioning that occur over the life span, the psychological clinician is prepared to talk with patients in a manner that helps reveal their particular struggles. An appreciation of how focal and diffuse injuries to the brain negatively affect neuropsychological and psychosocial activities further helps the clinician inquire about predictable neuropsychological disturbances the patient may or may not be experiencing. Objective assessment of the patient's neuropsychological functioning, via examination procedures, helps further clarify the patient's actual neuropsychological status.

This forms the first activity that can substantially contribute to the patient's psychological care. It is the provision of a medically necessary and clinically relevant neuropsychological consultation/examination.

The second activity is closely related to the first activity. It is the provision of information to the patient and family that goes beyond assessment and includes ongoing educational consultations. Most patients and family members do not fully understand the neuropsychological impairments associated with various brain disorders and what to expect in the future. Thus, they frequently require ongoing consultations to help educate them and guide them to avoid unnecessary frustrations and poor decision-making. Although this clinical service is required in various situations, the consultation services that can be provided to patients who undergo successful neurosurgery are considered in Part III.

The third activity is the actual provision of psychological treatments or interventions to reduce patients' psychological suffering and aid in their recovery and adaptation to the effects of their brain disorder. It requires a good understanding of human nature and the factors that foster resiliency to deal with life's struggles. A review of several of these activities is provided in Chapter 12.

10

A MEDICALLY NECESSARY AND PERSONALLY RELEVANT NEUROPSYCHOLOGICAL CONSULTATION AND EXAMINATION

INTRODUCTION

A medically necessary neuropsychological examination addresses the basic question of whether the patient's higher integrative brain functions (HIBFs) are within the normal range given the patient's age, educational level, occupational history, cultural background, and history of psychosocial functioning. The answer should be a straightforward "yes" or "no," with only an occasional "maybe." In cases of uncertainty, a clear rationale has to be communicated as to why a definitive answer could not be given at the time the patient was seen. It also requires a statement of what additional information would be needed to arrive at an answer to this question (e.g., repeated follow-up examinations to determine consistency of findings or signs of improved or worsening neuropsychological status with time and/or treatment).

If the answer is "yes" (i.e., the neuropsychological examination of the person suggests normal HIBFs) and the patient and family member are not reporting cognitive or affective disturbances, then the consultation provides reassuring information. In those instances, however, in which the patient and/or family member are reporting cognitive, affective, or behavioral difficulties and the neuropsychological examination findings are within the normal range, then some reasonable explanation as to the nature of the patient's subjective complaints has to be addressed. Chapter 24 of this book demonstrates how this might be done when a person complains of memory impairments and when their memory appears to be within the normal range and compatible with their age and educational background.

If the answer is "no" (i.e., the neuropsychological examination findings for a given individual are not considered to be normal and most likely reflect an underlying brain disorder or impairment of some type), then a second question needs to be addressed: Are the neuropsychological examination findings compatible with the patient's neurological/medical history? For example, in a right-handed, middle-aged male with 12 years of formal education who speaks English and was raised in the United States and who is now 6 months post a right middle cerebral artery infarction, are there predictable impairments in visual–spatial memory and visual–spatial problem-solving skills? Are there reduced attentional skills with possible diminished awareness of residual cognitive difficulties? Are there left-handed motor performance difficulties? If the answers to these questions are in the affirmative, then the examination findings are compatible with the known medical history of the patient and so should be stated.

If the findings are compatible with the patient's history, then a third question has to be addressed: What is the extent (i.e., severity level) of the difficulties and what would be reasonable treatment or management recommendations (in light of the patient's overall neuropsychological status and psychosocial situation) to help the patient (and, in some cases, family members)?

There are also instances in which the patient has a history of unequivocal brain disorder but the findings are highly atypical for the disorder documented in the medical records. These cases pose very interesting and, occasionally, challenging diagnostic dilemmas. Two brief examples are given. First, a right-handed adult male with 12 years of formal education and no history of learning disability suffered a small subcortical stroke within the right internal capsule. He reported no significant motor difficulties other than subtle problems of coordination with the left hand, but he reported significant cognitive deficits that precluded him from working. Although he was perfectly conversant in the interview and drove himself to the appointment without difficulty, on formal language testing, he could name only very few objects visually presented to him. He could not repeat three- or four-word sentences, and he complained of a decline in his ability to spell and read. He had difficulties recalling three words with distraction and stated he did not recognize these three words when they were repeated to him after the test was administered. He was bilaterally very slow when asked to rapidly tap his fingers, but he performed other hand–eye coordination tasks without difficulty.

It was the clinical impression of the examiner that the patient wanted to convince the examiner he was severely impaired in order to qualify for medical disability. The examination was stopped, and the examiner talked with him about the unusual nature of the findings. The patient insisted he was putting forth his best effort. It was explained to the patient that the examiner could write a report describing these highly unusual findings or the patient could return the next day and retake many of the tests. The patient appeared somewhat embarrassed but agreed to do so. The next day, he showed no unusual language or memory difficulties and only mild slowness of finger movements in the left hand. Without admitting his apparent attempt to feign impairments, his performance was now within the normal range on language and memory tasks with mild perceptual motor abnormalities. Further physical and occupational therapy was recommended, and with these therapies he improved and returned to work 3 months later.

Unusual examination findings, however, do not always suggest feigning of deficits. An 80-year-old woman had a large glioma removed from her left hippocampus. She and her husband reported no decline in memory after the surgery. The neurosurgeon requested a neuropsychological examination because it was difficult for him to believe that this was case. On examination, this ambidextrous woman had average intellectual abilities, with average verbal and nonverbal memory performance on a variety of memory tasks. Yet, her left hippocampus was totally removed, as noted previously. After the examination was completed and findings were reviewed with them, the patient and her husband indicated that in the past this woman had a clearly "superior" or above average memory. Many examples were given to support this viewpoint. Her average memory scores for her age seemed to reflect a drop from premorbid estimates even though they were within the average range. Average, of course, does not always mean normal for some individuals. Repeat testing revealed a further decline in both verbal and nonverbal memory performance as her malignant brain tumor began to grow following her initial neurosurgery.

Finally, there are instances in which the neuropsychological findings indicate an underlying disturbance in HIBFs but a diagnosis has not yet been established by the patient's physician. In these cases, it is appropriate and necessary to state whether the findings are compatible with a presumed or suspected diagnosis. Again, the rationale has to be clearly explained.

When the answers to the questions listed above are appropriately answered, the findings typically justify that the clinical neuropsychological examination was "medically necessary" (i.e., warranted as an important part of the patient's medical care).

However, the neuropsychological consultation/examination should also be personally relevant to the patient. This is achieved when the examination experience (which includes the clinical interview, neurobehavioral screening, psychometric neuropsychological tests, and at times psychological tests, and a clinically sensitive feedback session) results in the patient and/or family member experience that the examination process was worth it for them. Did they sense that the examining clinical neuropsychologist was interested in helping them? Were the examination findings and the explanations provided by the clinical neuropsychologist truly helpful to them (not just their doctors)? If these questions can be answered in the affirmative, the neuropsychological examination can also be regarding as "personally relevant."

As a result of this experience, the patient and family member now have a better understanding of the patient's personal experiences; the patient's neuropsychological symptoms; and probable causes for cognitive, affective, or behavioral difficulties they experience. They should also have an improved understanding of the next step in the patient's care (Prigatano & Morrone-Strupinsky, 2010).

A medically necessary and personally relevant clinical neuropsychological examination requires a careful record review (medical and psychosocial) in order to prepare for the neuropsychological examination procedures that may be most helpful in revealing the patient's neuropsychological status. It can also provide clues regarding how to best approach the patient and family members when they are greeted and how to initiate the clinical interview. It requires skilled interviewing based on the examiner's knowledge of the expected medical, neuropsychological, and psychosocial consequences of different types of brain disorders occurring over the life span. Although there are areas of functioning inquired about with most adults and children, particular questions are asked given the patient's known or suspected medical (neurological) diagnosis. The interview process requires concise and clinically sensitive questions asked in a sensible manner during the interview. It is the author's experience that this is the most challenging task for beginning clinical neuropsychologists. Although often well trained in administering and interpreting neuropsychological test findings, they are less prepared to conduct a clinical interview that is experienced as helpful by both the patient and family. The same is true when providing clinical feedback. Consequently, these two activities are discussed in more detail later.

The manner in which the patient responds to questions in the clinical interview often provides the first neurobehavioral observations regarding their clinical status. Certain "screening tests" of HIBFs, however, can provide further information about areas of functional difficulties that need to be more thoroughly evaluated via psychometric neuropsychological measures.

Those measures should allow for more detailed information concerning the patient's HIBFs. If possible, they should be selected on the basis of their ability to adequately hold the interest of the patient when attempting to perform the tasks.

New and/or unexpected information may come to light during the interview process and neurobehavioral screening, which is relevant to how the examination may best proceed. Patients may appear confused by certain questions or have difficulties understanding a simple instruction. They may quickly make disparaging comments about themselves or the value of "tests." They may become visibly upset if they cannot perform what seems to be a relatively simple task. Some behave in a manner that makes the administration of standardized test very difficult. If a test cannot be administered in a standardized manner, the apparent reasons should be noted for purposes of interpreting psychometric findings and understanding the patient's phenomenological state. This often requires that the clinical neuropsychologist observes first-hand "what the patient did" when asked to complete neuropsychological tasks they could or would not perform under standardized instructions.

When an adequate sample of the HIBFs has been obtained via psychometric testing of neuropsychological functions, the integrating/interpretation of the findings should take place and these should be relayed to the patient (and, in some instances, family members) in a manner that helps them. The "art" of clinical feedback regarding neuropsychological examination findings often requires synthesizing neuropsychological information in a manner that reflects a reasonable understanding of the patient's conscious and unconscious psychological features. This allows the patient (and often family members) to "hear" what is being said. When this is done in a clinically accurate and sensitive manner, the maximum value of the psychometric testing is experienced by the patient, family members, and clinical neuropsychologist.

MEDICAL AND PSYCHOSOCIAL HISTORIES OBTAINED FROM HEALTH CARE RECORDS

In light of the previous discussions regarding the natural plan of the central nervous system (CNS), human nature, and normal neuropsychological and psychological features of human beings over the life span, what should be reviewed from the health care records before seeing a patient? Box 10.1 outlines several sources of information that should be obtained from the health care records for late adolescents and adults.

The examining clinical neuropsychologist must be alert to many different sources of information prior to seeing the adolescent or adult patient (and possibly their family members). For any given patient, some of the information listed in Box 10.1 may be more important than other information. Much depends on the complexity of the clinical situation and the type of information sought from the neuropsychological evaluation. At a minimum, the record review should focus on the following: (1) Who is this patient? (2) What diagnostic or management questions have been asked? (3) How does one best approach the patient in the interview in light of their medical and psychosocial history? and (4) What neuropsychological tasks/tests should be attempted with the patient to potentially reveal the most important information for understanding this individual and his or her neuropsychological status?

Box 10.2 reviews a modification of the same information that should be obtained from the health records when examining school-age children (i.e., ages 6–14 years). Here, greater emphasis is on understanding the child's neurological and neuropsychological development and the challenges the child faces in light of his or her clinical status. It also requires a clear understanding of what the parents are hoping to learn from the examination and how to assist their child in the future. As is true with an adult patient, there are many areas of information relevant to the

> Box 10.1. Medical and Psychosocial History to Consider When Reviewing Health Care Records for Late Adolescents and Adults
>
> 1. Reason for referral (explicitly stated vs. implied given the referral source) and name of referring physician and physician's area of practice
> 2. Patient-reported symptoms or concerns versus family members' concerns about certain behaviors or symptoms
> 3. Patient name, age, sex, handedness, educational history, marital history, present and past work status, and race and cultural background
> 4. Relevant medical history (that may help explain expected and unexpected examination findings), which includes multiple past and present diagnoses and various medications prescribed versus actually taken
> 5. Relevant development history, including histories of learning disabilities and age at time of onset of the known or suspected brain abnormality
> 6. Neuroimaging findings
> 7. Neurophysiological findings (e.g., electroencephalogram, electrocardiogram, and electromyogram)
> 8. Genetic findings
> 9. Physical findings regarding the patient's present health status that might negatively impact the actual examination process (i.e., height, weight, restricted motor movements, visual deficits, hearing impairments, elevated blood pressure, breathing difficulties, excessive fatigue, headache, sensitivity to noise or sound, etc.)
> 10. Past and present history of smoking, alcohol use, and nonprescribed drug usage
> 11. Family history of medical or psychiatric illnesses (including psychosocial difficulties)
> 12. Cognitive, behavioral, or cultural/psychosocial characteristics of the patient that may impact how the interview and examination procedures should be conducted (English as a second language, limited formal education, different cultural backgrounds between the patient and the examiner, below average intellectual abilities, hostile reaction to being examined, history of paranoid ideation, history of imprisonment or ongoing litigation, etc.)
> 13. Reports in the medical records of any "bad experiences" the patient and family have voiced regarding contact with other health care professionals
>
> *Note:* Missing details should be obtained in a nonthreatening manner during the interview or by obtaining further records.

examination, including an understanding of the cultural background of the child, the child's ability to understand questions and instructions, and the child's overall intellectual level. Their willingness to adequately engage examination procedures has to be constantly monitored. Neuroimaging findings and relevant genetic information are also important when attempting to understand neuropsychological test performance and behavior during the interview.

GREETING THE PATIENT (AND FAMILY MEMBERS) AND THE CLINICAL INTERVIEW

The patient is first greeted by the physical surroundings in which your office is located. The

Box 10.2. Medical and Psychosocial Information To Be Considered When Reviewing Health Care Records of School-Age Children

1. Reason for referral
2. Actual referral source (physician request, parental request via the physician request, school district personnel request, etc.)
3. Present age of the child and grade level
4. Presenting diagnosis; if a clearly documented acquired brain injury (vs. development disorder) occurred, age at injury
5. Medical history regarding pregnancy, birth process, and aftermath
6. Developmental achievements and time frames during the first 5 years of life
7. Present family situation (who lives in the home; parents' marital status; for divorced parents, who has legal custody and how often the child sees the parent not living in the home; occupations and educational level of both parents; age and sex of siblings; etc.)
8. Present educational setting for the child (home school, public school, private school, special education services, speech and language services, occupational therapy services, physical therapy services, etc.)
9. Genetic findings
10. Neuroimaging findings
11. Neurophysiological findings
12. Previous academic history and test findings regarding academic achievement levels obtained at different ages
13. Previous measures of intellectual functioning or past neuropsychological evaluation reports
14. Previous and present medications and degree of adherence to present medications
15. Past and multiple diagnoses of the child
16. Cognitive, behavioral, or cultural characteristics that might influence the interview and examination process (see Box 10.1)
17. Physical characteristics that might influence the interview and examination process (see Box 10.1)
18. Identification of what the parents wish to obtain from the neuropsychological examination of their child

patient is then greeted by the secretarial staff, which acknowledge the patient and obtain registration information, including authorization to provide services. The patient's (and family members') impression of you can also be negatively influenced by difficulties in parking, cluttered or unclean hallways, dirty carpets, scratches on the walls leading to your office, or a loud and noisy environment. Clean, easily accessible environments that have a professional appearance are crucial to establishing the first sense of trust.

The secretarial staff that greet the patient also indicate much about you. Are they friendly but professional in their manner of welcoming the patient and putting the patient at ease? Are they well groomed and dressed in a professional manner? Many patients are not eager to have a neuropsychological examination. It is a highly personal experience that may reveal painful information. Thus, they must be comfortable with the surroundings and ancillary staff before they meet you.

The clinical neuropsychologist is encouraged to take the time and make the effort to greet the patient in the waiting room. Before entering the waiting room, one should know where the patient is seated and who is with the patient. Walking up to the patient in a friendly but professional manner and introducing oneself should be done calmly and with a sense of respect to the patient and family member. When greeting an adult patient, for example, it is a common courtesy to extend one's hand in greeting, followed by saying, for example, "Hello, Mr. [or Mrs.] . . ., I am Dr. [your last name]. It is a pleasure to meet you. Please follow me back to my office. Let me lead the way." Never refer to the person by their first name until given permission to do so by the patient and when you feel comfortable doing so. A certain level of formality can be especially important during problematic interviews.

Always greet the patient first (even if they are a minor). It conveys that you are there to see them and help them first. Then greet the accompanying family members or friends. In the case of children, it is the cultural norm to call them by their first name and extend your hand in greeting. Be careful, however, not to invade children's personal space, which may be overwhelming to them. Again, attend to who you are greeting and make an effort to make them feel comfortable being in your office setting.

Your office also "greets" the patient and their family. How you organize the furniture, the appearance of your desk, the pictures on the wall, and the display of your professional credentials gives the patient (and the family members) a sense of who you are. If it is cramped, cluttered, or in a disorganized state, so might your thinking and manner of preparation. Your office must foster a further sense of professional trust. Directing patients where to sit, at times, actually helps orient them to the beginnings of a safe environment. This has to be done, of course, in a nonthreatening manner. For example, one might say, "Please have a seat in one of the brown chairs against the wall or wherever you are most comfortable."

A few words to put the patient at ease are sometimes valuable. For example, if an adult patient is late for an appointment and the secretary informs you that the patient stated they experienced heavy traffic getting to your office, a comment about how unpredictable the traffic can be may allow for a sharing of common experiences between you and the patient and family members. If the patient is distressed about being late, reassuring them that it is not a problem can be important. In contrast, if they are very late and make no apology for their tardiness, it may say something about their impaired social judgment or a long-standing personality trait that reveals a lack of concern about any inconveniences they may produce for others. What is initially said between you, the patient, and family members sets the tone of the interview. You must try to make that tone as positive as possible and observe the reactions you get from the patient and family members. It can provide important diagnostic information.

The actual clinical interview of an adult or adolescent often begins with the clinical neuropsychologist clarifying their understanding of why the person is being seen. Next, it is often helpful for the clinical neuropsychologist to inquire whether this was the patient's and family member's understanding. For example, one might say,

> Mr. Jones, perhaps I could begin with my understanding of why I am seeing you today. Dr. H. asked me to see you today. He indicates that you have been diagnosed with multiple sclerosis, and recently you have reported a decline in your memory. He asked that I examine you today to better understand the nature of that memory problem and to see if there is anything we can do to further help you. Is that your understanding?

If the patient responds "yes," then one should check on the family member's understanding of the purpose of the examination. Several interesting scenarios can unfold at this time. The patient's wife, for example, may say that memory itself is not the major problem. She may say the patient has had trouble meeting job responsibilities at work and does not seem to take seriously the feedback he is getting from his supervisor. The patient's reaction to his wife's opinion may be crucial in understanding the clinical situation. The patient may say that the problem is in his memory only. He may argue that his supervisor is just "out for him" or that the supervisor is an idiot and he is not concerned about the supervisor's opinions. He knows he does good work. He just needs help improving his memory for "little things" at home or at work. In this scenario, the referral to evaluate "memory complaints" may have justified authorization for the services with the insurance company, but the real problem may be a lack of awareness of declining cognitive functioning.

Again, several scenarios are possible, and the clinician must listen carefully to the patient's perceptions/experiences/convictions as well as to the family member's viewpoint. During this time, the "real" referral question or problem may reveal itself. Sometimes it is straightforward, and sometimes it is not. The clinical examples provided in later chapters of this book highlight some of the different scenarios and how they might be handled to foster psychological care.

Assuming that some basic understanding of why the patient is being seen has been established, the clinical interview can proceed. The clinical interview should provide an opportunity for the patient to describe in more detail what they are experiencing. What the patient chooses to describe, how they describe themselves or their difficulties, and the history they provide concerning those difficulties can be of maximum importance in arriving at a diagnosis and formulating how clinical feedback should proceed. As noted previously, the family member is next given an opportunity to more fully explain or expand on their perceptions. Does the family member appear cautious in what they say? Conversely, are they harsh and blunt? Is their viewpoint presented in a thoughtful and supportive manner? How does the patient respond verbally and nonverbally to the words of the family member?

This initial dialogue between the patient, the clinical neuropsychologist, and the family member will determine how the interview proceeds. The clinical neuropsychologist now has a sense of how to direct questions, when to limit responses, and when to inquire about specific areas of functioning. Certainly, the questions about specific functional abilities are in large part dictated by the patient's known or suspected diagnosis. The questions may well vary depending on whether one is interviewing a 16-year-old disinhibited boy with a history of severe traumatic brain injury (TBI), a 50-year-old man with a malignant brain tumor in the left temporal lobe, or a 73-year-old man with the probable beginnings of dementia of the Alzheimer's type. Yet, there are specific domains of functioning that are worth exploring in a clinical interview, if possible. They are listed in Box 10.3 and are briefly reviewed here.

Begin with nonthreatening topics. It is often helpful to explain to the patient that although you have reviewed their records, it is helpful to you to hear directly from the patient about certain background information. Inquire as to the person's current age, date of birth, handedness, educational background, and work status. Explore the patient's work history to determine the level of past accomplishments and responsibilities. Compare the work history with the level of academic achievement, and estimate the patient's premorbid level of cognitive functioning. Tell the patient (and family member) that you are now going to switch topics.

Inquire as to the patient's sleep patterns. What time do they go to bed and what time do they awaken each morning? Do they have trouble falling asleep or returning back to

> Box 10.3. The Clinical Interview with Adults or Older Adolescents
>
> 1. Begin by explaining your understanding of why the person is being seen by you for a clinical neuropsychological examination.
> 2. Ask the patient and a family member (if present) if they have the same understanding. If there is a difference of opinion, note the difference in opinion(s) but make sure the patient and family member (if present) understand what you will attempt to do. Their permission to proceed is obviously necessary.
> 3. Ask the patient to describe in more detail their view of their functioning and if there are any areas of difficulty they wish to expand upon. Obtain a clear understanding of what the patient seems to be experiencing.
> 4. Obtain a similar description from a family member (if present).
> 5. Inquire about basic demographic information necessary for purposes of checking on reported records and for test selection and interpretation of test findings (e.g., age, date of birth, handedness, sex, educational level, school and/or work history, primary and secondary languages, and living circumstances).
> 6. Inquire about sleep patterns, appetite, vision, hearing, and strength.
> 7. Inquire about medications.
> 8. Inquire about other medical or psychosocial facts relevant to the patient's known or suspected medical diagnosis that would be relevant to the neuropsychological examination. These questions will vary greatly depending on the clinical status of the patient, the patient's ability answer the questions, and the family member's ability to provide supplementary information.
> 9. Ask the patient to make subjective ratings on perceived levels of difficulty in memory, concentration, word finding, irritability, anxiety, depression, fatigue, and problems with directionality in space (see text for details). If a significant other is present, obtain similar ratings regarding their perception of the patient's level of functioning in each of the domains listed here.
> 10. Ask whether there is anything else that the patient (and, later, family member) wishes to bring to the attention of the examiner that was not earlier asked about or discussed.

sleep if they wake up during the night? If they do awaken, roughly how many times a night, and what is the patient's understanding of the causes of multiple awakenings? Are there any diagnosed sleep disorders? Are there any persistent worries or concerns that keep the patient up at night or are on the patient's mind when they awaken? Do they dream when sleeping? Do they have any confusion upon awaking?

Next, inquire about the patient's appetite. Do they experience any difficulties with appetite? Do they eat three meals a day? Do they get hungry? Do they say they just do not feel like eating most of the time, or do they forget to eat? Inquire as to whether there has been any change in how food tastes or smells. Ask if there has been any change in their vision or hearing. Do they notice any lateralized or generalized weakness? Any spontaneous information regarding falls, driving accidents, or needing to turn the television volume up to hear what is being said can also provide important information about the patient's sensory–motor functioning that has implications for their ability to undergo a standard neuropsychological examination.

Ask the patient about their current medications and whether they take them as prescribed. Note the number of medications and the class of medications that may influence cognitive or behavioral functioning. Tell the patient and family member that you are going to switch topics again. Explain to them that you would like to get their perceptions of how much difficulty the patient may be experiencing in a number of areas. Indicate to the person that they may have no difficulty in some areas and some difficulty in other areas. Explain that you will ask the patient to first make ratings on a scale from 0 to 10 to help describe their level of perceived difficulties. You will then get the family member's perceptions. A rating of 0 means no difficulty, and a rating of 10 indicates a severe level of difficulty. Emphasize that if they give different ratings, it does not necessarily mean one is right or one is wrong. If they see it quite differently, you would like to better understand the basis for the different opinions because it may be helpful in better understanding a person's functioning. Different functional dimensions can be evaluated, but the average level of perceived difficulty in day-to-day memory for what a person wants to remember is inquired about first. Next, inquire about ratings concerning the following: concentration difficulties; word finding difficulties; difficulties with irritability, anxiety, depression, and fatigue; and problems with directionality in space (for further details on this rating system and its clinical utility, see Denney & Prigatano, 2019; Prigatano et al., 2014).

After this is done, it may be helpful to explore family history, including whether the patient's parents are still living and, if so, whether the patient continues to communicate with parents and siblings. If there is no communication with living (close) relatives, this may reveal important interpersonal difficulties and, occasionally, a history of physical or sexual abuse. It is also helpful to explore marital history and whether the patient has children. This is a delicate area of inquiry and should be done cautiously. The goal is to obtain some sense of the patient's past and present interpersonal bonding and relationships. In this context, explore if there is a history of neurological or psychiatric disorders in the immediate and extended family. Wait to explore relevant details as a working alliance develops between you and the patient.

Other topics of potential inquiry are also listed in Box 10.3 and can be explored as clinically indicated. However, it is often helpful to conclude the interview with a question regarding whether there was anything else that you (the examiner) had not inquired about that the patient or family member wants to bring to your attention. This gives them an opportunity to provide any concluding comments they wish to make.

After conducting the interview (which normally lasts 30–60 minutes), explain the examination procedures. For example, it may useful to indicate that you will ask the person to carry out a series of tasks, some of which will be very easy to do and others may be very challenging. Note that no one is able to complete all tasks easily. Some tests are made to be difficult, and that provides a "yardstick" for determining a person's relative strengths and weaknesses, which is important for diagnosis and treatment planning. Indicate who will be examining the patient; when the examination will most likely end; and that you will discuss, in a summary fashion, the findings after the examination is completed.

THE CLINICAL NEUROPSYCHOLOGICAL EXAMINATION

One of the major points of this book has been to emphasize that to provide useful clinical neuropsychological services for an individual, we must first have an informed understanding of basic human nature and how brain development over time determines the nature of HIBFs. The impact of the educational/cultural environment on brain development also has to be considered to validly estimate normal neuropsychological functioning for a given individual. Only when this is determined can the question of whether or not the patient's neuropsychological status suggests impairments in functioning indicative of an underlying brain disorder be addressed. In light of this perspective, what are the essential ingredients of a neuropsychological examination, and how should it proceed?

As noted in Chapter 2, the evolution of the human CNS allows us to experience feelings (basic emotions and motivations) that are often associated with visually guided movements that include the capacity to point to, and later grasp and manipulate, objects with our hands. As visual and auditory systems evolve, the infant is able to recognize familiar objects (including people). This is followed by vocalizations that convey feelings and, later, verbalization necessary for effectively communicating with others. This implies the capacity to form intentions and some beginning capacity to learn from "doing" or performing various activities. This further implies that normal brain function allows for the modification of behavior as the social situation requires.

Thus, motor skills, language skills, and learning and memory skills must be assessed in every examination. As it matures, the CNS also allows for the development of "higher order" symbolic representations reflected in such activities as an expanded vocabulary and the capacity to understand mathematical concepts as well as other abstract concepts or principles embedded in various storytelling. This ultimately culminates in having an expanded knowledge base regarding the self and the world that aids surviving and thriving in different complex social environments at different stages of development. Thus, Box 10.4 suggests the HIBFs that should be assessed in a clinical neuropsychological examination in light of the natural plan of the CNS. When these functions are disrupted, a large literature (briefly touched on in Chapters 6–8, this volume) reveals classical signs of neuropsychological impairments that cannot be explained on the basis of age, education, or cultural background.

The actual activities or tasks that comprise the neuropsychological examination may vary depending on the patient's diagnosis, clinical state, and the questions that are being asked of the clinical neuropsychologist. Box 10.5 lists some of the neuropsychological tests and tasks that can provide useful information when examining HIBFs. These and other tests, however, measure multiple functions at a single point in time and therefore do not provide a pure measure of any of these functions.

In light of the previous observations, how should the examination proceed? First, an attempt is made to determine the patient's level of understanding of basic verbal instructions. The second task is to determine the level of cooperation of the patient during the different phases of the examination process. The third task is to provide neuropsychological activities that are age and culturally appropriate. The fourth task is to choose neuropsychological tests that may best reveal important information about the state of the patient's higher integrative brain functions. When possible, these tasks should also have the potential to help localize or at least regionalize underlying regions of the brain that appear compromised. This, in fact, makes them "neuropsychological tests." However, for many patients and family members, the ultimate value of these tests is to help further document and explain how both cognitive and affective functions are compromised and the implication of these changes for adaptive daily functional activities.

Currently, it is fashionable to include "tests of adequate effort" or "validity checks" during standard neuropsychological examinations. The problem with this approach is that these "validity tests" are typically based on normal subjects asked to feign impairments or put forth inadequate effort during psychometric testing. The tests have never been adequately standardized on malingerers involved in litigation or who are unjustly seeking financial benefits by feigning deficits. Knowing what is a normal level and pattern of performance on existing neuropsychological tests

Box 10.4. Higher Integrative Brain Functions Sampled in a Clinical Neuropsychological Examination

1. Auditory (and written if necessary) comprehension of instructions (simple and complex)
2. Visual and tactile recognition of familiar objects (given adequate sensory processing skills)
3. Performance of finger–hand movements necessary for expressing intentions, grasping (drawing and writing if age and culturally appropriate), and exploring the immediate environment for effective problem-solving
4. Inhibitory control of certain motor movements when requested to carry out other motor movements
5. Demonstration of basic associative learning, which may include contradictory actions (e.g., if this, then that; if that, then this)
6. Demonstration of "incidental learning" (remembering important information when not explicitly instructed to do so)
7. Focused and divided attention to presenting stimuli
8. Maintaining a "mental representation" of information necessary for problem-solving (i.e., "working memory")
9. Learning and remembering information upon request—with and without practice for verbal, nonverbal, and tactile information
10. Performance of higher order language skills (fluency, naming, sentence repetition, and auditory comprehension with associated reading, spelling, and calculation skills relative to age and educational experiences)
11. Demonstration of planning skills when asked to solve simple and complex tasks
12. Efficient (i.e., age-appropriate) processing speeds when performing cognitive tasks
13. Perceptual accuracy/understanding when examining relationships between objects (including people) and events that have practical (judgment) and theoretical (abstract reasoning) significance for immediate and later problem-solving
14. Demonstration of adequate expression and perception of emotions
15. Demonstration of spontaneously experienced positive and negative emotions
16. Demonstration of adequate awareness of one's functional state (and environment; i.e., self-awareness)
17. Demonstration of adequate awareness of another person's state of mind (i.e., theory of mind)
18. Demonstration of sustained mental energy/effort when fatigued
19. Demonstration of exploration and seeking new opportunities/environments as well as novel learning situations
20. Demonstration of socially acceptable behaviors during the examination and in everyday activities (in light of the patient's age and educational and cultural background)

Box 10.5. Commonly Employed Psychometric Tests and Questionnaires Used to Assess Higher Integrative Brain (i.e., Neuropsychological) Functions

1. BNI Screen for Higher Cerebral Functions (adult and school-age children versions)
2. Wechsler Intelligence Scales (adult and child versions)
3. Rey Auditory Verbal Learning Test (RAVLT)
4. Brief Visual Memory Test–Revised form (BVMT-R)
5. Immediate and delayed recall of short stories (from the Wechsler Memory Scale–Fourth Edition [WMS-IV] or the Childrens' Memory Scale [CMS])
6. Trail Making Test Parts A and B
7. Halstead Finger Tapping Test
8. Grooved Pegboard Test
9. Word Fluency from Multilingual Aphasia Exam or from the NEPSY-II
10. Tower of London or the Halstead Category Test
11. Tactual Performance Test
12. Calculation and Passage Comprehension subtests of the Woodcock–Johnson III (WJ-III)
13. Patient Competency Rating Scale (PCRS)
14. Patient Competency Rating Scale–Relatives (PCRS-R; for children, the Child Behavioral Checklist)

for persons of different ages, educational/cultural backgrounds, and known medical history provides perhaps the most reasonable method of clinically determining whether reliable and valid assessment of higher brain functions is being obtained.

If the patient is judged by the examiner to show adequate emotional control and a desire (intention) to cooperate, the next step is to ensure that the patient properly understands various testing instructions. Although this can often be assessed in the clinical interview, various screening tests can be used. For example, on the Barrow Neurological Institute Screen for Higher Cerebral Functions (BNIS; Prigatano, Amin, & Rosenstein, 1995), the patient is first asked to carry out a one-step instruction ("Please touch the yellow circle") to ensure basic auditory–verbal comprehension. This is followed by a two-step auditorily presented request: "Please touch the small red circle and the large white square." If the patient can perform these tasks, then testing for other basic functions can proceed, including an assessment of naming, sentence repetition, reading, writing, and spelling skills. These simple functional measures help determine if an underlying aphasic syndrome exists (Kertesz, 1985) and, if so, reveal dimensions of language that need further assessment. Once it is established that the patient's emotional and motivational state is conducive to the examination process and the patient understands basic auditorily presented instructions, various examination procedures can proceed in different ways depending on the patient's clinical condition.

It is helpful to establish whether the person is adequately oriented to time and place. This provides important information about memory functions and incidental learning. It is also a potential marker of the severity of a possible underlying brain disorder, and it aids in the differential diagnosis. Basic assessment of right–left orientation and constructional praxis in both hands follows because these abilities reflect not only the capacity to perform a verbally requested motor response but also the ability to control or inhibit movements when carrying out those responses (Prigatano et al., 1995).

The patient is next asked to perform a simple memory task of recalling three words. Memory capacity is frequently compromised after various brain lesions (Schoenberg et al., 2006). Importantly, the patient is also asked to judge or predict how many of three words they can recall after a 5- to 10-minute delay. Luria (1966) noted that this capacity to realistically judge one's memory performance can reveal important information about self-monitoring. This function is thought to be heavily mediated by frontal lobe systems of the brain as they mature during adolescent and adult stages of life.

Following the previously mentioned basic assessments, it can be helpful to briefly assess basic mathematical skills because they can reflect a limited educational background and/or true dyscalculia.

Visual scanning, visual sequencing of information, and adequate pattern copying are assessed to reveal basic visual–motor skills. This is followed by a pattern recognition task that allows for assessment of the patient's problem-solving skills. All of these activities are assessed by many commonly used neuropsychological measures. Frequently missing, however, are two very important aspects of neuropsychological functioning that are clinically relevant. What will a person naturally do to improve their performance on a more challenging memory task? If allowed, will they write down what they need to learn? Will they practice or rehearse what they need to learn? Conversely, will they impulsively or with inadequate effort begin to perform the task? Normally functioning individuals often take time to rehearse or write down information they want to learn, whereas brain dysfunctional (and some psychiatric) patients do not (Prigatano, Amin, & Jaramillo, 1993). This should be directly assessed to determine how the patient goes about learning or preparing to perform a challenging task. This is observed on the BNIS. In addition, their spontaneous reactions to the task can provide important information. Are they overwhelmed by the task? Do they like the challenge? Do they give up quickly because it seems "too hard"?

Also, the direct assessment of the patient's emotional expression and perceptual skills is typically lacking in neuropsychological assessments. Frankly, this can be a major mistake not only in terms of its evolutional significance but also because such assessments allow for a direct observation of patients' emotionally guided behaviors. No competent neuropsychologist would report a patient has a memory impairment based solely on the patient's answering questions about their memory on a standardized questionnaire. They would want to examine the patient's memory directly. Yet, neuropsychologists commonly report the patient is "mildly or moderately depressed" or anxious based on the patient's responses to standardized questionnaires. I prefer to directly assess emotional functioning, via screening items, in three ways.

First, I ask the person to say the following sentence in a happy tone of voice: "They won the game!" Then, I ask the person to say it in an angry tone. Many depressed patients have difficulty with this simple task. Although some patients with right hemisphere lesions have difficulty with prosody of speech (Ross, 1985), their vocal responses are often monotone or "flat." In contrast, depressed patients raise the pitch of the voice when trying to say the sentence with a happy tone, and no perceptual quality of happiness can be perceived. When asked to say the sentence in an angry tone, some depressed patients may simply respond, "I do not do anger." This probably contributes to their depressed mood because getting angry can be quite emotionally healthy in the right circumstances.

Next, the patient is asked to verbally identify three facial affects. The first two are easily identifiable: They are drawings of an angry and a happy face. The third facial affect is more ambiguous and can be perceived as either fear or surprise. The response to the third face often reveals the emotional, phenomenological state of the person. Some demented patients respond, "confused." Some patients with mild cognitive impairment of the amnestic type respond, "wondering, she is thinking it over. She is undecided." Patients with anxiety disorders who do not self-perceive their own level of anxiety have been noted to describe the third face as "normal, no specific feeling." Depressed patients may say the third face shows sadness or a feeling of giving up. Many patients with a history of significant cognitive difficulties several months post severe TBI have been noted to respond, "She is frustrated." This task highlights the lost art and value of projective measures in the assessment of brain dysfunctional patients (Baker, 1956; Piotrowski & Rock, 1963).

Finally, the clinical neuropsychologist should attempt to evoke an emotional response that is appropriate to the examination process. I have attempted to do this in a standardized way by showing patients a familiar sign/symbol (i.e., the no smoking sign) and asking them to tell me what it means. They are then shown either an unfamiliar sign/symbol that has a specific meaning to a specific age group in the United States (e.g., for those aged 60 years or older, a picture of a lemon with a line through it like the line through the picture of the cigarette) or a simple incongruent stimulus. In both cases, the goal is to produce a smile or laughter. Although it is not always effective, the intent of the item is important. Can the patient show spontaneous affect when the situation normally stimulates such a response? Theoretically, this is an important evolutionary based higher brain function (Darwin, 1859; Luria, 1966).

In the tradition of the American psychometric approach to briefly assessing several HIBFs (language, visual–spatial abilities, orientation, memory, self-monitoring, bilateral motor control, and attention/working memory), a number is given for the level of performance (i.e., the total BNIS score), and this score is converted to an age-adjusted T score (Prigatano et al., 1995) and, in some instances, an age- and educational level-adjusted T score (Prigatano, Souza, & Braga, 2017). Also, in keeping with the life span perspective encouraged by this approach, an adult and a child version of the same test have been constructed for the purpose of evaluating these functions from the beginning of formal schooling (at approximately age 6 years) through the retirement years (into the 80s; Prigatano et al., 1995; Prigatano & Gagliardi, 2005).

After the initial screening of higher integrative brain functions, the neuropsychological examination/testing can proceed in many different ways. The psychometric tests listed in Box 10.5 are some commonly used measures that provide comparable assessments across school-age years into the eighth and ninth decades of life. A major limitation of many of the existing neuropsychological measures is that they may fail to hold the interest of the patient; this is especially the case for children (Prigatano, 2011). Future testing methods, for example, should explore in more detail whether memory performance for information that has personal appeal to the patient (at a conscious and unconscious level) versus information that is boring to the patient reveals different levels of performance.

THE CLINICAL INTERVIEW AND EXAMINATION PROCESS FOR YOUNGER ADOLESCENTS AND SCHOOL-AGE CHILDREN

The procedures for conducting a clinical interview with younger adolescents or school-age children and their parents are heavily influenced by the language skills of the child or adolescent, the cooperation level of the child or adolescent, and their level of intelligence. Sometimes it is very clear that the child or adolescent does not wish to be seen or evaluated. For example, a 14-year-old girl made it clear to the office personnel at the time of registration that she was not happy to be seen. Given this information, the patient and her mother were greeted as noted previously. In this instance, the clinical neuropsychologist asked the mother for permission to first speak with her daughter privately. The mother gave verbal permission to do so.

When the patient was seen privately, she made it clear that she did not want to be "tested." The clinical neuropsychologist assured her that she had the right to refuse testing, but he asked if she could explain why she did not want to be seen. The patient then stated that she believed her mother wanted to prove that "something was wrong with her, when nothing was wrong." After listening to the patient's comments and acknowledging her concerns, common areas of interest were touched upon. Both the clinical neuropsychologist and the patient had a dog, and the value and pleasure dogs can provide were commented on. The patient smiled for the first time. Some rapport was established, and she agreed to a brief assessment that, in fact, revealed normal neuropsychological status, which was expected given the patient's medical history. The patient and mother were then spoken to in a manner that seemed to defuse the patient's anger with her mother and left the "door open" for a possible future consultation. The patient and her mother appeared satisfied with the brief consultation.

When children or adolescents are more amenable to the neuropsychological consultation/examination, it is often best to begin by talking with both the child and parent together. This allows for natural observations regarding the child's level of psychosocial functioning and the bonding relationship they have with their parent(s). It is helpful to talk directly to the child and explain why you are seeing them. The child's level of understanding of what is being said will determine what questions are asked of them and how soon the examination process will begin. If the child can provide reasonable answers concerning their school and home life, these areas should be explored first. One can gently inquire about any difficulties with regard to schoolwork or getting along with siblings. Asking if the child has any pets is often beneficial because pets represent a natural subject for relating common experiences between the examiner and the child, thus helping engage the child in dialogue.

Further exploration with regard to sleep, appetite, taste, smell, vision, hearing, and motor functioning can be done as outlined previously for adults. Then, the child can be introduced to either a resident in clinical neuropsychology or a neuropsychology technician to begin the testing, and the parent can be further spoken to privately. Choosing a resident or technician skilled in interacting with children is vital. They must make the child feel comfortable, engage the child in the examination procedures, and manage any behaviors that seem to distract the child from participating in the examination process. The child's vocabulary level should be quickly determined in order to plan what tests will be given and in what order. The Peabody Picture Vocabulary Test can help accomplish this task in a nonthreatening manner. If the child's language skills are very limited, beginning with a "fun" activity such as drawing or coloring might be attempted. Once rapport is established, the HIBFs listed in Box 10.4 are explored using age-appropriate neuropsychological measures as suggested in Box 10.5.

While the child undergoes neuropsychological testing, the parent or parents are spoken to privately. Their concerns are first inquired about, followed by any comments they wish to make about their child. Typically, questionnaires concerning the child's medical and development history are completed before the patient and family are seen. The clinical neuropsychologist reviews that information with the parent(s) to further clarify or address relevant content areas covered in Box 10.2. Being clear as to what the parents are hoping to obtain from the examination/consultation deserves considerable discussion. Unrealistic expectations need to be addressed early so as not to foster misunderstanding of what can and cannot be done as a result of the examination findings. This often is very helpful in fostering a realistically supportive bond between the parent(s) and the clinical neuropsychologist.

SUMMARY COMMENTS ABOUT THE INTERVIEW AND EXAMINATION

Information obtained during the interview should provide a better understanding of the patient's present and past functioning than can be gleaned solely from the medical records. It should help the clinical neuropsychologist better understand the patient's (and, in some cases, the parents' or spouse's) questions and concerns. This information is invaluable when deciding how to best communicate with these individuals during the feedback session.

An effective clinical interview typically leads seamlessly to a discussion of examination procedures. The procedures not only attempt to reveal "objective" information regarding the patient's neuropsychological status but also provide information that helps the patient (and spouse or parents) better understand whatever disturbances in brain–behavior relationships are present and how to best cope with them.

Although clinical neuropsychologists are routinely trained to review medical records and identify important "facts" regarding the patient's medical history that are potentially relevant to interpreting clinical neuropsychological test findings, they are seldom trained to ask the following questions: How should I approach a specific patient after reviewing their medical records? What information in the records would be especially important to review and in what order? How do I explain the purpose of the examination while putting the patient at ease? How do I best manage a "difficult" patient or family member in the interview? What are the personality and behavioral characteristics of the patient that need to be considered when examining the patient? and What personality characteristics of the patient and family member should be considered when providing meaningful feedback? Attention to these questions prepares the clinical neuropsychologist to proceed in a manner that is likely to build a therapeutic relationship. Although details of how this is done are typically reviewed and practiced by residents in clinical neuropsychology who are seeing patients with different brain disorders, specific clinical guidelines are provided in Part IV of this book when clinical cases are reviewed. Some general guidelines are considered next.

THE FEEDBACK SESSION AND ITS IMPORTANCE

No matter how thorough the record review is, how skillfully the clinical interview is conducted, and how informative the neuropsychological examination findings are, it is all meaningless if the clinical neuropsychologist cannot condense the most important bits of information obtained from these activities and convey them in a manner that is helpful to the patient, the family member, and the referring physician. What does it all mean?

Many observations and findings are obtained in the course of a clinical neuropsychological consultation/examination. One must ask the following: What are the major findings? How do they relate to the patient's history? How do they help explain the patient's subjective experiences and ongoing difficulties observed by others? What are the diagnostic impressions? Moreover, how should these insights be verbally presented at the end of the examination? Once these questions are addressed, what are the clinical implications of the findings that need to be considered? What are the potentially relevant recommendations that flow from this information? How will the recommendations be viewed by the patient and family member? How do you help them accept and act on the recommendations?

Many clinical neuropsychologists struggle with answering some of these questions. Some lack sophistication in understanding human nature and the important psychological (psychodynamic) characteristics of the patient (and, occasionally, family members). Others have not had adequate clinical experience providing rehabilitation and psychotherapy services to make practical recommendations.

Others remain too "test oriented" in the description of the findings. Some lack conciseness in their communications when attempting to thoroughly explain the clinical picture. Finally, many do not take the time to explain their thought process concerning the major findings and their implications. This can leave the patient, family member, and referring physician with a less than optimal understanding of what has been learned by the consultation/examination. Table 10.1 presents five general guidelines for providing feedback to patients and their family members. They are based on the five "C's" of communication for providing feedback mainly to parents of school-age children (Prigatano & Gray, 2011). They are summarized here in a manner that, it is hoped, can be used when providing feedback to an adult patient, their family members, and the parents of children. A more extensive description of the findings can and should be included in the final written report.

It is often wise to begin the verbal feedback session with a brief (to the point) summary of why the patient was seen and the questions that were being raised by the physician to the clinical neuropsychologist. The language should be clear and easy to understand (C1). The basic findings (no more than three key points) then need to be verbally expressed in a concise (C2) and accurate (i.e., correct) manner (C3). This should be done with a sense of conviction and compassion. If done properly, this frequently results in a comforting (C4) experience. The patient and family now have a better understanding of what is "wrong" and what should be done next to help deal with whatever problems have been revealed by the consultation/examination. This constitutes a corrective experience (C5).

The training of clinical neuropsychologists to provide such feedback requires that they be properly educated to understand both the neuropsychological status of the patient and the patient's personality features. They must understand the patient's phenomenological state. They must have a "working understanding" of why the patient, and occasionally the family member, may resist or discount what is being communicated to them during the feedback session. They must have the resilience to reinterpret or describe their findings in a manner that "makes sense" to the patient and family member given the clinical situation that is encountered.

The nature of the feedback given to a school-age child is heavily dependent on the child's ability to understand what is being said.

Table 10.1 Guidelines for Providing Feedback of Neuropsychological Examination Findings and Their Implications

1. Clear	Language should be clear and easy to understand.
2. Concise	Limit what is said to a few important main points.
3. Correct (accurate)	Feedback should accurately describe major findings and conclusions from the examination.
4. Comforting	Feedback must be framed in a manner that takes into consideration the neuropsychological status and the probable psychodynamic features of the patient. It should attempt to reduce anxiety and negative affect.
5. Corrective (helpful)	Recommendations made should be practical and helpful to the patient and the family, particularly as they relate to psychological care issues.

Source: Modified and adapted from Prigatano, G. P., & Gray, J. A., Conducting Feedback for Pediatric Neuropsychological Assessment, in A. S. Davis (Ed.), Handbook of pediatric neuropsychology, 2011, p. 495–499, by permission of Springer Publishing Company.

Recognizing the child's hard work, pointing out their performance on tests in which they were most successful, and at the same time talking about what was "hard" for the child provide understandable feedback that can also foster a working or therapeutic relationship with the child. If the child expresses a spontaneous willingness to return in the future for a repeat examination, this is often an indication that the experience for the child was positive. It is important to tell the child and parent that a report will be sent to the referring doctor and the parent. The parent is encouraged to return and discuss the report if they have any questions.

THE WRITTEN REPORT

Neuropsychological reports can be written in many styles. Physicians often complain about the length of neuropsychological reports, which often have unclear conclusions or less-than-helpful recommendations. They want the basic facts; the data that support those facts; and recommendations for further treatment, management, or care. They want informed opinions and the logic behind those opinions. They do not want a re-description of all the medical information about the patient that they already know. They do want to be alerted to any information or observations they may have overlooked in either diagnosing or treating the patient. They also want the patient and family member to experience a clinical service that was meaningful to them. Finally, they want a timely report (usually within 7 days of seeing the patient).

Parents of children who are undergoing a neuropsychological examination want the same information, but not uncommonly they want more. They want detailed instructions on how to best help the child that they and teachers can follow like a recipe. This is often problematic. On the basis of a single examination, one cannot provide numerous recommendations when the home and educational environments are not fully understood and may change due to unexpected circumstances. Although providing as many reasonable recommendations as possible is important, it is more important that the parent really understand the neuropsychologist's appraisal of their child. This may require the parent to return and ask further questions or receive clarification after they have read and studied the clinical neuropsychological report. This has often been my practice when examining children who present with complicated histories and examination findings.

Written reports should be prepared as technical, professional documents with use of the appropriate terminology. The summary, recommendations, and conclusions sections, however, should be the most easily understood by the referring doctor and the patient (or the patient's family members). In this regard, patients often want (and deserve) a copy of their neuropsychological report. Great care needs to be taken to state the truth about what the neuropsychological examination findings revealed and recommendations for future treatments. This has to be done, however, in a manner that the patient and family can "hear" and are not offended by. This means choosing words carefully in light of what the patient and family experience.

REFERENCES

Baker, G. (1956). Diagnosis of organic brain damage in the adult. In B. Klopfer (Ed.), *Developments in the Rorschach technique* (Vol. 2, pp. 318–375). New York, NY: World Book Company.

Darwin, C. (1859). *The origin of species by means of natural selection*. London, UK: Murray.

Denney, D., & Prigatano, G. (2019). Subjective ratings of cognitive and emotional functioning in patients with mild cognitive impairment and patients with subjective memory complaints but normal cognitive functioning. Advance on line publishing: doi.org/10.1080/13803395.2019.1588229.

Kertesz, A. (1985). Aphasia. In P. Vinken, B. Bruyn, H. Klawans, & J. Frederiks (Eds.), *Handbook of clinical neurology* (Vol. 45, pp. 287–332). Amsterdam, the Netherlands: Elsevier.

Luria, A. (1966). *Higher cortical functions in man*. New York, NY: Basic Books.

Piotrowski, Z. A., & Rock, M. R. (1963). *The Perceptanalytic Executive Scale*. New York, NY: Grune & Stratton.

Prigatano, G. P. (2011). *Making the neuropsychological examination interesting to school-age children: A challenge for our field*. Paper presented at the annual meeting of the Institute of Child Health, London.

Prigatano, G. P., Amin, K., & Jaramillo, K. (1993). Memory performance and use of a compensation after traumatic brain injury. *Neuropsychological Rehabilitation, 3*(1), 53–62.

Prigatano, G. P., Amin, K., & Rosenstein, L. (1995). *Administration and scoring manual for the BNI Screen for Higher Cerebral Functions*. Phoenix, AZ: Barrow Neurological Institute.

Prigatano, G. P., & Gagliardi, C. (2005). *The BNI Screen for Higher Cerebral Functions in School Age Children: A manual for administration and scoring*. Phoenix, AZ: Barrow Neurological Institute.

Prigatano, G. P., & Gray, J. A. (2011). Conducting feedback for pediatric neuropsychological assessment. In A. S. Davis (Ed.), *Handbook of pediatric neuropsychology* (pp. 495–499). New York, NY: Springer.

Prigatano, G. P., Montreuil, M., Chapple, K., Tonini, A., Toron, J., Paquet, C., . . . Truelle, J. L. (2014). Screening for cognitive and affective dysfunction in patients suspected of mild cognitive impairment. *International Journal of Geriatric Psychiatry, 29*(9), 936–942.

Prigatano, G. P., & Morrone-Strupinsky, J. (2010). Advancing the profession of clinical neuropsychology with appropriate outcome studies and demonstrated clinical skills. *The Clinical Neuropsychologist, 24*(3), 468–480.

Prigatano, G. P., Souza, L., & Braga, L. W. (2017). Performance of a Brazilian sample on the Portuguese Translation of the BNI Screen for Higher Cerebral Functions. *Journal of Clinical and Experimental Neuropsychology, 40*(2), 173–182.

Ross, E. D. (1985). Modulation of affect and nonverbal communication by the right hemisphere. In M.-M. Mesulam (Ed.), *Principles of behavioral neurology* (pp. 239–257). Philadelphia, PA: Davis.

Schoenberg, M. R., Dawson, K. A., Duff, K., Patton, D., Scott, J. G., & Adams, R. L. (2006). Test performance and classification statistics for the Rey Auditory Verbal Learning Test in selected clinical samples. *Archives of Clinical Neuropsychology, 21*(7), 693–703.

11

NEUROPSYCHOLOGICAL CONSULTATION BEFORE AND AFTER NEUROSURGERY

INTRODUCTION

As noted in Chapter 1, a neuropsychological consultation and examination can be used for a variety of purposes. When requested for clinical purposes, they should be both medically necessary and personally helpful to the patient and family members (see Chapter 10, this volume). Although clinical neuropsychological consultations and examinations often have an educational component, the most frequent goal is to describe the higher integrative brain functions (HIBFs) for purposes of diagnosis and clinical management. Neuropsychological examinations are also used for research purposes. For example, neurosurgeons might request a "baseline" neuropsychological examination of patients prior to surgery. Often, the goal is to determine whether a particular surgical procedure carries less neuropsychological morbidity or if the surgeries performed resulted in a desired clinical outcome. Unfortunately, this approach is not always utilized in routine clinical practice. It may be viewed as medically unnecessary (i.e., the pre-surgical neuropsychological examination is not relevant to the operation that will be undertaken), it may be clinically impossible because the patient's acute or current medical status precludes adequate participation in neuropsychological examination procedures, or it may be needlessly expensive and may even be emotionally upsetting for some patients.

Yet, many patients undergoing neurosurgery (and their families) do not know what to expect regarding probable immediate, intermediate, and long-term neuropsychological consequences. It is important for clinical neuropsychologists to become involved in providing consultation services before and after neurosurgery, as this chapter demonstrates. A growing literature also suggests that advances in neuroimaging combined with a focused neuropsychological examination may be especially helpful to patients and their surgeons as they contemplate a specific operation (Lang, 2017).

Undoubtedly, there are patients who undergo neurosurgical procedures and have little or no regret that they never saw a clinical neuropsychologist prior to their operation. Others, however, lament not doing so when significant cognitive and behavioral impairments are unexpectedly experienced post-surgery. Some are outright angry with their neurosurgeon even though they greatly respect the surgeon's skill and are thankful for being alive. This chapter highlights these realities and provides examples of how neuropsychological consultations and examinations may be helpful to patients before and after a neurosurgical operation.

TWO CLASSIC CLINICAL EXAMPLES

A patient was seen post-surgery following successful removal of a cavernous malformation. After being evaluated post-surgery for residual neuropsychological difficulties, the patient was encouraged to write about his experience. The nature of his reaction has been observed in several other patients throughout the years. He wrote the following (as cited in Prigatano, 1995):

> On May 10, 1994 I had a craniotomy of the left parietal occipital region for a cavernous malformation. Everything happened in quick fashion prior to that. An episode of amnesia, a possible seizure at work (no one knows, I was in a remote warehouse at the time), several hours bumbling around in my office not fully comprehending nor being able to communicate adequately with other people. My adept office staff never caught on. Thankfully, someone from outside the office thought I had acted strange and pressured my absent boss to take me to my doctor. The doctor ordered magnetic resonance (MR) imaging, which revealed a malformation that had bled or was bleeding. A top-notch neurosurgeon from an acclaimed institution was enlisted, rather quickly I might add, to conduct surgery. Eight days later in the intensive care unit my neurosurgeon was extremely pleased with how things were going and full recovery was to be expected.
>
> Four days later I was home and obviously a little giddy about having dodged a big bullet. Everything seemed to be right on track. Heal up a little, go back to work, and forget that this bad dream ever happened. This was my thinking anyway, until six days postoperative my wife asked me what I was doing. My response was a total blank! I had a complete inability to express in words what I was doing! I stood stunned for a bit, and then turned away quickly so she wouldn't notice the tears.
>
> Let me preface my experience by saying how grateful I am to be alive and functional. The gratitude I have for my doctors in the speed, skill, and professional manner in which they acted is a real tribute to the medical community. I'm still amazed how such a delicate organ as the brain can be taken for granted, when even a slight malfunction can be the difference between life and death. Thankful? You bet! My wife, too. The experience has elevated us to a whole new level in our relationship. One that I hope will keep us bonded forever.
>
> Having said all that let me tell you why I'm angry. Angry at you!
>
> When I was told I would need surgery, my neurosurgeon was of course very matter-of-fact. The malformation was very reachable and there was no need to be too concerned. The downside was a 3% chance of death and a 5% chance of some type of therapy being needed.

"Alright, death." I said to myself, "That's everyone's ultimate concern." Therapy, well I can do that. A couple of sessions of leg lifts, a few bicep curls, maybe some whirlpool time and presto! I'll be as good as new!

There was no way I could have even imagined the actual inability to either comprehend or communicate with anything less than I had ever had before. No attempt, other than a few stats, was ever mentioned to me about what a *real life experience* might be like. Turning numbers around, difficulty in reading, complete memory lapses and tedious tasks? Forget it! Perhaps I should count my blessings considering the state other patients are in. Perhaps. But just perhaps my pain is no less heartfelt than those of others. What I wanted was an informed decision prior to surgery. The outcome would've been the same but with a hell of a lot less agony. (pp. 5–6)

It is probable that with even the best pre-surgical education, patients (and their family members) may not fully appreciate the real-life consequences of their brain lesion and/or the surgical interventions. However, as the ancient Chinese proverb states, "Forewarned is forearmed!" Patients and their families deserve to have written materials provided to them regarding the temporary and immediate symptoms frequently observed after neurosurgery. They should routinely review these symptoms with their neurosurgeon and in some instances with a consulting neuropsychologist. A focused baseline neuropsychological examination, when possible, would provide patients and their families with objective information regarding their current functioning. Repeat examinations post-surgery would not only provide objective information about recovery or the lack of it but also put the patient and their family members in contact with a clinical neuropsychologist who knows them and is willing to answer questions and provide further guidance.

Certainly, no one can exactly predict what a person will experience coming out of anesthesia and a neurosurgical procedure. Varied and complex neuropsychological and neuropsychiatric symptoms do occur and can be overwhelming even if informed about them ahead of time. Yet, that information can be helpful not only to the patient but also to family members. A simple brochure, such as that shown in Figure 11.1, should be provided to them on a regular basis.

The brochure in Figure 11.1 lists common immediate and temporary symptoms as well as symptoms that may change with time. In some instances, the symptoms can be permanent. Clearly, the goal is not to frighten the patient or family members but, rather, to make it clear to them that neuropsychological disturbances are common and to some degree expected. If the patient can tolerate it, a routine, focused clinical neuropsychological examination based on the patient's diagnosis should be planned prior to surgery. The patient and family should never feel alone in trying to understand disturbances in HIBFs and what steps may be useful in managing them if they occur.

The second example highlights the potential value of a post-surgical neuropsychological consultation. The patient was a 63-year-old man who suffered a ruptured cerebral aneurysm with subarachnoid hemorrhage. His case is described in more detail in Chapter 17. For the purposes of this chapter, however, note that he was close to death, and a very experienced and skilled neurosurgeon successfully re-clipped the aneurysm with no obvious neurological sequelae (i.e., no motor, sensory, or language deficits were recorded). The patient and his wife were told he would make a good recovery, but it would take time.

A year later, the patient continued to present with dense anterograde amnesia, loss of initiative, and "changed personality." He had significantly diminished self-awareness of the extent of his memory impairments. He could no longer practice in his profession. His creative and intelligent wife tried everything she knew to help him improve, but his

NEUROPSYCHOLOGICAL SYMPTOMS AFTER BRAIN SURGERY

Temporary and immediate symptoms

Brain surgery can cause mental (or neuropsychological) symptoms that can confuse you or your family.

It is difficult to predict exactly what neuropsychological symptoms you might experience after brain surgery.

General anesthetic and manipulation of the brain and blood vessels during brain surgery can cause immediate neuropsychological symptoms.

These symptoms are often temporary and include:

- Confusion about time and place
- Failure to recognize family members or friends
- Difficulty speaking and keeping thoughts clear
- Difficulty in remembering visitors or information
- Fear that mental functioning is impaired permanently

These are *normal* changes that often fade with time when there have been no complications during surgery or when the brain has not been significantly injured.

Temporary or permanent symptoms

Your neurosurgeon will do all he or she can to avoid prolonged or permanent changes in mental (neuropsychological) functioning.

Depending on the type of operation, what part of the brain is operated on, and other complications, some symptoms might persist or even be permanent.

You might have a difficult time:

- Remembering recent events
- Learning new information
- Communicating clearly
- Reading, writing, or doing arithmetic
- Paying attention
- Planning activities
- Controlling your emotions, particularly when frustrated
- Sustaining mental energy while thinking or doing problem-solving tasks

BARROW NEUROLOGICAL INSTITUTE®

Neuropsychological symptoms are complicated and although some can be related to certain types of brain dysfunction, they are not easily predicted.

Individuals can be alarmed if they have a neuropsychological symptom and have not been warned about it ahead of time. If you notice any change in your mental functioning, do not be afraid to ask and to obtain more information about it.

Talk to your neurosurgeon, neurologist, or consulting neuropsychologist if you have any mental symptoms that worry you.

Often with time and rehabilitation, many symptoms improve and even disappear. It can take, however, several weeks or even months to know if a symptom will be permanent. If a symptom does become permanent, rehabilitation physicians, psychologists, and therapists at the Barrow Neurological Institute® are available to help you learn to cope with difficulties as much as possible.

St. Joseph's Hospital and Medical Center
Mercy Healthcare Arizona

©1995 Barrow

FIGURE 11.1 Brochure listing common immediate and temporary symptoms of brain surgery as well as symptoms that may change with time.

Source: Courtesy of Barrow Neurological Institute.

neuropsychological impairments persisted. One year post-surgery, the patient's wife asked for a referral for a clinical neuropsychological consultation/examination.

The clinical neuropsychological examination documented in many ways what the patient's wife already knew. However, the "numbers" associated with her husband's memory and intellectual functioning were sobering to her. More important, the findings led to subsequent discussions about the patient's neurocognitive disturbance. The pattern of findings was common in some patients with an anterior cerebral ruptured aneurysm. It was emphasized that such patients often do not seem to be aware of or concerned about any change in their HIBFs. They are often apathetic and seem to lose their interest in people and the world around them. The patient's wife was visibly relieved by these discussions. She now had a much better understanding of her husband and began to take realistic steps to cope with the long-term consequences of such a devastating neuropsychological syndrome.

She greatly appreciated what she learned from repeated neuropsychological consultations and examinations of her husband. She no longer felt alone in trying to understand her husband's behavior and changed personality. Although very appreciative of the neurosurgeon's skills, she was also openly critical of the neurosurgeon. She believed that the neurosurgeon had given her a false sense of hope and did not recognize or describe to her the potential neuropsychological consequences of her husband's condition.

The patient's wife, along with many others throughout the years, reported not being adequately prepared to understand the cognitive and behavioral difficulties a spouse or partner may experience after a very technically satisfying neurosurgical procedure. They have repeatedly expressed a desire that someone (preferably a clinical neuropsychologist) talk with them in detail before and after the operation so that they will be better able to manage and understand potential (and, in some cases, probable) neuropsychological sequelae of short- or long-term (permanent) duration. Although neurosurgeons have certainly improved in providing this information, more can be done.

WHAT SHOULD BE DISCUSSED WITH THE PATIENT AND THE FAMILY?

As the patient with the cavernous malformation indicated, he was not aware of or prepared for the language difficulties he experienced after surgery. He was not aware that his mind might "go blank" at unexpected times, nor was he prepared for this to happen. He was not aware of or prepared for how frightening these experiences can be. These potential difficulties should be discussed with the patient and family members both before and after surgery. They should be forewarned.

In addition, some patients awaken from surgery quite confused as to what has happened. They may have difficulty explaining perceptual disturbances, orientation difficulties, and difficulty understanding what is said to them. For some, there may be a secret fear that they are "going crazy," as in the case of the patient described in the introductory comments in Chapter 1. It is very important to reassure the patient and the family that cognitive confusion can occur in many forms and is quite common after brain surgery. In most instances, it resolves within a relatively short period of time (often within hours to days) if there are no surgical complications, but not always.

Another common problem is fatigue. After brain surgery, patients fatigue easily with any physical or mental activity. One of the most important benefits of rehabilitation therapies (i.e., physical therapy, occupational therapy, and speech and language therapy) is to improve the mental and physical endurance of patients as they perform both physical and cognitive tasks. This can be easily overlooked if there are no obvious neurological impairments. Educating the patient and family members before and after neurosurgery regarding the important problem of fatigue should be done routinely.

In addition to the general consequences of disturbing any brain function, there are specific neuropsychological sequelae that should be considered in individual cases. Depending on the region of the brain that has been compromised secondary to a ruptured aneurysm, cavernous malformation, or brain tumor, specific long-term (and possibly permanent) neuropsychological consequences must be openly discussed but with a sense of supportive hope. Residual language and arithmetic difficulties are common following left parietal lobe lesions, but they can improve with time and therapy. Residual memory problems are common when lesions involve the temporal lobes of the brain, particularly the anterior portions, which may impact hippocampal function. Residual problems with abstract reasoning, attention, problem-solving, and subjective awareness of neuropsychological and behavioral difficulties are often associated with frontal lobe lesions. Subtle and not-so-subtle changes in personality also have to be considered, but these are not as easily predicted or described. They are often related to some significant change in cognitive functioning (Lishman, 1968; Max et al., 2000). Lesions to the right side of the brain are in some ways more unpredictable. They can include poorly defined visual–spatial disturbances and problems with attention. Lack of social judgment, social disinhibition, and failure to "seeing the big picture" are commonly observed with patients who have right frontal and parietal lobe dysfunctions.

Patients should be informed that lesions to certain areas of the brain more predictably lead to motor, visual, and language difficulties. However, the complex neuropsychological functions are not so easily localized. The graphic illustration of the relation between lesion location and functional connectivity deficits after stroke, as illustrated in Figures 7.3 and 7.4, may be shown to some patients and family members so that they can better understand the complexity of the clinical situation.

They can be helped to better understand the causes of the symptoms that persist after brain surgery for different brain lesions.

Related to this important clinical observation is the work of Sutterer et al. (2016). They demonstrated that impaired decision-making, which is common in many brain dysfunctional patients, is often correlated with a complex disruption of neural networks involving the limbic system and prefrontal regions of the brain. For example, poor performance on the Iowa Gambling Task was associated with disruption of neurocircuits interconnecting insula, somatosensory, and motor regions of the brain. It is very important for the patient and family to realize that a brain disorder often affects both affect and cognition. This needs to be expected and managed if disturbances in both areas of functioning are present. Patients and families often appreciate having these insights explained to them in simple, direct language. In light of these general observations, the potential value of a neuropsychological consultation and examination for three patient groups is described in more detail in the following sections.

NEUROPSYCHOLOGICAL CONSULTATIONS/ EXAMINATIONS FOR PATIENTS WITH CEREBRAL ANEURYSMS

Small nonruptured cerebral aneurysms are typically not associated with neuropsychological deficits. Large aneurysms are more likely to be associated with neurological or neuropsychological deficits because they compress cranial nerves or brain tissue. The major concern for neurosurgeons, however, is the risk of rupture, which can result in mortality and significant neurological morbidity (Towgood, Ogden, & Mee, 2004). Successful surgical clipping or coiling of unruptured cerebral or cerebellar aneurysms would be expected to produce no lasting neuropsychological consequences. What, however, do empirical studies report?

As would be expected, different viewpoints and findings are reported in the literature.

Tuffiash, Tamargo, and Hillis (2003) report, for example, that clipping of an unruptured cerebral aneurysm results in no neuropsychological impairments for the vast majority of patients. However, they report that a few patients do show a decline on measures sampling memory and speed of hand–eye coordination (as measured by the Grooved Pegboard Test). They note that "only 3 of 25 patients showed significant deterioration. All but 1 patient returned to baseline by the 3-month follow-up" (p. 2195). If you were one of those patients, however, the experience of those deficits could be quite alarming, particularly if they were not expected. Another study reported that 44% of patients (17 out of 39) evidenced cognitive impairments 1 week after coiling of an asymptomatic unruptured intracranial aneurysm (Kang, Hwang, Kim, Bae, & Lee, 2013). The percentage dropped to 19% (7 out of 37) at 4 weeks. Cognitive impairments again were specifically noted in memory and processing speed. Long-term outcomes were not reported.

Ohue et al. (2003) conducted neuropsychological testing on 43 patients with unruptured cerebral aneurysms before surgery and followed some patients up to 6 months post-surgery. They report that 40% of their patients (17 out of 43) showed a decline in neuropsychological test performance 1 month after surgery compared to their pre-surgery performance. By 6 months post-surgery, "6 showed complete recovery, 5 showed partial recovery, and 3 still showed cognitive deterioration" (p. 269). They further note that older patients with anterior communicating artery aneurysms may be at greater risk for a decline in their neuropsychological status post-surgery. As neurosurgeons, they emphasize the importance of neuropsychological evaluations after neurosurgery for this patient population. They make the important observation that all of their patients were considered to have made a "good neurosurgical outcome" as measured by the Glasgow Outcome Score. Nevertheless, some of their patients demonstrated clear neuropsychological impairments, particularly on tests of memory.

The cognitive and personality changes associated with "uncomplicated" aneurysmal surgery following subarachnoid hemorrhage (SAH) make an even more convincing argument for the need of neuropsychological consultation for this patient group. Again, early reports of cognitive and personality disturbance in this patient group tended to minimize the true neuropsychological and psychosocial sequelae common in this patient population (Maurice-Williams, Willison, & Hatfield, 1991). Later studies, however, left little doubt that substantial cognitive, emotional/motivational, and psychosocial difficulties were common in this group of patients. In a review of 61 empirical studies, Al-Khindi, Macdonald, and Schweizer (2010) note that memory, "executive dysfunction," and language impairments are commonly observed in this patient group. Although they are most frequently observed during the first 3 months after the SAH, Al-Khindi et al. note that these deficits can persist for long periods of time and may be permanent. They make the important observations that 50% of patients with SAH do not survive. Consequently, it is natural for neurosurgeons to describe patients as having a "good outcome" or only moderate disability if they survive and have no obvious neurological deficits. Yet these patients' lives and the lives of their families may be permanently altered. An extraordinarily insightful paper clearly makes this point.

Buchanan, Elias, and Goplen (2000) studied the outcome of SAH from the perspective of the patient, the relative, and the neurosurgeon. They interviewed in depth 28 patients surgically treated for SAH and their relatives. They note that "19 months after surgery for SAH, the majority of the patients reported significant negative neurobehavioral changes and negative changes in employment, energy levels, tolerance to mild stressors, leisure activities, and social and sexual relationships" (p. 831). Family members reported substantial negative changes in the relationship to the person and severe distress in caring for them. Yet, again, all patients were classified from a neurosurgeon's perspective as having either a good recovery or moderate disability. The authors emphasize that they are not blaming the neurosurgeons for the medical classification of the outcome based purely on neurological standards. However, a much broader range of outcome measures have to be considered when describing the "real-world outcome" for these patients.

How can these patients and their families be helped? What practical role can the neuropsychologist play in their psychological care? Al-Khindi et al. (2010) make the important point that some of the surviving patients with SAH secondary to a ruptured aneurysm may be too sick or impaired to undergo formal psychometric testing. However, the clinical neuropsychologist can talk to them about their experiences and concerns and help guide them and their family members to reduce the disabling difficulties they experience in everyday life. Again, the first patient described in this book (in Chapter 1) underwent no formal or standardized neuropsychological testing. A clinical neuropsychologist simply talked to him, listened to his concerns, and provided information that substantially reduced his anxiety. The second patient described in this chapter had significantly impaired self-awareness, and his wife was overwhelmed with this problem as well as his severe memory difficulties. By meeting with them conjointly and separately over a series of psychotherapeutic and cognitive rehabilitation activities (with an experienced clinical neuropsychologist and a resident in training in clinical neuropsychology), they were provided guidance and insight that were especially helpful to the spouse. Again, she was not alone with the burden of her husband's care.

Providing the patient and family members with a list of possible neuropsychological and behavioral consequences of SAH following ruptured cerebral aneurysm *before* they leave the hospital and return home is important. Despite reassurances that the patient will improve with time, family members are often very distressed when they observe significant cognitive and behavioral problems in a loved one.

They need the name and information of a clinical neuropsychologist whom they can contact when questions arise concerning the patient's neuropsychological status. This resource needs to be clearly identified for the patient and the family. Box 11.1 lists common neuropsychological, personality, and psychosocial difficulties that can exist weeks and months post SAH following a ruptured cerebral aneurysm.

NEUROPSYCHOLOGICAL CONSULTATIONS/EXAMINATIONS FOR PATIENTS WITH A HYPOTHALAMIC HAMARTOMA

Although hypothalamic hamartoma (HH) is a rare condition, the pre-surgical and post-surgical neuropsychological evaluations of children and adults with HH have provided much valuable information. This patient group can be quite heterogeneous in terms of neurocognitive and neurobehavioral disturbances. Examining these patients before surgery and providing objective information concerning their neuropsychological status and how it may relate to previous diagnoses have been invaluable for some families. For example, a relatively high functioning 21-year-old patient with an HH had been diagnosed with attention deficit disorder (ADD) during his childhood. His neuropsychological test findings did not reveal many of the classic signs of this condition. Rather, the neuropsychological examination revealed a circumscribed disturbance in working memory. After this information was presented to the patient and his parents, they better understood the patient's functioning and why previous medications for ADD were ineffective. They were greatly appreciative of having this information. It was "a real educational experience" for them (by their report).

Hypothalamic hamartomas involve a region of the brain that is less than 1% of total brain volume. However, it is an extremely important brain region (Prigatano, 2007). HHs are defined as non-neoplastic malformations resembling gray matter and contain varying

> **Box 11.1. Common Neuropsychological, Personality, and Psychosocial Difficulties Weeks and Months Post Subarachnoid Hemorrhage Following a Ruptured Cerebral Aneurysm**
>
> 1. Fatigue
> 2. Loss of drive or initiative (i.e., apathy)
> 3. Memory impairment (mild to profound)
> 4. Immature or more childlike behavior (even in a person who was very sophisticated prior to the subarachnoid hemorrhage)
> 5. Difficulties planning and organizing
> 6. Impaired language skills (in talking and writing)
> 7. Increased dependence of the spouse with a decrease in the sexual drive of the spouse
> 8. Loss of sexual drive
> 9. Reduced interest patterns
> 10. Reduced social judgment
> 11. Impaired sleep (sleeping too much or having multiple awakenings)
>
> All of these changes can exist even when the person has had a relatively good physical recovery (see Buchanan et al., 2000).

proportions of neurons, glia, and fiber bundles (Nguyen, Singh, & Zaatreh, 2003). They are frequently associated with epileptogenic disorders that originate as gelastic seizures, and these patients can go on to develop secondary epilepsy (Valdueza et al., 1994) and are thus frequently candidates for neurosurgery.

The hypothalamus has long been recognized as a crucial integrative brain structure that helps regulate such basic brain-mediated functions as sleep, dreaming, eating, drinking, temperature control, and reproductive and sexual behavior (Saper, 2004). As such, the hypothalamus is important for "fight and flight" reactions necessary to sustain survival.

Patients with HH can demonstrate mild to severe cognitive and behavior disorders. Presurgical neuropsychological assessment of these patients revealed IQ scores in the range of severe intellectual impairments (IQ estimates in the 50s for those who could be examined) to normal and, in some cases, bright normal levels of intellectual functioning (Prigatano et al., 2008). What was striking for this patient group was that early onset of a seizure disorder was not strongly related to estimates of intellectual functioning when examined prior to surgery. However, the size of the HH, its neuroanatomical features, and the number of anti-epileptic drugs or medications the patient was taking prior to surgery were clearly associated with the patient's level of intellectual functioning.

Not captured by such psychometrically driven studies was the equally wide range of affective and behavioral features of these children and adults. The medical records of these patients often referred to histories of ADD, "autistic spectrum disorders," bipolar disorder, and/or aggressive or "acting out" behavioral disorders. Even in the higher intellectually functioning subgroup of this patient population, there were subtle difficulties with social interaction and subjective reports of ongoing difficulties with attention and irritability. Irrespective of their seizure history, many could not complete a formal education or maintain gainful employment. Interestingly, the parents of children with HH described their child as not showing the typical "bonding" experiences that their other children showed. Children with HH were less easily "cuddled" or consoled when something upset them. It appeared that this subcortical brain dysfunction had profound effects not only on behavioral development but also on intellectual development.

Subsequent follow-up neuropsychological testing of these children and adults post-surgery revealed other important findings (Wethe et al., 2013). As a group, improvement in intellectual functioning post-surgery was observed primarily in patients who were functioning in the mental retardation range (but were "testable"). Duration of epilepsy and age at surgery were also related to outcome. Quite sobering was the fact that memory functioning did not seem to improve in the majority of patients. Some patients actually showed a worsening of their memory post-surgery. This was often associated with small thalamic infarcts assumed to be secondary to the neurosurgical interventions. These realities should be discussed with the patient and family prior to neurosurgery. The patient and family are often appreciative of this information and, when possible, return for further neuropsychological consultations particularly if residual cognitive or behavioral disturbances are present even in the absence of seizures.

NEUROPSYCHOLOGICAL CONSULTATIONS/ EXAMINATIONS FOR PATIENTS WITH PARKINSON'S DISEASE UNDERGOING DEEP BRAIN STIMULATION

The discovery that electrical stimulation of the subthalamic nucleus (STN) of the brain could reduce motor impairments in some patients with Parkinson's disease has been described as "the most important innovation for treatment of advanced Parkinson's disease" (Fasano et al., 2010, p. 2664). However, relatively early observations regarding the neuropsychological functioning of Parkinson's disease patients undergoing such deep brain stimulation (DBS) suggested that this treatment could have negative neuropsychological consequences (Saint-Cyr, Trépanier, Kumar, Lozano, & Lang, 2000). Declines in verbal fluency, working memory, and various "executive" functions were noted. Older patients (aged 69 years or older) were also considered to be especially at risk for negative neuropsychological consequences, but these findings were reported on a limited number of individuals. Voon, Kubu, Krack, Houeto, and Tröster (2006) provided an extensive review of the early literature regarding the potential negative neuropsychological and neuropsychiatric effects of DBS of the STN. They highlighted a number of methodological limitations in studies that reported adverse neuropsychological consequences of this procedure. They stated, "At present the evidence is inconclusive" (p. S321).

In the first multicenter randomized controlled trial that compared the motor and neuropsychological outcomes of DBS versus "best medical therapy" for patients with Parkinson's disease, Weaver et al. (2009) reported improved motor outcomes and improved quality of life for Parkinson's disease patients receiving DBS (approximately half of the patients receiving stimulation of the globus pallidus and the other half receiving stimulation of the STN). However, they reported "mild decrements in performance" in the DBS group on measures of verbal fluency, processing speed, and certain aspects of memory. They reported no significant age effects (i.e., whether older patients had worse neuropsychology comorbidity).

In an 8-year follow-up study of selected patients who underwent DBS of the STN, Fasano et al. (2010) reported sustained motor efficacy in the STN group, with some decline when comparing patients 5 and 8 years post-surgery. Ongoing cognitive impairments were noted on measures of verbal fluency and memory. However, the authors commented that the difficulties were "mild" and "did not have a clinically meaningful effect on daily living activities" (p. 2668). It is not known what the patients and families experienced in their everyday lives. The fact that this and other reports have mentioned the development of dementia in some Parkinson's disease patients receiving STN stimulation also raised other concerns.

Fields (2015) summarizes an extensive literature on the effects of DBS aimed at controlling motor abnormalities. She and others (e.g., Voon et al., 2006) appropriately caution that any adverse effects cannot be immediately assumed to be related to the surgical procedure. Fields refers, however, to a series of recommendations made by a consensus panel concerning possible exclusionary criteria for DBS (Bronstein et al., 2011). They include evidence of dementia and significant psychiatric disorders. Neuropsychological findings of "mild cognitive impairment" and/or executive dysfunction should also alert the clinician that the patient may be more at risk for post-surgical cognitive and behavioral difficulties. The advantages of pre-surgical neuropsychological consultation and examination for this patient group are listed by Fields and reproduced in Box 11.2.

Applying these insights to specific patients requires a careful assessment of the patient's neuropsychological and psychiatric status. Fields (2015) notes that the patient can be so focused on the potential of getting relief from motor symptoms that they may underreport comorbid psychiatric difficulties. Such was the case of a 68-year-old man who suffered from tremor and was seeking surgical relief of this disabling condition. He reported being anxious in the past, but now he emphasized that it was "not a problem." Post successful surgery for his tremor, he and his family members noted that he had to be hospitalized for uncontrollable anxiety and suicidal ideation. Eventually, the anxiety diminished with the aid of medication, but during the 2 years he was followed, the

---

Box 11.2. Potential Benefits of Pre-Surgical Neuropsychological Consultations and Examinations of Persons with Parkinson's Disease Who Are Being Evaluated for Deep Brain Stimulation

1. Determine the presence and pattern of deficits that warrant caution.
2. Assess the ability to comply with pre-, peri-, and postoperative treatment demands.
3. Assess the risk of postoperative confusion and future decline.
4. Evaluate surgical candidacy in the context of providing input to a multidisciplinary DBS team.
5. Provide the patient and family with as much information as possible to make an informed decision regarding surgery.
6. Delineate strengths and weaknesses to help guide the patient and family making appropriate accommodations to work, home, and social environment pre- and post-surgically.
7. Gain insight into patient's capacity for important decision making and consent to treatment.
8. Establish a baseline prior to intervention that allows the measurement of treatment outcomes.

Source: Reprinted from Fields, J., Effects of deep brain stimulation in movement disorders on cognition and behavior, in A. Tröster (Ed.), *Clinical Neuropsychology and Cognitive Neurology of Parkinson's Disease and Other Movement Disorders*, 2015, p. 332–375, by permission of Oxford University Press.

patient remained more anxious post-surgery than he appeared pre-surgery.

Following the insightful study of Buchanan et al. (2000) on differing perspectives on outcome after SAH, future research might focus on the patient's and family member's reports of the positive and negative effects following DBS, especially of the STN, in addition to obtaining the perspectives of neuropsychologists and neurologists.

In this regard, Tröster (2017) emphasizes that a neuropsychological examination prior to DBS for patients with Parkinson's disease can provide information that helps the patient and caregivers "assess the risk–benefit ratio of the procedure within the patient's framework of desired outcomes, hopes and expectations" (p. 812). In other words, it can provide useful information regarding the capacity for informed consent. It also helps prepare the patient and family for probable outcomes in light of their expectations. Tröster, Ponce, and Moguel-Cobos (2018) also note that postoperative confusion is common and that a neuropsychological consultation prior to surgery can help prepare the patient and family to deal with this reality when it occurs.

In a review of several studies, however, Tröster (2017) emphasizes that persistent severe neuropsychological adverse events following successful DBS surgery are not common. Mild to moderate verbal fluency declines are the most commonly reported neuropsychological disturbance following surgery. However, psychiatric consequences may be more substantial, especially an increase in depression. Preparing patients and their families for the potential of these realities is an important service that clinical neuropsychologists can provide.

ADVANCES THAT MAY HELP PREDICT POST-SURGICAL NEUROPSYCHOLOGICAL OUTCOMES

Warren et al. (2014) noted that regions of the default mode network have been considered to represent important "cortical hubs" for integrating several neuropsychological functions. This point has been made several times in this book. Just because a specific region of the brain has a number of connections with other regions does not automatically mean, however, that that region or "hub" plays some unique or especially important role in complex neuropsychological abilities. It may not be just the number of connections but, rather, the degree to which those connections participate in other neural networks underlying various complex neuropsychological functions. Relatively small lesions to these complex "target" regions (regions that demonstrate a high degree of "participation coefficient" with other important neural networks) may produce more devastating neuropsychological outcomes. If this can be demonstrated, it has important implications for predicting the neuropsychological consequences of relatively focal lesions being removed during brain surgery.

Figure 11.2, from Warren et al. (2014), color codes the various brain neural networks or "systems" that have been identified through various neuroimaging techniques (some of which were described in Chapter 5, this volume). It also captures areas of overlap (again color coded) between various systems and points to "target" areas that demonstrate higher participation coefficients. Warren et al. then tested the hypothesis that more severe neuropsychological disturbances will be observed when these target areas are damaged than when nontargeted, control regions are affected. Table 11.1 summarizes the various cognitive domains sampled. Warren et al. demonstrated that patients with lesions in these target zones clearly were more impaired on a number of neuropsychological dimensions compared to patients whose brain lesions did not involve these target zones (Figure 11.3).

Although these findings are preliminary, they open up a new level of inquiry that may be very helpful to the neuropsychologist and neurosurgeon when they consult with a patient regarding the potential neuropsychological

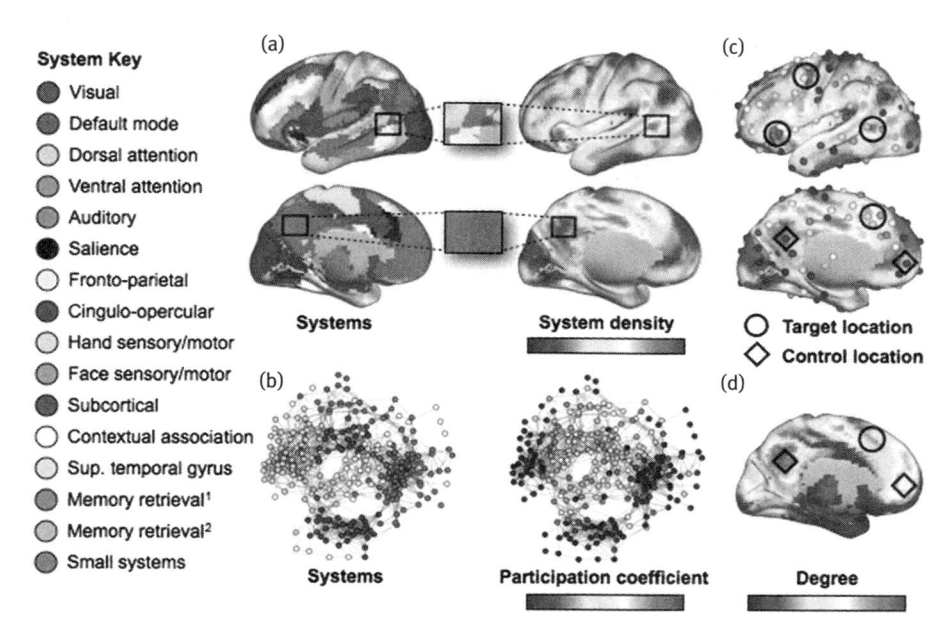

FIGURE 11.2 Network measures. (A) Consensus communities (systems; left) and plot of the density of these systems across the cortex (right). The blowup boxes illustrate how certain cortical locations contain many systems (top; a target location) or few systems (bottom; a control location). (B) Communities (systems) in a brain-wide network (left) and node participation coefficients (right), with warmer colors denoting nodes that display spontaneous blood oxygen level-dependent activity that correlates with multiple systems. (C) Plots of system density and participation coefficients overlaid. Target locations (circles) show where lesions might produce multisystem impairment. Control locations (diamonds) are predicted not to produce widespread impairment. Only four of six target locations are shown (those in the left hemisphere). (D) Node degree, with warmer colors indicating higher degree. Note that regions with high degree (D) may have low system density and/or participation coefficient (C) (See color plates).

Source: Reprinted from Warren, D. E., Power, J. D., Bruss, J., Denburg, N. L., Waldron, E. J., Sun, H., . . . Tranel, D., Network measures predict neuropsychological outcome after brain injury, *Proceedings of the National Academy of Sciences of the USA*, 111(39), 2014, p. 14247–14252, by permission of United States National Academy of Sciences.

consequences of a given surgery. Lesions involving the dorsal medial prefrontal cortex, the left posterior middle frontal gyrus, the left anterior insula, the right anterior insula, and the left posterior middle temporal gyrus resulted in more severe and widespread neuropsychological impairments as reported by Warren et al. (2014). Other studies need to determine the consistency of these findings. Nevertheless, this work represents an important advancement in understanding potential complex neuropsychological deficits following brain surgery. It encourages neurosurgeons to expand their view of what is "eloquent cortex." Eloquent cortex does not reflect purely sensory, motor, and language functions. It should include the concept of "cognitive (and I might add behavioral/affect) eloquence" that needs to be considered when an operation is being contemplated (Lang, 2017).

SUMMARY

There is certainly growing evidence that pre- and post-neurosurgical consultation with a clinical neuropsychologist may be advantageous to the patient and their family. It can provide information that is important for anticipating patient needs in the future and help to avoid needless frustrations after surgery. By

Table 11.1 Cognitive Domains, with Descriptions and/or Characteristic Examples

COGNITIVE DOMAIN[a]	DESCRIPTION
Orientation/attention	"... awareness of self in relation to one's surroundings ..." "... abilities for focused behavior ..."
Perception	"... involves active processing of the continuous torrent of sensations as well as their inhibition or filtering from consciousness."
Memory	"... the capacity to retain information and utilize it for adaptive purposes."
Verbal functions/language skills	"... the two-way translation mechanism between ... the organized manipulation of mental representations which constitutes thought, and the organized processing of verbal symbols and grammatical rules which constitutes sentences."
Construction/motor performance	"... combines perception with motor response ... has a spatial component."
Concept formation/reasoning	"... quality or process of thinking more than the content ..." "... thinking with a conscious intent to reach a conclusion."
Executive functions	"... (1) volition; (2) planning and decision making; (3) purposive action; and (4) effective performance."
Personal adjustment/emotional function	"... common direct effects of brain injury on personality are emotional dulling, disinhibition, diminution of anxiety with associated emotional blandness or mild euphoria, and reduced social sensitivity."
Adaptive functions	"The usual criterion of good outcome for younger adults ... is return to gainful employment." "For older people ... degree of independence, self-care, and whether the patient could return home rather than to a care facility."

[a]For each domain, the following rating scale was used: 0 = no impairment, meaning no significant impairment; 1 = moderate impairment, neuropsychological performance 1.5–2 standard deviations (SD) below normative expectations and some effect on activities of daily living; and 2 = severe impairment, neuropsychological performance at least 2 SD and typically ≥3 SD below normative expectations that substantially affect activities of daily living. Quotations describing each domain were drawn (whenever available) from corresponding chapter introductions in Lezak, Howieson, Bigler, and Tranel (2012) and from Warren et al. (2014).

Source: Reprinted from Warren, D. E., Power, J. D., Bruss, J., Denburg, N. L., Waldron, E. J., Sun, H., ... Tranel, D., Network measures predict neuropsychological outcome after brain injury, *Proceedings of the National Academy of Sciences of the USA*, 111(39), 2014, p. 14247–14252, by permission of United States National Academy of Sciences.

integrating neuropsychological observations regarding key behavioral and cognitive features of the patient pre-surgically with neuroimaging findings, a more informed view of what changes can be expected post-surgery is becoming a reality. Such consultations help establish a trusting relationship between the clinical neuropsychologist, the patient and family, and the neurosurgeon. That relationship can be used to help guide the patient and provide future psychological care, as demonstrated in Part IV of this book.

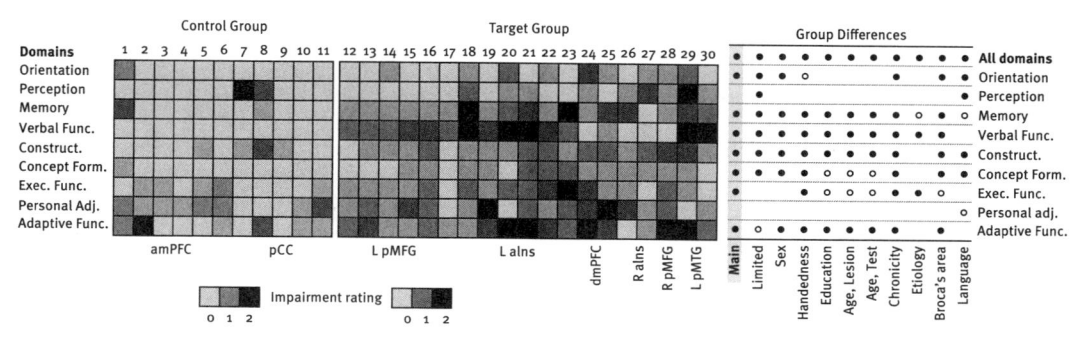

FIGURE 11.3 Individual mean ratings for impairment and analysis summary. (Left) Neuropsychological impairment across nine cognitive and behavioral domains for the control ($n = 11$) and target ($n = 19$) groups. Control cases are at left in shades of blue, target cases are at right in shades of red. Ratings of cognitive impairment for each case by domain were as follows: 0 = no impairment (gray), 1 = moderate impairment (light), and 2 = severe impairment (dark). Intermediate colors represent a score of 0.5 or 1.5 from averaging across two raters. Note the concentration of moderate and severe cognitive impairments among target cases. (Right) Summary of main analysis and follow-up analyses controlling for demographic, attribute, and lesion variables. Follow-up analyses controlling for several variables (see column labels) revealed a pattern broadly similar to the main analysis (leftmost data column, highlighted), with significant impairments of the target group always evident in at least two of nine cognitive domains. Main refers to the main analysis; Limited, results for less frequently sampled target locations only; Sex, mixed-sex locations only; Handedness, fully right-handed participants only; Education, years of education, controlled by regression (R); Age, Lesion, age at injury in years, R; Age, Test, age when tested, R; Chronicity, years between injury and test, R; Etiology, etiology of stroke only; Broca's area, no damage to Broca's area; Language, no impairment in verbal functions; solid circles, target group significantly impaired relative to control group ($p < .05$); open circles, marginal impairment ($p < .10$) (See color plates).

Source: Republished by permission of United States National Academy of Sciences, from Network measures predict neuropsychological outcome after brain injury, Warren, D. E., Power, J. D., Bruss, J., Denburg, N. L., Waldron, E. J., Sun, H., . . . Tranel, D., *Proceedings of the National Academy of Sciences of the USA*, 111(39), 2014; permission conveyed through Copyright Clearance Center, Inc.

REFERENCES

Al-Khindi, T., Macdonald, R. L., & Schweizer, T. A. (2010). Cognitive and functional outcome after aneurysmal subarachnoid hemorrhage. *Stroke*, 41(8), e519–e536.

Bronstein, J. M., Tagliati, M., Alterman, R. L., Lozano, A. M., Volkmann, J., Stefani, A., . . . Krack, P. (2011). Deep brain stimulation for Parkinson disease: An expert consensus and review of key issues. *Archives of Neurology*, 68(2), 165.

Buchanan, K. M., Elias, L. J., & Goplen, G. B. (2000). Differing perspectives on outcome after subarachnoid hemorrhage: The patient, the relative, the neurosurgeon. *Neurosurgery*, 46(4), 831–840.

Fasano, A., Romito, L. M., Daniele, A., Piano, C., Zinno, M., Bentivoglio, A. R., & Albanese, A. (2010). Motor and cognitive outcome in patients with Parkinson's disease 8 years after subthalamic implants. *Brain*, 133(9), 2664–2676.

Fields, J. (2015). Effects of deep brain stimulation in movement disorders on cognition and behavior.
In A. Tröster (Ed.), *Clinical neuropsychology and cognitive neurology of Parkinson's disease and other movement disorders* (pp. 332–375). New York, NY: Oxford University Press.

Kang, D.-H., Hwang, Y.-H., Kim, Y.-S., Bae, G. Y., & Lee, S. J. (2013). Cognitive outcome and clinically silent thromboembolic events after coiling of asymptomatic unruptured intracranial aneurysms. *Neurosurgery*, 72(4), 638–645.

Lang, S. (2017). Cognitive eloquence in neurosurgery: Insight from graph theoretical analysis of complex brain networks. *Medical Hypotheses*, 98, 49–56.

Lezak, M. D., Howieson, D. B., Bigler, E. D., & Tranel, D. (2012). *Neuropsychological assessment*. New York, NY: Oxford University Press.

Lishman, W. A. (1968). Brain damage in relation to psychiatric disability after head injury. *British Journal of Psychiatry*, 114(509), 373–410.

Maurice-Williams, R., Willison, J., & Hatfield, R. (1991). The cognitive and psychological sequelae of uncomplicated aneurysm surgery.

Max, J. E., Koele, S. L., Castillo, C. C., Lindgren, S. D., Arndt, S., Bokura, H., . . . Sato, Y. (2000). Personality change disorder in children and adolescents following traumatic brain injury. *Journal of the International Neuropsychological Society, 6*(3), 279–289.

Nguyen, D., Singh, S., & Zaatreh, M. (2003). Hypothalamic hamartomas: Seven cases and review of the literature. *Epilepsy Behavior, 4,* 246–258.

Ohue, S., Oka, Y., Kumon, Y., Ohta, S., Sakaki, S., Hatakeyama, T., . . . Ohnishi, T. (2003). Importance of neuropsychological evaluation after surgery in patients with unruptured cerebral aneurysms. *Surgical Neurology, 59*(4), 271–277.

Prigatano, G. P. (1995). Preparing patients for possible neuropsychological consequences after brain surgery. *BNI Quarterly, 11*(4), 4–8.

Prigatano, G. P. (2007). Cognitive and behavioral dysfunction in children with hypothalamic hamartoma and epilepsy. *Seminars in Pediatric Neurology, 14*(2), 65–72.

Prigatano, G. P., Wethe, J. V., Gray, J. A., Wang, N., Chung, S., Ng, Y.-T., . . . Kerrigan, J. F. (2008). Intellectual functioning in presurgical patients with hypothalamic hamartoma and refractory epilepsy. *Epilepsy & Behavior, 13*(1), 149–155.

Saint-Cyr, J. A., Trépanier, L. L., Kumar, R., Lozano, A. M., & Lang, A. (2000). Neuropsychological consequences of chronic bilateral stimulation of the subthalamic nucleus in Parkinson's disease. *Brain, 123*(10), 2091–2108.

Saper, C. B. (2004). The hypothalamus. In G. Paxinos & J. K. Mai (Eds.), *The human nervous system* (pp. 513–550). Amsterdam, the Netherlands: Elsevier.

Sutterer, M. J., Bruss, J., Boes, A. D., Voss, M. W., Bechara, A., & Tranel, D. (2016). Canceled connections: Lesion-derived network mapping helps explain differences in performance on a complex decision-making task. *Cortex, 78,* 31–43.

Towgood, K., Ogden, J. A., & Mee, E. (2004). Neurological, neuropsychological, and psychosocial outcome following treatment of unruptured intracranial aneurysms: A review and commentary. *Journal of the International Neuropsychological Society, 10*(1), 114–134.

Tröster, A., Ponce, F., & Moguel-Cobos, G. (2018). Deep brain stimulation for Parkinson's disease: Current perspectives on patient selection with an emphasis on neuropsychology. *Journal of Parkinsonism and Restless Legs Syndrome, 8,* 33–48.

Tröster, A. I. (2017). Some clinically useful information that neuropsychology provides patients, carepartners, neurologists, and neurosurgeons about deep brain stimulation for Parkinson's disease. *Archives of Clinical Neuropsychology, 32*(7), 810–828.

Tuffiash, E., Tamargo, R. J., & Hillis, A. E. (2003). Craniotomy for treatment of unruptured aneurysms is not associated with long-term cognitive dysfunction. *Stroke, 34*(9), 2195–2199.

Valdueza, J. M., Cristante, L., Dammann, O., Bentele, K., Vortmeyer, A., Saeger, W., . . . Herrmann, H.-D. (1994). Hypothalamic hamartomas: With special reference to gelastic epilepsy and surgery. *Neurosurgery, 34*(6), 949–958.

Voon, V., Kubu, C., Krack, P., Houeto, J. L., & Tröster, A. I. (2006). Deep brain stimulation: Neuropsychological and neuropsychiatric issues. *Movement Disorders, 21*(Suppl. 14), S305–S327.

Warren, D. E., Power, J. D., Bruss, J., Denburg, N. L., Waldron, E. J., Sun, H., . . . Tranel, D. (2014). Network measures predict neuropsychological outcome after brain injury. *Proceedings of the National Academy of Sciences of the USA, 111*(39), 14247–14252.

Weaver, F. M., Follett, K., Stern, M., Hur, K., Harris, C., Marks, W. J., . . . Moy, C. S. (2009). Bilateral deep brain stimulation vs. best medical therapy for patients with advanced Parkinson disease: A randomized controlled trial. *JAMA, 301*(1), 63–73.

Wethe, J. V., Prigatano, G. P., Gray, J., Chapple, K., Rekate, H. L., & Kerrigan, J. F. (2013). Cognitive functioning before and after surgical resection for hypothalamic hamartoma and epilepsy. *Neurology, 81*(2), 1044–1050.

12

THE MULTIFACETED NATURE OF PSYCHOLOGICAL TREATMENTS

> When you want to establish the existence of something large, such as the San Andreas Fault, you need to stand back and take a picture from a distance. A microscope can tell you about the soil in and around the fault or the nature of the rocks in the area. But you cannot establish that the fault exists in the first place, or the nature of the phenomenon that you need to explain, with a microscope. You need a telescope, or a Landsat photo, to get the larger picture.
>
> —Donald (2001, p. 9)

SO IT is when describing various psychological treatments that can contribute substantially to the psychological care of a person after a brain disorder. The neuroscientific "lens" of brain imaging of different patient groups and the detailed behavioral and neuropsychological analyses of those groups provide fascinating details for the clinical neuropsychologist. Yet, those details need to be integrated with a "telescopic view of human nature," knowledge of how different brain disorders typically affect people at different stages of psychosocial development, and knowledge of how methods used to reduce human suffering and aid psychological adjustment after a brain disorder must be modified in light of the person's psychodynamics and cultural background. This perspective was explicitly stated in Chapter 1. In this chapter, the focus is on describing multiple sources of information that have relevance to providing psychological care interventions beyond that of diagnosis and education following a brain disorder. This chapter sets the stage for how the approach advocated in this book can be applied to the psychological care of individuals with different brain disorders occurring at different stages in the life span (discussed in Part IV of this volume).

PSYCHOLOGICAL CARE AND THE ADJUSTMENT PROCESS FOLLOWING A BRAIN DISORDER

Psychological care is aimed at helping patients improve their psychological adjustment following a brain disorder by minimizing the direct and indirect effects of their neuropsychological disturbances in everyday life. As indicated in Chapter 1, psychological care to improve a sense of well-being and aid the psychological adjustment process can include a wide variety of activities and potential psychological treatments. Those interventions should help maintain and protect cognitive and affective aspects of brain (i.e., neuropsychological) functioning in a manner that aids adjustment to the "external" world in which the person lives and the "internal" subjective world the person experiences.

Psychological adjustment is a dynamic process that can at times appear satisfactory (or positive) and at other times seems nonexistent (or negative) given how the person describes himself or herself and how the individual functions in relation to others (Prigatano, 2018). Because individuals tend to fluctuate in their subjective sense of personal well-being, the adjustment process is never static. It is constantly changing (in minor to major ways), depending on the patient's conscious awareness of his or her cognitive and affective strengths and weakness, unconscious (or nonconscious) methods of coping (or behaving when faced with different choices), and the adjustment problems faced in the "real world" (e.g., perceived and actual ability to successfully meet academic requirements, skills at being gainfully employed, driving a car, making and maintaining friendships, and sustaining self-care activities). Box 12.1 lists common features of positive psychological adjustment observed in patients several months or years after moderate to severe traumatic brain injury (TBI), and Box 12.2 lists common features of negative psychological adjustment in the same population (Prigatano, 2018). These positive and negative features are also seen in various patient groups who have suffered a brain disorder.

The question is, What psychological methods seem to foster a positive psychological adjustment in different subgroups of patients with varying brain disorders? The process of psychological adjustment is highly individualized and can draw on several different psychological treatment methods of care. However, whatever methods are applied,

---

Box 12.1. Common Features of Positive Psychological Adjustment After Moderate to Severe Traumatic Brain Injury

1. Progressive and, at times, slow recognition of how a person has been affected by the TBI
2. Expressed sadness and, at times, anger and anxiety with the situation
3. A willingness to talk to others about what the person experiences and fears for the future
4. An active effort to use compensatory strategies to cope with functional limitations
5. A capacity to express appreciation over what the person has retained (not lost), and a capacity to express a sincere "thank you" to those who help the individual
6. A capacity to experience "real" satisfaction in personal accomplishments, no matter how disparate they are compared to previous levels of accomplishment
7. An experience of joy or satisfaction when helping others
8. A capacity not to be preoccupied with "how I used to be"
9. An active engagement in what makes life purposeful for the person
10. Expanding, not contracting, social interactions
11. Accepting help from others (often via rehabilitation or psychotherapy)

Source: Reprinted from Prigatano, G. P., Psychological adjustment to the effects of a moderate to severe traumatic brain injury, in J. M. Silver, T. W. McAllister, & D. B. Arciniegas (Eds.), *Textbook of Traumatic Brain Injury*, 3rd ed., pp. 817–829, 2018, by permission of American Psychiatric Association Press.

Box 12.2. Common Features of Negative Psychological Adjustment After Moderate to Severe Traumatic Brain Injury

1. A "flight into health"—"I am 100% back to normal" within a short period of time after the TBI
2. Failure (or inability) to recognize and verbally describe negative changes in functional capacity caused by the TBI
3. Persistent angry feelings about the events surrounding the TBI and life's present circumstances
4. Glib discussion about what the person experiences and no expressed concerns for the future
5. Failure to embrace compensatory strategies on a daily basis
6. Constant dissatisfaction with life experiences and accomplishments (often signaling severe depression)
7. A self-centered approach to life without having any joy in helping others
8. Constant preoccupation of how "things used to be" or "what life was like for me in the past"
9. An inability to experience activities that give a sense of "purpose to my life"
10. Progressive social isolation
11. Failure to make changes necessary to effectively work with those who want to help the person

Source: Reprinted from Prigatano, G. P., Psychological adjustment to the effects of a moderate to severe traumatic brain injury, in J. M. Silver, T. W. McAllister, & D. B. Arciniegas (Eds.), *Textbook of Traumatic Brain Injury*, 3rd ed., pp. 817–829, 2018, by permission of American Psychiatric Association Press.

they must be experienced as personally relevant to each individual given the person's age, gender, psychosocial and cultural background, level of cognitive functioning, and personality. Churchill et al. (2010) note that four basic psychological treatment approaches have been clinically used to help people improve their psychological well-being: the psychoanalytic/dynamic approach (Freud, 1900; Jung, 1964; Leichsenring & Klein, 2014), the humanistic approach (May, 1953, 1969; Rogers, 1951, 1961), the behavioral approach (Skinner, 1953; Wolpe, 1958; Wolpe & Lazarus, 1966), and the cognitive–behavioral approach (Beck, 1976; McKay, Davis, & Fanning, 2007). In addition to these approaches, there has been considerable interest in and scientific work done on two factors that may impact the effectiveness of medical and psychological care: the "placebo effect" (Diederich & Goetz, 2008) and the "resiliency" features of the individual (Richardson, 2002).

Finally, observations from literature, history, and the general study of humanities provide poignant insights into human behavior that are potentially relevant to psychological care interventions. Some of those insights are reviewed in this chapter. The point of departure for this chapter, however, is a closer examination of placebo effects.

PLACEBO EFFECTS IN SCIENCE AND HEALTH CARE

Benedetti, Mayberg, Wager, Stohler, and Zubieta (2005) note that there is no single placebo effect; rather, there are many. The concept of a placebo effect emerges when one observes that patients report or demonstrate some benefit in symptom reduction when the treatment provided was not a "real treatment" (i.e., applying an agent of change known to target or produce a specific biological or pathophysiological change associated with a disease and its symptom manifestations; Miller, Colloca, & Kaptchuk, 2009). Benedetti et al. also note that "the study of the placebo effect, at its core, is the study of how the context of beliefs and values shape brain processes related to perception and emotions and, ultimately, mental and physical health" (p. 10390). Thus, the study of placebo effects is very relevant to the process of providing psychological care.

Placebo effects have been clearly recognized in pharmacological research aimed at pain relief and the reduction of depression (Benedetti et al., 2005; Diederich & Goetz, 2008). In these studies, analyses of cerebrospinal fluid and neuroimaging blood flow changes in the brain repeatedly show that "placebo responders" have consistently higher concentrations of endorphins and patterns of brain activation suggestive of some modification of limbic and paralimbic appraisal of pain. Benedetti et al. make two very important points: Placebo effects appear to be associated with either past conscious or unconscious (possibly classically conditioned) learning, and they "enhance the specific effect of a treatment" (p. 10391). An early study by Desharnais, Jobin, Côté, Lévesque, and Godin (1993) illustrates Benedetti et al.'s second point. When young adults were enrolled in an exercise program aimed at improving aerobic fitness, the experimental group was told the program would also improve psychological well-being. The control group was simply informed of the potential physical benefits of the exercise program. Both groups achieved improved fitness scores of equal magnitude. Both groups also reported higher self-esteem scores (a measure of psychological well-being), but the effect was substantially greater in the experimental group.

In an attempt to explain placebo effects, Moerman and Jonas (2002) proposed that the placebo effect in medicine reflects how people interpret or extract meaning from what their doctor tells them will be the most likely benefit of a given treatment. For those who doubt that such verbal communications make any difference in the real world, Moerman and Jonas asked their scientific readers to reflect on their emotional (including physical) reactions when being told by someone that "I love you" versus hearing from a granting agency that their grant proposal has been rejected after they had spent several months of hard work developing it. Words clearly affect our sense of psychological well-being, but the impact may be different depending on who is saying those words.

In this regard, Miller et al. (2009) propose that it is the relationship between the doctor and the patient that ultimately influences the placebo effects. They emphasize that all of medicine has repeatedly observed this "interpersonal component of healing" (p. 518). They suggest that this component specifically produces symptom relief but does not halt the underlying disease process. Only "natural healing" (e.g., skin repair after a cut) or "technological healing" (e.g., surgical repair of a brain aneurysm) directly triggers the underlying pathophysiological changes necessary to reverse or stop a disease process. These investigators also ask the following important question: Why does the nature of this relationship matter so much in reducing symptoms? Citing the work of Humphrey (2002), they suggest that the relationship can trigger a sense of hope. Miller et al. go on to speculate that "as social animals, we are attuned from infancy to look to authoritative or protective figures—initially, our parents—to intervene to relieve distress" (p. 531). Note how important the experience of hope is in the Eriksonian model of psychological coping with different psychological crises (described in Chapter 4, this volume). Also note that the nature of the relationship between the health care provider and the patient can and does influence symptom relief. Reducing symptoms is often an essential feature of psychological care after a brain disorder.

Thus, to the degree to which it is possible, the psychological care provider should foster a sense of (realistic) hope. Also to the degree to which it is possible, the psychological care provider should strive to develop a professional relationship with the patient that helps the person make positive behavioral choices. This requires an understanding of the patient's phenomenological experiences and how past interpersonal relationships have or have not helped the individual make good choices in life. These activities can foster a positive therapeutic alliance between the treating clinician and the patient. As important as such an alliance can be, much more than a therapeutic alliance is needed to practically help a patient. When evaluating treatment size effects of the therapeutic alliance on psychotherapy outcome, D. Martin, Garske, and Davis (2000) reported an average mild size effect of approximately .22. As some of the case examples presented in Part IV of this volume illustrate, however, the strength of the therapeutic alliance with a person with a brain disorder may well determine the outcome of psychological care interventions. Moreover, there are certain qualities of a person that can have an even greater effect. Some of these qualities are summarized by the term *resiliency*.

RESILIENCY AND PSYCHOLOGICAL CARE

The topic of resiliency is important in the discussion of psychological care because it especially addresses the questions of how and why some people make a good psychological adjustment to very adverse events in life, whereas others do not (Fletcher & Sarkar, 2013). Like placebo effects, resiliency effects tell us much about human behavior that is relevant to psychological care. Research on resiliency has not been able to adequately answer the question of whether resiliency is an inherent personality trait of the individual, a process that evolves only when adequate support systems are in place, or simply a term to refer to unexplained "good outcomes after the fact." For example, patients with a history of acquired brain injury who demonstrate behaviors indicative of a good psychological adjustment are often described as "more resilient" (Neils-Strunjas et al., 2017). Is this an independent predictor of outcome or simply a defining feature of a good outcome?

Early psychoanalytic work on resiliency was greatly influenced by attachment theory as proposed by Bowlby (1969, 1973, 1980). Acknowledging this influence, Fonagy, Steele, Steele, Higgitt, and Target (1994) suggested that "resilience is *normal* development under difficult conditions" (p. 233). This ability to develop normally in individuals without brain dysfunction is heavily influenced by the quality of attachment the person experienced with primary caretakers early in life. Infants who could be readily comforted and return to play after being briefly separated from their parents were described as having a "secure attachment." This form of attachment was considered predictive of a resilient child. These clinician–researchers also emphasized the role of a "reflective self-function" in the development of resiliency (p. 233). That is, persons who can stop and reflect on what they think, feel, and do are in a better position to cope with life's adversities. They are more "psychologically minded." They have more impulse control. This capacity for impulse control or the ability to delay gratification in childhood has been clearly related to later academic success (Casey et al., 2011; see also Chapter 4, this volume).

Fonagy et al. (1994) listed several of the empirical correlates of "resiliency" as documented by other researchers, including (but not limited to) higher IQ; higher socioeconomic status; higher education; "easy temperament"; younger age; a better network of friendships or relationships; involvement in organized religious activities; good interpersonal awareness and empathy; a history of self-efficacy; a higher sense of self-worth; and, quite interestingly, a sense of humor. Unfortunately, brain injury often negatively affects many of these characteristics, but some of them do survive the effects of brain injury. Recall that in Chapter 8, it was mentioned that Kirk Douglas wrote about the role of humor, the loving relationship he had with his mother early in life, and his ability to help address the needs of others as important factors in reducing his depression and fostering a successful adaptation to his stroke.

More recent scientific observations on resiliency emphasize many of the same points (Bethell, Newacheck, Hawes, & Halfon, 2014; Stewart & Yuen, 2011). However, there is a growing interest in the potential underlying neurobiological correlates of resiliency. For example, Feder, Nestler, and Charney (2009) review animal research that suggests that different neural circuitry underlies the fear response, the response to reward, and the regulation of emotion. They suggest that a complex array of interactions between cortical and subcortical functions modulates the individual's response to stress. Southwick and Charney (2012) reiterate that "resilience to stress is a complex multidimensional construct" (p. 79) that is not easily defined, but genetic factors interact with environmental experiences to produce either nonresilient or resilient individuals. Depressive symptomatology, for example, has repeatedly been linked to low resiliency levels in people (Schure, Odden, & Goins, 2013). What is interesting about Southwick and Charney's analysis is their approach, which clarifies the potential interplay between "environmental stressors and genetic predisposition" in putting an individual "at risk for depression" and the impact of potential therapeutic interventions that result in greater "resilience protective factors" (p. 81). Figure 12.1 summarizes many of these potential interactions.

	Depression risk factors	Therapeutic intervention	Resilience protective factors
Cognitive/behavioral	Weak executive function: weak coping self-efficacy; negative attention bias; cognitive inflexibility	Cognitive behavioral therapy with cognitive reappraisal; positive emotion excercises, coping skill development, and training; well-being therapy	Strong executive function; high coping self-efficacy; positive emotions; realistic optimism; cognitive flexibility
Emotion regulation	Weak regulation (e.g., anhedonia; slow stress recovery)	Mindfulness; training; antidepressant medications	Strong regulation (e.g., delay gratification; rapid stress recovery)
Social	Weak social skills; minimal social network; no resilient role models	Social emotional training; network support treatment	Strong social skills; diverse social network; resilient role models
Physical health	Sleep deprivation; poor cardiovascular fitness; poor nutrition; obesity	Teach sleep hygiene; excercise regimen; improve diet	Strong sleep habits; physically fit; good nutrition
Neurobiology	Dysregulated HPA axis and SNS in response to stress; attenuated prefontal cortical executive function and stress-induced limbic system hyperactivity	Neural circuit training; novel medications (corticotropin-releasing factor, NPY, GABA, glutamate)	Effective regulation of HPA axis and SNS in response to stress; robust prefrontal cortical executive function and capacity to regulate limbic reactivity to stress

Environmental stressors and genetic predisposition

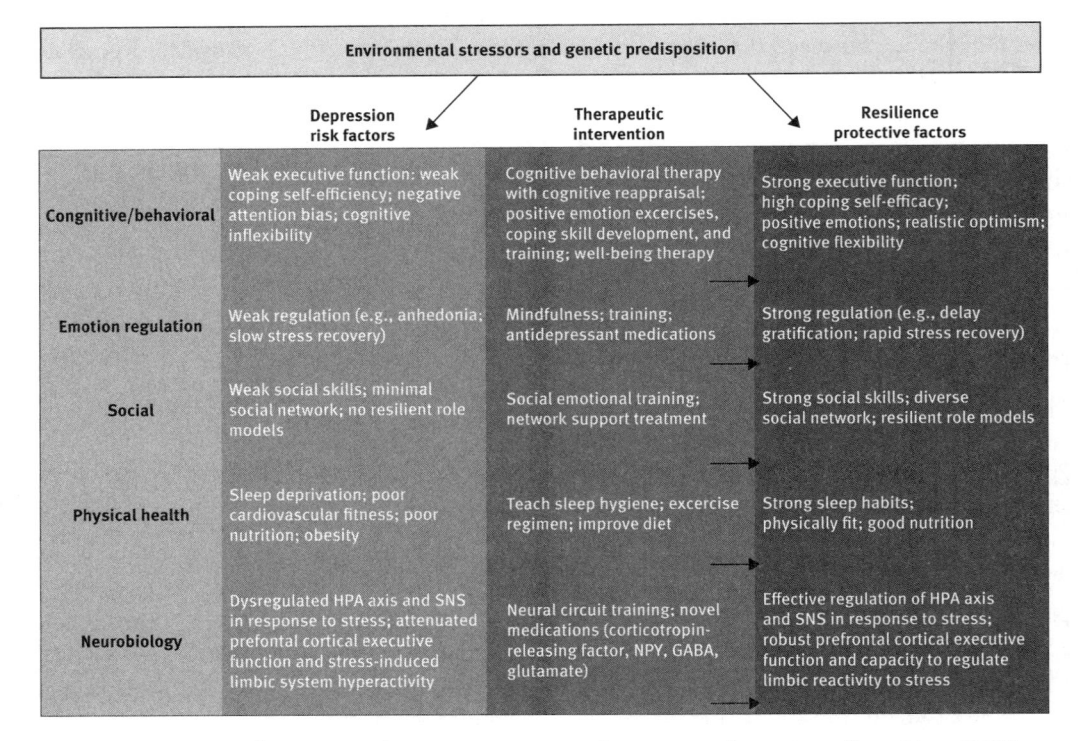

FIGURE 12.1 Potential interactions between environmental stressors and genetic predisposition. GABA, γ-aminobutyric acid; HPA, hypothalamic–pituitary–adrenal axis; NPY, neuropeptide Y; SNS, sympathetic nervous system (See color plates).

Source: Reprinted from Southwick, S. M., & Charney, D. S., The science of resilience: Implications for the prevention and treatment of depression, *Science*, *338*(6103), 2012, p. 79–82, by permission of American Association for the Advancement of Science.

Southwick and Charney (2012) note that at the physical health level, sleep deprivation, poor nutrition, obesity, and poor cardiovascular fitness place one at risk for depression. Direct interventions aimed at improving each of these dimensions result in "resilience protective factors." That is, persons can cope with adversity much better if they get restful and adequate sleep, have a healthy diet, lose weight, and improve their cardiovascular fitness. Regulating one's emotional responsiveness is also important. Cognitive–behavioral therapy, mindfulness training, and psychotropic medications appear helpful in this regard. Pet therapy or lovingly taking care of a pet may also reduce levels of stress. Finally, improving coping skills by fostering "cognitive flexibility" and the reappraisal of life's circumstances can also lead to improved psychological functioning. This latter goal is often the focus of psychodynamic forms of psychotherapy (Prigatano & Salas, 2017).

Similar to the earlier observations of Fonagy et al. (1994), Southwick and Charney (2012) list several psychosocial factors that have been associated with resiliency:

> Psychosocial factors that have been associated with resilience include positive emotion and optimism, loving caretakers and sturdy role models, a history of mastering challenges, cognitive flexibility including the ability to cognitively reframe adversity in a more positive light, the ability to regulate emotions, high coping self-efficacy, strong social support, disciplined focus on skill development, altruism, commitment to a valued cause or purpose, capacity to extract meaning from adverse situations, support from religion and spirituality, attention to health and good cardiovascular fitness, and the capacity to rapidly recover from stress. (p. 80)

The relevance of the previously discussed literature for the psychological care of persons with a brain disorder is that several domains of functioning have to be developed and reinforced to aid their psychological adjustment. Further efforts at education (despite cognitive limitations) appear important. Learning skills to establish friendships and increasing one's awareness of others' personal needs and struggles are important. Developing self-efficacy skills, no matter how basic, can be important for sustaining a sense of dignity and self-worth. Ongoing efforts at self-control are important. Improved diet, sleep, and cardiovascular fitness should also not be overlooked. Perhaps most interesting, however, is the special role of humor in resiliency.

Having a "sense of humor" may certainly be related to managing stress (R. Martin & Lefcourt, 1983; R. Martin, Puhlik-Doris, Larsen, Gray, & Weir, 2003), including the stress associated with life-threatening illnesses (Cousins, 1979). The type of humor, however, may well be associated with different attachment styles and is effective in lowering stress, as demonstrated by Besser, Luyten, and Mayes (2012). These investigators described both adaptive and maladaptive humor. Maladaptive humor is most often applied when a person's attachment relationships have been associated with a history of either anxiety or avoidance. Adaptive humor, on the other hand, often uses humor to facilitate interpersonal relationships and reduce interpersonal conflict or tension. The latter type of humor was described as the only type of humor associated with low levels of distress. It was considered an important potential feature for fostering resiliency. Again, this type of humor is reflected in the writings of Kirk Douglas (see Chapter 8, this volume).

A joke is often humorous when two opposing lines of reason clash and an unexpected "message" or moral to the story is recognized (McGhee & Pistolesi, 1979). Humor involves insight and knowledge about the human condition. It allows people to not be too serious about themselves and others. But at its core, humor involves "insight." People cannot spontaneously laugh at a joke if they do not "get it." The ability and *desire* to obtain insight into the truths about one's life often play a key role in establishing a positive psychological adjustment to any adversity one must face. An unwillingness to face the truth about one's life often is associated with a poor psychological adjustment outcome (see Chapters 19 and 21, this volume). To highlight this reality, the topic also needs to be approached from the perspective of literature and the study of the humanities.

GANDHI'S EXPERIMENTS WITH TRUTH

Mohandas K. Gandhi had a profound effect on the lives of many people. He is, of course, best known for his ability to produce and sustain a political movement that led to freeing India from British rule using nonviolent means. His life story, however, has been an inspiration to many people (e.g., see Erikson, 1969). Key to Gandhi's success was his preoccupation/obsession with understanding the truth about himself and the truth about how people treat each other; his autobiography is subtitled *The Story of My Experiments with Truth* (1957/1963). Based on his life, several individuals have highlighted and summarized some of Gandhi's astute observations. They can be readily found on the internet. Those observations have special relevance for understanding what can be involved when helping a person achieve a positive psychological adjustment to life's problems. The adjustment often requires sacrifice (and delayed gratification) and assistance to others.

In previous chapters, man's animal nature was documented. One does not have to be "Freudian" in orientation to life to readily observe that all animals (including humans) display sexual and aggressive behaviors on a regular basis. These behaviors can be life sustaining or destructive. They are powerful forces that need some "balance" or "control" to sustain human physical and psychological development. Gandhi, who was an expert at using nonviolent means to make important personal and political changes, had much to say about the "roots of violence." He is credited with a number of observations about human nature and what aspects of human beings seem to foster violence, which are discussed next.

Experiencing the benefits associated with wealth without earning that wealth can have devastating interpersonal consequences. One may perceive oneself as "entitled" to a "privileged life" and view others as not as "worthy." This produces a cancerous source of self-perceived superiority over others and a tendency to mistreat them. Aggression and violent behavior often follow. Pleasure obtained without conscience also frequently leads to violence. That is, obtaining the pleasures of sexuality in a manner that is consistent with one's moral code is crucial in order not to destroy marriages and not to produce harm to oneself and others. Interestingly, Gandhi suggested that "knowledge without character" may predispose a person to actions that can lead to violent behavior. "Knowledge is power," and not using power with a sense of responsibility is dangerous. Related to this observation was the dictum that "commerce without morality" leads to wealth for some and poverty for others. It was a moral injustice that sooner or later would produce a violent response. For the scientist reading this book, Gandhi proposed that "science without humanity" also predisposed us to use the knowledge resulting from scientific endeavors in ways that are not necessarily helpful to our fellow human beings. The developments of gunpowder, dynamite, and nuclear weapons demonstrate this reality.

Although religious beliefs may help people cope with life's problems and treat each other in a more supportive way, Gandhi also observed that "worship without (personal) sacrifice" can readily lead to violence. The need for self-control (or self-sacrifice) was crucial for developing a truly spiritual sense to one's life. Wars within and between religious groups highlight how destructive religious beliefs can be if individuals practicing those religious beliefs have not developed a personal sense of spirituality based on self-sacrifice. Finally, Gandhi noted that "politics without principles" was a sure recipe for civil wars and wars between nations. One cannot govern or rule groups of people based on untruths for very long. Gandhi was profoundly sensitive to the issues of fairness and the unmet needs of people less fortunate than himself. His work gave special meaning to everyone's life because he focused on trying to help others in need. The importance of this experience for a personal sense of psychological well-being is also seen in the work of a less well-known South African.

DR. BENJAMIN'S WORK IN PROVIDING COMFORT TO HIS PATIENTS

In 1985, I traveled to South Africa for the first time to give lectures and provide a workshop on neuropsychological rehabilitation. During that trip, I asked to visit a hospital to observe the typical care provided to patients with neurological disorders. I did not fully realize the political implications of my request. It was the time of apartheid, and my hosts found the request a little uncomfortable. Finally, I was allowed to visit a state hospital for patients who had a mixture of severe psychiatric disorders and some ill-defined neurological diseases. The patients were a mix of White and Black individuals. I will never forget this experience. It had a profound personal and professional impact on me.

I met a "physically small, but big-hearted" Jewish psychiatrist named Dr. Benjamin. Working in a very impoverished setting in which minimal psychotropic medications were available, he was in charge of caring for clearly psychotic patients. To help his patients, he provided them with psychodrama exercises that proved very effective. For example, he asked patients to imagine they were waiting for a bus to take them into the fields to work early in the morning. It was cold and damp, but they had to stay there in order to make enough money to care for their families. To take their minds off their suffering, they should sing a song together. He then stood between two large Black female nurses (archetypical mother figures) who began to clap their hands in a rhythm that was "truly out of Africa." It stimulated in me and others a soothing primordial state of comfort.

As the nurses clapped their hands, they began to sing a beautiful song, and some of the severely impaired patients began to look up and begin singing as well. During this time, there was a sense of inner peace and community in all of us. When the event was over, Dr. Benjamin asked if I wished to say a few words to his patients and nursing staff. Usually I am not at a loss to say something, but on this occasion I was so moved by what I had just experienced that all I could say was that I wished I could sing them a country-western song (I had been living in Oklahoma City just prior to my visit). I eventually said a few words, but I do not remember what I said. I acutely remember, however, what was said to me by Dr. Benjamin. He made the comment that the purpose of life is simply to provide some comfort to others while we are all alive. This comment by Dr. Benjamin highlights what I find most meaningful in my work as a psychologist with clinical and neuropsychology interests. Although having a scientific understanding of the various psychological and neuropsychological phenomena that we observe is very rewarding, enjoyable, and exciting, this "pure knowledge" does not do much unless it reduces the suffering of another human being. This is the first and final goal of psychological care.

Csikszentmihalyi (1999) also made an important observation relevant to Dr. Benjamin's insight. He notes, as many others have, that the experience of happiness in life can be fleeting. When a person is completely engrossed in a creative activity that is personally meaningful, there is often a subjective sense of "flow" in one's personal energies or insights. These experiences are often associated with a sense of happiness and personal well-being. When being taken up with these experiences, one is often not focused on the tragedies of life but, rather, on the joys of life. The experiences may vary greatly across individuals, depending on their personal interests, training, and childhood upbringing. For certain scientists, the experience of discovering a predictive law of nature may produce such an exhilarating feeling in their life. For physicians, it might be associated with being totally engrossed in a surgical operation that saves a person's life. For a pet owner, it may be being totally absorbed in playing with one's dog and experiencing the dog's insightful reactions to events even though the animal cannot talk. The important point here is that helping people experience moments of being engrossed in meaningful creative activities may be quite relevant to their psychological care.

FURTHER PSYCHOLOGICAL INSIGHTS FROM THE STUDY OF THE HUMANITIES

In *Fiddler on the Roof*, the main actor, Tevye, states that "tradition" tells man who he is and what God expects of him (Stein, 1964). By following (religious and cultural) "tradition," we can live stable lives and endure suffering because it is God's plan for us. This theme is alive and well and can be readily observed on television each day as various preachers tell us to trust in God and to do God's will. If we do so, they assure us, everything will be okay. The continued experience of wars, constant interpersonal conflict, and struggles by all humanity has, however, led some people to the sober thought that religion may not hold all the answers about how to live and maintain a sense of psychological well-being.

In *Zorba the Greek*, the repressed and somewhat neurotic Englishman asks Zorba to "teach me to dance" (Kazantzakis, 1952), by which he means teach him how best to live and enjoy life. One of Zorba's dictums is to say, "In work I am your man, but in play [meaning playing the satori, a musical instrument], I am my own—I mean free!" (pp. 14–15). One of the messages of this literary masterpiece is that work is important for survival, but one should remain free in spirit. Live the life you want to live—not the life others say you should live. This latter approach can have a profound personal and political impact. The US Declaration of Independence and the US Constitution are based in part on this principle and grant human beings "inalienable rights," including freedom of speech and freedom to seek out personal happiness. Gandhi (1957/1963) also emphasized that true happiness and contentment in life come from harmonizing what we think, say, and do. Hypocrisy and slavery are doomed to make a person unhappy. Science has not yet articulated these insights.

PSYCHODYNAMIC APPROACHES TO PSYCHOLOGICAL CARE

In the preceding sections of this chapter, several potential "ingredients" to psychological care were introduced, including establishing a sense of hope, developing a therapeutic relationship, providing comfort, encouraging the desire to reflect on oneself and others, and recognizing the importance of self-control. Facing the truth in one's life and finding happiness via honesty are a recurring theme in many contemporary and historical writings on psychological well-being and psychological care. However, there may be other factors necessary for effective psychological care. These efforts have undergone scientific scrutiny.

Thomas Szasz (1978) argued that psychotherapy was not a true therapy in the medical sense of the word because it did not deal with physiological interventions. It was merely a "talk therapy" that helped people learn to live life better. Some even argued that psychotherapy was nothing but the "purchase of friendship" (Schofield, 1964), and its effectiveness was based primarily on persuasion techniques (Frank & Frank, 1991). These are oversimplified but important criticisms to address when arguing that psychological care, which at times includes various forms of psychotherapy, is an important clinical service that is medically necessary.

The health psychology literature provides numerous examples of how the psychosocial and psychological state of the person is intricately related to major medical problems. A few examples are given here. There is an extensive literature on the connection between anxiety, depression, obesity, and diabetes (Everson, Maty, Lynch, & Kaplan, 2002; Scott et al., 2007). In large epidemiological studies, anxiety and depression have been linked to excessive weight gain (Brumpton, Langhammer, Romundstad, Chen, & Mai, 2013). Obesity has been closely linked with the development of type 2 diabetes and depression (De la Cruz-Cano et al., 2015). Diabetes, in turn, has been associated with multiple health problems, including the risk for a heart attack and stroke (Wolf, 2004). Psychological treatments for depression and anxiety can help reduce obesity (Wilfley et al., 2002). These psychological treatments often focus on stress management and changes in lifestyle. However, obese patients can resist talking about the causes of their anxiety and depression. They can explain away why they could not follow specific behavioral programs to reduce weight. Understanding this "natural resistance" (a part of human nature) is crucial in effective psychological care, and psychodynamic approaches are attuned to this problem.

Book (1998) recognized that traditional psychoanalytic approaches to psychological care may extend into many years of treatment. Although this is not necessarily bad (e.g., it takes many years of training to become a neurosurgeon, and it may take many years of self-exploration and efforts at self-control to understand how to best cope with important life problems), the contemporary influences of insurance companies demand briefer and evidence-based treatments. Consequently, Book developed a manual to guide clinicians to conduct a brief but systematic approach for focusing on recurring "core conflictual" issues that appear in relationships. Using a psychoanalytic framework, he helps individuals consciously identify their desired "wishes" and verbalize their reactions to others when their desires are not met. Book then helps patients explore their typical reactions and what internal forces or personal experiences drive those reactions. Insight into "unspoken components" that underlie repeated conflicts becomes "spoken" or consciously expressed. Individuals can thus begin to better understand their motivations and how these are tied to their reactions. They can try different behavioral scenarios as they better understand their motivations and ways of interacting with others. Book makes it clear that the goal of this treatment is purely symptom relief and not "meaningful character change" (p. 47).

Although the approach of psychodynamic, brief psychological care can vary, Abbass et al. (2014) note that short-term psychodynamic psychotherapies have in common methods that focus on the "triangle of conflict (the link between feelings, anxiety, and defense) and the triangle of person (the link between past, therapist, and current people) as key linkages to examine in the therapeutic process" (p. 3).

When this approach is applied to the psychological care of persons with a brain disorder, the focus is to understand the "complete fabric" of a person's life and not just the neuropsychological impairments. The goal is to have a collaborative dialogue that helps clarify the existentially relevant questions a person faces after the brain injury in light of who the person is now and who he or she was in the past (Prigatano & Salas, 2017). This level of insight (on the part of the psychotherapist and the patient) can (but does not always) lead to a more meaningful discussion of what the person experiences and what he or she can do to promote a positive psychological adjustment. It is an approach to psychological care that focuses on past and present relationships and the conscious and not-so-conscious motivations of a person throughout a lifetime. Some of those motivations can be driven out of conscious awareness by anxiety. The efficacy of this approach after the onset of a brain disorder has not been systematically assessed (Prigatano & Salas, 2017) but appears promising in light of the evidence-based support of the value of short-term psychodynamic therapies for a wide variety of psychological problems (Abbass et al., 2014; Leichsenring & Klein, 2014; Shedler, 2012). A recent article by Moore, Salas, Dockree, and Turnbull (2017) illustrates that psychoanalytic psychotherapy with an amnesic patient secondary to cerebral anoxia can foster improved psychological adjustment to a rehabilitation environment. Despite the patient's severe memory disturbance, a therapeutic relationship was established and guided by psychodynamic insights. The patient looked forward to the psychotherapeutic interviews even when he could not remember the content of what had been previously said. This psychotherapeutic relationship helped the patient improve his relationship with nursing staff, which was very problematic prior to the psychoanalytically oriented treatment (C. Salas, personal communication, August 23, 2018).

BEHAVIORAL AND COGNITIVE–BEHAVIORAL APPROACHES AND PSYCHOLOGICAL CARE

Another South African psychiatrist, Joseph Wolpe, had a profound influence on the development of behavioral approaches to psychological care. His initial work was to help soldiers who demonstrated "war neurosis" (today we refer to this phenomenon as post-traumatic stress disorder) overcome their symptoms. He found the psychodynamic model of his times not very helpful and decided to focus on how specific anxiety reactions could be reduced. His basic insight or principle was that one could inhibit anxiety by producing feeling states or responses that were not compatible with anxiety. His first book was therefore titled *Psychotherapy by Reciprocal Inhibition* (Wolpe, 1958).

Wolpe went on to develop a form of therapy called systematic desensitization (Wolpe & Lazarus, 1966). It utilized his model of reciprocal inhibition but did so systematically by ranking the degree of anxiety for a specific experience or thought. Wolpe then suggested that the person evoke or produce that thought, during which time Wolpe would teach the person to carry out relaxation exercises to interfere with the anxiety experience. The patient progressively went "up the ladder" with increasingly more anxiety-provoking images and experiences and used relaxation responses to inhibit them and eventually decondition the self from reacting with anxiety to such subjective experiences. Herbert Benson (1975) later systematically studied the physiological correlates of the relaxation response and showed its clinical value in reducing the impact of different stresses experienced in everyday life. Thus, "relaxation exercises" have been incorporated in many behavioral approaches to managing stress of various types (Mohr, 2010; Safren, Gonzalez, & Soroudi, 2007).

A second related behavioral approach attempted to help patients re-evaluate and restructure their perceptions and cognitive beliefs that appear to perpetuate maladaptive anxiety and related depressive reactions. This approach became known as cognitive–behavioral therapy (CBT) and was championed by Arnold Beck (1976). Like psychoanalytic theorists, Beck posited that early childhood experiences could make individuals misperceive the intentions and actions of others toward them. These "core" unhelpful beliefs could be a trigger anytime in life under stressful conditions. These beliefs, by their nature, perpetuated difficulties in making decisions and led to disturbed interpersonal relationships. Beck emphasized the importance of helping individuals critically re-evaluate their belief systems and, in so doing, achieve greater relief from depression and associated emotional disturbances. Hunot et al. (2010) document the value of CBTs in reducing depression for patients without brain dysfunction.

CBT to reduce anxiety and depression has also been attempted in patients with moderate to severe TBI, even though their cognitive deficits might limit its effectiveness. Hsieh, Ponsford, Wong, and McKay (2012) reported on a pilot investigation of this type. Their results indeed revealed a modest relationship between brain injury severity and the ability to reduce anxiety via CBT. The worse the injury (and assumed cognitive deficits), the less effective were the observed treatment effects. Helping patients with a brain disorder to be objective about their cognitive and behavioral difficulties has remained a central feature of holistic approaches to neuropsychological rehabilitation (Ben-Yishay & Diller, 2011; Prigatano, 1999b). "Noncognitive" restructuring exercises may be of more value in this patient group.

Clinically, I have experienced patients who can symbolize what they are experiencing in drawings and music and who often show some reduction in their anxiety and depression by recalling favorite movies or fairy tales from childhood (Prigatano, 1986, 1999b, 2012). The reduction of these symptoms may take place for different reasons for different patients. Nevertheless, the importance of analyzing one's cognitive perceptions as a way to understand how they may perpetuate negative affective responses can certainly be helpful, and that is the major message of CBT. It is interesting that Carl Jung many years ago reportedly stated, "If you think along the lines of nature, you think properly. And if you think properly, you may feel considerably better." Although his insights have not been quoted by modern cognitive–behavioral therapists, they are at the root of this approach to facilitating a sense of psychological well-being.

HUMANISTIC OR CLIENT-CENTERED PSYCHOTHERAPY AND PSYCHOLOGICAL CARE

Dissatisfied with both psychodynamic and behavioral approaches to psychotherapy, Carl Rogers (1951) proposed another, more fundamental way of fostering psychological care in individuals without brain dysfunction. His approach was as much philosophical as it was practical. Agreeing with the insights of Abraham Maslow (1954) regarding the need of people to actualize their potential once basic physiological and safety needs are met, Rogers and colleagues developed a technique in which they carefully listened to what patients were saying about themselves and then attempted to repeat back what was said so the patients might hear what they were saying. The ability of patients to benefit from such an approach and thereby "move on in life" and actualize their potential was studied intensively by Rogers and colleagues while he was in academia. Whatever one's theoretical orientation as a psychotherapist, I suspect few would disagree with Rogers' (1965) insightful comments:

> As our experience has moved us forward, it has become increasingly evident that the probability of therapeutic movement in a particular case depends primarily not upon the counselor's personality, nor upon his techniques, nor even upon his attitudes, but upon the way all these are experienced by the client in the relationship. The centrality of the client's perception of the interviews has forced itself upon our recognition. It is the way it seems to the client which determines whether resolution of conflict, reorganization, growth, integration—all the elements that comprise therapy—will occur. (p. 65)

This clinical reality has been one of the main reasons for studying the phenomenon of anosognosia and related disorders of impaired self-awareness after various forms of brain disorder (Prigatano, 1999b, 2010, 2014). It is what patients experience that counts and what will dictate how psychological care can proceed. Without knowing what patients perceive (irrespective of the cause), the therapist cannot "enter their phenomenological field" and begin to engage them in verbal or nonverbal dialogue that initiates the learning processes involved in rehabilitation and ultimately a reasonable psychological adjustment to the effects of their particular brain disorder. Because self-awareness is such a complicated phenomenon, it requires an understanding of patients at multiple levels (neurological, neuropsychological, psychological, psychodynamic, and sociocultural).

THE NATURE OF EVIDENCE REGARDING THE EFFECTIVENESS OF DIFFERENT PSYCHOLOGICAL TREATMENT APPROACHES TO PSYCHOLOGICAL CARE

The nature of evidence supporting or not supporting the clinical usefulness of psychological treatments that are aimed at improving psychological adjustment and well-being has varied throughout the years. Currently, there is a very strong bias to consider randomized controlled trials (RCTs) as providing the only scientifically convincing evidence for the efficacy of a treatment (Sackett, Straus, Richardson, Rosenberg, & Haynes, 2000). This method is aimed at controlling selection bias of which persons receive a certain treatment, controlling for placebo effects, and providing the most stringent test of treatment size effects. It has been most successfully applied to studying the effectiveness of pharmacological agents in treating various disease states, but it has been expanded to behavioral intervention studies as well (Braga, Da Paz, & Ylvisaker, 2005).

Several medical researchers, however, have questioned the wisdom of this approach given the costs of conducting RCTs. Carefully selected control subjects in observational studies produce findings similar to those of RCTs with no evidence that RCTs necessarily provide a more accurate estimate of treatment size effects (K. Benson & Hartz, 2000; Concato, 2004; Concato, Shah, & Horwitz, 2000). The wisdom of RCTs in behavioral studies also has to be seriously considered. Given the seductive nature of even the term "randomized controlled study," one may get the impression that such a study provides especially useful information. This can be clearly wrong if the persons conducting the RCTs do not properly understand the nature of the phenomena they are studying. What can be observed is "randomized controlled nonsense" versus a truly important insight regarding treatment effectiveness (Prigatano, 1999a, 2000).

For several years, psychologists have attempted to study the effectiveness of various psychological treatments by comparing some measurable outcome in two or more different treatments on similar patients with similar symptoms. Control groups often have included a "wait list control" (i.e., a group waiting to receive treatment) and some form of "placebo control group." The findings are interesting and bolster the argument that such treatments are valuable and practical. They also provide leverage to have insurance companies pay for such treatments (Prigatano & Pliskin, 2003).

Is there another source of evidence that the clinician can use when providing psychological care in the most reasonable and responsible way? In an extraordinary paper, Erik Erikson again leads the way. In 1957, he was asked to give a talk at the Massachusetts Institute of Technology regarding the nature of clinical evidence when working as a psychoanalyst. When describing his views on clinical evidence, Erikson (1964) explicitly stated that the appreciation voiced by the patient to the psychoanalyst for the care provided is not, in itself, clinical evidence for the effectiveness of the treatment. What is clinical evidence is the observable phenomenon of the patient being able to talk more completely and thoroughly about a problematic area in his or her life when the psychoanalyst's comments (or interpretation) to the patient seem to open such dialogue. The converse must also be true. If the comments, interpretation, or actions of a psychotherapist or psychological caregiver result in less talk or exploration of an important topic in the patient's life, the treatment is not only ineffective but also may be counterproductive.

Bettelheim (1989) expanded on this insight when he made the following comment: "Psychoanalysis was created to enable man to accept the problematic nature of life without being defeated by it, or giving in to escapism" (p. 8). The important point is that truly effective psychotherapy or, more broadly defined, psychological care should increase patients' "commitment to life" by their demonstrated efforts to continually try to improve coping with the problems of *their* life without "giving in to escapism," which is often seen in addictions or any other behavior that reflects maladaptive ways of dealing with anxiety, depression, and anger. A greater commitment to life and dealing with life's problems is often observed by changes in patients' behavior at work and in their interpersonal lives. Do they now engage in work (or any productive activity) with a greater sense of personal satisfaction concerning work efforts and production? Do significant others report less irritability in a patient, more spontaneous joy in the patient's relationships, and greater commitment to daily life activities? If the answers to these questions are in the positive, they provide the clinician (and ultimately science) with the evidence needed to sustain these psychological services.

There is another source of evidence that has clinical relevance but has been abandoned by many scientifically oriented psychologists and psychiatrists. Patients' dreams often reflect a complex mixture of their physiological state, their fears, their motivations, and their beliefs that are not always consciously recognized. Listening carefully to patients' descriptions of their dreams and how they may change during the course of treatment can provide another source of evidence. Shifts in the nature of the struggles reappearing in dreams often reflect changes in behavior or attitudes that may not be immediately obvious. The dream content can reveal less censured subjective experiences that patients are not always able to verbally or consciously report (Solms, 1997; Solms & Turnbull, 2002). The discussion in Chapter 19 of the psychological care of a young woman who suffered a moderate TBI in adolescence at least partially demonstrates this reality. One further topic that is foreign to scientifically oriented psychologists is the role of spirituality in the psychological care of persons who have neurological or neuropsychological disturbances.

SPIRITUALITY AND PSYCHOLOGICAL CARE

Religious beliefs and/or spiritual convictions have been recorded throughout history as important determiners of a person's behavior. Despite whatever scientific understanding a person has about how a brain injury has affected an individual, the patient's own religious interpretations of the meaning of the brain injury must be understood when attempting psychological care interventions. The psychological interventions must be compatible with the patient's religious and spiritual values. Carl Jung (1957) repeatedly emphasized this point. In fact, he emphasized that spiritual problems can produce, in and of themselves, significant psychiatric disturbances. According to Jung, this was perhaps most obvious in persons with alcohol addiction. In a letter written to William Wilson, cofounder of Alcoholics Anonymous, on January 30, 1961, Jung referenced his earlier psychotherapeutic work with a person who was an alcoholic and known to Wilson as Mr. Roland H (Alcoholics Anonymous World Services, 2001). Jung's comments included the following: "His craving for alcohol was the equivalent on a low level of the spiritual thirst of our being for wholeness, expressed in medieval language: the union with God." Jung then discussed the important role of a "higher education of the mind beyond the confines of mere rationalism." People, by their human nature, seek meaning in their life, which comes from the pursuit and practice of behaviors that foster the truth about themselves as they understand it within a given culture, religious orientation, and time in history. This seeking of meaning is not a purely cognitive or rational act.

The psychiatrist C. Robert Cloninger (2004), in his text *Feeling Good: The Science of Well-Being*, states that "authentic happiness requires a coherent way of living including the human processes that regulate the sexual, material, emotional, intellectual, and spiritual aspects of experience" (p. vi). He also states that "well-being only arises when a person learns how to let go of struggles, to work in the service of others, and to grow in awareness" (p. v). Seligman (2002), in his book *Authentic Happiness*, argues that insights of "positive psychology" are the answer for facilitating a sense of well-being. He denounces the insights of Freudian psychology as too negative and as having no scientific evidence to support them (he is, incidentally, wrong—see research on psychoanalytic psychotherapy referenced in this chapter), especially the concept of sublimation, which underlies some of our most altruistic behaviors. Bridging his insights as a psychologist with those from various religious and philosophical perspectives, Seligman suggests that there are six "core virtues" that lead to an authentically happy life: wisdom and knowledge, courage, love and humanity, justice, temperance, and spirituality and transcendence. One can see from the scientific and nonscientific writings of several recent authors a return to the "old wisdom" of Freud, Jung, Skinner, Rogers, Hebb, Gandhi, and others.

SUMMARY

There are many insightful observations on how human beings have successfully struggled to have a psychological sense of well-being and to maintain a positive state of psychological adjustment to life's problems. It is extremely important to note, however, that there is no "simple formula" for providing or fostering psychological well-being and care in another. Much depends on how a given individual has dealt with the basic struggles of life and what activities the person has engaged in to foster a sense of happiness and satisfaction with life prior to a brain injury.

A number of insightful behavioral scientists and neuroscientists, including Karl Pribram (1971), have noted four basic behaviors observed in primates, including humans. The first is the constant search for food to sustain life (i.e., the feeding response). This search often puts animals (and humans) in conflict with one another. This conflict underlies, in part, the establishment of "territories" by all animals (and humans). It can result in the responses of "flight" (a fear response) or "fight" (an aggressive but not necessarily violent response). These responses are necessary to maintain an individual's human existence. They are necessary to maintain survival via maintaining territories while searching for food and handling threats. The establishment of territories also has a direct bearing on another (fourth) basic response: searching for a receptive sexual mate. This drive for sexual intercourse is experienced as "pleasure seeking." It is aimed, from a biological perspective, at achieving procreation, which is crucial to the continuation of life.

Freud (see Pribram & Gill, 1976) proposed, of course, that the sexual and aggressive drives influence mental development and adult mental functioning and character. Not properly managed, they are responsible for some of the psychiatric symptoms observed in patients. Freud argued that neurosis was, in large part, driven by a lack of adequate sublimation of those basic drives to maintain a civilized society (see Freud's 1961 translated book, *Civilization and Its Discontents*). These basic drives, however, are modified in their expression by the conscious influence of language and culture as they socially transmit what is expected of a person at different times in the individual's psychosocial development. Jung (1964) brought attention to the fact that these influences produce "symbols of the libido." These symbols spontaneously emerge and can be observed across time and cultures. They reflect a complex mixture of both conscious and unconscious ways of perceiving and interpreting human experience. These symbols must be included in the psychological care of persons with a brain disorder to produce the most effective and sustaining sense of well-being (Prigatano, 1999b).

Finally, as noted in Chapter 2, Watzlawick (1993) reminds us of the natural human tendency to also promote misery (i.e., unhappiness) in life. As previously discussed in this chapter, Csikszentmihalyi (1999) notes that humans can be happy, but this sense of happiness and personal well-being is fleeting. It seems to occur primarily when a human being is totally engaged in activities the person finds meaningful. These perspectives are necessary for "seeing the big picture" regarding human nature and what can and cannot be done in the process of psychological treatment of persons after a brain disorder. It keeps in focus that it is not just the direct and indirect effects of a brain disorder that have to be treated/managed (Prigatano, 1999b). The treating clinician must have a basic understanding and acceptance of human nature and how it is manifested in a given person in light of the person's brain disorder and his or her particular psychodynamic and psychosocial situation. All of this has to be understood and dealt with on a constant basis in order to sustain efforts at psychological care during moments of discouragement.

Different brain disorders at different stages of psychosocial functioning produce specific challenges to psychological well-being that have to be understood, as briefly described in Chapters 6–8. The neuropsychological and neurological effects of the brain disorder often make psychosocial adjustments very difficult. They can greatly limit the natural plan of the central nervous system by diminishing one's memory, the ability to think logically, the ability to control impulses, and the ability to use words for effective problem-solving. They seriously limit one's academic successes and later one's ability to work, love, maintain friendships, and "live the life you want to live." In light of these observations, an outline of the recurring observations is offered as a guide to the psychological care of persons with a brain disorder.

RECURRING OBSERVATIONS RELEVANT TO PSYCHOLOGICAL TREATMENTS AFTER A BRAIN DISORDER

In light of the discussion in previous chapters, it should be abundantly clear that the first step to providing effective psychological treatment is obtaining an accurate understanding of what the person experiences regarding how the brain disorder or brain disease has affected the individual. This understanding guides what is said to the patient and family members. The next step is to obtain an accurate understanding of what the person (or patient) wants help with regarding how the brain disorder or brain disease has affected the individual. This can vary greatly depending on the nature of the underlying brain disorder and the patient's personality. This is why knowledge of neuropsychology and psychodynamic theory is so important. Sometimes the patient is acutely aware of how he or she has been affected by the brain disorder, and sometimes the patient is not. Some patients focus on their physical limitations; others focus on cognitive and behavioral changes. Still others may simply be concerned about the impact of their brain disorder on achieving personal aspirations or goals without clarifying their concerns about any specific neuropsychological disturbance. There is also a group of patients who focus on life and death issues and the impact of their illness on their families. Finally, there are patients who believe that their adjustment problems are caused by others and that the effects of their brain injury are essentially modest. Whatever patients' perceptions are, the correct understanding of what they want helps determine what the treating clinician can do to address their perceived needs and to reduce their frustrations and associated states of confusion (Prigatano, 1999b).

Interestingly, there can be a change in the focus of the discussion between the treating clinician and a patient after the patient's initial perceived needs are adequately addressed. This shift of focus often reflects an increased sense of trust and the revealing of even more basic, private concerns of the individual. Persons with and without a brain disorder will discuss their concerns sooner or later if the initial efforts at improving their psychological well-being have been successful. Helping patients

Box 12.3. Suggested "Targets" of Psychological Treatment Interventions with Persons with a Brain Disorder

1. Reduce the physical symptoms that cause discomfort or pain for the patient. This may include medications, receiving physical therapy, teaching stress management techniques, helping restore normal sleep patterns, and fostering adequate rest and a healthy diet.
2. Reduce anxiety, depression, and angry outbursts by altering environmental demands to a level the patient can adequately meet in light of his or her neuropsychological status.
3. Help reinforce "self-control" and reduce impulsive responding. Behavioral techniques and cognitive–behavioral therapy may help in this regard.
4. Reduce/and or manage addictive behaviors the person engages in to "soothe myself." (This is a further step in self-control and may require psychodynamically oriented psychotherapy, supportive care via Alcoholics Anonymous, etc.)
5. Continue to reduce anxiety and depression, and avoid the development of angry outbursts by spending time with the patient and talking with the individual about what he or she experiences (i.e., building the therapeutic alliance). The patient should not feel "alone with my problems." The patient should be helped to understand why these reactions are present and what may be done to reduce or control them. This continues to foster a realistic sense of hope and improves attachment styles.
6. Slowly return (when possible) the person to a state of productive activity (i.e., work) in order to re-establish a sense of self-efficacy. This often is a team effort best carried out in the context of milieu-oriented neuropsychological rehabilitation (Ben-Yishay & Diller, 2011; Prigatano et al., 1986).
7. Slowly return (when possible) the person to greater independence in the home and the community, which also fosters a sense of self-efficacy.
8. Provide guidance for improving intimate relationships (i.e., love) with the associated pleasures and responsibilities. This needs to be done without damaging the person's "individuality" (regarding work, love, and play, see Prigatano, 1999b).
9. Provide experiences that help the patient realize the importance of providing help and comfort to others (Benjamin, 1985).
10. Foster a better understanding of the person's "human nature" and in so doing help the individual learn "self-sacrifice" or "self-control" (Gandhi, 1957/1963), which aids the adaptive process of "philosophical patience in the face of suffering" (Jung, 1964).
11. Guide the person to make wise choices in light of his or her neuropsychological status, psychodynamic features, and cultural and religious values.
12. In this regard, explore the important symbols that motivate the person on a conscious and unconscious level (e.g., stories or fairy tales to which the individual personally relates [Bettelheim,1989], historical figures or heroes the person wishes to emulate, and music or artwork that "speaks to me").
13. Help the person feel "more alive" in daily activities and thereby find or re-establish meaning in the individual's personal life using scientific as well as literary sources.

> **Box 12.4. Questions That Guide Psychological Treatment Interventions with Persons with a Brain Disorder**
>
> 1. What does the person experience regarding how the brain disorder or brain disease has affected him or her?
> 2. What does the person want help with as it relates to how the brain disorder has affected him or her?
> 3. What is the initial focus of the discussion between the treating clinician and the patient, and does that focus (or content) change with time and attempted psychological care interventions? If so, what are the reasons behind this change in focus?
> 4. What forms of psychological care or intervention seem most appropriate and helpful for the patient? What is the clinical evidence that the intervention is helpful to the patient?
> 5. How does one foster resiliency in the patient (and, at times, family members), which can improve the quality of life in light of the patient's brain disorder, personal history, and psychosocial stage of life?

understand and deal with their more basic and private concerns often results in the establishment of a long-term psychological consultation relationship that can be of help to patients throughout life.

Box 12.3 lists several targets of psychological treatment intervention that can improve the psychological care of persons with a brain disorder. They reflect a wide range of activities, from symptom reduction to the establishment of meaning in one's life after sustaining a brain disorder. In choosing the targets with a patient who has a brain disorder, the treating psychological clinician might find it helpful to repeatedly ask and answer a few basic questions that can help guide psychological care interventions. These questions are listed in Box 12.4. They will repeatedly arise, and they are described in Part IV of this volume.

REFERENCES

Abbass, A. A., Kisely, S. R., Town, J. M., Leichsenring, F., Driessen, E., De Maat, S., . . . Rusalovska, S. (2014). *Short-term psychodynamic psychotherapies for common mental disorders.* San Francisco, CA: Wiley.

Alcoholics Anonymous World Services. (2001). *Alcoholics Anonymous: The story of how many thousands of men and women have recovered from alcoholism* (4th ed.). New York, NY: Author.

Beck, A. T. (1976). *Cognitive therapy and the emotional disorders.* New York, NY: Penguin.

Benedetti, F., Mayberg, H. S., Wager, T. D., Stohler, C. S., & Zubieta, J.-K. (2005). Neurobiological mechanisms of the placebo effect. *Journal of Neuroscience, 25*(45), 10390–10402.

Benson, H. (1975). *The relaxation response.* New York, NY: Morrow.

Benson, K., & Hartz, A. J. (2000). A comparison of observational studies and randomized, controlled trials. *New England Journal of Medicine, 342*(25), 1878–1886.

Ben-Yishay, Y., & Diller, L. (2011). *Handbook of holistic neuropsychological rehabilitation: Outpatient rehabilitation of traumatic brain injury.* New York, NY: Oxford University Press.

Besser, A., Luyten, P., & Mayes, L. C. (2012). Adult attachment and distress: The mediating role of humor styles. *Individual Differences Research, 10*(3), 153–164.

Bethell, C. D., Newacheck, P., Hawes, E., & Halfon, N. (2014). Adverse childhood experiences: Assessing the impact on health and school engagement and the mitigating role of resilience. *Health Affairs, 33*(12), 2106–2115.

Bettelheim, B. (1989). *The uses of enchantment: The meaning and importance of fairy tales.* New York, NY: Vintage.

Book, H. E. (1998). *How to practice brief psychodynamic psychotherapy.* Washington, DC: American Psychological Association.

Bowlby, J. (1969). *Attachment and loss, Volume I: Attachment*. New York, NY: Basic Books.

Bowlby, J. (1973). *Attachment and Loss, Volume II: Separation*. New York, NY: Basic Books.

Bowlby, J. (1980). *Attachment and Loss, Volume III: Loss*. New York, NY: Basic Books.

Braga, L. W., Da Paz, A., Jr., & Ylvisaker, M. (2005). Direct clinician-delivered versus indirect family-supported rehabilitation of children with traumatic brain injury: A randomized controlled trial. *Brain Injury, 19*(10), 819–831.

Brumpton, B., Langhammer, A., Romundstad, P., Chen, Y., & Mai, X. (2013). The associations of anxiety and depression symptoms with weight change and incident obesity: The HUNT study. *International Journal of Obesity, 37*(9), 1268–1274.

Casey, B., Somerville, L. H., Gotlib, I. H., Ayduk, O., Franklin, N. T., Askren, M. K., . . . Teslovich, T. (2011). Behavioral and neural correlates of delay of gratification 40 years later. *Proceedings of the National Academy of Sciences of the USA, 108*(36), 14998–15003.

Churchill, R., Davies, P., Caldwell, D., Moore, T. H., Jones, H., Lewis, G., & Hunot, V. (2010). Humanistic therapies versus other psychological therapies for depression. *Cochrane Database of Systematic Reviews, 2010*(9), CD008700.

Cloninger, C. R. (2004). *Feeling good: The science of well-being*. New York, NY: Oxford University Press.

Concato, J. (2004). Observational versus experimental studies: What's the evidence for a hierarchy? *NeuroRx, 1*(3), 341–347.

Concato, J., Shah, N., & Horwitz, R. I. (2000). Randomized, controlled trials, observational studies, and the hierarchy of research designs. *New England Journal of Medicine, 342*(25), 1887–1892.

Cousins, N. (1979). *Anatomy of an illness as perceived by the patient: Reflections on healing and regeneration*. New York, NY: Norton.

Csikszentmihalyi, M. (1999). If we are so rich, why aren't we happy? *American Psychologist, 54*(10), 821–827.

De la Cruz-Cano, E., Tovilla-Zarate, C. A., Reyes-Ramos, E., Gonzalez-Castro, T. B., Juarez-Castro, I., López-Narváez, M. L., & Fresan, A. (2015). Association between obesity and depression in patients with diabetes mellitus type 2: A study protocol. *Faculty of 1000 Research, 4*, 7.

Desharnais, R., Jobin, J., Côté, C., Lévesque, L., & Godin, G. (1993). Aerobic exercise and the placebo effect: A controlled study. *Psychosomatic Medicine, 55*(2), 149–154.

Diederich, N. J., & Goetz, C. G. (2008). The placebo treatments in neurosciences: New insights from clinical and neuroimaging studies. *Neurology, 71*(9), 677–684.

Donald, M. (2001). *A mind so rare: The evolution of human consciousness*. New York, NY: Norton.

Erikson, E. H. (1964). *Insight and responsibility*. New York, NY: Norton.

Erikson, E. H. (1969). *Gandhi's truth*. New York, NY: Norton.

Everson, S. A., Maty, S. C., Lynch, J. W., & Kaplan, G. A. (2002). Epidemiologic evidence for the relation between socioeconomic status and depression, obesity, and diabetes. *Journal of Psychosomatic Research, 53*(4), 891–895.

Feder, A., Nestler, E. J., & Charney, D. S. (2009). Psychobiology and molecular genetics of resilience. *Nature Reviews Neuroscience, 10*(6), 446–457.

Fletcher, D., & Sarkar, M. (2013). Psychological resilience. *European Psychologist, 18*(1), 12–23.

Fonagy, P., Steele, M., Steele, H., Higgitt, A., & Target, M. (1994). The Emanuel Miller Memorial Lecture 1992: The theory and practice of resilience. *Journal of Child Psychology and Psychiatry, 35*(2), 231–257.

Frank, J. D., & Frank, J. B. (1991). *Persuasion and healing: A comparative study of psychotherapy*. Baltimore, MD: Johns Hopkins University Press.

Freud, S. (1900). *The interpretation of dreams*. London, UK: Hogarth.

Freud, S. (1961). *Civilization and its discontents*. New York, NY: Norton.

Gandhi, M. (1963). *Autobiography: The story of my experiments with truth*. Boston, MA: Beacon. (Original work published 1957)

Hsieh, M.-Y., Ponsford, J., Wong, D., & McKay, A. (2012). Exploring variables associated with change in cognitive behaviour therapy (CBT) for anxiety following traumatic brain injury. *Disability and Rehabilitation, 34*(5), 408–415.

Humphrey, N. (2002). Great expectations: The evolutionary psychology of faith healing and the placebo effect. In N. Humphrey (Ed.), *The mind made flesh: Frontiers of psychology and evolution* (pp. 255–287). New York, NY: Oxford University Press.

Hunot, V., Moore, T. H., Caldwell, D., Davies, P., Jones, H., Furukawa, T. A., . . . Churchill, R. (2010). Cognitive behavioural therapies versus treatment as usual for depression. *Cochrane Database of Systematic Reviews, 2010*(9), CD008699.

Jung, C. G. (1957). *The practice of psychotherapy: Essays on the psychology of the transference and other subjects*. Princeton, NJ: Princeton University Press.

Jung, C. G. (1964). *Man and his symbols*. London, UK: Aldus.

Kazantzakis, N. (1952). *Zorba the Greek* (C. Wildman, Trans.). New York, NY: Simon & Schuster.

Leichsenring, F., & Klein, S. (2014). Evidence for psychodynamic psychotherapy in specific mental disorders: A systematic review. *Psychoanalytic Psychotherapy, 28*(1), 4–32.

Martin, D. J., Garske, J. P., & Davis, M. K. (2000). *Relation of the therapeutic alliance with outcome and other variables: A meta-analytic review*. New York, NY: American Psychological Association.

Martin, R. A., & Lefcourt, H. M. (1983). Sense of humor as a moderator of the relation between stressors and moods. *Journal of Personality and Social Psychology, 45*(6), 1313.

Martin, R. A., Puhlik-Doris, P., Larsen, G., Gray, J., & Weir, K. (2003). Individual differences in uses of humor and their relation to psychological well-being: Development of the Humor Styles Questionnaire. *Journal of Research in Personality, 37*(1), 48–75.

Maslow, A. (1954). *Motivation and personality* (2nd ed.). New York, NY: Harper.

May, R. (1953). *Man's search for himself*. New York, NY: Norton.

May, R. (Ed.). (1969). *Existential psychology* (R. May, Ed.; 2nd ed.). New York, NY: Random House.

McGhee, P. E., & Pistolesi, E. (1979). *Humor: Its origin and development*. San Francisco, CA: Freeman.

McKay, M., Davis, M., & Fanning, P. (2007). *Thoughts and feelings: Taking control of your moods and your life* (3rd ed.). Oakland, CA: New Harbinger.

Miller, F. G., Colloca, L., & Kaptchuk, T. J. (2009). The placebo effect: Illness and interpersonal healing. *Perspectives in Biology and Medicine, 52*(4), 518–539.

Moerman, D. E., & Jonas, W. B. (2002). Deconstructing the placebo effect and finding the meaning response. *Annals of Internal Medicine, 136*(6), 471–476.

Mohr, D. (2010). *The stress and mood management program for individuals with multiple sclerosis: Workbook*. New York, NY: Oxford University Press.

Moore, P. A., Salas, C. E., Dockree, S., & Turnbull, O. H. (2017). Observations on working psychoanalytically with a profoundly amnesic patient. *Frontiers in Psychology, 8*, 1418.

Neils-Strunjas, J., Paul, D., Clark, A. N., Mudar, R., Duff, M. C., Waldron-Perrine, B., & Bechtold, K. T. (2017). Role of resilience in the rehabilitation of adults with acquired brain injury. *Brain Injury, 31*(2), 131–139.

Pribram, K. H. (1971). *Languages of the brain: Experimental paradoxes and principles in neuropsychology*. Englewood Cliffs, NJ: Prentice-Hall.

Pribram, K. H., & Gill, M. M. (1976). *Freud's "Project" re-assessed: Preface to contemporary cognitive theory and neuropsychology*. New York, NY: Basic Books.

Prigatano, G. P. (Ed.). (1986). *Neuropsychological rehabilitation after brain injury*. Baltimore, MD: Johns Hopkins University Press.

Prigatano, G. P. (1999a). Commentary: Beyond statistics and research design. *Journal of Head Trauma Rehabilitation, 14*(3), 308–311.

Prigatano, G. P. (1999b). *Principles of neuropsychological rehabilitation*. New York, NY: Oxford University Press.

Prigatano, G. P. (2000). Rehabilitation for traumatic brain injury. *JAMA, 284*(14), 1783–1784.

Prigatano, G. P. (2010). *The study of anosognosia*. New York, NY: Oxford University Press.

Prigatano, G. P. (2012). Jungian contributions to successful neuropsychological rehabilitation. *Neuropsychoanalysis, 14*(2), 175–185.

Prigatano, G. P. (2014). Anosognosia and patterns of impaired self-awareness observed in clinical practice. *Cortex, 61*, 81–92.

Prigatano, G. P. (2018). Psychological adjustment to the effects of a moderate to severe traumatic brain injury. In J. M. Silver, T. W. McAllister, & D. B. Arciniegas (Eds.), *Textbook of traumatic brain injury* (3rd ed., pp. 817–829). Washington, DC: American Psychiatric Association Press.

Prigatano, G. P., Fordyce, D. J., Zeiner, H. K., Roueche, J. R., Pepping, M., & Wood, B. C. (1986). *Neuropsychological Rehabilitation after Brain Injury*. The Johns Hopkins University Press, Baltimore.

Prigatano, G. P., & Pliskin, N. H. (2003). *Clinical neuropsychology and cost outcome research: A beginning*. New York, NY: Psychology Press.

Prigatano, G. P., & Salas, C. (2017). Psychodynamic psychotherapy after severe traumatic brain injury. In R. Wood, T. McMillan, & A. Worthington (Eds.), *Neurobehavioral disability and social handicap following traumatic brain injury* (pp. 188–201). Philadelphia, PA: Taylor & Francis.

Richardson, G. E. (2002). The metatheory of resilience and resiliency. *Journal of Clinical Psychology, 58*(3), 307–321.

Rogers, C. R. (1951). *Client-centered therapy: Its current practice, implications, and theory, with chapters*. Boston, MA: Houghton Mifflin.

Rogers, C. R. (1961). *A therapist's view of psychotherapy: On becoming a person*. Boston, MA: Houghton Mifflin.

Rogers, C. R. (1965). *Client-centered therapy*. Boston, MA: Houghton Mifflin.

Sackett, D. L., Straus, S. E., Richardson, W. S., Rosenberg, W., & Haynes, R. B. (2000). *Evidence-based medicine: How to practice and teach EBM*. London, UK: Churchill Livingstone.

Safren, S., Gonzalez, J., & Soroudi, N. (2007). *Coping with chronic illness: A cognitive–behavioral approach for adherence and depression: Therapist guide*. New York, NY: Oxford University Press.

Schofield, W. (1964). *Psychotherapy: The purchase of friendship*. Englewood Cliffs, NJ: Prentice-Hall.

Schure, M. B., Odden, M., & Goins, R. T. (2013). The association of resilience with mental and physical health among older American Indians: The native elder care study. *American Indian and Alaska Native Mental Health Research, 20*(2), 27.

Scott, K., Bruffaerts, R., Tsang, A., Ormel, J., Alonso, J., Angermeyer, M., . . . De Graaf, R. (2007). Depression–anxiety relationships with chronic physical conditions: Results from the World Mental Health Surveys. *Journal of Affective Disorders, 103*(1), 113–120.

Seligman, M. E. (2002). *Authentic happiness: Using the new positive psychology to realize your potential for lasting fulfillment*. New York, NY: Free Press.

Shedler, J. (2012). The efficacy of psychodynamic psychotherapy. *The American Psychologist, 65*, 98–109.

Skinner, B. F. (1953). *Science and human behavior*. New York, NY: Macmillan.

Solms, M. (1997). *The neuropsychology of dreams: A clinico-anatomical study*. Mahwah, NJ: Erlbaum.

Solms, M., & Turnbull, O. (2002). *The brain and the inner world: An introduction to the neuroscience of subjective experience*. New York, NY: Other Press.

Southwick, S. M., & Charney, D. S. (2012). The science of resilience: Implications for the prevention and treatment of depression. *Science, 338*(6103), 79–82.

Stein, J. (1964). *Fiddler on the roof*. New York, NY: Washington Square Press.

Stewart, D. E., & Yuen, T. (2011). A systematic review of resilience in the physically ill. *Psychosomatics, 52*(3), 199–209.

Szasz, T. (1978). *The myth of psychotherapy: Mental healing as religion, rhetoric, and repression*. Syracuse, NY: Syracuse University Press.

Watzlawick, P. (1993). *The situation is hopeless, but not serious: The pursuit of unhappiness*. New York, NY: Norton.

Wilfley, D. E., Welch, R. R., Stein, R. I., Spurrell, E. B., Cohen, L. R., Saelens, B. E., . . . Matt, G. E. (2002). A randomized comparison of group cognitive–behavioral therapy and group interpersonal psychotherapy for the treatment of overweight individuals with binge-eating disorder. *Archives of General Psychiatry, 59*(8), 713–721.

Wolf, P. A. (2004). Epidemiology of stroke. In J. P. Mohr, D. W. Choi, J. C. Grotta, & P. A. Wolf (Eds.), *Stroke: Pathophysiology, diagnosis, and management* (4th ed., pp. 13–34). Philadelphia, PA: Churchill Livingstone.

Wolpe, J. (1958). *Psychotherapy by reciprocal inhibition*. Stanford, CA: Stanford University Press.

Wolpe, J., & Lazarus, A. A. (1966). *Behavior therapy techniques*. Oxford, UK: Pergamon.

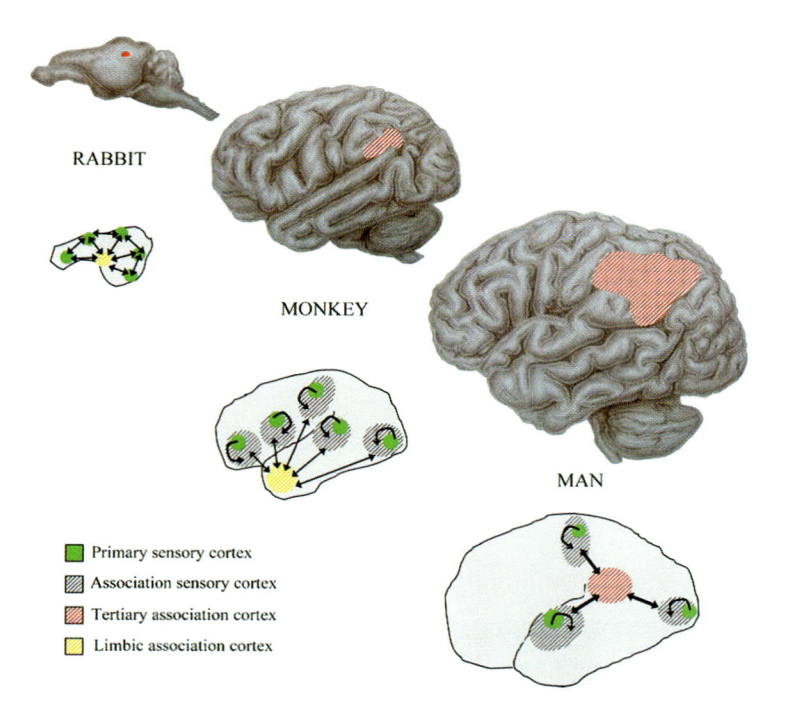

FIGURE 2.2   The top diagonal sequence shows the expansion of inferior parietal cortex from rabbit through monkey to man. The bottom diagonal sequence shows the differences in brain circuitry between the species. In man, the majority of intermodality connections are mediated by higher order association cortex in the parietal lobe.

Source: Reprinted from Catani and ffytche (2005), *Brain, 128*(10), p. 2230 with permission from Oxford University Press.

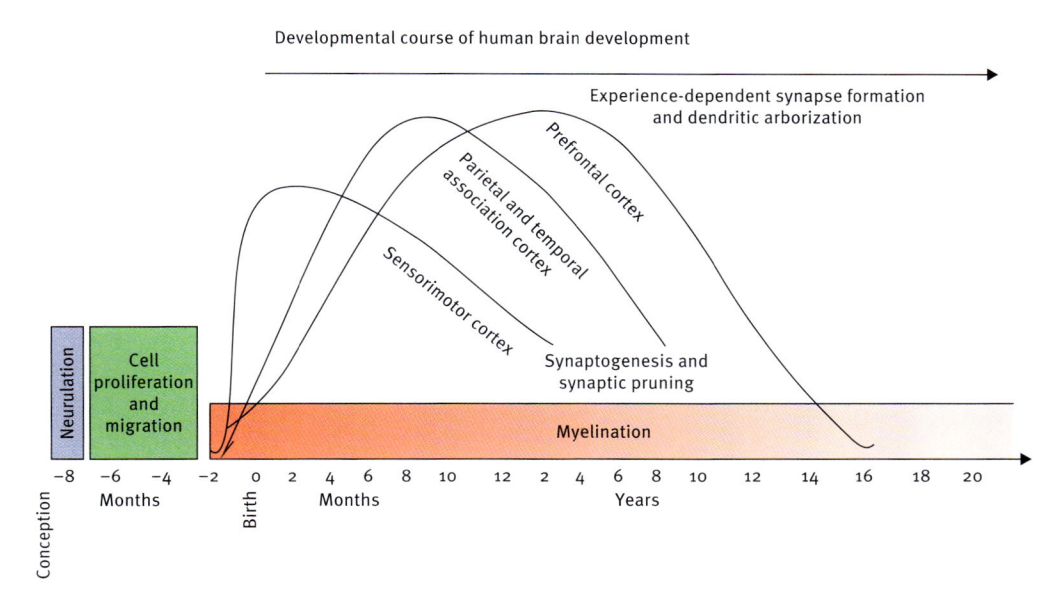

FIGURE 3.1   Schematic illustration of the complex changes in human brain anatomy occurring over time as summarized by Casey, Tottenham, et al. (2005).

Source: Reprinted from *Trends in Cognitive Sciences, 9*(3), Casey, B., Tottenham, N., Liston, C., & Durston, S., Imaging the developing brain: What have we learned about cognitive development?, p. 104–110, Copyright (2005), with permission from Elsevier.

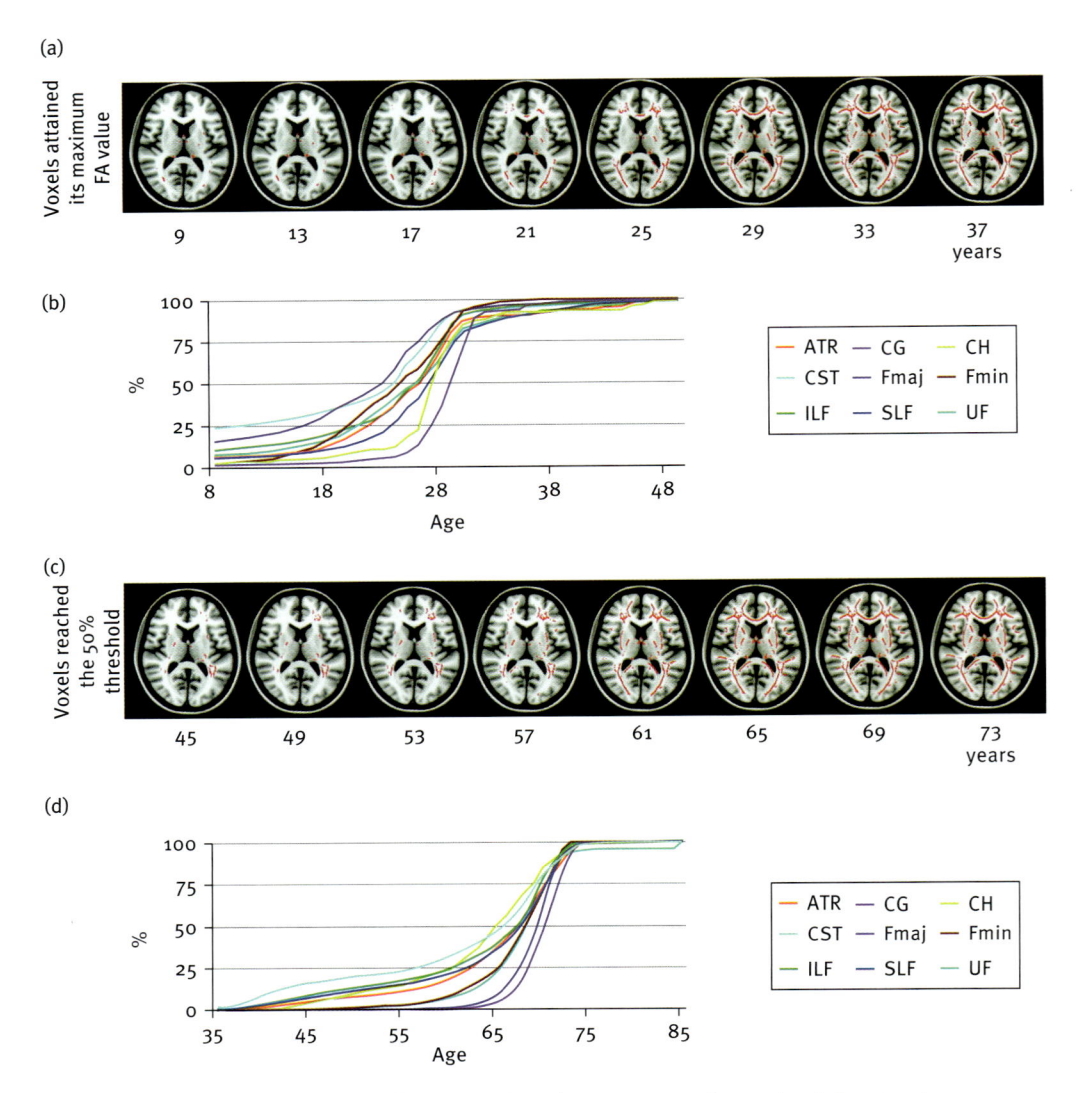

FIGURE 3.2 Regional variability in white matter (WM) maturation and age-related deterioration. (A) Skeleton voxels (red) having attained maximum fractional anisotropy (FA) value at different stages of chronological development in years (as estimated by regression locally estimated scatterplot smoothing). The skeleton voxels are superimposed on a transversal section of a T_1-weighted Montreal Neurological Institute template ($z = 83$). Only voxels showing a significant inverse U pattern across the life span were included in the peak estimations. Relatively early maturation (<21 years) is seen in occipital and frontal areas. (B) Percentage of voxels per tract having reached maximum FA value as a function of age (8–49 years). (C and D) Estimated age-related deterioration as indexed by age when FA fell below the value equal to 50% of the difference between maximum FA and FA at maximum age. Parts of the SLF reached the threshold at approximately 30 years of age, followed by areas encompassing F_{min} in the late 40s and posterior areas, including the occipital lobes, in the early 60s. As indicated by the cumulative curves (D), the vast majority of voxels reached the threshold in the 60s.

Source: Reprinted from Westlye, L. T., Walhovd, K. B., Dale, A. M., Bjørnerud, A., Due-Tønnessen, P., Engvig, A., . . . Fjell, A. M., Life-span changes of the human brain white matter: Diffusion tensor imaging (DTI) and volumetry, *Cerebral Cortex*, 20(9), 2009, p. 2055–2068, by permission of Oxford University Press.

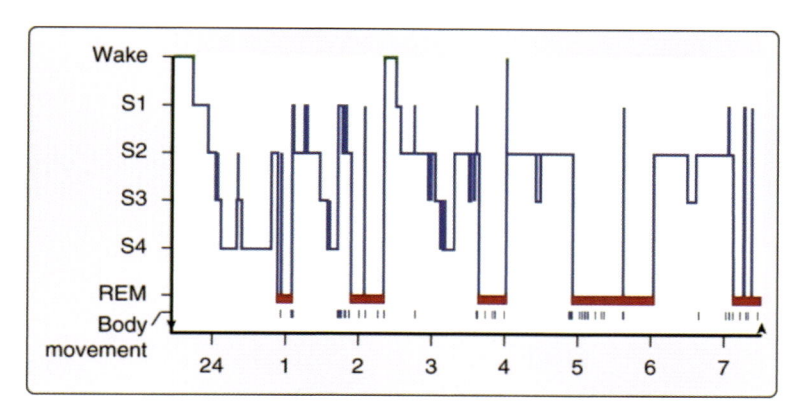

FIGURE 5.2 The progression of sleep stages across a single night in a normal young adult volunteer is illustrated in this sleep histogram. The text describes the "ideal" or "average" pattern. This histogram was drawn on the basis of a continuous overnight recording of electroencephalogram, electro-oculogram, and electromyogram in a normal 19-year-old man. The record was assessed in 30-second epochs for the various sleep stages. REM, rapid eye movement.

Source: Reprinted from Normal human sleep: An overview, Carskadon & Dement, in M. H. Kryger, T. Roth, & W. C. Dement (Eds.), *Principles and Practice of Sleep Medicine* (5 ed.), p. 16–26, Copyright (2010), with permission from Elsevier.

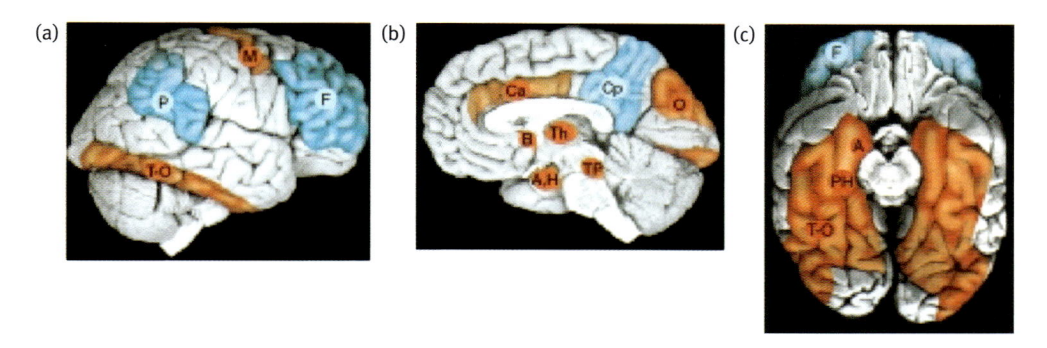

FIGURE 5.3 Schematic representation of the relative increases and decreases in neural activity associated with rapid eye movement (REM) sleep. Regions colored in red are those in which regional cerebral blood flow (rCBF) increases during REM sleep; those in blue correspond to rCBF decreases. (a) Lateral view, (b) medial view, and (c) ventral view. A, amygdala; B, basal forebrain; Ca, anterior cingulate gyrus; Cp, posterior cingulate gyrus and precuneus; F, prefrontal cortex; H, hypothalamus; M, motor cortex; P, parietal supramarginal cortex; PH, parahippocampal gyrus; O, occipital–lateral cortex; Th, thalamus; T-O, temporo-occipital extrastriate cortex; TP, pontine tegmentum.

Source: Reprinted from Schwartz, S., & Maquet, P., Sleep imaging and the neuro-psychological assessment of dreams, *Trends in Cognitive Sciences*, 6(1), p. 23–30, Copyright (2002), with permission from Elsevier.

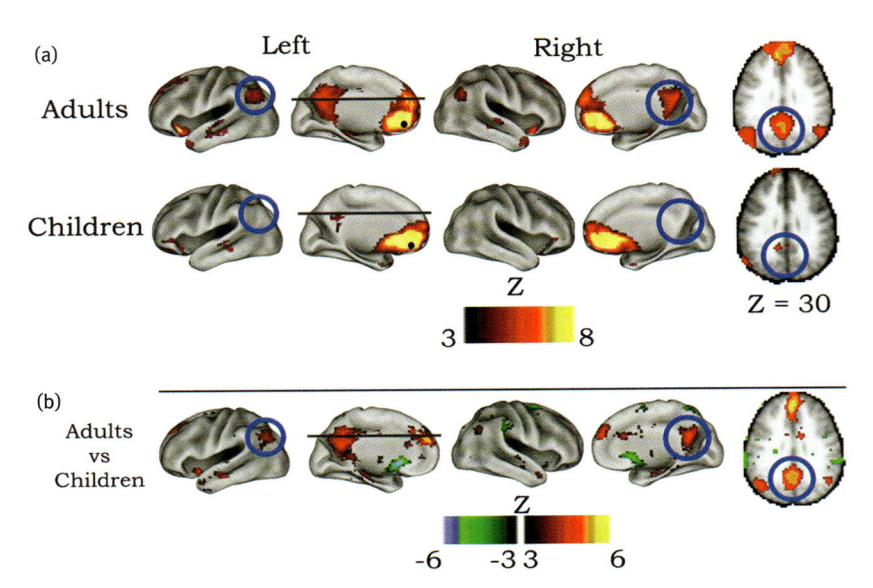

FIGURE 6.1 Voxelwise resting-state functional connectivity maps for a seed region (black circle) in the medial prefrontal cortex (mPFC; ventral: -3, 39, -2). (A) Qualitatively, the resting state functional connectivity MRI map for the mPFC (ventral) seed region reveals the commonly observed adult connectivity pattern of the default network (9, 18, 19). The connectivity map in children, however, significantly deviates from that of adults. Functional connections with regions in the posterior cingulate and lateral parietal regions (blue circles) are present in the adults but absent in children. (B) These qualitative differences between children and adults are confirmed by the direct comparison (random effects) between adults and children. mPFC (ventral) functional connections with the posterior cingulate and lateral parietal regions are significantly stronger in adults than in children.

Source: Reprinted from Fair, D. A., Cohen, A. L., Dosenbach, N. U., Church, J. A., Miezin, F. M., Barch, D. M., . . . Schlaggar, B. L., The maturing architecture of the brain's default network. *Proceedings of the National Academy of Sciences of the USA*, 105(10), p. 4028–4032, with permission. Copyright (2008) National Academy of Sciences, U.S.A.

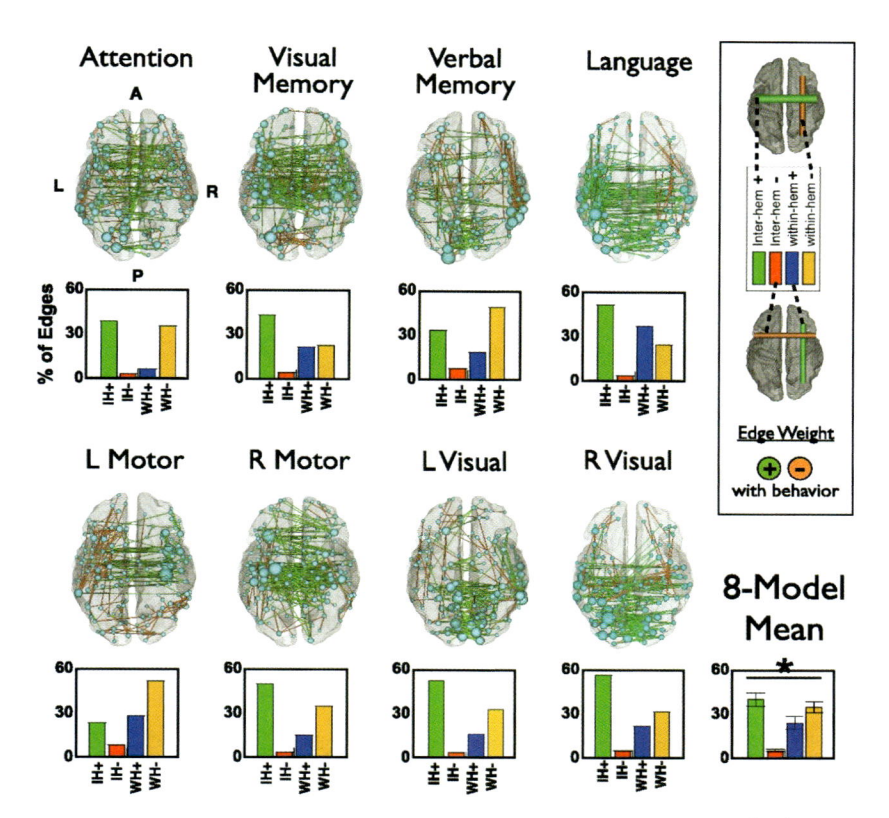

FIGURE 7.4 Most predictive connections and nodes for each functional connectivity (FC)-deficit model. (Top) The top 200 connections driving each FC-behavior model are projected back onto a semitransparent cerebrum (Population-Average, Landmark-, and Surface-based [PALS] atlas). Green connections indicate positive weights (increased FC predicts better performance), and orange connections indicate negative weights (increased FC predicts worse performance). The subset of the 324 parcels included in the top 200 weights are displayed as spheres, sized according to their contribution to the model. (Bottom) Weights from each FC-behavior model are divided into four groups: interhemispheric positive, interhemispheric negative, intrahemispheric positive, and intrahemispheric negative. Bars indicate the average contribution of each of the four groups. The average across models is shown at the bottom right. Analysis of variance (ANOVA) indicates a significant difference in contribution of the four connection types ($p = 1.6 \times 10^{-6}$).

Source: Reprinted from Siegel, J. S., Ramsey, L. E., Snyder, A. Z., Metcalf, N. V., Chacko, R. V., Weinberger, K., ... Corbetta, M., Disruptions of network connectivity predict impairment in multiple behavioral domains after stroke, *Proceedings of the National Academy of Sciences of the USA*, 113(30), 2016, p. E4367–E4376, by permission of United States National Academy of Sciences.

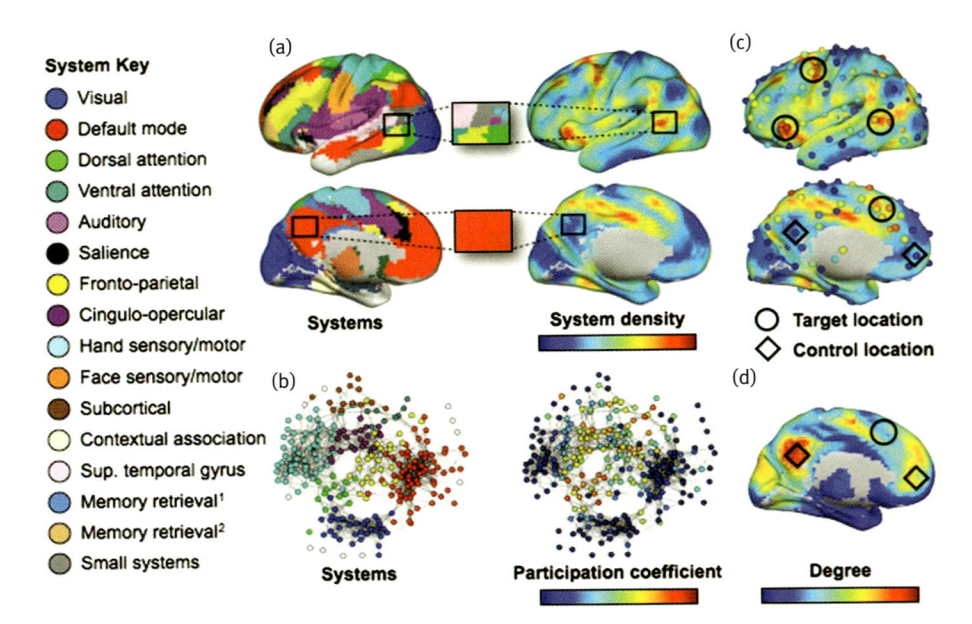

FIGURE 11.2 Network measures. (A) Consensus communities (systems; left) and plot of the density of these systems across the cortex (right). The blowup boxes illustrate how certain cortical locations contain many systems (top; a target location) or few systems (bottom; a control location). (B) Communities (systems) in a brain-wide network (left) and node participation coefficients (right), with warmer colors denoting nodes that display spontaneous blood oxygen level-dependent activity that correlates with multiple systems. (C) Plots of system density and participation coefficients overlaid. Target locations (circles) show where lesions might produce multisystem impairment. Control locations (diamonds) are predicted not to produce widespread impairment. Only four of six target locations are shown (those in the left hemisphere). (D) Node degree, with warmer colors indicating higher degree. Note that regions with high degree (D) may have low system density and/or participation coefficient (C).

Source: Reprinted from Warren, D. E., Power, J. D., Bruss, J., Denburg, N. L., Waldron, E. J., Sun, H., ... Tranel, D., Network measures predict neuropsychological outcome after brain injury, *Proceedings of the National Academy of Sciences of the USA*, 111(39), 2014, p. 14247–14252, by permission of United States National Academy of Sciences.

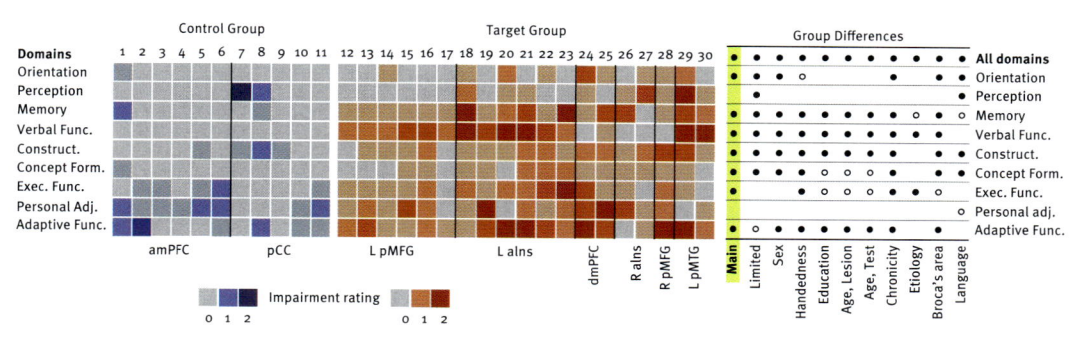

FIGURE 11.3   Individual mean ratings for impairment and analysis summary. (Left) Neuropsychological impairment across nine cognitive and behavioral domains for the control ($n = 11$) and target ($n = 19$) groups. Control cases are at left in shades of blue, target cases are at right in shades of red. Ratings of cognitive impairment for each case by domain were as follows: 0 = no impairment (gray), 1 = moderate impairment (light), and 2 = severe impairment (dark). Intermediate colors represent a score of 0.5 or 1.5 from averaging across two raters. Note the concentration of moderate and severe cognitive impairments among target cases. (Right) Summary of main analysis and follow-up analyses controlling for demographic, attribute, and lesion variables. Follow-up analyses controlling for several variables (see column labels) revealed a pattern broadly similar to the main analysis (left-most data column, highlighted), with significant impairments of the target group always evident in at least two of nine cognitive domains. Main refers to the main analysis; Limited, results for less frequently sampled target locations only; Sex, mixed-sex locations only; Handedness, fully right-handed participants only; Education, years of education, controlled by regression (R); Age, Lesion, age at injury in years, R; Age, Test, age when tested, R; Chronicity, years between injury and test, R; Etiology, etiology of stroke only; Broca's area, no damage to Broca's area; Language, no impairment in verbal functions; solid circles, target group significantly impaired relative to control group ($p < .05$); open circles, marginal impairment ($p < .10$).

Source: Republished by permission of United States National Academy of Sciences, from Network measures predict neuropsychological outcome after brain injury, Warren, D. E., Power, J. D., Bruss, J., Denburg, N. L., Waldron, E. J., Sun, H., . . . Tranel, D., *Proceedings of the National Academy of Sciences of the USA, 111*(39), 2014; permission conveyed through Copyright Clearance Center, Inc.

	Depression risk factors	Therapeutic intervention	Resilience protective factors
Congitive/behavioral	Weak executive function: weak coping self-efficiency; negative attention bias; cognitive inflexibility	Cognitive behavioral therapy with cognitive reappraisal; positive emotion excercises, coping skill development, and training; well-being therapy	Strong executive function; high coping self-efficacy; positive emotions; realistic optimism; cognitive flexibility
Emotion regulation	Weak regulation (e.g., anhedonia; slow stress recovery)	Mindfulness; training; antidepressant medications	Strong regulation (e.g., delay gratification; rapid stress recovery)
Social	Weak social skills; minimal social network; no resilient role models	Social emotional training; network support treatment	Strong social skills; diverse social network; resilient role models
Physical health	Sleep deprivation; poor cardiovascular fitness; poor nutrition; obesity	Teach sleep hygiene; excercise regimen; improve diet	Strong sleep habits; physically fit; good nutrition
Neurobiology	Dysregulated HPA axis and SNS in response to stress; attenuated prefontal cortical executive function and stress-induced limbic system hyperactivity	Neural circuit training; novel medications (corticotropin-releasing factor, NPY, GABA, glutamate)	Effective regulation of HPA axis and SNS in response to stress; robust prefrontal cortical executive function and capacity to regulate limbic reactivity to stress

FIGURE 12.1 Potential interactions between environmental stressors and genetic predisposition. GABA, γ-aminobutyric acid; HPA, hypothalamic–pituitary–adrenal axis; NPY, neuropeptide Y; SNS, sympathetic nervous system.

Source: Reprinted from Southwick, S. M., & Charney, D. S., The science of resilience: Implications for the prevention and treatment of depression, *Science,* 338(6103), 2012, p. 79–82, by permission of American Association for the Advancement of Science.

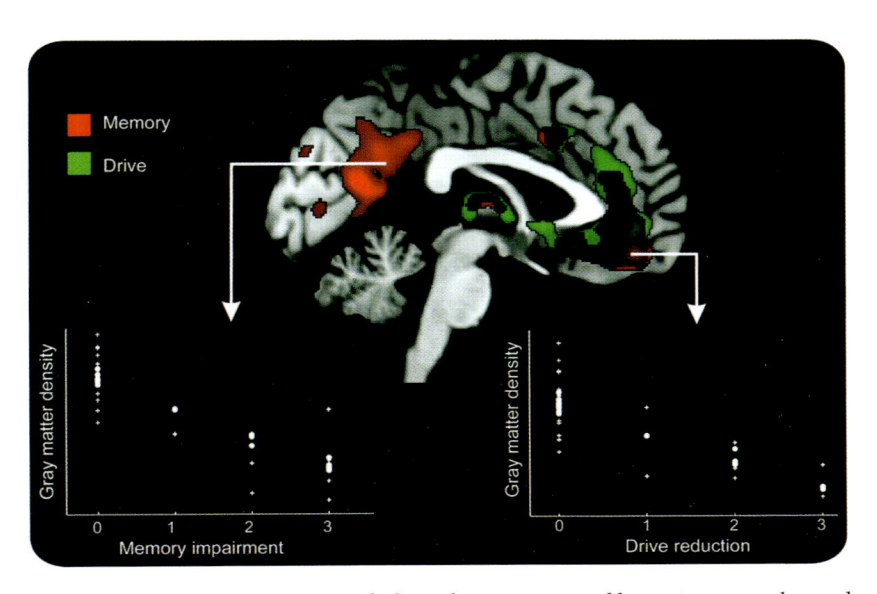

FIGURE 13.1 Correlation between neuropsychological impairment and brain tissue atrophy rendered onto a single subject brain. Memory: $p < .005$, corrected; drive: $p < .05$, corrected. Voxel size: $1 \times 1 \times 1$ mm. Circles, adjusted data; crosses, plus error.

Source: Reprinted from Horstmann, A., Frisch, S., Jentzsch, R. T., Müller, K., Villringer, A., & Schroeter, M. L., Resuscitating the heart but losing the brain: Brain atrophy in the aftermath of cardiac arrest, Neurology, 74(4), 2010, p. 306–312, with permission from Wolters Kluwer Health, Inc. www.neurology.org.

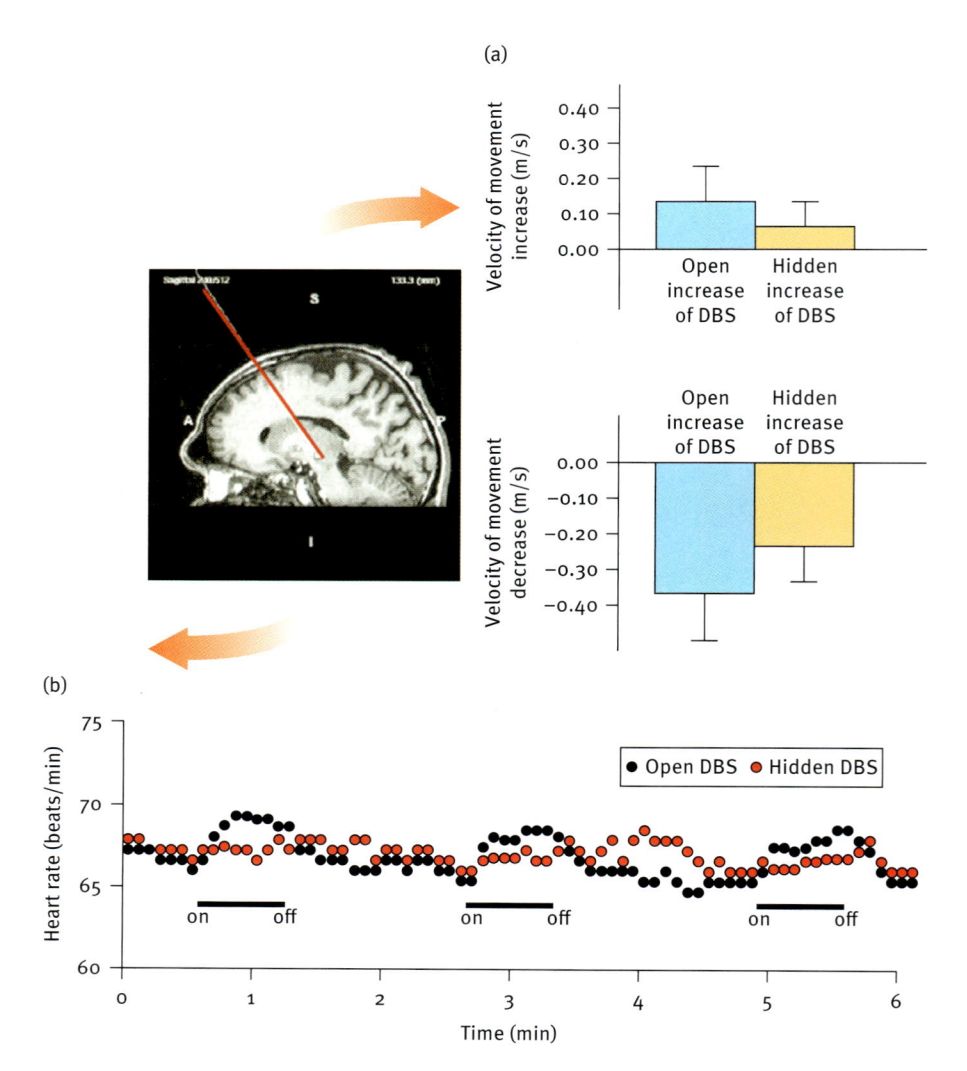

FIGURE 14.1 (A) The effects of open and hidden deep brain stimulation (DBS) on the velocity of hand movement. In all cases, hidden DBS is less effective than open DBS. (B) Heart rate responses of a patient with Parkinson's disease receiving three sequential stimulations (horizontal bars) of the ventral limbic portion of the subthalamic region overtly and covertly. The hidden stimulations are ineffective (there is no matching between stimulus on–off and heart rate changes), suggesting that heart rate increases after the open stimulations do not result from the stimulation itself but, rather, from other factors, such as attention, arousal, and expectation.

Source: Reprinted from Colloca, L., Lopiano, L., Lanotte, M., & Benedetti, F., Overt versus covert treatment for pain, anxiety, and Parkinson's disease, *The Lancet Neurology*, 3(11), 2004, p. 679–684, Copyright (2004), by permission of Elsevier.

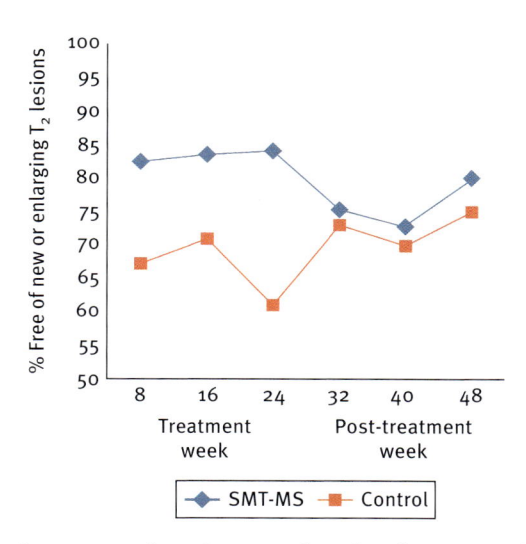

FIGURE 15.2 Percentage of participants free of new or enlarged T2 lesions at each time point by treatment group.

Source: Reprinted from Mohr, D. C., Lovera, J., Brown, T., Cohen, B., Neylan, T., Henry, R., . . . Pelletier, D., A randomized trial of stress management for the prevention of new brain lesions in MS, *Neurology*, 79(5), 2012, p. 412–419, by permission of Wolters Kluwer Health, Inc. www.neurology.org.

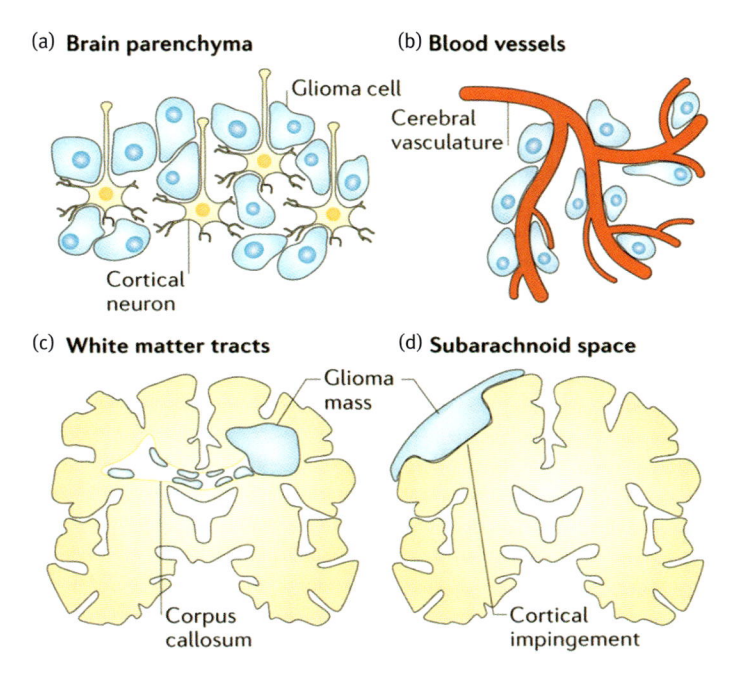

FIGURE 16.1 Pathways of glioma cell invasion: (a) the brain parenchyma, (b) pre-existing blood vessels, (c) white matter tracts (perifascicularly, intrafascicularly, or interfibrillary), and (d) the subarachnoid space below the meningeal covering of the brain.

Source: Reprinted from Cuddapah, V. A., Robel, S., Watkins, S., & Sontheimer, H., A neurocentric perspective on glioma invasion, *Nature Reviews Neuroscience*, 15(7), 2014, p. 455–465, by permission of Springer Nature.

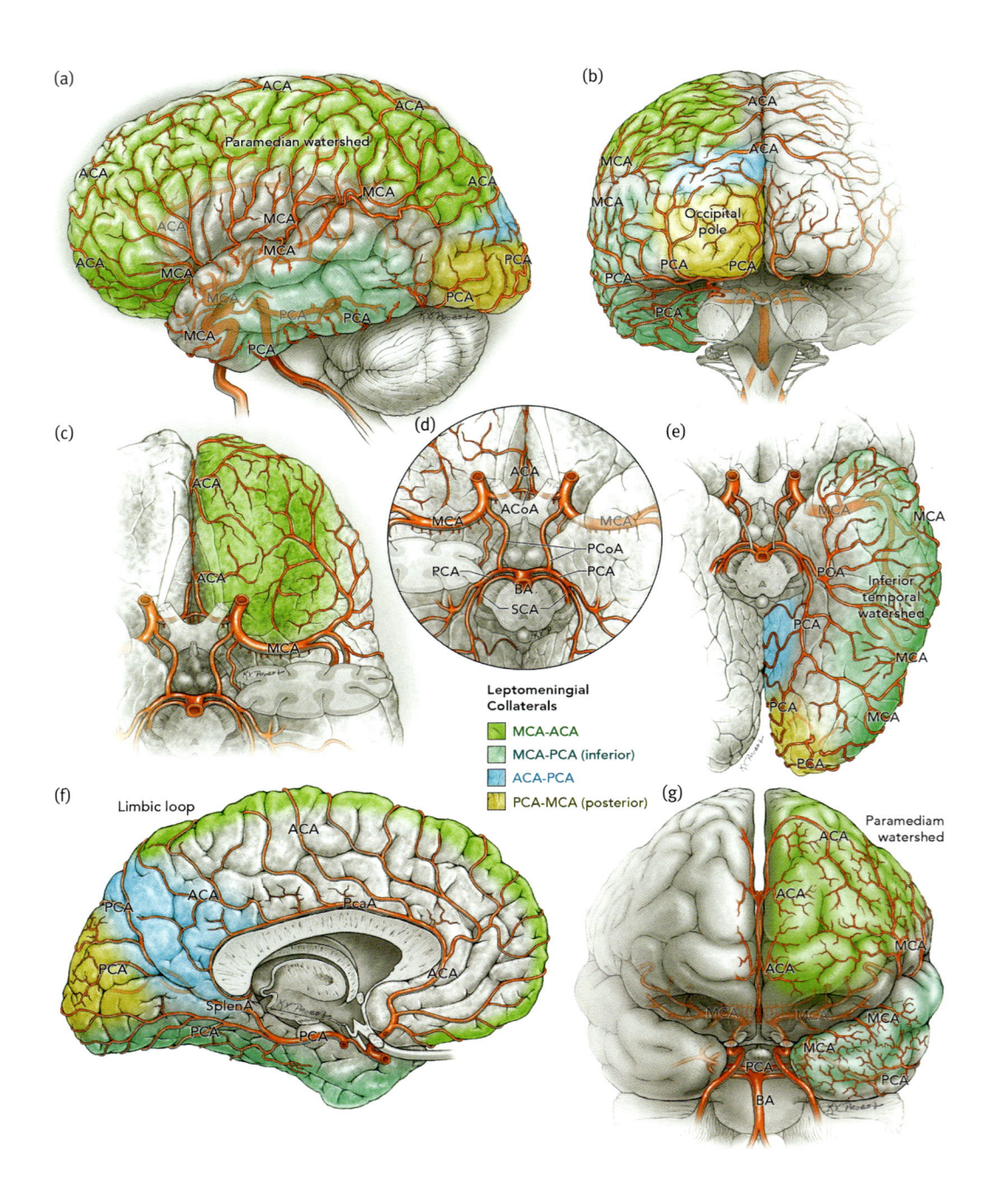

FIGURE 17.1 ACA, anterior cerebral artery; ACoA, anterior communicating; BA, basilar; MCA, middle cerebral artery; PCA, posterior cerebral artery; PcaA, pericallosal; PCoA, posterior communicating; SCA, superior cerebellar; SplenA, splenial.

Source: Reprinted from Lawton, M. T., *Seven Bypasses: Tenets and Techniques for Revascularization*, 2018, by permission of Thieme Medical Publishers. Illustration by Kenneth Xavier Probst, MA, CMI.

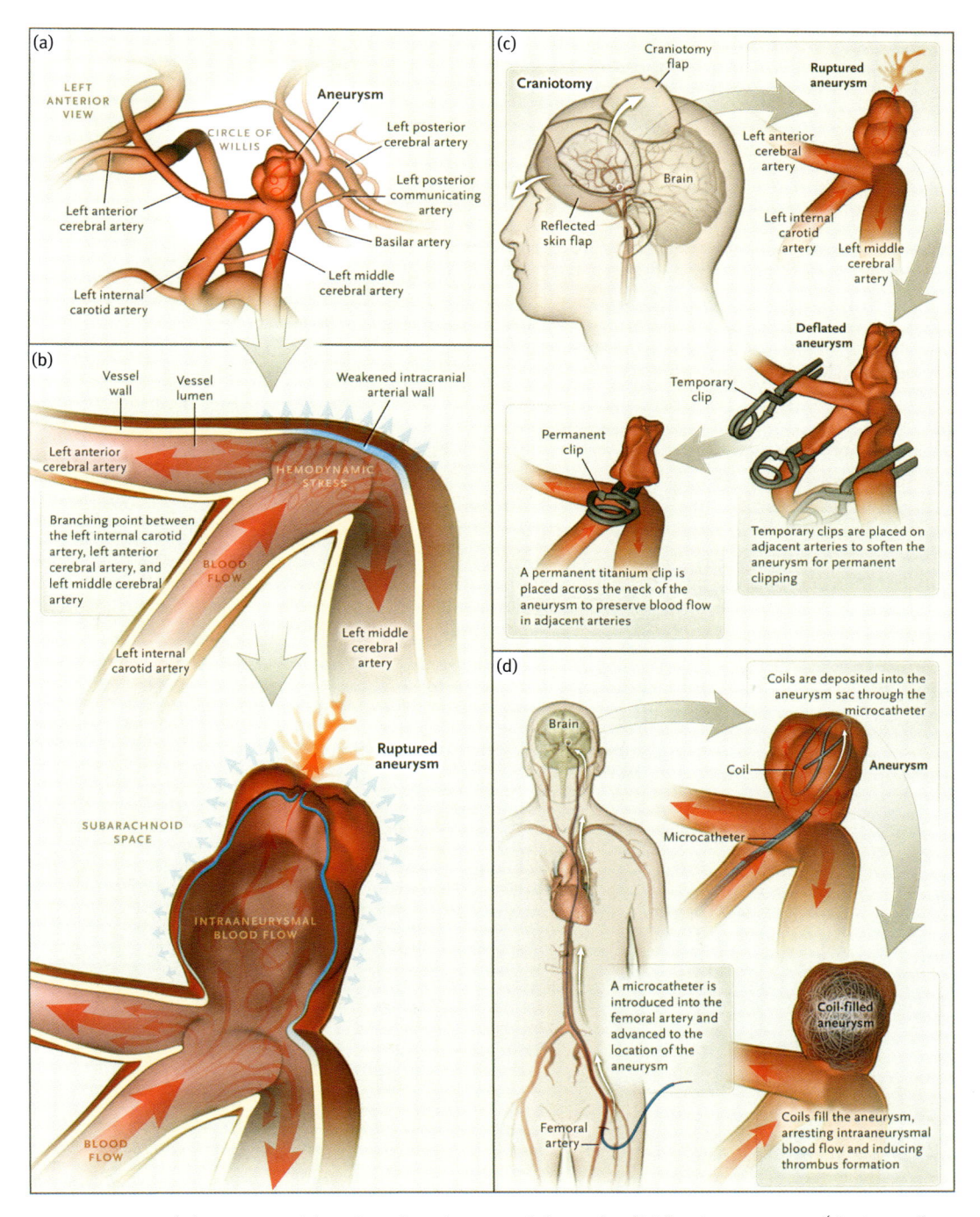

FIGURE 17.2 (A) Anatomy of the subarachnoid space and the circle of Willis. A major artery (the internal carotid artery) enters the skull from below and then follows a course through the subarachnoid space, giving off

(*continued*)

FIGURE 17.2 Continued

perforating branches that supply the parenchyma. (B) High pulsatile pressure at branching points of the proximal artery (arrow) soon after the arterial wall sheds much of its supporting adventitia can promote the formation of saccular aneurysms in susceptible persons. In such cases, an aneurysm forms at the branch point of an artery, where the arterial pulsation stress is maximal. Most lesions remain silent until rupture occurs, at which time blood is rapidly released into the subarachnoid space, leading to early effects, such as intracranial pressure elevation, parenchymal irritation, edema, and hydrocephalus, and delayed effects, such as vasospasm and delayed cerebral ischemia. (C) Open surgical repair of such an aneurysm involves exposing the aneurysm and the adjacent normal arteries so that the surgeon can apply a titanium clip on the neck of the aneurysm, which effectively excludes it from the arterial circulation. Removal of portions of the skull base provides improved access and operative exposure for the surgeon without the need for substantial brain retraction. The aneurysm is then collapsed and the field inspected to ensure that no branches are compromised by the clip placement. The inner walls of the aneurysm base are approximated by the clip, which generally provides a lifelong cure of the lesion. (D) Endovascular repair of such an aneurysm involves the navigation of an intra-arterial catheter through the circulation under fluoroscopic guidance until the catheter tip is in the lumen of the aneurysm. With the use of the catheter, platinum coils are delivered and packed into the lumen of the aneurysm, which slows or prevents blood flow into the aneurysm and leads to thrombus formation, effectively blocking arterial blood from entering the aneurysm. Angiographic examination of the results confirms flow through the normal arterial branches. Not all aneurysms can be treated with endovascular repair (some will have to be treated with surgery), but endovascular repair can treat many aneurysms without a visible scar.

Source: From Lawton, M. T., & Vates, G. E., Subarachnoid hemorrhage, *New England Journal of Medicine, 377*(3), p. 257–266, Copyright © 2017. Reprinted with permission from Massachusetts Medical Society.

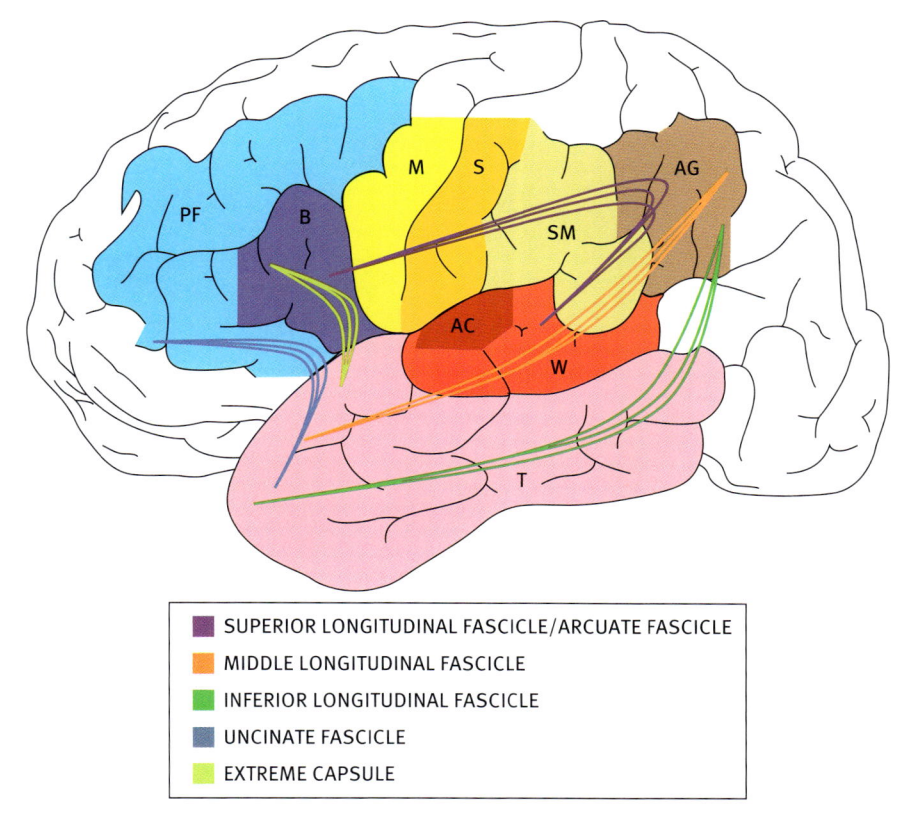

FIGURE 18.1 Vascular territories of language areas. Middle cerebral artery superior and inferior division territories, and middle cerebral artery–anterior cerebral artery (ACA) and middle cerebral artery–posterior cerebral artery watershed territories. AC = primary auditory cortex; AG = angular gyrus; B = Broca's area; M = motor networks in the precentral gyrus; PF = prefrontal networks; S = sensory networks in the postcentral gyrus; SM = supramarginal gyrus; T = inferior temporal networks and temporal pole; W = Wernicke's area.

Source: Reprinted from Oliveira, F. F., Marin, S. M, & Bertolucci, P. H., Neurological impressions on the organization of language networks in the human brain, *Brain Injury*, 31(2), 2017, p. 140–150, by permission of Taylor & Francis Ltd.

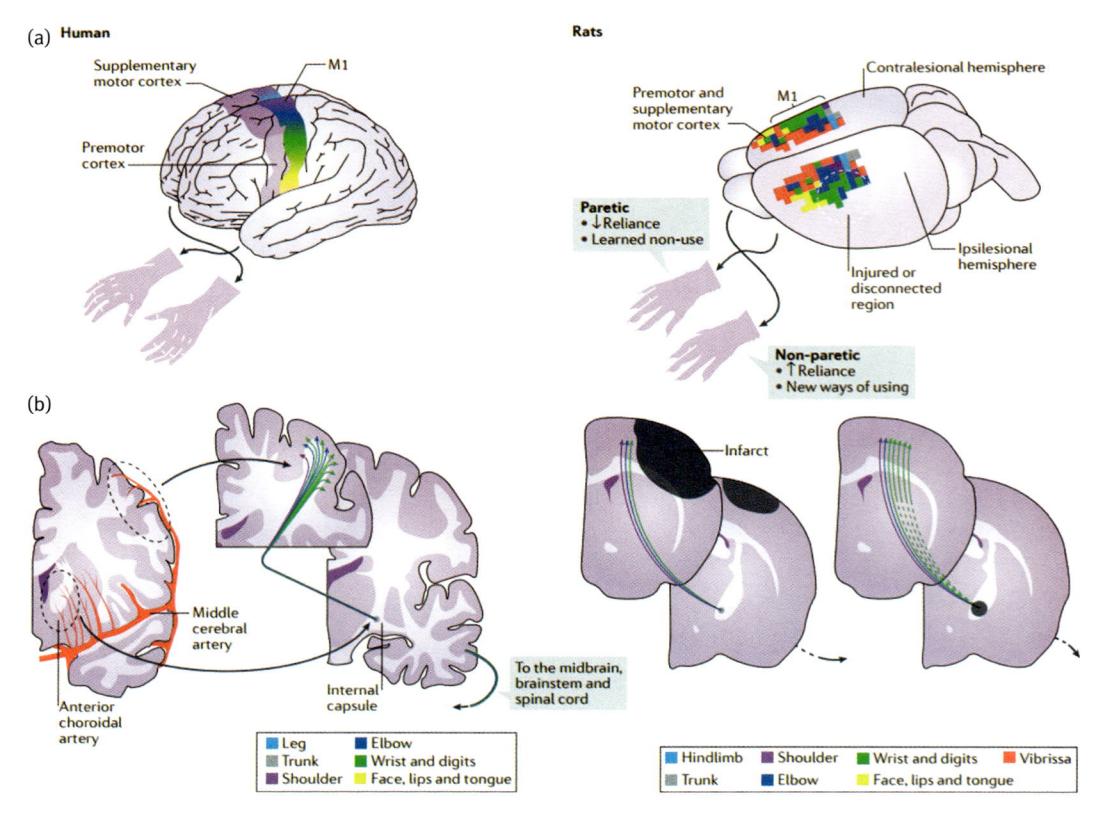

FIGURE 19.1 The motor cortex and its descending projection pathways are often affected by strokes that result in upper extremity impairments. (a) Simplified illustrations of motor cortical regions of a human (left) and a naive rat, derived using intracortical microsimulation (right), are shown. The colors show the cortical territories that are responsible for the movement of different body parts. The motor cortical control of the upper limbs is mostly crossed, such that the left hemisphere controls movement of the right side and vice versa. (b) Occlusions or ruptures in the cerebral vasculature (red) that supplies motor cortical regions (the distal middle cerebral artery) and its projection pathways (e.g., the anterior choroidal and striate arteries) position strokes (the dark gray regions on the rat coronal sections on the right) that either kill the cortical neurons that control upper limb movement or disconnect their projections to the spinal cord and other subcortical structures, such as the red nucleus and reticular formation. The degree of disruption of the descending motor cortical pathway due to either cortical or subcortical strokes predicts the severity of motor impairment. The colors of the corticospinal neurons correspond to the body parts that they control as in the motor cortical regions in panel a. The rat coronal sections show the locations of ischemic infarcts that have been used to model post-stroke upper extremity impairments; these infarcts are located in the forelimb region of the primary motor cortex (M1, which is supplied by the distal middle cerebral artery) and in the posterior limb of the internal capsule (which is supplied by the anterior choroidal artery). The dashed lines indicate the disconnection of descending cortical projections.

Source: Reprinted from Jones, T. A., Motor compensation and its effects on neural reorganization after stroke, *Nature Reviews Neuroscience*, 18(5), 2017, p. 267–280, by permission of Springer Nature.

PART IV

CLINICAL APPLICATIONS

PART IV demonstrates the clinical application of the approach advocated throughout this text. Fostering a positive psychological adjustment to any brain disorder is a highly individual process that requires different approaches depending on the unique features of a given individual (Prigatano, 2018; Prigatano & Salas, 2017). However, understanding the nature of the underlying brain disorder and how it affects neuropsychological functioning is a key component to providing effective psychological care. Understanding the person's individual expression of human nature at different times in his or her life cycle is also crucial to the process of providing effective psychological care. Integrating this knowledge with an understanding of the unique personal (i.e., psychodynamic) and interpersonal (including cultural) situation of the individual often determines the successfulness of such care at multiple levels of observation. Demonstrating "how this is done" and revealing events that either fostered a good psychological adjustment or failed to result in the desired outcome are the major goals of Part IV. Thus, it was the most challenging part of the book to write and yet the most important.

To facilitate this process, a "template" is followed to provide some structure when discussing how different brain disorders affect different individuals and how various forms of psychological care interventions are applied. Although group data are certainly important to review, they are ultimately important only if that knowledge can be effectively applied to the psychological care of specific individual patients.

The template includes background information concerning the brain disorder being considered, followed by a brief description of the neuropsychological impairments and psychiatric disturbances common to the clinical condition being considered. Then a case presentation (or case vignettes) is presented. The case presentation is organized in a manner that allows the reader to evaluate which aspects of psychological care (as discussed particularly in Chapters 1 and 12) appeared most important in determining the clinical outcome for specific individuals. Twenty clinical features relevant to the psychological care of patients with a brain disorder are included in each chapter. These 20 clinical features vary somewhat depending on the central problem that the patient is facing—for example, the problem of lost normality, the problem of not developing normally, and the problem of progressive decline in one's competency. The clinical features are referred to when evaluating which factors appear to positively or negatively correlate with the psychological care outcomes for the different patients discussed. Each chapter also includes a brief summary of approaches described in the literature when providing psychological (and related) care of persons with the specific brain disorder being considered.

REFERENCES

Prigatano, G. P. (2018). Psychological adjustment to the effects of a moderate to severe traumatic brain injury. In J. M. Silver, T. W. McAllister, & D. B. Arciniegas (Eds.), *Textbook of traumatic brain injury* (3rd ed., pp. 817–829). Washington, DC: American Psychiatric Association Press.

Prigatano, G. P., & Salas, C. (2017). Psychodynamic psychotherapy after severe traumatic brain injury. In R. Wood, T. McMillan, & A. Worthington (Eds.), *Neurobehavioral disability and social handicap following traumatic brain injury* (pp. 188–201). Philadelphia, PA: Taylor & Francis.

13

PSYCHOLOGICAL CARE OF PERSONS WITH CEREBRAL ANOXIA SECONDARY TO CARDIAC ARREST

BACKGROUND INFORMATION

Blood supply to the brain is achieved via several routes, but the internal carotid arteries, the basilar artery, and the vertebral arteries are of central importance (Blumenfeld, 2010). Occlusion of the blood supply to the brain typically produces unconsciousness after 10 seconds. It has long been recognized, however, that the brain stem is "more resistant" to oxygen deprivation compared to the cerebral cortex (Ganong, 1981). The entire cerebral cortex has a high demand for both oxygen and glucose to maintain normal activity (with an estimated consumption of 3.5 mL of oxygen and 5.5 mg of glucose per 100 g of brain tissue). The brain does not store energy; therefore, a constant supply of oxygen and glucose is needed to maintain normal brain activity (Nieuwenhuys, Donkelaar, & Nicholson, 1998). When that flow is interrupted, brain functioning decreases by altering the electrical activity of the brain (Nieuwenhuys et al., 1998) and can result in neuronal death (Caine & Watson, 2000), including ultimately brain death (Anderson & Arciniegas, 2010). Regions of the brain that are compromised by decreased blood flow, which results in hypoxic injury, vary as a function of age and duration and severity of insult (Huang & Castillo, 2008). Note, however, that 60% of patients die from cardiac arrest (Horstmann et al., 2010).

The adult brain is approximately 2% of the total body weight, but it utilizes an estimated 20% of the oxygen supply that is available (Ganong, 1981). It receives approximately 15% of the cardiac output (Caine & Watson, 2000). Although there are physiological autoregulation systems in place to protect the brain when oxygen supply is low, those systems cannot withstand prolonged oxygen deprivation. It is estimated that after 4–8 minutes of complete loss of oxygen, neuronal death is likely (Caine & Watson, 2000).

Although all brain regions obviously need oxygen (and related glucose metabolism) to function normally, different time courses and sensitivity to impaired oxygen uptake may exist for different regions of the brain. Caine and Watson (2000) note, for example, that neuropathological change after anoxic episodes is commonly observed in the hippocampus, basal ganglia, cerebellum, visual–motor cortex, and the "watershed regions" of the cortex. Horstmann et al. (2010) have extended this list to include gray matter loss in the anterior, medial, and posterior cingulate cortex as well as in the precuneus, the insular cortex, and the dorsomedial thalamus. Thus, multiple neuropsychological deficits can be observed in patients with a history of oxygen deprivation to the brain (Anderson & Arciniegas, 2010; Hopkins & Haaland, 2004).

The term *anoxia* refers to a complete loss of oxygen, whereas the term *hypoxia* refers to a reduced supply, but not complete loss, of oxygen. Various events can compromise oxygen supply to the brain. An important distinction has been made in the literature between ischemic causes of anoxic brain injury (ABI) and hypoxemic causes of ABI (Hopkins & Haaland, 2004; Thaler et al., 2013). In the former case, there is an abrupt loss of blood supply to the brain, as is seen in cases of cardiac arrest (Lim, Alexander, LaFleche, Schnyer, & Verfaellie, 2004) or ischemic strokes (Zola-Morgan, Squire, & Amaral, 1986). In the latter case, the loss of oxygen is due to some disruption of breathing in which blood oxygen saturation decreases but blood supply to the brain is not substantially interrupted. This can occur in cases of near drowning (Suominen & Vähätalo, 2012), untreated sleep apnea (Gale & Hopkins, 2004), or choking/hanging (Matthey, 1996; Medalia, Merriam, & Ehrenreich, 1991).

Lung disorders can also reduce the amount of oxygen in the bloodstream. When that reduction is below normal saturation points, the condition is referred to as *hypoxemia*. Hypoxemia has been shown to be associated with neuropsychological dysfunction even when direct evidence of structural brain abnormalities is not present (Grant et al., 1987). Acute (Hornbein, 2001) and chronic exposure to high altitudes (Davis et al., 2015) in which there is less oxygen in the air may also alter certain neuropsychological functions (especially learning, memory, and speed of motor performance).

NEUROPSYCHOLOGICAL CONSEQUENCES OF ANOXIA, HYPOXIA, AND HYPOXEMIA

Given the multiple mechanisms by which oxygen deprivation to the brain can occur, the variable duration of oxygen deprivation, and the potential vulnerability of different brain regions, a wide range and severity of neuropsychological impairments have been reported in this complex patient group (Anderson & Arciniegas, 2010; Caine & Watson, 2000). Severe memory impairment immediately following cerebral anoxia and hypoxia is most commonly reported (Caine & Watson, 2000). The memory disturbance can be mild to severe. It can present as an amnesic syndrome that may be permanent. Such a case was described by Zola-Morgan et al. (1986). These investigators suggested that severe anterograde amnesia can exist independent of other serious neuropsychological disturbances, particularly when neuropathological changes are specifically identified bilaterally in "the entire CA1 field of the hippocampus" (p. 2950). Allen, Tranel, Bruss, and Damasio (2006) also reported that anoxic patients with severe amnesia had significant hippocampal volume loss compared to age-matched peers.

However, in a systematic review of the literature, Caine and Watson (2000) reported that memory impairment following cerebral anoxia is often associated with other cognitive impairments. Their literature review suggests that fewer than one in five patients (i.e., 20%) showed memory impairment with no other cognitive impairments being reported. Given that multiple brain regions have a high need for oxygen to function properly, it would be anticipated that other cognitive (and perhaps personality) deficits would also be common. Caine and Watson also noted that visuospatial deficits are commonly observed (in at least 30% of the patients studied), as well as language difficulties. Naming and verbal fluency problems are common. Finally, personality changes are often reported, particularly after cardiac arrest. They include emotional lability, impulsivity, and difficulties in expressing emotions. Some patients are also described as apathetic or lacking concern regarding their clinical status. Still others have been characterized as having impaired "insight" or self-awareness. This latter observation is important and helps explain why it is not uncommon to note a striking discrepancy in how functional capacities are reported by persons with an anoxic brain injury compared to significant others who know them well (Pußwald, Fertl, Faltl, & Auff, 2000). These patients often underestimate their actual level of impairment/disability.

The review by Caine and Watson (2000) did not describe potential psychomotor or related finger–hand movement difficulties in this patient population. Given that the basal ganglia are frequently compromised secondary to hypoxic injury, this is an important omission. Lim et al. (2004) noted, for example, that following cardiac arrest the most common pattern of impairment in their patients was "a combination of memory and motor deficits with variable executive impairment" (p. 1774). Hopkins and Haaland (2004) also emphasized that a variety of motor disturbances have been reported in cases of anoxia due to heterogeneous causes. Thaler et al. (2013) further noted that motor dexterity disturbances were commonly observed in a series of six children with anoxic brain injury due to varying causes. Long-term follow-up studies of children with perinatal hypoxic–ischemic encephalopathy have also emphasized that common motor impairments are frequently observed (van Schie et al., 2015). Finally, there are case reports of delayed-onset dystonia following cerebral anoxic injury (Kuoppamäki, Bhatia, & Quinn, 2002). These reports are important because they suggest that the effects of anoxic brain injury may not be "static" for some individuals.

In addition to the adverse effect on motor movements and psychomotor speed, damage to the striatum could negatively affect frontal lobe systems of the brain, and various disorders of "executive functioning" have also been reported (Hopkins & Haaland, 2004). Anderson and Arciniegas (2010) specifically brought attention to this broad class of disturbances and also linked them to disorders of motivation (i.e., apathy) and impaired self-awareness.

Horstmann et al. (2010) correlated memory impairments and clinical estimates of apathy with brain tissue atrophy in 12 patients who suffered cardiac arrest. They noted, "On the medial surface, atrophy of the precuneus/retrospenial cortex was demonstrated to correlate with the severity of memory impairment, whereas atrophy of the ventromedian anterior cingulate cortex and dorsomedial thalamus was correlated with both apathy and memory impairments" (p. 308). Figure 13.1 illustrates the correlations observed in one of their patients.

Even in the absence of cerebral hypoxia/anoxia, neuropsychological impairments have been reported in patients who have chronic obstructive pulmonary disease (COPD) with associated hypoxemia (Grant et al., 1987; Prigatano, Parsons, Levin, Wright, & Hawryluk, 1983). In an initial study, Prigatano et al. reported that patients with mild hypoxemia (PaO_2 mean value of 66.3) were especially slow in carrying out neuropsychological tasks requiring a psychomotor response (e.g., the Tactual Performance Test and the Digit Symbol subtest of the Wechsler Adult Intelligence Scale). These findings were replicated in a larger group of COPD patients with varying degrees of hypoxemia. It was observed that the

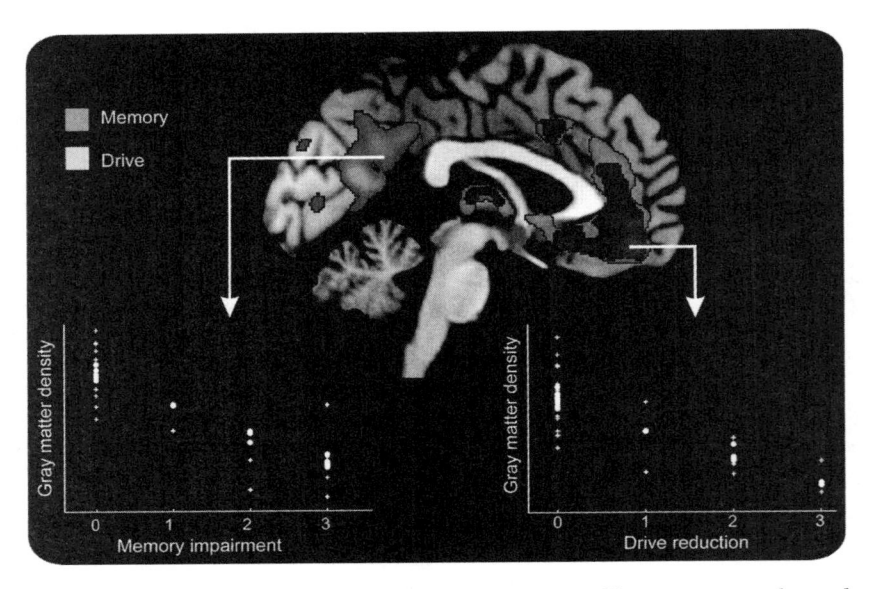

FIGURE 13.1 Correlation between neuropsychological impairment and brain tissue atrophy rendered onto a single subject brain. Memory: $p < .005$, corrected; drive: $p < .05$, corrected. Voxel size: $1 \times 1 \times 1$ mm. Circles, adjusted data; crosses, plus error (See color plates).

Source: Reprinted from Horstmann, A., Frisch, S., Jentzsch, R. T., Müller, K., Villringer, A., & Schroeter, M. L., Resuscitating the heart but losing the brain: Brain atrophy in the aftermath of cardiac arrest, Neurology, 74(4), 2010, p. 306–312, with permission from Wolters Kluwer Health, Inc. www.neurology.org.

greater the degree of hypoxemia, the greater the incidence of neuropsychological impairments (Grant et al., 1987). Interestingly, these negative effects seem to be accentuated in older individuals who have less education. Recall that as noted in Chapter 12, younger individuals with higher levels of education have been linked to the construct of "resiliency."

PSYCHIATRIC DISTURBANCES ASSOCIATED WITH CEREBRAL ANOXIA SECONDARY TO CARDIAC ARREST

Psychiatric disturbances associated with any brain disorder can be classified in different ways. Some of the disturbances appear to be in reaction to the cognitive and motor limitations caused by the brain disorder. Other disturbances may be directly related to the nature of the underlying brain pathology/pathophysiology. A third class of disturbances can be identified as existing prior to the onset of the brain disorder or clinical condition (Prigatano, 1986). The first category of problems can be broadly described as "reactionary problems." Not uncommonly, they include anxiety, depression, and irritability. They can also include angry outbursts, the development of specific phobias or anxiety attacks, a loss of hope, and social isolation/withdrawal. The second category of problems can be described as "neuropsychological mediated" or "neuropsychiatric" in nature. Emotional lability, impulsiveness, lack of "insight," and apathy as described in the review article by Caine and Watson (2000) are classified within this category. The findings reported by Horstmann et al. (2010) certainly support this view as it specifically relates to the problem of apathy. Finally, certain personality or psychiatric problems appear from the patient's history to be "premorbid"—that is, they existed before the onset of the brain disorder. Pre-existing depression and anxiety disorders, psychopathic or sociopathic behavioral disorders, and/or obsessive–compulsive disorders are present in some patients prior to cardiac arrest and associated anoxic injury. These can broadly be referred to as pre-existing personality or characterological disturbances. In some instances, they may have contributed to the onset of the brain disorder (e.g., bipolar depression that led to a suicide attempt that led to cerebral anoxia). To the degree to which it is possible, evaluating the psychiatric problems as potentially reactionary, neuropsychiatric, or premorbid in nature at times helps the clinician plan a more informed approach to the patient's psychological care.

Depression and Anxiety

Frasure-Smith and Lespérance (2008) studied the possible role of depression and anxiety in predicting negative outcomes of coronary artery disease (CAD), including cardiac arrest. As a part of their prospective investigation, they obtained estimates of major depressive disorder (MDD) and generalized anxiety disorder (GAD) in patients who were described as having "stable CAD" (p. 63). They then followed their patients for 2 years. At baseline testing, 57 of their 804 patients met criteria for MDD (7.1%), and 43 met criteria for GAD (5.3%). The two conditions often overlapped (i.e., they were commonly associated with each other). These figures are fairly comparable to what has been reported in the general population (Hiott & Labbate, 2002; Kessler et al., 2003). In Frasure-Smith and Lespérance's study, depression and anxiety were not found to predict later major adverse cardiac events when controlling for such variables as age and diastolic blood pressure.

In an earlier prospective drug treatment study that attempted to improve cognitive functioning following cardiac arrest, Roine, Kajaste, and Kaste (1993) reported that 35% of their patients showed "depressive symptoms" 3 months after cardiac arrest and 31% continued to show the same pattern 12 months after cardiac arrest. However, they reported severe depression in only 8% of their patients—a percentage similar to that reported by Frasure-Smith and Lespérance (2008).

The role of depression in predisposing a person to CAD was evaluated in a review article by Lett et al. (2004). They suggested that "depression confers a relative risk between 1.5 and 2.0 for the onset of CAD in healthy individuals, whereas depression in patients with existing CAD confers a relative risk between 1.5 and 2.5 for cardiac morbidity and mortality" (p. 305). However, not all studies support this claim. Some of the studies used to arrive at these estimates appeared not to control for comorbid medical conditions associated with depression. Lett et al., however, provided a useful "biobehavioral model" to help explain the potential complicated relationship between depression and CAD. Their model suggests that depression (and most likely the comorbid problem of anxiety) can be linked to alcohol use, physical inactivity, diabetes, obesity, and hypertension (Figure 13.2). These factors certainly can contribute to heart disease. Lett et al.'s simple model provides a good "teaching tool" for some patients.

Wachelder et al. (2009) reported on the long-term daily functioning and quality of life of patients who were, on average, 3 years post cardiac arrest. They did not specifically identify patients with known cerebral hypoxic insults but, rather, studied reports of cognitive functioning, emotional status, and participation in daily activities. Among their findings was the observation that reports of anxiety and depression were present in more than one-third of the patients studied. Although their findings are also compatible with those of an earlier report by Roine et al. (1993), the authors acknowledge that their patient sample tended to be older (mean age, 60.2 years) and age could have contributed to some of their findings.

Finally, the well-established relationships between level of depression, quality of life, and measures of "resiliency" in patients following cardiac arrest have been reported. For example, Toukhsati et al. (2017) found that cardiac arrest survivors who report high levels of

Depression

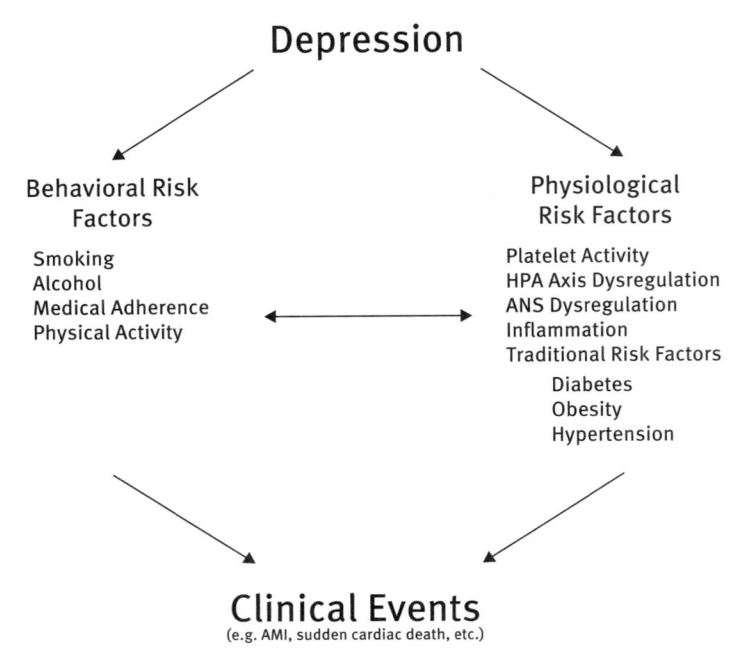

Behavioral Risk Factors
Smoking
Alcohol
Medical Adherence
Physical Activity

Physiological Risk Factors
Platelet Activity
HPA Axis Dysregulation
ANS Dysregulation
Inflammation
Traditional Risk Factors
  Diabetes
  Obesity
  Hypertension

Clinical Events
(e.g. AMI, sudden cardiac death, etc.)

FIGURE 13.2 Biobehavioral model for the relationship between depression and coronary artery disease clinical events. AMI, acute myocardial infarction; ANS, autonomic nervous system; HPA, hypothalamic–pituitary–adrenal axis.

Source: Reprinted from Lett, H. S., Blumenthal, J. A., Babyak, M. A., Sherwood, A., Strauman, T., Robins, C., & Newman, M. F., Depression as a risk factor for coronary artery disease: Evidence, mechanisms, and treatment, *Psychosomatic Medicine*, 66(3), 2004, p. 305–315, by permission of Wolters Kluwer Health, Inc. www.neurology.org.

depression also appear to have less resiliency in coping with the consequences of their cardiac condition ($r = -.79, p < .001$).

Post-Traumatic Stress Disorder

A literature review by Vilchinsky, Ginzburg, Fait, and Foa (2017) noted that, on average, 12% of patients with cardiac disease show behavioral signs of post-traumatic stress disorder (PTSD). Multiple forms of cardiac disease were reviewed and thus the authors did not directly compare cardiac arrest patients with patients who had other cardiac conditions. However, their findings are interesting in light of the fact that the patients' perceived level of severity of cardiac illness was predictive of PTSD symptoms. Demographic variables were not predictive of such symptoms. Pre-existing measures of resiliency were a predictive factor.

As might be expected from other studies dealing with the "resiliency factor," low levels of depression, good social support, and the ability to return to work were associated with an absence of PTSD.

Psychosomatic Difficulties

Given the elevated anxiety that an experience of cardiac arrest can produce in patients, it would be expected that psychosomatic difficulties might be common in patients after cardiac arrest. No prospective study or review article could be located that addresses this question. The earlier work of Ladwig et al. (1999), however, made several important points regarding psychosomatic difficulties. Ladwig et al. noted that persistent problems with concentration, intrusive thoughts about what happened, and fear of another cardiac arrest contributed to greater somatic complaints and anxiety in the patients they studied following cardiac arrest. Interestingly, Pußwald et al. (2000) reported that 60% of spouses of cardiac arrest patients showed evidence of psychosomatic difficulties. Pußwald et al. noted that the spouse often shoulders the burden of care, and increased emotional distress is common in family members.

Apathy, Impaired Self-Awareness, and Psychotic Reactions

Depending on the severity of anoxic injury to the brain, a wide range of neuropsychiatric disturbances can be observed. Lishman (1987) noted that the patient with severe anoxic injury who is unaware of the extent of his or her cognitive difficulties can "develop a dangerous fixity of purpose from which he [or she] cannot be dissuaded" (p. 549). Such patients are often easily agitated and emotionally labile. Persistent delusional thought patterns, behavioral dyscontrol, and paranoid ideation can exist when the level of cognitive impairment secondary to cerebral anoxia is severe.

As previously mentioned, apathy is very common and can be correlated with specific regions of brain volume loss (see Figure 13.1). Therefore, apathy may be more clearly identified as a neuropsychiatric disorder, whereas MDD often appears to exist premorbidly in patients with cardiac arrest. The development of depressive symptoms, however, can clearly be reactionary in nature.

Because the problem of impaired self-awareness (ISA) was discussed in detail in previous chapters, here it is only important to note that brain regions linked to apathy have also been linked to ISA in different patient populations. In this regard, damage to the ventromedian anterior cingulate cortex (an important component of the default mode network; see Chapter 9, this volume) is related to both disturbances. In classical neurology, some patients with anosognosia for hemiplegia demonstrated anosodiaphoria (a lack of concern about their condition). The phenomenon now referred to as apathy may in fact be the same phenomenon referred to as anosodiaphoria.

Social Isolation and Quality of Life

Most studies that have attempted to measure quality of life associated with cerebral anoxia/hypoxia secondary to cardiac arrest have noted a tendency for patients to become socially isolated with time. Wachelder et al. (2009) noted that the majority of their 63 patients were not participating in social activities. More recent reviews of the literature on quality of life after cardiac arrest tend to report more favorable outcomes, but details regarding which patients may not have a good return to normal daily living are often not clearly described (Elliott, Rodgers, & Brett, 2011). Again, the problem of impaired insight or awareness of one's limitations may skew the reported findings (Pußwald et al., 2000).

Middelkamp et al. (2007) studied quality of life in patients with hypoxic brain injury secondary to cardiac arrest. They reported that the period of post-traumatic (i.e., postanoxic) amnesia was strongly correlated with both daily functioning skills ($r = -.70, p < .01$) and measures of quality of life ($r = -.70, p < .01$). The degree of residual cognitive impairments correlated with these two outcome measures at a comparable level. The worse the level of cognitive functioning, the more compromised the quality of life—perhaps an obvious finding to clinicians and family members. The important point of these studies, however, is that ongoing problems with anxiety, depression, and cognitive dysfunction are not uncommon when there is hypoxic injury to the brain secondary to cardiac arrest. The literature, however, is limited in providing important details relevant to the psychological care of these persons. For example, motor disturbances are common in patients who suffer anoxic brain injury secondary to cardiac arrest (Lim et al., 2004). The specific impact of residual motor disturbances on quality of life in this patient group has not been clearly reported. However, in other patient groups who suffer brain injury (e.g., traumatic brain injury [TBI]), the correlation of impaired motor functions and quality of life measures is often quite high (Williams & Willmott, 2012).

PSYCHOLOGICAL CARE OF A PERSON WITH ANOXIC BRAIN INJURY SECONDARY TO CARDIAC ARREST: OBSERVATIONS OVER 26 YEARS

Before describing this case (and others in later chapters), certain types of information are important to consider in light of the discussion in Chapter 12. First, salient features of the patient's medical history are presented. This is followed by a short description of the key neuropsychological findings, including test findings, for given patients who are discussed. However, equally important (from the perspective of psychological care) is an explicit understanding of what the patient experiences regarding how the brain disorder has or has not affected them. Next, it is crucial to understand what the patient (or, in some instances, family members) "wants" regarding psychological care or rehabilitation interventions at different time periods in the patient's life. The nature of the dialogue between the treating clinician and the patient (and family members as the case may be) has to be understood in light of these considerations. Changes in what the patient and family members want at different times in the course of a patient's care often reflect changes in the patient's clinical condition and what he or she perceives as most important at that time. It clearly will affect what type of psychological care efforts or interventions are attempted at any given time. For each patient, the ultimate goal is to improve his or her psychological resilience in dealing with the direct and indirect effects of a brain disorder (Goldstein, 1942) in light of the facts of human nature and the patient's specific psychodynamic and psychosocial stage in life. The degree to which this goal can be achieved for different patients naturally leads to suggestions for improving psychological care for patients with similar medical, neuropsychological, and psychodynamic/psychosocial features.

Medical History

A 22-year-old, single, left-handed man suffered a cerebral anoxic insult secondary to cardiac arrest. Seven years prior to that event, he underwent an aortic valve replacement and implantation of an automatic cardioverter defibrillator. A single-photon emission computed tomography scan of the brain, obtained 22 days after the anoxic event, revealed diminished perfusion in both frontal lobes and the left occipital lobe. Neurologically, the patient was described at that time as showing severe anoxic encephalopathy. It was noted that he demonstrated "severe restriction of all higher cerebral functions without pattern of focal impairment." He received traditional inpatient neurorehabilitation to improve his functional capacities. He regained his strength (but he was excessively fatigued) and had no focal deficits (e.g., motor or visual impairments) on his neurological examination by 3 weeks after onset.

Severe memory impairment persisted, which was observed by his treating physicians, therapists, and family members. The patient appeared to be demonstrating a classical amnestic syndrome. He was quiet and compliant with the requests of his physicians and therapists. Given his obvious memory impairments, a neuropsychological examination/consultation was requested.

Neuropsychological Findings

The patient was initially evaluated while in the hospital. One month after his anoxic episode, he was asked about his memory. He reported having "some" memory difficulties but did not perceive a severe problem. He did not report any other cognitive or physical limitations. He was cooperative but quiet, as noted previously.

He did not initiate any conversation but simply answered questions. He appeared mildly apathetic, but clearly he was not depressed or anxious.

After talking with the patient for approximately 20 minutes, I excused myself to talk to his parents and get their perspective on his functioning and any changes they may have noticed. I spoke with them for approximately 15 minutes and then returned to the patient's room to do a brief assessment of his neuropsychological functioning. When I returned, the patient had no memory of who I was or that I had previously spoken with him. He was alert with no obvious language difficulties. He demonstrated what appeared to be a severe amnestic disorder. No further neurobehavioral assessment was done at that time.

Five months later, neuropsychological testing was conducted. On the Wechsler Adult Intelligence Scale–Revised form (WAIS-R), the patient obtained a Verbal IQ of 80 with a Performance IQ of 76 and a Full Scale IQ of 77. All age-adjusted subtest scale scores ranged from 5 to 8 (Block Design = 6, Similarities = 8, and Digit Symbol = 5). On the Wechsler Memory Scale–Revised form, recall of short stories was at the 6th percentile level for immediate recall and the 2nd percentile level for delayed recall. Visual spatial recall was at the 62nd percentile level for immediate recall but at the 18th percentile level for delayed recall. On the California Verbal Learning Test, he was able to recall 10 words by the 5th learning trial, but he could recall only 5 words at the time of long-term, free recall. On the Halstead–Reitan Neuropsychology Test Battery, he made 61 errors on the Category Test and was overwhelmed with the Tactual Performance Test. It was consequently discontinued. He made 4 errors on the Speech Perception Test and only 2 errors on the Seashore Rhythm Test. His average speed of finger tapping on the Halstead Finger Tapping Test was 52.4 taps with the dominant left hand and 47.2 taps with the right hand. These latter scores were within the normal range.

These findings are important insofar as they document the patient's impairment in overall problem-solving abilities. At the time of his cardiac arrest and anoxic injury, he was getting average grades at a major university and was taking premedicine courses. He most likely had premorbid intellectual abilities in the bright normal range. It is also important to note that he demonstrated severe memory impairments with no apparent decline in speed of simple finger movement (or tapping) tasks. Speed of information processing, however, was compromised (note the Digit Symbol scale score of 5).

After the previous findings were obtained, the patient underwent 9 months of intensive neuropsychological rehabilitation as described in detail elsewhere (Prigatano, 1986, 1999). Important aspects of his behavior during this rehabilitation program are described later in this chapter.

The permanency of this young man's neuropsychological difficulties was perhaps not fully appreciated at the time he was initially seen. It is of some value, therefore, to jump ahead and consider his neuropsychological functioning over time to obtain a more informed understanding of what needed to be addressed in his rehabilitation and long-term psychological care.

Approximately 13 years after the patient's original neuropsychological evaluation, repeat testing was done primarily for research purposes. At that time, on the WAIS-III, he obtained a Verbal IQ of 88 with a Performance IQ of 80, yielding a Full Scale IQ of 84. Age-adjusted subtest scale scores ranged from 5 to 10 (Block Design = 9, Similarities = 10, and Digit Symbol = 5). On the Wechsler Memory Scale–Revised (WMS-R), his recall of short stories was at the 24% level for immediate recall and 22% for delayed recall. Recall of visuospatial information was at the 98% level for immediate recall and 20% for delayed recall. On the California Verbal Learning Test, he was able to recall 11 words by the fifth trial and 8 words on the long-term free recall trial.

On this latter measure, his age-adjusted T score was 30, which is 2 standard deviations (SD) below average. On the Halstead–Reitan Neuropsychological Test Battery, he made only nine errors on the Halstead Category Test. He was able to complete the Tactual Performance Test. His left-hand score was 7 minutes and 2 seconds, and his right-hand score was 7 minutes and 58 seconds; the score for both hands was 3 minutes and 47 seconds. His Memory score was 7, and his Location score was 2. On the Speech Perception Test, he made four errors. On the Seashore Rhythm Test, he made three errors. His left-hand speed of finger tapping was 49.2 taps per 10 seconds, and he tapped an average of 45.2 taps per 10 seconds with his right hand.

Sixteen years after his initial neuropsychological examination, the patient was re-examined for clinical purposes (described in more detail later). At that time, his WAIS-IV Verbal Comprehension Index score was 95, and his Perceptual Reasoning Index score was 86. His Working Memory Index score was 83, and his Processing Speed Index score was 81. His Full Scale IQ was measured at 84. Age-adjusted scale scores now ranged from 5 to 12 (however, Block Design = 6, Similarities = 9, and Coding [Digit Symbol] = 6). On the Logical Memory subtest of the WMS-IV, his immediate scale score was 6, and his delayed scale score was 5. His left-hand speed of finger tapping was measured at 49.2 taps per minute, and his right-hand speed of finger tapping was measured at 50 taps per minute.

These neuropsychological findings highlight three important points in relation to this patient's neuropsychological status and psychological care issues. First, he initially demonstrated and continues to demonstrate unequivocal, persistent memory impairment, which has not substantially changed over the several years he has been followed. Second, there has been gradual improvement in some areas of cognitive functioning and problem-solving over time, but his level of intelligence remains compromised compared to his estimated premorbid intellectual abilities. Third, although his motor skills always appear unaffected from the anoxic event (i.e., finger tapping scores), his speed of new learning and psychomotor performance has also remained virtually unchanged and significantly below average (note the Digit Symbol or Coding scores). Helping the patient and his family members to understand these findings and to recognize that he had and has more than a "memory problem" was and is important in his psychological care.

The Patient's Experience and Efforts at Psychological Care During and After an Intensive Neuropsychological Rehabilitation Program

Approximately 4 months after his anoxic brain insult, the young man was enrolled in a day treatment, neuropsychologically oriented rehabilitation program. At that time, he did not report any specific "wants," but he expressed a desire to get better and was willing to engage in a day treatment program that consisted of approximately 5 or 6 hours of therapies or therapeutic activities during a 5-day week. His parents had a similar "want," but they were especially interested in whether his memory would adequately improve to allow him to continue his studies. He remained in the neuropsychological rehabilitation program for approximately 9 months, as noted previously. At the end at that time, he elected to return to his academic studies despite the advice of his therapists. He wanted to determine if he could successfully complete his studies. He "wanted to try."

The program in which he was enrolled was intended to help post-acute TBI patients whose cognitive and behavioral problems precluded them from returning to some form of productive lifestyle (for details regarding the program, see Prigatano, 1999). He was involved in this program so soon after his brain insult because it was the only program available at the time to specifically attempt to improve cognitive and behavioral functioning and awareness of one's neuropsychological strengths and limitations. The program also provided guided/protective work trials to help persons become as functional as possible in light of their residual neuropsychological impairments. It also provided educational and support services for family members. His parents, both professional individuals, were eager for him to obtain such treatments and were active participants in all activities asked of them. They, too, were unsure what to do at the end of their son's rehabilitation program, but they agreed it was time for him to attempt to resume his studies.

The patient's participation in this day program was one of compliance and cooperation. However, he did not always appear "motivated" to engage in all therapeutic activities. He acknowledged his memory difficulties, but he did not want to rely on a member notebook system to aid his recall in everyday life. He wanted to "exercise" his memory in the hope that it would improve with time. He worked at all cognitive retraining tasks, participated in all group therapy tasks, and eagerly involved himself in physically oriented therapies. His course of rehabilitative care was essentially uneventful until one emotionally charged event occurred.

The patient had an assignment to remember to buy and bring a certain food item for a planned picnic. The assignment had been discussed with the patient several times by a very dedicated staff member. The patient stated he would remember to get the food item, but he resisted writing down his assigned responsibility. The staff member went along with his decision, knowing that he would most likely forget his assignment. On the morning of the picnic, the staff member asked the patient if he had remembered to bring in the food item. The patient immediately had a sense of panic because he had forgotten the assignment. He requested permission to immediately go to the store and get the item. The therapist said that he could not do so, and he would simply have to tell people at the picnic that he had forgotten to get this important food item. The intent of the staff member was to teach the patient the important lesson of writing things down that he needed to do. The patient was very emotionally distressed for the entire morning prior to the picnic. Just before the picnic, the staff member told the patient that she had purchased the food item because she knew the patient would most likely forget it. The patient had a mixture of conflicting feelings. He was relieved to know the item was there, but he was angry with the staff member for making him suffer for several hours.

When this situation was brought to my attention, I first spoke with the staff member and others about not having the patient suffer in such a manner even if the intention was eventually to help him "learn his lesson." Certain staff members were not especially pleased with my request that an apology be made to the patient in a group meeting, but they complied with my request. As a result, the patient formed a very positive working alliance with me. He recognized that the program viewed his personal suffering as important and that the goal of all treatment was to reduce, not increase, that suffering. The beginning of a strong therapeutic alliance was established.

When the patient left the neuropsychological rehabilitation program, he and his parents were appreciative of the efforts of his therapists and believed he had improved cognitively and physically. His endurance was better, he was more prone to use a memory notebook, and he did not report any significant depression or anxiety. He seemed to have some lack of insight into his condition, but it was not clear if this was a method of psychologically coping or a subtle form of ISA. In any event, both he and his parents believed it was time to determine if he could resume his studies even if he had not returned to his premorbid level of cognitive and memory functioning. The patient was clear in stating that he wanted to end his formal rehabilitation and attempt to return to his academic studies. Consequently, he returned to his university upon leaving the rehabilitation program despite the collective opinion of his therapists that this did not appear to be a wise decision.

Within 6 months of leaving his neuropsychological rehabilitation program, the young man began to experience severe panic attacks when driving a car on the freeway. He also began having severe headaches. He left the university setting, which was in another state, and returned home. He and his parents now wanted help reducing his headaches and panic attacks (which appeared to be reactionary problems). He was now seen for a series of weekly outpatient psychotherapy sessions. The psychotherapy sessions focused on his frustrations and his fears of not being successful in life and of not living up to parental expectations. The sessions also focused on interpersonal issues he had with an older brother who appeared more successful and intelligent than he perceived himself to be. During some of these sessions, he was able to cautiously voice his anger over his cardiac arrest, although it was difficult for him to do so. He was secretly frightened that another cardiac arrest might occur. His doctor's reassurance was not adequate. The doctor had been wrong the first time, having told the patient that his pacemaker would most likely enable him to avoid a heart attack, and therefore the patient did not trust the doctor's opinion. The patient felt some comfort in meeting on a regular basis to discuss his feelings, worries, and frustrations. He said he felt good about his ability to "voice out loud" what he was experiencing.

Prior to psychotherapy and prior to returning home, the patient tried several medications to reduce his panic attacks and headaches, but to no avail. During this time, the patient perceived no connection between his residual cognitive difficulties (and how they resulted in poor academic performance) and his somatic and affective disturbance. Based on the strong therapeutic alliance established previously, however, the patient was slowly guided to give up his studies at the major university he had attended and begin academic studies at another university with lower academic standards. He was also guided to change his course of study and focus on an area related to his interest in sports. In this new setting, he was able to obtain passing grades in school and started again to experience some sense of competency. This circumstance is a reminder of Erikson's (1964) statement quoted in Chapter 4 that "if life is to be sustained hope must remain, even where confidence is wounded, trust impaired" (p. 115). This was certainly true for this patient.

During this time of psychological care in which the patient had a renewed sense of confidence in himself and trusted the guidance of his psychotherapist, hope in a better future naturally emerged. His headaches and panic attacks gradually disappeared. This was achieved by altering his environment and helping him accept functioning in the less demanding environment. This "acceptance" did not come easy. Understanding his basic personality, interests, and human need to be successful at something helped him make the change because he trusted the advice of the treating clinical neuropsychologist. However, his "lack of insight" persisted, even when his physical and psychological symptoms were successfully treated. It was now approximately 2 years after his anoxic event.

When the patient graduated from college and left the educational setting, he attempted to find employment, and his headaches and anxiety reactions (not full panic attacks) returned. Again, psychotherapeutic interventions were initiated to help guide him to take a certain type of job (compatible with his overall cognitive abilities, including memory impairment). This resulted in a substantial reduction of his symptoms. He simply followed the psychotherapeutic advice because he trusted the clinical neuropsychologist. This pattern has been observed during the 26 years that I have followed and periodically worked with this patient. His "denial" of his cognitive difficulties appears to me to be related to a lack of adequate awareness secondary to underlying brain dysfunction (i.e., "organic unawareness"). As he was guided to follow certain behavioral choices (based on the therapist's understanding of his neuropsychological difficulties and psychodynamic relationships with his parents and siblings), the symptoms began to disappear until a new, unexpected set of environmental problems occurred.

The patient's initial psychological difficulties focused on "identity" issues. Could he be the person he wanted to be before his cardiac arrest and anoxic brain injury? If not, how would he deal with the anxiety caused by this existential crisis? Throughout the years, other psychological adjustment problems emerged and seemed highly correlated with his stage of life (as described in Chapter 4, this volume). For example, after he married in his early 30s, relationship issues with his wife became a major focus of psychological interventions. He now wanted help in his marriage and assistance in knowing how to explain to his wife his cognitive limitations. Discussions with him and his wife before and after the marriage helped clarify his cognitive strengths and weaknesses. This led to important discussions about their economic future, including opportunities to address the patient's anger and resentment that re-emerged regarding his belief that he was not able to earn as good an income as his parents did when he was a child. Knowledge of this long-standing issue allowed for a re-evaluation of how it might be influencing some impulsive decisions on his part. This discussion was especially important for him when he wanted to leave a job to obtain a higher paying job, even though he most likely could not successfully meet the new job responsibilities because of his cognitive limitations. He was able to avoid this potential catastrophe with the guidance of a clinical neuropsychologist whom he trusted and who understood his psychosocial and psychodynamic circumstances.

Later in life (in his early 50s), the patient returned because of a new issue. He was always reluctant to tell employers about his medical history and associated memory difficulties. When a recent change of supervisors at work required him to take on more work responsibilities, he was unable to meet them, even with some accommodations. At this time, his headaches again reappeared, and his job security was threatened. Realizing in his adult years that disclosure of his medical condition was important, he approached me again for guidance and support. Given his limited awareness of his cognitive limitations and tendency to not fully recognize the severity of his memory difficulties, he was again guided to take specific steps to inform his supervisor. Although this was certainly difficult for him (like many other people with and without a brain disorder, earlier life problems had to be reckoned with as he got older), he was able to appropriately explain his cognitive difficulties to his supervisor and ultimately to a new job manager. As a result, he was assigned to another job within the company. Eventually, the patient left that company and reviewed with me in detail the job responsibilities of a position for which he had applied at a new company. It appeared that he would be able to handle these responsibilities and therefore he applied and obtained the position, which was more satisfying to him.

Having an ongoing consulting relationship with a clinical neuropsychologist who also served as a psychotherapist was valuable for this man and his family. It kept him working, allowed his psychiatric symptomatology to be adequately managed, reduced social isolation, and continued to foster the sense of hope that he could handle life's problems with adequate support. Perhaps most important, however, he did not harbor long-standing feelings of "resentment" about his changed neuropsychological abilities. He was able to get many of his personal needs in life met via ongoing support of his family and the long-standing consulting relationship with a clinical neuropsychologist. His "resiliency" was truly multifactorial in nature.

Table 13.1 summarizes 20 clinical features that appeared relevant to this man's psychological care. A retrospective "checking off" (yes or no) of whether a feature was clearly present in his case was made. In some instances, the feature was only occasionally or partially present. When that was the case, it was "checked off."

In light of this case presentation and the review of the neuropsychological and psychiatric

Table 13.1 Clinical Features Relevant to the Psychological Care of a Person with Cognitive Impairments Secondary to Cerebral Anoxia Caused by Cardiac Arrest

CLINICAL FEATURE	YES	NO	PARTIALLY
1. The dialogue between the patient and the clinical neuropsychologist was not rushed.	✓		
2. The patient was able to express or clearly convey his personal concerns.	✓		
3. The content of the concerns varied over time.	✓		
4. The patient experienced a sense of "realistic" hope in coping with his life situation.	✓		
5. The patient and the clinical neuropsychologist developed a positive therapeutic relationship that helped the patient sustain adaptive activities during difficult times.	✓		
6. Somatic symptoms (which appeared to be indirect effects of a brain disorder) were substantially reduced during periods of psychological care.	✓		
7. Anxiety/depression/anger and/or apathy were substantially reduced during periods of psychological care.	✓		
8. The patient was able to follow the guidance of the clinical neuropsychologist to improve functioning in everyday life activities.	✓		
9. The patient was able to control impulses and delay gratification.	✓		
10. The patient developed a new sense of competency or "mastery" following the brain disorder.	✓		
11. The patient was able to "self-reflect" or "be more aware" of personal "strengths" and "limitations."			✓
12. The patient experienced enjoyment in the care or help of other living things (people, animals, the environment, etc.).	✓		
13. The patient had an improved understanding of the "problematic nature of life" (given his psychosocial state of life) and was not overwhelmed or defeated by it or readily gave in to escapism to cope with life (Bettelheim, 1989).			✓
14. The patient could "live with" the restrictions produced by a brain injury "without resentment" (Goldstein, 1952).			✓

Table 13.1 Continued

CLINICAL FEATURE	YES	NO	PARTIALLY
15. The patient was able to obtain new insights into self by attending to why certain songs, stories, fairy tales, movies, tattoos, etc. had a special personal meaning that initially he did not understand.		✓	
16. The patient's dreams or artwork often heralded changes in behavior that aided in psychological adjustment before the consciously mediated changes occurred.		✓	
17. The psychological care interventions (including the dialogue) between the patient and the clinical neuropsychologist resulted in the patient talking more openly about problems and demonstrating self-directed efforts at improving psychological adjustment to the direct and indirect effects of the brain disorder.	✓		
18. The psychological care interventions were in harmony with the patient's cultural background and religious orientation.	✓		
19. The psychological care interventions were appropriate for the patient's psychosocial stage of development and facilitated psychosocial development/adaptation in later stages of life.	✓		
20. The patient and family experienced two basic facts of life: (a) The individual's state of subjective sense of personal well-being fluctuates and (b) the psychological adjustment process is never static and therefore hope should never be abandoned.			✓
Total	14	2	4

disturbances seen in patients with cerebral anoxia, a brief review of some of the approaches to rehabilitation and psychological care described in the literature is presented next.

APPROACHES TO THE REHABILITATION AND PSYCHOLOGICAL CARE OF PERSONS WITH ANOXIC BRAIN INJURY SECONDARY TO CARDIAC ARREST

Given the wide range of cognitive and motor deficits observed in this patient group, equally wide and varied approaches to interventions have been suggested and utilized. The most common first line of care is to provide traditional neurorehabilitation services to address the physical, cognitive, behavioral, and emotional impairments observed in this patient group. Cullen, Crescini, and Bayley (2009) compared functional outcomes of 15 patients with anoxic brain injury (AnBI), 7 (47%) of which had experienced cardiac arrest, with outcomes of demographically matched patients with a history of TBI following traditional inpatient neurorehabilitation (Table 13.2). Patients in both groups were relatively acute insofar as they were within 5 months of their initial hospitalization. In general, the functional outcome of the AnBI group was worse than that of the TBI group. The AnBI group also appeared to need

Table 13.2 Review of Selected Studies and Case Reports Relevant to the Psychological Care of Persons with Cerebral Anoxia

INTERVENTION	STUDY SAMPLE	MAJOR FINDINGS	CONCLUSIONS
Traditional inpatient neurorehabilitation to improve functional outcome following AnBI (Cullen et al., 2009). Interventions included an average of 3 hours of therapy per weekday, including physical therapy, speech therapy, and occupational therapy included in "individualized care plans."	Fifteen adult patients with AnBI (7 of the 15 had anoxia secondary to cardiac arrest) were compared to 15 patients with TBI. All patients were within 5 months of onset of the neurological condition and matched on relevant demographic variables.	AnBI patients had an average of 87.5 days of rehabilitation vs. 51.8 days for those with TBI. Given the variability of length of rehabilitation stay between patients, the difference did not reach traditional levels of statistical significance. Using the FIM scores, the total gains on the FIM were less in the AnBI group compared to the TBI group. FIM motor subscale scores were especially lower in the AnBI group.	Functional outcomes were worse for the AnBI group compared to the TBI group. It also appeared that patients in the AnBI group tended to need longer time periods to recover and were especially impaired in the motor domain, although on some comparisons they also demonstrated worse cognitive functioning.
Hyperbaric oxygen therapy to improve cognitive and motor functioning after AnBI (Hadanny et al., 2015). Therapy consisted of 60 daily sessions, 5 days per week exposure to 100% oxygen.	Retrospective analysis of cognitive functioning in 11 patients with anoxia secondary to cardiac arrest. Patients were between 5 months and 7.5 years post-cardiac arrest. Mean age was 45.6 years. No control group was studied.	Pre- vs. post-cognitive and motor performance following hyperbaric oxygen therapy were compared. Mild improvements on tests of executive functioning were reported. There were no reliable differences on measures of memory or motor functioning.	The absence of a control group makes interpretation of the findings challenging. Improvements on neuropsychological tests were rather mild, and the issue of practice effects was not adequately addressed.
Music therapy to engage anoxic patients in rehabilitation activities that may help foster recovery (Fürst, 2015; Seibert et al., 2000).	The use of music therapy has been reported in individual cases following severe AnBI after cardiac arrest. No group studies using music therapy for this patient group could be identified.	Although level of cognitive functioning may not necessarily improve with the use of music, "music enjoyment is universal" (Seibert et al., 2000, p. 296). Playing music to severely anoxic patients may have a calming effect and improve social interaction. Using melodies and rhythms may help improve some skills.	Activities that are phenomenologically important to the patient and tend to be universally enjoyed by humans are a natural starting point for engaging severely impaired patients in ways that may improve recovery and adaptation. This appealing idea, however, has not been empirically demonstrated in group studies.

The treatment impact of including psychotherapy, support group activities, and artistic activities in ongoing residential rehabilitation activities in patients with cerebral anoxia (Tazopoulou et al., 2016). The goal was to determine to what degree these additional therapeutic activities would influence cognitive and affective functioning, including self-reports regarding quality of life.	Provided specific psychotherapy, support group activities, and artistic activities over a 2-month period of time to 20 patients with cerebral anoxia (11 of which had a history of cardiac arrest). Pre- vs. post-treatment comparisons made on a number of variables. No control group was included in the study.	Major finding was that there was an improvement in the patients' social participation and quality of life when the effect of these combined therapies was assessed. No change in cognitive functioning was reported.	Group and case study findings suggest that improvement in "life satisfaction" and greater social interaction can be achieved in this group of patients when they are given an opportunity to engage in psychotherapy, support group activities, and artistic activities. This basic finding has been reported for other groups of patients (Prigatano, 1999), but no control group studies have empirically demonstrated the reported effect.
"Holistic" neuropsychological rehabilitation program for improving self-awareness after acquired brain injury (with a few patients having anoxic brain damage; Smeets et al., 2017).	Self-awareness of cognitive and behavioral functioning was assessed in 78 patients with acquired brain injury (35 with TBI, 17 with vascular lesions, 10 with tumors, 5 with anoxia, and 11 with "other causes") before and after the patients underwent an intensive, holistic form of neuropsychological rehabilitation. No control group was included.	Patients who underestimated their cognitive and behavioral functional abilities tended to report higher levels of depression at the start of rehabilitation. They showed enhanced self-awareness after this form of rehabilitation. This was associated with reduced self-reported depression. Patients who tended to overestimate their abilities (which occurs in anosognosia or true ISA) tended not to report high levels of depression before treatment. They showed no change in awareness after this form of rehabilitation. They were described as also reporting less depression after rehabilitation with "no significant changes in psychological or physical dysfunction" (p. 127).	Intensive, holistic neuropsychological rehabilitation programs do not seem to improve impaired self-awareness as traditionally defined (i.e., the patient who is overestimating his or her true functional abilities). For depressed brain-injured patients who underestimate their true functional abilities, such programs may help them become more realistic and in so doing reduce their depression. This may be true for anoxic patients, but this study included only a few such patients and no control group comparisons. The study is important insofar as it reinforces earlier observations that such programs may help reduce the indirect effects of a brain disorder with less or no effect on the direct effects of an acquired brain disorder.

(*continued*)

Table 13.2 Continued

INTERVENTION	STUDY SAMPLE	MAJOR FINDINGS	CONCLUSIONS
Cognitive training for hypoxemic COPD patients (Incalzi et al., 2008). A randomized controlled study that included cognitive training exercises in the standard components of care for this patient group (which included pharmacological therapy, health education, respiratory therapy, oxygen therapy, etc.).	Fifty-three COPD patients were in the intervention group and 52 were in the control group. Cognitive training exercises included group and individual therapy sessions to improve attention, learning, and logical-deductive thinking. Activities focused on "drill and practice" to determine if neuropsychological test scores would improve after such cognitive training. Cognitive training lasted 6 weeks with daily treatments. Patients were assessed at baseline, 6 weeks (the end of cognitive training), and again at 4 and 6 months.	No improvements on neuropsychological tests were observed pre- and post-treatment when comparing the intervention group with the standard care group. The investigators, however, reported that neither group showed a decline during the 6 months they were observed. They suggested that this may reflect the "cognitive-enhancing effect of the comprehensive care provided to both groups" (p. 245).	Not unexpectedly, the type of cognitive training provided did improve performance on neuropsychological tests pre- and post-treatment. However, comprehensive care, including oxygen therapy, was thought to contribute to the finding that no decline in functioning was observed during this 6-month study. Cognitive training faces an important paradox. Memory training, for example, is not like exercising a muscle. Practice does not seem to "make it stronger." Yet "use it or lose it" also seems to be true. Many persons working in the field of cognitive retraining have increasingly emphasized its important role in helping patients use compensatory activities to remain cognitively alert and responsible for completing certain tasks (Prigatano & Kime, 2003).

AnBI, anoxic brain injury; COPD, chronic obstructive pulmonary disease; FIM, Functional Independence Measure; ISA, impaired self-awareness; TBI, traumatic brain injury.

longer lengths of stay, in part related to their more severe motor limitations.

Hyperbaric oxygen therapy has also been employed with patients who have suffered cardiac arrest and AnBI (Hadanny et al., 2015). Although modest positive effects have been reported, the lack of adequate control groups limits the interpretation of these effects (see Table 13.2).

Case reports have been published on the use of music to help stimulate patients' interest and motivation to improve after very severe anoxic brain damage (Fürst, 2015; Seibert, Fee, Basom, & Zimmerman, 2000). Recall from Chapter 2 that the use of music stimulates the most primitive aspects of human nature. It involves feelings and movements that can motivate us to engage the environment and others in a more natural way. This approach has repeatedly been found helpful in working with many different patients who have suffered a brain disorder (Prigatano, 1986, 1999).

Behavioral modification programs have also been described to reduce perseverative responding in individuals who suffer AnBI (Matthey, 1996). Recall Fuster's (1997) observations (discussed in Chapter 3, this volume) about the value of basic operant learning or conditioning to guide the person to function as a member of a social group (i.e., "If this, then that; if that, then this"). This basic approach is very helpful with severely impaired individuals (Wood, 2017). Also, reality orientation training, used with patients with dementia, has been applied to the psychological care of individuals with AnBI who are severely impaired and present with an amnestic syndrome (Kaschel, Zaiser-Kaschel, Shiel, & Mayer, 1995).

Tazopoulou et al. (2016) investigated how specific psychological interventions may improve functional outcome in different domains in 20 post-acute patients with cerebral anoxia (11 of whom had a history of cardiac arrest) who were enrolled in five different care facilities. Tazopoulou et al. noted that their study was "observational" in nature insofar as they studied potential changes on cognitive, emotional, and quality-of-life measures before and after patients participated in psychotherapy, support group activities, and physical and artistic activities in addition to treatment they were already receiving in their respective residential treatment settings. The authors specifically noted that these therapeutic interventions have been shown to be helpful in holistic forms of neuropsychological rehabilitation (Ben-Yishay & Diller, 2011).

Tazopoulou et al. (2016) reported group findings and provided some clinical case examples. As a group, the patients showed a reduction in anxiety and depression after participating in weekly support group activities that attempted to foster the expression of feelings, concerns, hopes, and conflicts. Patients also reported greater life satisfaction following a combination of activities aimed at engaging them in discussions that fostered self-expression (a basic human need; see Chapters 2 and 3, this volume). Although the statistical effects were generally mild and no control group was included in their study, the important message of their work was to emphasize that even after severe cognitive and affective changes associated with AnBI, the patients' quality of life can be improved via a series of individual and group activities.

Although traditional approaches to neuropsychological rehabilitation have emphasized the importance of cognitive training or retraining activities, no group studies could be found on the effectiveness of such activities in improving cognitive functions following AnBI. However, Incalzi et al. (2008) reported on the effect of cognitive training for patients with hypoxemic COPD. Although the authors reported null results (i.e., the training activities did not result in improved neuropsychological test performance), the purpose of many cognitive training activities is to engage patients to begin to observe their cognitive strengths and limitations so that they can learn to use and accept compensation techniques to manage their cognitive limitations in everyday life

(Klonoff, 2010; Prigatano, 1999; Prigatano & Kime, 2003).

BUILDING RESILIENCY IN PATIENTS WITH ANOXIC/HYPOXIC BRAIN INJURY

Perhaps the major goal of all psychological care of persons with a brain disorder is to build and reinforce their resiliency to cope with direct and indirect effects of their disorder. A key component to building resiliency in patients with anoxic/hypoxic brain injury is to reduce their depression, anxiety, and anger. Building resiliency helps them feel "alive again" by having some purpose or meaning to their existence. This is a highly personal venture that requires understanding each individual's personality and psychosocial situation before and after the onset of the brain disorder. Building resiliency also requires understanding how severely impaired these persons are from a neuropsychological standpoint when helping them become as independent as possible in daily life activities and establishing a productive lifestyle. Both of these tasks aid in the development of a sense of competency and hope. Building resiliency also requires increasing the energy level of patients via physical and cognitive therapies. This is necessary to sustain the will to achieve and use necessary compensatory activities. Neuropsychological rehabilitation programs of the type described by Prigatano (1986, 1999), Klonoff (2010), and Ben-Yishay and Diller (2011) appear most helpful in achieving these goals. Consequently, these programs seem to substantially build resiliency in brain dysfunctional patients and in so doing improve their quality of life.

Such rehabilitation programs can also build resiliency in family members and substantially reduce their distress level and improve their quality of life. Although these programs have not been shown to reverse the direct effects of a brain disorder, they have often been shown to reduce the indirect effects (e.g., angry outbursts, depression, social isolation, and unemployment). A recent study on the relationship between changes in self-awareness and mood following intensive holistic neuropsychological rehabilitation for patients with acquired brain injury (including a few patients with anoxic brain damage) also emphasizes this point (Smeets, Vink, Ponds, Winkens, & van Heugten, 2017).

The cognitive changes and some of the personality changes caused by AnBI are usually permanent (although some positive change can occur), and these permanent changes in the higher integrative brain functions have to be contended with throughout life, as illustrated by the case example discussed previously. After formal rehabilitation efforts end, these patients need to be monitored and managed from both behavioral and phenomenological standpoints (Fürst, 2015; Prigatano & Salas, 2017). When environmental changes challenge the person's ability to cope with those changes, psychological care services are often needed to aid the patient and the family and thereby avoid further declines in psychological and psychosocial adjustment. This is best done if a long-standing positive therapeutic alliance exists between the patient, family members, and the treating clinical neuropsychologists.

SUMMARY

Anoxic/hypoxic injuries to the brain can have substantial consequences in terms of the patient's cognitive, motor, behavioral, and personality functioning. Many of these patients could benefit from neuropsychologically oriented rehabilitation programs of the type described by Prigatano (1986) and Ben-Yishay and Diller (2011). These programs were especially designed to help post-acute patients, many of them with a history of moderately severe TBI, return to a productive lifestyle, including a return to work. As suggested in this chapter, these types of programs appear to be very helpful in improving resiliency after a brain disorder and have a clear economic "payoff" when the person returns to work or an independent lifestyle after such treatments. However, these and related programs have not been shown to substantially alter the cognitive impairments of such patients. They are most helpful in modifying the indirect effects of a brain disorder. This benefit, however, is very important given the relative permanence of the cognitive deficits observed in this patient group.

Unfortunately, many patients with brain dysfunction are unable to receive this type of intensive care for a variety of reasons. Their clinical condition may reflect a progressive decline in cognitive and personality functioning that makes a return to work impossible. Some do not have the financial resources for such care. Others have life circumstances that make such intensive forms of care impractical. Yet their need for psychological care is obvious, and different approaches can be instituted depending on their clinical condition and life circumstances, as the following chapters demonstrate.

REFERENCES

Allen, J. S., Tranel, D., Bruss, J., & Damasio, H. (2006). Correlations between regional brain volumes and memory performance in anoxia. *Journal of Clinical and Experimental Neuropsychology, 28*(4), 457–476.

Anderson, C. A., & Arciniegas, D. B. (2010). Cognitive sequelae of hypoxic–ischemic brain injury: A review. *NeuroRehabilitation, 26*(1), 47–63.

Ben-Yishay, Y., & Diller, L. (2011). *Handbook of holistic neuropsychological rehabilitation: Outpatient rehabilitation of traumatic brain injury.* New York, NY: Oxford University Press.

Blumenfeld, H. (2010). *Neuroanatomy through clinical cases.* Sunderland, MA: Sinauer.

Caine, D., & Watson, J. D. (2000). Neuropsychological and neuropathological sequelae of cerebral anoxia: A critical review. *Journal of the International Neuropsychological Society, 6*(1), 86–99.

Cullen, N. K., Crescini, C., & Bayley, M. T. (2009). Rehabilitation outcomes after anoxic brain injury: A case–controlled comparison with traumatic brain injury. *PM&R, 1*(12), 1069–1076.

Davis, J. E., Wagner, D. R., Garvin, N., Moilanen, D., Thorington, J., & Schall, C. (2015). Cognitive and psychomotor responses to high-altitude exposure in sea level and high-altitude residents of Ecuador. *Journal of Physiological Anthropology, 34*(1), 2.

Elliott, V. J., Rodgers, D. L., & Brett, S. J. (2011). Systematic review of quality of life and other patient-centred outcomes after cardiac arrest survival. *Resuscitation, 82*(3), 247–256.

Erikson, E. H. (1964). *Insight and responsibility.* New York, NY: Norton.

Frasure-Smith, N., & Lespérance, F. (2008). Depression and anxiety as predictors of 2-year cardiac events in patients with stable coronary artery disease. *Archives of General Psychiatry, 65*(1), 62–71.

Fürst, E. L. (2015). Coming back to oneself: A case of anoxic brain damage from a phenomenological perspective. *Culture, Medicine, and Psychiatry, 39*(1), 121–133.

Fuster, J. M. (1997). *The prefrontal cortex: Anatomy, physiology, and neuropsychology of the frontal lobe* (3rd ed.). Philadelphia, PA: Lippincott–Raven.

Gale, S. D., & Hopkins, R. O. (2004). Effects of hypoxia on the brain: Neuroimaging and neuropsychological findings following carbon monoxide poisoning and obstructive sleep apnea. *Journal of the International Neuropsychological Society, 10*(1), 60–71.

Ganong, W. (1981). *Review of medical physiology.* Los Altos, CA: Lange.

Goldstein, K. (1942). *Aftereffects of brain injuries in war: Their evaluation and treatment. The application of psychologic methods in the clinic.* New York, NY: Grune & Stratton.

Grant, I., Prigatano, G. P., Heaton, R. K., McSweeny, A. J., Wright, E. C., & Adams, K. M. (1987). Progressive neuropsychologic impairment and hypoxemia: Relationship in chronic obstructive pulmonary disease. *Archives of General Psychiatry, 44*(11), 999–1006.

Hadanny, A., Golan, H., Fishlev, G., Bechor, Y., Volkov, O., Suzin, G., . . . Efrati, S. (2015). Hyperbaric oxygen can induce neuroplasticity and improve cognitive functions of patients suffering from anoxic brain damage. *Restorative Neurology and Neuroscience, 33*(4), 471–486.

Hiott, D. W., & Labbate, L. (2002). Anxiety disorders associated with traumatic brain injuries. *NeuroRehabilitation, 17*(4), 345–355.

Hopkins, R. O., & Haaland, K. Y. (2004). Neuropsychological and neuropathological effects of anoxic or ischemic induced brain injury. *Journal of the International Neuropsychological Society, 10*(7), 957.

Hornbein, T. F. (2001). The high-altitude brain. *Journal of Experimental Biology, 204*(18), 3129–3132.

Horstmann, A., Frisch, S., Jentzsch, R. T., Müller, K., Villringer, A., & Schroeter, M. L. (2010). Resuscitating the heart but losing the brain: Brain atrophy in the aftermath of cardiac arrest. *Neurology, 74*(4), 306–312.

Huang, B. Y., & Castillo, M. (2008). Hypoxic–ischemic brain injury: Imaging findings from birth to adulthood. *Radiographics, 28*(2), 417–439.

Incalzi, R. A., Corsonello, A., Trojano, L., Pedone, C., Acanfora, D., Spada, A., . . . Rengo, F. (2008). Cognitive training is ineffective in hypoxemic COPD: A six-month randomized controlled trial. *Rejuvenation Research, 11*(1), 239–250.

Kaschel, R., Zaiser-Kaschel, H., Shiel, A., & Mayer, K. (1995). Reality orientation training in an amnesic: A controlled single-case study (n = 572 days). *Brain Injury, 9*(6), 619–633.

Kessler, R. C., Berglund, P., Demler, O., Jin, R., Koretz, D., Merikangas, K. R., . . . Wang, P. S. (2003). The epidemiology of major depressive disorder: Results from the National Comorbidity Survey Replication (NCS-R). *JAMA, 289*(23), 3095–3105.

Klonoff, P. S. (2010). *Psychotherapy after brain injury: Principles and techniques.* New York, NY: Guilford.

Kuoppamäki, M., Bhatia, K. P., & Quinn, N. (2002). Progressive delayed-onset dystonia after cerebral anoxic insult in adults. *Movement Disorders, 17*(6), 1345–1349.

Ladwig, K.-H., Schoefinius, A., Dammann, G., Danner, R., Gürtler, R., & Herrmann, R. (1999). Long-acting psychotraumatic properties of a cardiac arrest experience. *American Journal of Psychiatry, 156*(6), 912–919.

Lett, H. S., Blumenthal, J. A., Babyak, M. A., Sherwood, A., Strauman, T., Robins, C., & Newman, M. F. (2004). Depression as a risk factor for coronary artery disease: Evidence, mechanisms, and treatment. *Psychosomatic Medicine, 66*(3), 305–315.

Lim, C., Alexander, M., LaFleche, G., Schnyer, D., & Verfaellie, M. (2004). The neurological and cognitive sequelae of cardiac arrest. *Neurology, 63*(10), 1774–1778.

Lishman, W. A. (Ed.). (1987). *Organic psychiatry: The psychological consequences of cerebral disorder* (3rd ed.). Oxford, UK: Blackwell.

Matthey, S. (1996). Modification of perseverative behaviour in an adult with anoxic brain damage. *Brain Injury, 10*(3), 219–228.

Medalia, A. A., Merriam, A. E., & Ehrenreich, J. H. (1991). The neuropsychological sequelae of attempted hanging. *Journal of Neurology, Neurosurgery, and Psychiatry, 54*(6), 546–548.

Middelkamp, W., Moulaert, V. R., Verbunt, J. A., van Heugten, C. M., Bakx, W. G., & Wade, D. T. (2007). Life after survival: Long-term daily life functioning and quality of life of patients with hypoxic brain injury as a result of a cardiac arrest. *Clinical Rehabilitation, 21*(5), 425–431.

Nieuwenhuys, R., Donkelaar, H. J., & Nicholson, C. (1998). *The central nervous system of vertebrates* (Vol. 1). New York, NY: Springer.

Prigatano, G. P. (Ed.). (1986). *Neuropsychological rehabilitation after brain injury.* Baltimore, MD: Johns Hopkins University Press.

Prigatano, G. P. (1999). *Principles of neuropsychological rehabilitation.* New York, NY: Oxford University Press.

Prigatano, G. P., & Kime, S. (2003). What do brain dysfunctional patients report following memory compensation training? *NeuroRehabilitation, 18*(1), 47–55.

Prigatano, G. P., Parsons, O., Levin, D. C., Wright, E., & Hawryluk, G. (1983). Neuropsychological test performance in mildly hypoxemic patients with chronic obstructive pulmonary disease. *Journal of Consulting and Clinical Psychology, 51*(1), 108.

Prigatano, G. P., & Salas, C. (2017). Psychodynamic psychotherapy after severe traumatic brain injury. In R. Wood, T. McMillan, & A. Worthington (Eds.), *Neurobehavioral disability and social handicap following traumatic brain injury* (pp. 118–201). Philadelphia, PA: Taylor & Francis.

Pußwald, G., Fertl, E., Faltl, M., & Auff, E. (2000). Neurological rehabilitation of severely disabled cardiac arrest survivors: Part II. Life situation of patients and families after treatment. *Resuscitation, 47*(3), 241–248.

Roine, R. O., Kajaste, S., & Kaste, M. (1993). Neuropsychological sequelae of cardiac arrest. *JAMA, 269*(2), 237–242.

Seibert, P. S., Fee, L., Basom, J., & Zimmerman, C. (2000). Music and the brain: The impact of music on an oboist's fight for recovery. *Brain Injury, 14*(3), 295–302.

Smeets, S. M., Vink, M., Ponds, R. W., Winkens, I., & van Heugten, C. M. (2017). Changes in impaired self-awareness after acquired brain injury in patients following intensive neuropsychological rehabilitation. *Neuropsychological Rehabilitation, 27*(1), 116–132.

Suominen, P. K., & Vähätalo, R. (2012). Neurologic long term outcome after drowning in children. *Scandinavian Journal of Trauma, Resuscitation and Emergency Medicine, 20*(1), 55.

Tazopoulou, E., Miljkovitch, R., Truelle, J.-L., Schnitzler, A., Onillon, M., Zucco, T., . . . Montreuil, M. (2016). Rehabilitation following cerebral anoxia: An assessment of 27 patients. *Brain Injury, 30*(1), 95–103.

Thaler, N. S., Reger, S. L., Ringdahl, E. N., Mayfield, J. W., Goldstein, G., & Allen, D. N. (2013). Neuropsychological profiles of six children with anoxic brain injury. *Child Neuropsychology, 19*(5), 479–494.

Toukhsati, S., Jovanovic, A., Dehghani, S., Tran, T., Tran, A., & Hare, D. (2017). Low psychological resilience is associated with depression in patients with cardiovascular disease. *European Journal of Cardiovascular Nursing, 16*(1), 64–69.

van Schie, P. E., Schijns, J., Becher, J. G., Barkhof, F., van Weissenbruch, M. M., & Vermeulen, R. J. (2015). Long-term motor and behavioral outcome after perinatal hypoxic–ischemic encephalopathy. *European Journal of Paediatric Neurology, 19*(3), 354–359.

Vilchinsky, N., Ginzburg, K., Fait, K., & Foa, E. B. (2017). Cardiac-disease-induced PTSD (CDI-PTSD): A systematic review. *Clinical Psychology Review, 55*, 92–106.

Wachelder, E. M., Moulaert, V., van Heugten, C., Verbunt, J. A., Bekkers, S. C., & Wade, D. T. (2009). Life after survival: Long-term daily functioning and quality of life after an out-of-hospital cardiac arrest. *Resuscitation, 80*(5), 517–522.

Williams, G., & Willmott, C. (2012). Higher levels of mobility are associated with greater societal participation and better quality-of-life. *Brain Injury, 26*(9), 1065–1071.

Wood, R. L. (2017). Disorders of impulse control after TBI. In T. M. McMillan & R. L. Wood (Eds.), *Neurobehavioural disability and social handicap following traumatic brain injury* (2nd ed., pp. 43–56). New York, NY: Routledge.

Zola-Morgan, S., Squire, L. R., & Amaral, D. (1986). Human amnesia and the medial temporal region: Enduring memory impairment following a bilateral lesion limited to field CA1 of the hippocampus. *Journal of Neuroscience, 6*(10), 2950–2967.

14

PSYCHOLOGICAL CARE OF PERSONS WITH PARKINSON'S DISEASE

BACKGROUND INFORMATION

Although adequate supply of oxygen and glucose to the brain is crucial for maintaining the life of neuronal and glial cells, these energy sources do not directly allow for communication within the central nervous system. Communication between neurons and supportive glia cells of the brain is achieved via electrical and chemical signals. The chemical substances that facilitate neuronal communication are referred to as neurotransmitters. The most important neurotransmitters discovered to date are acetylcholine, dopamine, norepinephrine, epinephrine, serotonin, histamine, γ-aminobutyric acid, glycine, and glutamate (Kolb & Whishaw, 2009; Murley & Rowe, 2018).

Parkinson's disease (PD) is a neurodegenerative disorder in which there is a progressive depletion of the neurotransmitter dopamine within the brain, with associated neuronal loss in the substantia nigra. This condition produces a cluster of motor symptoms referred to as parkinsonism. They include "slowness of movement (bradykinesia), difficulty initiating movement (akinesia), hypokinetic speech, masked facies, muscular rigidity, a shuffling or unsteady gait, abnormal gait, abnormal posture, and disturbances of equilibrium" (McPherson & Cummings, 2009, p. 199). Ultimately, the disease negatively impacts the functional integrity of the basal ganglia and frontostriatal circuits of the brain. As such, it can negatively impact both motor and nonmotor functions of the brain. In addition, Fuster (1997) noted that depletion of dopamine can have quite negative effects on sustaining motivated behavior, associated attentional skills, and the ability to flexibly engage in a sequence of problem-solving steps involved in many cognitive functions.

The epidemiology, genetics, neuropathology, neurophysiology, and the motor and neuropsychological disturbances associated with PD have been studied extensively and have recently been reviewed by Tröster and Garrett (2018). In their review article, Tröster and Garrett note that PD seldom occurs before age 50 years. Younger patients (i.e., those in their 50s) reportedly have less severe cognitive impairments and their motor difficulties are more responsive to L-DOPA therapy (Getz & Levin, 2017). Older individuals (aged 65 years or older) are more likely to demonstrate more significant neurocognitive impairments, including Lewy body dementia (Fields, 2017). In her review of the literature of dementia in patients with PD, Fields (2017) reports that "the mean duration of PD symptom onset to dementia ranges from 6 to 10 years" (p. 788). However, it is important to note that the duration can be considerably longer in some individuals.

If PD symptoms occur in the early to late 50s, the negative impact of the disease might be first felt in meeting demanding job responsibilities. As noted in Chapter 4, the median age of high-level executives is 55 years. If PD symptoms occur in the mid- to late 60s, the person may have other comorbid health problems that further complicate the quality of their life and plans for the future (see Chapter 8, this volume). In the older population, achieving the goals of retirement, enjoying outdoor activities, and physically and socially interacting with grandchildren may become seriously threatened. Regular tactile (and sexual) contact with one's mate is often reduced. Enhanced dependency on others becomes inevitable. Depression, which is common in the elderly, may become quite severe.

NEUROPSYCHOLOGICAL CONSEQUENCES OF PARKINSON'S DISEASE

Schmand and Tröster (2015) reviewed reports on neuropsychological test performance obtained in several studies on nondemented patients with PD. They state,

> The picture that emerges from this research seems to point at the existence of a continuum of cognitive symptoms with two clusters marking the extremes. . . . The first cluster is of a frontal-executive nature and is primarily found in patients with a relatively young age of onset. . . . The motor symptoms of these patients respond well to dopaminergic medications.
>
> With increasing age on onset, and with increasing age in patients with long-standing disease, the second cluster of memory and visuospatial symptoms encroaches on the first, probably due to the gradual involvement of posterior brain areas. (p. 219)

It is not uncommon to observe subtle attentional difficulties in patients with early onset of PD. However, as McPherson and Cummings (2009) note, it is not a problem of "simple attention" such as reflected in the ability to repeat verbally presented digits in the forward direction. The problem is more in self-initiated and sustained attention that requires effort. This is associated with difficulties attending to information that may have a high priority for the individual at a given time and place. Clinically, patients with PD often have subjective complaints of fatigue and problems in completing work in a time-efficient manner. Some of the underlying cognitive difficulties may also include organizational skills.

Reduced speed of problem-solving and speed of "flexibility" in shifting the thought processes (or reactions) is also quite common. This is frequently revealed by poor performance on tests such as the Trail Making Test Part B and verbal fluency measures (Schmand & Tröster, 2015).

Memory is also affected, but again in complex ways. A very interesting observation is that prospective memory (i.e., remembering to do something in the future) may be especially compromised (McPherson & Cummings, 2009). This is a very important observation as it relates to the psychological care of persons with PD. Their performance on traditional tests of learning and memory may be only mildly affected in the early stages of the disease, but in everyday life they may consistently forget to perform tasks they have committed to doing. As the disease progresses, for example, they may agree to ask for help when walking to avoid falls but "forget" to do so to the chagrin of their caregivers. The patient is often frustrated and humiliated by such "errors of memory."

Patients' ability to verbally communicate is usually unaffected, but classically they can be slow in responding to questions. They often need more time to do so before assuming they either do not understand a question or do not have the answer. Judgment, however, is often affected, and this can also be especially frustrating and humiliating to patients with good intelligence. Patients' ability to plan and organize sequential steps necessary to achieve certain goals and to rapidly recognize that a certain course of action may not be in their best interest is negatively affected. This is attributed to the common "executive" dysfunction seen in nondemented PD patients (McPherson & Cummings, 2009). As the disease progresses, certainly visual–spatial difficulties may well increase, and this is consistent with the hypotheses proposed by Schmand and Tröster (2015).

Although dementia may be the ultimate outcome for many patients with PD (not all of them), these patients often show "islands of cognitive strength." Clinically, as patients worsen in their cognitive functioning, there is often a progressive decline in problem-solving abilities with increased problems with attention and increased fatigue. Clearly, new learning and memory become less efficient. Patients are slower in performing motor and cognitive tasks. Although remaining oriented to time and place, many patients' families note that patients have increased difficulties with time perception. They may perceive themselves involved in a task for a much shorter time than they actually spend trying to accomplish the task. This type of disturbance is not typically measured by standard psychometric instruments used in neuropsychological assessments, but it is an important area of dysfunction to understand.

Related to the difficulty with time perception is an important behavioral change key to the management of these patients. Many PD patients have difficulty in the "timely" starting and stopping of activities in everyday life. For example, when shaving, they may repetitively (some would say compulsively) shave the same regions of the face repeatedly without the ability to monitor what they are doing and stop it as needed. This can cause great frustrations to caregivers and again needs to be considered when providing psychological care.

Finally, the phenomenological experiences of patients with PD are often not adequately assessed. What do they experience? How do they view themselves? What impact on others do they have from their perspective? This type of phenomenological or "subjective" information may be very important in both the diagnosis and the management of PD patients, particularly as the patients' cognitive, affective, and motor function decline with time. In the clinical case presented later in this chapter, it is noted that during his last neuropsychological examination, the patient described a fearful or surprised face as "perplexed." This appeared to be an ongoing psychological or subjective experience for this person. He was often "perplexed" by the nature of his cognitive problems. Psychological care, in part, attempted to reduce that perplexity and aid the adjustment process for him and his wife.

PSYCHIATRIC DISTURBANCES ASSOCIATED WITH PARKINSON'S DISEASE

Depression

Marsh and Dobkin (2015) emphasize an important feature about depression—namely that it can affect multiple domains of functioning. Depression can be reflected in cognitive disturbance (e.g., poor concentration and difficulties in decision-making), affect or mood disturbance (e.g., feeling "down" or hopeless and loss of pleasure from activities that are normally associated with pleasure), and disturbances in vegetative functions (e.g., sleep and appetite changes). In addition, a variety of somatic or bodily symptoms can and often do reflect depression (e.g., excessive muscle tension, gastrointestinal symptoms, and erectile dysfunction in men).

Marsh and Dobkin (2015) note that depression in patients with PD is common, with reportedly up to 50% of patients with PD demonstrating clinically significant depression at some point in their illness. These authors further note that the depressive symptoms are often chronic and recurring. They suggest that depressed PD patients demonstrate greater cognitive dysfunction, particularly in "executive" functions. As would be expected, such patients report significantly poorer quality of life and greater impairments in daily living tasks. Family members and caregivers may also experience more distress in attempting to help these patients.

There are many causes of depression, including a reaction to the diagnosis, increased physical disabilities, progressive loss of social status and independence, and altered cognitive functioning, which can adversely affect coping strategies. There are also possible underlying neurotransmitter disturbances that lead to depression. Marsh and Dobkin's (2015) review of the literature brings attention to the fact that "loss of dopaminergic neurons as well as noradrenergic and serotonergic neurons" impacts the "mood and reward systems" of the brain that may cause depression in some PD patients (p. 270). The exact brain mechanisms are unknown, but disturbances in orbitofrontal–basal ganglia–limbic circuits are thought to most likely underlie depressive symptomology in many PD patients (Aarsland, Påhlhagen, Ballard, Ehrt, & Svenningsson, 2012).

Treatments for depression in PD patients have been mainly pharmacological in nature, with a few studies measuring the effect of cognitive–behavioral therapy (CBT). Dobkin et al. (2011) conducted the first randomized controlled trial on CBT for depression in PD. Note, however, that other services were provided in addition to CBT services. Dobkin et al. stated that "treatment incorporated exercise, behavioral activation, thought monitoring and restructuring, relaxation training, worry control, and sleep hygiene" (p. 4). In addition, individual caregiver educational sessions were provided. A main outcome measure was ratings on the Hamilton Depression Rating Scale (HAM-D) pre- versus post-treatment. Results were compared to those of a group of PD patients who were simply clinically monitored during a 10-week training program. The treated PD patients reported significantly less depression on the HAM-D compared to the nontreated PD patients. There was also self-reported improvement in anxiety, social functioning, and "positive reframing." The actual degree of improvement for specific patients is often not reported in such research studies. However, these researchers indicated that 56% of their treatment group met criteria for a treatment response compared to 8% in the control (clinical monitoring) group. Although the findings are clearly encouraging, it is difficult to know the overall clinical significance of these findings for the patient and family. Note, however, that their treatment approach included many different types of activities and recognized the importance of educating family members about the nature of the patient's behavioral as well as medical problems.

Anxiety

Pontone et al. (2009) conducted a prospective study of anxiety disorders in 127 patients with idiopathic PD. Considering all anxiety disorder classifications, they estimate that 50% of their sample had an anxiety disorder sometime in their life. Anxiety disorder not otherwise specified (NOS) was the most common diagnosis (25–30%), with post-traumatic stress disorder being the least common diagnosis (<2% over the course of the person's lifetime). They estimated that generalized anxiety disorder (GAD) was represented in approximately 3% of their population. Phobic reactions were also relatively common (i.e., for combined social phobias with specific phobias, the estimates were between 20% and 28%).

In a relatively recent review, Dissanayaka et al. (2014) summarize findings from multiple studies regarding anxiety disorders in PD patients. Like depression, anxiety disorders are common in PD patients but are frequently overlooked. Dissanayaka et al. make the important observation that it is difficult to estimate the prevalence of anxiety disorders in this group, in part due to the fact that the typical psychometric scales available for rating anxiety may not be easily applied to PD. For many of the scales, the person rates somatic symptoms that are common to both anxiety and PD (e.g., palpitations, shortness of breath, sweating, and trembling). However, Dissanayaka et al. note that phobic reactions are common, as is anxiety disorder NOS (also estimated to be approximately 25%). GAD is not especially prevalent, often being reported in the range of 3–8%.

Dissanayaka et al. (2014) make several clinically relevant points concerning the evaluation and care of PD patients. First, patients with GAD tend to have a premorbid history of anxiety disorder. Second, fear of falling and fears of embarrassment when walking and eating in public are perhaps most common in this group of individuals. Finally, fear of dying (via choking or falling) is commonly expressed and should be appropriately recognized and treated when possible.

Dissanayaka and colleagues (2017) have also recently reported that CBT may be helpful for reducing anxiety in PD patients.

Psychosomatic Difficulties

Given the multiple physical problems associated with PD, it is especially challenging to evaluate the presence of psychosomatic difficulties in this patient population. Nevertheless, some authors argue that psychosomatic difficulties are more common in PD than is clinically recognized. Carrozzino et al. (2017) note the human tendency to experience and report somatic symptoms in response to psychological distress even if the person has an underlying physical illness. In their review of others' research, they estimate that somatization as a psychogenic movement disorder occurs in 10–15% of neurological patients with a documented "organic movement disorder" (p. 23).

A major problem in evaluating psychosomatic difficulties in PD patients is defining exactly what a psychosomatic difficulty might look like in individuals with PD. Theoretically, it would be a physical symptom that cannot be explained on the basis of the known pathophysiological features of the disease. This might include headache, nausea, vomiting, and sensitivity to light and sound. The literature on PD does not typically report such psychosomatic difficulties (McPherson & Cummings, 2009; Tröster & Schmand, 2015).

Apathy, Impaired Self-Awareness, and Psychotic Reactions

In contrast to the literature on psychosomatic difficulties in PD, there is a rich literature on apathy and psychotic reactions in these patients, with a growing literature on impaired self-awareness (ISA). Some authors report a relationship between apathy and disease progression, especially motor symptoms (Pedersen, Larsen, Alves, & Aarsland, 2009), whereas others do not (Pluck & Brown, 2002).

Weintraub and Goldman (2015) note that apathy is difficult to study because it frequently overlaps with depression and cognitive impairment. They suggest that apathy be defined as "a lack of motivation, manifested as a decrease goal-directed behavior, verbalization, and emotional expression" (p. 302). Defined in this way, apathy is frequently "accompanied by diminished self-awareness" (p. 303). However, apathy is often associated with a subjective sense of a decreased interest or pleasure when preforming activities that once were pleasurable or interesting to the person. The neuropathophysiology underlying apathy remains difficult to define, but depletion of dopamine and noradrenaline may contribute to this clinical phenomenon (Weintraub & Goldman, 2015). Pagonabarraga and Kulisevsky (2017) note that apathy has been consistently related to impaired executive functions, which are often associated with damage or disruption of the dorsolateral prefrontal cortex.

Psychosis has been reported to frequently occur in PD patients, affecting approximately one-third of them (Weintraub & Goldman, 2015). It, too, has been linked to dopaminergic medications, which are thought to be "stimulating or inducing hypersensitivity of mesocorticolimbic dopamine receptors" (p. 310). Visual hallucinations are perhaps the most common symptoms. They frequently are recognized by the patient as hallucinations but nevertheless appear "real."

Although ISA is common in many cases of dementia (Prigatano, 2010), there is a growing appreciation that nondemented, nondepressed PD patients have subtle ISA for their specific motor impairments (Maier & Prigatano, 2017). Such patients may be aware of their overall functional competencies in everyday life but not experience specific motor limitations when carefully examined. This ISA for motor difficulties may represent a previously undetected neuropsychological disturbance in this patient group.

Social Isolation and Quality of Life

As the disease progresses, most patients with PD prefer not to go out in public or be involved in social interactions. In addition to moving slowly, having problems with balance, and an increased tendency for falls, patients also report embarrassment in not being able to properly hold food when eating. They report frustrations with regard to others asking them to speak more loudly and not understanding that their loss of volume when speaking is a common feature of their illness. They further report that their fatigue and cognitive difficulties make it increasingly more difficult to sustain social interactions. Therefore, they tend to withdraw from social interactions and may be viewed by others as "self-absorbed" or not interested in others.

Research on social interaction and quality of life in PD patients often supports these contentions. For example, Rahman, Griffin, Quinn, and Jahanshahi (2008) noted that "difficulty in dressing, difficulty walking, falls, depression and confusion" (p. 1428) were related to decreased social interactions and reduced quality of life. They also importantly mentioned that "autonomic disturbances particularly urinary incontinence, unpredictable on/off fluctuations, and sensory symptoms such as pain" (p. 1428) further compromised their quality of life and resulted in a tendency to stay at home and socially disengage from others.

The quality of life for caregivers of persons with PD often (if not always) declines. They take on increasingly more responsibilities for domestic and home care issues. One manifestation of this reduced quality of life for caregivers is frequently reported sleep disturbances (Happe & Berger, 2002).

In addition to the previously mentioned expected problems, some PD patients have also been noted to engage in behaviors that were atypical for them before the disorder, such as gambling, excessive spending, or a preoccupation with pornography. Weintraub and Goldman (2015) suggest that these behavioral problems might be generally termed impulse control problems (ICDs). Although multiple factors may contribute to these behaviors, they have been linked to dopamine replacement therapy. Specifically, the use of dopamine agonist treatments increased the odds ratio for developing an ICD by 2–3.5. Discontinuing such therapies often decreased these behaviors, but they can cause significant social adjustment problems for PD patients and their family members.

Although PD is observed worldwide, it is most prevalent in North America, Europe, and Australia (Getz & Levin, 2017). One of the symptoms of parkinsonism is facial masking, which can give the impression of apathy, social disengagement, and cognitive impairment (Tickle-Degnen, Zebrowitz, & Ma, 2011). There may be cultural differences with regard to how people respond to facial masking in PD patients. Tickle-Degnen et al. demonstrated, for example, that clinical practitioners in the United States were more likely to judge a PD patient with facial masking as more cognitively impaired than were clinical practitioners in Taiwan. In the Chinese culture, failure to show facial emotion is not considered an abnormal social feature. This study clarifies how cultural biases can influence one's perceptions of a person with PD, which in turn can influence the PD patient's quality of life.

In this regard, it is important to also note that professional biases have existed when attempting to understand symptoms associated with parkinsonism. For a period of time, there was a search for premorbid personality features common to patients with PD (Todes & Lees, 1985). This was in part stimulated by an influential article by Booth (1948) in which he attributed certain motivational and behavioral characteristics of the patient to psychodynamic causes. Sexual and aggressive impulses were thought to contribute to the patient's physical symptomology. Clearly this was wrong, and a more informed neuroscientific understanding of these patients' motor impairments eventually prevailed. Although PD patients may show a greater frequency of certain personality features (Santangelo et al., 2018), the explanation for these findings is not always clear. There is not a specific premorbid personality type for patients with PD or parkinsonism.

PSYCHOLOGICAL CARE OF A PERSON WITH ATYPICAL PARKINSONISM WHO WAS FOLLOWED FOR 8 YEARS

Medical History

At age 55 years, a prominent professional individual noted increasing difficulty completing his professional work by the expected time. He also noted poorly defined challenges in walking. He continued in his professional work despite these limitations, which were considered to be more "annoyances" than a true impairment or disability. His condition progressively worsened, and he began to experience excessive fatigue with concern about a reduction in his cognitive abilities. Over the course of the next 8 years, repeated evaluations revealed several medical problems and related diagnoses.

By age 63 years, he was diagnosed with PD, depression, sleep apnea, and mild cognitive impairment of the amnestic type. He was later described as demonstrating an akinetic rigid PD. He was placed on a series of medications to address his multiple health problems.

As expected with PD, he had episodes of gait "freezing" when his carbidopa–levodopa medication effects were "wearing off." He became more prone to falls. With time, he developed other motor symptoms, including tongue protrusion and dystonic dyskinesia. He began to complain of visual disturbances, which were difficult to define. Initially, he had intermittent diplopia, but later it became persistent. He had trouble with depth perception and judging distances.

He also had a sleep disturbance that was not completely corrected by using continuous positive airway pressure (CPAP) therapy for his obstructive sleep apnea. He complained of excessive daytime somnolence. He had sleep parasomnia with no evidence of REM sleep disorder.

He was especially aware of and concerned about his nonmotor symptoms, which included fatigue, decreased concentration, poor attention, and problems with planning. He noted that he was easily distracted. His depressed mood initially improved with medications (i.e., Lexapro), and he became more engaging with others. As he began to physically and cognitively decline, however, his depression fluctuated. At times, he was doing "reasonably well," and other times he experienced severe depression.

His wife was also becoming emotionally overwhelmed with his progressive decline in multiple domains of functioning and his associated multiple needs. She initially viewed him as unwilling to follow suggested compensatory guidelines to lessen the burden of his care. Yet, he often simply "forgot" to take his medications, ask for help when walking, and argued with her over a variety of issues. A series of behavioral problems she (and he) did not understand also emerged (discussed later). It was at this time (approximately 12 years after onset of his initial symptoms) that he was referred for psychotherapy and "emotional support."

He was now 67 years old, and his diagnosis had been modified in light of his changing and evolving clinical picture. He did not show a robust responsiveness to levodopa therapy. He showed axial more than appendicular symptomatology, and cognitive decline was characterized by increased difficulties with attention and starting and stopping various thought patterns. He reported, for example, "getting lost in daydreams" only to suddenly become aware that he was daydreaming while awake and in a standing position. The nature and frequency of his falls also changed. In addition to falling forward, he now was falling backward on a more regular and frequent basis. He complained of worsening vision and at times said "I cannot see." This typically meant he could not move his eyes in the typical conjugate directions and consequently had trouble locating objects in space. He had notable and progressive difficulties sustaining his visual gaze for any length of time. He found it easier to close his eyes when talking in order not to be distracted by his visual disturbances.

Eventually, he was diagnosed as have atypical parkinsonism with progressive supranuclear palsy and cognitive disorder.

Neuropsychological Examination Findings

The patient was first seen for a neuropsychological consultation and examination at age 60 years (Table 14.1). At that time, the diagnosis of PD had not been established, but it was considered probable. The patient was aware of decreased memory and energy level, which was making it more difficult to meet job responsibilities. He also noted a reduced volume in his normal speaking voice and change in his handwriting. When writing, he was making his letters smaller. At the time, he was placed on antidepressant medication (Cymbalta) and believed it was of substantial help to him. He was also placed on a medication (Provigil) that reportedly improved his alertness and energy level. He was taking carbidopa–levodopa and reported improvement in motor functioning, particularly walking. He also reported having sleep apnea and was treated via CPAP. Initially, he reported considerable benefit with increased energy level upon awaking.

He reported mild decline in vision and also mild decline in hearing. He believed these were likely age-related.

The patient was asked to rate (on a scale from 0 to 10, with 0 meaning no problem and 10 meaning a severe problem) his level of difficulty with memory and fatigue (as described in Chapter 10). He rated himself a 3 or 4 for memory difficulties and a 5 for fatigue. His wife gave ratings of 3 and 4, respectively. Both agreed that his level of depression was low (rated a 1 by the patient and 3 by his wife).

His neuropsychological examination findings at the time were essentially within the normal range and compatible with his occupational background (e.g., a Vocabulary scale score of 14 and a Verbal IQ of 121; Matrix Reasoning scale score was 11, and Performance IQ was 102; for details, see Table 11.1). Verbal

Table 14.1 Serial Neuropsychological Test Findings from a Patient with Atypical Parkinson's Disease

DATE	6/3/2009	12/2/2009	6/8/2010	12/10/2010	11/26/2013	1/13/2015	3/15/2017
BNI SCREEN	45/50, T = 55	—	43/50, T = 50	—	—	—	43/50, T = 50
DEMENTIA RATING SCALE	—	—	—	—	138/144, SS = 10	141/144, SS = 12	—
WECHSLER INTELLIGENCE SCALES	WAIS-III	WAIS-III	WAIS-III	WAIS-III	WASI-II	WASI-II	WAIS-IV
Verbal subtests							
Vocabulary	ss = 14	—	ss = 13	ss = 15	T = 80	T = 80	ss = 13
Similarities	ss = 15	—	ss = 13	ss = 16	—	—	ss = 11
Arithmetic	ss = 13	—	—	—	—	—	—
Digit Span	ss = 12	ss = 14	ss = 14	ss = 14	—	—	ss = 10
Forward Span	8 (61T)	8 (61T)	8 (61T)	7 (55T)	—	—	7 (54T)
Backward Span	4 (47T)	6 (59T)	5 (53T)	6 (59T)	—	—	4 (46T)
Information	ss = 12	ss = 14	ss = 12	ss = 13	—	—	—
Performance subtests							
Picture Completion	ss = 11	ss = 14	ss = 13	—	—	—	—
Digit Symbol Coding	ss = 9	ss = 7	ss = 10	ss = 8	—	—	—
Block Design	ss = 9	ss = 12	ss = 9	ss = 11	—	—	ss = 9
Matrix Reasoning	ss = 11	—	ss = 13	ss = 15	T = 56	T = 54	ss = 8

Picture Arrangement	ss = 12	—	—	ss = 10	—	—	—
Symbol Search	ss = 10	—	ss = 10	—	—	—	—
Composite scores							
FSIQ	113	—	—	—	131, 98th %ile	129, 97th %ile	—
VIQ	121	—	—	—	—	—	—
PIQ	102	—	—	—	—	—	98, 45th %ile
List learning	RAVLT	RAVLT	CVLT	HVLT (list 1)	HVLT (list 2)	HVLT (list 1)	RAVLT
Learning trials	6, 10, 12, 11, 13	6, 8, 11, 14, 12	7, 9, 12, 15, 13	8, 11, 11	7, 8, 11	7, 11, 12	5, 6, 7, 8, 11
Total recall	52/75, $T = 65$	38/75	56/80, $T = 67$	30/36, $T = 55$	26/36, $T = 49$	30/36, $T = 62$	37/75, $T = 49$
Short delay (free recall)	11/15, $T = 64$	10/15, $T = 60$	14/16, $T = 65$	—	—	—	9/15, $T = 57$
Long delay (free recall)	11/15, $T = 61$	10/15, $T = 59$	14/16, $T = 65$	11/12, $T = 56$	10/12, $T = 53$	11/12, $T = 60$	7/15, $T = 51$
Recognition trial	—	—	16/16 w/3 f+, $T = 50$	12/12 w/0 f+, $T = 60$	12/12 w/2 f+, $T = 45$	11/12 w/2 f+, $T = 42$	13/15 w/7 f+
BVMT-R	Form 1	Form 1	Form 2	Form 3	Form 1	Form 2	Form 1
Learning trials	5, 9, 8	4, 6, 12	6, 8, 12	8, 10, 12	3, 4, 7	4, 5, 5	5, 5, 8
Total recall	22/36, $T = 49$	22/36, $T = 49$	26/36, $T = 57$	30/36, $T = 64$	14/36, $T = 36$	14/36, $T = 36$	18/36, $T = 44$
Long delay	7/12, $T = 43$	11/12, $T = 61$	7/12, $T = 43$	12/12, $T = 66$	7/12, $T = 45$	6/12, $T = 40$	6/12, $T = 41$
Wechsler Memory Scale	WMS-R		WMS-R				
Logical Memory I	27, 76th %ile	—	27, 76th %ile	—	—	—	37, ss = 12
Logical Memory II	23, 75th %ile	—	40, 99th %ile	—	—	—	17, ss = 9

(continued)

Table 14.1 Continued

DATE	6/3/2009	12/2/2009	6/8/2010	12/10/2010	11/26/2013	1/13/2015	3/15/2017
Visual Reproduction I	38, 98th %ile	—	39, 99th %ile	—	—	—	—
Visual Reproduction II	27, 48th %ile	—	23, 33th %ile	—	—	—	—
Phonemic fluency	COWAT	COWAT	COWAT	COWAT	FAS	FAS	—
	38 words, 25–75%	44 words, 25–75th %ile	45 words, 77–89th %ile	47 words, 77–89th %ile	48 words, $T = 53$	35 words, $T = 42$	—
Semantic fluency (animals)	17 words, $T = 47$	22, $T = 59$	21 words, $T = 57$	—	13 words, $T = 31$	17 words, $T = 43$	—
Wisconsin Card Sorting Test							
Categories	6, >16th %ile	—	6, >16th %ile	—	3, >16th %ile	4, >16th %ile	6/6, >16th %ile
Total errors	11, $T = 54$	—	8, $T = 56$	—	7, $T = 59$	10, $T = 59$	12, $T = 57$
Perseverative responses	6, $T = 53$	—	4, $T = 55$	—	3, $T > 80$	5, $T > 80$	6, $T = 55$
Set loss	2, >16th %ile	—	0, >16th %ile	—	2	1	3, 6–10th %ile
Finger Tapping							
Right (dominant)	53.8 taps, $T = 50$	54.8 taps, $T = 55$	55.2 taps, $T = 55$	54.2 taps, $T = 55$	—	50.8 taps, $T = 46$	42.7 taps, $T = 38$
Left	43.6 taps, $T = 43$	48.6 taps, $T = 51$	48.2 taps, $T = 51$	43.2 taps, $T = 44$	—	32.4 taps, $T = 30$	18 taps, $T = 9$

BNI, Barrow Neurological Institute; BVMT-R, Brief Visuospatial Memory Test–Revised; COWAT, Controlled Oral Word Association Test; CVLT, California Verbal Learning Test; FAS, Fatigue Assessment Scale; FSIQ, Full Scale IQ; HVLT, Hopkins Verbal Learning Test; PIQ, Performance IQ; RAVLT, Rey Auditory Verbal Learning Test; ss, scaled score; VIQ, Verbal IQ; WAIS, Wechsler Adult Intelligence Scale; WMS-R, Wechsler Memory Scale–Revised; %ile, percentile rank.

memory test scores were above average and compatible with IQ estimates. Yet he did report memory difficulties in everyday life that may in part have been related to prospective memory problems not sampled by the tests used to examine him. His abstract reasoning skills or executive functions appeared intact, although he complained of fatigue and reduced problem-solving abilities. It is noteworthy that he was slightly slow in terms of speed of finger tapping in his left, nondominant hand.

At this time, the patient was especially concerned about his ability to meet professional job responsibilities. Given the psychometric findings, it was judged he could continue to function at his current job.

Given his concerns and certain inefficiencies in neuropsychological functioning, he was serially followed during the next year. Although his neuropsychological status did not substantially worsen, there was a tendency for his concentration and memory performance to show "some decline." However, as for many patients, his performance was variable over time (see Table 14.1). He began reporting worsening memory, fatigue, and depression (e.g., ratings of 6, 8–9, and 6–7, respectively). His wife viewed his memory as slightly worse (rating of 3–5), with fatigue being worst (rating of 7) but no worsening of his depression (rating of 2). With these findings, he continued to work with no change in professional responsibilities. However, with time, he felt increasingly overwhelmed with work responsibilities. He was getting increasingly "behind" in meeting job responsibilities.

The patient was seen by another neuropsychologist 3 years later. At that time, the diagnosis of akinetic rigid PD was established. Somewhat different neuropsychological testing methods were employed. As can be seen from Table 14.1, his Vocabulary and Matrix Reasoning scale scores had not declined. However, he was having more difficulty on tests of executive functioning, and it was judged that there was a decline in his visual reasoning, visual memory, and verbal recognition.

The patient was described as reporting "moderate symptoms of depression" with increased impulsivity and compulsive behaviors. By this time, he was 65 years old, and he sought medical retirement. He was referred for "rehabilitation counseling."

The patient continued to be monitored with neuropsychological testing for another year. There continued to be a decline in his executive functioning with associated decline in memory and concentration. He became especially slow in terms of his speed of finger tapping in the left versus the right hand (see Table 14.1). His fatigue and depression also appeared to worsen, and he and his wife were now referred for psychotherapy.

Efforts at Psychological Care

The patient's formal psychotherapy began approximately 3 months after his last neuropsychological examination. However, the patient had a very brief series of psychotherapy visits in 2009 and 2010. He decided to stop those sessions given his work schedule and energy level, but a good rapport was established during that time. Thus, when he was referred for psychotherapy a few years later, he requested to see the same clinical neuropsychologist. If one develops a good psychotherapeutic or working alliance with a patient during psychotherapy, this often results in the patient returning when their psychological needs become more urgent.

The patient has continued to be actively involved in psychotherapeutic treatment since originally seen in 2015. He has been seen weekly and has missed very few sessions. The typical treatment session consists of meeting with him and his wife conjointly for approximately 20 minutes, followed by 20–30 minutes with the patient alone and the remaining time with his spouse alone. This approach has proven very helpful in his case (but not in other cases, as described in Chapter 20, this volume).

It is important to review the recurring themes or issues the patient and his wife experienced that brought them "into psychotherapy" and appear relevant to their sustaining their motivation to continue in psychotherapy. During the first psychotherapy session, the patient stated he wanted to "learn to die gracefully." His wife was very vocal in expressing her anger and frustration with her husband's behavior and her view about his "aptitudes." She wanted me "to talk to him" about what frustrates her the most. He was using poor judgment in spending money they did not have. From her viewpoint, he had many excuses as to why he was behaving in that manner. She agreed that this behavior had gotten worse with his PD, but she believed these were long-standing personality or behavioral characteristics of her husband that had simply worsened with time. She viewed her husband as self-absorbed and often not willing to talk to others at the dinner table.

With time, these long-standing themes were modified somewhat, but the basic issues remained. The patient's wife did not understand her husband's behavior and eventually voiced her long-standing resentment about events that occurred earlier in their marriage. She wanted to have more insight into her husband's past and present behavior. Providing an informed neuropsychological opinion about the probable causes of his problematic behaviors seemed to have a calming effect, and the verbal bantering back and forth between the two began to subside slightly. Her concerns were now more focused on safety issues as her husband's falls became more prevalent. She would chide him for not using agreed upon safety steps in the home and outside of the home. He often would say he simply "forgot" to do what she asked (again, a probable reflection of a prospective memory problem). His wife also now wanted me to talk to him about letting her take over monitoring his medication usage because of his failure to take them as prescribed.

The patient's depression has repeatedly gone through "ups and downs." There were days he felt more positive and he enjoyed various outdoor activities. Other days, he experienced increasingly more limitations in his daily activities. This clearly increased his depressive symptomology. At such times, he would report excessive fatigue, poor sleep, and disturbing dreams. He also had a tendency to close his eyes when talking about topics that disturbed him. This typically occurred when his physical independence had reduced and his opinion about what he needed and wanted was discounted by family members. He noted that in the past he used to be highly independent and made decisions for others. The situation now had totally reversed. This was his personal or phenomenological experience.

Progressively he complained of increasing problems with vision and wore several different types of glasses in an effort to improve his vision. He wanted his physicians to consider surgery to help correct his visual problems. When he was told the visual problems could not be corrected by surgery, he became increasingly quiet and discouraged.

An important behavioral feature that developed for him was difficulty in judging how much time had passed while performing various activities. He might stand in front of a mirror and brush and floss his teeth for more than 1 hour—to the amazement and frustration of his wife. He and his wife did not understand that with his probable frontostriatal difficulties, he had increased problems initiating and stopping repetitive behaviors. It was an "eye opener" when this was explained to them from a neuropsychological perspective.

During the course of psychotherapy, a series of educational discussions were held that the patient greatly appreciated. He did not know why he was doing what he was doing. Having a neuropsychologist explain the probable causes of some of his behavioral difficulties was emotionally relieving to him and his wife. It helped their relationship. His wife started to view him as less of a "Mr. Excuse" and more as an intelligent man who had increasingly less control of his thought processes and behavior than was previously believed. Such discussions led to less conflict between the patient and his wife.

However, his high level of dependence on his wife was clearly difficult for her despite a better intellectual and empathetic understanding of his neurological and neuropsychological difficulties. Efforts were made to have an occupational therapist help set up a daily schedule for the patient to follow. This was partially effective, but it was difficult for the patient (and his wife) to follow the schedule. The goal was to have the patient follow a specific behavioral regime each morning in preparing for the day. Start and stop times were identified and mutually agreed upon by the patient and his wife. Despite the best efforts of the occupational therapist and the patient and his wife, this routine was very difficult to follow. He had difficulties starting on time by himself. He had difficulties stopping on time by himself. He had different thoughts that entered his mind at different times that distracted him from the tasks at hand (i.e., problems with the control of internal attentional processes). He did not understand (or perceive at the time) what was happening. He later recognized that he had gotten "lost in a certain thought or mental problem" and somehow could not detach himself from these consuming mental states. This appeared to reflect a problem of shifting his attention or cognitive set as the situation demanded.

For example, he might find himself drifting into solving a mathematic problem using a math formula he learned in high school. For some reason, he was absorbed with trying to figure out the solution to the math problem even though it appeared totally irrelevant to what he was doing at the time. Later, it seemed (to the psychotherapist) that he was trying to use his mind productively and demonstrate to himself that he could still think and solve problems. The patient, however, did not experience it that way. He simply was trapped in solving a mental problem and could not consciously or willfully disentangle himself from this mental exercise.

Relatively early in the psychotherapeutic discussion, sexuality became an important topic. He was sexually impotent, and this greatly disturbed him. He began to have more interest in looking at sexually explicit materials. This, of course, was disturbing to his wife. Physical touch and sexual contact were no longer present between him and his wife. Cognitive and behavioral difficulties interfered with expressing his love toward his wife. This was also discussed openly between him and his wife. The patient was encouraged to start each morning, before beginning his daily self-care routine, by saying out loud (so his wife could hear) that he was trying to lessen the burden of care on his wife because he loved her. Her prescribed response was to give him a kiss on the cheek. These behavioral prescriptions seemed to have an important but modest effect on the couple's comfort level with each other.

During a series of sessions, the topic of anger and depression with regard to his PD was discussed. The patient often spontaneously stated that he felt better after these sessions, in which he could openly talk about what he was experiencing. However, the recurring preoccupation about death, how he will die, and that he wants to die (perhaps by a fall) to avoid a long and painful protracted illness remains at the heart of the continued efforts at psychological care of this patient.

Two other features of his psychological care are important to note. Despite his cognitive limitations and the fact that he is no longer working in his profession, I always addressed him by his professional title. He commented once that he was not sure why I was doing this because he no longer held a certain esteemed position in society. I remarked that he deserves the title given what he accomplished professionally in his life. A second important component to his care was listening to his experiences of being discriminated against as a young boy. This led to a desire for social justice, which influenced his professional work and political orientation. Understanding this important feature of his personality appeared to strengthen the therapeutic relationship that I had with him. It highlights how understanding certain features of a person's psychodynamics can greatly aid the therapeutic alliance.

Howard Book (1998) made an important comment when writing about "in-press countertransference." He talked insightfully about the realities of what can happen when a psychotherapist wishes to write about their work with a patient while they are still working with the patient. Read carefully what he has to say:

> Because I knew that I would be using material from a patient's, "Ms. Benton's" treatment to illustrate this book, I was continually wrestling with a unique countertransference dynamic: I wished Ms. Benton's treatment to be successful for *my* benefit in order that it seamlessly illustrates the benefits of BPP (Brief Psychodynamic Psychotherapy) for this book. I had a fear, however, that Ms. Benton would bring up material that would make me look less than competent in illustrating the effectiveness of the CCRT (the Core Conflictual Relationship Theme) method. As a result, I was continually tempted to avoid exploring material that might end up making me, the book, and the CCRT method appear confusing and ineffective. My desire to write a successful book frequently conflicted with my wish to offer Ms. Benton competent psychotherapy. It was a wish that I constantly monitored and that I hope I have been able to contain. (p. 16)

This type of honesty is often missing in reports about the effectiveness of different types of psychological care with patients with and without brain disorders. Book reminds us that we may not always "tell the whole story" in the interest of getting our point across to the reader. I mention this point to highlight that the "whole story" regarding the patient I just described is not complete. His psychological care is ongoing, and I may have omitted information that the reader wished I would have included. What I wanted to outline in this section, however, are some of the real issues faced by patients with PD and their spouses as they struggle to cope with this disease. I also wanted to illustrate how I approached this patient and the wide variety of behavioral suggestions/interventions and personal topics discussed with him. I hope that it provides an example of how various factors have to be considered in the psychological care of persons with PD.

Table 14.2 lists the 20 clinically relevant features of psychological care described in Chapter 13. Here, they are applied to summarize this patient's care to date. Although there are different areas of overlap, two important similarities are noted. As a result of the psychological care, the person was able to openly discuss his personal concerns and with time other related concerns emerged. Second, the psychotherapeutic relationship has been and continues to be very positive, and it appears to help the patient and his wife sustain their efforts at psychological adjustment during difficult times.

APPROACHES TO PSYCHOLOGICAL CARE WITH PATIENTS WITH PARKINSON'S DISEASE

A wide range of approaches to the psychological care of persons with PD have been reported in the literature (Table 14.3). The studies listed in Table 14.3 are not all-inclusive but, rather, highlight different approaches and the typical findings that are reported. Studies employing cognitive–behavioral approaches, often in conjunction with anti-depressant medications, are most frequently reported.

Behavioral therapies, mindfulness training, group psychodrama, exercise, music and dance therapies, and even straightforward cognitive training have all been studied as means to reduce depression and/or increase quality of life in PD patients. When positive findings are reported, the effect sizes are often in the mild range. This should be expected given that these treatments typically are applied for relatively short periods of time. Typically, there are 12–16 sessions, and most treatment programs do not last longer than 6 months, with several

Table 14.2 Clinical Features Relevant to the Psychological Care of a Person with Atypical Parkinsonism

CLINICAL FEATURE	YES	NO	PARTIALLY
1. The dialogue between the patient and the clinical neuropsychologist was not rushed.	✓		
2. The patient was able to express or clearly convey his personal concerns.	✓		
3. The content of the concerns varied over time and reflected the patient's stage of decline.	✓		
4. The patient experienced a sense of "realistic" hope that he and his wife could better cope with their life's situation. They also did not experience "being alone" with their problem(s).	✓		
5. The patient and the clinical neuropsychologist developed a positive therapeutic relationship in which the patient's dignity was maintained even in the face of significant physical and cognitive declines.	✓		
6. Somatic symptoms (which appeared to be indirect effects of a brain disorder) were substantially reduced during periods of psychological care.			✓
7. Anxiety/depression/anger and/or apathy were substantially reduced during periods of psychological care.			✓
8. The patient was able to follow the guidance of the clinical neuropsychologist to improved functioning in everyday life activities.			✓
9. The patient was able to control impulses and delay gratification.			✓
10. The patient actively worked at developing "self-efficacy skills" in the face of his declining abilities.			✓
11. The patient attempted to "self-reflect" or "be more aware" of personal "strengths" and "limitations."	✓		
12. The patient experienced enjoyment in the care or help of other living things (people, animals, the environment, etc.).	✓		
13. The patient had an improved understanding of the "problematic nature of life" (given his psychosocial state of life) and was not overwhelmed or "defeated" by it or readily gave in to escapism to cope with life (Bettelheim,1989).			✓
14. The patient could "live with" the restrictions produced by a brain injury "without resentment" or loss of hope (Goldstein, 1952).			✓

(continued)

Table 14.2 Continued

CLINICAL FEATURE	YES	NO	PARTIALLY
15. The patient was able to obtain new insights into self by attending to why certain songs, stories, fairy tales, movies, tattoos, etc. had a special personal meaning that he initially did not understand.		✓	
16. The patient's dreams or artwork often heralded changes in behavior that aided in psychological adjustment before the consciously mediated changes occurred.		✓	
17. The psychological care interventions (including the dialogue) between the patient and the clinical neuropsychologist resulted in the patient talking more openly about problems and demonstrating self-directed efforts at improving psychological adjustment to the direct and indirect effects of the brain disorder.	✓		
18. The psychological care interventions were in harmony with the patient's cultural background and religious orientation.	✓		
19. The psychological care interventions were appropriate for the patient's psychosocial stage of development and facilitate adaptation in the later stages of life (an ongoing process).	✓		
20. The patient and family experienced two basic facts of life: (a) The individual's state of subjective sense of personal well-being fluctuates and (b) the psychological adjustment process is never static and therefore hope should never be abandoned.	✓		
Total	11	2	7

ending within 3 months. Detailed descriptions of what occurs during these various forms of treatment and the degree of impact on individual patients (and family members) are not reported. Most studies report, however, some attempt to modify the standardized treatment protocol to the individual needs of the patient. How that is done is typically not reported.

A meta-analysis comparing the effectiveness of CBT with that of short-term psychodynamic therapy for depression in PD patients reported greater treatment size effects for the psychodynamic-treated patients (Xie et al., 2015). No major differences were found between the two groups on the Parkinson's Disease Questionaire-39 scale.

No studies could be identified in which the quality of the patients' interpersonal relationship *before* the onset of the disease impacted their response to various treatments for depression in PD patients and/or caregiver burden. This appears to be a fruitful area for future investigations.

BUILDING RESILIENCY IN PATIENTS WITH PARKINSON'S DISEASE AND THEIR CAREGIVERS

Given that resiliency is an important variable in the psychological care of persons with brain disorders, what determines resiliency in PD patients? Robottom et al. (2012) reported that

Table 14.3 Review of Selected Studies and Meta-Analyses Relevant to the Psychological Care of Persons with Parkinson's Disease

INTERVENTION	STUDY SAMPLE	MAJOR FINDINGS	CONCLUSIONS
Group psychodrama to reduce depression and anxiety and improve quality of life in PD patients (Sproesser, Viana, Quagliato, & Pedroso de Souza, 2010)	16 idiopathic PD patients were randomized to a treatment (or experimental) group vs. a control group. Therapy was for twelve 90-minute sessions during a 6-month period of time.	Quality of life (as judged by the Parkinson's Disease and Quality of Life measure) improved in the treatment group. The control group showed greater anxiety post treatment compared to the treated group.	Group-oriented psychotherapy sessions extended for 6 months may improve quality of life in PD patients. The lack of such group experience may be associated with increased anxiety over time. This study highlights the possibility that without some form of psychological care, patients may have enhanced psychiatric symptoms as the disease progresses.
CBT+ for depression (Dobkin et al., 2011; see text for more details)	40 PD patients randomized to CBT+ compared to 39 PD patients who were clinically monitored. CBT+ treatments included many activities, such as relaxation exercises, sleep hygiene interventions, and individual educational sessions for caregivers. Treatment was for 10 weeks in 60- to 75-minute sessions.	CBT+ group demonstrated less self-reported depression on the Hamilton Depression Rating Scale in addition to improvements in other domains (e.g., anxiety) compared to the clinically monitored group.	PD patients receiving CBT+ had a greater treatment response (56%) compared to those simply monitored (8%). The actual impact on patients' day-to-day functioning is undetermined.
Self-control vs. other controlled motor practice at improving balance and avoiding falls (Chiviacowsky, Wulf, Lewthwaite, & Campos, 2012)	28 PD patients were randomized to a balance task in which they could choose using a balance pole to aid balance on a balance platform or not (i.e., self-control group) or were simply yoked to whatever the self-control group decided to do (i.e., the control group).	The self-control PD group demonstrated more effective motor learning compared to the control group. On a simple questionnaire, patients in the self-control PD group reported more motivation to learn the task and were less "nervous."	Although this study does not meet the standards for a systematic assessment of psychological improvement, it supports a very basic psychological insight. The more "self-control" or, better stated, the more "self-choice" PD patients have, the more likely they are to subjectively report greater motivation to learn and less anxiety in the learning process. This may apply to the effects of various forms of psychological interventions.

(continued)

Table 14.3 Continued

INTERVENTION	STUDY SAMPLE	MAJOR FINDINGS	CONCLUSIONS
CBT for pathological gambling in PD (Jimenez-Murcia et al., 2012)	15 patients with PD who also had pathological gambling (PG+PD) were compared to 45 patients with pathological gambling and no PD (PG–PD) in terms of clinical characteristics and response to 16 weeks of CBT. The treatments, however, were not identical because different topics were emphasized in the PD group.	The PG+PD group was older, tended to play more bingo, and was less hostile than the PG–PD group. Rates of relapses and dropouts were higher in the PG+PD group. Levels of compliance with the treatment protocol were equivalent between the two groups but were low.	Although lacking methodological rigor, this study is important for at least two negative reasons. If a treatment has a low compliance rate as well as a high dropout rate, it suggests that the treatment was not experienced by the person as being helpful. Second, equating patients on demographic as well as personality features (e.g., level of hostility) is important when attempting to understand the presence or absence of treatment effects.
Meta-analysis of the effects of music-based movement (MbM) therapy on gait and quality of life (deDreu, van der Wilk, Poppe, Kwakkel, & Wegen, 2012)	168 PD patients from six articles were reviewed to determine the effect of music-based movement on gait-related activities, with two studies measuring potential impact on quality of life.	Significant positive effects on walking velocity for gait were noted, but not on dance-related activities. No significant changes on the UPDRS motor scale were reported; however, there was a reported trend for improved quality of life (particularly a "happiness" measure).	MbM therapy improves gait and may reduce the risk of falls. It is also associated with mild improvement in quality of life, but it does not appear to change the underlying motor limitations of PD patients.
Meta-analysis review of various psychosocial interventions for depression and anxiety in PD patients (Yang, Sajatovic, & Walter, 2012)	281 idiopathic PD patients in varying Hoehn and Yahr stages were studied using various research designs, including RCTs and prospective uncontrolled studies.	CBT was shown to lower depression, via rating on the HAM-D scale. Also, patient educational programs were shown to improve quality of life, and behavioral therapy was shown to improve posture and gait.	This study summarizes evidence that multiple types of interventions may improve depression and anxiety in PD patients. It is noted the findings applied to "acute effects" and the long-term benefits remained unclear.

Meta-analysis review of pharmacologic and behavioral interventions for depression (Bomasang-Layno, Fadlon, Murrary, & Himelhoch, 2015)	893 idiopathic PD patients with depression studied in 20 RCT studies using various forms of treatments were included in the meta-analysis. Comparison of findings with those of other similar reviews was considered.	Antidepressant medications, especially SSRIs, improve depression in PD patients. Behavioral interventions (especially CBT+) also improve depression.	Treatment size effects are quite variable. The sustainability of behavioral interventions remains undetermined. The same is true for medication effects. Placebo effects are also noted and again related to possible release of dopamine. The quality of the patient–doctor relationship in influencing placebo effects was not considered.
Meta-analysis review of the effect of cognitive training on PD patients (Leung et al., 2015)	272 PD patients with Hoehn & Yahr stages 1–3 treated with cognitive training exercises in seven RCTs were studied concerning the effects of such training on specific cognitive functions as well as on measures of depression and quality of life.	Cognitive training had significant effects in different domains, with the greatest size effects occurring for working memory, processing speed, and "executive functions." No associated improvements in depression, independence in daily living activities, or quality of life were reported.	The implication of this meta-analysis (which is based on only a few studies in light of the requirement that only RCTs were included) is that modest improvement in cognitive functioning does not correlate with a reduction of depression or improvement in quality of life. However, other studies (referenced previously) have argued for the importance of cognitive appraisal of disabilities as a mediator of depression.
Mindfulness-based lifestyle program to improve quality of life and reduce depression in PD patients (Advocat et al., 2016)	80 Hoehn and Yahr stage 2 PD patients were randomized to a 6-week (2 hours per group session) mindfulness-based lifestyle intervention vs. a wait-list control group.	No improvement in quality of life (as measured by the PDQ-39) was reported. Depression and anxiety also did not change. Reportedly, stress significantly increased in the intervention group upon completion of the program. However, at 6-month follow-up, a small effect size for decreased stress was reported in this PD intervention group. A statistically significant but small relationship was found for increased depression and adherence.	Although the findings of this study are not encouraging, they have a potential take-home message relevant to psychological care: Attempts at psychological care can be ineffective and at times distressing to the patient. A frank discussion of when this occurs is often missing in the scientific literature, but it is an extremely important observation that can guide further care activities.

(continued)

Table 14.3 Continued

INTERVENTION	STUDY SAMPLE	MAJOR FINDINGS	CONCLUSIONS
Meta-analysis comparing CBT and psychodynamic therapy for depression in Parkinson's disease (Xie et al., 2015)	766 patients diagnosed with PD and with comorbid depression from 12 studies were compared regarding the relative effectiveness of CBT vs. psychodynamic therapy of relatively short duration.	Self-ratings on the HAM-D showed greater improvement in the psychodynamic therapy patients compared to those receiving CBT. There were no differences on the PDQ-39 scale.	The findings are interesting in light of greater size of treatment effects in the psychodynamic-treated patients vs. those receiving CBT. Such comparisons are seldom seen in patients with known brain disorders. The findings are limited, however, to patients treated in China vs. Europe or the United States.

CBT, cognitive–behavioral therapy; HAM-D, Hamilton Depression Rating Scale; PD, Parkinson's disease; PDQ-39, Parkinson's Disease Questionaire-39; RCT, randomized controlled trial; SSRIs, selective serotonin reuptake inhibitors; UPDRS, Unified Parkinson's Disease Rating Scale.

resiliency in PD patients was not associated with disease severity. It did correlate, however, with fewer psychiatric symptoms (i.e., patients described as less depressed and less anxious were described as more resilient). It was also associated with less fatigue. These investigators raise the question of whether resilience can be "cultivated." They suggest that involving patients in more artistic or creative activities may help in this regard (which was also noted for patients with anoxia and described in Chapter, 13, this volume). They suggest that improving social support networks for patients can also be very helpful.

Resiliency in caregivers, however, may be related to several, and at times different, variables. Lawson et al. (2016) noted that the number of hours spent caregiving, caregiver's depression, and PD motor severity all contributed to significant caregiver's burden. Interestingly, attentional deficits (which were clearly noted in the patient described previously) accounted for the largest portion of variance for caregiver's quality of life. Sanders-Dewey, Mullins, and Chaney (2001) noted that as the disease progresses, family members (who are often caregivers) may experience greater burden as their responsibilities in taking care of the patient increase. They noted that family caregivers are especially distressed by not knowing what to expect regarding the progression of the disease and what problems they will need to manage. The tendency to negatively emotionally react to the patient's limitations and needs was related to the distress level of the caregivers.

In the case example described previously, the more the patient's wife became emotionally upset with the patient's cognitive, motor, and affective disturbances, the more she seemed to require additional support from the clinical neuropsychologist. Building resiliency in her appeared directly tied to how much support and knowledge she received from the psychotherapy sessions. Occasionally, she would jokingly state that the psychologist should have the patient during his vacation times so he could really understand what she was going through.

Monin and Schulz (2009) note that the caregiver's emotional responses to a suffering family member often reflect differences in emotional coping mechanisms, but caregivers often feel many of the same emotions as those experienced by the care recipients. Often, family members want the treating psychotherapist or psychological caregiver to experience what they experience with a family member who has a progressive illness requiring increasingly more care. This seems to relieve their burden, even if for a short period of time.

A final set of observations about caregiver burden related to PD is also relevant to the discussion about the patient briefly described in this chapter. Schrag, Hovris, Morley, Quinn, and Jahanshahi (2006) noted that caregivers often experience higher levels of distress or burden with their PD spouse when significant psychiatric symptoms are present and the patient is prone to falls. They also report, however, that the degree of marital satisfaction that often predated the development of the disabilities associated with PD significantly correlates with caregiver burden. This observation has important clinical implications. It may be helpful to assess, in as brief and nonintrusive manner as possible, the quality of the marital relationship. This may help the clinician gain a better understanding of how to best manage the patient and the spouse when levels of depression and anger are high. Hendrick (1988) provides a brief scale for assessing the strength of marital or partner relationships that may be helpful in this regard.

PLACEBO EFFECTS IN THE CARE OF PERSONS WITH PARKINSON'S DISEASE

Colloca, Lopiano, Lanotte, and Benedetti (2004) report very interesting findings concerning a possible placebo effect in the treatment of this patient group. Summarizing research findings from previous studies (Benedetti et al., 2003; Pollo et al., 2002), they note that the therapeutic response to deep brain stimulation (DBS) of the subthalamic nucleus in PD patients is influenced by physician comments. Treatment effects differ when patients are told they are receiving the stimulation (the so-called open DBS) versus not being told they are receiving such stimulation (the so-called hidden DBS). The treatment effects are enhanced in the open condition (Figure 14.1).

They note that "awareness of the treatment, the presence of the therapist, and the expectation of the outcome are likely to be very important" (p. 682) for treatment outcome, even if the treatment is medical/surgical in nature versus psychological in nature. This is an important finding for all treating clinicians.

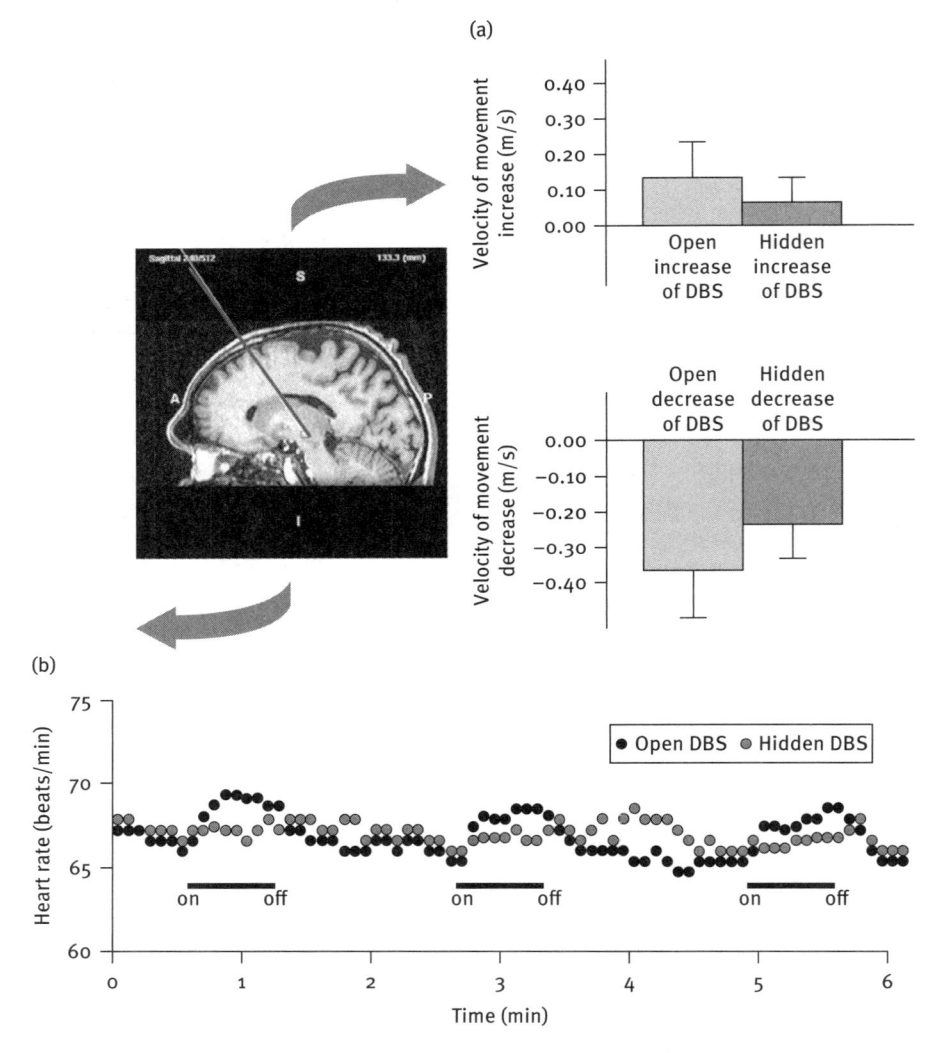

FIGURE 14.1 (A) The effects of open and hidden deep brain stimulation (DBS) on the velocity of hand movement. In all cases, hidden DBS is less effective than open DBS. (B) Heart rate responses of a patient with Parkinson's disease receiving three sequential stimulations (horizontal bars) of the ventral limbic portion of the subthalamic region overtly and covertly. The hidden stimulations are ineffective (there is no matching between stimulus on–off and heart rate changes), suggesting that heart rate increases after the open stimulations do not result from the stimulation itself but, rather, from other factors, such as attention, arousal, and expectation (See color plates).

Source: Reprinted from Colloca, L., Lopiano, L., Lanotte, M., & Benedetti, F., Overt versus covert treatment for pain, anxiety, and Parkinson's disease, *The Lancet Neurology*, 3(11), 2004, p. 679–684, Copyright (2004), by permission of Elsevier.

In earlier research, De la Fuente-Fernández et al. (2001) demonstrated that placebo therapies can induce the release of endogenous dopamine in the striatum. When the instructions to the placebo group are somewhat different than those to the experimental group and it is not clear if the treatment is presented in a manner that leads to the expectation of benefits, placebo effects may not occur in some PD patients (Lomarev et al., 2006).

SUGGESTIONS REGARDING THE PSYCHOLOGICAL CARE OF PERSONS WITH PARKINSON'S DISEASE

Based on the literature regarding the neuropsychological features of persons with PD and the methods used to aid in their psychological care, some suggestions relevant to this patient group can be made. These suggestions, however, have to be tailored to the individual needs of the person. They are listed in Box 14.1 as a

---

Box 14.1. Suggestions to Consider for the Psychological Care of Persons with Parkinson's Disease

1. Diagnostic and educationally relevant (periodic) neuropsychological consultation with the patient and family/caregivers is crucial. Traditional psychometric test findings may not capture several important neuropsychological disturbances common to PD patients.
2. Foster resilience in PD patients and their caregivers. There is often an educational and psychotherapeutic component to this process. Addressing conscious and perhaps nonconscious needs of both parties can be very helpful to this process.
3. Maximize placebo effects in the context of ethical practices. This includes fostering the experience of hope at appropriate times irrespective of the patient's clinical condition.
4. Cognitive-behavioral approaches (which often include relaxation exercises) may be helpful in reducing early symptoms of anxiety and depression in PD.
5. Psychodynamic approaches to reduce core conflictual relationships may be helpful for some patients and their spouses. Attention to the personal emotional needs of the patient and spouse is important irrespective of the psychotherapeutic model used.
6. Utilize humanistic or client centered approaches to understand what the patient (and at times the spouse/caregiver) actually perceive or experience concerning their clinical status and their perceptions of the psychological care interventions that are being employed.
7. Utilize symbolic expressions (including dreams, music, drawings, artwork, fairy tales) to better understand the personality features of person and their existential concerns and reactions that they may not be able to easily verbalize (this is one feature of a Jungian approach to facilitating psychological care and well-being in PD patients).
8. Explore the role of music, dance therapies and singing therapies in the psychological care of the person to improve motor and voice functioning in PD.
9. Facilitate awareness of motor limitations and institute steps to avoid falls and enhance or maintain daily functional independence in as many areas as possible.
10. Help coordinate care between physical, occupational and speech therapy if possible. It conveys to the patient and spouse your willingness to take an active interest in the patient's overall functioning which improves the quality of their life and promotes a positive psychological adjustment.

potential resource for the reader. Note that many of these suggestions can be applied to other patient groups as well.

SUMMARY

In the preceding chapters, the point was made several times that effective psychological care is predicated on integrating basic knowledge about human nature with an understanding of how a brain disorder affects the "natural plan" of the patient's central nervous system. It was stated that these two knowledge bases have to be integrated with an understanding of the different types of interventions that may foster psychological care and well-being in patients after a brain disorder. Do the case described in this chapter and the empirical findings reviewed from several studies support this contention? First, it is natural (i.e., a part of human nature) for older people to think about how they will die, particularly when they have a progressive neurodegenerative disorder. It is not necessarily part of a clinical depression, although the patient described has fluctuated in his depressive symptoms over time. This existential issue also existed, side by side, with ongoing daily struggles with a loss of independence and emotional disagreements with his wife regarding his behavior and his repeated failure to use compensatory strategies to reduce his burden of care on others. In addition, he suffered from a variety of physical difficulties, including difficulties walking, getting up from a chair, holding food in his hands without dropping it, chewing and swallowing food, and speaking too softly to be heard by others. Most significant, he had several serious falls in which he would fall backwards. He also had ongoing sleep disturbance. A number of functioning difficulties could foster anger and depression as a *natural* response to these progressive difficulties.

Second, his neuropsychological disturbances (which were only partly reflected in psychometric test performance but became more fully understood by speaking to him on several occasions concerning what he experienced while performing a variety of activities) significantly limited him with regard to using compensatory techniques. The impact of these neuropsychological disturbances was often not obvious to him or his wife. For example, he could not easily stop and start a behavior according to an agreed upon time schedule with his wife and the occupational therapist because of underlying frontal lobe system dysfunction. That dysfunction negatively altered the verbal control of behavior. His wife's verbal prompting to begin or end an action often had no impact, to the frustration of both parties. This automatic function of starting and stopping a behavior with verbal self-instruction or the verbal instruction of another was simply not working. Also, the basic perception of how much time had passed while engaged in an activity was altered. He needed someone to respectfully physically guide him (with a touch or guided hand movement) to start an action and to respectfully touch him and behaviorally guide the next needed action. The clinical neuropsychologist's explanation of the underlying neuropsychological difficulties and specific behavioral recommendations to help counter his functional difficulties were experienced by the patient and his wife as extremely helpful. It helps to clarify the nature of the underlying neuropsychological problem. The patient was not trying to be "difficult," nor was he demented. He was an intelligent person with frontostriatal difficulties who needed to be understood and worked with to the degree that was possible. This led to a reduction of tension in the interpersonal relationship between the patient and his wife, which is one marker of effective psychological care.

Third, the patient would periodically report feeling "relieved" and less depressed after certain insightful sessions regarding his neuropsychological functioning, its impact on his daily activities, and his personal reactions to his illness. Occasionally, he would speak of his professional life and activities that gave him joy during times of recreation. He sensed the desire of the clinical neuropsychologists to be of help to him and his wife. He recognized the time commitment that was made for him in an effort to be of assistance to him and his wife. He was immensely grateful for the psychological care provided.

As Erik Erikson (1964) clearly pointed out, however, the patient's expressed gratitude to the therapist is not evidence of effective treatment per se. What is convincing evidence is the patient's ongoing willingness (and his wife's ongoing willingness) to engage in each psychotherapy session with openness and an eagerness to try any activity that may further help him cope with his illness and its related disabilities. His subjective feeling of comfort regarding someone taking interest in him and helping him deal with his declining health was perhaps the most important outcome measure. To some degree, his wife had a similar feeling. She was not alone in understanding her husband or trying to take care of his needs. As stated previously, his psychotherapy is not complete. Yet the progress achieved to date is encouraging.

REFERENCES

Aarsland, D., Påhlhagen, S., Ballard, C. G., Ehrt, U., & Svenningsson, P. (2012). Depression in Parkinson disease—Epidemiology, mechanisms and management. *Nature Reviews Neurology, 8*(1), 35–47.

Advocat, J., Enticott, J., Vandenberg, B., Hassed, C., Hester, J., & Russel, G. (2016). The effects of a mindfulness-based lifestyle program for adults with Parkinson's disease: a mixed methods, wait list controlled randomized control study. *BMC Neurology, 16*, 166–176.

Benedetti, F., Pollo, A., Lopiano, L., Lanotte, M., Vighetti, S., & Rainero, I. (2003). Conscious expectation and unconscious conditioning in analgesic, motor, and hormonal placebo/nocebo responses. *Journal of Neuroscience, 23*(10), 4315–4323.

Bettelheim, B. (1989). *The uses of enchantment: The meaning and importance of fairy tales.* New York, NY: Vintage.

Bomasang-Layno, E., Fadlon, I., Murrary, A., & Himelhoch, S. (2015). Antidepressive treatments for Parkinson's disease: A systematic review and meta-analysis. *Parkinsonism and Related Disorders, 21*, 833–842.

Book, H. E. (1998). *How to practice brief psychodynamic psychotherapy.* Washington, DC: American Psychological Association.

Booth, G. (1948). Psychodynamics in parkinsonism. *Psychosomatic Medicine, 10*(1), 1–14.

Carrozzino, D., Bech, P., Patierno, C., Onofrj, M., Morberg, B. M., Thomas, A., . . . Fulcheri, M. (2017). Somatization in Parkinson's disease: A systematic review. *Progress in Neuro-Psychopharmacology and Biological Psychiatry, 78*, 18–26.

Chiviacowsky, S., Wulf, G., Lewthwaite, R., & Campos, T. (2012). Motor learning benefits of self-controlled practice in persons with Parkinson's disease. *Gait & Posture, 35*, 601–605.

Colloca, L., Lopiano, L., Lanotte, M., & Benedetti, F. (2004). Overt versus covert treatment for pain, anxiety, and Parkinson's disease. *Lancet Neurology, 3*(11), 679–684.

deDreu, M., van der Wilk, A., Popper, E., Kwakkel, G., & van Wegen, E. (2012). Rehabilitation, exercise therapy and music in patients with Parkinson's disease: a meta-analysis of the effects of music-based movement therapy on walking ability, balance, and quality of life. *Parkinsonism and Related Disorders,* (18S1), S114–S119.

De la Fuente-Fernández, R., Ruth, T. J., Sossi, V., Schulzer, M., Calne, D. B., & Stoessl, A. J. (2001). Expectation and dopamine release: Mechanism of the placebo effect in Parkinson's disease. *Science, 293*(5532), 1164–1166.

Dissanayaka, N. N., Pye, D., Mitchell, L. K., Byrne, G. J., O'Sullivan, J. D., Marsh, R., & Pachana, N. A. (2017). Cognitive behavior therapy for anxiety in Parkinson's disease: Outcomes for patients and caregivers. *Clinical Gerontologist, 40*(3), 159–171.

Dissanayaka, N. N., White, E., O'Sullivan, J. D., Marsh, R., Pachana, N. A., & Byrne, G. J. (2014). The clinical spectrum of anxiety in Parkinson's disease. *Movement Disorders, 29*(8), 967–975.

Dobkin, R. D., Menza, M., Allen, L. A., Gara, M. A., Mark, M. H., Tiu, J., . . . Friedman, J. (2011). Cognitive–behavioral therapy for depression in Parkinson's disease: A randomized, controlled trial. *American Journal of Psychiatry, 168*(10), 1066–1074.

Erikson, E. H. (1964). *Insight and responsibility.* New York, NY: Norton.

Fields, J. A. (2017). Cognitive and neuropsychiatric features in Parkinson's and Lewy body dementias. *Archives of Clinical Neuropsychology, 32*(7), 786–801.

Fuster, J. M. (1997). *The prefrontal cortex: Anatomy, physiology, and neuropsychology of the frontal lobe* (3rd ed.). Philadelphia, PA: Lippincott–Raven.

Getz, S. J., & Levin, B. (2017). Cognitive and neuropsychiatric features of early Parkinson's disease. *Archives of Clinical Neuropsychology, 32*(7), 769–785.

Goldstein, K. (1952). The effect of brain damage on the personality. *Psychiatry, 15*(3), 245–260.

Happe, S., & Berger, K. (2002). The association between caregiver burden and sleep disturbances in partners of patients with Parkinson's disease. *Age and Ageing, 31*(5), 349–354.

Hendrick, S. S. (1988). A generic measure of relationship satisfaction. *Journal of Marriage and the Family, 50*(1), 93–98.

Jimmenez-Murcia, S., Bove, F., Israel, M., Steiger, H., Fernandez-Aranda, F., Alvarez-Moya, E., . . . Menchon, J. (2012). Cognitive-behavioral therapy for pathological gambling in Parkinson's disease: A pilot controlled study. *European Addiction Research, 18*, 265–274.

Kolb, B., & Whishaw, I. Q. (2009). *Fundamentals of human neuropsychology*. New York, NY: Freeman.

Lawson, R., Yarnall, A., Johnston, F., Duncan, G., Khoo, T., Collerton, D., . . . Burn, D. (2016). Cognitive impairment in Parkinson's disease: Impact on quality of life of carers. *International Journal of Geriatric Psychiatry, 32*(12), 1362–1370.

Leung, I., Walton, C., Hallock, H., Lewis, M., Valenzuela, M., & Lampit, A. (2015). Cognitive training in Parkinson disease: a systematic review and meta-analysis. *Neurology, 85*, 1843–1851.

Lomarev, M. P., Kanchana, S., Bara-Jimenez, W., Iyer, M., Wassermann, E. M., & Hallett, M. (2006). Placebo-controlled study of rTMS for the treatment of Parkinson's disease. *Movement Disorders, 21*(3), 325–331.

Maier, F., & Prigatano, G. P. (2017). Impaired self-awareness of motor disturbances in Parkinson's disease. *Archives of Clinical Neuropsychology, 32*(7), 802–809.

Marsh, L., & Dobkin, R. D. (2015). Depression and anxiety in Parkinson's disease. In A. Tröster (Ed.), *Clinical neuropsychology and cognitive neurology of Parkinson's disease and other movement disorders* (pp. 265–290). New York, NY: Oxford University Press.

McPherson, S. E., & Cummings, J. L. (2009). Neuropsychological aspects of Parkinson's disease and parkinsonism. In I. Grant & K. M. Adams (Eds.), *Neuropsychological assessment of neuropsychiatric and neuromedical disorders* (3rd ed., pp. 199–222). Oxford, UK: Oxford University Press.

Monin, J. K., & Schulz, R. (2009). Interpersonal effects of suffering in older adult caregiving relationships. *Psychology and Aging, 24*(3), 681–695.

Murley, A. G., & Rowe, J. B. (2018). Neurotransmitter deficits from frontotemporal lobar degeneration. *Brain, 141*(5), 1263–1285.

Pagonabarraga, J., & Kulisevsky, J. (2017). Apathy in Parkinson's disease. *International Review of Neurobiology, 133*, 657–678.

Pedersen, K. F., Larsen, J. P., Alves, G., & Aarsland, D. (2009). Prevalence and clinical correlates of apathy in Parkinson's disease: A community-based study. *Parkinsonism & Related Disorders, 15*(4), 295–299.

Pluck, G., & Brown, R. (2002). Apathy in Parkinson's disease. *Journal of Neurology, Neurosurgery, and Psychiatry, 73*(6), 636–642.

Pollo, A., Torre, E., Lopiano, L., Rizzone, M., Lanotte, M., Cavanna, A., . . . Benedetti, F. (2002). Expectation modulates the response to subthalamic nucleus stimulation in Parkinsonian patients. *Neuroreport, 13*(11), 1383–1386.

Pontone, G. M., Williams, J. R., Anderson, K. E., Chase, G., Goldstein, S. A., Grill, S., . . . Margolis, R. L. (2009). Prevalence of anxiety disorders and anxiety subtypes in patients with Parkinson's disease. *Movement Disorders, 24*(9), 1333–1338.

Prigatano, G. P. (2010). *The study of anosognosia*. New York, NY: Oxford University Press.

Rahman, S., Griffin, H. J., Quinn, N. P., & Jahanshahi, M. (2008). Quality of life in Parkinson's disease: The relative importance of the symptoms. *Movement Disorders, 23*(10), 1428–1434.

Robottom, B., Gruber-Baldini, A., Anderson, K., Reich, S., Fishman, P., Weiner, W., & Shulman, L. (2012). What determines resilience in patients with Parkinson's disease? *Parkinsonism & Related Disorders, 18*(2), 174–177.

Sanders-Dewey, N. E., Mullins, L. L., & Chaney, J. M. (2001). Coping style, perceived uncertainty in illness, and distress in individuals with Parkinson's disease and their caregivers. *Rehabilitation Psychology, 46*(4), 363–381.

Santangelo, G., Garramone, F., Baiano, C., D'Iorio, A., Piscopo, F., Raimo, S., & Vitale, C. (2018). Personality and Parkinson's disease: A meta-analysis. *Parkinsonism & Related Disorders, 49*, 67–74.

Schmand, B., & Tröster, A. I. (2015). Earliest cognitive changes and mild cognitive impairment in Parkinson's disease. In A. Tröster (Ed.), *Clinical neuropsychology and cognitive neurology* of *Parkinson's disease and other movement disorders* (pp. 205–238). New York, NY: Oxford University Press.

Schrag, A., Hovris, A., Morley, D., Quinn, N., & Jahanshahi, M. (2006). Caregiver-burden in Parkinson's disease is closely associated with psychiatric symptoms, falls, and disability. *Parkinsonism & Related Disorders, 12*(1), 35–41.

Sproesser, E., Viana, M., Quagliato, E., & Pedroso de Souza, E. (2010). The effect of psychotherapy in patients with PD: A controlled study. *Parkinsonism and Related Disorders, 16,* 298–300.

Tickle-Degnen, L., Zebrowitz, L. A., & Ma, H.-i. (2011). Culture, gender and health care stigma: Practitioners' response to facial masking experienced by people with Parkinson's disease. *Social Science & Medicine, 73*(1), 95–102.

Todes, C. J., & Lees, A. J. (1985). The pre-morbid personality of patients with Parkinson's disease. *Journal of Neurology, Neurosurgery, and Psychiatry, 48*(2), 97–100.

Tröster, A., & Garrett, R. (2018). Parkinson's disease and other movement disorders. In J. E. Morgan & J. H. Ricker (Eds.), *Textbook of clinical neuropsychology* (2nd ed., pp. 507–559). New York, NY: Routledge.

Weintraub, D., & Goldman, J. G. (2015). Impulse control disorders, apathy, and psychosis. In A. Tröster (Ed.), *Clinical neuropsychology and cognitive neurology of Parkinson's disease and other movement disorders* (pp. 291–331). New York, NY: Oxford University Press.

Xie, C.-L., Wang, X.-D., Chen, J., Lin, H.-Z., Chen, Y.-H., Pan, J.-L., & Wang, W.-W. (2015). A systematic review and meta-analysis of cognitive behavioral and psychodynamic therapy for depression in Parkinson's disease patients. *Neurological Sciences, 36*(6), 833–843.

Yang, S., Sajatovic, M., & Walter, B. (2012). Psychosocial interventions for depression and anxiety in Parkinson's disease. *Journal of Geriatric Psychiatry and Neurology, 25*(2), 113–121.

15

PSYCHOLOGICAL CARE OF PERSONS WITH MULTIPLE SCLEROSIS

BACKGROUND INFORMATION

In addition to having adequate energy sources and the appropriate balance of neurotransmitter activity for neurons to function properly, neuronal "signals" require fast communication between large neural networks. Myelin is a substance (white in appearance) that surrounds the axons of nerve cells and facilitates rapid communication within the nervous system. The process of myelination is important to brain development and contributes to child behavioral development, particularly walking and crawling early in life (see Chapter 3, this volume). Myelination occurs at different rates and locations throughout development (Menkes, Sarnat, & Maria, 2006). Disruption of myelin, via axonal damage secondary to traumatic brain injury, is common (Bigler, 2011). It is often associated with neuropsychological impairments marked by slow and inefficient information processing. However, disruption of myelin sheaths in the brain can be caused by many factors, including multiple sclerosis (MS).

Multiple sclerosis is a chronic inflammatory autoimmune and neurodegenerative disease that affects the central nervous system (brain and spinal cord; Sospedra & Martin, 2005; Steenwijk et al., 2016). It can produce a wide range of deficits in sensory and motoric functions, autonomic functions, and neurocognitive functions (Sospedra & Martin, 2005). As a progressive demyelinating disease, focal white matter lesions are most commonly observed on neuroimaging studies. Progressively, neurons can be affected. There is clear evidence that gray matter involvement (i.e., neurons) is also an important feature of this disease (Dutta & Trapp, 2007; Steenwijk et al., 2016). Dutta and Trapp suggest that axonal loss is "clinically silent early because of the compensatory capacity of the CNS" (p. S24). However, prolonged axon degeneration in MS patients has been associated with ion imbalance, which impacts the energy resources of the brain. This may be a major contributing factor to the fatigue commonly reported in MS patients, particularly as the disease progresses.

Multiple sclerosis is characterized by episodes of focal disorder involving the optic nerve, spinal cord, and brain (Ropper & Samuels, 2009). There are various patterns or clinical manifestations of MS. The most common has been described as relapsing–remitting (RR-MS), which is estimated to occur in 85–90% of MS patients (Sospedra & Martin, 2005). Most of these patients go on to develop what has been described as secondary progressive MS. When this latter condition occurs first in the disease process, the MS patient is described as having primary progressive MS, and some investigators suggest this typically accounts for approximately 10% of MS patients (Dutta & Trapp, 2007). Confavreux and Vukusic (2006) propose, however, that MS is a single disease process with different clinical phenotypes.

Recent magnetic resonance imaging (MRI) studies of MS patients noted subtle gray matter damage in both the thalamus and the cortex of patients. Frontal and temporal lobe lesions were frequently observed when cortical involvement was present (Steenwijk et al., 2016).

Onset of multiple sclerosis often occurs between ages 20 and 40 years, and it can have profound personal and socioeconomic effects (Sospedra & Martin, 2005). During this time period, the individual often begins a family and embarks on a career. Cognitive and interpersonal skills are needed to maintain relationships and work. Unemployment figures for this group of individuals are relatively high (estimated between 56% and 58%; Julian, Vella, Vollmer, Hadjimichael, & Mohr, 2008). Unemployment has been associated with a number of factors, including problems of physical mobility, reduced hand function, fatigue, and poor cognitive functioning. Clinically, many of these patients experience marital problems as they find it increasingly more difficult to meet the responsibilities of work and marriage.

NEUROPSYCHOLOGICAL IMPAIRMENTS ASSOCIATED WITH MULTIPLE SCLEROSIS

Estimates of the frequency of cognitive dysfunction in persons with MS vary, but typically they are reported to be 40–50% (Rao, Leo, Bernardin, & Unverzagt, 1991; Thornton & DeFreitas, 2009). However, some studies report that up to 70% of MS patients may demonstrate cognitive impairments (Roy & Benedict, 2018).

What was recognized early in the neuropsychological study of persons with MS is the heterogeneity of cognitive deficits these patients demonstrate (Rao et al., 1991). The variability is often related to lesion location and lesion "load," although measures of overall brain atrophy have also been associated with overall severity of neuropsychological dysfunction (Benedict et al., 2004) and degree of long-term disability (Brex et al., 2002).

Most commonly, however, MS patients demonstrate disturbance in information processing speed as measured by various tests (DeLuca, Chelune, Tulsky, Lengenfelder, & Chiaravalloti, 2004). This, of course, is to be expected given the high prevalence of axonal damage (involving the myelinated sheaths) in this neurological disorder. Disturbances in other areas of neuropsychological functioning have also been observed. Memory, visual–spatial abilities, and a variety of "executive functions" involving planning and response inhibition can also be negatively affected (Thornton & DeFreitas, 2009). Roy and Benedict (2018) have emphasized the high incidence of episodic memory disturbances in this patient group. Again, lesion location as well as the relative amount of brain tissue directly or indirectly damaged often correlate with the diverse pattern of neuropsychological disturbances that can be seen in this patient group. Appreciating the diverse patterns of neuropsychological impairment is important when examining patients and providing diagnostic insights as to what they are experiencing.

PSYCHIATRIC DISTURBANCES ASSOCIATED WITH MULTIPLE SCLEROSIS

Psychiatric disturbances are common and equally diverse as cognitive changes observed in MS patients. Depression (Arnett, Cadden, Roman, & Guty, 2018) as well as anxiety disorders, bipolar affective disorder, euphoria, and pseudobulbar affect have been reported in MS patients (Feinstein & Pavisian, 2018). Only a brief review of the psychiatric characteristics is presented in light of the great diversity of clinical presentations.

Depression is frequently reported (Feinstein, 2011), with estimates typically in the 50% range or higher for patients with MS. Depression is often associated with (but most likely different from) fatigue in the MS population (Kinsinger, Lattie, & Mohr, 2010). In fact, some patients can appear joyful or even euphoric (Fishman, Benedict, Bakshi, Priore, & Weinstock-Guttman, 2004), whereas others are "indifferent" to their physical symptoms. Some can present with unawareness of their neurocognitive deficits, depending again on lesion location and the presence of bilateral cerebral atrophy (Prigatano, Hendin, & Heiserman, 2014). A few patients may even present with psychotic symptoms, including hallucinations and delusional thinking. For example, Diaz-Olavarrieta, Cummings, Velazquez, and Garcia de al Cadena (1999) reported in their prospective study of 44 patients with MS that 10% presented with hallucinations and 7% evidenced delusions. It should also be kept in mind that persons who develop MS have varied psychosocial backgrounds with equally varied premorbid levels of intelligence and personality characteristics. These realities further complicate not only diagnostic understanding of the patient's symptoms but also approaches to their psychological care.

Given that patients with MS can present with different neuropsychological profiles, can display comorbid psychiatric features, and come from different psychosocial backgrounds, a single case is not presented in this chapter. Rather, four brief case examples are described that attempt to illustrate the broad range of psychological care services that may be helpful.

Case Vignette 15.1

At age 17 years, an adolescent male was noted to have problems with walking and ill-defined sensory changes. His mother also began to notice a decline in his memory. Neurological workup described a slow, broad-based gait with instability. He had "coarse saccades on gaze bilaterally, mild dysmetria, and mild slurring." It was noted that he had sleep disturbance and appeared at times anxious. His mother noted he needed encouragement to exercise and to do his schoolwork. She believed that he might be depressed. He eventually was diagnosed as having RR-MS.

MRI of the brain at age 25 years revealed multiple regions of abnormal fluid-attenuated inversion recovery signal within the periventricular and deep white matter consistent with a history of a demyelinating process. Abnormal hyperintense lesions were noted bilaterally in the middle cerebellar peduncles, the left midbrain, the right frontal subcortical white matter, the right basal ganglia, and the left temporal periventricular white matter.

Neuropsychological examination findings revealed at that time a pleasant and cooperative patient but one who seemed to be somewhat childlike in his manner given his age. He recognized mild to moderate memory difficulties (on a self-report memory rating scale described in Chapter 10, he rated his difficulty a 5–6; his mother rated it a 7). He reported mild to moderate anxiety (self-rating of 6) but no depression (self-rating of 0). His mother rated his anxiety higher (rating of 8) but could not judge his level of depression. Both agreed that his level of fatigue was severe (patient rated it a 7; mother rated it a "10+").

On examination, he was severely impaired. On the BNI Screen for Higher Cerebral Functions (BNIS), his total score was 29/50 points, resulting in an age-adjusted T score of <1. He had no obvious language impairment, but he had subtle difficulties in auditory comprehension and spelling. He also had difficulty adding and subtracting numbers. He could only recall one of three words with distraction and was showing slight inability to copy a picture of a Greek cross with both his right and left hands, suggesting subtle visuospatial difficulties (Figure 15.1).

He had difficulty generating affect in his tone of voice and perceiving facial affect. He described a fearful/surprised face as "shocked."

On the Wechsler Adult Intelligence Scale–Third Edition (WAIS-III), he had a Verbal Comprehension Index Score of 78, a Perceptual Reasoning Index Score of 65, a Working Memory Index Score of 57, and a Processing Speed Index Score of 63. His Full Scale IQ was estimated to be 65. Prior to the development of his MS (in his teenage years), his intelligence level was considered in the average range because he was attending normal classes in a public school.

By age 29 years, his BNIS total score was 18/50 points (age-adjusted T score of <1), with a Full Scale IQ of 52. At this time, he could not draw a Greek cross with either hand. He continued to have difficulty generating affect in his voice, but now he described a fearful/surprised face by saying, "I don't know what to say." He had notable difficulties with auditory comprehension, naming, sentence repetition, and spelling. He was unable to do any mathematic problem-solving and appeared dyscalculic. He continued to be friendly and cooperative but clearly childlike in his manner given his age.

When asked to make subjective ratings about his cognitive and affective functioning, he would smile and simply say he was "okay." He now had considerable difficulty following what was being asked of him using this rating system.

The patient was not in any apparent distress by this time and was not asking for any help. He appeared content being with his mother during the day when she worked. His mother, in contrast, was in a great deal of distress and was seeking help to determine what more she could do to help her adult child and improve the quality of his life.

Detailed discussions of his neuropsychological findings were held whenever the patient was seen for a neuropsychological consultation. The patient's mother appeared in some ways relieved with the information but certainly saddened by it. She wanted her other children to talk with the clinical neuropsychologist about her son's neuropsychological status and encourage the young man's brothers to engage him in as many social activities as they could. Such a consultation took place, but the extent of the patient's neurocognitive difficulties made it clear that typical social interactions beyond the immediate family environment would be difficult for the patient. The brothers, who were very supportive of their mother and brother,

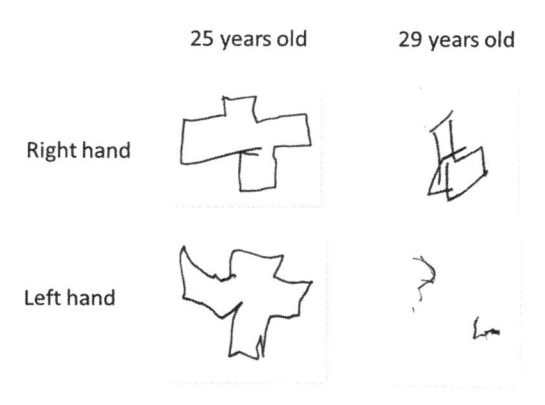

FIGURE 15.1 Attempted drawings of a Greek cross by a patient with multiple sclerosis over time (Case Vignette 1).

spontaneously gave examples of the patient avoiding social interactions because he could not follow what was happening in those social situations and often "did not know what to say."

This feedback helped the mother understand that simple, one-on-one social and recreational activity with the brothers was the most meaningful way to assist her son. She had a realistic sense of discouragement, but she continues to be vested in maintaining her son's independence with the necessary daily supports.

She brings the patient in for 6-month evaluations, during which she has time to talk about her son's status and also receives emotional support regarding how best to cope with her son's deteriorating condition. Each session not only provides educational information but also helps build her resiliency in coping with the daily demands she faces. She does not feel alone in helping her son. The therapeutic alliance with the patient's mother continues to be strengthened as a result of these consultations.

Case Vignette 15.2

A 39-year-old man was seen for a neuropsychological consultation and examination after being diagnosed with a history of RR-MS. He reported that his symptoms began approximately 10 years earlier with associated problems in fatigue and vision. He reported no ongoing problems with gait or balance. More recently, he was concerned about a possible decline in his memory. He was quick to add, however, "I never had a great memory." His wife believed that the decline in his memory started approximately 4 or 5 years prior to the examination.

On examination, he reported mild to moderate memory difficulties (using the self-report method, his score was a 4). His wife believed the memory difficulties were more substantial (she rated them an 8–9). He rated anxiety a 5 and depression a 3. Again, his wife viewed the problems as more substantial, rating them 7–8 and 10, respectively. Both concurred, however, that fatigue was very high (he rated it a 9; his wife rated it a 10).

On examination, his BNIS total score was 42/50 points, producing an age-adjusted T score of 27. He could recall only one of three words with distraction, but language functions were normal with no evidence of constructional dyspraxia or dyscalculia. He had mild difficulty generating affect in his tone of voice, but he could perceive facial affect with no difficulty on this screening test. On the WAIS-III, he had a Verbal IQ of 116, a Performance IQ of 98, and a Full Scale IQ of 108. Compatible with his educational background and professional work, his Vocabulary age-adjusted scale score of 13 and Matrix Reasoning score of 12 were above average for his age. On tests of speed of information processing, his scores were in the average range (Symbol Search = 9 and Coding = 9). His performance on tests of memory showed mild memory difficulties but no substantial problems. For example, on the Rey Auditory Verbal Learning Test (RAVLT), he learned 56 words over five trials (T score = 54) and remembered 9 words after a 20-minute delay (T score = 47). Given his Verbal IQ score of 116, this was interpreted as showing mild but "real" difficulties with memory. His subjective ratings of his memory difficulties were compatible with his self-reported memory but not with his wife's ratings.

Throughout the clinical interview and feedback session, his wife seemed especially critical of him. He had difficulty verbally "defending" himself when she was openly critical of how he functioned at home. One area of contention was her belief that he could take over the management of their children when he returned home from work despite his severe fatigue. Although he attempted to do so, he was often exhausted. He briefly sought out individual psychotherapy consultation, but because his wife opposed this form of treatment, he discontinued it.

This case vignette highlights the reality that attempts at psychological treatment of people with MS may only progress if important family members support such activities. If there is considerable marital distress, patients with MS may become overwhelmed with the demands of work and family life. They do not have the energy to "fight" for their psychological needs.

Case Vignette 15.3

A 38-year-old woman was referred for a neuropsychological examination because a recent MRI of her brain revealed abnormal cortical atrophy. She was described by her referring physician as showing "atypical multiple sclerosis." When asked to describe her daily functioning, she had a halting quality to her speech. She stated this was very embarrassing for her. She noted difficulties reading and comprehending what she read. She believed that her vocabulary had declined, and she had difficulty understanding what people were saying to her. She emphasized that she was anxious most of the time. She also was severely depressed. She reported that on many days, she would not leave the house. She found it very difficult to get out of bed most mornings because of her mood.

As the history unfolded, she reported a period of time in her life when she heavily consumed alcohol. According to her, this occurred after losing a child during childbirth because the attending doctor at the time did not come to the hospital as requested. She spontaneously noted that she "did not like doctors." Her subjective reports indicated moderate memory difficulties (self-reported memory difficulty was a 5–6) but substantial problems with anxiety and depression (ratings of 9 and 8, respectively). Fatigue was also rated as severe (rating of 9–10). There was no significant other to provide an impression of her functioning from another's point of view.

Her BNIS total score was 48/50 points, which was above average for her age (T score = 56). She had no difficulty generating affect in her tone of voice or perceiving facial affect. On the WAIS-IV, her Verbal Comprehension Index score was 100, Perceptual Reasoning Index score was 96, Working Memory Index score was 119, and Processing Speed Index Score was 92. Her Full Scale IQ was measured at 101. Memory scores were within the normal range and not disparate with verbal and nonverbal problem-solving skills. For example, on the RAVLT, she recalled 56 words ($T = 53$), and after a brief distraction she recalled 14 words ($T = 60$). The Halstead Finger Tapping test showed that she had very slow speeds in the right hand (mean score, 28.1 taps; $T = 27$), with mild slowing in the left hand (mean score, 38.2 taps; $T = 41$).

These findings led to a discussion of how to best help her. She agreed to seek out physical therapy to improve motor function and reduce fatigue. She also agreed to receive speech and language therapy to improve articulation and fluency in speech. In addition, she agreed to undergo occupational therapy to try to improve fine motor/finger control in the right hand. The possible connection between her halting speech and right-hand finger speed difficulties was explained, and she was appreciative of the explanation. Finally, she agreed to a trial of antidepressant medications and to undergo psychotherapy with a person familiar with the type of adjustment problems she had in her past as well as the physical and neuropsychological consequences of possible MS. She expressed appreciation for the consultation and stated that her dislike of doctors did not extend to the present neuropsychologist. Follow-up consultation will obviously be needed to determine if she benefited from this consultation.

Case Vignette 15.4

A 59-year-old medically retired engineer diagnosed with RR-MS was seen for a neuropsychological consultation because of complaints of memory difficulties. This occurred in 1972 when cognitive difficulties were often underestimated in patients diagnosed with RR-MS. The patient's medical history is not available at this time because he was seen more than 45 years ago. At the time he was seen, however, he had had MS for a number of years. He was walking with a cane and reported problems with fatigue, balance, and a decline in his memory capacity.

On the WAIS, his overall IQ was in the 120s. On the Wechsler Memory Scale, his Memory Quotient was 89. The findings were reviewed with his attending neurologist. The neurologist, who initially believed that the patient's memory complaints were secondary to depression, now accepted the psychometric test findings as documenting "true memory difficulties" in the patient. Because he thought that his doctors did not always believe he was "objective" in reporting cognitive symptoms, the patient was relieved by the findings and felt vindicated by the fact that there was now objective evidence of his memory difficulties.

Most interesting about this patient, however, were his responses to the Rorschach inkblot test (which at the time was occasionally included in neuropsychological examinations). Again, there are no longer detailed records regarding his responses on each card, but I have a clear memory of his response to card VIII. This is the so-called "mother card." He looked at it for a short time and then turned it face down and asked for the next card. He showed no emotion and had nothing to say about what this card look liked to him. The remainder of his responses did not seem to reflect anything unusual.

Because my neuropsychological consultation and examination findings "validated" his concerns about memory difficulties, he asked me to help him adjust to the MS. In addition to his cognitive concerns, he was getting progressively more unsteady in his gait and walked with a cane, as noted previously. He worried about having to use a wheelchair and wondered how he would die. He also did not know how to talk to his wife regarding his worries and consequently wanted to talk to me privately.

He stated that he had a good relationship with his wife, but he was always uncomfortable talking to women. He did not understand this reaction, but this had been occurring all of his adult life. During the course of several psychotherapy sessions, a good therapeutic alliance was established and many topics were discussed. Then, unexpectedly, during one session he asked me to again show him the Rorschach cards. He looked at each one until he found card VIII.

He now wanted to tell me about his previous reaction to this card. He remembered that when he was an adolescent, his mother dressed in a negligee when his father left the house. One day, she approached him dressed in the negligee and asked him to rub her back. He was both sexually excited and frightened at the same time. He uncomfortably rubbed her back but then excused himself as quickly as possible. He could now "connect the dots." His uncomfortableness with women was tied to this experience.

This insight also helped him understand his preoccupation with the play *Rigiletto*, in which a father is furious with his daughter for being sexually seduced by a young lover. He could now discuss these feelings with me and could do so later with his wife present in the psychotherapy sessions. He felt a sense of relief and appreciation. Although he first wanted to talk about his reaction to his illness, he ultimately wanted to talk about a long-standing psychological issue unrelated to his illness but equally important to him. It is not uncommon for patients who have an underlying brain disorder to begin talking about their reaction to their illness. If a psychotherapeutic dialogue evolves into a truly intimate, professional trusting relationship, then other important issues in the patient's life often emerge that require psychotherapy, as noted in Chapter 12. This was an important fact in this patient's psychological care. Unfortunately, the scientific literature does not always consider this reality when discussing resiliency, quality of life, and/or efficacy of psychological treatments. Table

15.1 summarizes the 20 clinically relevant features in this patient's care. Note that in addition to discussing his immediate concerns (i.e., he had an "objective memory problem"), he eventually wanted to discuss more important personal concerns as a result of the therapeutic relationship/dialogue. Responding to the Rorschach cards and later relating his personal difficulties with his previously unexplained preoccupation with the play *Rigiletto* were essential features of his psychological care.

Table 15.1 Clinical Features Relevant to the Psychological Care of a Person with Multiple Sclerosis (Case Vignette 15.4)

CLINICAL FEATURE	YES	NO	PARTIALLY
1. The dialogue between the patient and the clinical neuropsychologist was not rushed.	✓		
2. The patient was able to express or clearly convey his personal concerns.	✓		
3. The content of the concerns varied over time and reflected the patient's stage of decline.	✓		
4. The patient experienced a sense of "realistic" hope that he and his wife could better cope with their life's situation. The patient did not experience "being alone" with his problem(s).	✓		
5. The patient and the clinical neuropsychologist developed a positive therapeutic relationship in which the patient's dignity was maintained even in the face of significant physical and cognitive declines.	✓		
6. Somatic symptoms (which appeared to be indirect effects of a brain disorder) were substantially reduced during periods of psychological care.		✓	
7. Anxiety/depression/anger and/or apathy were substantially reduced during periods of psychological care.			✓
8. The patient was able to follow the guidance of the clinical neuropsychologist to improve functioning in everyday life activities.	✓		
9. The patient was able to control impulses and delay gratification.	✓		
10. The patient actively worked at developing "self-efficacy skills" in the face of his declining abilities.		✓	
11. The patient attempted to "self-reflect" or "be more aware" of personal "strengths" and "limitations."	✓		
12. The patient experienced enjoyment in the care or help of other living things (people, animals, the environment, etc.).			✓

(*continued*)

Table 15.1 Continued

CLINICAL FEATURE	YES	NO	PARTIALLY
13. The patient had an improved understanding of the "problematic nature of life" and was not overwhelmed or defeated by it or readily gave in to escapism to cope with life (Bettelheim, 1989).	✓		
14. The patient could "live with" the restrictions produced by a brain injury "without resentment" or loss of hope (Goldstein, 1952).	✓		
15. The patient was able to obtain new insights into self by attending to why certain songs, stories, fairy tales, movies, tattoos, etc. had a special personal meaning that he initially did not understand.	✓		
16. The patient's dreams or artwork often heralded changes in behavior that aided in psychological adjustment before the consciously mediated changes occurred.		✓	
17. The psychological care interventions (including the dialogue) between the patient and the clinical neuropsychologist resulted in the patient talking more openly about problems and demonstrating self-directed efforts at improving psychological adjustment to the direct and indirect effects of the brain disorder.	✓		
18. The psychological care interventions were in harmony with the patient's cultural background and religious orientation.	✓		
19. The psychological care interventions were appropriate for the patient's psychosocial stage of development and facilitated adaptation in the later stages of life (an ongoing process).			✓
20. The patient and family experienced two basic facts of life: (a) The individual's state of subjective sense of personal well-being fluctuates, and (b) the psychological adjustment process is never static and therefore hope should never be abandoned.	✓		
Total	14	3	3

RESILIENCY IN PATIENTS WITH MULTIPLE SCLEROSIS AND THEIR CAREGIVERS

Given the variability of neurological, neuropsychological, and psychosocial difficulties that MS patients and their caregiver face, are there specific variables that correlate with resiliency in this patient population? In a correlational study, Tan-Kristanto and Kiropoulos (2015) examined the statistical relationship between different measures of resiliency and different measures of self-efficacy, depression, anxiety, and coping styles. Expectedly, various measures of resilience correlated with measures of depression and anxiety. The less the depression and anxiety reported, the higher the self-reported resilience indices. The magnitude of the correlates ranged from .20 to .69, suggesting that resilience in this patient group could not be explained purely on the basis of these variables. As also expected, self-reported anxiety level in MS patients was correlated with a tendency to use denial as a method of coping and to rely on substance use to control anxiety. Behavioral disengagement from others was also related to anxiety level in the MS patients they studied.

Other investigators have empirically shown that levels of depression, optimism, and "benefit-finding" are interrelated in MS patients (Hart, Vella, & Mohr, 2008). Patients who are naturally more optimistic may be less depressed; conversely, less depressed patients may report (not unexpectedly) more positive affect and more optimistic views about themselves and life in general. Optimism has been related to more successful management of a number of chronic health care conditions (Schiavon, Marchetti, Gurgel, Busnello, & Reppold, 2016). It may therefore be an additional component to resiliency in MS patients.

Resiliency has been related to stable and supportive interpersonal relationships (see Chapter 12, this volume). Boland, Levack, Hudson, and Bell (2012) noted that divorce is twice as common in couples in which one partner has MS. In a phenomenological study, they reported several interesting findings. When the coping styles of the two individuals within a couple differ, conflict clearly emerges (again, as would be expected). However, when the couple agreed on shared responsibilities within the home, a more normalized lifestyle persisted and the couple "shared a sense of pride" (p. 4). This might be one measure of self-efficacy for a couple that is related to a "resilience" factor. That is, the experience of working together and having pride in one's accomplishments may well be an important component of resilience in MS patients and their partners.

The couple's sense of having their lives "intertwined" was also an important theme. The sense that they live life together helped them with the "ups and downs" of losses and emotional reactions to the disabilities caused by MS. Especially interesting in light of Case Vignette 15.4 was Boland et al.'s (2012) observation that some MS patients felt relief when their diagnosis was confirmed. Objective evidence that they were "not nutty" (p. 4) but, rather, had "true" impairments due to a medical condition validated their symptoms. Finally, learning more about themselves and life in light of their illness (i.e., benefit-finding) was also an emergent theme related to positive coping in these individuals.

Resiliency and lack of depression are not the same, but they do overlap. As such, it would be expected that both measures would relate to quality of life findings. Mitchell, Benito-León, González, and Rivera-Navarro (2005) reported that depression was the most significant predictor of low or poor quality of life in MS patients. They note that it impairs motivation and interest in staying physically active, which is important for possibly limiting the progression of the illness. They also note that depression can impact decision-making and produces a sense of impaired self-efficacy. By definition, self-efficacy reflects the beliefs people have about their ability to handle different situations (Hughes et al., 2015). As noted previously, low self-efficacy scores in MS patients correlate the highest with measures of depression. Thus, building resiliency in MS patients and their caregivers requires staying physically active, working together to solve problems, and finding adaptive ways of reducing depression and anxiety. Although this is certainly not a new "message," it may be especially relevant for MS patients in light of the fact that adaptive stress reduction activities have been shown to prevent the occurrence of new brain lesions in these patients (Mohr et al., 2012), as discussed more thoroughly later in this chapter.

It is also important to note that caregivers of individuals with MS have very specific stresses related to this illness. Because the illness often occurs relatively early in adult life, employment is adversely affected and therefore so is the economic status of the family. Financial worries are common and a source of distress. The unpredictableness of the disease course is also a factor that can erode resiliency in caregivers. Finally, MS patients who have impaired self-awareness for their cognitive limitations may impose a special burden on caregivers. Caregivers' life satisfaction and ability to cope with the family member who has MS with associated significant cognitive and affective disturbances are adversely affected (Waldron-Perrine, Rapport, Ryan, & Harper, 2009).

In some cases, the "unawareness" of cognitive deficits may seem like a "blessing," particularly if the patient is young. Younger patients with severe cognitive impairments appear content to be cared for by a parent (see Case Vignette 15.1). Adults who have moderate cognitive deficits and who are unaware place an especially difficult burden on their adult partner (Prigatano, 2014).

PLACEBO EFFECTS IN PATIENTS WITH MULTIPLE SCLEROSIS

Placebo effects have been reported in MS patients, as they have in those with other neurological or medical conditions. In a randomized controlled trial (RCT) on the efficacy of cannabinoids to reduce spasticity in MS patients, no objective evidence (using the Ashworth score of spasticity) of improved spasticity was observed compared to placebo treatments (Zajicek et al., 2003). However, 53% of patients treated with cannabis self-reported improvement in spasticity, and 37% of placebo-treated patients also reported improvement in spasticity. Both groups reported less fatigue and less depression, with no difference in the percentages of the two groups reporting benefits.

Although fatigue can be modestly improved in MS patients with modafinil (Provigil), placebo effects are also noted (Rammohan et al., 2002). The relationship between depression and fatigue has long been recognized in the study of patients with MS. Treatment of depression appears to result in improved mood, which leads to reporting less symptoms of fatigue in MS patients (Mohr, Hart, & Goldberg, 2003).

Sertraline (Zoloft) has been studied extensively for the treatment of depression in multiple clinical conditions. In a relatively early comparison study, Mohr, Boudewyn, Goodkin, Bostrom, and Epstein (2001) compared the effectiveness of sertraline versus cognitive–behavioral therapy (CBT) and supportive–expressive group psychotherapy in treating depression. They reported that all three treatments reduced depression in patients with MS, with CBT and sertraline having the greatest effects. Unfortunately, there was no control group to assess possible placebo effects. Interestingly, at 6-month follow-up there was no difference in self-reported depression on the Beck Depression Inventory (BDI) between the three treatment groups. No study could be identified that specifically assessed the effects of sertraline versus placebo on treating depression in patients with MS. However, a study comparing sertraline and placebo in patients with post-traumatic stress disorder reported a familiar finding seen in many such drug studies (Davidson, Rothbaum, van der Kolk, Sikes, & Farfel, 2001): 60% of patients demonstrated a positive treatment response with the drug versus 38% of placebo-treated patients also reporting a positive response.

Are placebo effects observed in various forms of psychological treatment for affective disturbances in MS patients? In a recent systematic review of various treatments for depression and anxiety in persons with MS, Fiest et al. (2016) report a very interesting trend. Although their findings are based on just a few published studies, they note that placebo effects for psychological and pharmacological treatments are typically seen when there is an "active comparator" versus an "inactive comparator." That is, if a treatment is compared to a wait-list control group (e.g., no attempt to actively engage the patient in some type of treatment that could potentially foster hope or an ongoing relationship with a treating clinician), then placebo effects are not observed. When

APPROACHES TO PSYCHOLOGICAL CARE OF PATIENTS WITH MULTIPLE SCLEROSIS

Table 15.2 summarizes a wide range of approaches to the psychological care of persons with MS. Again, these studies are not all-inclusive, but they provide a representative sample of the different treatment approaches that have been attempted in light of the diverse symptoms for this patient group. Before reviewing the findings, however, two points need to be made explicit. First, the treatment of depression in this patient group has been the major target of psychological interventions/care. Because RCTs are currently considered the most effective way of determining "true treatment effects," the length of treatments is typically relatively short (often not exceeding 16 weeks of psychological care). This relatively "brief" form of psychological intervention is often used to reveal treatment effects, but again, it does not provide a treating clinician with details necessary to really understand the intermediate- and long-term effects of such interventions. Second, as Fiest et al. (2016) eloquently and systematically note, changes in self-reported measures of depression on brief rating scales (e.g., the BDI) do not reveal the magnitude of change and its clinical relevance to individual patients. In light of these important observations, four basic types of psychological interventions have been reported in the literature: CBT, group therapy with a focus on affect expression and obtaining social support from others, mindfulness training, and stress and mood management techniques that often combine several sources of behavioral (and psychotherapeutic) interventions.

Crawford and McIvor (1985) provided a brief report on the effectiveness of a group psychotherapy intervention for reducing emotional distress, particularly depression, in patients with MS. The psychotherapy sessions were held twice weekly for 1 hour per session, extending over a 6-month period. Patients treated with psychotherapy were compared to MS patients involved in reviewing current events (i.e., providing some social interaction and possible support) versus a no treatment condition. Depression was significantly lower in the psychotherapy group compared to the other two conditions, but details regarding effect sizes and long-term outcomes were not available. It is important to note that this approach advocated an insight-oriented form of psychotherapy that encouraged verbalization and confrontation of conflicts in the person's life.

Mohr, Goodkin, Islar, Hauser, and Genain (2001) limited the number of supportive–expressive group (SEG) psychotherapy sessions to 16 weekly sessions and compared the effectiveness of this approach to reducing depression to that of a CBT approach. A third treatment condition was also compared. This group received an antidepressant medication (i.e., sertraline). There was no difference between the CBT and drug treatment groups, but both groups reported less depression on the BDI compared to the SEG-treated condition. As noted previously, however, there was no difference in self-reported depression between the three groups at 6-month follow-up.

Grossman et al. (2010) compared the effectiveness of mindfulness-based training (MBT) on reducing depression and improving quality of life in patients with MS. Utilizing an RCT study design, they randomized MS patients to this form of treatment versus "usual care"—meaning no specific active (or placebo) intervention. Those receiving MBT reported less depression and improved quality of life compared to the usual care, non-intervention group. Effect sizes were greater during the post-intervention assessment period and reduced at the 6-month follow-up period, but significant differences remained. Effect size (ES) varied across different measures, but one measure of

Table 15.2 Review of Selected Individual Studies and Meta-Analyses Relevant to the Psychological Care of Persons with Multiple Sclerosis

INTERVENTION	STUDY SAMPLE	MAJOR FINDINGS	CONCLUSIONS
Insight-oriented group psychotherapy to reduce depression and anxiety in MS patients (Crawford & McIvor, 1985)	32 MS patients considered to have mild to moderate cognitive deficits were randomly assigned to one of three groups: traditional psychotherapy vs. current events group vs. a control, nontreatment group. 50 therapy sessions during the course of 6 months, with twice-weekly, 1-hour sessions.	Depression (as measured by the MMPI) was reduced significantly more in the psychotherapy group compared to the two other conditions. No change in self-reported anxiety was seen across groups.	Insight-oriented group psychotherapy may help reduce depression in MS patients, but the magnitude of the effect is unclear. Anxiety was not reduced by such treatments. The length of therapy appeared adequate for the treatment modality being studied, but it was longer than is currently employed by other treatment approaches.
CBT was compared to SEG psychotherapy and sertraline to reduce depression in MS patients (Mohr et al., 2001)	63 patients with MS and major depressive disorder were randomly assigned to one of three treatment conditions as noted previously. All treatments were limited to 16 weekly sessions. CBT was based on a manualized model for use with older adults. SEG therapy attempted to facilitate emotional expressions and interpersonal group interactions regarding feelings and personal reactions to the illness. Sertraline, which is a serotonin-specific reuptake inhibitor, was initiated at 50 mg/day. Side effects were regularly monitored by a psychologist. Dosage was increased to facilitate optimal dosing.	11 patients dropped out of treatments, leaving 52 completers. There was no difference in dropout percentages across treatment conditions. BDI ratings at the end of treatments were related to pretreatment ratings and varied across groups. SEG therapy was "significantly less effective in reducing BDI scores than CBT . . . and sertraline" (p. 946). However, there was no significant treatment difference on the BDI at 6-month follow-up.	CBT and sertraline treatments reduced self-reported depression on the BDI more than did the SEG condition. However, CBT was a one-on-one treatment, and the sertraline treatment included one-on-one monitoring of depression. The SEG treatment was a group experience that was shorter in duration than is typical. The immediate benefits of the first two treatment conditions were clear, but these were not present at follow-up. BDI scores appeared to show a slight increase in all three conditions after treatment stopped and a follow-up evaluation was conducted. The findings raised the possibility that ongoing treatment for depression may be necessary to substantially reduce self-reported symptoms of depression.

MBI was compared to a no training or "usual care" (UC) condition for improving quality of life in MS patients (Grossman et al., 2010).	150 MS patients were randomly assigned to the intervention (*n* = 76) vs. UC (*n* = 74). Intervention attrition rate was low (5%). MBI consisted of 8 weekly, 2½-hour classes to reduce stress and develop skills/body postures to facilitate "moment-to-moment" nonjudgment awareness of the self and the environment. Activities included dynamic yoga postures.	Several findings were reported, but noteworthy was the observation that fatigue and mood improved at the end of treatment and persisted at 6-month follow-up. Effect size (ES) was substantial at the end of the intervention on a measure of quality of life used in chronic conditions (ES = .86) but reduced to a moderate level at 6-month follow-up (ES = .51).	MS patients appear to benefit from MBI, and this was noted irrespective of the patients' neuropsychological status. Importantly, the amount of practice of MBI between therapy sessions (i.e., homework activities) was related to improvements in self-reported quality of life and on measures of depression and fatigue. The absence of "active control" experiences or exercises precluded assessing potential placebo effects.
SMT-MS for potentially reducing new gadolinium-enhancing (Gd+) lesions in MS patients was compared to a wait-list control condition (Mohr et al., 2012).	121 RR-MS patients were randomly assigned to a SMT-MS treatment or a wait-list control condition in a multisite study. 16 (50-minute) individual SMT-MS sessions were provided during a 24-week period. SMT-MS was based on a manualized stress management therapy program, but it is important to note that it attends to the individual needs/perceptions of patients and monitors and resolves issues associated with the therapeutic alliance or the "collaborative relationship" between the patient and the therapist, as noted in the manual (Mohr, 2010). Seven PhD-level licensed psychologists and one very experienced social worker familiar with CBT served as therapists.	60 MS patients received SMT-MS therapy, with 50 patients completing the training (83.3% compliance). These patients had significantly fewer new enhancing Gd+ lesions compared to the wait-list control patients during the time of treatment. 76.8% of MS patients were free of any new lesions during treatment compared to 54.7% of controls. These effects were not maintained after the therapy ended. Finally, it is important to note that during the time of treatment, the STM-MS group also reported a significantly greater reduction in stress levels from baseline to post-treatment.	This appears to be the first study to show that SMT-MS treatment may influence the number of new lesions occurring during the course of the illness. It is important to note that the effect was only seen during the course of treatment; it ended when treatment ended. This is another example of the potential importance of continuing such psychological care activities to obtain maximum benefit for patients. Having experienced therapists conduct this form of treatment may be vital to its success.

(continued)

Table 15.2 Continued

INTERVENTION	STUDY SAMPLE	MAJOR FINDINGS	CONCLUSIONS
Systematic review and meta-analysis of psychological and pharmacological interventions for depression and anxiety in persons with MS (Fiest et al., 2016).	Reviewed in detail 24 studies that systematically evaluated different psychological and pharmacological interventions for depression or anxiety in persons with MS. Described the nature of the intervention, who provided the intervention, and the methods used to evaluate the effectiveness of the intervention. Psychological interventions included CBT, acceptance and commitment therapy, and telephone-delivered physical activity counseling (with motivational interviewing).	Several important findings were reported. Psychological treatments for major depression appear to be effective, with varying treatment effect sizes. On average, the treatment effect sizes were considered "moderate." Treatment effects were most clearly demonstrated when there was an "inactive comparator" vs. an "active comparator" control group. Pharmacotherapy studies reviewed used medications not commonly prescribed for the treatment of depression. Treatment effects were modest, if any. Anxiety did not seem to improve with the therapies they studied.	Psychological interventions are helpful, but the degree to which they are clinically helpful is not always obvious from the empirical findings reported. These reviewers make the very important point that self-reported symptoms on different questionnaires, such as the BDI, do not provide adequate information as to the magnitude of change and the clinical significance in individual patient's lives. The need for an "active control" group in assessing the effectiveness of psychological interventions for reducing depression in patients with MS is clearly needed.
Systematic review and meta-analysis of the effects of yoga on symptom reduction and improvement in quality of life for persons with MS (Cramer et al, 2014).	Nine articles involving seven RCTs assessing the effects of yoga in 670 patients were reviewed in-depth.	Short-term positive effects on self-reported fatigue and mood were observed when comparing the relative effects of yoga vs. UC (or an inactive comparator). When the effects of yoga are compared to the effects of exercises programs, more variable findings are reported. Often, the effects appear similar.	There are two important implications from this and the previous review. Positive effects in improving mood and fatigue are seen when the patients are involved in some active program of care vs. remaining inactive. However, it is difficult to determine if this is related to a specific effect of the treatment or a placebo effect. Second, effects are only maintained if the activity is maintained.

BDI, Beck Depression Inventory; CBT, cognitive–behavioral therapy; MBI, mindfulness-based intervention; MMPI, Minnesota Multiphasic Personality Inventory; MS, multiple sclerosis; RCT, randomized controlled trial; RR, relapsing–remitting; SEG, supportive–expressive group therapy; SMT-MS, stress management therapy for MS patients.

depression reflected an ES of .36 at follow-up. Quality of life measurement revealed an ES of .51 at follow-up. The approach clearly seemed promising.

The most exciting interventional study to date was reported by Mohr et al. (2012) on the effectiveness of a stress and mood management (SMT) program for helping MS patients. Before reviewing those findings, it is important to understand the treatment approach and activities associated with this form of care. Mohr (2010) describes in very useful detail what is involved. He emphasizes several important features, including careful screening of each patient and understanding the complexity and severity of their MS-related difficulties. He describes the need to foster realistic hope and a collaborative relationship (this traditionally has been called a therapeutic alliance) and to understand the patient's personal experiences of their problems and how they experience the various therapy sessions. Active resolution of negative experiences during the therapy sessions becomes the focus of further discussions and interventions. These are essential features of psychotherapy emphasized by many different theorists and practitioners. He also describes cognitive–behavioral analyses of the different problems the patient faces and the need to engage the patient in homework activities that reinforce what is learned during any given treatment session. He emphasizes again that it is the practice of the activities outside of the treatment hour that often determines the success of the interventions. This is also a common feature of various successful psychotherapeutic endeavors. Does the patient think about and practice what they have discussed or learned during a previous psychotherapy session? If the answer is yes, progress is more likely.

Clearly, one of the major advantages of this approach is the use of a "workbook" in which the patient and the therapist track how well homework assignments were or were not successfully completed. Reducing the barriers that interfere with the application of a learned strategy is an ongoing process and also predictive of the success of this approach. Mohr (2010) emphasizes that although the course of treatment is typically 16 sessions (2 devoted to assessment and introducing the patient to the type of treatment that will follow and 14 actual therapy sessions), the number of sessions can be expanded as needed for a given patient.

In an RCT, Mohr et al. (2012) demonstrated that such training was associated with preventing new brain lesions from occurring in the treated MS patients. The findings are astounding, and they are depicted in Figure 15.2. This effect occurred while the patients were actively engaged in such training activities. The effects were not maintained after training terminated. The "take-home message" was that to maintain these benefits, daily engagement in SMT activities may be necessary.

In the previously mentioned review and meta-analysis of the treatment of depression in MS patients, Fiest et al. (2016) conclude that psychological treatments for major depression

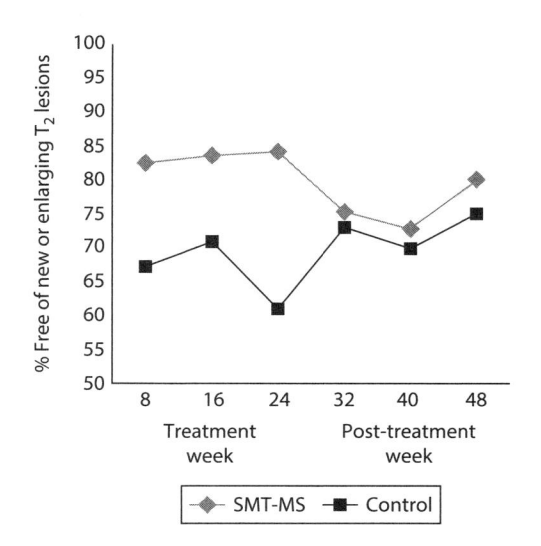

FIGURE 15.2   Percentage of participants free of new or enlarged T2 lesions at each time point by treatment group (See color plates).

Source: Reprinted from Mohr, D. C., Lovera, J., Brown, T., Cohen, B., Neylan, T., Henry, R., . . . Pelletier, D., A randomized trial of stress management for the prevention of new brain lesions in MS, *Neurology*, 79(5), 2012, p. 412–419, by permission of Wolters Kluwer Health, Inc. www.neurology.org.

in MS patients are indeed effective. The effect sizes are considered to be between mild and moderate. They also note that selective serotonin reuptake inhibitors and tricyclic antidepressants are also effective treatments. They emphasize that pharmacological treatment for depression can also substantially improve symptoms of fatigue.

WELLNESS AND MULTIPLE SCLEROSIS

It is interesting to note that recent research on psychological well-being in MS patients has emphasized the importance of approaching the topic of "wellness" from different and multiple perspectives (Motl et al., 2017). Promoting wellness in MS certainly should include attempts at improving psychological well-being by reducing depression and anxiety. However, to be maximally effective, changes in lifestyle may be especially important because they further enhance resiliency. These changes include efforts to establish a healthy diet and make exercise programs (including yoga) a part of everyday life. Such activities/exercise programs not only improve aerobic capacity but also can reduce symptoms of fatigue and depression (Motl et al., 2017). They may also have a positive impact on some aspects of cognitive functioning, but a recent extensive review of the literature on this topic notes the multiple methodological problems in interpreting this literature (Sandroff & Motl, 2018). However, given that food choices and dietary activities impact the course of multiple health problems (see Chapter 12, this volume), these are now considered important in the care of MS patients.

SUGGESTIONS REGARDING THE PSYCHOLOGICAL CARE FOR PERSONS WITH MULTIPLE SCLEROSIS

Multiple sclerosis is a neurodegenerative disease affecting a relatively young population and for which no cure exists. The primary approach of psychological care is often focused on symptom reduction (i.e., reducing depression, anxiety, fatigue, etc.). As described in this chapter, multiple methods can be used. However, available studies often do not provide detailed information regarding how to help different patients with different disease-related difficulties and with different premorbid personality characteristics living in different psychosocial situations. The four case vignettes in this chapter highlight a small subsample of the patients encountered and the great variability of their neuropsychological disturbances. It is crucial for patients to remain active in their efforts to reduce depression, anxiety, and fatigue. Inactivity or an indifferent attitude to trying to *daily* improve emotional and physical functioning may result in a worsening of symptoms over time, with perhaps worsening of the underlying disease process (Mohr et al., 2012). Understanding who patients were before the diagnosis of MS and communicating with them in a manner that is sensitive to their unique personalities and neuropsychological status may improve the likelihood of establishing an effective therapeutic alliance that aids the patients in their daily struggles.

The initial neuropsychological consultation, if it is to be clinically meaningful to the patient and family, should lead to a discussion of how to foster resiliency in the patient and relevant family members. Case Vignette 15.1 revealed that the patient was too cognitively impaired to appreciate what needed to be done. His mother, on the other hand, benefited greatly from the consultation and was able to help other family members engage the patient in activities from which he could benefit. Realistic expectations were set in place.

Case Vignette 15.2 highlights that the psychosocial situation of the patient can help or interfere with proper symptom management and reduction. When a spouse, for whatever reason, does not understand and accept the need of an MS patient to avoid excessive fatigue, for example, the outcome is not positive.

Working with the spouses of MS patients is an area not adequately addressed in the psychological intervention/care literature, but it has emerged as an extremely important area of clinical intervention.

Case Vignette 15.3 also emphasizes a major point: coexisting psychiatric difficulties in MS patients have to be recognized and greater efforts are needed to substantially help this group of patients. Problems of addition and/or severe premorbid depression require aggressive interventions above and beyond the typical CBT methods often prescribed in the scientific literature. These patients require more time and resources from treating clinicians.

Although the first efforts of psychological care for persons with MS understandably focus on symptom reduction, Case Vignette 15.4 illustrates that more is needed for some patients. When a patient with a degenerative brain disorder has established a trusting, professional relationship with a clinical neuropsychologist who understands their neurocognitive impairments, there can be a natural desire to talk about "other problems" the patient has struggled with all their life. It is extremely important to be open to these discussions and to provide a forum for the patient to now work on other problems that are not directly related to MS but may become important to discuss in light of their illness. This may be a benefit-finding experience for the patient. Faced with the disabilities and impairments of this disease, patients may want help resolving psychological problems they may have never thought to discuss with a psychologist until the disease brought them into a (clinical neuro) psychologist's office.

SUMMARY

The psychological care of persons with MS perhaps most clearly demonstrates the central thesis of this book. Knowledge about human beings and their nature (which includes understanding the psychological need for hope and the experiencing of a satisfactory bonding relationship with caregivers early and later in life) is often the beginning point for providing psychological care. Understanding where the person is in their life cycle (e.g., young adulthood with the desire to be productive and have a committed relationship and satisfying family life) helps clarify major existential crises the person is most likely facing. Understanding the patient's neurocognitive impairments, which frequently include inefficiency in the learning and memory processes, helps the clinician provide medically necessary and clinically relevant information in response to patient questions regarding diagnosis and patient care/management. If the patient can understand their cognitive strengths and limitations, there is often a sense of being understood and not "alone with the problem." The patient's emotional reactions to their illness (e.g., depression and anxiety) and their spouse's reactions have to be understood in terms of the couple's life history and personality strengths and weaknesses. Bolstering resiliency in both individuals may be very important in the psychological care venture. Finally, understanding the patient's physical limitations (sensory and motor impairments, fatigue, sleep disturbance, etc.) also aids the decision regarding what forms of psychological care should be attempted (supportive and psychodynamic insight work, CBT, mindfulness training, etc.).

This process is obviously highly individualized depending on the person, their psychosocial situation, their medical status, their neuropsychological status and their specific personal needs at the time they are seen by a clinical neuropsychologist who attempts to provide psychological care.

REFERENCES

Arnett, P. A., Cadden, M., Roman, C., & Guty, E. (2018). Cognition and depression in multiple sclerosis. In J. DeLuca & B. M. Sandroff (Eds.), *Cognition and behavior in multiple sclerosis* (pp. 89–111). Washington, DC: American Psychological Association.

Benedict, R. H., Weinstock-Guttman, B., Fishman, I., Sharma, J., Tjoa, C. W., & Bakshi, R. (2004).

Prediction of neuropsychological impairment in multiple sclerosis: Comparison of conventional magnetic resonance imaging measures of atrophy and lesion burden. *Archives of Neurology, 61*(2), 226–230.

Bigler, E. D. (2011). Structural imaging. In J. M. Silver, T. W. McAllister, & S. C. Yudofsky (Eds.), *Textbook of traumatic brain injury* (2nd ed.). Washington, DC: American Psychiatric Publishing.

Boland, P., Levack, W. M., Hudson, S., & Bell, E. M. (2012). Coping with multiple sclerosis as a couple: "Peaks and troughs"—An interpretative phenomenological exploration. *Disability and Rehabilitation, 34*(16), 1367–1375.

Brex, P. A., Ciccarelli, O., O'Riordan, J. I., Sailer, M., Thompson, A. J., & Miller, D. H. (2002). A longitudinal study of abnormalities on MRI and disability from multiple sclerosis. *New England Journal of Medicine, 346*(3), 158–164.

Confavreux, C., & Vukusic, S. (2006). Natural history of multiple sclerosis: A unifying concept. *Brain, 129*(3), 606–616.

Cramer, H., Lauche, R., Azizi, H., Dobas, G., & Langhorst, J. (2014). Yoga for Multiple Sclerosis: A Systematic Review and Meta-Analysis. *Plos One, 9*(11), e112414. doi:10.1371/journal.pone.0112414

Crawford, J. D., & McIvor, G. P. (1985). Group psychotherapy: Benefits in multiple sclerosis. *Archives of Physical Medicine and Rehabilitation, 66*(12), 810–813.

Davidson, J. R., Rothbaum, B. O., van der Kolk, B. A., Sikes, C. R., & Farfel, G. M. (2001). Multicenter, double-blind comparison of sertraline and placebo in the treatment of posttraumatic stress disorder. *Archives of General Psychiatry, 58*(5), 485–492.

DeLuca, J., Chelune, G. J., Tulsky, D. S., Lengenfelder, J., & Chiaravalloti, N. D. (2004). Is speed of processing or working memory the primary information processing deficit in multiple sclerosis? *Journal of Clinical and Experimental Neuropsychology, 26*(4), 550–562.

Diaz-Olavarrieta, C., Cummings, J. L., Velazquez, J., & Garcia de al Cadena, C. (1999). Neuropsychiatric manifestations of multiple sclerosis. *Journal of Neuropsychiatry and Clinical Neurosciences, 11*(1), 51–57.

Dutta, R., & Trapp, B. D. (2007). Pathogenesis of axonal and neuronal damage in multiple sclerosis. *Neurology, 68*(22 Suppl. 3), S22–S31.

Feinstein, A. (2011). Multiple sclerosis and depression. *Multiple Sclerosis Journal, 17*(11), 1276–1281.

Feinstein, A., & Pavisian, B. (2018). Cognition and neuropsychiatric disorders in multiple sclerosis. In J. DeLuca & B. M. Sandroff (Eds.), *Cognition and behavior in multiple sclerosis* (pp. 113–126). Washington, DC: American Psychological Association.

Fiest, K., Walker, J., Bernstein, C., Graff, L., Zarychanski, R., Abou-Setta, A., . . . Marriott, J. (2016). Systematic review and meta-analysis of interventions for depression and anxiety in persons with multiple sclerosis. *Multiple Sclerosis and Related Disorders, 5,* 12–26.

Fishman, I., Benedict, R. H., Bakshi, R., Priore, R., & Weinstock-Guttman, B. (2004). Construct validity and frequency of euphoria sclerotica in multiple sclerosis. *Journal of Neuropsychiatry and Clinical Neurosciences, 16*(3), 350–356.

Grossman, P., Kappos, L., Gensicke, H., D'Souza, M., Mohr, D. C., Penner, I. K., & Steiner, C. (2010). MS quality of life, depression, and fatigue improve after mindfulness training: A randomized trial. *Neurology, 75*(13), 1141–1149.

Hart, S. L., Vella, L., & Mohr, D. C. (2008). Relationships among depressive symptoms, benefit-finding, optimism, and positive affect in multiple sclerosis patients after psychotherapy for depression. *Health Psychology, 27*(2), 230.

Hughes, A. J., Beier, M., Hartoonian, N., Turner, A. P., Amtmann, D., & Ehde, D. M. (2015). Self-efficacy as a longitudinal predictor of perceived cognitive impairment in individuals with multiple sclerosis. *Archives of Physical Medicine and Rehabilitation, 96*(5), 913–919.

Julian, L. J., Vella, L., Vollmer, T., Hadjimichael, O., & Mohr, D. C. (2008). Employment in multiple sclerosis. *Journal of Neurology, 255*(9), 1354–1360.

Kinsinger, S. W., Lattie, E., & Mohr, D. C. (2010). Relationship between depression, fatigue, subjective cognitive impairment, and objective neuropsychological functioning in patients with multiple sclerosis. *Neuropsychology, 24*(5), 573.

Menkes, J., Sarnat, H., & Maria, B. (2006). *Child neurology* (7th ed.). Philadelphia, PA: Lippincott Williams & Wilkins.

Mitchell, A. J., Benito-León, J., González, J.-M. M., & Rivera-Navarro, J. (2005). Quality of life and its assessment in multiple sclerosis: Integrating physical and psychological components of wellbeing. *Lancet Neurology, 4*(9), 556–566.

Mohr, D. C. (2010). *The stress and mood management program for individuals with multiple sclerosis.* New York, NY: Oxford University Press.

Mohr, D. C., Boudewyn, A. C., Goodkin, D. E., Bostrom, A., & Epstein, L. (2001). Comparative outcomes for individual cognitive–behavior therapy, supportive–expressive group psychotherapy, and sertraline for the treatment of depression in multiple sclerosis. *Journal of Consulting and Clinical Psychology, 69*(6), 942.

Mohr, D. C., Goodkin, D. E., Islar, J., Hauser, S. L., & Genain, C. P. (2001). Treatment of depression is associated with suppression of nonspecific and antigen-specific TH1 responses in multiple sclerosis. *Archives of Neurology, 58*(7), 1081–1086.

Mohr, D. C., Hart, S. L., & Goldberg, A. (2003). Effects of treatment for depression on fatigue in multiple sclerosis. *Psychosomatic Medicine, 65*(4), 542–547.

Mohr, D. C., Lovera, J., Brown, T., Cohen, B., Neylan, T., Henry, R., . . . Pelletier, D. (2012). A randomized trial of stress management for the prevention of new brain lesions in MS. *Neurology, 79*(5), 412–419.

Motl, R. W., Mowry, E. M., Ehde, D. M., LaRocca, N. G., Smith, K. E., Costello, K., . . . Giesser, B. (2017). Wellness and multiple sclerosis: The National MS Society establishes a Wellness Research Working Group and research priorities. *Multiple Sclerosis Journal, 24*(3), 262–267.

Prigatano, G. P. (2014). Anosognosia and patterns of impaired self-awareness observed in clinical practice. *Cortex, 61,* 81–92.

Prigatano, G. P., Hendin, B. A., & Heiserman, J. E. (2014). Denial or unawareness of cognitive deficit associated with multiple sclerosis? A case report. *Journal of Clinical and Experimental Neuropsychology, 36*(4), 335–341.

Rammohan, K. W., Rosenberg, J., Lynn, D., Blumenfeld, A., Pollak, C., & Nagaraja, H. (2002). Efficacy and safety of modafinil (Provigil) for the treatment of fatigue in multiple sclerosis: A two centre phase 2 study. *Journal of Neurology, Neurosurgery, and Psychiatry, 72*(2), 179–183.

Rao, S. M., Leo, G. J., Bernardin, L., & Unverzagt, F. (1991). Cognitive dysfunction in multiple sclerosis: I. Frequency, patterns, and prediction. *Neurology, 41*(5), 685–691.

Ropper, A., & Samuels, M. (2009). *Adams and Victor's principles of neurology* (9th ed.). New York, NY: McGraw-Hill.

Roy, S., & Benedict, R. H. (2018). Assessment of cognitive impairment in multiple sclerosis. In J. DeLuca & B. M. Sandroff (Eds.), *Cognition and behavior in multiple sclerosis* (pp. 7–31). Washington, DC: American Psychological Association.

Sandroff, B. M., & Motl, R. W. (2018). Exercise, physical activity, physical fitness, and cognition in multiple sclerosis. In J. DeLuca & B. M. Sandroff (Eds.), *Cognition and behavior in multiple sclerosis* (pp. 293–319). Washington, DC: American Psychological Association.

Schiavon, C. C., Marchetti, E., Gurgel, L. G., Busnello, F. M., & Reppold, C. T. (2016). Optimism and hope in chronic disease: A systematic review. *Frontiers in Psychology, 7,* 2022.

Sospedra, M., & Martin, R. (2005). Immunology of multiple sclerosis. *Annual Review of Immunology, 23,* 683–747.

Steenwijk, M. D., Vrenken, H., Jonkman, L. E., Daams, M., Geurts, J. J., Barkhof, F., & Pouwels, P. J. (2016). High-resolution T1-relaxation time mapping displays subtle, clinically relevant, gray matter damage in long-standing multiple sclerosis. *Multiple Sclerosis Journal, 22*(10), 1279–1288.

Tan-Kristanto, S., & Kiropoulos, L. A. (2015). Resilience, self-efficacy, coping styles and depressive and anxiety symptoms in those newly diagnosed with multiple sclerosis. *Psychology, Health & Medicine, 20*(6), 635–645.

Thornton, A. E., & DeFreitas, V. G. (2009). The neuropsychology of multiple sclerosis. In I. Grant & K. M. Adams (Eds.), *Neuropsychological assessment of neuropsychiatric and neuromedical disorders* (pp. 280–305). New York, NY: Oxford University Press.

Waldron-Perrine, B., Rapport, L. J., Ryan, K. A., & Harper, K. T. (2009). Predictors of life satisfaction among caregivers of individuals with multiple sclerosis. *The Clinical Neuropsychologist, 23*(3), 462–478.

Zajicek, J., Fox, P., Sanders, H., Wright, D., Vickery, J., Nunn, A., Thompson, A.; UK MS Research Group. (2003). Cannabinoids for treatment of spasticity and other symptoms related to multiple sclerosis (CAMS study): Multicentre randomised placebo-controlled trial. *Lancet, 362*(9395), 1517–1526.

16

PSYCHOLOGICAL CARE OF PERSONS WITH A PRIMARY MALIGNANT BRAIN TUMOR

BACKGROUND INFORMATION

With the application of functional and structural brain imaging techniques coupled with mathematic modeling such as graph theory, the intercorrelations of various regions of the brain underlying complex neuropsychological functions (Warren et al., 2014; see also Chapters 7 and 11, this volume) have become clearer. These interneural connections are highly complex and require a constant energy supply for their effective communication. The cellular basis for that energy supply relies on intact neurons and glial cells (Laughlin & Sejnowski, 2003).

Although neurons have traditionally been considered "the basic units of signaling in the nervous system" (Blumenfeld, 2010, p. 17) and therefore are very important for learning and problem-solving, the role of glial cells in maintaining the integrity of all the higher integrative brain functions has progressively become more clearly recognized (Jäkel & Dimou, 2017). Herculano-Houzel (2014) noted that glial cells have been considered "key players in brain physiology, metabolism, development and even neurological diseases" (p. 1377). Their functions include influencing synaptic formation, providing metabolic support to axons, regulating blood flow, and controlling synaptic transmission.

Glial cells have historically been described as microglia, astrocytes, and oligodendrocytes (Jäkel & Dimou, 2017). When glial cells begin to grow and divide in an uncontrollable manner, they are described as "malignant" and are referred to as a glioma of the brain. Cuddapah, Robel, Watkins, and Sontheimer (2014) have summarized several interesting facts about how gliomas negatively affect brain function. Figure 16.1 illustrates some of the classic ways that gliomas are thought to migrate throughout the brain. The authors note that their observations reaffirm the early insights of Scherer (1938).

Gliomas can directly invade the brain parenchyma (Figure 16.1a), alter the course of pre-existing blood vessels (Figure 16.1b), disturb the white matter tracts of the brain (Figure 16.1c), and invade the subarachnoid space below the meningeal covering (Figure 16.1d). As Scherer (1938) suggested, glioma cells can "assume the physical shape of the structure they occupy rather than each cell having a characteristic form" (as cited in Cuddapah et al., 2014, p. 19). Greenberg (2010) noted that the most common primary intra-axial brain tumor is an astrocytoma.

Depending on the dominant cell features, an astrocytoma is further subdivided into "types." Within the context of the World Health Organization's (WHO) system (van den Bent et al., 2017), four grades of astrocytoma are identified. Grade I refers to more circumscribed tumors (e.g., pilocytic astrocytoma). Grade II refers to a diffuse but still "low-grade" astrocytoma. Grades III and IV are considered to be malignant astrocytomas. Grade III is referred to as an anaplastic astrocytoma, and Grade IV is called a glioblastoma. In this chapter, the neuropsychological and psychiatric features of adults presenting with gliomas are briefly considered, with primary emphasis on both Grade III and Grade IV astrocytomas. Common psychiatric features of patients with Grades III and IV astrocytomas are also summarized. The complex psychological care of patients with brain gliomas is then discussed.

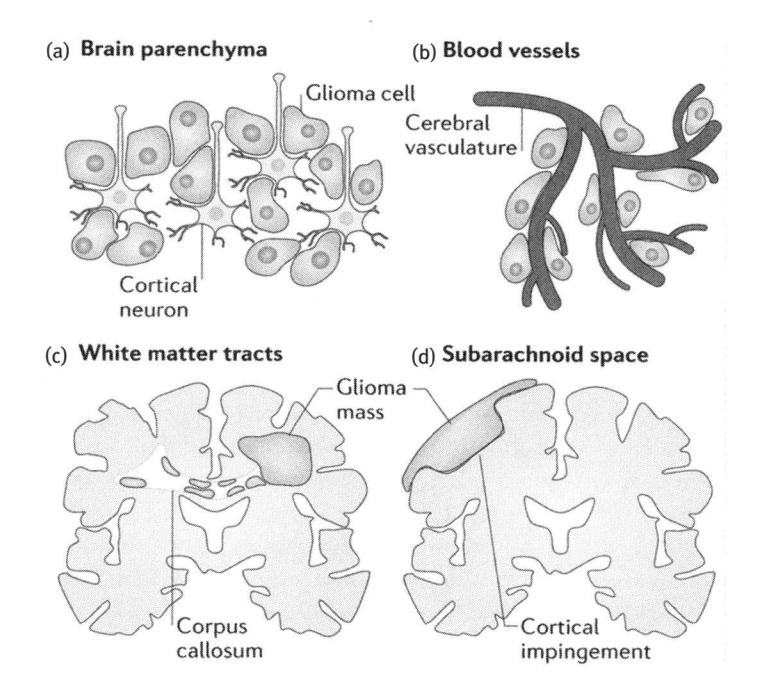

FIGURE 16.1 Pathways of glioma cell invasion: (a) the brain parenchyma, (b) pre-existing blood vessels, (c) white matter tracts (perifascicularly, intrafascicularly, or interfibrillary), and (d) the subarachnoid space below the meningeal covering of the brain (See color plates).

Source: Reprinted from Cuddapah, V. A., Robel, S., Watkins, S., & Sontheimer, H., A neurocentric perspective on glioma invasion, *Nature Reviews Neuroscience*, 15(7), 2014, p. 455–465, by permission of Springer Nature.

ASTROCYTES AND THEIR IMPACT ON BRAIN FUNCTION

Volterra and Meldolesi (2005) note that there has been a revolution in the understanding of the nature of astrocytes, with the realization that they have a much more important role than merely providing "supportive tissue" for neurons and thereby serving as "brain glue." Volterra and Meldolesi provide convincing evidence that astrocytes play a key role in the release of neurotransmitters and as such greatly influence synaptic transmission between neurons, as noted previously. This latter fact may help explain why a single seizure, in what appears to be a typically functioning adult, often raises concern about an underlying astrocytoma (Greenberg, 2010).

Astrocytes also have been implicated in water transport and in maintaining the blood–brain barrier (Booth, Hirst, & Wade-Martins, 2017).Clinically, a glioblastoma is often associated with significant cerebral edema given the disruption of water transport within the brain. Thus, astrocytes produce "pressure effects" that may result in headaches. Persistent headaches are also commonly observed in this patient group at the time of diagnosis.

Depending on the location and size of the astrocytes, a variety of other symptoms can be observed, including lateralized motor weakness, apraxia, aphasia, agnosia, memory impairments, personality changes, and visual and auditory hallucinations (Greenberg, 2010). These dramatic changes in brain function can bring such patients to the attention of clinical neuropsychologists. However, given that the life expectancy of such patients is often short (approximately 95% of patients with a malignant glioma succumb to the disease within 5 years of diagnosis; Cuddapah et al., 2014), many of these patients are not routinely referred for neuropsychological assessment or consultation. For patients who are referred, however, multiple skills are required to provide psychological care for this group of individuals.

NEUROPSYCHOLOGICAL IMPAIRMENTS OF PATIENTS WITH MALIGNANT BRAIN GLIOMAS

Correa and Root (2018) reviewed and summarized the diverse neuropsychological test findings reported in studies of patients with cancerous brain tumors. As expected, patients with right-sided tumors demonstrated substantial visuospatial disturbances. Patients with left cerebral hemisphere tumors not only demonstrated language difficulties but also were noted to be especially slow in visual scanning and showed greater interference effects on a variety of tasks. Clearly, the grade of tumor and treatment effects (e.g., from antiepileptic medications, radiation therapy, and chemotherapy) contributed to the severity of the neuropsychological disturbances.

Neuropsychological studies of patients with brain gliomas have also focused on the potential usefulness of neuropsychological test findings for predicting survival (Johnson, Sawyer, Meyers, O'Neill, & Wefel, 2012; Meyers & Cantor, 2003). In a collaborative enterprise, Johnson et al. studied patients with glioblastomas. The mean survival rate of their patient group was 20.7 months. They further noted that there was no relationship between length of survival and whether the tumor was on the right or the left side of the brain. However, older individuals typically succumbed sooner than younger individuals. The authors reported a relationship between level of impaired neuropsychological test performance and average length of survival in the patients they studied. They found that four neuropsychological measures (i.e., Similarities and Digit Span subtests of the Wechsler Intelligence Scale, the Trail Making Test Part B, and the Controlled Oral Word Association [COWA] Test) were related to average length of survival. Figure 16.2 plots the relationship between impaired versus unimpaired performance and months of survival on each of these four measures. The average length of survival was much

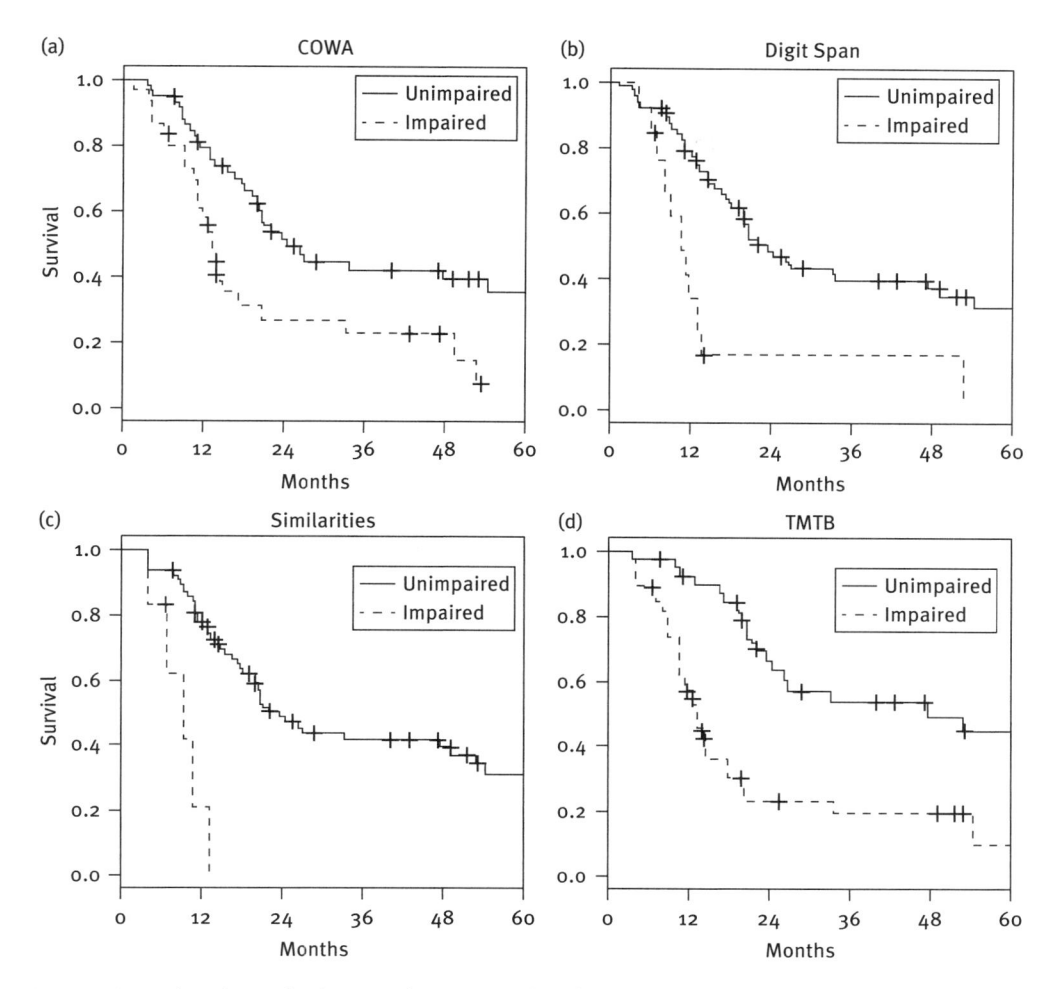

FIGURE 16.2 The relationship between longevity and performance on specific neuropsychological measures for patients with malignant glioma. Kaplan–Meier plot of survival by impairment on (a) Controlled Oral Word Association (COWA), $p = .0029$; (B) Digit Span, $p = .0003$; (C) Similarities, $p < .0001$; and (D) Trail Making Test Part B (TMTB), $p < .001$.

Source: Reprinted from Johnson, D. R., Sawyer, A. M., Meyers, C. A., O'Neill, B. P., & Wefel, J. S., Early measures of cognitive function predict survival in patients with newly diagnosed glioblastoma, Neuro-oncology, 14(6), 2012, p. 808–816, by permission of Oxford University Press.

shorter in individuals whose level of performance was considered in the impaired range on the Similarities subtest versus normal scores on this measure (i.e., median survival for impaired individuals was 9.1 months vs. 23.6 months for those who were not impaired). The investigators noted, however, that cognitively impaired patients often have impaired performance on multiple tests. Thus, they compared survival curves for individuals who showed no impairment on these four tests (i.e., 0–4) with those of individuals who were impaired on one of the four measures and those of individuals impaired on at least two of the four measures. Figure 16.3 illustrates their findings. Clearly, individuals who showed impaired neuropsychological performance on two or more of the four measures had a shorter length of survival.

Meyers, Hess, Yung, and Levin (2000) demonstrated that decline in neurocognitive functioning of individuals with such tumors often appeared before neuroimaging evidence

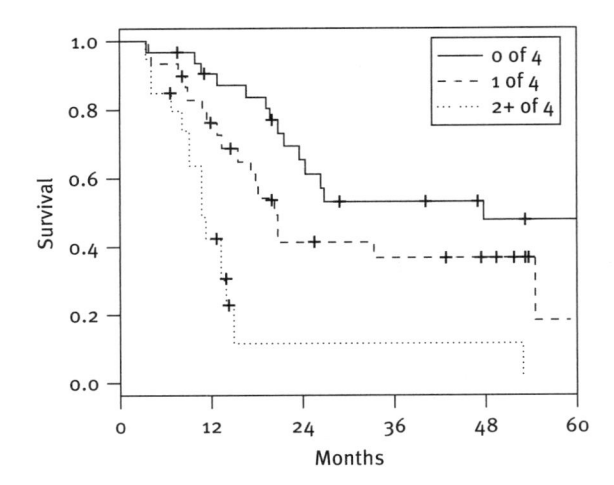

FIGURE 16.3 The relationship between longevity and the number of tests (out of four) on which a glioma patient performed in the impaired range. Kaplan–Meier plots of survival by number of tests in impaired range among Controlled Oral Word Association (COWA), Digit Span, Similarities, and Trail Making Test Part B (TMTB).

Source: Reprinted from Johnson, D. R., Sawyer, A. M., Meyers, C. A., O'Neill, B. P., & Wefel, J. S., Early measures of cognitive function predict survival in patients with newly diagnosed glioblastoma, Neuro-oncology, 14(6), 2012, p. 808–816, by permission of Oxford University Press.

of tumor progression was observed with magnetic resonance imaging (MRI). This finding was at times clinically useful to the treatment team when it faced difficult management issues with patients (Meyers & Cantor, 2003).

Adult patients with Grade III and Grade IV astrocytomas often show greater neuropsychological impairments on standardized neuropsychological tests compared to patients with Grade II tumors (Correa & Root, 2018). In another review article, van Kessel, Baumfalk, van Zandvoort, Robe, and Snijders (2017) noted that prior to surgery, 68.9% of patients with high-grade gliomas showed neuropsychological impairments compared to 31.1% of patients with low-grade gliomas. These authors made the important point that such tumors "can give rise to neurocognitive deficits through many mechanisms, such as local mechanical effects of the tumor mass and thereby ischemic changes, but also cell death by tumor-released excitotoxins and disturbances in synaptic transmission" (p. 10).

Summarizing the research findings of various investigators, van Kessel et al. (2017) further noted that the common cognitive disturbances in this diverse group of patients are problems with "word-finding, short-term memory, and carrying out complex tasks" (p. 9). Lesion location and size of lesion, however, clearly contribute to the more classic neuropsychological and neurological syndromes such as aphasia or anosognosia for hemiplegia, as noted previously. When dramatic neurological symptoms or syndromes are present, they may overshadow the detection of less obvious neurocognitive difficulties that affect a person's functioning in everyday life.

MULTIPLE CORRELATES OF QUALITY OF LIFE IN PATIENTS WITH A BRAIN GLIOMA

Reijneveld, Sitskoorn, Klein, Nuyen, and Taphoorn (2001) noted that measuring quality of life (QOL) in patients with glioma is especially relevant given that "these patients cannot be cured and nearly all will eventually die of their disease" (p. 618). These patients naturally experience considerable anxiety and depression, and both of these variables have been linked to poor QOL reports. Giovagnoli,

Silvani, Colombo, and Boiardi (2005) reported that levels of anxiety and depression were higher in patients with Grade III and Grade IV gliomas compared to patients with chronic neurological disease (e.g., multiple sclerosis, polyneuropathies, and myasthenia gravis). They also reported that overall QOL (as measured by the Functional Living Index–Cancer) significantly correlated with self-reported levels of anxiety and depression. Neuropsychological impairments correlated with this QOL measure but to a lesser degree.

In a prospective study of QOL in a large number of patients with "newly diagnosed high-grade gliomas," Brown et al. (2005) reported that the fatigue level of the patient, but not depression per se, was significantly correlated with QOL measures (i.e., the greater the fatigue, the worse the QOL). Interestingly, fatigue was also an independent predictor of overall survival. Performance on the Mini-Mental State Examination was an additional predictor of length of survival, but this measure correlated with both increased fatigue and depression.

Ediebah et al. (2017) noted that level of cognitive impairment in low-grade glioma patients seemed to influence the degree of disparity between what a patient reported about level of functioning and a relative's or significant other's reports about the patient's functioning. Their findings are complex, but basically patients reported "worse level of symptoms and better level of functioning than their proxies" (p. 872). Clinically, it is not uncommon to observe depressed patients reporting more symptomatology than family members report regarding them (Prigatano & Hill, 2018). However, underreporting of cognitive and functional limitations is associated with impaired self-awareness secondary to an underlying brain disorder (Prigatano, 2014; see also Chapter 9, this volume). This may also be the case in patients with a malignant brain tumor.

PSYCHIATRIC FEATURES OF PATIENTS WITH A BRAIN GLIOMA

A wide variety of personality changes have been observed in adult patients with a brain glioma (Zwinkels et al., 2016). Size of brain tumor, location of brain tumor, the underlying nature of the pathology, and associated cerebral edema seem to influence the neuropsychiatric disturbances observed (Price, Goetz, & Lovell, 2010). Self-reports of depression are often high, but so are reports of being more irritable and quick to anger. As the disease progresses, anxiety may become more prevalent (Langbecker & Yates, 2016). Progressive loss of competency and impending death are common concerns of this patient group.

An especially disturbing neuropsychiatric symptom can be the development of psychoses with both paranoid ideation and hallucinations. The content of the delusional thinking as well as the nature of the hallucinations may, in part, be related to premorbid personality features or concerns. Tumors of the temporal lobe are often associated with psychotic symptomatology (Price et al., 2010), but psychotic symptoms can occur when various regions of the brain are losing their functional integrity. Delirium is also common and is frequently present in patients near the end of life (Breitbart & Alici, 2008).

Changes in personality and the emergence of severe psychiatric symptoms are major sources of distress for the family and caregivers (Langbecker & Yates, 2016; Zwinkels et al., 2016). Spouses and children are often perplexed by these changes, and they often require assistance in understanding them and managing them as much as possible.

Next, two clinical cases are described that highlight important psychological care issues when working with adult patients with a brain glioma.

PSYCHOLOGICAL CARE OF AN ADULT MALE WITH A GLIOBLASTOMA WHO DECLINED TREATMENT FOLLOWING NEUROSURGERY

Medical History

A successful 58-year-old right-handed businessman began to demonstrate difficulties performing typical work projects from home. A family member noted that the patient would often "sit and stare," which was highly unusual for this self-directed entrepreneur. The patient did not notice any major cognitive impairment, but he did report increased fatigue with recent weight loss. With time, he noted difficulties with word finding, but he reported no other cognitive impairment. His wife noted that in retrospect he may have begun showing subtle problems with memory 6 months before he was brought to medical attention.

Because of his fatigue, weight loss, and subtle difficulties in word finding, he was neurologically evaluated. An MRI of the brain revealed a brain tumor. The histology report indicated a WHO Grade IV glioblastoma—a large mass regionalized to the left frontal lobe. The radiology report noted that this large frontal lobe lesion compressed the left lateral ventricle and displaced the third ventricle. An approximately 9-mm midline shift from left to right was noted. At the time of this radiological study, the patient had notable difficulties initiating speech with appropriate word finding. His neurologist described him as presenting with Broca's aphasia.

The patient underwent a surgical resection of the large mass a few days following his diagnosis. A post-surgical resection radiology report noted that the mass previously seen on imaging was completely resected. However, medical recorders noted at that time that his "speech was worse after surgery." He was begun on radiation and chemotherapy, but he decided to terminate treatment after 5 days.

The patient's history was also significant for chronic headaches. After diagnosis and surgical treatment, he was described as suffering from depression, insomnia, and fatigue, and he had repeated falls. There was a brief time during which he demonstrated a right hemiparesis, but it improved with time. The patient was referred for a neuropsychological examination to determine if he could begin driving his car again.

Neuropsychological Examination Findings

The examination was conducted approximately 7 months after the patient's diagnosis and surgery. He was pleasant and cooperative but quiet in his demeanor. When asked about his present functioning, he reported only problems with word finding that at times resulted in stuttering. At the time he was evaluated, the classic signs of Broca's aphasia were not present. The patient did not perceive (or self-report upon questioning) any major change in his memory, language comprehension, or mood. He reported no unusual difficulties with motor coordination.

His wife agreed with his report, but she noted that he tended to sleep much more than he had in the past. She described him as having a substantial decline in memory. When his wife described her view of his memory difficulties in his presence, he appeared surprised. She went on to note that he seemed emotionally more detached from family members than he had been in the past. She stated that he could become very confused at night. For example, he sometimes had difficulty finding the bedroom after awaking from his sleep to use the bathroom.

Table 16.1 lists the patient's psychometric test scores and his and his wife's subjective ratings regarding his cognitive and affective functioning. It is interesting to note that both he and his wife identified substantial difficulties in word finding, but his wife appeared to underestimate his substantial difficulties with fatigue. Both reported that he had mild difficulties with memory and no major problem with depression. However, his wife reported that he had

Table 16.1 Subject Ratings of Cognitive and Affective Functioning and Neuropsychological Test Performance in a 59-Year-Old Patient with a Glioblastoma Who Succumbed from His Illness Approximately 5 Months After Testing Was Conducted and 12 Months After His Diagnosis

Patient ratings		Vocabulary	ss = 7	Trails A	T = 32
Memory	3	Information	ss = 10	Time, errors	46 seconds, 2 errors
Concentration	3	Block Design	ss = 8		
Word finding	8	Matrix Reasoning	ss = 9	Trails B	T = 25
Irritability	3	Picture Completion	ss = 6	Time, errors	206 seconds, 0 errors
Anxiety	3	Digit Span	ss = 7		
Depression	3	Arithmetic	ss = 8	Phonemic Verbal Fluency (3 × 1 minute)	10 words, <1st %ile
Fatigue	5	Coding	ss = 6		
Directionality	3	Symbol Search	ss = 4	Semantic Verbal Fluency	T = 13
Family ratings		**RAVLT**			
Memory	3	Learning	4, 5, 6, 9, 9	Animals (words in 1 minute)	6 words
Concentration	7	Total words	33/75, T = 32	Boston Naming Test	49/60, T = 32
Word finding	9				
Irritability	9	Immediate recall	5/15, T = 36	MAE Sentence Repetition	9/14
Anxiety	6				
Depression	3	Delayed recall (20 minutes)	4/15, T = 34	**WCST-64**	
Fatigue	9			Total categories	0/6
Directionality	8	Recognition	15/15, 4 f+	**Finger Tapping**	
BNI Screen	40/50, T = 36	**BVMT-R**		Dominant right hand	41.4, T = 31
WAIS-IV		Trial 1	T = 33	Nondominant left hand	51.6, T = 56
Verbal IQ	91	Trial 2	T = 45		
Performance IQ	86	Trial 3	T = 44	Patient Competency Rating Scale: Patient	114/150
Working Memory IQ	86	25-minute delay	T = 38		
Processing Speed IQ	74	**WMS-IV**		Patient Competency Rating Scale: Family	98/150
Full Scale IQ	81	Logical Memory I	ss = 4		
Similarities	ss = 8	Logical Memory II	ss = 5		

BNI, Barrow Neurological Institute; BVMT-R, Brief Visuospatial Memory Test–Revised; RAVLT, Rey Auditory Verbal Learning Test; ss, scaled score; WAIS-IV, Wechsler Adult Intelligence Scale–Fourth Edition; WCST-64, Wisconsin Card Sorting Test-64; WMS-IV, Wechsler Memory Scale–Fourth Edition; %ile, percentile rank.

increased (and severe) irritability, with substantial problems getting lost in space (i.e., the ratings on directionality).

On standardized psychometric testing, the patient demonstrated multiple neuropsychological difficulties in light of his educational and occupational background. His cognitive difficulties were not limited to language and memory tasks. It is important to note that his lesion location involved the dorsomedial prefrontal cortex, affected the left posterior middle frontal gyrus, and invaded or at least compressed the left anterior insula. These regions have been described as important areas of neural network interconnections. When they are damaged, several domains of neuropsychological functioning are frequently compromised (Warren et al., 2014; see also Chapter 11, this volume). This seems to account for the multiple cognitive and behavioral changes observed in this patient.

On formal testing, the speed of information processing and generating answers to a variety of questions was substantially slow (see Table 16.1). Of the four measures related to longevity that were used by Johnson et al. (2012), the patient demonstrated impaired performance on three of them based on age-based normative data (Digit Span, COWA, and Trail Making Test Part B). It is important to note that his memory performance was severely impaired on three different measures (the Rey Auditory Verbal Learning test, the Brief Visual Memory Test–Revised form, and the Logical Memory of the Wechsler Memory Scale–Fourth Edition). He also demonstrated severe difficulties when attempting to perform a novel problem-solving task (i.e., categories achieved on the Wisconsin Card Sorting Test were "0"). In addition, the patient underestimated his functional capacities in everyday life on the Patient Competency Rating Scale (PCRS) relative to his wife's ratings of his functional capacities as measured by this scale (see Table 16.1). He clearly was too impaired to work or safely drive a car. During the actual examination process, he made a comment to the examiner that he could not believe that he had developed a malignant brain tumor. He said this with no emotion in his tone of voice. On the BNI Screen for Higher Cerebral Functions, he was shown drawings depicting three facial affects. He was asked to identify each affect. He easily identified pictorial representations of angry and happy faces. When he was shown a somewhat ambiguous facial affect (i.e., which is frequently described as either fear or surprise), he stated that the facial picture showed "no emotion." Whether this reflected his phenomenological state or was an error in the perception of common facial emotions remains unclear. However, his wife noted that he was more detached and less involved with family members than he had been in the past. Given his religious background, involvement with family members' lives was very important to him.

Discussion of Findings with the Patient and His Wife

After the neuropsychological examination was completed, the test findings and clinical observations were reviewed. Both husband and wife showed little outward emotion. When the specific question of safety in driving was addressed, again no outward emotional reaction was displayed. The patient expressed mild disappointment in the recommendation that he should not drive a car in light of his neuropsychological status. However, he said very little. Neither the patient nor his wife inquired about any form of psychological support given his diagnosis and neuropsychological condition. They thanked the examiner for his efforts and reported they would consult further with their physicians regarding his future medical care.

Events Leading to the Patient's Death

The patient and his wife were quite religious and sought emotional support from church teachings, other members of the church, close friends, and selected family members. The patient appeared resigned to his terminal condition and showed little emotion regarding his diagnosis. After talking with friends (including some physicians), he and his wife decided that he would not undergo further medical treatments. They were aware that such treatments (radiation therapy and chemotherapy) might substantially interfere with his quality of life during the expected short duration of his life that remained. He traveled with his wife and attempted to engage in as many pleasurable activities as he could enjoy given his severe fatigue. He eventually became obtunded, slipped into a coma, and succumbed from his illness 12 months after the diagnosis.

This case highlights an important clinical reality. When faced with imminent death, some individuals and families simply wish to be left alone and deal with their personal situation without the help of any professional caregivers. They may not seek out or welcome any form of psychological care. This has to be understood and respected.

PSYCHOLOGICAL CARE OF AN ADULT MALE WITH AN ANAPLASTIC OLIGODENDROGLIA TUMOR WHO OBTAINED MEDICAL, SURGICAL, AND PSYCHOLOGICAL TREATMENTS

Medical History

A 46-year-old right-handed businessman had a generalized seizure while on vacation with his family. He was taken to a nearby hospital and underwent a left frontal craniotomy for partial resection of an anaplastic oligodendroglioma (WHO Grade III). Prior to his seizure, he and his wife noted no cognitive difficulty. His wife, however, believed that he had become more irritable several months prior to his seizure. He was placed on seizure medications, and he returned home.

The patient was then followed by a local neurosurgeon who performed a second surgery to further resect a left frontal residual tumor in the premotor cortex. Radiology reports indicated a large lesion resection that included the left dorsolateral cortex up to and including part of the anterior cingulate gyrus. Broca's area (Brodmann area 44 or the pars opercularis) was spared, as were the inferior portions of the left frontal lobe.

He was referred for a neuropsychological examination to document his higher integrative brain functions and also to help him and his wife understand his cognitive and affective difficulties. He also expressed a cautious interest in speaking with a clinical neuropsychologist regarding his emotional state and the impact of his diagnosis and health problems on his family.

Neuropsychological Examination Findings

When seen for his neuropsychological examination, the patient was asked to describe his present difficulties. He noted that he struggled to find words when communicating. He also noted that others had described him as being emotionally distant. His wife added that he was having considerable difficulty with his "short-term memory" and was quick to become frustrated and irritable. She noted that in the past this was atypical for him.

On formal examination, the patient demonstrated neuropsychological impairments in multiple domains. For example, his Verbal Comprehension Index was 74, and his Perceptual Reasoning Index was 81. His Full Scale IQ was 75. As Table 16.2 illustrates, his levels of performance on tests of memory, concentration, processing speed, and abstract reasoning were all below what would be expected of a man with a presumed premorbid normal level of intelligence given his occupational and educational history. What was interesting, however, was his level of daily functioning as rated by him and his wife on the PCRS. Both agreed that his daily functioning was affected, but he clearly was more functional in his daily life than the previously discussed patient: The PCRS-R score for this patient was 115/150,

Table 16.2 Neuropsychological Test Performance in a 46-Year-Old Male 3 Months After Being Diagnosed with an Anaplastic Oligodendroglioma

BNI Screen	40/50, $T = 36$	Trial 3	$T = 36$
WASI-II		25-minute delay	$T = 32$
Verbal Comprehension Index	74	**Trails A**	$T = 31$
		Time, errors	46 seconds, 0 errors
Perceptual Reasoning Index	81		
Full Scale IQ	75	**Trails B**	$T = 33$
Similarities	$T = 32$	Time, errors	112 seconds, 0 errors
Vocabulary	$T = 36$	**Phonemic Verbal Fluency (3 × 1 minute)**	26 words, $T = 37$
Block Design	$T = 35$		
Matrix Reasoning	$T = 42$	**Semantic Verbal Fluency**	$T = 37$
WAIS-IV		Animals (words in 1 minute)	14 words
Digit Span	ss = 10	**Boston Naming Test**	45/60, $T = 29$
Coding	ss = 6	**WCST-64**	
RAVLT		Total categories	1/6
Learning	5, 7, 8, 9, 8	Perseverative responses	14, $T = 37$
Total words	37/75, $T = 38$	**Finger Tapping**	
Immediate recall	3/15, $T = 28$	Dominant right hand	37.4, $T = 26$
Delayed recall (20 minutes)	4/15, $T = 34$	Nondominant left hand	38.4, $T = 34$
BVMT-R		**Patient Competency Rating Scale: Patient**	110/150
Trial 1	$T = 35$		
Trial 2	$T = 41$	**Patient Competency Rating Scale: Family**	115/150

BNI, Barrow Neurological Institute; BVMT-R, Brief Visuospatial Memory Test–Revised; RAVLT, Rey Auditory Verbal Learning Test; ss, scaled score; WAIS-IV, Wechsler Adult Intelligence Scale–Fourth Edition; WASI-II, Wechsler Abbreviated Scale of Intelligence–Second Edition; WCST-64, Wisconsin Card Sorting Test-64.

whereas that for the prior patient was only 98/150. Most normally functioning individuals are rated by relatives at approximately 125+/150 points on the PCRS-R.

Although the patient's processing speed was similar to that of the previous patient (both had age-corrected Coding subtest scores of 6), he did not show impaired performance on the Digit Span (he had an age-adjusted score of 10, whereas that of the previous patient was 7). This patient also had better verbal fluency: as measured by the FAS phonemic verbal fluency test, he had a raw score of 26 words and a T score of 37, whereas the previous patient had a score of 10 words and a T score of less than 20. This patient performed in the impaired range on the Trail Making Test Part B, but he did better than the previous patient. The total time for this patient was 112 seconds with no errors and a T score of 33 versus 206 seconds with no errors and a T score of 25 for the previous patient. Thus, although this patient also had evidence of impaired performance on three of the four measures utilized by Johnson et al. (2012) to predict longevity, his level of performance was clearly higher considering age and educational norms.

When his neuropsychological test findings were discussed, the patient and his wife both showed "controlled concern." The patient was aware that he was reporting fewer cognitive difficulties than what his wife was describing concerning his functioning. The patient was also able to convey (not in the presence of his wife) severe depression. He was not apathetic; he was concerned about his health, life, and family.

When these findings were discussed, both the patient and his wife agreed that the patient should receive speech and language therapy, occupational therapy, and physical therapy. They were both open to the possibility of receiving supportive psychotherapy and psychotropic medications to reduce depression.

Efforts at Psychological Care

Within 2 weeks of the neuropsychological examination/consultation, the patient was seen for his initial supportive psychotherapy sessions. During the first session, his wife was also present. She wanted a better understanding of how to respond to her husband's cognitive and affective difficulties at home. She was especially concerned about his "lost filter" as it related to his expression of anger. The patient always wanted help to become less angry at home, but he hinted at wanting to have help with his depression and his severe (understandable) anxiety, which he attempted to hide from his wife and children. He wanted to be strong for them, but secretly he was very worried and depressed.

In the initial sessions, specific behavioral recommendations were made to the patient's wife regarding management of her husband's angry outbursts, but they were made in light of the patient's unspoken worries. For example, the patient's wife was encouraged to acknowledge her husband's worries about his health and the long-term consequences for the family but at the same time to gently touch him to express her concern and closeness to him during these very tumultuous times. She asked him in a quiet but loving voice to try to be less angry. She was also educated about the fact that with frontal lobe impairments, the control of emotional expressions can be compromised. Thus, she had a better understanding of her husband and was less critical of him and less overwhelmed by him because she understood the probable cause of his "loss of filter" when upset.

As the patient was able to begin expressing his anxiety and depression, he did not feel "alone with his problem." He became open to taking an antidepressant medication. Importantly, in later sessions he explained why he was initially hesitant to take the medication. In his younger days, he consumed alcohol in excessive amounts to cope with his problems. He did not want to become dependent on the antidepressant medication as he was once dependent on alcohol to help deal with some major life disappointments. This important issue, however, did not come to light initially. It emerged several sessions later after a close working relationship with the patient was established.

How was such a relationship achieved? When the patient's emotional reactions to his tumor and medical treatments were initially discussed, the clinical neuropsychologist noted that his responses were often short, without any elaboration of how he was actually feeling. The topic was shifted to important relationships in his life, such as his father and mother. Again, his responses were brief. This was accepted without further probing.

Following sessions of speech therapy and physical therapy, the patient slowly began to talk about his experiences. He noted how fatigued he was and how his level of fatigue surprised him. He also noted a decline in his sexual drive and did not know how to talk to his wife about this issue. He then began talking about other issues in his life (not directly related to his tumor or medical condition). He had difficulty communicating with his daughter from a previous marriage. He wanted help with knowing how to talk to her.

A series of sessions (some of which included his wife) ensued to especially conjointly develop strategies for dealing with the daughter and ongoing difficulties dealing with his previous spouse. Not all strategies proved to be helpful, but some were. Perhaps more important, the patient and his wife experienced the clinical neuropsychologist as willing to help them with whatever adjustment issues were experienced. The patient was grateful for those efforts and began to trust the clinical neuropsychologist with more private details of his life.

When the patient began taking an antidepressant medication and engaging in activities in the psychotherapy sessions, his affect improved and he became more talkative. He began to talk about his concerns regarding what a recent MRI of his brain might reveal. He had undergone a series of radiation and chemotherapy treatments and was hoping that the tumor would not regrow. His wife had raised concerns that his memory had worsened during the past few weeks, and this clearly bothered him. It was agreed to do a brief assessment of his language and memory functions to determine if any decline had occurred. Fortunately, no decline was observed in his memory, but verbal fluency showed a slight decline. There was no major change in his neuropsychological status.

The patient progressively began to talk more openly about his fears and anxieties. This led to a discussion of what had given him relief from anxiety in the past. He mentioned that his work helped him greatly reduce his anxiety. He also spoke of his favorite books and movies. He indicated that watching comedy was especially helpful to him when his anxiety was high.

For several sessions, the patient's mood was more positive, but then there was an unexpected intense angry reaction concerning his children from a previous marriage. It was especially difficult for him that they did not seem to show supportive concern for him and his medical condition. For the first time, he expressed feelings of anger from the perspective of concerns about his death. The patient was asked "to say out loud what you are feeling." Rules regarding confidentiality were reviewed and emphasized. The therapeutic alliance seemed to become stronger.

During the course of 20 one-hour psychotherapy sessions, he discussed his tumor, work, death, his children (from a previous marriage), and his current wife. The dialogue became progressively more expansive, and several important issues came to light. One fascinating comment that the patient made during his psychotherapy was that he had had a tattoo on his shoulder (which he had not previously mentioned) changed. The original tattoo was Felix the Cat holding his hand up "giving the finger" to the world. He obtained this tattoo in his younger days when he was drinking alcohol heavily. He had the tattoo changed to show Felix the Cat holding his hand up with the universal peace sign.

During the remaining sessions, the patient spoke more about increasing his hours at work and feeling physically better as he completed his course of chemotherapy. We talked more about looking forward to the future and steps he could take in building his relationship with his wife and the one child who was repeatedly distant from him. Repeat MRIs of the brain showed no tumor growth approximately 15 months after his tumor was initially discovered and treated. The patient was feeling better and consequently he was discharged from psychotherapy with the understanding that the "door was always open" if he wished to return at any time.

Clinical Features Relevant to the Person's Psychological Care

There are several important features of this patient's psychological care. Not only was the dialogue with this patient not rushed but also the patient was not forced to engage in extensive dialogue about his concerns until he was ready to do so. He had some limitations of language functions, but they were not a barrier to the dialogue. Practical suggestions were made to his wife to manage his angry outbursts. The complex factors contributing to his angry outbursts were only progressively revealed and discussed. Although the psychotherapeutic dialogue was supportive in nature, the patient revealed how earlier issues in his personal life influenced his resistance to taking antidepressant medications. He also talked about his need to project his "strength" to the world for the sake of his children and family. When he did not experience their support with regard to how he was secretly trying to protect them, he exploded into angry outbursts. He had a gradual shift in his behavior and symbol representations of how he perceived the world (note the change in hand gesture on the tattoo on his shoulder) as a result of two factors. First, his tumor did not regrow, and he had an opportunity to talk about and better understand his most personal and private reactions to a devastating diagnosis. Second, and more important, the nature of his psychological care allowed him to talk more completely and thoroughly about the problems he faced in his life (for a discussion of this important point, see Chapter 12, this volume). This repeated phenomenon becomes an essential feature of clinically meaningful psychological adjustment to a brain disorder. Table 16.3 reviews several of the important features of this person's psychological care.

APPROACHES TO PSYCHOLOGICAL CARE OF PERSONS WITH A PRIMARY MALIGNANT BRAIN TUMOR

Given the two rather extreme examples of how a malignant brain tumor can affect persons and their methods of adjustment to this life-threatening diagnosis, it should be obvious that the psychological needs and approaches to psychological care can be very different for different people with malignant brain tumors. However, a review article by Ford, Catt, Chalmers, and Fallowfield (2012) provides several interesting observations relevant to psychological care of persons with a malignant brain tumor. The authors note that there is a high incidence of affective disturbances in both the patient and, at times, caregivers. They emphasize the repeated observation that patients and caregivers voice their dissatisfaction with health care providers regarding how they communicate with them and the type of information they provide. Although patients are informed about the various medical and surgical treatments available, their doctors often do not discuss patients' psychosocial and personal care needs. Patients and family members are often shocked by their diagnosis. They need time to process the information and their reactions before they can ask important questions about future care. They often find decision-making difficult when they have incomplete knowledge about their diagnosis and prognosis. An extremely important point that these authors make is that the treating physicians should strive to honestly deliver the prognosis with compassion, empathy, and some semblance of hope. A key issue is that patients want to be treated "as a person" and not "just numbers in the system" (Ford et al., 2012, p. 394).

In light of their diagnosis and prognosis, many patients seek out complementary

Table 16.3 Clinical Features Relevant to the Psychological Care of Persons with an Anaplastic Oligodendroglioma

CLINICAL FEATURE	YES	NO	PARTIALLY
1. The dialogue between the patient and the clinical neuropsychologist was not rushed.	✓		
2. The patient was able to express or clearly convey his personal concerns.	✓		
3. The content of the concerns varied over time.	✓		
4. The patient experienced a sense of "realistic" hope that he could better cope with his life situation. He did not experience "being alone" with his problem(s).	✓		
5. The patient and the clinical neuropsychologist developed a positive therapeutic relationship over time.	✓		
6. Somatic symptoms (e.g., fatigue, which may be both a direct and an indirect effect of a malignant brain tumor) were substantially reduced during periods of psychological care.		✓	
7. Anxiety and depression were substantially reduced during periods of psychological care. This resulted in fewer angry outbursts.	✓		
8. The patient was able to follow the guidance of the clinical neuropsychologist to improve functioning in everyday life activities.			✓
9. The patient was able to control impulses, delay gratification, and sustain his work efforts when fatigued.	✓		
10. The patient actively sought out work and recognized how it and comedy reduced his anxiety.	✓		
11. The patient attempted to "self-reflect" or "be more aware" of personal "strengths" and "limitations."			✓
12. The patient experienced enjoyment in the care or help of other living things (people, animals, the environment, etc.).			✓
13. The patient experienced an understanding of the "problematic nature of their unique life" and was not overwhelmed or "defeated" by it or readily gave in to escapism to cope with life (adapted from Bettelheim, 1989).			✓
14. The patient could "live with" the restrictions produced by a brain injury "without resentment" or loss of hope (adapted from Goldstein, 1952).			✓

Table 16.3 Continued

CLINICAL FEATURE	YES	NO	PARTIALLY
15. The patient was able to obtain new insights into self by attending to why certain songs, stories, fairy tales, movies, tattoos, etc. had a special personal meaning to him that initially he did not understand.	✓		
16. The patient's dreams or artwork often heralded changes in behavior that aided in psychological adjustment before the consciously mediated changes occurred.	✓		
17. The psychological care interventions (including the dialogue) between the patient and the clinical neuropsychologist resulted in the patient talking more openly about problems and demonstrating self-directed efforts at improving psychological adjustment to the direct and indirect effects of the brain disorder.	✓		
18. The psychological care interventions were in harmony with the patient's cultural background and religious orientation.	✓		
19. The psychological care interventions facilitated a personal discussion about death and issues of meaning in life.			✓
20. The patient and family experienced two basic facts of life: (a) The individual's state of subjective sense of personal well-being fluctuates and (b) the psychological adjustment process is never static and therefore hope should never be abandoned.			✓
Total	12	1	7

therapies, including homeopathy, vitamin supplements, herbs, meditation, psychotherapy, and "faith healing." The goal is often "to do something" to build both their physical and their psychological resiliency. Although there is limited research on the effectiveness of different forms of complementary therapies for improving mood and personality changes in this patient group, this is an area of inquiry that needs to be further explored.

Ford et al. (2012) note that the typical course of care for patients in oncology centers is to do repeat brain imaging to monitor possible tumor recurrence and to monitor medical/surgical treatment effects. Although patients with malignant brain tumors are frequently referred to speech therapy and physical therapy, these authors note that "the least accessible service was clinical psychology" (p. 396). Thus, the personal, psychological needs of this patient group often receive less attention. Helping these patients reduce fatigue and increase word-finding skills is more readily addressed.

The needs of caregivers and family members are often neglected. When family members are given the chance to talk about the concerns that are most troubling to them, Ford et al. (2012) note that they might begin with questions concerning the tumor, prognosis, and end-of-life issues. However, with time, they talk about "topics that had nothing to do with the patient or the illness" (p. 397). This is an extremely important observation and needs to be kept clearly in focus when working with any patient with a brain disorder and/or the patient's family members. Family members have a variety of personal needs that may require special help when an important family member is severely compromised by a neurological condition. Being prepared for this reality and allowing the family members to have such dialogue is "medically necessary" if the goal is to improve the quality of life for the patient and the family members.

Various studies have been performed on the effectiveness of certain forms of rehabilitation to aid this patient group. In an early retrospective study, Sherer, Meyers, and Bergloff (1997) evaluated the clinical outcome of 13 patients with a primary malignant brain tumor who were enrolled in a day-treatment program based on the clinical model described by Ben-Yishay, Silver, Piasetsky, and Rattok (1987) and Prigatano et al. (1984). Note that this was the same model employed to help the patient with cerebral anoxia described in Chapter 13. In the study by Sherer et al., 9 out of the 13 patients had a diagnosis of anaplastic glioma. Outcomes varied, but some patients were able to return to either gainful employment or volunteer work. Others remained nonproductive, but the overall impression was that such intensive neuropsychological and psychosocially oriented rehabilitation could potentially be helpful to such patients. Unfortunately, no other research on the effectiveness of such programs for patients with anaplastic glioma could be found in the literature.

Although fatigue is a common problem for patients with a malignant brain tumor (Langbecker & Yates, 2016), no studies could be found that specifically evaluated the effectiveness of rehabilitation for improving fatigue level. The research focus is often on documenting the extent of fatigue in this patient group and evaluating the different methods available for measuring fatigue in glioma patients (van Coevorden-van Loon, Coomans, Heijenbrok-Kal, Ribbers, & van den Bent, 2017).

However, Khan, Amatya, Physio, Drummond, and Galea (2014) did evaluate the effectiveness of an "integrated multidisciplinary rehabilitation" approach for improving cognitive, motor, communication, and psychosocial outcome for patients with primary brain tumors. Patients included those with Grades I–IV gliomas, with approximately half of the patients (54.1%) being diagnosed with Grade III or IV gliomas. Three months after rehabilitation (which lasted on average only 21 days), there were significant and positive differences between patients receiving rehabilitation and wait-list controls on several dimensions. The effect sizes were described as ranging from small to moderate. At 6-month follow-up, significant improvements were maintained on selected measures (i.e., sphincter control, communication, and psychosocial and cognitive status). In a later Cochrane review article on the effectiveness of multidisciplinary rehabilitation after primary brain tumor, Khan, Amatya, Ng, Drummond, and Galea (2015) concluded,

> We found "low-level" evidence to support high-intensity ambulatory (outpatient) multidisciplinary rehabilitation in reducing short- and long-term motor disability . . . when compared with standard outpatient care. We found improvement in some domains of disability (continence, communication) and psychosocial gains were maintained at six months follow-up. (p. 2)

They also noted that they found no evidence for improved quality of life.

A few studies have formally addressed the role of cognitive rehabilitation in the care of patients with gliomas (Day et al., 2016; Gehring et al., 2009). The findings are mixed, with relatively small treatment effect sizes (Table 16.4). Studies on psychological care interventions for specifically improving the quality of life

Table 16.4 Review of Selected, Representative Studies Relevant to the Psychological Care of Persons with a Malignant Brain Tumor

INTERVENTION	STUDY SAMPLE	MAJOR FINDINGS	CONCLUSIONS
Multifaceted CRP to reduce subjective complaints of cognitive dysfunction and improve objective performance on neuropsychological tests in patients with a primary brain tumor (Gehring et al., 2009)	140 adult patients with low-grade and anaplastic gliomas were recruited from 11 hospitals in the Netherlands. 70 patients were enrolled in a CRP program (which included both cognitive retraining and cognitive compensation training) for 6 weeks with two individual hourly sessions per week. The focus was on attention training. They were compared to 70 wait-list control patients.	Findings were multiple and complex; however, positive short-term effects were observed on certain attention and memory tasks. Effects tended to diminish with time, with no statistically significant group differences in self-reported cognitive function at a 6-month follow-up examination. However, at 6-month follow-up, "the CRP group exhibited continued improvement in objective cognitive performance, whereas the control group did not" (p. 3720).	Although the percentage of patients in the CRP who showed reasonable effect sizes of treatment tended to be greater than that of control group patients, the overall treatment benefits appeared modest but potentially clinically useful.
Pilot investigation of a neuropsychological (and psychosocial) rehabilitation day treatment program for return to work and increase independence in patients with a primary brain tumor (Sherer et al., 1997)	This study was a retrospective chart review of 13 patients with a primary malignant brain tumor (9 of whom had an anaplastic glioma) who underwent on average a 2.6-month post-acute day treatment program. No control group was examined.	Although the sample size was very small, as a group, patients were more productive and independent at the end of their rehabilitation program compared to their status at entry into the rehabilitation program. The relationship between neuropsychological status of the patients and/or their psychiatric status to outcome was not reported.	A holistic, post-acute rehabilitation approach to the patient's physical, cognitive, and emotional/motivational needs would seem most helpful to this patient group. However, the lack of a control group and further exploration of why some patients improved and others did not make the interpretation of the reported findings difficult. As the authors indicated, however, it was intended only as a pilot investigation. No further research using this approach with glioma patients could be identified in a literature search.

(*continued*)

Table 16.4 Continued

INTERVENTION	STUDY SAMPLE	MAJOR FINDINGS	CONCLUSIONS
Integrated individualized multidisciplinary outpatient rehabilitation program for improving functional independence in multiple areas, including communication and psychosocial functioning in patients with a primary brain tumor (Khan et al., 2014)	106 patients were allocated to an intervention group (IG; $n = 53$) or a wait-list control group (CG; $n = 53$). The IG group received comprehensive individualized multidisciplinary rehabilitation for 6–8 weeks. Controls received no rehabilitation per se but were followed by their physicians and appropriate health care providers. Measures of functional status and depression, anxiety, and psychological well-being were obtained at 3- and 6-month follow-up.	At the 3-month follow-up, the IG was functioning higher on each of the FIMs (i.e., FIM subtest scores) compared to the CG. By 6 months, the effects were maintained in "sphincter" control, communication, and psychosocial and cognition subtests. Effects were mild to moderate. On specific measures of anxiety and depression using the DASS-21, positive statistical findings were reported mainly for anxiety and expressing less stress, but not depression per se. It should be noted that Grade I-IV glioma patients were included in this study, with 54% of the sample having Grade III and IV. Given the sample size, the impact of grade of glioma on outcome measures was not reported.	Even with a relatively short period of individualized comprehensive rehabilitation activities, positive treatment effects were noted in the psychological functioning of this heterogeneous group of brain tumor patients. The findings are encouraging and suggest that patients with malignant brain tumors can be helped to reduce their emotional distress by attending to their individual rehabilitation needs.

CRP, cognitive rehabilitation program; DASS-21, Depression Anxiety Stress Scale–21 items; FIMs, Functional Independence Measures.

in patients with Grade III and IV gliomas are striking in their absence from the literature. Studies on helping each patient face death with the least amount of anxiety are also missing.

SUMMARY

The psychological care of persons with a primary malignant brain tumor is one of the most challenging and at the same time potentially rewarding experiences for a clinical neuropsychologist. This brain disorder is fatal, so the ability to sustain the patient's hope (a key ingredient in effective psychological care) often seems lost. But this does not have to be the case. The review article by Ford et al. (2012) provides many helpful suggestions for psychologically aiding these patients. The manner of communication, the exploration of the patient's and family members' personal concerns, and an understanding of the multiple factors that can contribute to cognitive and affective dysfunction can positively influence the person's psychological adjustment and thereby reduce anxiety and depression. Because the issue of mortality is faced by all who are involved in the patient's care, the passing from life to death can be achieved with considerably less agony. Much of the care involves addressing meaningful experiences in the person's life and what is meaningful to the person now as he or she passes from life to death. This is a highly individual process and brings into sharp focus how personal psychodynamic features of the individual and his or her cultural and religious values must be woven into end-of-life psychological care.

REFERENCES

Ben-Yishay, Y., Silver, S. M., Piasetsky, E., & Rattok, J. (1987). Relationship between employability and vocational outcome after intensive holistic cognitive rehabilitation. *Journal of Head Trauma Rehabilitation, 1,* 35–48.

Blumenfeld, H. (2010). *Neuroanatomy through clinical cases.* Sunderland, MA: Sinauer.

Booth, H. D., Hirst, W. D., & Wade-Martins, R. (2017). The role of astrocyte dysfunction in Parkinson's disease pathogenesis. *Trends in Neurosciences, 40*(6), 358–370.

Breitbart, W., & Alici, Y. (2008). Agitation and delirium at the end of life. *JAMA, 300*(24), 2898–2910.

Brown, P. D., Maurer, M. J., Rummans, T. A., Pollock, B. E., Ballman, K. V., Sloan, J. A., . . . Buckner, J. C. (2005). A prospective study of quality of life in adults with newly diagnosed high-grade gliomas: The impact of the extent of resection on quality of life and survival. *Neurosurgery, 57*(3), 495–504.

Correa, D. D., & Root, J. C. (2018). Cognitive functions in adults with central nervous system and non-central nervous system cancers. In J. Morgan & J. Ricker (Eds.), *Textbook of clinical neuropsychology* (2nd ed., pp. 560–586). New York, NY: Taylor & Francis.

Cuddapah, V. A., Robel, S., Watkins, S., & Sontheimer, H. (2014). A neurocentric perspective on glioma invasion. *Nature Reviews Neuroscience, 15*(7), 455–465.

Day, J., Gillespie, D. C., Rooney, A. G., Bulbeck, H. J., Zienius, K., Boele, F., & Grant, R. (2016). Neurocognitive deficits and neurocognitive rehabilitation in adult brain tumors. *Current Treatment Options in Neurology, 18*(5), 22.

Ediebah, D. E., Reijneveld, J. C., Taphoorn, M. J., Coens, C., Zikos, E., Aaronson, N. K., . . . Klein, M. (2017). Impact of neurocognitive deficits on patient–proxy agreement regarding health-related quality of life in low-grade glioma patients. *Quality of Life Research, 26*(4), 869–880.

Ford, E., Catt, S., Chalmers, A., & Fallowfield, L. (2012). Systematic review of supportive care needs in patients with primary malignant brain tumors. *Neuro-oncology, 14*(4), 392–404.

Gehring, K., Sitskoorn, M. M., Gundy, C. M., Sikkes, S. A., Klein, M., Postma, T. J., . . . Kappelle, A. C. (2009). Cognitive rehabilitation in patients with gliomas: A randomized, controlled trial. *Journal of Clinical Oncology, 27*(22), 3712–3722.

Giovagnoli, A., Silvani, A., Colombo, E., & Boiardi, A. (2005). Facets and determinants of quality of life in patients with recurrent high grade glioma. *Journal of Neurology, Neurosurgery, and Psychiatry, 76*(4), 562–568.

Goldstein, K. (1952). The effect of brain damage on the personality. *Psychiatry, 15*(3), 245–260.

Greenberg, M. (2010). *Handbook of neurosurgery.* Tampa, FL: Greenberg Graphics.

Herculano-Houzel, S. (2014). The glia/neuron ratio: How it varies uniformly across brain structures and species and what that means for brain physiology and evolution. *Glia, 62*(9), 1377–1391.

Jäkel, S., & Dimou, L. (2017). Glial cells and their function in the adult brain: A journey through the history of their ablation. *Frontiers in Cellular Neuroscience, 11,* 24.

Johnson, D. R., Sawyer, A. M., Meyers, C. A., O'Neill, B. P., & Wefel, J. S. (2012). Early measures of cognitive function predict survival in patients with newly diagnosed glioblastoma. *Neuro-oncology, 14*(6), 808–816.

Khan, F., Amatya, B., Ng, L., Drummond, K., & Galea, M. (2015). Multidisciplinary rehabilitation after primary brain tumour treatment. *Cochrane Database Systematic Reviews, 2013*(1), CD009509.

Khan, F., Amatya, B., Physio, B., Drummond, K., & Galea, M. (2014). Effectiveness of integrated multidisciplinary rehabilitation in primary brain cancer survivors in an Australian community cohort: A controlled clinical trial. *Journal of Rehabilitation Medicine, 46*(8), 754–760.

Langbecker, D., & Yates, P. (2016). Primary brain tumor patients' supportive care needs and multidisciplinary rehabilitation, community and psychosocial support services: Awareness, referral and utilization. *Journal of Neuro-oncology, 127*(1), 91–102.

Laughlin, S. B., & Sejnowski, T. J. (2003). Communication in neuronal networks. *Science, 301*(5641), 1870–1874.

Meyers, C., & Cantor, S. (Eds.). (2003). *Neuropsychological assessment and treatment of patients with malignant brain tumors.* New York, NY: Psychology Press.

Meyers, C. A., Hess, K. R., Yung, W. A., & Levin, V. A. (2000). Cognitive function as a predictor of survival in patients with recurrent malignant glioma. *Journal of Clinical Oncology, 18*(3), 646–646.

Price, T., Goetz, K., & Lovell, M. (2010). Neuropsychiatric aspects of brain tumors. In S. C. Yudofski & R. E. Hales (Eds.), *Essentials of neuropsychiatry and behavioral neurosciences* (2nd ed., pp. 473–497). Washington, DC: American Psychiatric Publishing.

Prigatano, G. P. (2014). Anosognosia and patterns of impaired self-awareness observed in clinical practice. *Cortex, 61,* 81–92.

Prigatano, G. P., Fordyce, D. J., Zeiner, H. K., Roueche, J. R., Pepping, M., & Wood, B. C. (1984). Neuropsychological rehabilitation after closed head injury in young adults. *Journal of Neurology, Neurosurgery, and Psychiatry, 47*(5), 505–513.

Prigatano, G. P., & Hill, S. W. (2018). Cognitive complaints, affect disturbances, and neuropsychological functioning in adults with psychogenic nonepileptic seizures. In W. C. LaFrance, Jr., & S. C. Schachter (Eds.), *Gates & Rowan's non-epileptic seizures* (4th ed., pp. 158–164). Cambridge, UK: Cambridge University Press.

Reijneveld, J., Sitskoorn, M., Klein, M., Nuyen, J., & Taphoorn, M. (2001). Cognitive status and quality of life in patients with suspected versus proven low-grade gliomas. *Neurology, 56*(5), 618–623.

Scherer, H. (1938). Structural development in gliomas. *American Journal of Cancer, 34*(3), 333–351.

Sherer, M., Meyers, C. A., & Bergloff, P. (1997). Efficacy of postacute brain injury rehabilitation for patients with primary malignant brain tumors. *Cancer, 80*(2), 250–257.

van Coevorden-van Loon, E. M., Coomans, M. B., Heijenbrok-Kal, M. H., Ribbers, G. M., & van den Bent, M. J. (2017). Fatigue in patients with low grade glioma: systematic evaluation of assessment and prevalence. *Journal of Neuro-oncology, 133*(2), 237–246.

van den Bent, M. J., Weller, M., Wen, P. Y., Kros, J. M., Aldape, K., & Chang, S. (2017). A clinical perspective on the 2016 WHO brain tumor classification and routine molecular diagnostics. *Neuro-oncology, 19*(5), 614–624.

van Kessel, E., Baumfalk, A. E., van Zandvoort, M. J., Robe, P. A., & Snijders, T. J. (2017). Tumor-related neurocognitive dysfunction in patients with diffuse glioma: A systematic review of neurocognitive functioning prior to anti-tumor treatment. *Journal of Neuro-oncology, 134*(1), 9–18.

Volterra, A., & Meldolesi, J. (2005). Astrocytes, from brain glue to communication elements: The revolution continues. *Nature Reviews Neuroscience, 6*(8), 626.

Warren, D. E., Power, J. D., Bruss, J., Denburg, N. L., Waldron, E. J., Sun, H., . . . Tranel, D. (2014). Network measures predict neuropsychological outcome after brain injury. *Proceedings of the National Academy of Sciences of the USA, 111*(39), 14247–14252.

Zwinkels, H., Dirven, L., Vissers, T., Habets, E. J., Vos, M. J., Reijneveld, J. C., . . . Taphoorn, M. J. (2016). Prevalence of changes in personality and behavior in adult glioma patients: A systematic review. *Neuro-Oncology Practice, 3*(4), 222–231.

17

PSYCHOLOGICAL CARE OF PERSONS WITH A HISTORY OF ANEURYSMAL SUBARACHNOID HEMORRHAGE

BACKGROUND INFORMATION

The psychological care of a person with a ruptured aneurysm in the posterior cerebral artery (PCA) was briefly discussed in Chapter 1. In Chapter 11, the neuropsychological consultation with a patient and his wife after the patient underwent surgical clipping of a ruptured aneurysm of the right pericallosal anterior cerebral artery (ACA) was briefly described. In this chapter, the psychological care of patients who have suffered a subarachnoid hemorrhage (SAH) secondary to a ruptured cerebral aneurysm is discussed in more detail.

SUBARACHNOID HEMORRHAGE AND INTRACRANIAL ANEURYSMS

Lawton and Vates (2017) note that SAH "without a preceding trauma is caused by the rupture of an intracranial aneurysm in 80% of cases" (p. 257). Intracranial aneurysms occur in 1% or 2% of the population and typically form at branch points along intracranial arteries (p. 257). Lawton and Vates state,

> When an aneurysm ruptures, it is an intracranial catastrophe. Blood pushes into the subarachnoid space at arterial pressure until the intracranial pressure equalizes across the ruptured site and stops the bleeding, with thrombus formation at the bleeding site. The reported case fatality rate is 25 to 50%. (p. 258)

Atangana et al. (2017) note that SAH can produce both primary and secondary forms of damage to the brain. Immediately after SAH, there is a sudden rise of intracranial pressure, which often results in a decrease in cerebral perfusion with associated hypoxia. In addition, global cerebral edema occurs. Accumulation of blood in multiple cisterns or fissures (Kreiter et al., 2002), in addition to accumulation in the subarachnoid space, can produce further pressure effects and brain herniation. If pressure effects are not reduced via medication and/or surgery, death can result. Using an experimental animal model, Atangana et al. suggest that there can be secondary effects of SAH. They note that in their study, SAH was associated with microglia changes, which contributed to neuronal cell death. These changes can be focal or widespread, depending on the location and extent of the SAH.

BLOOD SUPPLY TO THE BRAIN AND THE IMPACT OF RUPTURED ANTERIOR AND POSTERIOR ARTERY ANEURYSMS

The two ACAs supply oxygenated blood to most midline portions of the frontal lobes and superior medial parietal lobes. The two middle cerebral arteries (MCAs), with their multiple branches, supply oxygenated blood to most of the lateral cerebral cortex, including the frontal, parietal, and temporal structures. The MCAs are also the major blood supply to the anterior temporal lobes and the insular cortices. The two PCAs supply oxygenated blood primarily to the occipital cortex but also to the medial surfaces of the thalami, the inferior temporal gyri, the fusiform gyrus, the fornix, and brain regions beneath the splenium of the corpus callosum in addition to other important brain structures. Figure 17.1 provides a color representation of the exquisite manner in which these major arteries ensure adequate energy sources to the entire brain.

Although saccular aneurysms are most commonly found in the anterior circulation systems of the brain (estimated 86.5%; Ferguson, 1989), on average 30% are found in the distribution of the ACAs. In contrast, only approximately 1% are found in the distribution of the PCAs (Ciceri, Klucznik, Grossman, Rose, & Mawad, 2001). When these aneurysms rupture, mortality is quite high, as noted previously. Greenberg (2010) reported that more than 50% of patients die within the first 2 weeks of SAH. Figure 17.2 illustrates several important features of ruptured cerebral aneurysms and neurosurgical approaches to repair a ruptured cerebral aneurysm after SAH (Lawton & Vates, 2017). The neuropsychological and psychiatric morbidity of surviving patients can be substantial and greatly reduces the quality of life for many of them.

NEUROPSYCHOLOGICAL CONSEQUENCES OF ANEURYSMAL SUBARACHNOID HEMORRHAGE

Patients who survive aneurysmal SAH (aSAH) typically have some form of residual neuropsychological impairment. Kreiter et al. (2002) reported that for a group of 113 aSAH patients, performance on several cognitive tests was typically below normative standards. However, older age, less education, global edema, and a left cerebral hemisphere infarction at the time of hospital admission were predictive of poor neuropsychological test performance. The authors noted that the most common impairments were in verbal memory and motor functioning. The impairments, however, were generally in multiple domains, including reaction times, confrontational naming, rapidly and accurately shifting the cognitive set, and other measures of executive functioning. Interestingly, patients with posterior circulation aneurysms showed better neuropsychological test performance compared to other groups. Kreiter et al. suggested that this may be because "posterior circulation aneurysms generally result in less SAH coming in contact with the cortical surface of the brain" (p. 207).

Vilkki et al. (2004) also reported greater verbal memory deficits in patients who had a left versus a right aSAH. However, patients with bilateral medial or basal frontal lesions also performed very poorly on verbal memory tests.

Early studies noted that confusion and amnestic syndromes were common immediately

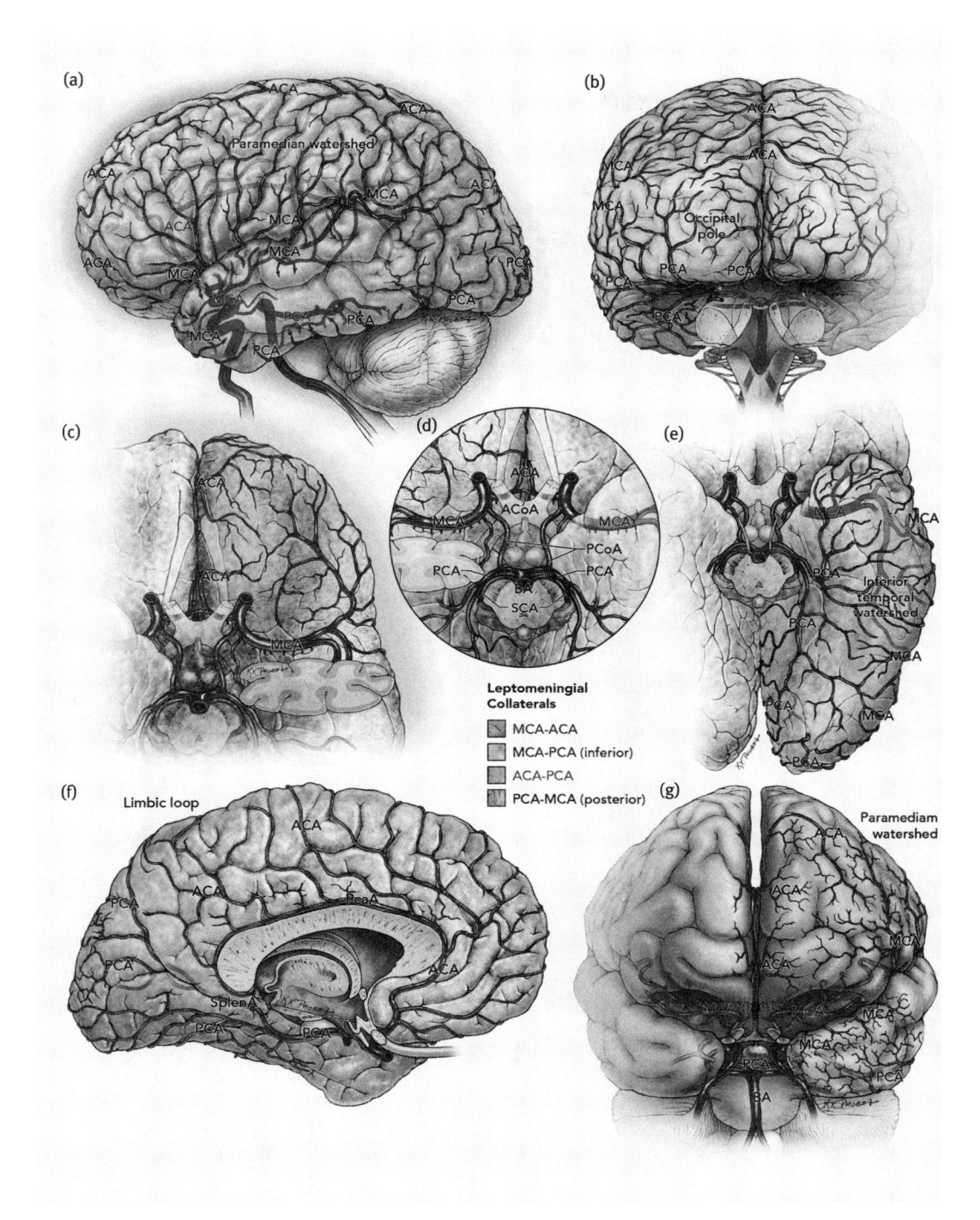

FIGURE 17.1 ACA, anterior cerebral artery; ACoA, anterior communicating; BA, basilar; MCA, middle cerebral artery; PCA, posterior cerebral artery; PcaA, pericallosal; PCoA, posterior communicating; SCA, superior cerebellar; SplenA, splenial (See color plates).

Source: Reprinted from Lawton, M. T., *Seven Bypasses: Tenets and Techniques for Revascularization*, 2018, by permission of Thieme Medical Publishers. Illustration by Kenneth Xavier Probst, MA, CMI.

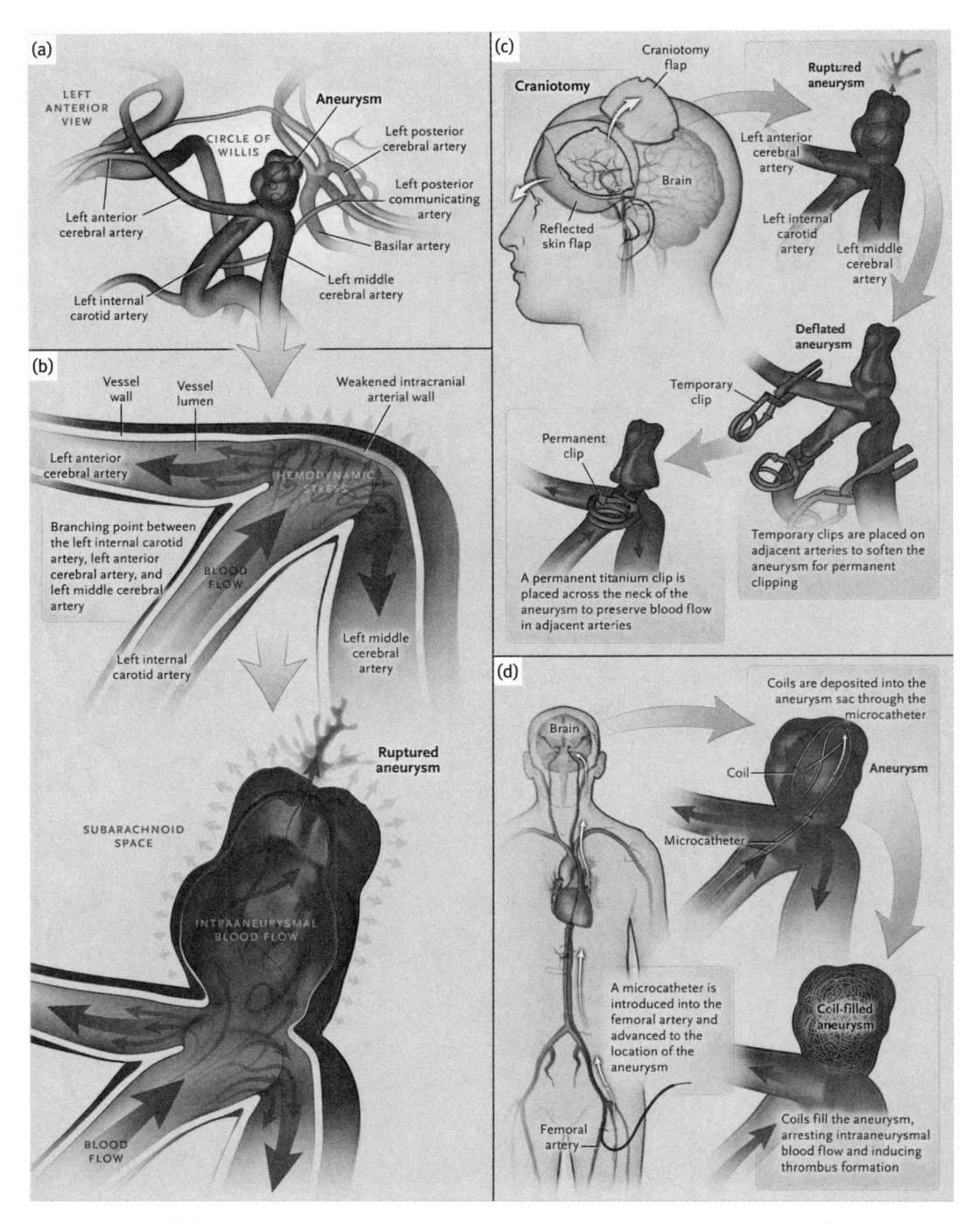

FIGURE 17.2 (A) Anatomy of the subarachnoid space and the circle of Willis. A major artery (the internal carotid artery) enters the skull from below and then follows a course through the subarachnoid space, giving off perforating branches that supply the parenchyma. (B) High pulsatile pressure at branching points of the proximal artery (arrow) soon after the arterial wall sheds much of its supporting adventitia can promote the formation of saccular aneurysms in susceptible persons. In such cases, an aneurysm forms at the branch point of an artery, where the arterial pulsation stress is maximal. Most lesions remain silent until rupture occurs, at which time blood is rapidly released into the subarachnoid space, leading to early effects, such as intracranial pressure

326 • CLINICAL APPLICATIONS

after ruptured aneurysms of the anterior communicating artery (ACoA; Gade, 1982; Volpe & Hirst, 1983). It was also noted that the hemorrhage often extended beyond frontal lobe structures and frequently extended to deep brain structures, including the thalamus, fornix, and hypothalamus (Gade, 1982). This helped explain the complex set of neurological and neuropsychological symptoms often observed in this particular patient group. Sleep disturbances, changes in mood and affect, and memory and intellectual impairments are often reported (Kreitschmann-Andermahr et al., 2007).

Various investigators also noted that the amnestic syndrome observed in ACoA patients often persisted. These patients showed the classic signs of an amnestic syndrome, which included severely impaired free recall of both visual and verbal information. Recognition memory was also impaired, but less than free recall. In general, measures of overall intelligence were within the normal range.

Later studies with this group of patients revealed less obvious but important cognitive disturbances frequently associated with frontal lobe dysfunction. For example, patients with ruptured ACoAs often made poor decisions while performing a risk-taking task (Mavaddat, Kirkpatrick, Rogers, & Sahakian, 2000), even in the presence of normal IQ scores. They did not appear to be impulsive but, rather, used poor judgment when making decisions that carried different magnitudes of reward and punishment. In common parlance, family members might describe these patients as not thinking through the consequences of their actions despite their normal intelligence.

In addition, patients with aSAH have been described as having problems with "social cognition" (Buunk et al., 2017). That is, these patients have difficulty recognizing emotional reactions in others. They also are frequently described as showing less empathy for others and have difficulty understanding the actions and intentions of others (i.e., they perform poorly on theory of mind tests). These difficulties have been associated with impaired self-awareness (ISA). Clinically, spouses often describe these individuals as apathetic and less motivated to engage others or to become involved in new tasks. They have considerable difficulty organizing their day and showing appropriate initiative in various social situations. This is often in striking contrast to their functioning prior to the SAH.

FIGURE 17.2   Continued

elevation, parenchymal irritation, edema, and hydrocephalus, and delayed effects, such as vasospasm and delayed cerebral ischemia. (C) Open surgical repair of such an aneurysm involves exposing the aneurysm and the adjacent normal arteries so that the surgeon can apply a titanium clip on the neck of the aneurysm, which effectively excludes it from the arterial circulation. Removal of portions of the skull base provides improved access and operative exposure for the surgeon without the need for substantial brain retraction. The aneurysm is then collapsed and the field inspected to ensure that no branches are compromised by the clip placement. The inner walls of the aneurysm base are approximated by the clip, which generally provides a lifelong cure of the lesion. (D) Endovascular repair of such an aneurysm involves the navigation of an intra-arterial catheter through the circulation under fluoroscopic guidance until the catheter tip is in the lumen of the aneurysm. With the use of the catheter, platinum coils are delivered and packed into the lumen of the aneurysm, which slows or prevents blood flow into the aneurysm and leads to thrombus formation, effectively blocking arterial blood from entering the aneurysm. Angiographic examination of the results confirms flow through the normal arterial branches. Not all aneurysms can be treated with endovascular repair (some will have to be treated with surgery), but endovascular repair can treat many aneurysms without a visible scar (See color plates).

Source: From Lawton, M. T., & Vates, G. E., Subarachnoid hemorrhage, *New England Journal of Medicine*, 377(3), p. 257–266, Copyright © 2017. Reprinted with permission from Massachusetts Medical Society.

NEUROPSYCHOLOGICAL CONSEQUENCES OF A RUPTURED POSTERIOR COMMUNICATING ARTERY

Given that approximately 1% of all intracranial ruptured aneurysms involve the PCA, the neuropsychological consequences of these lesions have been less studied. However, various neuropsychological symptoms have been reported after ruptured PCA aneurysms. Visual disturbances are perhaps most common. This is expected in light of the role of the PCA in supplying blood to the occipital lobe (see Figure 17.1). However, given that the PCA provides "feeders" to the fusiform gyrus and has segments that supply blood to the thalamus, hippocampus, and parietal regions of the brain, other neuropsychological deficits can be observed in this patient group. These deficits, however, often involve some sort of visual disturbance or higher order visual–spatial recognition difficulties, including visual neglect (Bird et al., 2006). In rare cases, a special form of amnesia is seen, which is referred to as "reduplicative paramnesia" (recall the patient described in Chapter 1, this volume).

Reduplicative paramnesia (RA) is a clinical condition in which the person "asserts the presence of two or more places with nearly identical attributes, while only one exists in reality" (Patterson & Mack, 1985, p. 111). This phenomenon is often short-lived, but it can persist even after the initial period of confusion disappears following aSAH. It is not associated with global amnesia, but it seems specific to reduplicative phenomena (Patterson & Mack, 1985). Not uncommonly, these lesions are in the right cerebral hemisphere in right-handed individuals. It has been reported, however, that RA can occur following a left hemisphere stroke in left-handed persons (Budson, Roth, Rentz, & Ronthal, 2000). Although clinical evidence often suggests bilateral cerebral dysfunction associated with frontal lobe pathology (Pisani, Marra, & Silveri, 2000), investigators have noted that damage or disruption of the ventral visual system (i.e., temporal–occipital pathways) involving the nondominant cerebral hemisphere may play a key role in RA (Budson et al., 2000).

Another syndrome associated with disturbed blood flow to both occipital regions of the brain is cortical blindness without subjective awareness of that blindness. The syndrome is referred to as Anton's syndrome (see Chapter 9, this volume). Although Anton's syndrome can be permanent (Maddula, Lutton, & Keegan, 2009), it typically resolves if the disruption of blood flow to the occipital lobes and associated surrounding cortex is short-lived (Argenta & Morgan, 1998).

PSYCHIATRIC CONSEQUENCES OF ANEURYSMAL SUBARACHNOID HEMORRHAGE

Persistent changes in personality and mood state after aSAH have been repeatedly reported (Hütter & Kreitschmann-Andermahr, 2014). Some of the studies in the field that have implications for psychological care for this patient group are reviewed here.

Depression and Anxiety

In a prospective study, Powell, Kitchen, Heslin, and Greenwood (2002, 2004) evaluated psychosocial outcome in 52 adult patients with a good neurological recovery after aSAH during an 18-month period. Their work is especially interesting because they included in their analyses measures of pre- and postmorbid functional status on several dimensions. They also matched individual patients with healthy controls on age, sex, and occupation. The location of the ruptured aneurysms, however, was not reported. Powell et al. reported clinically significant depression and anxiety (as measured by the Hospital Anxiety and Depression scale) in 14% and 16% of patients, respectively, in the two studies. Depression and anxiety did not decrease during an 18-month follow-up period. Behavioral indicators of anxiety were most prominent (an estimated 1 in 5 patients demonstrated significant anxiety). Other investigators have reported similar findings and emphasize that the incidence of anxiety may be even higher in this population of patients. For example, Visser-Meily, Rhebergen, Rinkel, van Zandvoort, and Post (2009) reported that 2–4 years after aSAH, 32% of patients reported anxiety and 23% reported depression. Sixty-seven percent reported ongoing difficulties with fatigue. Recent research emphasizes anxiety as a predictor of limited social activities following aSAH (Huenges Wajer et al., 2017).

Although Powell et al. (2002) noted that a composite "mood disturbance" score was related to pre-existing mental health difficulties (accounting for 15% of the variance), other variables were also important. Level of physical health accounted for 12% of the variance, the presence of dysphasia accounted for 8%, and residual memory difficulties (as measured by prose recall) accounted for 5%.

One of the most interesting observations by Powell et al. (2002) was that patients with a history of aSAH often demonstrated intrusive thoughts regarding their medical condition and often avoided talking about anything that reminded them of their SAH. The authors noted that at one point, more than 60% of their sample was considered to show symptoms of post-traumatic stress disorder (PTSD).

Post-Traumatic Stress Disorder

In their 18-month follow-up study, Powell et al. (2004) reported that "full blown post-traumatic stress disorder" was observed in only 3 of the 49 patients they were able to follow. However, they noted that intrusive thoughts regarding the experience of SAH presented in 22% of their study population. Although increased dependence on others, loss of organizational skills, and loss of employment were common in this group of patients, "very little variance in outcome was predicted by demographic variables, neurological or cognitive impairment, prior life stress or mood" (p. 1119).

The great variability of outcomes remained somewhat of a mystery.

The observation that the level of cognitive and physical (neurological) impairments may not easily explain reduced functional capacity led other investigators to consider alternative explanations. Noble et al. (2008), for example, investigated the incidence of PTSD in a group of 105 adults with a history of SAH, the majority of whom had aSAH. On average, the study sample was 109 days post-SAH for their first assessment. Noble et al. reported that 37% of their patient sample met diagnostic criteria for PTSD. These patients often had the worst quality-of-life scores. Maladaptive coping strategies were reported to "increase the probability of PTSD" (p. 1101). This was indirect evidence that for some patients with SAH, PTSD may contribute to their functional outcomes.

Visser-Meily et al. (2013) also attempted to measure the frequency of PTSD in 94 patients with aSAH. They reported that 3 years post aSAH, 1 out of 4 patients had PTSD and that having a passive coping style appeared to put a patient at risk for PTSD. What produces a passive coping style is an important issue. Such a style may be a result of anxiety, depression, or apathy. It may relate to the level or nature of cognitive impairments, which in turn is related to lesion location. A passive coping style may also be related to pre-existing personality characteristics. Unfortunately, the study by Visser-Meily et al. did not address this important question, but some interesting trends were observed in their data. Although only 14 of their 94 patients (15%) had aneurysms in the posterior circulation, 7 of these 14 patients (50%) were described as presenting with PTSD. Eighty of the 94 patients had aneurysms in the anterior circulation (i.e., 85% of the study sample). Of these 80 patients, 17 (21.5%) showed signs of PTSD.

Hütter and Kreitschmann-Andermahr (2014) conducted structured clinical interviews to determine the presence of PTSD in 45 patients with a history of aSAH. At approximately 4 years post-hemorrhage, 27%

of the patients were diagnosed with PTSD. Interestingly, the authors scored sleep disturbance only if the patients' sleep problems were clearly related to thoughts or worries regarding their bleeding, treatment, or later sequelae. Fear of recurring hemorrhage was more common in the PTSD group. Those in the PTSD group also showed a greater tendency to avoid thinking or talking about their hemorrhage. They had more intrusive thoughts about the SAH experience. For this group, measures of avoidance and intrusion significantly and positively correlated with the Beck Depression Inventory: The correlations were $r = .45$ and $r = .52$, respectively ($p < .001$ for each). The findings suggest that patients with a history of aSAH who have adequate cognitive skills to experience anxiety and depression may be prone to PTSD.

PSYCHOTIC SYMPTOMS AFTER ANEURYSMAL SUBARACHNOID HEMORRHAGE

Psychotic symptoms are rare after aSAH, but they do occur. In a four-center research project conducted in Hong Kong, Wong et al. (2014) asked spouses or caregivers to describe neuropsychiatric outcomes of 103 patients who had a history of aSAH. Patients were at least 1 year post-SAH. Delusions and hallucinations were reported in only 2% of the sample the authors studied. Agitation/aggression, depression, apathy/indifference, and irritability/lability were the most common neuropsychiatric symptoms reported by significant others. Interestingly, the neuropsychiatric symptoms of this patient group were related to the presence of chronic hydrocephalus that required shunt implantation.

A case report of persistent delusional behavior following aSAH caused by a ruptured basilar artery aneurysm in a 48-year-old woman was reported by Anderson, Camp, and Filley (1998). The nature of the delusion was the belief that "a physician at the hospital where she worked was in love with her. She based this belief on the 'special' look he had given her in the hospital cafeteria" (p. 331). There was no evidence, however, that this was in fact the case. This type of delusion, known as erotomania, has been described in patients with different brain abnormalities, including severe traumatic brain injury, seizure disorder, and brain tumors (Anderson et al., 1998). It is interesting to note that it often occurs in patients with a premorbid history of depression and dissatisfaction in their personal lives.

The patient described by Anderson et al. (1998) also had a history of persisting hydrocephalus. More than 30 years ago, Roberts, Trimble, and Robertson (1983) described a series of case studies in which delusional symptoms were observed in some patients with hydrocephalus secondary to aqueduct stenosis. They speculated that compression of the diencephalon might place a person at risk for delusional symptoms. More recently, Kito et al. (2009) reported that more than 12% of a sample of patients with normal pressure hydrocephalus showed evidence of delusions. The neuroanatomical correlates of the delusions were difficult to identify.

SOCIAL ISOLATION, APATHY, IMPAIRED SELF-AWARENESS, AND QUALITY OF LIFE AFTER ANEURYSMAL SUBARACHNOID HEMORRHAGE

As noted in Chapter 11, Buchanan, Elias, and Goplen (2000) found that descriptions of the quality of life of patients following aSAH can be quite different depending on whether one asks the patient, the family member, or the neurosurgeon. Depending on their reference point, these individuals can describe a "good" or "favorable" outcome, but some do not. By the nature of their neurocognitive difficulties, patients with aSAH may have ISA, as noted previously. They tend to underreport their actual functional difficulties (Buunk et al., 2017). Many of these patients (especially those with frontal lobe dysfunction) are also apathetic (Buunk et al., 2017) and report no distress or depression, which can give a false impression about the actual quality of their life. These patients may appear "content" or "nondistressed," but their caregivers (especially spouses) can be quite distressed secondary to the significant cognitive and behavioral changes they witness daily. Observing no neurological deficits, the neurosurgeon may consider both a noncomplaining and a compliant patient as having a good quality of life because they survived the potential lethal effects of aSAH.

Early studies on a mixed group of patients with ruptured cerebral aneurysms (including ACoA, internal carotid, and MCA aneurysms but not PCA aneurysms) reported that patients had a wide range of impairments on tests of intellectual functioning, memory, visual–spatial abilities, and processing of information (Ljunggren, Sonesson, Säveland, & Brandt, 1985). These studies noted that patients who made a good neurological recovery (e.g., no hemiparesis or aphasia) often presented with measurable cognitive impairments that appeared to negatively affect quality of life.

Following this mixed group of patients for 20–28 years post aSAH, Sonesson, Kronvall, Säveland, Brandt, and Nilsson (2018) reported that "more than half of the patients with SAH who had early good neurological recovery experienced reintegration difficulties after >20 years" (p. 785). Sleep disturbances, fatigue, and residual cognitive problems in memory function and executive functions were noted. Throughout the years, other investigators have emphasized the problem of fatigue in this patient group and the overall decrease in the quality of life given the physical and neuropsychological disturbances commonly observed (Visser-Meily et al., 2009). Collectively, these findings clearly make an argument for the need for continued and long-term psychological care for patients with aSAH and mostly likely their spouses as well.

PSYCHOLOGICAL CARE OF A PERSON WITH A RUPTURED ANTERIOR CEREBRAL ARTERY ANEURYSM WITH SUBARACHNOID HEMORRHAGE

Medical History

At 59 years of age, a successful practicing attorney suffered a small SAH secondary to a ruptured aneurysm on the right pericallosal anterior cerebral artery. The aneurysm was successfully surgically clipped, and the man returned to his normal work and home activities without any obvious impairment following a course of neurorehabilitation. Five years later, he presented with an acute change in his mental status. Computed tomography of the brain revealed extensive SAH as well as intraventricular hemorrhage. He also had a right frontal intraparenchymal hematoma with enlargement of both lateral ventricles. He underwent surgical reclipping of that pericallosal aneurysm.

Approximately 8 days after surgery, there was again an acute decline in the patient's neurological status witnessed by the onset of a seizure and worsening mental status. Neuroimaging of the brain revealed a recurrence of aSAH adjacent to the left pericallosal artery. There was also downward tentorial herniation. Reclipping was again performed. It was noted that there was mild vasospasm of both anterior cerebral arteries as well as the posterior cerebral arteries. Hydrocephalus developed, and a ventriculoperitoneal shunt was inserted.

The patient's course during hospitalization was further characterized by a series of medical complications, including respiratory failure, pneumonia, dysphagia, and a small pulmonary embolism. He remained in the hospital for approximately 5 weeks after surgery and then was transferred to inpatient neurorehabilitation, which revealed many of the expected disturbances in higher integrative brain functioning, including hypoarousal, confused and confabulatory thinking, apraxia, severe memory impairments, and limited speech production. The patient often would not initiate communications or any other activity. At times, he would close his eyes for long periods but remained awake. It appeared that he was either overwhelmed with what was occurring in his environment or needed to reduce stimulus input when attempting to respond. The point of these observations is that the patient demonstrated severe and multiple neurocognitive impairments for several weeks after surgery.

Family education regarding the nature of frontal lobe dysfunction ensued during the course of inpatient neurorehabilitation, followed by discussions regarding caregiver burnout and the importance of caregiver self-care. The patient's wife was a highly intelligent woman, and after listening to these discussions, she said she believed that she could help her husband regain much of his cognitive capacity. This idea was reinforced when the skilled neurosurgeon involved in her husband's care assured her that with time, her husband would greatly improve (this was also mentioned in Chapter 11, this volume).

Outpatient Neuropsychological Examination Findings and Consultation

After approximately 1 year post aSAH, the patient's wife asked the attending neurologist, who was prescribing medications for seizure control, to refer the patient for a neuropsychological examination. The patient was never referred by the attending neurosurgeon. Despite the neurosurgeon's encouraging words that her husband would get better with time, the patient continued to be severely impaired from a neuropsychological perspective. The wife needed help understanding what was "wrong." Would he ever get better? What could be done to help him? What did the neuropsychological examination findings reveal?

During the clinical interview, the patient was quiet but pleasant and cooperative. He appeared alert with no obvious speech or language impairments. He had no obvious motor impairments. When specifically asked if he experienced any difficulties with his memory, he paused and with some reflection stated that he did not notice any difficulties. When asked about possible difficulties in sustaining his concentration, he again reported no difficulties. When answering these questions, he would frequently turn toward his wife in an apparent effort to see what her perceptions were regarding him and whether she appeared to agree with his answers.

The patient's wife noted his severe difficulties with memory and specifically noted equally severe difficulties with initiation and motivation to accomplish tasks in everyday life. This was in striking contrast to his functioning prior to his last aSAH and the surgical reclipping of his aneurysm, as described previously. The patient's wife was apparently trying to be positive and not reveal the depth of her frustration and sadness over her husband's condition.

The patient was administered various neuropsychological tests at different times following his aSAH to determine the extent of his neurocognitive difficulties and any indications of improved functioning over time. His major findings were as follows (and have not changed with time): His IQ scores were in the average to mildly above average range (Wechsler Adult Intelligence Scale–Second Edition Verbal Comprehension Index Score of 111, a Perceptual Reasoning Index score of 108, and an estimated Full Scale IQ of 108). His vocabulary score remained clearly superior using normative standards and was compatible with his occupation as an attorney. Visual–spatial problem-solving skills were repeatedly in the average range, as were verbal reasoning skills. It appeared that some decline in verbal problem-solving had occurred (given his occupational background) despite his average scores. It should be kept in mind that "average scores" do not necessarily reflect "normal functioning" for some individuals.

The patient's performance on memory tests revealed severe difficulties with new learning and retention of whatever information he could learn. For example, on the Rey Auditory Verbal Learning Test, he was able to recall 6 words on Trial 1, followed by 6 words on Trial 2. On Trials 3, 4, and 5, he recalled 6, 7, and 7 words, respectively. The total number of words he recalled was 32, producing an age-adjusted T score of 44. After a brief distraction, he could recall none of the words (T score = 26). Twenty minutes later, he could recall none of the words (T score = 32). His performance on the Wechsler Memory Scale–Revised form also revealed severe learning and memory difficulties for both verbal and visual memory, with delayed recall of both short stories and visual–spatial designs being at the first percentile.

Verbal fluency scores were within the average range, despite the patient's above-average vocabulary. His performance on the Trail Making Test Part B (which requires connecting numbers and letters in an alternating manner) was below normative expectations. He often took nearly 3 minutes to complete the task, and he made several errors. Speed of finger movements (as measured by the Halstead Finger Tapping Test) was consistently above average in both hands.

Thus, the patient had a true amnestic disorder with no aphasic or motor impairments. On psychometric assessment, he had subtle changes in executive functioning, but in everyday life he was quite impaired in his problem-solving abilities. Regarding his functional capacity in everyday life, he reported no major difficulties. In contrast, his wife reported that he had considerable difficulties with memory, attention span, problem-solving, and initiating behaviors to improve his daily functional capacity and also that he had an apparent loss of motivation. These latter findings also suggested definite ISA of his neuropsychological impairments. He showed no anxiety or defensiveness when performing neuropsychological tests. He showed no anxiety or depression when the test findings were reviewed with him and his wife. He appeared more subdued by the findings and apologetic for his level of performance. He did not appear to show any classical signs of denial of disability (see Chapter 9, this volume). He did not appear to show any signs of PTSD. Apathy (reduced motivation and initiative), social withdrawal, and a severe amnestic syndrome with ISA characterized his neuropsychological status, which remained permanent and did not improve with time. His wife now knew "what was wrong."

His wife also had an answer to the question regarding whether his condition would improve: He most likely would not get better over time. His clinical picture appeared permanent. The following question was now addressed: What can be done to help him now?

Efforts at Psychological Care

The patient's wife felt relieved with the neuropsychological explanation of her husband's difficulties. She now had a better understanding of "what was wrong." She also felt sad and experienced a sense of helplessness over whether he could be helped to further improve his cognitive functioning. She was a very accomplished woman and had viewed her husband's problems as a major challenge that she would help him overcome. She now recognized that she (and he) could benefit from some further external help. She was referred to a very experienced occupational therapist skilled in training patients to use a memory notebook to compensate for their memory difficulties in everyday life (Prigatano & Kime, 2003).

The patient and his wife saw the therapist for a series of training sessions. The patient began using his memory notebook. However, at times he forgot to use the notebook or forgot where he placed it. His entries in the notebook often gave unnecessary details and appeared to reflect problems with organizing his thoughts and summarizing the most important points that needed to be remembered. His wife was frustrated with this but continued to be supportive. She tried to give him gentle reminders of how he could become more functional in the home and use the notebook to greater advantage.

Despite these integrated and intensive efforts, the effectiveness of the intervention was modest, and the work with the occupational therapist ended.

The patient continued to be monitored from a neuropsychological perspective, and the wife's frustrations became more evident. She felt totally alone in helping her husband and discouraged not only with his persistent memory difficulties but also with his lack of initiative and difficulties interacting socially with family members and friends. Whereas in the past he had always attempted to be polite and sensitive to others, he was now observed sitting quietly for long periods of time in the presence of others and not engaging them in conversation. In social settings, he did not seem to respond well to established social cues. For example, if he liked a certain food in a buffet line at a dinner party, he would take more of the food item than would be socially correct given other people's potential desire for the same food item. When this was brought to his attention after the party was over, he could become angry and upset. On rare occasions, he would voice how "stupid" he was now. He would make occasional derogatory remarks about himself when his limited capacities were brought to his attention. These appeared to be "mini" catastrophic reactions, as Goldstein (1952) described them. He would often quickly "recuperate" after such reactions and return to being quiet and appreciative of his wife's care. In fact, during each time he was seen, he would routinely talk about how lucky he was to be married to his wife. He would say this with a somewhat boyish smile. He never voiced any frustration or anger toward her.

After his fourth neuropsychological examination (approximately 18 months after his initial evaluation and 30 months after his last aSAH), another attempt was made to provide psychological care for him and his wife. After some discussion, it was agreed that they would both be seen weekly by a clinical neuropsychologist and a clinical neuropsychology resident for 1-hour sessions. Typically, during the first part of the hour (approximately 10–15 minutes), the patient, his wife, the clinical neuropsychologist, and the resident in clinical neuropsychology would meet. A review of the week, including "successes" and "failures" at being more independent in a variety of activities, was performed. Then the resident would work with the patient with a renewed effort to monitor his mood, reinforce the use of a memory notebook and daytime planner, and train/guide him to carry out tasks that he enjoyed. During this time, the clinical neuropsychologist would talk to the patient's wife regarding a variety of topics related to her marriage with her husband and her positive and negative reactions toward him, in addition to providing suggestions for dealing with her frustrations with him in the most productive manner. With time, these discussions focused on other stressors the patient's wife experienced with other family members who required her attention as well. Toward the end of the 1-hour session (typically the last 10 minutes), all four individuals would meet to discuss what had been done or accomplished during the session. These discussions kept everyone informed and seemed to foster an important trusting relationship between all parties. The patient would often express appreciation to the psychologists for taking the time to help him and his wife. Note, however, that this schedule was not always followed. Occasionally, the clinical neuropsychologist spent more time talking directly to the patient about his life, his previous work as an attorney, his desires for the future, and his reaction to his medical condition.

The outcome from these interventions (which lasted more than 1 year) was that the patient again began using his memory notebook more regularly and the patient's wife had someone with whom to talk concerning the stresses she experienced in several domains. She appeared calmer with time, and the patient appeared to be content living his life without obvious resentments. His wife, however, experienced considerable resentment toward physicians who did not seem to take a real interest in how her husband had changed and her need for help when he left the hospital and ended formal rehabilitation programs.

The discussions with both the patient and his wife often focused on present-day functional concerns. Psychodynamic issues were not the focus of discussion. However, the patient's wife spontaneously recognized how her personality was similar to that of her mother when dealing with a spouse who required care following a brain disorder. This often resulted in a smile or a laugh as she recognized her need to never be defeated by any challenge. This seemed to help further bolster her resiliency. The discussions and interventions did not improve the patient's memory functioning and only modestly improved his ability to use a memory notebook. The discussions, however, provided continued professional contact to help address the concerns of the patient's wife and her need to feel supported by someone who understood her husband's medical condition and his neuropsychological status. She was no longer "alone" with the problems she experienced daily.

Table 17.1 summarizes the clinically relevant features of the patient's psychological care. Note that many of the features associated with improved psychological well-being seen in other patient groups are not positively checked off for this patient. His apathy, ISA, and cognitive impairments seem to preclude achievements in these areas. However, he was able to follow the guidance of his clinical neuropsychologist and expressed enjoyment in helping his wife at home. He could "live with" the restrictions produced by the brain disorder without any obvious resentment. Table 17.2 summarizes important features of his wife's psychological care. She felt supported and not alone when attempting to help her husband. She was able to maintain her resiliency in light of those supports. Although she was not especially hopeful that her husband's clinical condition would change, she was hopeful that she could handle his changed functional capacities.

APPROACHES TO PSYCHOLOGICAL CARE OF PERSONS WITH ANEURYSMAL SUBARACHNOID HEMORRHAGE

The literature on interventions aimed specifically at improving psychological care for adults with aSAH is considerably less extensive than that on other patient groups. For example, no studies could be located that evaluated the effects of cognitive–behavioral therapy (CBT) in reducing depression, anxiety, or PTSD after aSAH. No studies could be found that evaluated the potential use of brief psychodynamic psychotherapies for addressing these problems. In addition, no behavioral studies could be found concerning how to improve apathy, social isolation, or fatigue after aSAH. This is somewhat surprising in light of the rather large literature devoted to describing the neuropsychological and psychosocial problems of these patients. That literature emphasizes the importance of residual cognitive and emotional disturbances in significantly compromising the quality of life in patients with a history of aSAH (Buunk, Groen, Veenstra, & Spikman, 2015; Huenges Wajer et al., 2017).

The lack of specific literature on therapies aimed at improving psychological care of patients with aSAH may, in part, be due to the tendency to consider patients with aSAH as a "sub-type of stroke" (Stern, Chang, Odell, & Sperber, 2006, p. 679). For example, in a study of neuropsychiatric disturbances associated with aSAH, Wong et al. (2014) suggested that aSAH accounts for "only 3–5% of all strokes" (p. 1695). Furthermore, the rehabilitation interventions and needs of patients with aSAH appear identical to those reported in the stroke rehabilitation literature (Shukla, 2017).

The research on the efficacy of reducing depression and anxiety in broadly defined "stroke patients" is wanting. The Cochrane reviews on interventions for treating anxiety (Knapp et al., 2017) and depression (Hackett, Anderson, House, & Xia, 2008) do not give an adequate picture of what can be done psychologically to

Table 17.1 Clinical Features Relevant to the Psychological Care of a Person with a Subarachnoid Hemorrhage Following a Right Pericallosal Anterior Cerebral Artery Aneurysm

CLINICAL FEATURE	YES	NO	PARTIALLY
1. The dialogue between the patient and the clinical neuropsychologist was not rushed.	✓		
2. The patient was able to express or clearly convey his personal concerns.		✓	
3. The content of the concerns varied over time.		✓	
4. The patient experienced a sense of "realistic" hope in coping with his life situation.			✓
5. The patient and the clinical neuropsychologist developed a positive therapeutic relationship that helped the patient sustain adaptive activities during difficult times.			✓
6. Somatic symptoms (which appeared to be indirect effects of a brain disorder) were substantially reduced during periods of psychological care.			n/a
7. Anxiety/depression/anger and/or apathy were substantially reduced during periods of psychological care.		✓	
8. The patient was able to follow the guidance of the clinical neuropsychologist to improve his functioning in everyday life activities.	✓		
9. The patient was able to control impulses and delay gratification.			✓
10. The patient developed a new sense of competency or "mastery" following the brain disorder.		✓	
11. The patient was able to "self-reflect" or "be more aware" of personal "strengths" and "limitations."		✓	
12. The patient experienced enjoyment in the care or help of other living things (people, animals, the environment, etc.).	✓		
13. The patient had an improved understanding of the "problematic nature of life" (given his psychosocial state of life) and was not overwhelmed or "defeated" by it or readily gave in to escapism to cope with life (Bettelheim, 1989).		✓	
14. The patient could "live with" the restrictions produced by a brain injury "without resentment" (Goldstein, 1952).	✓		
15. The patient was able to obtain new insights into self by attending to why certain songs, stories, fairy tales, movies, tattoos, etc. had a special personal meaning that initially he did not understand.		✓	

Table 17.1 Continued

CLINICAL FEATURE	YES	NO	PARTIALLY
16. The patient's dreams or artwork often heralded changes in behavior that aided in psychological adjustment before the consciously mediated changes occurred.		✓	
17. The psychological care interventions (including the dialogue) between the patient and the clinical neuropsychologist resulted in the patient talking more openly about problems and demonstrating self-directed efforts at improving psychological adjustment to the direct and indirect effects of the brain disorder.		✓	
18. The psychological care interventions were in harmony with the patient's cultural background and religious orientation.	✓		
19. The psychological care interventions were appropriate for the patient's psychosocial stage of development and facilitated psychosocial development/adaptation in later stages of life.	✓		
20. The patient and family experienced two basic facts of life: (a) The individual's state of subjective sense of personal well-being fluctuates, and (b) the psychological adjustment process is never static and therefore hope should never be abandoned.			✓
Total	6	9	4

Table 17.2 Clinically Relevant Features of the Spouse of the Case Study Patient When Providing Psychological Care

CLINICAL FEATURE	YES	NO	PARTIALLY
1. Quality of the relationship before the onset of the brain disorder was good.	✓		
2. Spouse has adequate supports that help maintain her resiliency.	✓		
3. Spouse is personally offended by the behavioral problems of the patient.		✓	
4. Spouse has a good working (therapeutic) relationship with the clinical neuropsychologist.	✓		
5. Spouse understands the biological factors (and at times the psychological factors) underlying the behavioral problems of the patient.	✓		
6. Spouse does not feel "alone" in the care of the patient.	✓		
7. Spouse has some sense of "hope" that the behavioral problems will get better with time and/or there is "light at the end of the tunnel."		✓	
Total	5	2	

reduce these emotional disorders in patients and their family members. Limited studies are included in such reviews without detailed discussion of how specific patient types undergoing specific forms of psychotherapy were or were not helped from a psychological care perspective (for a further critique, see Prigatano, 2018). Strict reliance on randomized group studies seems to lead to the repetitive conclusion that "evidence is insufficient" for making recommendations or suggesting treatments that can indeed be helpful.

Clinicians in the field clearly recognize that any psychological intervention must be tailored to the individual needs of the person (Coetzer, 2014), including taking into account the underlying neurological disorder and associated neuropsychological and psychiatric deficits (Schmidt, Piliavska, Maier-Ring, van Husen, & Dettmers, 2017). As such, several studies that have the potential for improving efforts at psychological care of patients with aSAH are reviewed next.

Persson, Törnbom, Sunnerhagen, and Törnbom (2017) interviewed 16 patients who were on average 6 years post SAH. Eleven of the 16 patients had a history of a ruptured cerebral aneurysm with aSAH. Their findings are relevant to the topic of psychological care of persons (and family members) who have suffered aSAH. In their qualitative study, Persson et al. noted that these patients were very appreciative of the acute medical and surgical care they received. They were thankful for being alive. However, many voiced feeling "abandoned" by the medical community once their neurological problems were acutely treated. They were not prepared to understand and manage the various neurological and neuropsychological problems that would ensue. This was exactly the experience of the patient's wife described previously. Many patients (and most likely their family members) were not prepared to deal with the cognitive, emotional, and motivational problems that they would encounter in everyday life. These patients' perception of time was affected, as was their memory of when specific events occurred. This was also a key feature of the patient described previously, although it was not specifically mentioned as part of his amnestic difficulties.

Four coping strategies used by patients were described. These strategies helped reveal the natural response tendencies that members of this patient group used to reduce their psychological distress. First, after formal rehabilitation ended, many patients started to practice physical exercises on a daily basis. They also became more aware of their diet and began to eat in a more healthy manner. They were now "more health conscious." Trying to stay physically healthy was often the first "line of defense" in coping with the residual effects of aSAH, which often included fatigue.

A second coping strategy was to rely more on spouses, partners, or caregivers. This was also observed in the patient described previously. Many patients recognized the value of this support and regularly recognized their spouses for their help (also like the patient discussed previously). However, patients do not always fully appreciate the negative impact this can have on a spouse.

A third coping strategy was to concentrate on the positive and avoid negative thoughts. Again, this was observed in the patient described previously. It is an approach used in CBT for depression. It is unclear as to what patient characteristics naturally result in this approach to problems encountered in everyday life following aSAH.

A fourth common coping strategy of these patients was to "keep up appearances" by ceasing to engage in some activities that would reveal their deficits. By not engaging in activities that would reveal their cognitive, behavioral, or motor limitations, patients may avoid what Goldstein (1952) described as catastrophic reactions. This approach, however, can lead to increased social isolation for the patient and the spouse.

A Korean study reported decreased depression and anxiety in 11 patients with aSAH who underwent mindfulness-based interventions to reduce stress (Joo, Lee, Chung, & Shin, 2010). The multiple interventions included meditation exercises, such as "loving-kindness" meditation, "body scanning," and Hatha yoga. These approaches are based on Buddhist spiritual practices (Marchand, 2012) and thus represent a form of psychological intervention that blends philosophical and religious practices to aid psychological adjustment.

One case report demonstrated the potential usefulness of reducing anxiety and increasing social interaction/participation in a 42-year-old man with a history of SAH (Gracey, Oldham, & Kritzinger, 2007). Many of this patient's "panic" symptoms were successfully reduced by helping him verbally identify symptoms and restricting his cognitive appraisal of those symptoms.

A few studies have noted the potential role of emotional support in reducing subjective cognitive complaints of patients with aSAH (e.g., Toomela et al., 2004). Other studies, dealing with a heterogeneous group of stroke patients, have documented the potential role of family support in facilitating environmental change that fosters greater independence in the patient (Tsouna-Hadjis, Vemmos, Zakopoulos, & Stamatelopoulos, 2000).

SUMMARY

Given the variable locations of ruptured aneurysms and resultant severity of aSAH, forms of psychological care interventions can be quite diverse. Detailed case studies are needed to help clarify important changes in the neuropsychological and psychiatric functioning of this heterogeneous group of individuals. Understanding the dynamic interplay between the patient's premorbid personality and neuropsychological status, on the one hand, and what is observed in the clinical interview and on formal neuropsychological tests, on the other hand, is the beginning point of such interventions. Taking time to listen to the concerns of the patient and family is crucial to establishing a therapeutic alliance that can reduce the psychological suffering of the patient and, in many instances, that of family members as well. Although support groups and environmental restrictions of the patient's daily activities can be helpful, the permanency of the patient's neuropsychological difficulties should not be underestimated. The goal is not to give up hope that a better psychosocial adjustment can be achieved. Rather, the goal is to help the patient and family members build their resiliency in coping with the long-term effects of aSAH. Providing ongoing neuropsychological consultation after formal neurorehabilitation has ended often helps the patient's family not to feel alone with the care of the individual. This is especially true when the aSAH does not produce any obvious neurological deficit.

When hemiparesis, aphasia, and neglect are present following aSAH, or any other form of vascular accident within the brain, the need for continued rehabilitation activities and psychological care becomes obvious. These clinical conditions present formidable challenges to the patient, family, and rehabilitation team. Consequently, Chapters 18 and 19 consider the problems of aphasia and hemiplegia/hemiparesis from a psychological care perspective.

REFERENCES

Anderson, C. A., Camp, J., & Filley, C. M. (1998). Erotomania after aneurysmal subarachnoid hemorrhage: Case report and literature review. *Journal of Neuropsychiatry and Clinical Neurosciences, 10*(3), 330–337.

Argenta, P. A., & Morgan, M. A. (1998). Cortical blindness and Anton syndrome in a patient with obstetric hemorrhage. *Obstetrics & Gynecology, 91*(5), 810–812.

Atangana, E., Schneider, U. C., Blecharz, K., Magrini, S., Wagner, J., Nieminen-Kelhä, M., . . . Vajkoczy, P. (2017). Intravascular inflammation triggers intracerebral activated microglia and contributes to secondary brain injury after experimental subarachnoid hemorrhage (eSAH). *Translational Stroke Research, 8*(2), 144–156.

Bird, C. M., Malhotra, P., Parton, A., Coulthard, E., Rushworth, M. F., & Husain, M. (2006). Visual neglect after right posterior cerebral artery infarction. *Journal of Neurology, Neurosurgery, and Psychiatry, 77*(9), 1008–1012.

Buchanan, K. M., Elias, L. J., & Goplen, G. B. (2000). Differing perspectives on outcome after subarachnoid hemorrhage: The patient, the relative, the neurosurgeon. *Neurosurgery, 46*(4), 831–840.

Budson, A. E., Roth, H. L., Rentz, D. M., & Ronthal, M. (2000). Disruption of the ventral visual stream in a case of reduplicative paramnesia. *Annals of the New York Academy of Sciences, 911*(1), 447–452.

Buunk, A. M., Groen, R. J., Veenstra, W. S., & Spikman, J. M. (2015). Leisure and social participation in patients 4–10 years after aneurysmal subarachnoid haemorrhage. *Brain Injury, 29*(13–14), 1589–1596.

Buunk, A. M., Spikman, J. M., Veenstra, W. S., van Laar, P. J., Metzemaekers, J. D., van Dijk, J. M. C., ... Groen, R. J. (2017). Social cognition impairments after aneurysmal subarachnoid haemorrhage: Associations with deficits in interpersonal behaviour, apathy, and impaired self-awareness. *Neuropsychologia, 103*, 131–139.

Ciceri, E. F., Klucznik, R. P., Grossman, R. G., Rose, J. E., & Mawad, M. E. (2001). Aneurysms of the posterior cerebral artery: Classification and endovascular treatment. *American Journal of Neuroradiology, 22*(1), 27–34.

Coetzer, R. (2014). Psychotherapy after acquired brain injury: Is less more? *Revista Chilena de Neuropsicología, 9*(1), 8–13.

Ferguson, G. G. (1989). Intracranial arterial aneurysms—A surgical perspective. In P. J. Vinkin, G. W. Bruyn, & H. Klawans (Eds.), *Handbook of clinical neurology* (pp. 41–87). New York, NY: Elsevier.

Gade, A. (1982). Amnesia after operations on aneurysms of the anterior communicating artery. *Surgical Neurology, 18*(1), 46–49.

Goldstein, K. (1952). The effect of brain damage on the personality. *Psychiatry, 15*(3), 245–260.

Gracey, F., Oldham, P., & Kritzinger, R. (2007). Finding out if "The 'me' will shut down": Successful cognitive–behavioural therapy of seizure-related panic symptoms following subarachnoid haemorrhage: A single case report. *Neuropsychological Rehabilitation, 17*(1), 106–119.

Greenberg, M. (2010). *Handbook of neurosurgery*. Tampa, FL: Greenberg Graphics.

Hackett, M. L., Anderson, C. S., House, A., & Xia, J. (2008). Interventions for treating depression after stroke. *Cochrane Database of Systematic Reviews, 2008*(4), CD003437.

Huenges Wajer, I. M., Visser-Meily, J. M., Greebe, P., Post, M. W., Rinkel, G. J., & van Zandvoort, M. J. (2017). Restrictions and satisfaction with participation in patients who are ADL-independent after an aneurysmal subarachnoid hemorrhage. *Topics in Stroke Rehabilitation, 24*(2), 134–141.

Hütter, B.-O., & Kreitschmann-Andermahr, I. (2014). Subarachnoid hemorrhage as a psychological trauma. *Journal of Neurosurgery, 120*(4), 923–930.

Joo, H. M., Lee, S. J., Chung, Y. G., & Shin, I. Y. (2010). Effects of mindfulness based stress reduction program on depression, anxiety and stress in patients with aneurysmal subarachnoid hemorrhage. *Journal of Korean Neurosurgical Society, 47*(5), 345–351.

Kito, Y., Kazui, H., Kubo, Y., Yoshida, T., Takaya, M., Wada, T., ... Miyake, H. (2009). Neuropsychiatric symptoms in patients with idiopathic normal pressure hydrocephalus. *Behavioural Neurology, 21*(3–4), 165–174.

Knapp, P., Campbell Burton, C., Holmes, J., Murray, J., Gillespie, D., Lightbody, C. E., ... Lewis, S. R. (2017). Interventions for treating anxiety after stroke. *Cochrane Database of Systematic Reviews, 2017*(5), CD008860.

Kreiter, K. T., Copeland, D., Bernardini, G. L., Bates, J. E., Peery, S., Claassen, J., ... Mayer, S. A. (2002). Predictors of cognitive dysfunction after subarachnoid hemorrhage. *Stroke, 33*(1), 200–209.

Kreitschmann-Andermahr, I., Poll, E., Hutter, B. O., Reineke, A., Kristes, S., Gilsbach, J. M., & Saller, B. (2007). Quality of life and psychiatric sequelae following aneurysmal subarachnoid haemorrhage: Does neuroendocrine dysfunction play a role? *Clinical Endocrinology, 66*(6), 833–837.

Lawton, M. T., & Vates, G. E. (2017). Subarachnoid hemorrhage. *New England Journal of Medicine, 377*(3), 257–266.

Ljunggren, B., Sonesson, B., Säveland, H., & Brandt, L. (1985). Cognitive impairment and adjustment in patients without neurological deficits after aneurysmal SAH and early operation. *Journal of Neurosurgery, 62*(5), 673–679.

Maddula, M., Lutton, S., & Keegan, B. (2009). Anton's syndrome due to cerebrovascular disease: A case report. *Journal of Medical Case Reports, 3*(1), 9028.

Marchand, W. R. (2012). Mindfulness-based stress reduction, mindfulness-based cognitive therapy, and Zen meditation for depression, anxiety, pain, and psychological distress. *Journal of Psychiatric Practice, 18*(4), 233–252.

Mavaddat, N., Kirkpatrick, P. J., Rogers, R. D., & Sahakian, B. (2000). Deficits in decision-making in patients with aneurysms of the anterior communicating artery. *Brain, 123*(10), 2109–2117.

Noble, A. J., Baisch, S., Schenk, T., Mendelow, A. D., Allen, L., & Kane, P. (2008). Posttraumatic stress disorder explains reduced quality of life in subarachnoid hemorrhage patients in both the short and long term. *Neurosurgery, 63*(6), 1095–1105.

Patterson, M. B., & Mack, J. L. (1985). Neuropsychological analysis of a case of reduplicative paramnesia. *Journal of Clinical and Experimental Neuropsychology, 7*(1), 111–121.

Persson, H. C., Törnbom, K., Sunnerhagen, K. S., & Törnbom, M. (2017). Consequences and coping strategies six years after a subarachnoid hemorrhage—A qualitative study. *PLoS One, 12*(8), e0181006.

Pisani, A., Marra, C., & Silveri, M. (2000). Anatomical and psychological mechanism of reduplicative misidentification syndromes. *Neurological Sciences, 21*(5), 324–328.

Powell, J., Kitchen, N., Heslin, J., & Greenwood, R. (2002). Psychosocial outcomes at three and nine months after good neurological recovery from aneurysmal subarachnoid haemorrhage: Predictors and prognosis. *Journal of Neurology, Neurosurgery, and Psychiatry, 72*(6), 772–781.

Powell, J., Kitchen, N., Heslin, J., & Greenwood, R. (2004). Psychosocial outcomes at 18 months after good neurological recovery from aneurysmal subarachnoid haemorrhage. *Journal of Neurology, Neurosurgery, and Psychiatry, 75*(8), 1119–1124.

Prigatano, G. (2018). Psychotherapy and the practice of clinical neuropsychology. In J. E. Morgan & J. H. Ricker (Eds.), *Textbook of clinical neuropsychology* (2nd ed., pp. 1045–1053). New York, NY: Taylor & Francis.

Prigatano, G. P., & Kime, S. (2003). What do brain dysfunctional patients report following memory compensation training? *NeuroRehabilitation, 18*(1), 47–55.

Roberts, J., Trimble, M., & Robertson, M. (1983). Schizophrenic psychosis associated with aqueduct stenosis in adults. *Journal of Neurology, Neurosurgery, and Psychiatry, 46*(10), 892–898.

Schmidt, R., Piliavska, K., Maier-Ring, D., van Husen, D. K., & Dettmers, C. (2017). Psychotherapy in neurorehabilitation. *Neurology International Open, 1*(3), E153–E159.

Shukla, D. P. (2017). Outcome and rehabilitation of patients following aneurysmal subarachnoid haemorrhage. *Journal of Neuroanaesthesiology and Critical Care, 4*(4), 65.

Sonesson, B., Kronvall, E., Säveland, H., Brandt, L., & Nilsson, O. G. (2018). Long-term reintegration and quality of life in patients with subarachnoid hemorrhage and a good neurological outcome: Findings after more than 20 years. *Journal of Neurosurgery, 128*(3), 785–792.

Stern, M., Chang, D., Odell, M., & Sperber, K. (2006). Rehabilitation implications of non-traumatic subarachnoid haemorrhage. *Brain Injury, 20*(7), 679–685.

Toomela, A., Pulver, A., Tomberg, T., Orasson, A., Tikk, A., & Asser, T. (2004). Possible interpretation of subjective complaints in patients with spontaneous subarachnoid haemorrhage. *Journal of Rehabilitation Medicine, 36*(2), 63–69.

Tsouna-Hadjis, E., Vemmos, K. N., Zakopoulos, N., & Stamatelopoulos, S. (2000). First-stroke recovery process: The role of family social support. *Archives of Physical Medicine and Rehabilitation, 81*(7), 881–887.

Vilkki, J. S., Juvela, S., Siironen, J., Ilvonen, T., Varis, J., & Porras, M. (2004). Relationship of local infarctions to cognitive and psychosocial impairments after aneurysmal subarachnoid hemorrhage. *Neurosurgery, 55*(4), 790–803.

Visser-Meily, J., Rinkel, G., Vergouwen, M., Passier, P., Van Zandvoort, M., & Post, M. (2013). Post-traumatic stress disorder in patients 3 years after aneurysmal subarachnoid haemorrhage. *Cerebrovascular Diseases, 36*(2), 126–130.

Visser-Meily, J. A., Rhebergen, M. L., Rinkel, G. J., van Zandvoort, M. J., & Post, M. W. (2009). Long-term health-related quality of life after aneurysmal subarachnoid hemorrhage. *Stroke, 40*(4), 1526–1529.

Volpe, B. T., & Hirst, W. (1983). Amnesia following the rupture and repair of an anterior communicating artery aneurysm. *Journal of Neurology, Neurosurgery, and Psychiatry, 46*(8), 704–709.

Wong, G. K. C., Lam, S. W., Chan, S. S., Lai, M., Patty, P., Mok, V., . . . Wong, A. (2014). Neuropsychiatric disturbance after aneurysmal subarachnoid hemorrhage. *Journal of Clinical Neuroscience, 21*(10), 1695–1698.

18

PSYCHOLOGICAL CARE OF PERSONS WITH APHASIA SECONDARY TO A CEREBRAL VASCULAR ACCIDENT OR TRAUMATIC BRAIN INJURY

BACKGROUND INFORMATION

As noted in previous chapters of this book, the development of language is crucial for the development of the higher integrative brain functions, the control of behavior, and the establishment of interpersonal bonds. As a symbolic representation system, language conveys and defines experience (see Chapter 2, this volume). Also, the written word can be reviewed to expand our working memory when problem-solving (see Chapters 1 and 3, this volume). In light of these observations, the disruption of language development or the impairment of existing language skills secondary to a brain lesion can have an especially devastating effect on the psychological well-being of the person. Patients who experience impairment of language functions secondary to a brain insult are described as demonstrating *aphasia*.

Aphasia, however, literally means a complete loss of language function due to a brain insult. The term *dysphasia* refers to a partial loss of language function caused by a brain insult. In this chapter, the psychological care of patients with aphasia/dysphasia is considered, and the terms are used interchangeably.

Aphasia can be caused by various brain disorders and occurs at different times during the life span. This chapter reviews the various types of aphasia reported in the literature, followed by a brief discussion of how aphasia may affect the phenomenological state of the person. Three case vignettes are then presented: one of a 9-year-old girl, one of a 22-year-old man, and one of a 71-year-old man. These cases were selected because they highlight important considerations in the psychological care of persons when aphasia occurs at different times in the life cycle. These individuals were followed for several years and provide a longitudinal perspective that may be useful in the psychological care of persons with aphasia.

DISRUPTION OF BLOOD FLOW IN MIDDLE CEREBRAL ARTERIES AND NEUROLOGICAL/ NEUROPSYCHOLOGICAL CORRELATES

Given that the middle cerebral arteries (MCAs) supply blood to large regions of the cortex (i.e., the lateral surface of the frontal, parietal, and temporal lobes), infarctions or hemorrhages in either artery often produce dramatic neurological deficits. In right-handed individuals, when blood supply to the left hemisphere is compromised via a left MCA stroke, some form of an aphasic disturbance often results. Vascular lesions in the anterior distribution of the MCA (superior division) involving the posterior portion of the third (inferior) frontal gyrus often produce a clinical condition generally referred to as a nonfluent aphasic disturbance (Blumenfeld, 2010). This clinical condition is characterized by hesitant, agrammatic, spontaneous speech with very poor fluency. Auditory comprehension is relatively preserved. However, the individual has difficulty with sentence and word repetition as well as problems with naming (Kertesz, 1985). Classically, the condition has been referred to as Broca's aphasia.

When the vascular lesion occurs in the posterior distribution (inferior division) of the left MCA involving the superior temporal gyrus, a fluent aphasic condition often is observed (Blumenfeld, 2010). It has classically been described as Wernicke's aphasia. In this clinical condition, the spontaneous speech is characterized by paraphasic errors and jargon (i.e., nonsensical) words. Auditory comprehension, sentence and word repetition, and naming are also severely compromised (Kertesz, 1985). These patients often are not fully aware of their errors in language production.

Vascular lesions disturbing the connection between Broca's area and Wernicke's area produce a special type of aphasic speech in which the ability to repeat what is said is greatly disturbed. It is referred to as conduction aphasia (Blumenfeld, 2010). Finally, a region depicted in the "watershed territories" between the MCA and the anterior cerebral artery produces an aphasic condition referred to as transcortical motor aphasia. In this condition, the patient has to put forth considerable effort to speak, often with long latency response times. However, unlike patients with Broca's aphasia, these patients can repeat what they hear (Blumenfeld, 2010). When the watershed territories between the MCA and the posterior cerebral artery are compromised, a condition called transcortical sensory aphasia is said to exist. These patients have a fluent form of aphasia, but unlike patients with Wernicke's aphasia, they can repeat what they hear (Blumenfeld, 2010).

Other aphasic conditions have also been described. Table 18.1 lists the traditional classification of aphasic syndromes with associated neurological disorders and the typical lesion locations (Oliveira, Marin, & Bertolucci, 2017). Figure 18.1 illustrates, in an abbreviated form, key regions involved in language production and that, when damaged, result in different types of language disturbances (Oliveira et al., 2017).

When blood supply to the sensorimotor cortex is compromised, hemiplegia or hemiparesis predictably occurs on the side of the body contralateral to the lesion location in the brain. Vascular lesions in the distribution of the lenticulostriate arteries emerging from the proximal MCA can also produce hemiparesis secondary to damage to the internal capsule and surrounding basal ganglia structures.

It is also important to note that when blood supply to the entire left MCA is obstructed secondary to an occultation of the left carotid artery, a dense or "global" aphasic condition is produced. All aspects of language are compromised, and spontaneous speech is frequently characterized by stereotypic utterances

Table 18.1 Traditional Classification of Aphasic Syndromes

TYPE OF APHASIA	SPONTANEOUS SPEECH	FLUENCY	COMPREHENSION	REPETITION	NAMING	OTHER SIGNS	LESION LOCALIZATION (DOMINANT HEMISPHERE)
Broca's aphasia	Poor, with effort, paraphasias, agrammatism	Impaired	Preserved	Impaired	Impaired	Hemiparesis, apraxia of mouth and hand	Posterior–inferior frontal
Wernicke's aphasia	Logorrheic, with paraphasias and neologisms	Preserved	Impaired	Impaired	Impaired	Homonymous hemianopia, apraxia, anosognosia	Posterior-superior temporal
Conduction aphasia	Normal (phonemic mistakes)	Preserved	Preserved	Impaired	Preserved	Hemihypesthesia, apraxia, hemianopia	Arcuate fascicle–supramarginal gyrus
Global aphasia	Poor (mutism), restricted to simple verbal stereotypes	Impaired	Impaired	Impaired	Impaired	Hemiparesis, hemianopia, hemihypesthesia, apraxia	Perisylvian region (middle cerebral artery territory)
Semantic aphasia	Normal (difficulty finding words)	Preserved	Preserved	Preserved	Impaired	Homonymous hemianopia	Inferior parietal (angular gyrus)
Transcortical motor aphasia	Poor (mutism), with great latency at responses, echolalia, perseveration	Impaired	Preserved	Preserved	Impaired	Eventually hemiparesis (crural involvement) and grasp reflex	Anterior and superior to Broca's area (supplementary motor area)
Transcortical sensory aphasia	Normal (semantic jargon)	Preserved	Impaired	Preserved	Impaired	Eventually hemianopia and visual agnosia	Watershed areas of middle cerebral artery and posterior cerebral artery

Mixed transcortical aphasia	Mutism	Impaired	Impaired	Preserved	Impaired	Eventually hemianopia, visual agnosia and hemiparesis	Watershed areas of middle cerebral, anterior cerebral, and posterior cerebral arteries
Verbal deafness	Normal	Preserved	Impaired	Impaired	Preserved	Absent	Middle third of superior temporal gyrus
Thalamic aphasia	Normal or with paraphasias	Preserved	Preserved or discretely impaired	Preserved	Impaired	Dysarthria, initially with mutism	Thalamus in the dominant hemisphere
Subcortical aphasia (nonthalamic)	Poor, with great latency at responses, echolalia, perseveration	Preserved	Preserved	Preserved	Impaired	Dysarthria, hypophonia	Basal nuclei in the dominant hemisphere

Source: Reprinted from Oliveira, F. F., Marin, S. M., & Bertolucci, P. H., Neurological impressions on the organization of language networks in the human brain, *Brain Injury*, 31(2), 2017, p. 140–150, by permission of Taylor & Francis Ltd.

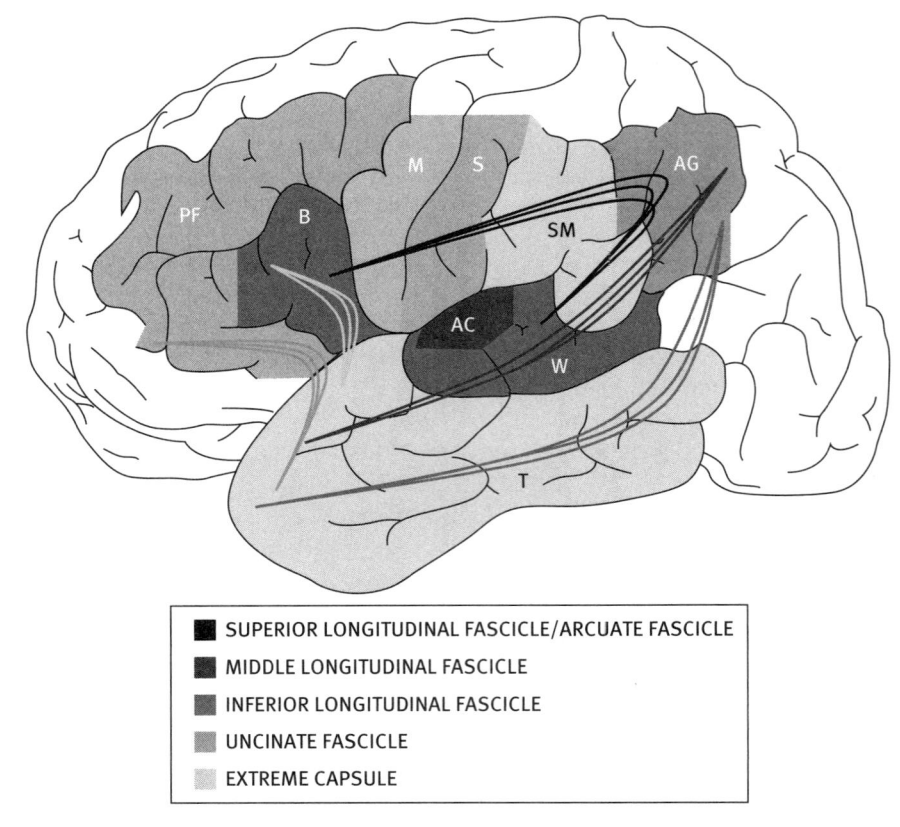

SUPERIOR LONGITUDINAL FASCICLE/ARCUATE FASCICLE
MIDDLE LONGITUDINAL FASCICLE
INFERIOR LONGITUDINAL FASCICLE
UNCINATE FASCICLE
EXTREME CAPSULE

FIGURE 18.1 Vascular territories of language areas. Middle cerebral artery superior and inferior division territories, and middle cerebral artery–anterior cerebral artery (ACA) and middle cerebral artery–posterior cerebral artery watershed territories. AC = primary auditory cortex; AG = angular gyrus; B = Broca's area; M = motor networks in the precentral gyrus; PF = prefrontal networks; S = sensory networks in the postcentral gyrus; SM = supramarginal gyrus; T = inferior temporal networks and temporal pole; W = Wernicke's area. (See color plates)

Source: Reprinted from Oliveira, F. F., Marin, S. M, & Bertolucci, P. H., Neurological impressions on the organization of language networks in the human brain, *Brain Injury, 31*(2), 2017, p. 140–150, by permission of Taylor & Francis Ltd.

(Kertesz, 1985). These patients inevitably have a right hemiplegia or hemiparesis involving the arm and the leg.

When a stroke occurs in the right MCA, involving either superior or inferior divisions, hemineglect of personal and extrapersonal space is often present. Attentional disturbances of various magnitudes also occur even when hemineglect is not present. A portion of these patients (an estimated one-third) acutely present with anosognosia for hemiplegia, as noted in Chapter 9.

With time and rehabilitation, improvement in these dramatic neurological disturbances is often observed. Unfortunately, language impairments can be permanent. Understanding the phenomenological state of aphasic patients is therefore perhaps the best place to start when considering their psychological care.

PHENOMENOLOGICAL EXPERIENCES OF APHASIC PATIENTS

Martha Taylor Sarno (1998) wrote insightfully about the phenomenological experiences of aphasic patients. She noted, "Aphasia strikes at the very heart of personhood. It is no wonder that its onset has a profoundly negative effect on a person's sense of self. Aphasia represents a loss of a part of the self, a changed identity" (p. 84). She added that most aphasic patients are deprived of the ability to share experiences with others and that others may avoid attempting to communicate with these patients because of their language difficulties. Social isolation and a feeling of insignificance are common experiences. Some patients with large left temporal–parietal lesions may find it very difficult to understand what people say to them. Thus, when a clinical neuropsychologist takes the time and exerts the effort to communicate with an aphasic patient, it can have a greater personal impact on the patient than is immediately obvious.

The phenomenological experiences of aphasic patients seem to be greatly influenced by the nature of their aphasic condition (and related neuropsychological dysfunctions), as well as their stage in life and previous life experiences. For example, a female nurse in her early 40s suffered an intracranial hemorrhage involving the left temporal–parietal region of the brain secondary to a bleed of an arterial venous malformation. Two years after the hemorrhage, she still had persistent difficulties understanding (i.e., verbally comprehending) what was said to her. Earlier in her life, she lived in impoverished conditions and was sexually assaulted as a young woman. Despite her husband's reassurance that she was safe in their home, she had difficulty following the logic of his verbal arguments (i.e., understanding the meaning of words and the logic of what he was saying). She progressively became increasingly more paranoid, and her comprehension deficits did not improve. She ultimately required psychiatric hospitalization for her paranoid ideation. Lishman (1987) brought attention to the fact that aphasic patients with language comprehension deficits are prone to experience paranoid reactions when severe comprehension deficits are present (p. 55).

A different pattern of emotional reactions/experiences may be present in patients who have relatively normal comprehension skills but have impairments in speech and language production. Lishman (1987) noted that these patients are more likely to experience frustration and depression. This was also observed in a recent case report by Salas and Yuen (2016) of a 72-year-old university professor who presented with primarily expressive language difficulties. However, Salas and Yuen provided some interesting additional insights when they described the phenomenological experiences of this professor, who suffered an ischemic stroke in the left anterior and middle cerebral arteries. Portions of the left dorsal medial prefrontal cortex and the intraparietal cortex were involved.

For purposes of this discussion, two of Salas and Yuen's (2016) observations are emphasized. First, their patient found it absolutely necessary to write down his thoughts in order to keep them clear and in "working memory." Otherwise, he often remained confused. An excerpt from the patient's personal experiences clarifies this point: "Writing is like putting words to the mess. If I don't write, everything goes to hell. If I think about it, but don't write, it goes away" (p. 94).

A second point made by Salas and Yuen (2016) regarding their patient is the effect of the patient's left dorsal medial frontal lesion on "inner speech." We talk to ourselves all the time (most of the time subvocally) about our reactions, our worries, our personal thoughts, and our future plans. Before his stroke, their patient believed he needed to do his absolute best when presented with a task. He had a strong work ethic and a strong sense of guilt if he did not do "the right thing" (i.e., live up to the expectations of a strong superego, to use Freudian terminology). The patient reported, in rather poetic fashion, that after his stroke and resultant aphasic condition, "the Greek chorus has gone quieter" (p. 95). Although he was still prone to guilt reactions and depression, the intensity of those reactions seemed to diminish as his ability to talk to himself—inner speech—was compromised. Research on inner speech has highlighted the role it plays in cognitive development and problem-solving during childhood and adulthood (Alderson-Day & Fernyhough, 2015). It also seems to play a role in depression.

Similar to the case report of Salas and Yuen (2016), Prigatano and Summers (1997) described the phenomenological experiences of a person who was severely depressed before his traumatic brain injury (TBI). The patient spontaneously reported that his "worry loop" (i.e., going over and over in his mind negative thoughts about himself) disappeared after his TBI. Surprisingly, he was less depressed. However, during this time he reported much more difficulty concentrating. This might have reflected some alteration in his working memory capacities. Collectively, these observations suggest that different aphasic conditions may be associated with different underlying neurocognitive deficits, which in turn result in different phenomenological experiences for the patient. Such experiences set the stage for what can be done to help these patients from a psychological care perspective. The following three case vignettes help demonstrate this point.

Case Vignette 18.1

Medical and Psychosocial History

An experienced 71-year-old skier was found on a ski slope by the ski patrol. By the time he was found (8 hours after he had last been seen), he was described as confused, combative, and incontinent. He subsequently had a generalized seizure. He underwent a craniotomy to evacuate a large left temporal lobe hematoma. He was transferred to a major neurological center for his neurorehabilitation and to manage his seizures. At that time, he was aphasic and appeared severely depressed.

Prior to his TBI-induced temporal lobe hematoma, he was an accomplished European businessman with 16 years of formal education and a history of being a military pilot. He was an accomplished musician and singer. He spoke several languages quite well, including English. He was married to his wife for nearly five decades prior to the accident. He divided his time living in Europe and the United States.

Repeated magnetic resonance imaging (MRI) scans of the brain obtained several months after the onset of his TBI revealed "extensive left temporal–parietal encephalomalacia suggestive of hemosiderin and atrophy." Repeated electroencephalogram recordings showed "markedly abnormal" findings, including persistent and frequent spike-waves over the left mid to posterior temporal head region. He was placed on a variety of seizure medications, which were successful in controlling his seizures. Visual field testing revealed a right upper quadrant hemianopia. There were no obvious motor impairments.

The Initial Neuropsychological Consultation

The patient was seen for his first neuropsychological consultation approximately 22 days after the onset of his aphasic condition while on an acute rehabilitation unit. A neuropsychological consultation was requested because the patient often refused to come out of his private room and involve himself in various rehabilitation activities. His room was noted to always be dark, and he was usually found in his bed with his head under the sheets.

Prior to entering the patient's room, I knocked on the door announcing my name and asking if I could enter. There was no verbal response. I again knocked, called out who I was, and asked if I could enter. When there was still no verbal response, I slowly opened the door to find the room dark and only the patient's head slightly emerging from under the bedsheets. After introducing myself again, I told the patient that I had visited his home city in Europe many times. The patient then made eye contact with me and appeared willing to interact with me.

The patient was very cooperative and polite but fearful, somewhat suspicious, and guarded. He was hesitant to attempt to talk. However, we exchanged a few ideas. The patient's speech was fluent with occasional paraphasic errors. There were obvious difficulties in word finding in "free speech" when he attempted to either answer a question or make a statement. The patient apologized for his language impairments, stating that he was significantly disappointed in himself. He blamed himself for his language and cognitive problems because he apparently had made a mistake while skiing. He was a very accomplished skier and could not believe he would ever make a mistake that would cause such a devastating accident. Note that he had always been a very self-reliant person who prided himself in his good judgment and independence. Although he now appeared depressed, he did not report depression per se. He reported only wanting to be left alone so that he could improve on his own without further embarrassment. He was concerned about how others would view him, especially family members and his doctors.

The patient agreed, however, to further assessment of his neuropsychological (including his language) functions to better understand his current cognitive strengths and limitations. A screening test was performed (i.e., the Barrow Neurological Institute Screen for Higher Cerebral Functions [BNIS]; see Chapter 10, this volume). He had difficulty with auditory comprehension (following a two-step command such as "Touch the small red circle and the large white square"), even though comprehension difficulties were not obvious when I was speaking with him. He had difficulty with confrontational naming and sentence repetition. His abilities to read and spell were also compromised, but to a less severe level. Moreover, he had difficulty with visual sequencing and pattern recognition tasks. He could draw a Greek cross with both hands and had no obvious motor impairment. He could recall only one out of four number/symbol associations. He was not willing to estimate how many of three words he would recall with distraction. When asked to give the words approximately 6 minutes after he repeated them, he could recall none. His total score on the BNIS was 28 out of 50 ($T = 6$), suggesting multiple and severe neurocognitive impairments in which aphasia was the most prominent and obvious symptom. This, of course, would be expected given the location and extent of his encephalomalacia.

Despite his significant cognitive and language impairments, the patient appeared progressively more comfortable talking to me, and a good working relationship was established. The patient agreed that he would come out of his room more frequently and engage in speech and language therapies as well as physical therapy (because he understandably often felt fatigued). After a short stay on the inpatient neurorehabilitation unit, he was discharged to outpatient rehabilitation services and continued to receive speech and language therapy. He also now began to see me for brief but repeated neuropsychological consultations/assessments to monitor his cognitive recovery. During such times, we talked about how he and his wife were personally doing in light of his injuries and associated impairments. He found the discussions helpful and expressed a desire for my consultations. He was followed in such a manner for the next 13 years.

Efforts at Psychological Care

Following the initial neuropsychological consultation with this patient, he would periodically be re-evaluated from a neuropsychological perspective, as noted previously. His first extensive follow-up examination was approximately 7 months after his injury. His BNIS total score was now 34 out of 50 points ($T = 24$). Progressive improvement occurred in functions thought to be mediated primarily via the right cerebral hemisphere. For example, visual search and sequencing tasks became easier to perform. Recall of number/visual symbol associations improved. However, language skills and verbal memory remained impaired. Auditory comprehension improved, but naming and sentence repetition remained quite compromised.

The patient now wanted more time to talk about what he was struggling with, and he wanted his wife to also have time to talk to me regarding her observations and concerns. During the 13 years he was followed, he expressed considerable gratitude for the time I was willing to spend talking with him and his wife. Several topics were discussed. Initially, the topic of prognosis was most important. How much would he improve with time and therapies? This is a delicate topic. One must be honest and realistic but positive in what is said. The following statement appeared to be helpful and was repeatedly used: "As long as the brain is alive, it can learn!" However, the extent of recovery of language function that would ultimately be achieved most likely would be less than what the patient wanted and what I would hope for the patient.

As his condition began to appear stable (by 2 years after the injury), the discussion turned to activities that he could still perform and enjoy doing. Playing the piano became an obviously important activity for him. Travel to Europe during the summers and enjoying the outdoors and "nature" (as Erikson pointed out; see Chapter 4, this volume) now became very satisfying. Yet he continued to struggle with depression. He was not and would never be the same intelligent, energetic, athletic man he was before. He could not operate a successful business as he could before. Although he was not concerned about financial matters, his loss of a sense of competency (and a previous sense of normality) haunted him on a daily basis. Repeat neuropsychological testing was done to give him and his wife an "objective" view of his skills, which helped him make important business decisions. For example, 6 years after the TBI-induced aphasia, his Wechsler Adult Intelligence Scale–Third Edition (WAIS-III) Block Design scale score was 14 and Coding was 10 for his age. Yet he continued to have substantial difficulties on tests of visual naming, sentence repetition, verbal fluency, auditory comprehension, and spelling. Given his persistent (but mildly improved) language difficulties, verbal sections of the WAIS-III were not administered. This would have only served to demoralize him and measure the obvious. Instead, these findings were reviewed with some emphasis on the skills he had retained.

He showed modest pleasure in hearing this news, but his aphasic condition continued to depress him.

About this time, he also became sexually impotent (he now was in his mid-70s). This bothered him greatly. His wife emphasized that it was not important to her that they be sexually active, but it disturbed him. Several discussions about sexuality, feeling "masculine," and a loss of confidence often found their way into each conversation. The patient repeatedly expressed appreciation for the time spent in talking about and thinking "out loud" with someone who understood his clinical (and existential) situation.

The patient often preferred not to be with others because of his inability to verbally communicate (e.g., finding words as needed and fully understanding what was being said if the person talked quickly or if multiple people were talking in the room). He still looked forward to long vacations with his wife and frequently would send me postcards from his various travels. He liked working in his garden and often got "lost in the activity." This latter experience helped him. In an unusually insightful article, Csikszentmihalyi (1999) asked (tongue in cheek), "If we are so rich, why aren't we happy?" He noted that wealth and economic security go only so far to produce a sense of personal satisfaction and happiness. He suggested that some people may experience happiness "when they are thoroughly involved in something that is enjoyable and meaningful to the person" (p. 825). This was certainly true for this patient and became an important lesson when I was working with other patients.

During the time of the patient's psychological care, his wife remained positive regarding her husband, but frankly at times she appeared somewhat guarded in describing her reactions toward her husband to me. Any negativity that was expressed might appear to betray her commitment to her husband. It might also be inadvertently conveyed to her husband (despite the rules of confidentiality). However, she continued to be supportive of her husband during the ensuing years. Their relationship had been good for more than 50 years, and it did not seem to change after the onset of his aphasic condition.

Approximately 13 years after the onset of his TBI-induced aphasia, the patient and his wife returned for a consultation because they were concerned that he might be declining in his cognitive functioning. They explicitly voiced concern that he might be experiencing the early signs of dementia. Although there was a mild decline in his naming ability (perhaps related to the aging process; he was now nearly 84 years old), there were no signs of dementia. He and his wife were relieved and returned to Europe to spend the rest of their lives together.

In many ways, this was a "successful" outcome in terms of the psychological care of this patient. His sadness over his aphasia and the impact it had on his life was a realistic response. He momentarily could overcome the sadness by getting lost in activities he enjoyed. Most important, he did not "feel alone" with his struggles and greatly appreciated that someone of professional stature would take time to meet with him and his wife to discuss their concerns/reactions. Table 18.2 lists some of the essential clinical features of his care, and Table 18.3 lists some of the features observed in his wife during that time.

Table 18.2 Clinical Features Relevant to the Psychological Care of an Older Individual with a Traumatically Induced Fluent Aphasia

CLINICAL FEATURE	YES	NO	PARTIALLY
1. The dialogue between the patient and the clinical neuropsychologist was not rushed.	✓		
2. The patient was able to express or clearly convey his personal concerns.	✓		
3. The content of the concerns varied over time.	✓		
4. The patient experienced a sense of "realistic" hope in coping with his life situation.			✓
5. The patient and the clinical neuropsychologist developed a positive therapeutic relationship that helped the patient sustain adaptive activities during difficult times.	✓		
6. Somatic symptoms (which appeared to be indirect effects of a brain disorder) were substantially reduced during periods of psychological care.			n/a
7. Anxiety/depression/anger and/or apathy were substantially reduced during periods of psychological care.	✓		
8. The patient was able to follow the guidance of the clinical neuropsychologist to improve functioning in everyday life activities.	✓		
9. The patient was able to control impulses and delay gratification.	✓		
10. The patient developed a new sense of competency or "mastery" in his life following the brain disorder.			✓

(*continued*)

Table 18.2 Continued

CLINICAL FEATURE	YES	NO	PARTIALLY
11. The patient was able to "self-reflect" or "be more aware" of personal "strengths" and "limitations."	✓		
12. The patient experienced enjoyment in the care or help of other living things (people, animals, gardening, the environment, etc.).	✓		
13. The patient had an improved understanding of the "problematic nature of life" (given his psychosocial state of life) and was not overwhelmed or "defeated" by it or readily gave in to escapism to cope with life (Bettelheim, 1989).			✓
14. The patient could "live with" the restrictions produced by a brain injury "without resentment" (Goldstein, 1952).			✓
15. The patient was able to obtain new insights into self by attending to why certain songs, stories, fairy tales, movies, tattoos, etc. had a special personal meaning that initially he did not understand.		✓	
16. The patient's dreams or artwork often heralded changes in behavior that aided his psychological adjustment before the consciously mediated changes occurred.		✓	
17. The psychological care interventions (including the dialogue) between the patient and the clinical neuropsychologist resulted in the patient talking more openly about problems and demonstrating self-directed efforts at improving psychological adjustment to the direct and indirect effects of the brain disorder.	✓		
18. The psychological care interventions were in harmony with the patient's cultural background and religious orientation.	✓		
19. The psychological care interventions were appropriate for the patient's psychosocial stage of development and facilitated psychosocial development/adaptation in later stages of life.	✓		
20. The patient and family experienced two basic facts of life: (a) The individual's state of subjective sense of personal well-being fluctuates and (b) the psychological adjustment process is never static and therefore hope should never be abandoned.	✓		
Total	13	2	4

n/a, not applicable.

Table 18.3 Clinically Relevant Features of a Wife When Providing Psychological Care for Her Husband, Who Has a Traumatically Induced Fluent Aphasia

CLINICAL FEATURE	YES	NO	PARTIALLY
1. The quality of the relationship before the onset of the brain disorder was good.	✓		
2. The wife has adequate supports that help maintain her resiliency.	✓		
3. The wife is personally offended by the behavioral problems of the patient.		✓	
4. The wife has a good working (therapeutic) relationship with the clinical neuropsychologist.			✓
5. The wife understands the biological factors (and at times the psychological factors) underlying the behavioral problems of the patient.	✓		
6. The wife does not feel alone in caring for the patient.	✓		
7. The wife has some sense of hope that the patient's behavioral problems will get better with time and/or there is "light at the end of the tunnel."			✓

Case Vignette 18.2

Medical and Psychosocial History

At age 22 years, a healthy young man suffered a blow to the neck while playing football that resulted in the dissection of his left carotid artery. This resulted in a massive ischemic injury to the entire left MCA. He was rendered completely aphasic, with a dense right hemiplegia. With time, his motor and language difficulties showed improvement, but he remained severely impaired. In an attempt to help him with possible further recovery and rehabilitation, he was referred for an intensive neuropsychological rehabilitation program (Prigatano, 1986). He was now 27 years old. He could ambulate with an assistive device placed on his right lower extremity. He could move his right shoulder and wrist, but he demonstrated severe spasticity in both the arm and the leg. He was diagnosed with a right spastic hemiplegia.

He often spoke in fragmented phrases with stereotypical responses. For example, when asked a question, he would frequently respond with the same phrase: "I think so." Previously, examiners described him as demonstrating a global aphasia. With time, his language difficulties appeared to be primarily nonfluent in nature and more closely resembled Broca's aphasia. However, even during this time, he had notable difficulties with language comprehension, repetition, and naming. He was married, and there was concern that his wife might financially exploit him, so a fiduciary was assigned by the courts to handle his financial matters. The relationship with his spouse was tense, and she avoided any involvement in his rehabilitation.

Neuropsychological Rehabilitation and Consultation

When first seen, the patient was cooperative and smiled much of the time. He had a somewhat immature look on his face, as if he either did not know what to say or what a given situation was going to demand of him. He was, however, eager to obtain more rehabilitation in hopes of greater language and motor recovery. He did not verbalize any specific needs, but when the goals of the rehabilitation program were described in short sentences, he nodded his head "yes." Interestingly, he reported no depression. His performance on various working memory tests was clearly below average.

His wife, who was present for the initial consultations, appeared guarded and volunteered very limited information about her husband or herself. She stated that she had to return home to another state to take care of their child. She would speak with the rehabilitation therapists over the phone, but she could not stay and be a part of his rehabilitative care.

At the time he was enrolled in the neuropsychological rehabilitation program, his Verbal IQ was 71 and Performance IQ was 91 as measured by the WAIS-R. It was noteworthy that his Similarities scale score was 2 and his Block Design scale score was 11. Thus, he could perform certain visual–spatial tasks within the normal range, but he could not perform verbal reasoning tasks adequately. Speed of finger tapping was 0 in the right hand (he could not perform the task), but 47 (which is normal) in the left hand. Interestingly, he made only 28 errors on the Halstead Category Test, suggesting that certain nonverbal abstract reasoning skills may not have been severely affected.

The patient engaged in an extensive day treatment/rehabilitation program for nearly a year and made modest gains in language, motor, and cognitive functioning. He was always cooperative and congenial, as noted previously. He expressed very little sadness or frustration with his life's circumstances. However, his marital situation deteriorated, and his wife refused any contact with the rehabilitation team. He eventually returned to his home state, where another clinical neuropsychologist attempted to provide continued psychological support and care. He was never able to return to work. Eventually, he divorced, but with time he remarried another woman who seemed sincerely interested in him and was willing to accept his cognitive and physical limitations.

Efforts at Psychological Care

This patient's psychological care was purely supportive in nature. He could not verbalize his concerns. He did not express anger or depression. He appeared helpless in interpersonal situations and simply followed the direction of others. He functioned much like an older child who was dependent on others for continued care. Due to his severe language impairments, he simply followed what others would outline for him to do. Tables 18.4 and 18.5 summarize the behavioral correlates associated with the psychological care efforts.

Long-Term Follow-Up Neuropsychological Consultation

Years later, when the patient was 45 years old, his attorney referred him for a follow-up neuropsychological examination to address two questions: Had there been any improvement in his neuropsychological status? Had his language skills improved to the point that he could answer questions in a court of law over allegations of sexual misconduct? It is unclear as to what happened, but it appeared that the patient may have done something of a sexually inappropriate nature.

The patient's cognitive and language functioning at the time of this follow-up examination did not reveal any positive or negative change since he was last seen. On the WAIS-III, his Verbal IQ was 70 and his Performance IQ was 92. These scores were almost identical to those obtained years earlier. His Similarities subtest scale score was now 5, but his Vocabulary scale score was 3 and his Block Design scale score was 10. His language performance on the Multilingual Aphasia Examination remained impaired in all domains, with verbal fluency being substantially worse than auditory comprehension. His Halstead Category score was 11, which remained within the normal range.

Table 18.4 Clinical Features Relevant to a Young Adult Man with a Global Aphasic Disturbance Secondary to Occlusion of the Left Carotid Artery

CLINICAL FEATURE	YES	NO	PARTIALLY
1. The dialogue between the patient and the clinical neuropsychologist was not rushed.	✓		
2. The patient was able to express or clearly convey his personal concerns.		✓	
3. The content of the concerns varied over time.		✓	
4. The patient experienced a sense of "realistic" hope in coping with his life situation.			✓
5. The patient and the clinical neuropsychologist developed a positive therapeutic relationship that helped the patient sustain adaptive activities during difficult times.		✓	
6. Somatic symptoms (which appeared to be indirect effects of a brain disorder) were substantially reduced during periods of psychological care.			n/a
7. Anxiety/depression/anger and/or apathy were substantially reduced during periods of psychological care.		✓	
8. The patient was able to follow the guidance of the clinical neuropsychologist to improve functioning in everyday life activities.		✓	
9. The patient was able to control impulses and delay gratification.	✓		
10. The patient developed a new sense of competency or "mastery" in his life following the brain disorder.		✓	
11. The patient was able to "self-reflect" or "be more aware" of personal "strengths" and "limitations."		✓	
12. The patient experienced enjoyment in the care or help of other living things (people, animals, the environment, etc.).			✓
13. The patient had an improved understanding of the "problematic nature of life" (given his psychosocial state of life) and was not overwhelmed or "defeated" by it or readily gave in to escapism to cope with life (Bettelheim, 1989).			✓
14. The patient could "live with" the restrictions produced by a brain injury "without resentment" (Goldstein, 1952).	✓		
15. The patient was able to obtain new insights into self by attending to why certain songs, stories, fairy tales, movies, tattoos, etc. had a special personal meaning that initially he did not understand.		✓	

(continued)

Table 18.4 Continued

CLINICAL FEATURE	YES	NO	PARTIALLY
16. The patient's dreams or artwork often heralded changes in behavior that aided psychological adjustment before the consciously mediated changes occurred.		✓	
17. The psychological care interventions (including the dialogue) between the patient and the clinical neuropsychologist resulted in the patient talking more openly about problems and demonstrating self-directed efforts at improving psychological adjustment to the direct and indirect effects of the brain disorder.		✓	
18. The psychological care interventions were in harmony with the patient's cultural background and religious orientation.	✓		
19. The psychological care interventions were appropriate for the patient's psychosocial stage of development and facilitated psychosocial development/adaptation in later stages of life.		✓	
20. The patient and family experienced two basic facts of life: (a) The individual's state of subjective sense of personal well-being fluctuates and (b) the psychological adjustment process is never static and therefore hope should never be abandoned.		✓	
Total	4	12	3

n/a, not applicable.

Table 18.5 Clinically Relevant Features of the Wife of a Global Aphasic Adult Patient When Providing Psychological Care

CLINICAL FEATURE	YES	NO	PARTIALLY
1. The quality of the relationship before the onset of the brain disorder was good.		✓	
2. The wife has adequate supports that help maintain her resiliency.		✓	
3. The wife is personally offended by the behavioral problems of the patient.			Unknown
4. The wife has a good working (therapeutic) relationship with the clinical neuropsychologist.		✓	
5. The wife understands the biological factors (and at times the psychological factors) underlying the behavioral problems of the patient.			Unknown
6. The wife does not feel alone in the care of the patient.			Unknown
7. The wife has some sense of hope that the patient's behavioral problems will get better with time and/or there is "light at the end of the tunnel."		✓	

It was determined that the patient continued to have impaired language skills and could not answer questions in a court of law. There was no clinical evidence of improved neuropsychological functioning nearly 20 years after his stroke. Again, the neuropsychological consultation served more to help protect the individual. The patient was appreciative of this help, but he was unable to verbally express any complicated feelings or reactions. After severe disruption of language occurred in this patient as a young adult, his personality did not appear to undergo expected changes (see Chapter 4, this volume) as he grew older.

APHASIA IN CHILDREN

Understanding the phenomenological experiences of children with an aphasic condition is an especially challenging task. Normally, the tendency for verbal rehearsal of what is said to the child increases as the child grows older (Alderson-Day & Fernyhough, 2015). This capacity has been linked not only to working memory but also to other aspects of language and cognitive development (Alderson-Day & Fernyhough, 2015). Therefore, disturbances of language systems during childhood that affect "inner" and "outer" (i.e., spoken) speech most likely affect both cognitive and emotional development.

Disruption of language functions affects the child's ability to communicate with parents and caregivers. This can also produce a deep sense of loneliness and loss of connectedness with family members. For example, one very intelligent adolescent male, who had substantial word-finding difficulties after his TBI, drew a picture that symbolically represented "his falling away" from family members after his brain injury (Prigatano, 1986, p. 86). Drawings of aphasic adolescents often highlight the difficulties they have in thinking and reflecting on their situation in life (Prigatano, 1986, p. 85).

Case Vignette 18.3

Medical and Psychosocial History
A 9-year-old right-handed girl began having difficulties with her speech and flexing her right arm after getting off an amusement park ride. It was also noted that she had trouble walking. She was transported to a local medical center, where an initial computed tomography scan of the brain was read as negative. However, her symptoms progressively worsened with an increase in intracranial pressure. An MRI and magnetic resonance angiography revealed an extensive acute infarction of the left MCA distribution, with high-grade stenosis and near occlusion of the origin of the left MCA. She had extensive mass effect with a midline shift.

A day later, the child underwent a left frontal temporal parietal craniotomy, and a left frontal lobectomy was performed. She received aggressive physical therapy, occupational therapy, and speech therapy. She was then transferred to a major neurological center for further care. Four weeks after the onset of her left MCA stroke, she continued to demonstrate significant language and motor deficits.

Prior to her stroke, she was functioning normally in school in the third grade. Following the stroke, she returned to school and received special education services in addition to continued physical, occupational, and speech therapies. She remained cooperative and appeared positive in her attitude. She developed an interest in drawing (with her "unaffected" left hand) and had an outgoing personality. There were no behavioral disturbances, but her parents wanted more information concerning her cognitive and language status. Thus, she was referred for a clinical neuropsychological examination at age 12 years, approximately 3 years after the stroke.

Neuropsychological Examination Findings
When initially seen for her neuropsychological examination, the girl's speech was effortful and nonfluent. She had difficulties in all domains

of language, but auditory comprehension, naming, and sentence repetition were notably affected. She now used her left hand to carry out all motor activities. On the Wechsler Intelligence Scale for Children–Fourth Edition, she obtained a Verbal Comprehension Index score of 67, a Perceptual Reasoning Index score of 79, a Working Memory Index score of 50, and a Processing Speed Index score of 50. Her language difficulties negatively affected her ability to carry out working memory tasks. Her use of her left (vs. right) hand resulted in slow processing speeds. Her Matrix Reasoning scale score was 8, her Block Design score was 7, and her Similarities score was 7. She had notable difficulties finding words to define the meaning of terms, and consequently her Vocabulary scale score was 1.

Similar to the previously described patient, the girl's abstract reasoning performance on some tasks was above average. For example, she obtained 6 out of 6 categories on the Wisconsin Card Sorting Test, with no failures to maintain set. She made only 25 perseverative errors, producing an age-adjusted T score of 41. Her hemiparetic right hand made it impossible to tap with the right index finger, but with the left hand she tapped 35.4 taps per 10 seconds ($T = 50$). Her arm/hand movements were substantially affected, but she could walk without difficulty. She was now considered to have a right spastic monoparesis.

The findings were reviewed with the patient and her mother. They appreciated the consultation and were subsequently followed for the next 5 years. The girl's ability to find words in free speech improved with time and therapy. Her auditory comprehension skills also improved. Interestingly, during this time of improvement, she became increasingly more interested in art and drew various pictures with increasing clarity and skill. She remained positive in her attitude and had no behavioral difficulties. She began wearing makeup and showed an interest in boys and dating.

By age 16 years, the girl was still receiving special education and resource services, but progressive gains in her cognitive and language functioning were noted, with no change in her motor functioning. Her motor and language dysfunction again continued to negatively affect her test performance on the WAIS-IV. However, subtle improvement was again noted. Her Verbal Comprehension Index score was 76, and her Perceptual Reasoning Index was 82. Her verbal memory was difficult to test because of her aphasic condition, but her visual–spatial memory was within the normal range. For example, on the Brief Visuospatial Memory Test, she had age-adjusted T scores of 55, 52, and 52 on Trials 1–3, respectively. Delayed recall was also within the average range ($T = 54$). Speed of left finger tapping showed normal developmental improvement (mean left hand score of 43.4; $T = 54$), but she continued to be unable to use the right hand to perform this task.

Continued Efforts at Psychological Care

As with the preceding patient, this patient displayed no obvious depression or anxiety. There were no behavioral problems. She was very motivated to interact with others and constantly tried new activities. As she aged, she took on responsibilities that allowed for expression of her needs as an adolescent female. Dating and work activities were very important to her. Given her lack of negative emotion and her hard-working attitude, she ingratiated herself to many people. Her desire to work in some capacity resulted in her beginning a holistic approach to neuropsychological rehabilitation. During this time, further development of language skills appeared to take place. She took on part-time paid employment and appears to be making an excellent psychosocial adjustment. Although her initial psychological care was primarily supportive in nature, it became more insightful in its efforts as she expressed a desire to engage activities that fostered the natural plan of her central nervous system (as discussed in previous chapters of this volume).

APPROACHES TO THE PSYCHOLOGICAL CARE OF PERSONS WITH APHASIA

Throughout the years, several approaches have been explored to aid in the psychological care of patients with aphasia secondary to a left MCA stroke or TBI. However, the academic and research communities continue to emphasize the need to develop methods to improve language and motor functioning after stroke and to enhance self-care and functional use of the arms and legs (Cramer et al., 2017; Dobkin, 2005). Specific attention to issues of psychological well-being is often not the focus of discussion. This is somewhat understandable because worse emotional well-being is often associated with continued physical and cognitive limitations in the stroke population (Clarke, Marshall, Black, & Colantonio, 2002).

However, it is noteworthy that very recent clinical practice guidelines for post-stroke aphasia rehabilitation include a recommendation to provide support at all stages of recovery with "relevant health professionals" (Shrubsole, Worrall, Power, & O'Connor, 2017, p. 14). The recommendation does not specifically mention the need for psychological support services to help build resiliency in the patient and family members. As noted previously, Sarno (1998) emphasized some important observations relevant to the psychological care of aphasic patients. These patients often feel "left out" of conversations, and some actively avoid social interactions because of their language difficulties. Later research has clearly linked loneliness and low satisfaction with one's social network as especially important predictors of psychological distress in stroke patients (Hilari et al., 2010). These factors also produce considerable family distress (Kitzmüller, Asplund, & Häggström, 2012). Thus, involving patients in activities they can perform often helps reduce social isolation and loneliness. It may also reduce family distress.

Having aphasic patients sing in a choir may help reduce social isolation and build confidence to interact with others (Tamplin, Baker, Jones, Way, & Lee, 2013). Likewise, music therapy or simply listening to a variety of music may be helpful. Särkämö et al. (2008) reported that patients with both right and left hemisphere strokes involving the MCA seemed to show enhanced cognitive recovery and improved mood following 2 months of daily listening to self-selected music or audio books. It has also been suggested that music therapy that requires stroke patients to move a hemiparetic limb to the beat of a musical sound pattern helps engage patients in activities that give a greater sense of personal competence and increase motivation to interact with others (Street et al., 2017). Recall that the first aphasic patient discussed in this chapter was also a musician who found great solace in playing a song on the piano and singing with friends. Thus, music therapy in one form or another may be very helpful for improving the psychological well-being of aphasic patients.

Kneebone (2016) reviewed a number of studies that suggest that the prevalence rate for prolonged depression after stroke is often in the range of 30%. He outlines a number of behavioral activation strategies to re-engage patients in activities that are pleasurable and allow them to experience competencies in domains of functioning that are not compromised. For example, rediscovering that one can play chess may add a sense of competency and reduce negative thoughts about the self. Kneebone (2016) draws attention to an important point that Beck (1979) made regarding the thought processes of depressed individuals. There tends to be "black-and-white" thinking, with no in-between choices. For example, a patient with a stroke may feel so changed that there is nothing positive left in life. This can be reinforced by disturbances in abstract thought and the tendency for concrete behavior after a stroke, as noted by Salas, Gross, Rafal, Viñas-Guasch, and Turnbull (2013). Helping patients rediscover that they are not helpless and that they have hope for a better future is often crucial. The child with the left MCA stroke described previously seemed to embody this approach naturally. She recognized what she could do and what the possibilities were for her in the future. She also experienced continued support and encouragement from her mother.

The senior adult patient described in Case Vignette 18.1 was in the later years of his life. Few new possibilities were in front of him, but he did take pleasure (with momentary reductions in depression) when he "lost himself" in playing the piano, singing with friends, and growing something beautiful in his garden. This seemed to periodically boost his resiliency.

When the aphasic patient is in the "middle years of life" or in young adulthood, building relationships, engaging in work to build self-confidence and self-esteem, and enjoying sexual relationships with a partner are perhaps most prominent (Lawrence, 2010; Nilsson, Fugl-Meyer, von Koch, & Ytterberg, 2017; Sorin-Peters, 2003). Overdependence on a spouse during this time frame, however, can be especially exhausting to the spouse, particularly when the spouse also needs to attend to the needs of children. Some of these patients may also appear somewhat childlike in how they approach a partner sexually. This further adds to the distress that both the patient and the partner experience. There is no easy way of dealing with these issues, but helping the patient be productive in some capacity is crucial. This not only builds the patient's sense of competency but also reduces the burden of care on the spouse. Unfortunately, building resiliency and fostering independence in this patient group are difficult but of course not impossible.

Psychodynamic issues between the young adult aphasic patient and his or her partner frequently have to be attended to as well. Not infrequently, however, these issues are overlooked. For example, one aphasic young woman became overly dependent on her husband. He secretly enjoyed her dependence on him, and when she was able to work as a hairdresser and become more independent, he exploded in angry outbursts. Thus, working to improve the psychological care of young adults with aphasia is perhaps the most complicated and challenging of all efforts in the psychological care of persons with a brain disorder.

Holistic approaches to neuropsychological rehabilitation have emphasized the need to engage aphasic (and nonaphasic) brain dysfunctional patients in a variety of individual and group therapy activities (Prigatano, 1986). In addition to receiving individual speech and language therapy, aphasic patients seem to benefit by observing and interacting with other patients with brain dysfunction. They often begin to recognize the permanency of some aphasic symptomatology and the need to be productive even if their aphasia persists. Some are able to re-establish meaning in their lives after aphasia, and this is often depicted in their artwork (Prigatano, 2012; Prigatano & Salas, 2017).

Although certainly not an exhaustive list, Table 18.6 provides some clinical reports that highlight various trends involved in helping reduce psychological distress in aphasic adults following a left MCA stroke.

SUMMARY

An acquired disturbance of language has profound effects on the psychological well-being of adults and children who have lost the ability to communicate thoughts and feelings to others. The sense of "loss of significance" and social/family position often predominates the psychological state of these individuals and frequently results in reduced contact with others and social isolation. Depression, anxiety, and angry outbursts can occur, but much depends on the premorbid personality characteristics of the person, the person's social situation, and the underlying neurocognitive systems that have or have not been affected. Suggestive clinical evidence points to a potentially important mediating role of working memory in persistent depression. Disruption of working memory functions may also reduce affective disturbances by interrupting inner speech. A reduction of inner speech may produce less verbal rehearsal

Table 18.6 Review of Selected Clinical Reports Relevant to the Psychological Care of Persons with Aphasic Conditions Secondary to a Left MCA Stroke

INTERVENTION	STUDY SAMPLE	MAJOR FINDINGS	CONCLUSIONS
Modified cognitive–behavioral approaches to reducing depression and related problems in aphasic patients after stroke (Kneebone, 2016)	A series of clinical case vignettes describing practical steps to help aphasic patients experience some sense of competency and to engage in personal and socially rewarding activities. Psychological interventions were often combined with occupational therapy activities.	Having patients experience that they have not lost all cognitive skills after stroke-induced aphasia is important for reducing inactivity. Having patients experience their changes in functioning in less concrete terms (e.g., "I lost myself" vs. "I lost some of my abilities") not only reduces depression but also helps patients become more involved in daily activities.	As a series of case vignettes, this article draws attention to the need to integrate psychological interventions, based in part on both cognitive–behavioral and behavioral theories, with the practical activities that occupational therapists employ to help patients become functional in daily life.
Psychodynamic psychotherapy to help reduce depression associated with a left hemisphere stroke (Salas & Yuen, 2016)	A case study of a 71-year-old university professor with an expressive (i.e., nonfluent) aphasic disturbance. Treatment extended for a 7-year period.	Writing down thoughts was very helpful to improve the patient's problem-solving skills and to express internal worries or concerns. Verbal thinking and inner speech (as described by Luria and Vygotsky) were compromised, reducing the patient's feelings of guilt (which always pervaded his life). However, disturbances in language functioning appeared to make the mourning process more difficult.	This case report draws attention to the complex interaction between the patient's premorbid personality characteristics and the brain lesion–based neuropsychological deficits to produce the clinical picture. It provides some insight into how to psychologically help the patient from a psychodynamic perspective.

(*continued*)

Table 18.6 Continued

INTERVENTION	STUDY SAMPLE	MAJOR FINDINGS	CONCLUSIONS
Holistic neuropsychological rehabilitation programs for helping aphasic and nonaphasic patients return to a productive lifestyle (Prigatano, 1986; see also Prigatano, 2012; Prigatano & Salas, 2017)	Case reports of patients undergoing intensive holistic neuropsychological rehabilitation programs for at least 6 months. Multiple forms of psychological interventions are included in such programs.	Individual aphasic patients can reconstruct a productive and meaningful life if they become progressively aware of their limitations, provided they have adequate cognitive functioning in domains outside of their speech and language deficits.	Combining traditional rehabilitation therapies (e.g., speech and language therapies) with various cognitive and psychotherapeutic activities may be helpful in restoring some sense of productivity after an aphasic disorder. At minimum, such activities may help avoid psychiatric deterioration on the part of the patient and the caregiving family member. The conclusions, however, are based on individual patients, and no systematic group studies have yet been conducted in this area.
Use of singing in a choir to reduce social isolation in aphasic patients after stroke (Tamplin et al., 2013)	Thirteen patients with aphasia following a stroke were recruited to sing in a community choir. They participated in a weekly 2-hour rehearsal. The amount of time spent in this activity varied across patients.	Qualitative analysis suggested that patients had an increased confidence in different domains, but most important, they felt connected to others and had a sense of belonging.	For some aphasic patients, singing in a group may help improve one's sense of self-confidence and reduce social isolation.

Listening to music to enhance cognitive recovery and mood after MCA stroke (Särkämö et al., 2008)	Sixty patients with a left or right hemisphere MCA stroke were randomly assigned to a music group, a language group, or a control group. Treatments lasted 2 months. Fifty-four patients completed the study.	Patients receiving music therapy not only reported less depression but also performed better on a test of verbal memory and attention. Improvement in attention was reported to occur primarily in the left MCA patients. The magnitude of changes appeared mild but statistically reliable.	The authors note that music, by its nature, "has strong connections to both attention and memory systems" (p. 872). It appears that music may be a useful adjunct for facilitating cognitive and affective functioning. This theme is more fully discussed when considering psychological care issues for persons with TBI.
Failure to discuss sexuality or sexual life after stroke (Nilsson et al., 2017)	Twelve patients were interviewed 6 years following stroke (2 were described as having speech impairments).	Qualitative analysis suggests that the topic of sexuality is seldom adequately discussed with patients following stroke during or after rehabilitation. Individual differences exist as to the importance of sexual dysfunction after stroke but in some instances may greatly influence the degree of intimacy between partners.	

MCA, middle cerebral artery; TBI, traumatic brain injury.

of worrisome thoughts. In some instances, the psychological care interventions for aphasic patients are more "active" and directly engage the patients in discussions and activities that help them deal with their disturbing existential situation. In other cases, the psychological care interventions appear more "passive" in nature when ongoing anxiety and depression seem strangely absent. These individuals, however, need ongoing external supports from others to reinforce their natural attempts at adaptation and avoidance of future harm.

Because language is so crucial for the development of one's unique expression of human nature, any disturbance of language seems to alter a person in a very significant way. For those of us who do not experience an aphasic disturbance, this may be difficult to understand. However, it should be remembered that language not only conveys experience but also defines experience (see Chapters 2 and 9, this volume). Thus, any disruption of language alters what the person actually experiences and thereby can change personality and behavior in complicated ways. Helping with the psychological adjustment of aphasic patients can be challenging for everyone involved, but it is perhaps most needed, given that patients themselves often cannot adequately ask for such help.

REFERENCES

Alderson-Day, B., & Fernyhough, C. (2015). Inner speech: Development, cognitive functions, phenomenology, and neurobiology. *Psychological Bulletin, 141*(5), 931–965.

Beck, A. T. (1979). *Cognitive therapy of depression*. New York, NY: Guilford.

Blumenfeld, H. (2010). *Neuroanatomy through clinical cases*. Sunderland, MA: Sinauer.

Clarke, P., Marshall, V., Black, S. E., & Colantonio, A. (2002). Well-being after stroke in Canadian seniors. *Stroke, 33*(4), 1016–1021.

Cramer, S. C., Wolf, S. L., Adams, H. P., Chen, D., Dromerick, A. W., Dunning, K., . . . Lansberg, M. G. (2017). Stroke recovery and rehabilitation research. *Stroke, 48*(3), 813–819.

Csikszentmihalyi, M. (1999). If we are so rich, why aren't we happy? *American Psychologist, 54*(10), 821–827.

Dobkin, B. H. (2005). Rehabilitation after stroke. *New England Journal of Medicine, 352*(16), 1677–1684.

Goldstein, K. (1952). The effect of brain damage on the personality. *Psychiatry, 15*(3), 245–260.

Hilari, K., Northcott, S., Roy, P., Marshall, J., Wiggins, R. D., Chataway, J., & Ames, D. (2010). Psychological distress after stroke and aphasia: The first six months. *Clinical Rehabilitation, 24*(2), 181–190.

Kertesz, A. (1985). Aphasia. In P. Vinken, B. Bruyn, H. Klawans, & J. Frederiks (Eds.), *Handbook of clinical neurology* (Vol. 45, pp. 287–332). Amsterdam, the Netherlands: Elsevier.

Kitzmüller, G., Asplund, K., & Häggström, T. (2012). The long-term experience of family life after stroke. *Journal of Neuroscience Nursing, 44*(1), E1–E13.

Kneebone, I. I. (2016). A framework to support cognitive behavior therapy for emotional disorder after stroke. *Cognitive and Behavioral Practice, 23*(1), 99–109.

Lawrence, M. (2010). Young adults' experience of stroke: A qualitative review of the literature. *British Journal of Nursing, 19*(4), 241–248.

Lishman, W. A. (Ed.). (1987). *Organic psychiatry: The psychological consequences of cerebral disorder* (3rd ed.). Oxford, UK: Blackwell.

Nilsson, M. I., Fugl-Meyer, K., von Koch, L., & Ytterberg, C. (2017). Experiences of sexuality six years after stroke: A qualitative study. *Journal of Sexual Medicine, 14*(6), 797–803.

Oliveira, F. F., Marin, S. M., & Bertolucci, P. H. (2017). Neurological impressions on the organization of language networks in the human brain. *Brain Injury, 31*(2), 140–150.

Prigatano, G. P. (Ed.). (1986). *Neuropsychological rehabilitation after brain injury*. Baltimore, MD: Johns Hopkins University Press.

Prigatano, G. P. (2012). Jungian contributions to successful neuropsychological rehabilitation. *Neuropsychoanalysis, 14*(2), 175–185.

Prigatano, G. P., & Salas, C. (2017). Psychodynamic psychotherapy after severe traumatic brain injury. In R. Wood, T. McMillan, & A. Worthington (Eds.), *Neurobehavioral disability and social handicap following traumatic brain injury* (pp. 188–201). Philadelphia, PA: Taylor & Francis.

Prigatano, G. P., & Summers, J. D. (1997). Depression in traumatic brain injury patients. In M. M. Robertson & C. L. E. Katona (Eds.), *Depression and physical illness* (pp. 341–358). New York, NY: Wiley.

Salas, C. E., Gross, J. J., Rafal, R. D., Viñas-Guasch, N., & Turnbull, O. H. (2013). Concrete behaviour and reappraisal deficits after a left frontal stroke: A case study. *Neuropsychological Rehabilitation, 23*(4), 467–500.

Salas, C. E., & Yuen, K. S. (2016). Revisiting the left convexity hypothesis: Changes in the mental apparatus after left dorso-medial prefrontal damage. *Neuropsychoanalysis, 18*(2), 85–100.

Särkämö, T., Tervaniemi, M., Laitinen, S., Forsblom, A., Soinila, S., Mikkonen, M., . . . Laine, M. (2008). Music listening enhances cognitive recovery and mood after middle cerebral artery stroke. *Brain, 131*(3), 866–876.

Sarno, M. T. (1998). Aphasia: Rehabilitation and recovery from loss. *Loss, Grief & Care, 8*(1–2), 83–91.

Shrubsole, K., Worrall, L., Power, E., & O'Connor, D. A. (2017). Recommendations for post-stroke aphasia rehabilitation: An updated systematic review and evaluation of clinical practice guidelines. *Aphasiology, 31*(1), 1–24.

Sorin-Peters, R. (2003). Viewing couples living with aphasia as adult learners: Implications for promoting quality of life. *Aphasiology, 17*(4), 405–416.

Street, A. J., Magee, W. L., Bateman, A., Parker, M., Odell-Miller, H., & Fachner, J. (2017). Home-based neurologic music therapy for arm hemiparesis following stroke: Results from a pilot, feasibility randomized controlled trial. *Clinical Rehabilitation, 32*(1), 18–28.

Tamplin, J., Baker, F. A., Jones, B., Way, A., & Lee, S. (2013). "Stroke a chord": The effect of singing in a community choir on mood and social engagement for people living with aphasia following a stroke. *NeuroRehabilitation, 32*(4), 929–941.

19

PSYCHOLOGICAL CARE OF PERSONS WITH HEMIPLEGIA/HEMIPARESIS SECONDARY TO A CEREBRAL VASCULAR ACCIDENT OR TRAUMATIC BRAIN INJURY

BACKGROUND INFORMATION

Given the importance of movement to sustain life, maintain social interactions, and develop higher integrative brain functions (see Chapters 2 and 3, this volume), the loss of motor skills following a cerebral vascular accident (CVA) or traumatic brain injury (TBI) can be psychologically devastating. When such an event occurs during adulthood, loss of employment, reduced sexual attractiveness, and physical dependence on others often result in important psychological adjustment issues. Although motor impairments are observed in different types of brain disorders, they are perhaps most common following a CVA. It has been estimated that 85% of stroke patients have some form of hemiparesis following a stroke (Mayo et al., 1999). Reportedly, 70–80% of stroke patients have upper extremity impairments (Krakauer & Carmichael, 2017). Although hemiplegia/hemiparesis is less common after severe TBI, Katz, Alexander, and Klein (1998) reported that approximately 30% of acutely admitted TBI patients present with paresis. Residual motor impairments strongly predict the quality of life in TBI patients (Klonoff, Costa, & Snow, 1986). In this chapter, the psychological care of persons with acquired hemiplegia and/or hemiparesis during childhood and adulthood is discussed.

HEMIPLEGIA AND HEMIPARESIS

Hemiplegia refers to a complete paralysis of one-half of the body caused by an underlying brain disorder. *Hemiparesis* refers to a partial paralysis of one side of the body. Although the primary feature of both hemiplegia and hemiparesis is weakness, this condition also includes impairments of motor movement and control. Even in cases of favorable recovery, "movements are slower and more variable" (Jones, 2017, p. 268). The organization of the human motor system is fairly well understood. It involves complex but predictable networks of interacting and reciprocal pathways within the brain and spinal cord (Blumenfeld, 2010, p. 230). Multiple feedback loops exist between the cerebral motor cortex, basal ganglia, thalamus, and cerebellum that allow for fine and gross motor movements necessary for independent living. Injury to any of these regions can produce motor impairments. However, direct damage to the motor cortex often results in upper extremity impairments (Jones, 2017). Figure 19.1 illustrates cortical motor control regions in humans and compares them to those observed in rats. Vascular occlusions of the distal middle cerebral artery and its projection pathways (i.e., the anterior choroidal artery and striate arteries) often result in hemiparesis or hemiplegia.

In adult humans, complete recovery from hemiplegia is rare. The majority of adult patients with hemiplegia demonstrate persistent residual difficulties in motor strength, movement, and control. Rehabilitation activities initially are aimed at recovery, but with time the focus is more on improving functional capacity in everyday life. This is often achieved by learning compensatory techniques. Whether there is neural reorganization in the recovery/rehabilitation process after a stroke has been open to debate. In a recent review article, Jones (2017) noted that subtle compensatory movement strategies are often misinterpreted as signs of actual motor recovery. Jones also commented that "although the movements of both the left and right hands are typically impaired after unilateral stroke, the non-paretic side is less severely so" (p. 268). Further recovery of the so-called nonaffected hand is often associated with improved functional recovery across many domains following inpatient neurorehabilitation (Prigatano & Wong, 1997).

A variety of strategies have been used to attempt to improve functional recovery in a hemiparetic hand and arm. They include traditional physical therapy (Dobkin, 2005), constraint-induced movement therapy (Kwakkel, Veerbeek, van Wegen, & Wolf, 2015), motor imagery training (Dunsky, Dickstein, Marcovitz, Levy, & Deutsch, 2008), music therapy (Street et al., 2017), yoga (Bastille & Gill-Body, 2004), and repetitive transcranial magnetic stimulation therapy (Sasaki, Mizutani, Kakuda, & Abo, 2013).

In addition, considerable research has been conducted on the neurobiology of motor recovery after stroke, as recently summarized by Krakauer and Carmichael (2017). They argue that building on the neurobiological changes associated with "spontaneous recovery," greater neural repair may occur with associated behavioral (i.e., motor) recovery. However, this would require that intensive efforts at physical therapy and various motor training programs be conducted during the early phases (not chronic phases) after stroke. Although there is certainly growing interest in understanding important neurobiological changes associated with hemiplegia, less attention has been focused on understanding the psychological care issues for patients with hemiplegia or hemiparesis.

THE PSYCHOLOGICAL IMPACT OF HEMIPLEGIA OR HEMIPARESIS

After describing the development and organization of the human brain, Moore (1986) noted the following:

> Granted, man uses one limb more precisely than the other for some specific functions, such as writing, and perhaps eating, and reaching for objects. But few individuals can get dressed, take part in sports, be musicians, painters or clinicians without utilizing the entire body in the activity. Everything man does on one side of the body immediately

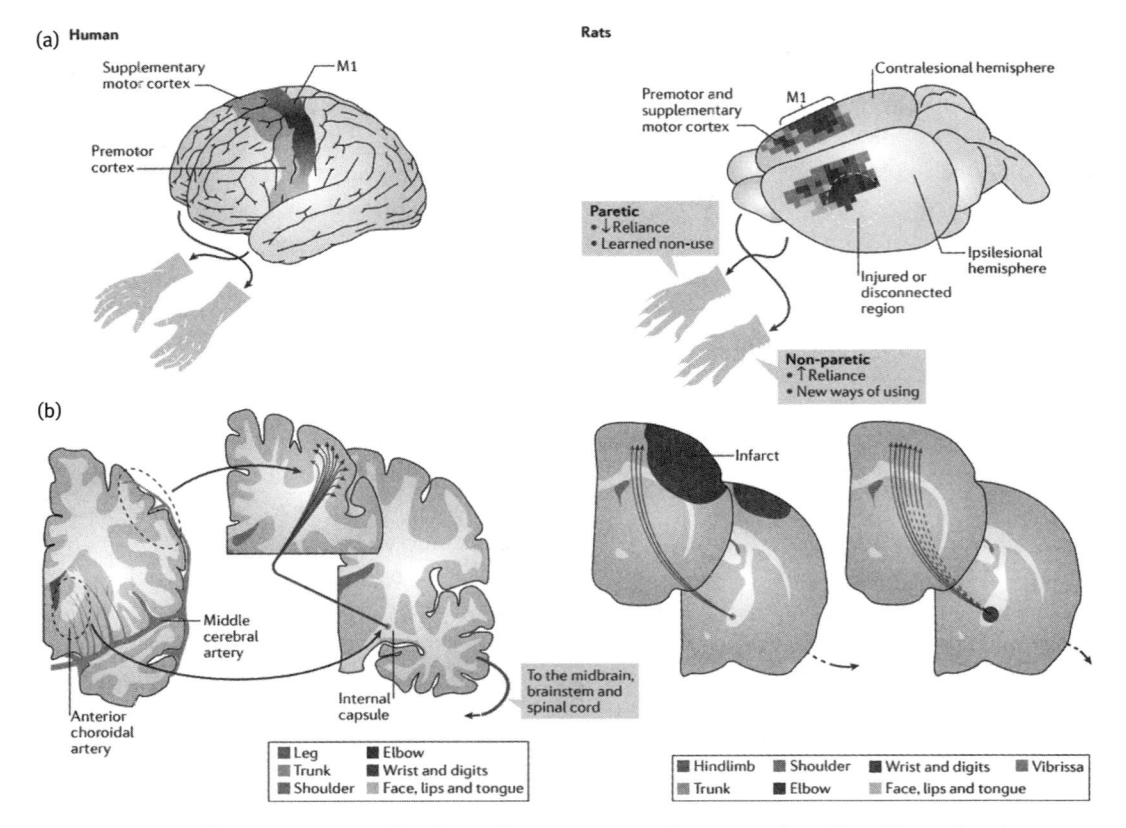

FIGURE 19.1 The motor cortex and its descending projection pathways are often affected by strokes that result in upper extremity impairments. (a) Simplified illustrations of motor cortical regions of a human (left) and a naive rat, derived using intracortical microsimulation (right), are shown. The colors show the cortical territories that are responsible for the movement of different body parts. The motor cortical control of the upper limbs is mostly crossed, such that the left hemisphere controls movement of the right side and vice versa. (b) Occlusions or ruptures in the cerebral vasculature (red) that supplies motor cortical regions (the distal middle cerebral artery) and its projection pathways (e.g., the anterior choroidal and striate arteries) position strokes (the dark gray regions on the rat coronal sections on the right) that either kill the cortical neurons that control upper limb movement or disconnect their projections to the spinal cord and other subcortical structures, such as the red nucleus and reticular formation. The degree of disruption of the descending motor cortical pathway due to either cortical or subcortical strokes predicts the severity of motor impairment. The colors of the corticospinal neurons correspond to the body parts that they control as in the motor cortical regions in panel a. The rat coronal sections show the locations of ischemic infarcts that have been used to model post-stroke upper extremity impairments; these infarcts are located in the forelimb region of the primary motor cortex (M1, which is supplied by the distal middle cerebral artery) and in the posterior limb of the internal capsule (which is supplied by the anterior choroidal artery). The dashed lines indicate the disconnection of descending cortical projections (See color plates).

Source: Reprinted from Jones, T. A., Motor compensation and its effects on neural reorganization after stroke, *Nature Reviews Neuroscience*, 18(5), 2017, p. 267–280, by permission of Springer Nature.

affects and is affected in turn by the opposite side. (p. 28)

Following the onset of hemiparesis or hemiplegia, the person is faced with a number of situations that challenge independent living. The person can "switch" hand dominance for eating and writing, but what about getting dressed, playing a sport, learning to be a musician, and functioning in jobs that routinely require the functional use of both hands (e.g., typing on a keyboard when working on the computer)? Hemiplegia or hemiparesis restricts daily life activities in substantial ways that (1) make the person more dependent on others to meet daily needs, (2) restrict many forms of new learning, and (3) substantially alter "body image" (Morin, Pradat-Diehl, Robain, Bensalah, & Perrigot, 2003). These factors limit the person's ability to engage in physical activities that can create a sense of pleasure and well-being.

The hemiparesis or hemiplegia makes one more physically and psychological vulnerable. Some men feel less able to carry out the traditional role of protection of loved ones; some women feel less feminine because they are no longer able to wear high heels with a skirt or dress. They are unable to dance and move in a seductive manner for a chosen partner. Children are restricted in sport activities, which are often important for successful peer interaction and developing a positive body image.

Takashima, Murata, and Saeki (2016) reported on the phenomenological experiences of many stroke survivors who experience hemiplegia or hemiparesis. They commented,

> Participants experienced changes resulting from hemiplegia, perceiving themselves differently from the way they did before the stroke. Living in a body impaired by hemiplegia was different from living in an able body before the stroke, so that participants experienced "inescapable dependence," a "sense of incompetence" and "lack of autonomy." (p. 1581)

It is of little wonder, therefore, that the presence of hemiplegia/hemiparesis is associated with a reduction in quality of life (Nichols-Larsen, Clark, Zeringue, Greenspan, & Blanton, 2005; Pulman & Buckley, 2013). How people emotionally react to this "inescapable dependence" appears to relate to premorbid personality features and/or the immediate frustrations experienced by the person with hemiplegia/hemiparesis. In 1974, MacDonald Critchley coined the term *misoplegia* or hatred of hemiplegia. The phenomenon is often associated with the patient talking in negative terms to an affected limb (Loetscher, Regard, & Brugger, 2006) or actually hitting or biting it, as is observed in some children. Brugger (2007) suggested that this reaction is more common following a right parietal lesion than a left parietal lesion.

Other reactions can be observed. One young adult TBI patient, with residual left hemiplegia, repeatedly stated that he was not handicapped by his motor condition. It was just "a damn inconvenience." His clinical presentation was also associated with persistent denial of his cognitive limitations. Despite repeated failures at employment, he explained each failure as a result of his employer's limitations rather than his own. In some cultures, patients avoid social contact because of a sense of shame regarding their clinical situation. They prefer to stay at home and do not want to explain to others what happened to them or appear dependent on others.

The degree to which hemiplegia/hemiparesis produces persistent depression is difficult to determine and again may be related to several factors. Early research by Robinson and Price (1982) concluded that the presence of different types of neurological symptoms following a stroke was not associated with depressive disorders 6–12 months after the stroke. For example, the presence of hemiparesis did not distinguish depressed versus nondepressed post-stroke individuals. However, the degree to which a person experienced reduced self-efficacy was strongly related to the degree of depression during the first month after the stroke (Robinson-Smith, Johnston, & Allen, 2000). At 6 months post-stroke, there was not a significant correlation between level of functional independence and degree of depression (Robinson-Smith et al., 2000).

However, Robinson and Price (1982) and later investigators (e.g., Rashid, Clarke, & Rogish, 2013) have demonstrated that depression is more common following left hemisphere strokes. In a well-designed study, Aström, Adolfsson, and Asplund (1993) conducted a 3-year longitudinal investigation of major depressive disorder in stroke patients. Acutely, major depression was associated with left anterior brain lesions. However, at 1 year post-stroke, major depression was primarily correlated with the degree to which the patient was socially isolated. At 3 years post-stroke, the most powerful predictor of major depression was the degree of cerebral atrophy. Perhaps with greater cortical atrophy, the patient had less "cognitive reserve" and sustained self-efficacy as it relates to self-care and maintaining interpersonal relationships. In this regard, Aström et al. noted that persistent aphasia (which is often associated with hemiplegia/hemiparesis) was consistently a predictor of depression after stroke.

BODY SCHEMA AND BODY IMAGE CHANGES ASSOCIATED WITH HEMIPLEGIA AND HEMIPARESIS

A fair amount of research has emanated from the neurosciences concerning brain disorders that alter a person's conscious recognition or perceptions regarding his or her body. Parietal lobe lesions and lesions involving the insular cortex are often associated with some negative alteration of a person's ability to perceive body parts and to consciously identify a body part (e.g., an arm and hand) as belonging to the person and moving in space (Bottini et al., 2010; Haggard, Rossetti, & Kawato, 2008; Karnath & Baier, 2010). There is also an appreciation of the importance of occipital–temporal brain regions for visually identifying body parts for oneself and others (Peelen & Downing, 2007). Disturbances of these types typically fall under the rubric of "disorders of the body schema." Such disorders are certainly common after stroke, particularly following a right hemisphere stroke (Prigatano, 2010).

Less well studied are the changes or disturbances in body image following a brain disorder that results from hemiplegia and hemiparesis. Body image is a complicated, multifactorial concept. Body image, however, reflects "how we feel" about our bodies. It includes a "valence of self-perceptions (i.e., ranging from highly negative to highly positive)" (Trapnell, Meston, & Gorzalka, 1997, p. 268). At some point, psychological care of persons with hemiplegia and hemiparesis has to focus on how the patients feel about their motor impairments. Frequently, studies that directly or indirectly focus on changes in body image do not address this important point. For example, Denes, Semenza, Stoppa, and Lis (1982) noted that patients with right-sided brain lesions and left hemiplegia demonstrated greater indifference toward their motor impairments compared to left-sided brain lesion patients with right hemiplegia. How this indifference is experienced by the patients was not included in the discussion.

Another issue that may not be readily discussed with patients is decreases in their libido and sexual activity following the onset of hemiparesis or hemiplegia. These are commonly reported problems (Binder, 1984; Korpelainen, Nieminen, & Myllylä, 1999; Nilsson, Fugl-Meyer, von Koch, & Ytterberg, 2017). When provided with an opportunity to discuss this issue, patients may privately report "not feeling good" about their bodies. Improving body image and helping patients and their spouses re-engage in sexual activity may have clear relevance to the psychological care of some patients.

In a study of body image in women following different forms of acquired brain disorder (including TBI and stroke), Howes, Edwards, and Benton (2005) demonstrated a clear relationship between disturbances in mobility (one feature of body image) and lower self-esteem ($r = -0.64$, $p < .05$). As expected, lower self-esteem was associated with a lack of social contact ($r = 0.65$, $p < .05$). Keppel and Crowe (2000) studied the relationship between body image and self-esteem in relatively young stroke patients (mean age, 36.7 years). They reported that body image was significantly negatively affected following stroke, but there was no specific comparison of stroke patients who had motor disorders with those who did not. Their findings, however, are relevant to this discussion insofar as the authors note that "before the stroke, only physical self-esteem and body image were correlated, however, after the stroke, all measures of self-esteem correlated with evaluations of body image" (p. 15).

In an internet-based study of personal reactions to impaired upper limb functioning following stroke, Poltawski et al. (2016) summarized several important findings relevant to psychological care of patients with hemiplegia/hemiparesis. They noted four broad themes: perceptions of the affected upper limb, reactions to the disability, experiences of therapy, and recovery and adaptation to the disability. These researchers specifically noted, "Objectification of the affected limb was common, with a range of terms used to describe it and express feelings towards it" (p. 947). Much like Critchley (1955, 1974) and other early investigators noted (e.g., Weinstein & Kahn, 1955), some individuals referred to the affected limit as "useless" or "not serving any purpose." Others described the limb as having an independent existence that often resisted the will of the individual. In some cases, the limb was not viewed as being a part of the person's body and was alien to the person. These latter descriptions are well known to the scientific community and are described by the term *somatoparaphrenia* (Invernizzi et al., 2013) or *alien limb syndrome* (Garbarini et al., 2015). The point is that there are different personal reactions to hemiplegia and hemiparesis that need to be considered when providing psychological care.

Regarding reactions to the disability, frustration was commonly reported (which again had been reported previously; see Prigatano, 1999). Next was the "distress at the realization that cherished activities could no longer be engaged in" (Poltawski et al., 2016, p. 948). Finally, "concern about appearance and associated behavior in social situations" was an important personal reaction to the disability. These dimensions must be integrated into any attempt to provide psychological care for such individuals.

In light of these observations, two clinical case examples are briefly reviewed next. The first case example highlights certain patent characteristics and responses to psychological interventions that were associated with apparently successful adaptation to the hemiplegia/hemiparesis. The second case example highlights features associated with nonsuccessful psychological adaptation.

PSYCHOLOGICAL CARE OF PERSONS WITH HEMIPLEGIA/HEMIPARESIS: TWO CASE VIGNETTES

Case Vignette 19.1

A 63-year-old man suffered a right middle cerebral artery stroke with resultant left hemiparesis and mild neglect. He had been an accomplished businessman who was married to his wife for more than 30 years. He and his wife appeared to have had a very good and mutually supportive relationship before his stroke, and they appeared to continue to do so after the stroke. The patient, however, suffered from pathological crying. That is, he often would break down in tears for no apparent reason. This was obviously embarrassing to him and his wife. As a consequence, he avoided all social contact.

Prior to his stroke, he was gregarious and enjoyed other people's company. He suffered from a left hemiparesis as a result of his stroke, but his motor impairments were not his major concern when first seen. What he wanted was help in controlling his unexplained negative emotional reactions.

This man was fluent in his speech, and his verbal intellectual abilities appeared unaffected except for occasional word-finding difficulties. He also demonstrated mild visual–spatial neglect. To compensate for this difficulty, he would consistently verbally self-cue himself to look to the left when walking and reading the newspaper. His personal history was to naturally try to be as self-sufficient as possible (a well-established marker of resiliency; see Chapter 12, this volume).

In the initial neuropsychological interview, he often broke into tears. When asked if he was sad or unhappy, his response was that he was not sad or unhappy. He just could not control his crying. Any time he would talk about something that had any emotional valence to it (positive or negative), he would begin to cry uncontrollably. It was suggested to him that when he began to sense he was about to cry, he should focus his attention on his shoes (Prigatano, 2011). Shoes (as least for men) tend to be fairly neutral stimuli. By focusing on this rather bland object, he was able to behaviorally inhibit his crying behavior. He was grateful for being taught this simple behavioral maneuver that proved very helpful to him. A positive professional relationship was established, and he felt comfortable raising another topic that concerned him.

He was secretly very distressed over his inability to get an erection and enjoy sexual relations with his wife. He often avoided having any physical contact with her because he was afraid she would expect it and would move into a more intimate expression of love and pleasure between the two. His wife repeatedly told him it was not an issue for her, but he felt differently. During a series of individual psychotherapy sessions, he spoke of the many happy days he had with his wife. When asked what he would typically do to please her in the past, he stated that he had a good sense of humor (perhaps another marker of resiliency; see Chapter 12, this volume) and could always make her laugh or smile. Many times, this was a precursor to lovemaking.

The treating clinical neuropsychologist suggested another idea that proved to be helpful. It was suggested to the patient that he could give his wife one "love note" each day. On the note, he would write something humorous or at least something sensitive about her uniqueness as a person that he appreciated. (More details of how this was done are provided elsewhere [Prigatano, 2011].) The patient immediately agreed to the idea and with the help of an aide began taking on this responsibility each day. It proved to be very beneficial and helped sustain a positive love (and romantic) relationship between him and his wife, even though he physically found it very difficult to obtain and sustain an erection. This couple did not go into details of how their sexual relationship changed after this intervention. However, they seemed to remain happy. Pertinent to the question of his psychological adjustment and reaction to his disability, the patient was less frustrated and irritated with his reduced motor independence. He found a way to stay actively involved in maintaining a mutually supportive relationship with his wife (another source of resiliency; see Chapter 12, this volume). This appeared to reduce the psychological burden of his motor and related functional limitations. Table 19.1 lists the clinical features associated with this man's psychological care, and Table 19.2 lists the clinically relevant features of his spouse when he was provided psychological care.

Table 19.1 Clinical Features Relevant to the Psychological Care of the Patient in Case Vignette 19.1

CLINICAL FEATURE	YES	NO	PARTIALLY
1. The dialogue between the patient and the clinical neuropsychologist was not rushed.	✓		
2. The patient was able to express or clearly convey his personal concerns.	✓		
3. The content of the concerns varied over time.	✓		
4. The patient experienced a sense of "realistic" hope in coping with his life situation.	✓		
5. The patient and the clinical neuropsychologist developed a positive therapeutic relationship that helped the patient sustain adaptive activities during difficult times.	✓		
6. Somatic symptoms (which appeared to be indirect effects of a brain disorder) were substantially reduced during periods of psychological care.			n/a
7. Anxiety/depression/anger and/or apathy were substantially reduced during periods of psychological care.		✓	
8. The patient was able to follow the guidance of the clinical neuropsychologist to improve functioning in everyday life activities.	✓		
9. The patient was able to control impulses and delay gratification.	✓		
10. The patient developed a new sense of competency or "mastery" in his life following the brain disorder.	✓		
11. The patient was able to "self-reflect" or "be more aware" of personal "strengths" and "limitations."	✓		
12. The patient experienced enjoyment in the care or help of other living things (people, animals, the environment, etc.).	✓		
13. The patient had an improved understanding of the "problematic nature of life" (given his psychosocial state of life) and was not overwhelmed or "defeated" by it or readily gave in to escapism to cope with life (Bettelheim, 1989).	✓		
14. The patient could "live with" the restrictions produced by a brain injury "without resentment" (Goldstein, 1952).	✓		
15. The patient was able to obtain new insights into self by attending to why certain songs, stories, fairy tales, movies, tattoos, etc. had a special personal meaning that he initially did not understand.			✓

(*continued*)

Table 19.1 Continued

CLINICAL FEATURE	YES	NO	PARTIALLY
16. The patient's dreams or artwork often heralded changes in behavior that aided his psychological adjustment before the consciously mediated changes occurred.		✓	
17. The psychological care interventions (including the dialogue) between the patient and the clinical neuropsychologist resulted in the patient talking more openly about problems and demonstrating self-directed efforts at improving psychological adjustment to the direct and indirect effects of the brain disorder.	✓		
18. The psychological care interventions were in harmony with the patient's cultural background and religious orientation.	✓		
19. The psychological care interventions were appropriate for the patient's psychosocial stage of development and facilitated psychosocial development/adaptation in later stages of life.	✓		
20. The patient and family experienced two basic facts of life: (a) The individual's state of subjective sense of personal well-being fluctuates and (b) the psychological adjustment process is never static and therefore hope should never be abandoned.	✓		
Total	16	2	1

n/a, not applicable.

Table 19.2 Clinically Relevant Features of the Patient's Wife in Case Vignette 19.1

CLINICAL FEATURE	YES	NO	PARTIALLY
1. The quality of the relationship before the onset of the brain disorder was good.	✓		
2. The wife has adequate supports that help maintain her resiliency.	✓		
3. The wife is personally offended by the behavioral problems of the patient.		✓	
4. The wife has a good working (therapeutic) relationship with the clinical neuropsychologist.	✓		
5. The wife understands the biological factors (and at times the psychological factors) underlying the behavioral problems of the patient.	✓		
6. The wife does not feel alone in the care of the patient.	✓		
7. The wife has some sense of hope that the patient's behavioral problems will get better with time and/or there is "light at the end of the tunnel."	✓		
8. The wife had a rewarding relationship with the patient before the onset of hemiplegia.	✓		

Case Vignette 19.2

A 16-year-old girl suffered what was considered at the time to be a moderate TBI. She demonstrated several of the cognitive and behavioral difficulties common to these injuries (see Chapter 6, this volume). Initially, she had no motor impairments, but several months after her TBI, she had a seizure that resulted in a probable embolic stroke. Unlike the patient described in the previous case, she had not yet established a history of self-sufficiency and self-reliance. In addition, she had a very problematic relationship with her father that made her doubt her competency *before* her brain injury and later onset of left hemiparesis. Both before and after her brain injury, she would frequently make choices that upset her father. This resulted in a further strained relationship.

The patient had been involved in a neuropsychological rehabilitation program as described previously (see Chapter 13, this volume). Initially, she reported little depression but considerable dissatisfaction with how others treated her. She eventually engaged in a number of impulsive relationships. The result was severe depression and a sense of hopelessness about her future. She would comment that the only thing she was good at after her left upper extremity hemiparesis was her ability to please men sexually. This, of course, ultimately left her feeling less self-worth. Unfortunately, the developmental experiences that help foster resiliency (a well-established history of self-sufficient behavior, enduring supportive relationships, and a pre-injury sense of self-worth) were not clearly established. Efforts to engage her in a series of activities that were intended to build resiliency were not successful. The ineffective efforts at psychological care appeared to be related to features found in both the patient and the psychotherapist. The patient's inability to sustain hope, to control impulsive behavior, and to live with the restrictions associated with her hemiparesis were major contributing factors. The psychotherapist's inability to help the patient successfully deal with both positive and negative feelings toward her father (that were transferred onto the male psychotherapist) also appeared to be an important contributing factor. The psychological adjustment process is not always straightforward or as helpful as one would like it to be. Continued dialogue with this patient throughout the years suggests that the therapeutic relationship has been of some help to her as she continues to struggle with depression. Her courage to do so is a further testimony of the human spirit to deal with personal losses in as productive manner as possible for the individual in light of their history and the effects of the brain injury on their life. Table 19.3 lists the clinical features that emerged during the period of time psychological care efforts were attempted.

Table 19.3 Clinical Features Relevant to the Psychological Care of the Patient in Case Vignette 19.2

CLINICAL FEATURE	YES	NO	PARTIALLY
1. The dialogue between the patient and the clinical neuropsychologist was not rushed.	✓		
2. The patient was able to express or clearly convey her personal concerns.	✓		
3. The content of the concerns varied over time.			✓

(continued)

Table 19.3 Continued

CLINICAL FEATURE	YES	NO	PARTIALLY
4. The patient experienced a sense of "realistic" hope in coping with her life situation.			✓
5. The patient and the clinical neuropsychologist developed a positive therapeutic relationship that helped the patient sustain adaptive activities during difficult times.			✓
6. Somatic symptoms (which appeared to be indirect effects of a brain disorder) were substantially reduced during periods of psychological care.		✓	
7. Anxiety/depression/anger and/or apathy were substantially reduced during periods of psychological care.		✓	
8. The patient was able to follow the guidance of the clinical neuropsychologist to improve functioning in everyday life activities.		✓	
9. The patient was able to control impulses and delay gratification.		✓	
10. The patient developed a new sense of competency or "mastery" in her life following the brain disorder.		✓	
11. The patient was able to "self-reflect" or "be more aware" of personal "strengths" and "limitations."			✓
12. The patient experienced enjoyment in the care or help of other living things (people, animals, the environment, etc.).		✓	
13. The patient had an improved understanding of the "problematic nature of life" (given her psychosocial state of life) and was not overwhelmed or "defeated" by it or readily gave in to escapism to cope with life (Bettelheim, 1989).		✓	
14. The patient could "live with" the restrictions produced by a brain injury "without resentment" (Goldstein, 1952).		✓	
15. The patient was able to obtain new insights into self by attending to why certain songs, stories, fairy tales, movies, tattoos, etc. had a special personal meaning that she initially did not understand.		✓	
16. The patient's dreams or artwork often heralded changes in behavior that aided her psychological adjustment before the consciously mediated changes occurred.		✓	
17. The psychological care interventions (including the dialogue) between the patient and the clinical neuropsychologist resulted in the patient talking more openly about problems and demonstrating self-directed efforts at improving psychological adjustment to the direct and indirect effects of the brain disorder.			✓

Table 19.3 Continued

CLINICAL FEATURE	YES	NO	PARTIALLY
18. The psychological care interventions were in harmony with the patient's cultural background and religious orientation.	✓		
19. The psychological care interventions were appropriate for the patient's psychosocial stage of development and facilitated psychosocial development/adaptation in later stages of life.		✓	
20. The patient and family experienced two basic facts of life: (a) The individual's state of subjective sense of personal well-being fluctuates and (b) the psychological adjustment process is never static and therefore hope should never be abandoned.		✓	
Total	3	12	5

APPROACHES TO THE PSYCHOLOGICAL CARE OF PERSONS WITH HEMIPLEGIA/HEMIPARESIS

The internet-based study by Poltawski et al. (2016) highlights two essential features relevant to psychological care following hemiplegia/hemiparesis. First, patients often described their discouragement about lack of motor recovery. However, those patients who could remain focused and committed to trying to improve motor functioning over several months and years after a stroke maintained a more active involvement in their rehabilitation. This involvement fostered a sense of personal responsibility (i.e., self-sufficiency) for their rehabilitation, which appears to bolster resiliency. Second, patients who noted small improvements in motor functioning were often encouraged by such improvements (sometimes even more than their therapists). The personal experience of some improvement in motor functioning, no matter how small, stimulated a sense of hope. This was the second major ingredient to sustain resiliency, as noted in previous chapters. In light of these observations, any therapy that can stimulate the patient's desire to continue to try to improve motor functioning should be encouraged. Ongoing traditional physical therapy, constraint-induced movement therapy, music therapy, dance therapy, yoga, walking, weightlifting, acupuncture, muscle relaxation exercises, and the use of transcranial stimulation all have a potential role to play in this regard. Table 19.4, from the work of Poltawski et al., is a useful chart to review with patients on a regular basis. It highlights the common themes that patients experience regarding their upper limb disabilities and provides a template for them to discuss their specific personal reactions and reflect on what they can do to enhance their recovery and adaptation.

Specific psychological interventions to improve psychological adaptation to hemiplegia and hemiparesis are difficult to find in the literature. Most research focuses on treatments that may promote neural repair after stroke (Cramer, 2018). Recently, it has been suggested that a combination of cognitive–behavioral therapy and task-oriented balance training may reduce the fear of falling in stroke patients (Liu, Ng, & Ng, 2018). Data have yet to be published to support this intriguing idea. A combination of repetitive transcranial magnetic stimulation and aerobic exercise has

Table 19.4 Descriptive Responses to Upper Limb Disabilities Made by Patients on the Internet

THEME	RESPONSES		
	EMOTIONAL	COGNITIVE	BEHAVIORAL/ PHYSICAL
Perceptions of the upper limb	• Revulsion	• UL as alien • UL as bad • UL as useless • UL as uncooperative • Trust/confidence in the UL	• Autonomous behavior by UL (moving independently of the individual's will)
Reactions to the upper limb problem	• Frustration • Emotional distress • Fear • Despair • Shock • Embarrassment, shame • Amusement	• Preferring one form of impairment or disability to another (e.g., UL amputation) • Mental fatigue due to concentration on UL tasks • Comparing self to others	• Hiding the effects of the impairment
Experience of recovery	• Hope—hopelessness • Disappointment • Sadness • Anxiety about the future • Excitement about changes	• Psychological significance of small changes • Beliefs and knowledge about condition and recovery • Comparing self to others with stroke • Determination • Recovering a sense of autonomy–independence • Regaining a sense of "normality" in use of UL • Developing a positive sense of self • Attitudes to therapy and therapists	• Self-management of upper limb therapy • Monitoring changes over time • Setting goals • Measuring recovery • Showing off improvements to others
Adaptation to upper limb problem	• Resistance to adaptation • Excitement about finding new ways of doing things	• Acceptance of disability • Reframing the experience of impairment • Valuing new experiences since stroke • Formation of a new sense of self-identity	• Learning compensatory strategies from others • Developing one's own compensatory strategies for tasks

UL, upper limb.
Source: Reprinted from Poltawski, L., Allison, R., Briscoe, S., Freeman, J., Kilbride, C., Neal, D., . . . Dean, S., Assessing the impact of upper limb disability following stroke: A qualitative enquiry using internet-based personal accounts of stroke survivors, *Disability and Rehabilitation, 38*(10), 2016, p. 945–951, with permissions under the terms of the Creative Commons Attribution License.

been reported to not only reduce depression but also increase walking capacity following stroke (VanDerwerker et al., 2018). The use of art therapy to improve kinesthetic–sensory experience and to explore feelings associated with change and loss after hemiplegic stroke has also been suggested (Reynolds, 2012). Again, data are missing to support this practical idea. Earlier work by Morin et al. (2003) supports the notion that self-portraits after stroke-induced hemiplegia can reveal the personal perceptions and struggles of the patient. How to use this information within the context of a psychotherapeutic dialogue needs to be further explored. A combination of educationally based interventions about emotional changes following stroke, ongoing physical therapy, and behavioral management interventions to reduce patients' anger over their clinical condition has been reported to reduce the expression of anger, as well as anxiety and depression. These positive changes were expectedly related to improved quality of life (Chang, Zhang, Xia, & Chen, 2011). Finally, in a review article on factors that improve health-related quality of life in stroke patients with limb hemiparesis, Pulman and Buckley (2013) noted several medically and physically based treatments that can have a positive effect. Their review indicates that botulinum toxin type A injections, constraint-induced movement therapy, robotic-assisted therapy, and acupuncture are all reported to improve quality of life in this patient group. In some studies, a positive placebo affect was also observed. These findings reinforce the idea that psychological care interventions in combination with other therapies that can even modestly improve motor functioning may be very helpful to this patient group. Understanding and effectively dealing with patients' personal reactions to their hemiplegia/hemiparesis in light of their personal history and past relationships with others remains an important area of inquiry. Unfortunately, no studies could be found that expressly address this important topic for treating clinicians. Table 19.5 summarizes some of the psychological care approaches reported in the literature on patients with hemiplegia or hemiparesis.

SUMMARY

Key components of patients' psychological care after they experience a vascular lesion to the brain include (1) providing a realistic sense of hope, (2) building on patients' premorbid skills that have fostered resiliency in their life (e.g., increasing self-sufficiency, establishing and building upon "secure" relationships, attending to the needs of others, and recognizing one's self-worth), (3) helping them to not feel abandoned after acute and subacute rehabilitation therapies end, and (4) taking steps to reduce depression and anxiety via whatever methods patients experience as useful. Continued efforts at trying to improve language functions as well as motor functions over a long period of time should also be encouraged. Within the context of a therapeutic relationship, patients must be reminded repeatedly that these efforts can extend several years.

Whereas aphasia and hemiplegia/hemiparesis are formidable problems that these patients face, anosognosia, impaired awareness, and apathy are especially burdensome for their spouses and ultimately to the patients. In a sense, these problems make patients more helpless. The patients do not recognize that a problem exists and often appear indifferent with regard to their clinical situation. Spouses can become exhausted and angry with patients for "not trying" or "denying" their problems. The spouse may not recognize the "organic" nature of these problems and believe the patient has just given up, is depressed, or is simply "selfish." Helping family members understand the neuropsychological bases of these problems can go a long way toward building the resiliency of family members or caregivers. In this regard, it is important for the clinical neuropsychologist who is functioning as the primary psychological caregiver to be available to speak with the patient's spouse and any other family

Table 19.5 Review of Selected Studies Relevant to the Psychological Care of Persons with Hemiplegia/Hemiparesis

INTERVENTION	STUDY SAMPLE	MAJOR FINDINGS	CONCLUSIONS
Effectiveness of knowledge and behavior therapy in patients with hemiplegic stroke (Chang, Zhang, Xia, & Chen, 2011)	66 patients with hemiplegic stroke ranging in ages from 34 to 84 years were randomly assigned to a control or experimental group. Both control and experimental groups received "regular therapies," including medications and physical therapy. The experimental group also received counseling, which included psychoeducation sessions and training in anger management. It was noted that "great care was given to establishing a therapeutic relationship between the client and counselor" (p. 529).	The treatment (or experimental group) not only showed significant improvement in controlling and experiencing anger but also reported less anxiety and depression. The treatment group also demonstrated greater achievements in activities of daily living.	Directly targeting angry reactions to hemiplegia is an important goal of psychological care of these individuals. Reducing angry feelings via a combination of psychological and educational methods may reduce anxiety and depression. These patients also showed greater gains on measures of daily living activities. Although the emphasis was on using a behavioral approach, the authors emphasize the importance of a strong therapeutic alliance in order to be of maximum help to the patient.
Combining rTMS with aerobic exercise to reduce post-stroke depression in patients with residual paresis (VanDerwerker et al., 2018)	Three individuals (aged 64, 58, and 82 years) were seen three times per week for 8 weeks and received a total of 24 sessions. Each session consisted of both aerobic exercise and rTMS. Two of the patients were considered to have probable major depressive disorder, and one patient had mild depression.	Each of the patients showed decreased depression and improved walking capacity (they had lower extremity paresis). Aspects of the patients' phenomenological experiences were included in the report. Some of the subjective reports were "I do not let things bother me like I used to" and "I am really laughing and smiling more."	Although the data presented were only on three cases, the outcomes suggest that a combination of rTMS and aerobic exercise may reduce depression in patients with residual hemiparesis. The lack of an appropriate control group does not allow for assessing possible placebo effects influencing outcome. This brief report, however, is important insofar as it includes an individualized approach and takes into consideration objective and subjective data in evaluating the efficacy of this combined treatment approach.

Yoga-based exercise program to improve balance, movement, and peace of mind (Bastille & Gill-Body, 2004)	Four individuals (aged 71, 49, 59, and 61 years) who ranged from 1.5 to 8 years post-stroke underwent an 8-week intervention program consisting of 1½-hour yoga sessions. Two patients had left hemiparesis, and two had right hemiparesis. The yoga activities included exercises to increase body awareness, control breathing to facilitate body awareness, and movement as well as guided imagery aimed at relaxation.	Patients varied with regard to their motor limitations and associated problems (e.g., pain). As would be expected, variable outcomes were reported, but three out of the four patients showed improvement in their balance. Patients reported improvement in their emotional state and social interactions.	No control group was used and therefore the role of placebo effects could not be determined. This multiple case series report, however, is important insofar as it emphasizes the need to engage patients in physically based activities that improve movement and therefore likely have a positive effect on their emotional well-being.
Home-based music therapy for arm hemiparesis following stroke (Street et al., 2017)	A pilot feasibility randomized controlled trial was performed to determine whether participation in a therapeutically intended music performance would improve arm function after stroke. A crossover design was employed; 14 subjects were studied. Ten patients completed their 12 scheduled sessions. Participants played 20–30 minutes per session.	Although patients often expressed concern or skepticism about engaging in music interventions, they all found it motivating. It was reported that "the facilitating music and instruments were supportive of target arm movements and that tolerance for TIMP (therapeutic instrument music performance) was high and fatigue low" (p. 5). While engaging in TIMP, patients tended to demonstrate improved hand–eye coordination/speed on a pegboard test.	Although the authors emphasize the limitations of their study, including biases in patient selection, their findings are important for at least two reasons. The first is that the therapeutic activity involved the affected hand/arm. This may be of special value given the evidence in favor of constraint-induced movement therapy after stroke (Kwakkel et al., 2015). Second, from an evolutionary standpoint (see Chapters 2 and 3, this volume), music often facilitates movement. This is often accompanied by an emotional experience, which can facilitate a psychological state of well-being.

rTMS, repetitive transcranial magnetic stimulation.

members about the need to reduce distress in the home environment. Not being alone with their problems (i.e., having the clinical neuropsychologist available to assist the spouse or family members as needed) has repeatedly been experienced as a key component of the psychological care of these patients. This is also true for patients who are in the early stages of a dementing condition and those with a history of moderate and severe TBI, as Chapters 20 and 21 illustrate.

REFERENCES

Aström, M., Adolfsson, R., & Asplund, K. (1993). Major depression in stroke patients: A 3-year longitudinal study. *Stroke, 24*(7), 976–982.

Bastille, J. V., & Gill-Body, K. M. (2004). A yoga-based exercise program for people with chronic poststroke hemiparesis. *Physical Therapy, 84*(1), 33–48.

Binder, L. M. (1984). Emotional problems after stroke. *Stroke, 15*(1), 174–177.

Blumenfeld, H. (2010). *Neuroanatomy through clinical cases.* Sunderland, MA: Sinauer.

Bottini, G., Paulesu, E., Gandola, M., Pia, L., Invernizzi, P., & Berti, A. (2010). Anosognosia for hemiplegia and models of motor control: Insights from lesional data. In G. Prigatano (Ed.), *The study of anosognosia* (pp. 363–379). New York, NY: Oxford University Press.

Brugger, P. (2007). Hostile interactions between body and self. *Dialogues in Clinical Neuroscience, 9*(2), 210–213.

Chang, K., Zhang, H., Xia, Y., & Chen, C. (2011). Testing the effectiveness of knowledge and behavior therapy in patients of hemiplegic stroke. *Topics in Stroke Rehabilitation, 18*(5), 525–535.

Cramer, S. C. (2018). Treatments to promote neural repair after stroke. *Journal of Stroke, 20*(1), 57–70.

Critchley, M. (1974). Misoplegia, or hatred of hemiplegia. *Mount Sinai Journal of Medicine, 41,* 82–87.

Denes, G., Semenza, C., Stoppa, E., & Lis, A. (1982). Unilateral spatial neglect and recovery from hemiplegia: A follow-up study. *Brain, 105*(3), 543–552.

Dobkin, B. H. (2005). Rehabilitation after stroke. *New England Journal of Medicine, 352*(16), 1677–1684.

Dunsky, A., Dickstein, R., Marcovitz, E., Levy, S., & Deutsch, J. (2008). Home-based motor imagery training for gait rehabilitation of people with chronic poststroke hemiparesis. *Archives of Physical Medicine and Rehabilitation, 89*(8), 1580–1588.

Garbarini, F., Fossataro, C., Berti, A., Gindri, P., Romano, D., Pia, L., . . . Neppi-Modona, M. (2015). When your arm becomes mine: Pathological embodiment of alien limbs using tools modulates own body representation. *Neuropsychologia, 70,* 402–413.

Goldstein, K. (1952). The effect of brain damage on the personality. *Psychiatry, 15*(3), 245–260.

Haggard, P., Rossetti, Y., & Kawato, M. (2008). *Sensorimotor foundations of higher cognition.* New York, NY: Oxford University Press.

Howes, H., Edwards, S., & Benton, D. (2005). Female body image following acquired brain injury. *Brain Injury, 19*(6), 403–415.

Invernizzi, P., Gandola, M., Romano, D., Zapparoli, L., Bottini, G., & Paulesu, E. (2013). What is mine? Behavioral and anatomical dissociations between somatoparaphrenia and anosognosia for hemiplegia. *Behavioural Neurology, 26*(1–2), 139–150.

Jones, T. A. (2017). Motor compensation and its effects on neural reorganization after stroke. *Nature Reviews Neuroscience, 18*(5), 267–280.

Karnath, H.-O., & Baier, B. (2010). Anosognosia for hemiparesis and hemiplegia: Disturbed sense of agency and body ownership. In G. Prigatano (Ed.), *The study of anosognosia* (pp. 39–62). New York, NY: Oxford University Press.

Katz, D. I., Alexander, M. P., & Klein, R. B. (1998). Recovery of arm function in patients with paresis after traumatic brain injury. *Archives of Physical Medicine and Rehabilitation, 79*(5), 488–493.

Keppel, C. C., & Crowe, S. F. (2000). Changes to body image and self-esteem following stroke in young adults. *Neuropsychological Rehabilitation, 10*(1), 15–31.

Klonoff, P. S., Costa, L. D., & Snow, W. G. (1986). Predictors and indicators of quality of life in patients with closed-head injury. *Journal of Clinical and Experimental Neuropsychology, 8*(5), 469–485.

Korpelainen, J. T., Nieminen, P., & Myllylä, V. V. (1999). Sexual functioning among stroke patients and their spouses. *Stroke, 30*(4), 715–719.

Krakauer, J. W., & Carmichael, S. T. (2017). *Broken movement: The neurobiology of motor recovery after stroke.* Cambridge, MA: MIT Press.

Kwakkel, G., Veerbeek, J. M., van Wegen, E. E., & Wolf, S. L. (2015). Constraint-induced movement therapy after stroke. *Lancet Neurology, 14*(2), 224–234.

Liu, T.-W., Ng, G. Y., & Ng, S. S. (2018). Effectiveness of a combination of cognitive behavioral therapy and task-oriented balance training in reducing the fear of falling in patients with chronic stroke: Study protocol for a randomized controlled trial. *Trials, 19*(1), 168.

Loetscher, T., Regard, M., & Brugger, P. (2006). Misoplegia: A review of the literature and a case without hemiplegia. *Journal of Neurology, Neurosurgery, and Psychiatry, 77*(9), 1099–1100.

Mayo, N., Wood-Dauphinee, S., Ahmed, S., Carron, G., Higgins, J., Mcewen, S., & Salbach, N. (1999). Disablement following stroke. *Disability and Rehabilitation, 21*(5–6), 258–268.

Moore, J. (1986). Neuroanatomical considerations relating to recovery of function following brain injury. In P. Bach-y-Rita (Ed.), *Recovery to function: Theoretical consideration for brain injury rehabilitation* (pp. 9–90). Toronto, Ontario, Canada: Huber.

Morin, C., Pradat-Diehl, P., Robain, G., Bensalah, Y., & Perrigot, M. (2003). Stroke hemiplegia and specular image: Lessons from self-portraits. *International Journal of Aging and Human Development, 56*(1), 1–41.

Nichols-Larsen, D. S., Clark, P., Zeringue, A., Greenspan, A., & Blanton, S. (2005). Factors influencing stroke survivors' quality of life during subacute recovery. *Stroke, 36*(7), 1480–1484.

Nilsson, M. I., Fugl-Meyer, K., von Koch, L., & Ytterberg, C. (2017). Experiences of sexuality six years after stroke: A qualitative study. *Journal of Sexual Medicine, 14*(6), 797–803.

Peelen, M. V., & Downing, P. E. (2007). The neural basis of visual body perception. *Nature Reviews Neuroscience, 8*(8), 636–649.

Poltawski, L., Allison, R., Briscoe, S., Freeman, J., Kilbride, C., Neal, D., . . . Dean, S. (2016). Assessing the impact of upper limb disability following stroke: A qualitative enquiry using internet-based personal accounts of stroke survivors. *Disability and Rehabilitation, 38*(10), 945–951.

Prigatano, G. P. (1999). *Principles of neuropsychological rehabilitation*. New York, NY: Oxford University Press.

Prigatano, G. P. (2010). *The study of anosognosia*. New York, NY: Oxford University Press.

Prigatano, G. P. (2011). The importance of the patient's subjective experience in stroke rehabilitation. *Topics in Stroke Rehabilitation, 18*(1), 30–34.

Prigatano, G. P., & Wong, J. L. (1997). Speed of finger tapping and goal attainment after unilateral cerebral vascular accident. *Archives of Physical Medicine and Rehabilitation, 78*(8), 847–852.

Pulman, J., & Buckley, E. (2013). Assessing the efficacy of different upper limb hemiparesis interventions on improving health-related quality of life in stroke patients: A systematic review. *Topics in Stroke Rehabilitation, 20*(2), 171–188.

Rashid, N., Clarke, C., & Rogish, M. (2013). Post-stroke depression and expressed emotion. *Brain Injury, 27*(2), 223–238.

Reynolds, F. (2012). Art therapy after stroke: Evidence and a need for further research. *The Arts in Psychotherapy, 39*(4), 239–244.

Robinson, R. G., & Price, T. R. (1982). Post-stroke depressive disorders: A follow-up study of 103 patients. *Stroke, 13*(5), 635–641.

Robinson-Smith, G., Johnston, M. V., & Allen, J. (2000). Self-care self-efficacy, quality of life, and depression after stroke. *Archives of Physical Medicine and Rehabilitation, 81*(4), 460–464.

Sasaki, N., Mizutani, S., Kakuda, W., & Abo, M. (2013). Comparison of the effects of high- and low-frequency repetitive transcranial magnetic stimulation on upper limb hemiparesis in the early phase of stroke. *Journal of Stroke and Cerebrovascular Diseases, 22*(4), 413–418.

Street, A. J., Magee, W. L., Bateman, A., Parker, M., Odell-Miller, H., & Fachner, J. (2017). Home-based neurologic music therapy for arm hemiparesis following stroke: Results from a pilot, feasibility randomized controlled trial. *Clinical Rehabilitation, 32*(1), 18–28.

Takashima, R., Murata, W., & Saeki, K. (2016). Movement changes due to hemiplegia in stroke survivors: A hermeneutic phenomenological study. *Disability and Rehabilitation, 38*(16), 1578–1591.

Trapnell, P. D., Meston, C. M., & Gorzalka, B. B. (1997). Spectatoring and the relationship between body image and sexual experience: Self-focus or self-valence? *Journal of Sex Research, 34*(3), 267–278.

VanDerwerker, C. J., Ross, R. E., Stimpson, K. H., Embry, A. E., Aaron, S. E., Cence, B., . . . Gregory, C. M. (2018). Combining therapeutic approaches: rTMS and aerobic exercise in post-stroke depression: a case series. *Topics in Stroke Rehabilitation, 25*(1), 61–67.

Weinstein, E. A., & Kahn, R. L. (1955). *Denial of illness: Symbolic and physiological aspects*. Springfield, IL: Charles C Thomas.

20

PSYCHOLOGICAL CARE OF PERSONS WITH PROGRESSIVE COGNITIVE DECLINE AND EARLY STAGE DEMENTIA

BACKGROUND INFORMATION

Although the diagnosis of a malignant brain tumor often produces a sense of shock in the patient followed by anxiety regarding the prospect of impending death, the diagnosis of probable dementia can be equally frightening. For some, however, it is an affirmation that their observed decline in memory is real and not just a part of normal aging or a reaction to stress or a by-product of depression. Others may be confused by the diagnosis and not know what it actually means. Still others have an immediate concern about what will happen to them, especially if they have observed a parent who suffered from dementia. Unless one has witnessed the gradual dementing process of another, the real impact of this clinical state may not be immediately obvious (Robinson, Ekman, & Wahlund, 1998). Finally, there are other patients who may deny (or be unaware of) their cognitive decline to the chagrin of their family members. The diagnosis is often quite alarming to the patient's family (Brodaty, Green, & Koschera, 2003).

Recall from Chapter 3 that the normal aging process is not associated with significant neuronal loss. Changes in the integrity of the white matter tracts do occur, and this often results in reduced processing speed and a decline in some aspects of problem-solving ability. The amount of information a person can learn and retain also declines in normal aging (see Chapter 8, this volume). Subtle decoupling of the default mode network has been linked to some of these neurocognitive changes (see Chapter 3, this volume). The knowledge of words and the ability to communicate do not deteriorate in normal aging (see Chapter 4, this volume). However, in the sixth and seventh decades of life, health does decline and fatigue is common (see Chapters 4 and 8, this volume). The need to sustain self-efficacy skills becomes very important during the aging process and has been repeatedly linked to the quality of life the person experiences, as previous chapters have noted. Dementia in its early and later forms compromises self-efficacy skills. This reality raises many concerns regarding how best to help these persons (and their family members) when a progressive decline in cognitive functioning is identified and associated with the dementing condition.

DEMENTIA IS A CLINICAL SYNDROME

Katzman (1992) noted that the term *dementia* refers to a clinical syndrome that can be caused by different forms of brain pathology. The most common form of dementia has typically been considered to be Alzheimer's disease. However, other forms of dementia have been recognized throughout the years, including frontotemporal dementia (or Pick's disease), Lewy body dementia, and vascular dementia (Smith & Butts, 2018). Some dementing conditions, however, are not easily classified. In the early stages of dementia of the Alzheimer's type (DAT), the patient is typically alert and awake but often has substantial difficulties learning new information (Katzman, 1992). With time, there is a substantial decline in memory with an associated decline in other higher integrative brain functions (HIBFs), including language and problem-solving abilities. These changes cannot be explained by the normal aging process or psychiatric illness.

A recent consensus panel commissioned by the National Institute of Aging (Leshner, Landis, Stroud, & Downey, 2017) emphasized the "mixed causes of dementia" even in patients clinically diagnosed as having DAT. Therefore, the panel recommended using the term clinical Alzheimer's-type dementia (CATD). In their review article, Querfurth and LaFerla (2010) estimated that DAT (or CATD) accounts for 50–56% of cases that come to autopsy and are studied in various clinical research investigations. They also reported that an additional 13–17% of patients had a combination of both DAT and cerebral vascular lesions. Barker et al. (2002) reported that although pathological findings definitive of DAT were identified in 77% of 382 brains that were examined, there was great overlap in the pathology observed in different brains. In brains that showed primarily Lewy bodies, 66% also showed pathological features of Alzheimer's disease. In brains with primarily vascular pathology, 77% also showed pathological features of Alzheimer's disease. Thus, for many forms of dementia, the underlying brain pathologies are indeed mixed. This may help explain why different dementing conditions often reveal different "neuropsychological signatures" (meaning specific neuropsychological functions may be somewhat differently affected in the different conditions; Salmon & Butters, 1992; Smith & Bondi, 2013).

PROGRESSIVE COGNITIVE DECLINE AND DEMENTIA

Some have suggested that the very early signs or stages of a dementing process can be described as mild cognitive impairment (MCI). Not all individuals with MCI progress to a dementing condition, but many do. The exact percentages are difficult to determine. Conversion figures appear to depend on the age of the patient when examined and when symptoms occurred, as well as the patient's educational background, psychiatric status, and the time frame in which the patient was followed. In one study that followed patients during a 3-year period, 64% of MCI patients showed probable signs of CATD (Ewers et al., 2012). Poor performance on the Trail Making Test Part B was a relatively sensitive marker of severe cognitive decline, resulting in the diagnosis of dementia. Other studies have also noted that simply the number of words an individual can recall over repetitive trials is also an important predictor of later dementia (M. Albert, Moss, Tanzi, & Jones, 2001). In their review article, Ward, Tardiff, Dye, and Arrighi (2013) noted that in two 5-year follow-up studies, MCI conversions to dementia were 68.3% and 77.1%, respectively. In a 6-year follow-up study, Brodaty et al. (2016) reported that 11% of their sample showed "stable MCI" (p. 581). If the conversion rates are, on average, 10% each year, then one would expect that in 10 years, all MCI patients would be diagnosed as demented. This has not been my clinical experience, but the available data do not seem to clearly resolve this issue.

What appears most relevant to the psychological care of these individuals is clear documentation of the extent and severity of various HIBFs. Next, clinical assessment of the probable interaction of premorbid cognitive and personality features with the patient's current neuropsychological status is necessary for patient management. It is also important to explain the neuropsychological test findings in a way that is understandable to the patient and family members. Conveying findings in an honest and supportive manner will often help these patients accept treatment recommendations. However, the cultural and, at times, religious background of patients and their families can influence how they perceive the neuropsychological findings and what recommendations they are likely to accept.

In this chapter, psychological care efforts for three different patients with progressive cognitive decline and early stages of dementia are described. The first patient was initially referred to evaluate MCI with probable early onset of a dementing condition. Her symptom picture was most compatible with CATD. The second patient had a mix of cognitive and motor problems that were not well understood, and a neuropsychological examination was initially requested to aid diagnosis and patient management. The third patient had a vascular dementia. He was diagnosed with cerebral autosomal dominant arteriopathy with subcortical infarcts and leukoencephalopathy (CADASIL). He was seen because he questioned the findings of two previous neuropsychological examiners and requested a third opinion. Each person presented with neuropsychological disturbances compatible with progressive cognitive decline suggestive of a dementing condition, but their methods of dealing with changes in their cognitive status differed considerably.

CLINICAL ALZHEIMER'S-TYPE DEMENTIA

Smith and Bondi (2013) reviewed in detail the biological and neuropsychological correlates of CATD (previously referred to as DAT). The classic pathological findings of this disease state are (1) neuritic plaques frequently found in the mesial temporal lobe structures but also observed in other areas of the neocortex (i.e., frontal and parietal regions), (2) neurofibrillary tangles found in these structures, and (3) amyloid angiopathy with no Lewy body pathology observed. Neuronal loss with generalized cerebral atrophy is eventually observed on neuroimaging of the brain. Specific loss of volume in the temporal lobes, especially the hippocampus, is perhaps most commonly reported.

Neuropsychological features of CATD include an insidious onset of cognitive impairment with gradual decline in several cognitive functions over time. Most prominent is progressive and severe memory loss, which includes both the inability to learn and the inability to retain new information even with repetition. The degree of memory impairment exceeds that of mild cognitive impairment of the amnestic type. Difficulties in other cognitive functions, including difficulties with working memory and subtle language and/or apraxic disturbances, may also be present. With time, these cognitive difficulties begin to negatively impact the person's ability to engage in independent living activities (e.g., driving a car or managing a checkbook).

In CATD, intellectual and memory functions continue to decline and ultimately become severely compromised. Performance on standardized tests of intelligence often reflects a generalized deterioration in problem-solving ability with relatively intact attention skills. Vocabulary level also remains reasonably intact for a fairly long period of time. Working memory, however, can be seriously compromised. Subtle and not so subtle language difficulties (e.g., verbal fluency) now are frequently observed, even though the vocabulary level of the individual does not appear to substantially change. However, the individual increasingly has more difficulty understanding complicated verbal instructions that negatively affects problem-solving (Oosterman et al., 2017). Progressive loss of insight or lack of self-awareness about the extent of cognitive impairment follows with a variety of behavioral changes, including apathy and at times paranoid ideation. Severe memory impairment continues, with a lost sense of familiarity about previously recalled or known information. During this time, disorientation for time and place is a common hallmark of CATD.

There is no known treatment for CATD. When methods to reduce cognitive and affective symptoms are considered, pharmacological interventions are often first mentioned. Their efficacy, however, is doubtful in light of group data on cognitive functioning (Raina et al., 2008). Clinically, some individuals do appear to show mild improvement and are therefore frequently given medications. More recently, nonpharmacological interventions have been attempted to reduce the impact of progressive cognitive deficits. These interventions include efforts at cognitive training, aerobic exercise, and a healthy diet. The efficacy of these approaches has also been called into question (Leshner et al., 2017), but engaging in activities that improve physical health and stimulate cognitive functioning has been reported to have beneficial results for older people at risk for cognitive decline (Ngandu et al., 2015) or who subjectively report memory difficulties (de Souto Barreto, Andrieu, Rolland, & Vellas, 2018). There is also a very large literature aimed at helping patients' caregivers (typically spouses) cope emotionally with the cognitive and behavioral problems observed in demented individuals (Mace & Rabins, 2011).

A few clinical reports have considered what patients experience. The limited research in this area focuses mainly on patients with early stage dementia (S. Albert et al., 1996; Russell, 1996). It suggests that the reactions and adjustments to dementia differ considerably across individuals. Therefore, professional care interventions should be guided by the individual's psychological state and needs (Holst & Hallberg, 2003). The three case vignettes described in this chapter highlight this reality.

Case Vignette 20.1

Summary of Neurological and Neuropsychological Findings

An 87-year-old woman reported to her physician that she was concerned about a decline in her memory. She was a nurse by training and successfully worked until age 70 years. However, during the preceding few years, she noticed a decline in her memory, which concerned her. She was especially concerned because three out of her six siblings had been diagnosed as having probable Alzheimer's disease. The patient's husband believed that his wife's memory difficulties were most likely simply related to her age. Her neurological examination did not reveal any abnormal findings. Magnetic resonance imaging (MRI) of the brain revealed generalized atrophy of brain structures compatible with her age. Consequently, she was referred for a neuropsychological examination.

As part of the initial clinical neuropsychological examination, the patient was asked to make subjective ratings regarding the relative degree of difficulty she experienced in a few cognitive and affective domains (see Chapter 10, this volume). Although she was quite conversant in the clinical interview and had a normal vocabulary, she experienced some confusion in keeping in mind the rating system. She repeatedly reversed the scale of 0–10 when making her ratings, thinking that 10 meant no problem instead of a severe problem, as was originally explained to her.

The patient's performance on the Barrow Neurological Institute Screen for Higher Cerebral Functions (BNIS) was significantly below average (raw score of 30 out of 50 points, $T = 12$). Despite her educational background, her Full Scale IQ, as measured by the Wechsler Abbreviated Scale of Intelligence–Second Edition, was 87. She had notable difficulties with all memory tasks presented to her. On the Rey Auditory Verbal Learning Test (RAVLT), she recalled 32 words, and for her age this produced a T score of 34. She had difficulty shifting her cognitive set without getting lost or confused. For example, on the Trail Making Test Part B, she completed the task in 300 seconds and made one error ($T = 21$). The patient acknowledged difficulties handling finances and understanding new instructions but otherwise reported no difficulties in a variety of daily activities. Her husband generally agreed, but he noted that at times she had "occasional disorientation to time" and "short-term memory lapses regarding a conversation they had." The patient and her husband agreed that she was active and independent in the home, but they agreed to restrict her driving because she did not feel safe and was worried about getting lost.

The patient was followed and re-examined every 6 months after the individual examination. Unfortunately, there was a progressive decline in her neuropsychological status. For example, her performance on the Trail Making Test Part B consistently declined on each follow-up examination. Her IQ scores and memory scores did not reveal much change until approximately 3 years after the initial neuropsychological examination. At that time, she was repetitively asking the same questions, was increasingly tangential in her comments, and could not maintain her cognitive set when attempting to complete the Trail Making Test Part B. The test had to be discontinued because she simply could not "keep in mind" the instructions necessary to complete the task.

Three years after the patient's initial neuropsychological evaluation, her husband noted some important behavioral changes, including a brief episode in which she could not recognize him as her husband. When they were getting ready to go to bed one night, she asked who he was. His initial reaction was that she was joking with him. It then became obvious that she did not recognize his face or voice. He eventually convinced her that he was her husband, and they went to bed. The next morning, she recognized him as her husband. Also during this time, she began to believe that someone was removing clothing from her closet and putting someone else's clothing in it. Despite all rational (and probable) explanations, she held on to this belief. It was at this point that a series of psychological intervention sessions began.

Efforts at Psychological Care

Given the progressive signs of neuropsychological decline, a frank but supportive discussion was held with the patient's husband. Her declining condition was reviewed, and the topic of residential care was broached. The husband recognized his wife's declining status, but he believed that she was safe and well cared for at home. He understood the concerns of the neuropsychologist and said that he would monitor his wife's situation and consult with the neuropsychologist on a regular basis regarding management issues. When a copy of the report was sent to the patient's neurologist, the patient and his wife were referred to an Alzheimer's treatment center for comprehensive care. They rejected the referral and wanted to continue to consult with the clinical neuropsychologist.

The patient and her husband were then seen for a series of psychological management/care consultation sessions. The sessions began on a biweekly basis but changed to a monthly basis, as discussed later. The patient was very clear in wanting to see the neuropsychologist. She stated (and repeated almost every session) that the clinical neuropsychologist talked directly to her and asked her opinions. She stated that other doctors asked her husband, her children, and even her grandchildren what they thought or perceived. They never directly talked to or recognized the importance of her experience. This not only made her angry but also minimized her personal sense of importance as an individual, not just a patient. This was an especially important issue for her, given her background and personality. She often felt pushed aside by other people's opinions at work and at home *before the dementing process occurred*. Having someone honestly interested in her opinion was crucial to establishing an effective therapeutic relationship with her and guiding her. It touches, however, on an important issue that many patients with dementia experience. Did the beginnings of dementia mean they had no value, no say, and no opinion worth listening to?

Listening to the patient enabled her to be willing to listen to the psychological caregiver. When the topic of clothing was discussed, the patient was asked to trust the psychological caregiver's viewpoint. It was very unlikely that her clothes were being taken and other clothes put in her closet. It was suggested that her memory difficulties might account for this repeated perception that was not shared by others. Although she was convinced that her experience was accurate (as all of us do, with or without dementia), she was willing to trust the opinion of the clinical neuropsychologist because she experienced him as taking an honest interest in her care and not diminishing the importance of her experiences. The clinical neuropsychologist was able to relate to her over a long-standing psychological issue, which was openly discussed as her cognitive functions declined. This was an essential component to her psychological care.

As time went on, both she and her husband had other medical illnesses that resulted in extensive outpatient rehabilitation. Neither was able to safely drive a car. Both were trying to help each other at home with their physical needs. During these times, the patient would call the clinical neuropsychologist's office and tell the office staff that she wanted to come in for an appointment but was unable to do so because of her husband's medical condition. A discussion with the patient over the phone revealed continued tangential thoughts and difficulties remembering what was said. The patient, however, gave the clinical neuropsychologist permission to speak with her primary care physician, whom she also trusted.

As a result of that discussion, the physician sent a medical social worker to the home to provide further guidance. As of this writing, the patient continues to reside in the home, and home health personnel come to her house on a regular basis. In the future, it is anticipated that her psychological care will include helping her make the transition from her home to an assisted living facility. Table 20.1 summarizes some of the important clinical features in her psychological care. Table 20.2 lists the characteristics of the patient's spouse during and between the psychological care sessions.

Table 20.1 Clinical Features Relevant to the Psychological Care of the Person with Early Stage Dementia Described in Case Vignette 20.1

CLINICAL FEATURE	YES	NO	PARTIALLY
1. The dialogue between the patient and the clinical neuropsychologist was not rushed.	✓		
2. The patient experienced that her personal opinion was important regarding diagnosis and management issues.	✓		

(*continued*)

Table 20.1 Continued

CLINICAL FEATURE	YES	NO	PARTIALLY
3. The content of the concerns was voiced and repeated out loud by the clinical neuropsychologist to the patient and family members.	✓		
4. The patient did not experience "being alone" with her problem(s). The patient experienced that the clinical neuropsychologist was honestly and respectfully taking "extra steps" to help her.	✓		
5. The patient and the clinical neuropsychologist developed a positive therapeutic relationship in which the patient's dignity was maintained.	✓		
6. The patient independently stated that she wanted to see the clinical neuropsychologist in repeated consultations.	✓		
7. Anxiety/depression/anger and/or apathy were substantially reduced during periods of psychological care.			✓
8. The patient was able to follow the guidance of the clinical neuropsychologist to improve functioning in everyday life activities and to avoid dangerous behaviors given her declining competencies (e.g., driving a car, attempting to handle finances, and walking without standby assistance).			✓
9. The patient was able to control impulses and delay gratification.	✓		
10. The patient actively worked at developing self-efficacy skills in the face of her declining abilities.	✓		
11. The patient attempted to self-reflect or be more aware of her personal strengths and limitations.		✓	
12. The patient experienced enjoyment in the care or help of other living things (people, animals, the environment, etc.).		✓	
13. The patient experienced an understanding of the "problematic nature of her unique life" and was not overwhelmed or defeated by it or readily gave in to escapism to cope with life (Bettelheim, 1989).			✓
14. The patient could "live with" the restrictions produced by a brain injury "without resentment" or loss of hope (Goldstein, 1952).	✓		
15. The patient was able to obtain new insights into herself by attending to why certain songs, stories, fairy tales, movies, tattoos, etc. had a special personal meaning that she initially did not understand.		✓	
16. The patient's dreams or artwork often heralded changes in behavior that aided psychological adjustment before the consciously mediated changes occurred.		✓	

Table 20.1 Continued

CLINICAL FEATURE	YES	NO	PARTIALLY
17. The psychological care interventions (including the dialogue) between the patient and the clinical neuropsychologist resulted in the patient talking more openly about problems and demonstrating self-directed efforts at improving psychological adjustment to the direct and indirect effects of the brain disorder.		✓	
18. The psychological care interventions were in harmony with the patient's cultural background and religious orientation.	✓		
19. The psychological care interventions facilitated psychosocial development/adaptation in the later stages of the patient's life.		✓	
20. The patient and family experienced two basic facts of life: (a) The individual's state of subjective sense of personal well-being fluctuates and (b) the psychological adjustment process is never static and therefore hope should never be abandoned.	✓		
Total	11	6	3

Table 20.2 Clinically Relevant Features of the Husband When His Wife was Receiving Psychological Care Described in Case Vignette 20.1

CLINICAL FEATURE	YES	NO	PARTIALLY
1. The quality of the relationship before the onset of the brain disorder was good.			✓
2. The husband has adequate supports that help maintain his resiliency.	✓		
3. The husband is personally offended by the behavioral problems of the patient.		✓	
4. The husband has a good working (therapeutic) relationship with the clinical neuropsychologist.	✓		
5. The husband understands the biological factors (and at times the psychological factors) underlying the behavioral problems of the patient.	✓		
6. The husband does not feel alone in the care of the patient.	✓		
7. The husband has some sense of hope that his wife's behavioral problems will get better with time and/or there is "light at the end of the tunnel."		✓	

POSTERIOR CORTICAL ATROPHY (DEMENTIA)

Benson, Davis, and Snyder (1988) initially described five patients with neuropsychological impairments involving a progressive decline in visual–spatial abilities but with relatively preserved memory, judgment, and self-awareness of their condition. These patients were described as having posterior cortical atrophy (PCA) underlying their dementia. This clinical condition is often considered to be a variant expression of Alzheimer's disease (Berthier, Leiguarda, Starkstein, Sevlever, & Taratuto, 1991; Nestor, Caine, Fryer, Clarke, & Hodges, 2003), but alternative causes have also been proposed, including dementia with Lewy bodies and corticobasal degeneration (Crutch et al., 2012).

The prevalence and incidence of PCA remain undetermined. However, in one study with patients suspected of Alzheimer's dementia, PCA represented approximately 5% of these patients (see Crutch et al., 2012). PCA is reported to be associated with an earlier age of onset (from the mid-50s to early 60s; Crutch et al., 2012). What is striking about the nature of the neuropsychological disturbances is the presence of apraxia, acalculia, agraphia, left–right orientation, and visual agnosia (Heber et al., 2016; McMonagle, Deering, Berliner, & Kertesz, 2006). This can occur even in a person who remains oriented to time and place and has relative preserved memory functions.

Note, however, that both visual and verbal memory can be compromised in these individuals when basic language functions are compromised. These patients may struggle to find words when speaking and turn toward a spouse to answer a question they did not fully understand or could not find the words to express themselves. It is also important to note that some of these patients have motor findings compatible with parkinsonism and can be quite anxious and depressed because of their awareness of their cognitive limitations and decline (Crutch et al., 2012).

Case Vignette 20.2

Summary of Neurological and Neuropsychological Findings

A 67-year-old businessman began to notice progressive difficulties with his speech and memory. He also noted that he had more difficulties handling finances and doing mechanical work on his cars. He used to perform these activities very well. Computerized tomography of the head did not reveal any signs of cortical atrophy. However, a positron emission tomography study suggested "mild posterior cortical hypo-metabolism and possible temporal hypo-metabolism." Repeated neurological examinations revealed memory loss, speech disorder, and visual loss. It was noted that the patient had rigidity and cogwheel rigidity in both right and left upper extremities. His family history was positive for both Alzheimer's dementia and Parkinson's disease in his mother. His neurologist diagnosed him as having dementia due to Alzheimer's disease as well as dementia with Lewy bodies. Repeat MRIs of the brain were interpreted as demonstrating "mild cerebral volume loss" with "chronic microvascular ischemic changes." No specific atrophy in the posterior regions of the cerebral hemispheres was reported.

To better characterize the patient's cognitive difficulties, a neuropsychological examination was requested. In his initial examination, he was fully oriented to time and place. He had subtle difficulties in word finding when talking in the interview. He had a good sense of humor (a long-standing personality trait), and he appeared quite aware of his cognitive, visual, and motor difficulties. The patient and his wife wanted answers to the following questions: What was causing these difficulties? Could anything be done to help him? What would be the natural course of his illness? They noted that they did not get answers to these questions when talking to several neurologists.

This man was a very successful businessman with undoubtedly above average intelligence. During the initial examination, his Full Scale IQ (measured by the Wechsler Abbreviated Intelligence Test) was 99. His score was average, but it was not normal for him. His verbal recall was also in the average range, but it was most likely a drop from premorbid levels of functioning (e.g., on the RAVLT, he recalled 39 words, producing a T score of 56). He recalled 7 words after a 20- to 25-minute delay, producing a T score of 48. His visual–spatial recognition skills were severely compromised. For example, on the Benton Facial Recognition Test (Short Form), he obtained a raw score of 17, producing a T score of 25. He also had difficulties carrying out arithmetic tasks and drawing simple designs. His findings were certainly compatible with posterior cortical atrophy/dysfunction. The final diagnosis, however, remained unclear.

The patient was subsequently followed from a neuropsychological and psychological care perspective for 5 years. Each year, there has been evidence of progressive decline in visual–spatial, visual recognition, and praxic functions. However, he has remained oriented to time and place, with relatively preserved verbal memory functions. Four years after first being examined, he was able to recall 34 words on the RAVLT ($T = 52$). He could recall 9 words with a 20-minute delay ($T = 63$). However, there was a progressive decline in his word finding, naming, and verbal reasoning skills. He could not perform the Trail Making Test Part B, having difficulties recognizing numbers and letters as well as locating them on the sheet of paper.

The patient's wife kept copious notes regarding his functioning in everyday life during a 7-year period. Her extensive notes are replicated (with her permission) in Box 20.1. They highlight the realities of this patient's situation as he went about his daily activities. They also highlight some of his personal reactions to his progressive neuropsychological impairments that are not always captured in neuropsychological reports.

Box 20.1. Wife's Notes About the Functioning of the Patient in Case Vignette 20.2 over a 7-Year Period

Difficulty findings "words" when speaking
Difficulty organizing thoughts, order of things to do
Difficulty remembering things to do; has started making lists, which helps; remembers things he thinks of better than things spouse thinks of
Dexterity has diminished; handwriting has become difficult
Difficulty with eye–hand coordination; fingers seem stiff
Easily frustrated, short temper when he can't do something
Unsteady walk; has had several falls when working in the car barn (watching for signs of Parkinson's)
Difficulty with time estimates, how long things will take
Driving difficulties: staying in lane, turning corners, parking "straight" in a space
Depth perception diminished
Tires easily, may work a few hours on a car but then rests several hours afterward
Sense of smell diminished
Difficulty finding items/tools, "not sure what they should look like"
Puts things in the wrong place occasionally, i.e., freezer instead of refrigerator

Easily "lost" or turned around in unfamiliar locations (5-2013)

Not driving at night due to cataracts

No longer reads the newspaper (type too small)

When telling an anecdote often gets lost in details, never gets to main point of story (10-2013)

No longer does much work on his old cars (6-2013)

Not able to do taxes (4-2014); not able to keep track of finances, paying bills (4-2014)

Eating has become difficult, a bit messy, food ends up on table/floor, finds it hard to cut with a knife, holding a sandwich is hard (6-2014)

Getting dressed is a challenge, has to really look carefully to find the front/back of shirts, pants

No longer writes things down, forming letters/words is difficult, cannot write on a line, signs name when necessary

Finding words when speaking is becoming even more difficult, cannot finish sentences; cannot get to the main point, may not realize he hasn't finished his whole thought, gets frustrated when he does

Has gained 20–30 pounds in past year; spends lots of time watching TV or playing games on computer

Takes a lot of naps when not actively doing something, easily falls asleep when watching TV

Now using a C-PAP machine when sleeping; sleeps more soundly and is much more rested (11-2014)

Depression is more severe since December 2014, more frequent angry outbursts

Mowing the lawn in straight rows and using the lawn mower is becoming difficult (6-2015)

Short-term memory has declined; must tell me things right away before he forgets

Can no longer key in the alarm code; difficulty finding the correct keys on TV remote

Driving less and less (9-2015); accident on 10-16-2015—ran over highway sign; did not drive for several weeks; only drives short distances

Dribbles on the floor when urinating (not every time), is unaware of it (11-2015)

Vision problems diagnosed by retinal specialist; an unnamed condition that may be related to Parkinson's. Decreased central vision, delayed reaction time, decreased depth perception; condition will very slowly progress as Parkinson's progresses (Jan-Feb 2016)

Depression seems to be better; fewer angry outbursts (2-2016)

Beginning to have vivid dreams; talks in sleep and jerks around in his sleep (2-2016)

Short-term memory has decreased unless it is something really important to him

Has stopped all driving out of the immediate neighborhood, usually only drives to the gym and back, which is less than a mile away

Very seldom reads a book in bed at night, usually goes right to sleep; says lines are wavy plus he forgets too much of the story to keep up with it (2-2016)

Cannot remember how to put on a T-shirt (3-18-2016); asked me to document this turn of events. We practiced for several days and within a week he was doing much better; not successful every time but knows he can do it when he concentrates.

At the gym he is not remembering how to use the machines and weights; paid for two sessions with a trainer in one month; in late April trainer suggested a class structured for older adults; is having success with this class; attends 2 in a row M-F (5-2016)

Has started getting up to use the bathroom during the night (6-2016)

Tremors in hands/arms at night when falling asleep (6-2016)

Tremors in hands more noticeable during the day (7-2016); small nicks on face when shaving

Beginning to exhibit difficulty with time frames; i.e., 30 minutes from now it will be 2:30

Tying shoe laces is difficult; it takes him several attempts (7-2016). He is now having me tie his shoes most of the time (8-2016). I now tie his shoes all of the time (12-2016).

Has lost 20 pounds since Feb. 2016 when we adjusted eating habits and added more exercise (9-2016)

Cannot empty dishwasher, silverware in wrong spots, dishes in wrong places (11-2016)

Had a struggle with depression between Christmas and New Year's, took him a few days to work his way through it (12-2016)

Vision bothering him, knows he has "blind spots," no peripheral vision (1-2017)

Has to stop and think about routine chores: steps to making coffee, finding bowl for cereal, making lunch, shaving (1-2017)

Difficulty using TV remote, not remembering station numbers, calls CNN TNN instead, channel 200 becomes 2nn (4-2017)

Cell phone becoming difficult to use, trouble with fine motor skills in opening flip phone, holds it to his ear upside down and cannot figure out how to turn it the other way, cannot see well enough to read who is calling

Reaction time from hearing information to responding is slowing down; takes more time to process information

Wants me with him when around other people to help him "find the words" or to finish a thought for him when he is stuck; has me order for him in a restaurant

When taking out trash from house will sometimes confuse which container is recycle/regular garbage

Has gained back the 20 pounds he lost last year, eats a lot of snacks and always wants dessert after dinner (5-2017)

Struggling to read his digital watch or bedside clock

Couldn't remember how to open his bathroom medicine cabinet today (6-21-2017); managed to laugh about it; remembered how to do it later in the day

Does not enjoy being with friends due to difficulty having a conversation; has to be in just the right frame of mind to be around others (6-2017)

Very slow and somewhat confused in the mornings, usually gets better as the day goes on (7-2017)

Attended a gathering of friends from his military reserve unit; discussed ahead of time that he wanted me near him in case he needed help with conversation . . . said later that he was very glad we went; relieved to see that others were also having health issues of their own (7-22-2017)

Decided that it is time to hire someone to mow the lawn; it is too tiring and difficult; he sometimes mows the same area multiple times before moving over to the next section (unaware of this) and cannot operate the mower without some help from me (7-2017)

Efforts at Psychological Care

The first efforts at psychological care with this patient began when he was seen for his second neuropsychological examination. The first examination was conducted by another examiner, who limited his role to "testing the patient" and helping provide a diagnosis. When seen by a second examiner, the patient was 71 years old. He was pleasant and cooperative. He began the interaction by telling a joke to the clinical neuropsychologist. He had a gleam in his eye and an apparent deep joy in interacting with others and making them laugh. This method of interacting has been repetitively observed as the patient has been followed multiple times during a 3-year period.

When the patient attempted to answer questions in the interview, his speech was fluent, but he struggled to find words. When speaking, he frequently made both phonemic and semantic paraphasic errors. He seemed to understand, however, what was being said and what he was being asked. He had good insight into his difficulties. At times, tears came to his eyes when describing his limitations. During such times, he would talk about working with animals on a farm as a boy and young man. He talked about how he knew that the animals knew when they were about to be killed for their meat. He stated that if he continued to decline, he would take his own life. He did not want to die, but it appeared to him a rational choice if he continued to decline and could not take care of himself. He felt worthless and ashamed of not being able to be "able-bodied." He revealed these thoughts only when he was talking privately with the clinical neuropsychologist and not in the presence of his wife.

During these times, the clinical neuropsychologist emphasized that "we don't want to lose you." This was said with sincere warmth and while looking the patient in the eyes. It was emphasized to the patient (and later to his wife in his presence) that they could call the clinical neuropsychologist anytime the depression, sense of hopelessness, or the impulse to kill himself was strongly felt. The patient emphasized his cowboy background and said that it was never his style to ask for such help. But he, too, looked the clinical neuropsychologist in the eyes and expressed how he appreciated the offer. As a successful businessman, he strongly believed in the need to take seriously the concerns of his customers. This was a long-standing personality and interpersonal trait. He appreciated that the clinical neuropsychologist was extending this type of service to him and his wife. He expressed that "it felt good" to talk to the clinical neuropsychologist because the clinical neuropsychologist seemed to be the only one willing to spend time with him in regard to what he was experiencing and to attempt to address his questions regarding his clinical condition and course. His wife also appreciated this clinical approach and religiously brought him in for his appointments.

The questions that this patient asked are important for many individuals with a dementing condition. One question was about his longevity, given his clinical condition. It was noted that no one could predict how long he would live. Another question was "how bad" would the situation become? The answer was that "time would tell"; right now, his condition was gradual, but he was showing severe neurocognitive impairments. It was emphasized that no matter how he might decline in the future, he and his wife would be given guidance to handle the situation and his declining functions. It was also mentioned that he might forget a lot about what was talked about, but he would not forget the relationship between himself and the consulting clinical neuropsychologist. That is, he would remember that the relationship was "a good one" and that both mutually enjoyed seeing and speaking with each other. He was comforted by those words.

As of this writing, he continues to be followed and re-examined on a regular basis.

His wife, who is very practical and intelligent, looks forward to the periodic discussions and emphasizes that the clinical neuropsychologist is the only one who takes the time to listen to them and to answer their questions. They have expressed their appreciation in several ways, including yearly Christmas cards. Table 20.3 summarizes some of the features of the patient's psychological care. Table 20.4 summarizes some of his wife's characteristics and reactions to the psychological care interventions.

Table 20.3 Clinical Features Relevant to the Psychological Care of the Person Described in Case Vignette 20.2

CLINICAL FEATURE	YES	NO	PARTIALLY
1. The dialogue between the patient and the clinical neuropsychologist was not rushed.	✓		
2. The patient experienced that his personal opinion was important regarding diagnosis and management issues.	✓		
3. The content of the concerns was voiced and repeated out loud by the clinical neuropsychologist to the patient and spouse.	✓		
4. The patient did not experience "being alone" with his problem(s). He experienced that the clinical neuropsychologist was honestly and respectfully taking "extra steps" to help him.	✓		
5. The patient and the clinical neuropsychologist developed a positive therapeutic relationship in which the patient's dignity was maintained even in the face of significant physical and cognitive losses.	✓		
6. The patient independently stated that he wanted to see the clinical neuropsychologist in repeated consultations.	✓		
7. Anxiety/depression/anger and/or apathy were substantially reduced during periods of psychological care.			✓
8. The patient was able to follow the guidance of the clinical neuropsychologist to improve functioning in everyday life activities and to avoid dangerous behaviors given his declining competencies (e.g., driving a car, attempting to handle finances, and walking without standby assistance).	✓		
9. The patient was able to control impulses and delay gratification.	✓		
10. The patient activity worked at developing self-efficacy skills in the face of his declining abilities.	✓		
11. The patient attempted to self-reflect or be more aware of his personal strengths and limitations.			✓

(continued)

Table 20.3 Continued

CLINICAL FEATURE	YES	NO	PARTIALLY
12. The patient experienced enjoyment in the care or help of other living things (people, animals, the environment, etc.).	✓		
13. The patient experienced an understanding of the "problematic nature of his unique life" and was not overwhelmed or defeated by it or readily gave in to escapism to cope with life (Bettelheim, 1989).	✓		
14. The patient could live with the restrictions produced by a brain injury without resentment or loss of hope (Goldstein, 1952).			✓
15. The patient was able to obtain new insights into himself by attending to why certain songs, stories, fairy tales, movies, tattoos, etc. had a special personal meaning that he initially did not understand.		✓	
16. The patient's dreams or artwork often heralded changes in behavior that aided psychological adjustment before the consciously mediated changes occurred.		✓	
17. The psychological care interventions (including the dialogue) between the patient and the clinical neuropsychologist resulted in the patient talking more openly about problems and demonstrating self-directed efforts at improving psychological adjustment to the direct and indirect effects of the brain disorder.	✓		
18. The psychological care interventions were in harmony with the patient's cultural background and religious orientation.	✓		
19. The psychological care interventions facilitated psychosocial development/adaptation in the later stages of life.		✓	
20. The patient and family experienced two basic facts of life: (a) The individual's state of subjective sense of personal well-being fluctuates and (b) the psychological adjustment process is never static and therefore hope should never be abandoned.			✓
Total	13	3	4

Table 20.4 Clinically Relevant Features of the Wife When Her Husband Was Provided Psychological Care as Described in Case Vignette 20.2

CLINICAL FEATURE	YES	NO	PARTIALLY
1. The quality of the relationship before the onset of the brain disorder was good.	✓		
2. The wife has adequate supports that help maintain her resiliency.	✓		
3. The wife is personally offended by the behavioral problems of the patient.		✓	
4. The wife has a good working (therapeutic) relationship with the clinical neuropsychologist.	✓		
5. The wife understands the biological factors (and at times the psychological factors) underlying the behavioral problems of the patient.			✓
6. The wife does not feel alone in the care of the patient.	✓		
7. The wife has some sense of hope that the behavioral problems will get better with time and/or there is "light at the end of the tunnel."		✓	

VASCULAR DEMENTIA, INCLUDING CADASIL

Vascular dementias are often considered the second most common form of dementia, particularly in the older population of individuals (Stephens et al., 2004). There are different causes of vascular dementia. Perhaps the most common cause has been traditionally referred to as "multifocal" or "multi-infarct" vascular lesions underlying the dementing condition (Seshadri, Economos, & Wright, 2016). As increasingly more focal vascular lesions occur, there is a progressive decline in neurocognitive and neurobehavioral status. However, with time, it has been recognized that single infarcts (typically large ones) can result in dementia if there is concomitant cortical atrophy at the time of the stroke or following it (Seshadri et al., 2016). It has been progressively recognized that a major contributing factor to dementia in patients with cerebral vascular disease is the presence of diffuse ischemic white matter hyperintensities (List et al., 2011). One genetically determined cerebral vascular disease, which produces multiple confluent white matter lesions in various regions of the brain, is CADASIL.

CADASIL often occurs in younger patients (e.g., those in their 30s or 40s) and is associated with quite diverse symptomatology, including mood disturbances, migraines, and a decline in several neuropsychological functions. Disturbances in memory and executive functions are most common (List et al., 2011). The disease typically progresses slowly, but by age 65 years, cognitive impairments are often severe and dementia is diagnosed. It is important to note that patients with CADASIL are occasionally misdiagnosed as having multiple sclerosis (Carone, 2017) or a psychiatric illness.

Case Vignette 20.3

Summary of Neurological and Neuropsychological Findings

A 55-year-old physician was diagnosed as having CADASIL and referred for a third opinion regarding his neuropsychological status and his ability to return to driving a vehicle. He had undergone two previous clinical neuropsychological examinations that documented multiple cognitive impairments. The findings were compatible with multiple vascular lesions detected on repeat MRI scans of the brain. The repeated recommendation of a previous neuropsychologist was for the patient to stop working as a physician and to stop driving a vehicle. The physician, however, was unconvinced that his cognitive problems were of such a magnitude. Although he recognized that he was "less sharp" in his thinking abilities and would not attempt to practice medicine at that time, he was hopeful and mildly confident that he might return to medical practice with time and therapy. His wife, who was also a physician, recognized his limitations and tried to convince him to accept the recommendations of his treating neurologist and consultant clinical neuropsychologist. He would hear none of this and wanted another opinion from a more experienced clinical neuropsychologist.

His neuropsychological examination revealed a cooperative man who was somewhat guarded in how he described his neurocognitive symptoms. He clearly underestimated his cognitive and affective difficulties compared to his wife's descriptions. On examination, the same impairments noted in previous neuropsychological examinations were again seen. On the BNIS, his total score was 34 out of 50 points, producing a T score of 18. He had cognitive impairments in multiple domains, including word finding and confrontational naming, with subtle problems in auditory comprehension. He made errors performing arithmetic calculations secondary to problems with attention and planning. On the WAIS-IV, his Similarities age-adjusted scale score was 5 and his Block Design score was 7. On the RAVLT, he could recall none of the words after a 20-minute delay. He could complete the Trail Making Test Part B, but it took him 135 second and he made one error. Finally, he had restricted movement and control of his left arm and was considered to have a "mild" left hemiparesis.

After the examination was completed and the results were reviewed with the patient and his wife, he became quiet and looked dejected. He acknowledged that perhaps he had more cognitive problems than he recognized, but he was willing to work in physical therapy, speech therapy, and occupational therapy in order to improve his functioning. He also expressed a willingness to begin seeing the clinical neuropsychologist (who conducted his third examination) in psychotherapy to deal with his emotional struggles and obtain guidance regarding how to improve his recovery.

Efforts at Psychological Care

The initial efforts at psychological care appeared promising. The patient began to talk about his depression and sense of personal loss in multiple domains in life. A therapeutic rapport seemed to be emerging. For several sessions, the patient noted that he wanted to improve his relationship with his wife and did not know how to do so. He could not discuss his marital situation in-depth and often seemed to give some details and then avoid any further discussion. In an effort to better understand the marital relationship, the clinical neuropsychologist asked the patient if he could speak to the patient's wife regarding her view of him and their marriage. The patient agreed to this request without much hesitation. As time went on, however, it became clear that this benign request had not so benign consequences.

The patient's wife spoke about substantial pre-existing marital difficulties. Prior to his illness, there was a strong sense that divorce was inevitable. With the onset of his CADASIL, divorce seemed out of the question for his wife, who had a strong sense of duty to care for him. Their religious and cultural backgrounds also required that they stay together. The patient's wife was committed to helping her husband, but she clearly was emotionally estranged from him. As noted previously, the patient wanted to improve his relationship with his wife, but when details were explored as to why the relationship had deteriorated, little direct, honest communication ensued. Statements were often vague and tangential anytime emotional topics were raised. The patient did not want to discuss these details.

The patient's cultural background and related premorbid personality characteristics appeared to cause him to believe that such personal discussions could be dangerous and result in a loss of dignity. He would therefore often shift his attention to other topics. He would talk of his growing interest in religious texts that were important to him in his life as a boy and young man. As he struggled with a combination of guilt and lost competencies, he became more preoccupied with the religious teachings. He was especially taken by religious writings that emphasized devotion to God and God's forgiveness of humans. He clearly wanted forgiveness, but he would not go into details about what needed to be forgiven.

The patient educated the psychotherapist about his religious background and the teachings of his religion. During this time, the patient's wife and daughter noted that the patient expressed a desire to see the clinical neuropsychologist on a regular basis. They were grateful for this and noted that he seldom would speak to anyone else about personal matters. They noted that before the onset of CADISAL, he would seldom talk to either of them when he returned from work. He characteristically preferred to listen to music, especially classical music and music from his native country, when he was stressed or worn down from his daily work.

As time went on, the family noted that the patient's depression was worsening. He did not want to get out of bed; he showed no interest in any activities; he would not express his feelings. When seen in a psychotherapy session, he noted that he became especially saddened after hearing from his speech therapist that his memory appeared to be worsening. He wanted a repeat neuropsychological examination to determine if this was true. A repeat examination indeed revealed further subtle decline. He was demoralized and again became very quiet.

Given that depression was worsening, the family asked his treating psychiatrist to re-evaluate his antidepressant medications. The medications were increased, and for a period of time his depression seemed to improve. At that time, he became more energetic but "manic." He spoke about his memory improving as he took dietary supplements. He wanted to take a medical refresher course to again determine if he could return to the practice of medicine. His wife noted that she had seen this pattern before when, after a burst of energy and unrealistic optimism, he would again become more depressed and withdrawn. This pattern, in fact, reoccurred.

The patient now talked about whether it was worth living or not. He stated that he was not suicidal, but he was ready to go anytime God wanted to take him. He no longer had any purpose in life; he had done all that he could as a physician. He began talking about reducing the frequency of psychotherapy sessions because he had come to grips with his existential situation. He was encouraged to continue, and he did so for a while, but he began either to be late for sessions or to find reasons why he could not keep scheduled psychotherapy visits. This type of pattern fluctuated during the next 12 months.

Seeing the wife's growing frustration and discouragement over her husband's situation, the clinical neuropsychologist asked the patient if he could speak with his wife for a series of sessions. The patient stated that he wanted "a break" from his psychotherapy sessions and agreed that the clinical neuropsychologist could speak with his wife. Although the sessions with the patient's wife were informative regarding several complex issues in their life, these sessions offended him. This reality was not immediately clear, but it came out in later sessions with the patient. Unlike the patients described in the first and second case vignettes, this patient believed that his opinion was no longer important to the clinical neuropsychologist. His wife's opinion was more important. This went against his cultural values, his premorbid personality characteristics, and his sense of dignity. He was personally offended that the clinical neuropsychologist talked to his wife over several sessions. The therapeutic relationship was now over for him. He decided to discontinue psychotherapy. His wife was in tears over this decision, but that is in fact how the psychological care efforts had stopped. Approximately 1 year after the patient's psychotherapy ended, his wife called to inform the clinical neuropsychologist that her husband had died suddenly of a massive stroke. Table 20.5 summarizes some of the major clinical features relevant to this patient's psychological care. Table 20.6 lists clinically relevant features of his spouse during the time that psychological care efforts were attempted.

Table 20.5 Clinical Features Relevant to the Psychological Care of the Person Described in Case Vignette 20.3

CLINICAL FEATURE	YES	NO	PARTIALLY
1. The dialogue between the patient and the clinical neuropsychologist was not rushed.	✓		
2. The patient experienced that his personal opinion was important regarding diagnosis and management issues.		✓	
3. The content of the concerns was voiced and repeated out loud by the clinical neuropsychologist to the patient and family members.	✓		
4. The patient did not experience "being alone" with his problem(s). He experienced that the clinical neuropsychologist was honestly and respectfully taking "extra steps" to help him.			✓
5. The patient and the clinical neuropsychologist developed a positive therapeutic relationship in which the patient's dignity was maintained.		✓	
6. The patient independently stated that he wanted to see the clinical neuropsychologist in repeated consultations.			✓
7. Anxiety/depression/anger and/or apathy were substantially reduced during periods of psychological care.		✓	
8. The patient was able to follow the guidance of the clinical neuropsychologist to improve functioning in everyday life activities and to avoid dangerous behaviors given his declining competencies (e.g., driving a car, attempting to handle finances, and walking without standby assistance).		✓	
9. The patient was able to control impulses and delay gratification.			✓

Table 20.5 Continued

CLINICAL FEATURE	YES	NO	PARTIALLY
10. The patient activity worked at developing self-efficacy skills in the face of his declining abilities.		✓	
11. The patient attempted to self-reflect or be more aware of his strengths and limitations.		✓	
12. The patient experienced enjoyment in the care or help of other living things (people, animals, the environment, etc.).		✓	
13. The patient experienced an understanding of the "problematic nature of his unique life" and was not overwhelmed or defeated by it or readily gave in to escapism to cope with life (Bettelheim, 1989).			✓
14. The patient could "live with" the restrictions produced by a brain injury "without resentment" or loss of hope (Goldstein, 1952).		✓	
15. The patient was able to obtain new insights into himself by attending to why certain songs, stories, fairy tales, movies, tattoos, etc. had a special personal meaning that he initially did not understand.		✓	
16. The patient's dreams or artwork often heralded changes in behavior that aided psychological adjustment before the consciously mediated changes occurred.		✓	
17. The psychological care interventions (including the dialogue) between the patient and the clinical neuropsychologist resulted in the patient talking more openly about problems and demonstrating self-directed efforts at improving psychological adjustment to the direct and indirect effects of the brain disorder.			✓
18. The psychological care interventions were in harmony with the patient's cultural background and religious orientation.		✓	
19. The psychological care interventions facilitated psychosocial development/adaptation in the later stages of life.		✓	
20. The patient and family experienced two basic facts of life: (a) The individual's state of subjective sense of personal well-being fluctuates and (b) the psychological adjustment process is never static and therefore hope should never be abandoned.			✓
Total	2	12	6

Table 20.6 Clinically Relevant Features of the Wife When Her Husband Was Provided Psychological Care Described in Case Vignette 20.3

CLINICAL FEATURE	YES	NO	PARTIALLY
1. The quality of the relationship before the onset of the brain disorder was good.		✓	
2. The wife has adequate supports that help maintain her resiliency.			✓
3. The wife is personally offended by the behavioral problems of the patient.	✓		
4. The wife has a good working (therapeutic) relationship with the clinical neuropsychologist.	✓		
5. The wife understands the biological factors (and at times the psychological factors) underlying the behavioral problems of the patient.	✓		
6. The wife does not feel alone in the care of the patient.			✓
7. The wife has some sense of hope that her husband's behavioral problems will get better with time and/or there is "light at the end of the tunnel."		✓	

APPROACHES TO PSYCHOLOGICAL CARE OF PERSONS WITH PROGRESSIVE COGNITIVE DECLINE AND EARLY STAGE DEMENTIA

The psychological care of patients with progressive cognitive decline and early stages of dementia is greatly influenced by the nature of the therapeutic alliance or relationship that can be established. However, many complex issues have to be faced and effectively dealt with to provide ongoing psychological care for these individuals, as the three case vignettes have demonstrated. In the last stage of life, hope is the essential virtue needed to deal with the crisis of loss of life and loss of cognitive abilities, as suggested by Erikson and Erikson (1998). How can one have a realistic sense of hope during this time if one has a dementing condition?

Much depends on the premorbid personality characteristics of the individual and the ability of the psychological care provider to work effectively with these characteristics in the face of the patient's declining neuropsychological functions. Often, one does not know what those characteristics are until one interacts with the patient and approaches the person with a sense of respect and clinical sensitivity to the individual's situation. In time, those features often reveal themselves. Listening to the patient's history and current concerns is crucial in this regard. Also, it must be recognized that the inevitable aspects of human nature that make psychological care efforts both rewarding and at times frustrating and discouraging to the provider and the patient must be dealt with constantly.

Although cognitive impairments are often the focus of neuropsychological assessments of these individuals, an understanding of what these patients perceive is just as important to their psychological care. Some lack a sense of physical touch and reassurance from loved ones. When a partner is not available, the touch and care of an animal may be very important for the patient. In fact, there is a literature suggesting that animal-assisted therapy can be helpful in the care of patients with cognitive impairments (Majić, Gutzmann, Heinz, Lang, & Rapp, 2013). The patient described in Case Vignette 20.3 was asked about his possible interest in having a pet to care for and interact with on a daily basis. He dismissed the idea, stating that he was never interested in animals. Music therapy has also been noted to help some patients with dementia reduce their anxiety and depression (Guetin et al., 2009; Svansdottir & Snaedal, 2006). Music, in fact, seemed to calm the third patient. Nevertheless, his depression remained extremely difficult to treat. He had lost his dignity; he had lost his profession; he had lost his freedom to do as he pleased. He had lost hope. Although religious teachings provided some initial relief, they could not sustain him. Ultimately, he lost important sustaining interpersonal relationships.

The patients described in Case Vignettes 20.1 and 20.2 felt a sense of trust in the clinical neuropsychologist, and a strong therapeutic bond was established and reinforced over several sessions. They openly discussed their most personal concerns. They were not evasive when difficult interpersonal topics emerged in the psychotherapy sessions. These factors appear to be of major importance when helping these patients from a psychological care perspective. Hope was sustained in patients with early dementing conditions when (1) a meaningful patient–doctor relationship could be established; (2) the patients could talk openly about what concerned them the most; and (3) the patients (and families) believed they would be cared for until the end. The three case vignettes highlight that the actions of the psychological caregiver can have unexpected positive or negative impacts, depending on the premorbid features of the individual, which are seldom considered in the neurological and clinical neuropsychological consultations of these patients.

The scientific approaches to the psychological care of patients with early stage dementia typically do not emphasize the points just made. However, a number of behavioral and psychological approaches found in the literature may help reduce some behavioral symptoms and produce a periodic sense of well-being. Regier and Gitlin (2017) reviewed a series of studies on the effects of physical exercises, cognitive rehabilitation, bright light therapy, aromatherapy, animal-assisted therapy, massage therapy, and music therapy to reduce anxiety, depression, and agitation. Under certain circumstance, these therapies may have modest, momentary effects.

Livingston et al. (2005) conducted an evidence-based review of the effectiveness of various psychological approaches to reducing neuropsychiatric symptoms in persons with dementia. They concluded that behavioral approaches may be especially helpful. Using the strict guidelines of evidence-based methods, they could neither endorse nor refute essentially humanistic approaches to the psychological care of these individuals, which are embedded in the approach outlined in this chapter.

Given that cognitive impairments greatly affect these persons' lives and may be especially distressing to them, efforts at cognitive rehabilitation have been the focus of some approaches to psychological care for patients with early stage CATD (Clare, 2003; Clare et al., 2000; Clare, Wilson, Carter, Roth, & Hodges, 2004). Although potentially promising, the treatment effects are typically modest. This line of research has noted, however, that patients with early stage CATD who have good awareness of their cognitive limitations often benefit the most from such training (Clare et al., 2004). Clare et al. (2004) noted that good awareness was positively correlated with depression. Other studies have also shown a correlation between lower depression and poor awareness (Jacus, 2017). The problem with these studies, however, is that they do not specifically try to separate organic unawareness from psychologically motivated denial (see Chapter 9, this volume). These are different phenomena that may underlie underreporting of cognitive and behavioral deficits in this patient group. In true denial, there are many signs of avoidance behavior. This was true of the patient described in Case Vignette 20.3. In true organic unawareness, patients show behavioral signs of apathy or perplexity when they are confronted with their cognitive limitations. They do not usually avoid discussing important topics. For example, in Case Vignette 20.1, the patient appeared to progressively become less aware of her cognitive limitations. During this time, she did not avoid discussing personal concerns about her relationship with her husband and her delusional beliefs.

A major issue that faces some patients with early stages of dementia is the question of whether they should end their life. Richman (1992) wrote insightfully about whether "preemptive suicide" or "rational suicide" is a viable option for elderly people who have declining health and depression—key features of many patients diagnosed as being in the early stages of dementia. He noted, "Conflicts arising from developmental processes do not appear only at the appointed life stage, but are revived at every developmental crisis. Problems with all the developmental tasks return in full force in the ill elderly" (p. 132). The patient's experience of distrust, disgust, and despair can lead to a "disconfirmation of life, the worth of the self, and relationships with others" (p. 132). Richman argued, with considerable psychotherapeutic experience and insight, that it is more rational to reaffirm the importance of life rather to reject life "even to the very end" (p. 132). Patients who have relationships with others that lead to a sense of trust that they will not be abandoned often choose life over death. This has been true for the patient described in Case Vignette 20.2. For individuals whose relationships with others are filled with distrust and who feel a sense of disgust with themselves, suicide becomes a more feasible option.

Richman (1992) noted,

Ours is ... an age of impersonality and dehumanization in medicine, where machines and laboratory tests have replaced the doctor who made home visits and had a special relationship with his patients. Life and death issues were a natural part of that relationship. (p. 134)

The psychological care of persons with dementia requires such relationships, which are never a waste of time no matter how discouraging some moments are experienced.

In an equally insightful article, Hasselkus (1998) described several important activities that can increase the personal sense of well-being in persons with dementia. She reviewed previous research findings and her own qualitative findings. Engaging patients in activities that they might enjoy is, of course, the first step. When these activities produce a smile on a patient's face, one knows that a greater sense of personal well-being is being experienced by the person, even for a short period of time. When the patient wants to spend more time doing the activities, this is another marker of an improved sense of well-being, even in a cognitively confused person. When patients remember past events with their caregivers and also remember activities they shared in an assisted living environment, they appear to experience less distress and present an enhanced sense of well-being. Finally, Hasselkus noted that the experience of greater independent functioning (e.g., remembering what activities follow each other) in the assisted living environment often was associated with an enhanced sense of well-being.

Because many patients with dementia progressively become unaware of their surroundings and their cognitive limitations, they often can make decisions that upset their caregivers. Clare and colleagues (2013) conducted a pilot study on the teaching of caregivers to become observant of signs suggesting impaired self-awareness in demented individuals. Such training may not only improve the quality of life

Table 20.7 Approaches to the Psychological Care of Patients with Dementing Conditions

INTERVENTION	STUDY SAMPLE	MAJOR FINDINGS	CONCLUSIONS
Literature review on psychosocial and environmental approaches for behavioral and psychological symptoms in dementia (Regier & Gitlin, 2017)	Initially identified 378 articles relevant to the topic. Excluded articles regarding caregiver focus, case studies, and nonrandomized controlled studies. Eventually reviewed 14 papers in detail.	"The efficacy of psychosocial and environmental treatment approaches to behavioral symptoms in dementia continue to be promising, yet the results are also mixed" (p. 95). Music therapy and animal-assisted therapy seem to hold some promise in reducing depression, anxiety, and agitation in individuals with dementia.	The focus of such scientific reviews continues to be on symptom reduction rather than on managing patients' personal reactions to their dementia and how to successfully cope with those changes over time.
Literature review of diverse approaches to the psychological care of persons with dementia, with particular emphasis on reducing or managing neuropsychiatric symptoms (Livingston et al., 2005)	Initially identified 1632 papers of any psychologically based therapy to reduce neuropsychiatric symptoms in persons with dementia. Again, based on typical criteria of evidence-based medicine, only 163 papers were included.	The authors note that several forms of psychological interventions included several different elements and therefore are difficult to classify. Behavioral management techniques are reported to be generally successful in reducing symptoms of a neuropsychiatric nature. Psychoeducation for caregivers was also noted to be helpful if provided individually and not just in a group format. Specific types of staff training and education were also noted to be helpful.	The authors recognize that various approaches may be helpful to the psychological care of persons with dementia, but they conclude with the typical proviso that limited evidence exists for humanistic or psychodynamic approaches to helping these individuals deal with their declining neuropsychological abilities.

(*continued*)

Table 20.7 Continued

INTERVENTION	STUDY SAMPLE	MAJOR FINDINGS	CONCLUSIONS
Clinically dealing with the issue of suicide in the sick elderly (Richman, 1992)	Philosophical and psychodynamically oriented review of the problems the sick elderly face and when the issue of suicide becomes a focus of their care.	The author notes that developmental issues that a person faced earlier in life are often re-experienced during the last stages of life when various types of illness prevail (including dementia). Experiences of distrust, disgust, and despair play a crucial role in a "disconfirmation of life" (p. 132). The author includes in his discussion some interesting observations about Bruno Bettelheim and his decision to commit suicide.	Not surprisingly, the quality of the doctor–patient relationship and the relationship that persons have with important people in their life often mitigate against the decision to take one's life.
Caregiver support in the psychological care of persons with dementing conditions (Mace & Rabins, 1981)	The authors describe the clinical experience of trying to help families cope with the wide range of problems a person with dementia faces.	Several important clinical insights and practical suggestions are presented in this internationally recognized book.	The need to care for the impaired family member while also caring for oneself is perhaps one of the most important points of this book.
Cognitive rehabilitation of patients with early stage dementia of Alzheimer's type (Clare et al., 2004)	The authors investigated the relationship between awareness of impairments and response to cognitive rehabilitation activities in 12 patients with early stage dementia.	Patients with better awareness had better cognitive outcomes from the cognitive retraining experiences. Importantly, the level of awareness was associated with depression but not performance on measures of executive functions.	Although not the focus of this article, the empirical findings suggest that noncognitive factors (those related to depression) may affect new learning experiences in early stages of dementia. The need for psychological care models that address this reality and separate "organic unawareness" from "psychological denial" may improve our understanding of how to provide better psychological care of these patients.

Assessment of activities conducted in traditional adult day care centers that foster a sense of well-being in persons with dementia (Hasselkus, 1998)	Interviews were successfully completed with staff members of 40 centers. Forty-two staff members were interviewed, and repeated themes that clinically suggested improved psychological well-being in demented patients in those centers were identified. The author also reviewed literature findings on therapeutic activities that helped improve quality of life in persons with dementia.	Several important observations are made in this article. Listening to patients' stories about their lives helped identify activities that might engage their interest. Having a "meeting of the minds" between the caregiver and the patient is an important first step. It reflects a respect for the patient's viewpoint. Activities the naturally produce a smile on the patient's face and the enjoyment of humor were noted as being especially important. This often led to a bond or warm relationship between the caregivers and the patients. This was further associated with moments of well-being. When patients wished to spend increasingly more time doing a task they enjoyed, moments of well-being were further achieved. Feeling helpful or competent, even in relatively small areas, can have a major impact on patients' sense of personal well-being.	This article deserves special attention because it provides very practical steps in helping demented individuals have moments of improved psychological well-being during times in which they need considerable assistance from others.
AwareCare training for staff caring for persons with dementia in residential settings (Clare et al., 2013)	The authors compared the impact of teaching staff to recognize impaired awareness in persons with dementia living in a residential setting. In a pilot randomized controlled study, the staff of four care homes received training and the staff of four care homes did not receive training. Training took place during an 8-week period involving 32 patients and 32 staff members.	Family members judged that quality of life was improved in the patients whose attending staff received the awareness training compared to patients in the control settings. The staff, however, did not report improved quality of life for these patients. Staff appeared to benefit from such training in different ways. Staff now appeared to better understand the patients' behaviors.	The findings of this research project are encouraging. They suggest that when residential staff understand the phenomena of impaired awareness in persons with dementia, they may in fact treat the patients in a manner that improves the patients' quality of life, even though this was not clearly demonstrated in this article.

for the patient but also provide the staff with a better understanding of the patient's cognitive limitations. Although not demonstrated in the research by Clare et al., I suspect that this enhanced insight can lower staff distress and increase their empathetic responses to patients. Table 20.7 summarizes the articles and insights mentioned in this chapter that are relevant to the psychological care of persons with early stage dementia as well as to helping family members and caregivers.

SUMMARY

The psychological care of individuals with early stage dementia requires a good understanding of their neuropsychological difficulties and an appreciation of what they subjectively experience regarding their dementing process. Even in cases in which patients are not fully aware of their limited cognitive capacities, their desires should be kept in mind in light of their premorbid methods of coping with loss and adversity. Understanding these patients from both neuropsychological and psychodynamic standpoints can help form a relationship with these patients that guides their care. Long-standing interpersonal and intrapsychological issues will inevitably emerge, and they need to be addressed as thoughtfully as possible. A variety of behavioral techniques can help reduce the distress level of these patients, leading to associated reductions in anxiety, agitation, and depression. However, the doctor–patient relationship, established over several years, will ultimately determine the real value of the psychological care interventions for these patients and their families.

Because dementia is a frightening diagnosis, sometimes individuals, even primary care providers, may avoid using that term in front of patients. Honest but sensitive dialogue is often needed. Because patients and their families are desperate to obtain any potential form of help, they are at risk of seeking out expensive proposed therapies that hold out some promise to help them. They often turn to the clinical neuropsychologist for advice during these times. The clinical neuropsychologist's combined training in the neurosciences and in psychology and psychotherapy can help patients and their families make informed decisions. Universally, they are grateful for such guidance.

REFERENCES

Albert, M. S., Moss, M. B., Tanzi, R., & Jones, K. (2001). Preclinical prediction of AD using neuropsychological tests. *Journal of the International Neuropsychological Society, 7*(5), 631–639.

Albert, S., Castillo-Castaneda, C., Sano, M., Jacobs, D., Marder, K., Bell, K., ... Albert, M. (1996). Quality of life in patients with Alzheimer's disease as reported by patient proxies. *Journal of the American Geriatrics Society, 44*(11), 1342–1347.

Barker, W. W., Luis, C. A., Kashuba, A., Luis, M., Harwood, D. G., Loewenstein, D., ... Sevush, S. (2002). Relative frequencies of Alzheimer disease, Lewy body, vascular and frontotemporal dementia, and hippocampal sclerosis in the State of Florida Brain Bank. *Alzheimer Disease & Associated Disorders, 16*(4), 203–212.

Benson, D. F., Davis, R. J., & Snyder, B. D. (1988). Posterior cortical atrophy. *Archives of Neurology, 45*(7), 789–793.

Berthier, M. L., Leiguarda, R., Starkstein, S. E., Sevlever, G., & Taratuto, A. L. (1991). Alzheimer's disease in a patient with posterior cortical atrophy. *Journal of Neurology, Neurosurgery, and Psychiatry, 54*(12), 1110–1111.

Brodaty, H., Green, A., & Koschera, A. (2003). Meta-analysis of psychosocial interventions for caregivers of people with dementia. *Journal of the American Geriatrics Society, 51*(5), 657–664.

Brodaty, H., Heffernan, M., Kochan, N. A., Draper, B., Trollor, J. N., & Sachdev, P. S. (2016). Incidence of MCI and dementia over six years in an Australian population sample. *Alzheimer's & Dementia, 12*(7 Suppl.), P581.

Carone, D. A. (2017). CADASIL and multiple sclerosis: A case report of prolonged misdiagnosis. *Applied Neuropsychology: Adult, 24*(3), 294–297.

Clare, L. (2003). Cognitive training and cognitive rehabilitation for people with early-stage dementia. *Reviews in Clinical Gerontology, 13*(1), 75–83.

Clare, L., Whitaker, R., Woods, R. T., Quinn, C., Jelley, H., Hoare, Z., ... Wilson, B. A. (2013). AwareCare: A pilot randomized controlled trial of an awareness-based staff training intervention to improve quality of life for residents with severe dementia in long-term care settings. *International Psychogeriatrics, 25*(1), 128–139.

Clare, L., Wilson, B. A., Carter, G., Breen, K., Gosses, A., & Hodges, J. R. (2000). Intervening with everyday memory problems in dementia of Alzheimer type: An errorless learning approach. *Journal of Clinical and Experimental Neuropsychology, 22*(1), 132–146.

Clare, L., Wilson, B. A., Carter, G., Roth, I., & Hodges, J. R. (2004). Awareness in early-stage Alzheimer's disease: Relationship to outcome of cognitive rehabilitation. *Journal of Clinical and Experimental Neuropsychology, 26*(2), 215–226.

Crutch, S. J., Lehmann, M., Schott, J. M., Rabinovici, G. D., Rossor, M. N., & Fox, N. C. (2012). Posterior cortical atrophy. *Lancet Neurology, 11*(2), 170–178.

de Souto Barreto, P., Andrieu, S., Rolland, Y., & Vellas, B. (2018). Physical activity domains and cognitive function over three years in older adults with subjective memory complaints: Secondary analysis from the MAPT trial. *Journal of Science and Medicine in Sport, 21*(1), 52–57.

Erikson, E. H., & Erikson, J. M. (1998). *The life cycle completed (extended version)*. New York, NY: Norton.

Ewers, M., Walsh, C., Trojanowski, J. Q., Shaw, L. M., Petersen, R. C., Jack, C. R., . . . Scheltens, P. (2012). Prediction of conversion from mild cognitive impairment to Alzheimer's disease dementia based upon biomarkers and neuropsychological test performance. *Neurobiology of Aging, 33*(7), 1203–1214.

Goldstein, K. (1952). The effect of brain damage on the personality. *Psychiatry, 15*(3), 245–260.

Guetin, S., Portet, F., Picot, M., Pommié, C., Messaoudi, M., Djabelkir, L., . . . Touchon, J. (2009). Effect of music therapy on anxiety and depression in patients with Alzheimer's type dementia: Randomised, controlled study. *Dementia and Geriatric Cognitive Disorders, 28*(1), 36–46.

Hasselkus, B. R. (1998). Occupation and well-being in dementia: The experience of day-care staff. *American Journal of Occupational Therapy, 52*(6), 423–434.

Heber, I. A., Costa, A. S., Werner, C. J., Schöne, U., Reich, A., Schulz, J. B., & Reetz, K. (2016). Posterior cortical atrophy: A case report of a 6-year natural progression. *Alzheimer Disease & Associated Disorders, 30*(3), 276–280.

Holst, G., & Hallberg, I. R. (2003). Exploring the meaning of everyday life, for those suffering from dementia. *American Journal of Alzheimer's Disease & Other Dementias, 18*(6), 359–365.

Jacus, J. P. (2017). Awareness, apathy, and depression in Alzheimer's disease and mild cognitive impairment. *Brain and Behavior, 7*(4), e00661.

Katzman, R. (1992). Neuropsychologic assessment of dementia in the elderly. In R. Katzman & J. W. Rowe (Eds.), *Principles of geriatric neurology* (pp. 167–206). Philadelphia, PA: Davis.

Leshner, A. I., Landis, S., Stroud, C., & Downey, A. (2017). *Preventing cognitive decline and dementia: A way forward*. Washington, DC: National Academies Press.

List, J., Duning, T., Meinzer, M., Kürten, J., Schirmacher, A., Deppe, M., . . . Flöel, A. (2011). Enhanced rapid-onset cortical plasticity in CADASIL as a possible mechanism of preserved cognition. *Cerebral Cortex, 21*(12), 2774–2787.

Livingston, G., Johnston, K., Katona, C., Paton, J., Lyketsos, C. G.; Old Age Task Force of the World Federation of Biological Psychiatry. (2005). Systematic review of psychological approaches to the management of neuropsychiatric symptoms of dementia. *American Journal of Psychiatry, 162*(11), 1996–2021.

Mace, N. L., & Rabins, P. V. (2011). *The 36-hour day: A family guide to caring for people who have Alzheimer disease, other dementias, and memory loss* (5th ed.). Baltimore, MD: Johns Hopkins University Press.

Majić, T., Gutzmann, H., Heinz, A., Lang, U. E., & Rapp, M. A. (2013). Animal-assisted therapy and agitation and depression in nursing home residents with dementia: A matched case–control trial. *American Journal of Geriatric Psychiatry, 21*(11), 1052–1059.

McMonagle, P., Deering, F., Berliner, Y., & Kertesz, A. (2006). The cognitive profile of posterior cortical atrophy. *Neurology, 66*(3), 331–338.

Nestor, P., Caine, D., Fryer, T., Clarke, J., & Hodges, J. (2003). The topography of metabolic deficits in posterior cortical atrophy (the visual variant of Alzheimer's disease) with FDG-PET. *Journal of Neurology, Neurosurgery, and Psychiatry, 74*(11), 1521–1529.

Ngandu, T., Lehtisalo, J., Solomon, A., Levälahti, E., Ahtiluoto, S., Antikainen, R., . . . Laatikainen, T. (2015). A 2 year multidomain intervention of diet, exercise, cognitive training, and vascular risk monitoring versus control to prevent cognitive decline in at-risk elderly people (FINGER): A randomised controlled trial. *Lancet, 385*(9984), 2255–2263.

Oosterman, J. M., Heringa, S. M., Kessels, R. P., Biessels, G. J., Koek, H. L., Maes, J. H., & van den Berg, E. (2017). Rule induction performance in amnestic mild cognitive impairment and Alzheimer's dementia: Examining the role of simple and biconditional rule learning processes. *Journal of Clinical and Experimental Neuropsychology, 39*(3), 231–241.

Querfurth, H., & LaFerla, F. (2010). Alzheimer's disease. *New England Journal of Medicine, 362*, 329–344.

Raina, P., Santaguida, P., Ismaila, A., Patterson, C., Cowan, D., Levine, M., . . . Oremus, M. (2008). Effectiveness of cholinesterase inhibitors and memantine for treating dementia: Evidence review for a clinical practice. *Annals of Internal Medicine, 148*(5), 379–397.

Regier, N. G., & Gitlin, L. N. (2017). Psychosocial and environmental treatment approaches for behavioral and psychological symptoms in neurocognitive disorders: An update and future directions. *Current Treatment Options in Psychiatry, 4*(1), 80–101.

Richman, J. (1992). A rational approach to rational suicide. *Suicide and Life-Threatening Behavior, 22*(1), 130–141.

Robinson, P., Ekman, S.-L., & Wahlund, L.-O. (1998). Unsettled, uncertain and striving to understand: Toward an understanding of the situation of persons with suspected dementia. *International Journal of Aging and Human Development, 47*(2), 143–159.

Russell, C. K. (1996). Passion and heretics: Meaning in life and quality of life of persons with dementia. *Journal of the American Geriatrics Society, 44*(11), 1400–1402.

Salmon, D. P., & Butters, N. M. (1992). Neuropsychologic assessment of dementia in the elderly. In R. Katzman & J. W. Rowe (Eds.), *Principles of geriatric neurology* (pp. 144–166). Philadelphia, PA: Davis.

Seshadri, S., Economos, A., & Wright, C. (2016). Vascular dementia and cognitive impairment. In J. Grotta, G. W. Albers, J. P. Broderick, S. E. Kasner, E. H. Lo, A. D. Mendelow, . . . L. K. S. Wong (Eds.), *Stroke: Pathophysiology, diagnosis, and management* (6th ed., pp. 253–267). New York, NY: Elsevier.

Smith, G., & Butts, A. (2018). Dementia. In J. E. Morgan & J. H. Ricker (Eds.), *Textbook of clinical neuropsychology* (2nd ed., pp. 717–741). New York, NY: Taylor & Francis.

Smith, G. E., & Bondi, M. W. (2013). *Mild cognitive impairment and dementia: Definitions, diagnosis, and treatment.* Oxford, UK: Oxford University Press.

Stephens, S., Kenny, R., Rowan, E., Allan, L., Kalaria, R., Bradbury, M., & Ballard, C. (2004). Neuropsychological characteristics of mild vascular cognitive impairment and dementia after stroke. *International Journal of Geriatric Psychiatry, 19*(11), 1053–1057.

Svansdottir, H., & Snaedal, J. (2006). Music therapy in moderate and severe dementia of Alzheimer's type: A case–control study. *International Psychogeriatrics, 18*(4), 613–621.

Ward, A., Tardiff, S., Dye, C., & Arrighi, H. M. (2013). Rate of conversion from prodromal Alzheimer's disease to Alzheimer's dementia: A systematic review of the literature. *Dementia and Geriatric Cognitive Disorders Extra, 3*(1), 320–332.

21

PSYCHOLOGICAL CARE OF PERSONS WITH COGNITIVE AND BEHAVIORAL DISORDERS SECONDARY TO TRAUMATIC BRAIN INJURY

BACKGROUND INFORMATION

Previous chapters in this book have summarized the behavioral and cognitive disturbances associated with traumatic brain injury (TBI) during childhood and adolescence (see Chapter 6), young adulthood (see Chapter 7), and the older years of life (see Chapter 8). In addition, previous chapters have noted that aphasia (see Chapter 18) and hemiplegia (see Chapter 19) are common neurological disturbances associated with TBI throughout the life span. This chapter presents a more focused discussion on how to provide psychological care for young adults with moderate to severe TBI. Understanding and managing the diverse cognitive and behavioral disturbances of these patients has been the focus of many neurological and neuropsychological rehabilitation programs (e.g., McMillan & Wood, 2017; Prigatano, 1999; Sherer & Sander, 2014; Silver, McAllister, & Yudofsky, 2011). Several approaches can be taken, but the approach advocated in this chapter stems from earlier work aimed at helping patients return to a productive lifestyle, improve interpersonal relationships, and avoid the development of new psychiatric disturbances. That work is summarized in Prigatano (1986) and Ben-Yishay and Diller (2011). More recent work germane to these early efforts is also considered in this chapter.

HISTORICAL AND RECENT OBSERVATIONS RELEVANT TO PSYCHOLOGICAL CARE AFTER MODERATE TO SEVERE TRAUMATIC BRAIN INJURY IN YOUNG ADULTS

The first step in providing psychological care is a thorough understanding of the neuropsychological and related personality or affective disturbances associated with moderate to severe TBI. These disturbances have been systematically related to neuropathological changes after TBI and the extent to which consciousness has been disturbed. Loss of consciousness has always been a marker of the severity of TBI, followed by the period of post-traumatic amnesia (Russell, 1971). The introduction of the Glasgow Coma Scale was an additional important advance in assessing coma (Jennett & Teasdale, 1981). It provided further quantification of the "depth of coma" by evaluating the motor responses of patients, their eye movements, and their verbalizations (or lack thereof). Neuroimaging studies of the brain have provided further information that has proven very valuable to clinical neuropsychologists. Both computed tomography (CT) and magnetic resonance imaging (MRI) scans of the brain can now readily identify damage to different regions of the cortex, white matter tracts, and subcortical structures. Following severe TBI secondary to motor vehicle accidents, MRI findings often reveal bilateral damage to the prefrontal cortex and the anterior portions of the temporal lobes, indicating neuronal damage (Bigler, 2011). Lesions to the white matter tracts of the brain, including the corpus callosum, are also commonly observed. Several months after an injury, enlarged lateral ventricles secondary to generalized volume loss of the brain are frequently reported (Bigler, 2011).

This combination of neuronal and white matter damage produces disturbances of synaptic integrity and alters the electrophysiological and neurotransmitter functions within the brain. The electrophysiological disturbances are often associated with seizures and/or the presence of diffuse slow wave activity associated with a state of reduced cortical activation or arousal (Arciniegas, Anderson, & Rojas, 2011). Sleep disturbances, endocrine dysfunction, and mood disorders are also common following severe TBI (Silver et al., 2011).

The neurotransmitter disturbances are especially obvious during the acute phase following a severe TBI (Arciniegas & Silver, 2011). During this period, a "neurotransmitter storm" is said to occur (Mcintosh, Juhler, Raghupathi, Saatman, & Smith, 1999). Although this "storm" can abate with time, neurotransmitter functions do not necessarily return to normal several months or years after brain trauma. Residual neurotransmitter disturbances have been implicated in the long-term neuropsychiatric disturbances of persons with severe TBI (Arciniegas & Silver, 2011). The complex combinations of lesion location and size with the degree of neuronal loss, white matter damage, and electrophysiological and neurotransmitter disorders underlie the myriad of neuropsychological disturbances that are associated with moderate to severe TBI several months after the injury.

Historically, memory disturbances, a loss of abstract reasoning, slow information processing, disturbances in attention, reduced tolerance for frustrations, enhanced irritability, childlike behavior, and impaired self-awareness of these changes have been noted (Goldstein, 1942; Meyer, 1904; Oddy, Coughlan, Tyerman, & Jenkins, 1985; Prigatano, 1986; Schilder, 1934; van Zomeren, 1981). This list has been refined to separate different types of attentional, memory, and abstract reasoning difficulties that this patient group demonstrates (McCullagh & Feinstein, 2011). Also, more recent neuroimaging studies have helped shed light on why young adults with moderate to severe TBI show so many complex (and overlapping) neuropsychological disturbances. In Chapter 11, the innovative work of Warren et al. (2014), which systematically related neuropsychological and emotional functioning to different lesion locations, was summarized. Recall that overlapping neural networks are especially rich in the frontal regions of the brain (see Figure 11.2). Damage to these areas is known to produce significant impairments in attention, response inhibition, social judgment, abstract reasoning, and the (verbal) control of behavior. These are, of course, common problems of persons with moderate to severe TBI. Damage to the orbital frontal regions and the anterior portions of the temporal lobe can produce errors in judging "salient" (meaning important) social cues as well as negatively affect the ability to learn and retrieve new information. Again, these are common sequelae of moderate to severe TBI. In Chapter 7, the innovative work of Corbetta and colleagues (especially the paper by J. Siegel et al., 2016) demonstrated that disturbances in functional connectivity, supported by the white matter tracts of the brain, are predictive of neuropsychological disturbances (see Figure 7.2). Again, it is not just the lesion location but also how that lesioned region disrupts communication patterns between multiple neuronal networks within and between cerebral hemispheres that produce the complex array of neuropsychological dysfunctions observed after moderate to severe TBI.

Although some neuropsychological functions improve following moderate to severe TBI in young adults, significant residual disturbances are common. The question thus becomes, Can anything be done to improve the functional and social outcomes for these individuals? Holistic neuropsychological rehabilitation programs (NRPs) have specifically addressed this question. By engaging patients in a series of group and individual training activities, it was demonstrated that improved psychosocial outcomes could be achieved (for a review of research supporting this claim, see Malec, 2014). As noted in Chapter 13, these intensive NRPs included several hours of treatment each day, 5 days a week, for 6–12 months (Ben-Yishay & Diller, 2011; Ben-Yishay et al., 1982; Prigatano, 1999; Prigatano et al., 1984). Thus, these intensive therapy programs allowed the opportunity to observe the cognitive and behavioral problems of such patients in an "up close and personal way." That is, the actual cognitive and behavioral problems were experienced daily by the treating staff (many of whom were clinical neuropsychologists) in both structured and unstructured settings. This allowed for a more naturalistic understanding of how the underlying cognitive and behavioral problems influenced the thought process, the ability to learn, the ability to stay focused, the ability to inhibit disruptive impulses, and the ability to self-recognize the nature and the extent of one's cognitive strengths and limitations. Providing a series of structured activities proved helpful in guiding the individual to higher levels of psychosocial functioning. This was the second step in providing psychological care services to this patient group.

The third step became more obvious when trying to understand why some patients benefited from this intensive holistic approach while others did not. The answer appeared to be related to some important individual differences among patients. The severity of neuropsychological impairments was certainly important, but so were the personality features of these individuals. Clinically, it appeared that pre-injury personality characteristics greatly influenced the clinical outcome for many patients. It has always been challenging to empirically support that clinical impression. The relatively recent work of Sela-Kaufman, Rassovsky, Agranov, Levi, and Vakil (2013), however, strongly supports this idea. Using structural equation modeling and multiple regression analyses, they replicated a well-established fact that severity of TBI is predictive of level of occupational outcome. They also were able to demonstrate that the attachment style of the patient (which reflects the nature of the emotional bond between the child and the parent) serves as a moderating variable in predicting outcome. One especially interesting finding was that low avoidance attachment style did not seem to influence the relationship between severity of TBI and occupational outcome (i.e., patients with less severe brain injuries typically had better occupational outcomes). This was not true for TBI patients who were judged to have high levels of avoidance attachment styles. Their level of occupation outcome was not related to severity of initial brain injuries. This is a highly important finding. Patients who had high avoidance attachment styles were less likely to return to higher levels of occupational outcome when they had milder brain injuries. In the course of conducting NRPs, researchers have found that these individuals also seem to have more difficulty establishing a therapeutic alliance with treating clinicians (for a more complete discussion of this clinical impression, see Prigatano, 1999). This latter finding and many similar clinical observations made it clear that the third step in the psychological care of persons who have cognitive and behavioral problems following moderate to severe TBI is to manage the patients in light of a more complete understanding of their premorbid personality characteristics.

It became progressively clearer that the psychological adjustment to the effects of a moderate to severe TBI was a highly individualized process. It had to take into consideration the patient's cultural background; age at injury; sex; educational level; nature and pattern of neuropsychological deficits; and premorbid methods of coping with anxiety, depression, and losses in life. This basic point was made several times, but it first came to light after working with patients within the context of holistic NRPs. It is well recognized today that multiple avenues of therapeutic interventions are potentially needed to adequately engage patients with moderate to severe TBI in rehabilitation experiences/exercises that have a reasonable chance of helping. Outcome studies of adults (Hoofien, Gilboa, Vakil, & Donovick, 2001; Ponsford et al., 2014) and children (Hawley, 2003) have repeatedly documented that the combination of physical, cognitive, behavioral, psychiatric, and psychosocial difficulties in fact does persist in these individuals despite rehabilitation efforts. Hoofien et al. made the important observation that ongoing professional assistance is therefore often needed to maintain a reasonable quality of life for these patients and their family members after formal rehabilitation efforts end. Intensive holistic NRPs often help patients by fostering self-sufficient behaviors, improving resiliency, and assisting them in becoming productive. Many of these patients, however, require different forms of long-term psychological care to maintain the gains achieved in NRPs. As noted in Chapter 9, for example, residual impairments in self-awareness (ISA) can persist in patients with moderate to severe TBI even after intensive holistic NRPs end; consequently, they too require continued management (Smeets, Vink, Ponds, Winkens, & van Heugten, 2017).

The long-term psychological care of persons with a history of moderate to severe TBI requires an integration of the seminal insights of Goldstein (1942, 1952, 1954) and his students (Ben-Yishay & Diller, 2016), as well as our expanding knowledge about human nature, psychodynamic theory, learning theory, and various observations emerging from the neurosciences (Carhart-Harris & Friston, 2010; Prigatano & Salas, 2017; R. Siegel, Miller, & Jemal, 2016; Wilson, 2002). These sources of knowledge have provided further insights into how to sustain a positive psychological adjustment several years after moderate to severe TBI (Prigatano, 2018).

BARRIERS TO SUCCESSFUL LONG-TERM PSYCHOLOGICAL CARE OF PERSONS WITH A MODERATE TO SEVERE TRAUMATIC BRAIN INJURY

In Chapter 12, features of a positive psychological adjustment to a moderate to severe TBI were summarized. In this chapter, factors that appear to foster a negative psychological adjustment are further clarified. They are listed in Table 21.1 (Prigatano, 2018). When a person does not subjectively experience important alterations in neuropsychological functioning, the individual tends to make poor choices in life. At times this type of disturbance is related to underlying brain pathology, and at other times it appears to reflect ineffective methods of coping (see Chapter 9, this volume). Whatever the cause, disturbances of self-awareness and denial pose major barriers to successful long-term psychological care and have to be addressed.

Table 21.1 Factors That Foster a Negative Psychological Adjustment

1. Unresolved anosognosia or severe ISA and DD
2. Unresolved anger and depression over life's circumstances
3. Reliance on addictive behaviors to "soothe oneself"
4. Poor pre-trauma interpersonal relationships that impede development of a therapeutic alliance with treating clinicians
5. Failure to have the support of close loved ones
6. Inability to establish or re-establish meaning in life
7. Resistance to any work activities that may help others
8. Significantly reduced ability to control emotional reactions when frustrated
9. Limited ability for empathy, which impedes the development of love relationships
10. Failure to foster their "individuality" "in the face of, not despite, their brain injury."
11. Failure to make "lifestyle changes" that contributed to the TBI
12. Failure to use compensatory aids to become more independent
13. Failure to "behaviorally give back" to family members who help them on a regular, if not daily, basis

DD, defensive denial; ISA, impaired self-awareness; TBI, traumatic brain injury.
Source: Reprinted from Prigatano, G. P., Psychological adjustment to the effects of a moderate to severe traumatic brain injury, in J. M. Silver, T. W. McAllister, & D. B. Arciniegas (Eds.), Textbook of Traumatic Brain Injury 3rd ed., p. 817–839, 2018, by permission of American Psychiatric Association Publishing.

Patients with moderate to severe TBI are also prone to angry outbursts and depression (Silver et al., 2011). Some patients develop addictive behaviors such as excessive alcohol use to "soothe" themselves. Poor pretrauma relationships interfere with the establishment of a therapeutic or working alliance that is crucial for maintaining long-term employment (Prigatano et al., 1994). Some patients have limited empathy skills (Williams & Wood, 2017) and are resistant to helping others. They may also resist using compensations and accepting lifestyle changes necessary to remain productive and to establish or re-establish a sense of meaning in their life. Thus, the psychological care of this particular group of individuals is especially challenging and requires psychological intervention skills to combat the barriers to successful long-term care.

THE IMPORTANCE OF DREAMS, MUSIC, ARTWORK, AND FAIRY TALES IN THE PSYCHOLOGICAL CARE OF PATIENTS WITH MODERATE TO SEVERE TRAUMATIC BRAIN INJURY

One of the unexpected benefits of participating in holistic or milieu-oriented NRPs was the observation and ultimately the recognition that a strict brain–behavior approach to neuropsychological rehabilitation was much too limited when helping these patients deal with the problems they faced in life (Prigatano et al., 1984). As I (2018) have stated elsewhere, "The patient's subjective experience of how they were affected by their brain injury influenced the process and outcome of rehabilitation and therefore the person's level of psychological adjustment. Their subjective experience is revealed in many different ways" (p. 822).

Although patients' verbal reports certainly are an important source of information about what they experience, some patients cannot easily put into words what they are struggling with on a daily basis. Their favorite choice of music, metaphors about life, and movies they watch repeatedly provide rich insights into what they are experiencing. Their dreams and favorite fairy tales read to them as a child often have special significance for their personal struggles in adult life after a TBI. Finally, their spontaneous drawings or artwork can give the psychological clinician insights regarding their phenomenological experiences that may not be obvious.

The first clear example came from working with adult patients with severe TBI at Presbyterian Hospital in Oklahoma City (Prigatano et al., 1984). Many of these patients had a "cowboy background." As such, they were not inclined to discuss personal feelings with anyone, especially not in groups. They clearly felt uncomfortable talking about how the brain injury had affected them. They were not as educated as the treating therapists, they often came from different cultural backgrounds, and consequently they felt awkward about revealing personal information. However, they all loved country-and-western music.

It was suggested that each person in the group, including the two clinical neuropsychologists/psychotherapists conducting the group, bring in their favorite song and let others listen to it. It was agreed that the group members would respond only to the feelings that the song stimulated in them. The person bringing in the favorite song did not have to say why he or she liked it. To "break the ice," an occupational therapist suggested to one of the psychotherapists that they might begin by playing Merle Haggard's song, "When Heaven Was a Drink of Wine." The song has many important lyrics, including the following: "That psycho-out psychologist asking about my drinking ways, but if the truth were known I never took a drink until she was gone and then Heaven was a drink of wine." Other lyrics include "Hey good doctor, I have something on my mind you can't find." The cowboys from Oklahoma loved this song, and they began to bring in their own favorite music, which often reflected their personal struggles and feelings. One song was "Big Wheels Turning," a song about a truck driver who returns home after a long night away from his wife. The patient was estranged from his wife after his brain injury, and the song was used to express his sadness and longing to be with her again. Another patient played "Sleeping Single in a Double Bed." The message was also clear: He was no longer with his wife and greatly missed her. Another song was "She Is Raising Cain in Texas and I Am Pulling Weeds in Tennessee." As the songs were played, a group cohesion often occurred as patients were able to talk about what was really bothering them. Generally, this led to valuable dialogue, which seemed to help patients become accepted in the group and ultimately to be more accepting of their situation in life.

The song a person picked, however, sometimes did not have this effect. At such times, it seemed to herald a poor clinical outcome. For example, one patient played his favorite song, "Bad to the Bone." The female patients and therapists were uncomfortable listening to this music and felt the hostility this patient had toward women. The patient could not accept his physical limitations caused by his TBI and became increasingly more violent. He was eventually placed in an inpatient psychiatric facility, and his wife divorced him because of his continued abusive behavior toward her.

Several years after severe TBI, songs and music often provide important insights into what a patient is experiencing following the brain injury. For example, a quiet, highly intelligent professional man suffered a moderate to severe TBI. During the first year following his TBI, he appeared to make an excellent (but not complete) neuropsychological recovery. His test scores suggested that he might be able to return to his professional responsibilities.

With the consent of his physicians and a clinical neuropsychologist, he did return to his demanding job. Within a few years, however, he experienced difficulties with organization and planning. He could not guide a team of co-workers as effectively as he once did. His professional empire deteriorated, and he found another job site to practice his trade. His thought was that other people were getting in his way and a new environment would most likely bring success. When this failed, he became deeply withdrawn and avoided social interaction with others. He was drawn to the movie *Beauty and Beast*.

Like the prince in the movie, the patient believed he had lost everything. He could not openly express his rage (not just anger) and retreated to the "west wing." This was a euphemism for isolating himself from others so that they would be spared his rage. Listening to the songs in this movie and going over the storyline helped him have an external set of images to which he could relate but could not verbally express despite his superior intelligence. As Dora Kalff (1980) noted, when the internal (or inner) problem is made exterior, it often points to the next step in development. This was certainly true in helping guide this person's psychological adjustment in a positive manner several years after the TBI.

Several years after formal neuropsychological rehabilitation, another, less favorable outcome was observed. A young woman with a moderate to severe TBI struggled with worsening depression. In an effort to help her, the treating clinical neuropsychologist emphasized her need to engage in a voluntary work trial. She believed that this was not necessary and in some ways was detrimental to her lifestyle. In the course of attempted psychotherapy, she dreamed that a doctor had given her a very large contact lens and asked her to place it in her eye. The task was impossible; the clinical neuropsychologist was asking too much of her. She eventually ended psychotherapy because the issue could not be resolved. Her long-term psychological adjustment did not appear positive.

In previous writings, I have given examples of how patients' drawings and favorite fairy tales help the clinician understand their reactions in neuropsychological rehabilitation and their ultimate adjustment (Prigatano, 1986, 1991, 1999; Prigatano & Salas, 2017). The point of these remarks is that entering the symbolic world of patients is important in their psychological care, particularly when they struggle with issues they cannot verbalize but that need to be addressed in order to help them. Not all patients communicate via artistic expressions, but many do if one listens to their songs, asks about their dreams, and looks at their spontaneous drawings.

As stated previously in this book, holistic forms of neuropsychological rehabilitation, if successful, build resiliency in patients. However, the patients still have to deal with the long-term struggles that are inevitable after moderate to severe TBI. This reality has become clearer with time by interacting with patients over several years. Next, three case vignettes are presented that reflect common features of positive and negative psychological adjustment following a moderate to severe TBI.

PSYCHOLOGICAL CARE OF YOUNG ADULTS WHO SUFFERED MODERATE TO SEVERE TRAUMATIC BRAIN INJURY AND UNDERWENT A HOLISTIC NEUROPSYCHOLOGICAL REHABILITATION PROGRAM

This section presents three case vignettes involving young adults who suffered severe TBI and who also underwent a holistic neuropsychologically oriented rehabilitation program as described by Prigatano (1986). The first case illustrates a positive outcome with continued psychological care supports. The second case illustrates an initial positive outcome with later decline despite efforts at continued psychological care. The role of premorbid personality characteristics and relationship issues with parents appeared to determine the long-term outcome for these two individuals. The third case vignette illustrates how a song greatly influenced the course of one patient's neuropsychological rehabilitation and continued to help her maintain a positive psychological adjustment after formal rehabilitation was complete.

Case Vignette 21.1

While serving in the military, a 21-year-old single man fell from a bridge and suffered the classic bilateral hemorrhagic injuries to the frontal cortex and tips of the temporal lobes often observed in severe TBI. At the time he was seen (1981), MRI scans were not in existence, but his CT scan revealed these injuries. He was involved in an NRP for approximately 1 year after the injury. At the time, he was cooperative but demonstrated a restriction in his range of affect. His emotional responses often appeared blunted. He moved slowly and talked slowly. His intellectual abilities and memory were severely compromised. He appeared to lack awareness of the extent of his cognitive and behavioral limitations. He had very unrealistic vocational goals. A summary of his course of rehabilitation is presented elsewhere (Prigatano, 1986, pp. 57–59).

Two seminal factors were important in this man's long-term, positive psychological adjustment. Although his vocational goals were unrealistic, he was guided to do volunteer work that he could adequately accomplish during his rehabilitation program. With this achievement, he was later helped to get part-time paid employment cleaning rooms in a hotel. Although he would periodically voice his disappointment that he could not do more in life, he experienced satisfaction related to two aspects of his work. First, he enjoyed interacting with co-workers, who seemed to like him and wanted him to be a part of their team. Second, he had a real sense of personal pride in doing his job well (although slowly). Previously, he had much greater aspirations in life, but in light of his cognitive and motor limitations and because of the two previously mentioned important job experiences he continued to enjoy, he was able to accept where he was in life.

As the patient was followed throughout the years, he would periodically voice his old desire to do other work. With the repetitive guidance of a clinical neuropsychologist and insightful parents, he was encouraged to continue with his current job. He maintained that job for several years while living with his parents, who continued to provide guidance for him, given his substantial neuropsychological impairments. He had a good relationship with both parents before and after the injury. He sensed that they were always trying to help him and consequently accepted their advice and guidance. He felt the same way toward the clinical neuropsychologist. These relationships seemed to foster resilience in dealing with his situation.

Another important neuropsychological feature was that he was not impulsive. He thought and acted slowly. Traditional efforts at psychotherapy were not attempted, but making time to talk with him, listening to his concerns and the concerns of his parents, and guiding him when he was faced with difficult life challenges seemed to greatly aid his overall positive psychological adjustment.

Continued periodic long-term consulting sessions with the patient and his parents helped him maintain his job and live with his parents without further psychiatric deterioration. Table 21.2 summarizes clinical features of his care. Table 21.3 summarizes clinical features of his mother, who worked most closely with the rehabilitation staff and the treating clinical neuropsychologist.

Table 21.2 Clinical Features Relevant to the Psychological Care of the Patient Described in Case Vignette 21.1

CLINICAL FEATURE	YES	NO	PARTIALLY
1. The dialogue between the patient and the clinical neuropsychologist was not rushed.	✓		
2. The patient was able to express his personal concerns with limited cognitive capacities and language skills.	✓		
3. The content of the concerns varied over time and reflected the patient's stage of functioning.			✓
4. The patient did not experience "being alone" with his problem(s).	✓		
5. The patient and the clinical neuropsychologist developed a positive therapeutic relationship in which the patient's dignity was maintained even in the face of significant physical and cognitive losses.	✓		
6. Somatic symptoms (which appeared to be indirect effects of a brain disorder) were substantially reduced during periods of psychological care.		✓	
7. Anxiety/depression/anger and/or apathy were substantially reduced during periods of psychological care.		✓	
8. The patient was able to follow the guidance of the clinical neuropsychologist to improve functioning in everyday life activities and avoid dangerous behaviors given his limited competencies (e.g., driving a car, and attempting to handle finances).	✓		
9. The patient was able to control impulses and delay gratification.	✓		
10. The patient actively worked at developing self-efficacy skills "in the face" of his impaired abilities.	✓		
11. The patient attempted to "self-reflect" or "be more aware" of personal "strengths" and "limitations."	✓		
12. The patient experienced enjoyment in the care or help of other living things (people, animals, the environment, etc.).	✓		
13. The patient experienced an understanding of the "problematic nature of their unique life" and was not overwhelmed or "defeated" by it or readily gave in to escapism to cope with life (Bettelheim, 1989).	✓		
14. The patient could "live with" the restrictions produced by a brain injury "without resentment" or loss of hope (Goldstein, 1952).			✓

(*continued*)

Table 21.2 Continued

CLINICAL FEATURE	YES	NO	PARTIALLY
15. The patient was able to obtain new insights into self by attending to why certain songs, stories, fairy tales, movies, tattoos, etc. had a special personal meaning that initially he did not understand.		✓	
16. The patient's dreams or artwork often heralded changes in behavior that aided psychological adjustment before the consciously mediated changes occurred.		✓	
17. The psychological care interventions (including the dialogue) between the patient and the clinical neuropsychologist resulted in the patient talking more openly about problems and demonstrating self-directed efforts at improving psychological adjustment to the direct and indirect effects of the brain disorder.	✓		
18. The psychological care interventions were in harmony with the patient's cultural background and religious orientation.	✓		
19. The psychological care interventions facilitated psychosocial development/adaptation in the later stages of life.			✓
20. The patient and family experienced two basic facts of life: (a) The individual's state of subjective sense of personal well-being fluctuates and (b) the psychological adjustment process is never static and therefore hope should never be abandoned.	✓		
Total	13	4	3

Table 21.3 Clinically Relevant Features of the Mother of the Patient Described in Case Vignette 21.1

CLINICAL FEATURE	YES	NO	PARTIALLY
1. The quality of the relationship before the onset of the brain disorder was good.	✓		
2. The mother has adequate supports that help maintain her resiliency.	✓		
3. The mother is personally offended by the behavioral problems of the patient.		✓	
4. The mother has a good working (therapeutic) relationship with the clinical neuropsychologist.	✓		
5. The mother understands the biological factors (and at times the psychological factors) underlying the behavioral problems of the patient.	✓		
6. The mother does not feel alone in the care of the patient.	✓		
7. The mother has some sense of hope that the behavioral problems will get better with time and/or there is "light at the end of the tunnel."			✓

Case Vignette 21.2

As a 30-year-old woman was driving her car along a mountain road, a large boulder fell and struck her vehicle, causing her to sustain a moderate to severe TBI. Certain clinical features of her case were described in Chapter 9. What is relevant to this discussion is her early reluctance to engage in certain forms of cognitive rehabilitation, even though her cognitive deficits were obvious to her and others. She wanted only physically oriented therapies. She also was cautious in discussing her personal situation with her parents and the treating clinical neuropsychologist. As noted in Chapter 9, she discussed her intense fear of her mother only toward the end of her holistic NRP. Finally, she struggled to engage in volunteer work. Although she expressed some enjoyment of the activity, she never seemed really satisfied with what she was doing or emotionally connected with the people in her work environment. Moreover, at the end of her formal rehabilitation program, she would not take any entry-level job in the same geographical location as her parents' home. Unlike the first patient described in this chapter, she was fearful and distrusted her mother. She viewed her father as somewhat impotent to deal with her mother's rage reactions. With the guidance of a clinical neuropsychologist and rehabilitation therapist, she began part-time employment in an area closer to one of her siblings but several hundred miles away from her parents.

The patient was provided with outpatient psychotherapy services in her home environment by a psychologist who was not a part of her original rehabilitation team. Her depression increased with time, and she began to drink alcohol heavily (a problem that existed prior to her brain injuries). She did not follow the guidance of the psychologist or other family members to avoid certain relationships that appeared exploitive. Her heavy drinking continued, and she eventually died of liver failure. Pre-existing relationship issues and an inability to trust in the guidance of others who attempted to help her were painfully obvious. Table 21.4 summarizes the clinical features relevant to this patient's psychological care. Clinical features of the patient's parents were quite different from each other and are separately described in Tables 21.5 and 21.6.

Table 21.4 Clinical Features Relevant to the Psychological Care of the Person Described in Case Vignette 21.2

CLINICAL FEATURE	YES	NO	PARTIALLY
1. The dialogue between the patient and the clinical neuropsychologist was not rushed	✓		
2. The patient was able to express or clearly convey her personal concerns.			✓
3. The content of the concerns varied over time.			✓
4. The patient experienced a sense of "realistic" hope in coping with her life's situation.		✓	
5. The patient and the clinical neuropsychologist developed a positive therapeutic relationship that helped the patient sustain adaptive activities during difficult times.			✓

(continued)

Table 21.4 Continued

CLINICAL FEATURE	YES	NO	PARTIALLY
6. Somatic symptoms (which appeared to be indirect effects of a brain disorder) were substantially reduced during periods of psychological care.			✓
7. Anxiety/depression/anger and/or apathy were substantially reduced during periods of psychological care.		✓	
8. The patient was able to follow the guidance of the clinical neuropsychologist to improve functioning in everyday life activities.			✓
9. The patient was able to control impulses and delay gratification.		✓	
10. The patient developed a new sense of competency or "mastery" in her life following the brain disorder.		✓	
11. The patient attempted to "self-reflect" or "be more aware" of personal "strengths" and "limitations."			✓
12. The patient experienced enjoyment in the care or help of other living things (people, animals, the environment, etc.).			✓
13. The patient experienced an understanding of the "problematic nature of their unique life" and was not overwhelmed or "defeated" by it or readily gave in to escapism to cope with life (Bettelheim, 1989).		✓	
14. The patient could "live with" the restrictions produced by a brain injury "without resentment" or loss of hope (Goldstein, 1952).		✓	
15. The patient was able to obtain new insights into self by attending to why certain songs, stories, fairy tales, movies, tattoos, etc. had a special personal meaning that initially she did not understand.			✓
16. The patient's dreams or artwork often heralded changes in behavior that aided psychological adjustment before the consciously mediated changes occurred.		✓	
17. The psychological care interventions (including the dialogue) between the patient and the clinical neuropsychologist resulted in the patient talking more openly about problems and demonstrating self-directed efforts at improving psychological adjustment to the direct and indirect effects of the brain disorder.		✓	
18. The psychological care interventions were in harmony with the patient's cultural background and religious orientation.	✓		

Table 21.4 Continued

CLINICAL FEATURE	YES	NO	PARTIALLY
19. The psychological care interventions were appropriate for the psychosocial stage of development/adaptation in later stages of life.		✓	
20. The patient and family experienced two basic facts of life: (a) The individual's state of subjective sense of personal well-being fluctuates and (b) the psychological adjustment process is never static and therefore hope should never be abandoned.		✓	
Total	2	10	8

Table 21.5 Clinically Relevant Features of the Mother of the Patient Described in Case Vignette 21.2

CLINICAL FEATURE	YES	NO	PARTIALLY
1. The quality of the relationship before the onset of the brain disorder was good.		✓	
2. The mother has adequate supports that help maintain her resiliency.		✓	
3. The mother is personally offended by the behavioral problems of the patient.			✓
4. The mother has a good working (therapeutic) relationship with the clinical neuropsychologist.			✓
5. The mother understands the biological factors (and at times the psychological factors) underlying the behavioral problems of the patient.		✓	
6. The mother does not feel alone in the care of the patient.	✓		
7. The mother has some sense of hope that the behavioral problems will get better with time and/or there is "light at the end of the tunnel."			✓

Table 21.6 Clinically Relevant Features of the Father of the Patient Described in Case Vignette 21.2

CLINICAL FEATURE	YES	NO	PARTIALLY
1. The quality of the relationship before the onset of the brain disorder was good.	✓		
2. The father has adequate supports that help maintain his resiliency.			✓
3. The father is personally offended by the behavioral problems of the patient.		✓	

(continued)

Table 21.6 Continued

CLINICAL FEATURE	YES	NO	PARTIALLY
4. The father has a good working (therapeutic) relationship with the clinical neuropsychologist.			✓
5. The father understands the biological factors (and at times the psychological factors) underlying the behavioral problems of the patient.		✓	
6. The father does not feel alone in the care of the patient.	✓		
7. The father has some sense of hope that the behavioral problems will get better with time and/or there is "light at the end of the tunnel."			✓

Case Vignette 21.3

A bright young college student with outstanding athletic skills was involved in a severe motor vehicle accident. She suffered the classic neuropathological lesions involving the frontal and temporal regions of the brain, as well as an injury to her cerebellum and upper brain stem. She was confined to a wheelchair, which she of course hated. She had trouble with basic truncal movements and could not stand up without losing her balance. Her dreams of being a professional athlete were gone. To add to this devastating situation, she had significant cognitive impairments and would often smile and behave in a childlike manner. These latter problems are frequently seen following significant bilateral frontal lobe injuries, which were evident on her neuroimaging studies.

Although the patient was originally cooperative with holistic neuropsychological rehabilitation activities, she began to become excessively aggressive, often expressing her anger and frustration when she was unable to perform basic activities of independent living. Her peers were estranged from her, and the likelihood of her having a long-term, intimate relationship with another seemed unlikely, if not impossible. Her expressions of anger escalated as she faced one frustrating situation after another when involved in physical therapy, speech therapy, occupational therapy, and cognitive retraining exercises. At one point, the therapists raised the question of whether the patient was too impaired to benefit from the type of rehabilitation program in which she was enrolled.

After several weeks of rehabilitation efforts, music was played in one group psychotherapy session in which the patient participated. All members of the group were asked to play their favorite song. The patient listened intently to the songs others played that emotionally touched them. The songs covered many different topics and associated feelings. One patient in the group played the Beatles' song, "Yesterday." The lyrics spoke of being half the man today that he was yesterday. This struck the patient, who had considerable cognitive difficulties, as being true for her as well. She struggled with the song she would play, and she eventually chose Michael Jackson's song, "Man in the Mirror." The message of the song was clear: If you want to make the world a better place, start by looking at the man (or woman you are) in the mirror—*and make a change*. This song was inspirational to her, and she recognized—with very limited cognitive resources but with a premorbid history of resiliency—that she had to change her attitude about herself and life. She began to control her emotional reactions and became less impulsively angry when something disturbed her. She began to recognize that she still could do some limited work, even if she could not finish college and be a professional athlete.

The patient's mother noted that an important change had occurred in her daughter, who eventually returned home to live with her parents and to work in a volunteer job setting in which she found satisfaction. Her story has not ended, but the role of music in helping her express feelings and aspirations she could not verbally express is undeniable. The right song at the right time helped this patient clarify a simple but important direction in her life. It made a world of difference in the outcome of her NRP. She continues to be active in her volunteer work and has fewer angry outbursts. Music continues to help her control her mood and behavior despite her persistent and severe cognitive impairments. Table 21.7 summarizes the clinical features relevant to this patient's psychological care.

Table 21.7 Clinical Features Relevant to the Psychological Care of the Person Described in Case Vignette 21.3

CLINICAL FEATURE	YES	NO	PARTIALLY
1. The dialogue between the patient and the clinical neuropsychologist was not rushed.	✓		
2. The patient was able to express her personal concerns with limited cognitive capacities and language skills.			✓
3. The content of the concerns varied over time and reflected the patient's stage of decline.			✓
4. The patient did not experience "being alone" with her problem(s).	✓		
5. The patient and the clinical neuropsychologist developed a positive therapeutic relationship in which the patient's dignity was maintained even in the face of significant physical and cognitive losses.	✓		
6. Somatic symptoms (which appeared to be indirect effects of a brain disorder) were substantially reduced during periods of psychological care.		✓	
7. Anxiety/depression/anger and/or apathy were substantially reduced during periods of psychological care.	✓		
8. The patient was able to follow the guidance of the clinical neuropsychologist to improve functioning in everyday life activities and avoid dangerous behaviors given her limited competencies (e.g., driving a car, and attempting to handle finances).			✓
9. The patient was able to control impulses and delay gratification.			✓
10. The patient actively worked at developing self-efficacy skills "in the face" of her impaired abilities.	✓		
11. The patient attempted to "self-reflect" or "be more aware" of personal "strengths" and "limitations."			✓

(continued)

Table 21.7 Continued

CLINICAL FEATURE	YES	NO	PARTIALLY
12. The patient experienced enjoyment in the care or help of other living things (people, animals, the environment, etc.).	✓		
13. The patient experienced an understanding of the "problematic nature of their unique life" and was not overwhelmed or "defeated" by it or readily gave in to escapism to cope with life (Bettelheim, 1989).	✓		
14. The patient could "live with" the restrictions produced by a brain injury "without resentment" or loss of hope (Goldstein, 1952).			✓
15. The patient was able to obtain new insights into self by attending to why certain songs, stories, fairy tales, movies, tattoos, etc. had a special personal meaning that initially she did not understand.	✓		
16. The patient's dreams or artwork often heralded changes in behavior that aided psychological adjustment before the consciously mediated changes occurred.		✓	
17. The psychological care interventions (including the dialogue) between the patient and the clinical neuropsychologist resulted in the patient talking more openly about problems and demonstrating self-directed efforts at improving psychological adjustment to the direct and indirect effects of the brain disorder.			✓
18. The psychological care interventions were in harmony with the patient's cultural background and religious orientation.	✓		
19. The psychological care interventions facilitated psychosocial development/adaptation in the later stages of life.			✓
20. The patient and family experienced two basic facts of life: (a) The individual's state of subjective sense of personal well-being fluctuates and (b) the psychological adjustment process is never static and therefore hope should never be abandoned.	✓		
Total	10	2	8

APPROACHES TO POST-ACUTE PSYCHOLOGICAL CARE OF PERSONS WITH MODERATE TO SEVERE TRAUMATIC BRAIN INJURY

Given the complexity and diversity of cognitive and behavioral problems associated with moderate to severe TBI in older adolescents and adults, it has become progressively clear that a comprehensive, holistic approach to neuropsychological rehabilitation is often necessary to help these individuals. Once patients with a history of post-acute moderate to severe TBI have completed formal neuropsychological rehabilitation, their long-term psychological adjustment can be positive, negative, or at times mixed. Much depends on the nature of the brain injury, premorbid personality features, and the ability to sustain adaptive efforts in the face of residual difficulties. The adjustment course typically fluctuates, but one can estimate whether overall the outcome was favorable to the patient and to the family.

Many variables contribute to the long-term psychological well-being of individuals with a moderate to severe TBI. There are hundreds of studies that directly and indirectly bear on this topic. Prigatano and Salas (2017) suggested that these studies can be grouped to address four levels of psychological care. The first level of care is to focus on symptom reduction. The goal is to primarily reduce disturbing symptoms, such as headaches, angry outbursts, depression, anxiety, irritability, and social withdrawal. The second level of care is to help patients avoid "escapism" from their clinical condition. For adolescents and adults, this often means helping them avoid various addictive behaviors (e.g., drug abuse, alcoholism, and sexual promiscuity) and reduce disruptive behaviors that interfere with school or work activities. The third level of care focuses on helping patients deal effectively with their "altered sense of self." This often involves efforts at improving interpersonal relationships, fostering self-control, enhancing competence skills, and establishing or re-establishing a sense of identify following the TBI. The fourth level of care is built on all three preceding levels of care. It directly attempts to help patients establish or re-establish a sense of meaning in life, given the losses they have experienced and the limitations they continue to face on a daily basis. The latter two levels of care often involve addressing both conscious and unconscious strivings as these patients deal with adversity and loss. All four levels of care can be observed at each stage of the life cycle after moderate to severe TBI. A sample of studies and clinical case reports that address these levels of care is summarized here.

Pharmacological interventions to control aggressive behavior and depression are often the first line of defense in the psychological care of persons with moderate to severe TBI (Arciniegas & Silver, 2011). However, such treatments are seldom adequate in and of themselves. Behavioral approaches have been shown to be helpful in controlling specific behavioral symptoms associated with TBI (McMillan & Wood, 2017). Several examples can be given regarding this first level of care. For example, Walker et al. (2010) developed a 12-week psychoeducational anger management program based on a cognitive–behavioral therapy (CBT) model to help adults with severe TBI control their aggression and expressions of anger. Expressions of anger before and after treatment were measured. No control group, however, was employed. Investigators reported a decrease in the expression of anger following these sessions.

Hsieh, Ponsford, Wong, and McKay (2012) reported on the potential effectiveness of reducing anxiety in adults with moderate to severe TBI using CBT approaches in addition to motivational interviewing. Although sample sizes were small, the combination of CBT with motivational interviewing resulted in greater treatment size effects compared to CBT without motivational interviewing. Motivational interviewing was viewed as potentially important for helping engage patients in the therapeutic activities.

Bédard et al. (2014) evaluated the potential effectiveness of a mindfulness-based cognitive therapy program in reducing depression in patients with a history of TBI. The authors compared self-report symptoms of depression in patients enrolled in a 10-week mindfulness-based cognitive therapy group versus a wait-list control group. There was greater self-reported reduction in the treated group versus the control group.

In another treatment versus wait-list control group study, Simpson, Tate, Whiting, and Cotter (2011) examined self-reported feelings of hopelessness following 10 weekly 2-hour sessions of a manualized group treatment program. This program involved multiple activities, but all activities seemed to focus on engaging the patients to understand the causes of their distress and take practical steps to reduce their social isolation. Small numbers of subjects were studied (eight in the treatment group and nine in the wait-list control). Perhaps the major value of this study was to demonstrate that without active treatment efforts, patients in the control group tended to show a worsening of their symptoms with time, whereas those receiving the treatment showed the opposite pattern.

There are fewer studies on the second level of care. Although drug and alcohol addictions are frequently reported in patients with a history of moderate to severe TBI, studies on the effectiveness of psychological treatments for reducing these problems in adults are very limited. In a recent report, mindfulness training seemed to help patients with substance abuse disorders and TBI (Kristofersson, Beckers, & Krueger, 2016). However, this remains the less explored area of psychological treatment for this patient group.

Holistic approaches to NRPs have focused on returning individuals to a protective lifestyle and thereby indirectly helping them with issues of self-acceptance and establishing a renewed sense of identity and personal meaning in life (Ben-Yishay & Diller, 2011; Klonoff, 2010; Prigatano, 1986). Holistic approaches have addressed all levels of care but have made explicit the need for third and fourth levels of care. Because the research findings of such programs are reasonably well known, only a brief summary of the findings is presented.

In the first study that compared TBI young adults with a matched group of TBI individuals who could not receive such rehabilitation (primarily because of financial constraints), Prigatano et al. (1984) reported three important findings. First, according to relatives' perceptions, patients undergoing such treatments showed considerably less emotional distress compared to nontreated patients. Second, patients' neuropsychological functions were not substantially improved following such interventions, but treated patients were more likely to be employed following rehabilitation compared to nontreated patients. Third, impaired self-awareness in TBI patients appeared to be a major barrier to successful rehabilitation.

Prigatano et al. (1994) replicated the employment findings described in the initial study by Prigatano et al. (1984). In addition, they demonstrated for the first time that the quality of the working alliance (or therapeutic relationship) between the therapist and the patient (and family members) correlated with which patients returned to work after their rehabilitation program: The better the relationship, the more likely the person was to be employed after such rehabilitation efforts.

Colleagues in Denmark followed up on this latter observation and reported similar findings (Schönberger, Humle, Zeeman, & Teasdale, 2006). The quality of the working alliance between the treating neuropsychologist and the patient did indeed correlate with employment status of the individuals in a larger group of patients with a history of either TBI or a cerebral vascular accident. Improving the working alliance between the treatment team and the patient thus became a very important feature of this form of rehabilitation.

Disturbances in self-awareness seemed to interfere with the development of a good working alliance with the patient. This clinical observation was also empirically demonstrated by colleagues in Denmark (Schönberger, Humle, & Teasdale, 2006). They further noted that patients who tended to overestimate their cognitive abilities (i.e., demonstrate ISA) often showed the same pattern at the end of their rehabilitation program. Smeets et al. (2017) further replicated this finding. The implication is clear: If one is to help patients with moderate to severe TBI sustain a productive lifestyle and thereby improve resiliency and their quality of life, a better understanding and better management of disorders of self-awareness are necessary. This often requires having a reasonable understanding of patients' neuropsychological status and their psychodynamic features and cultural background.

Table 21.8 Approaches to the Psychological Care of Persons with Cognitive and Behavioral Disorders After Traumatic Brain Injury

INTERVENTION	STUDY SAMPLE	MAJOR FINDINGS	CONCLUSIONS
Metaphoric identity mapping: facilitating goal setting and engagement in rehabilitation after TBI (Ylvisaker et al., 2008)	After reviewing the need to find a method of helping both children and adults improve their organizational skills and identify practical and achievable goals in rehabilitation that have appeal for them, these investigators report on the use of identity-oriented goal setting (IOG) to guide the rehabilitation efforts of five adults with a history of moderate to severe TBI. They emphasize, however, that the use of personally relevant metaphors about life as well as identifying a "metaphoric hero" in the person's life can meaningfully guide the IOG.	Having these individuals think of themselves as the kind of person they admire and establishing goals that have personal meaning to them were not only helpful in guiding rehabilitation goal setting but also led to engagement of these goals by their patients. The authors noted, however, that cognitive deficits often posed obstacles in following through on agreed upon goals. Despite the obstacles, revisiting the identity map at the beginning of each session resulted in greater engagement in the rehabilitation process and a stronger working alliance (or rapport) with the therapists. These were qualitative observations by the investigators.	Although phrased in cognitive–behavioral terminology, this paper highlights a key point made by clinicians involved in holistic neuropsychological rehabilitation programs that incorporate traditional forms of psychotherapy adjusted to the neuropsychological status of the patients. Namely, entering their phenomenological field and reducing their frustration and confusion by identifying goals that have both a conscious and an unconscious appeal results in a better working alliance and often a better treatment outcome (Prigatano, 1999). Helping a patient relate to a specific hero's journey may be especially important (Prigatano, 2012).
Neuropsychological rehabilitation after closed head injury in adults (Prigatano et al., 1984)	18 young adults with severe TBI who underwent a neuropsychological rehabilitation program modeled after the work of Ben-Yishay and Diller were compared to 17 adults who did not receive such care. Patients' neuropsychological, emotional, and employment status post treatment were compared.	There were no major changes in neuropsychological status between the two groups, but there was a trend for modest improvement in speed of performance and memory in the treated group. Treated patients had significantly fewer behavioral disturbances and were more frequently described by relatives as less socially withdrawn, less restless, and less helpless. Half of the patients were working after undergoing this form of neuropsychological rehabilitation compared to 36% of controls.	Findings suggested that treated patients had improved interpersonal skills and showed less emotional distress than untreated TBI patients. A good work history prior to TBI and a supportive social milieu outside of neuropsychological rehabilitation appeared to be related to a positive outcome. Ongoing problems with limited or impaired self-awareness of their difficulties seemed to negatively affect outcome.

(*continued*)

Table 21.8 Continued

INTERVENTION	STUDY SAMPLE	MAJOR FINDINGS	CONCLUSIONS
Productivity after neuropsychological-oriented milieu rehabilitation (Prigatano et al., 1994)	38 TBI patients who completed a neuropsychological rehabilitation program, as described by Prigatano et al. (1994), were compared to 37 TBI patients who did not undergo such a program.	Patients receiving this form of rehabilitation were more productive and at a similar level previously reported by Prigatano et al. (1984). Treated patients who were productive had a good/excellent working alliance with therapists, whereas nonproductive patients did not.	Not only were earlier reported figures of return to work after severe TBI replicated but also, for the first time, the importance of the therapeutic or working alliance for productivity outcome was demonstrated.
Working alliance and psychosocial outcome after undergoing a holistic neuropsychological rehabilitation program (Schonberger et al., 2006)	The study evaluated the hypothesis that the quality of the working alliance between the patient and treating psychological clinicians related to whether a person with a brain disorder was working at the end of a holistic neuropsychological rehabilitation program. Data were obtained on 98 patients undergoing this form of rehabilitation. 27% had a history of TBI, and 59% had a history of CVA.	A good/excellent working alliance with the treating neuropsychologist was clearly associated with employment, whereas a poor/fair working alliance was not. This replicated results from an earlier report by Prigatano et al. (1994).	This study reaffirms that the strength of the working alliance between the treating psychological clinician and the person with a moderate to severe brain injury clearly relates to whether the patient engages in employment after rehabilitation. As noted throughout this book, maintaining a productive lifestyle is clearly related to quality of life.
Changes in impaired self-awareness after acquired brain injury in patients following intensive neuropsychological rehabilitation (Smeets et al., 2017)	Smeets et al. studied different patterns of impaired self-awareness in brain dysfunctional patients undergoing a neuropsychological rehabilitation program modeled on the work of Ben-Yishay and Diller. The authors related those patterns to the patients' emotional status and quality of life. 78 patients were included in the study (44.9% had a history of TBI).	Several findings are reported. 20 patients overestimated their abilities, 35% of which had a history of TBI. Although a few patients who showed overestimation became more accurate in their self-appraisal of their neuropsychological abilities following such rehabilitation, the majority of overestimators did not. Elevated depression was observed in individuals who tended to underestimate their abilities.	The tendency to overestimate one's competencies after a brain disorder does not frequently change after intensive neuropsychological rehabilitation efforts. This may be why the quality of the working alliance is so important in guiding these patients' behavior before and after such rehabilitation efforts.

IOG, identity-oriented goal setting; TBI, traumatic brain injury.

One final observation is relevant to the discussion of the psychological care of adolescents and young adults with a history of moderate to severe TBI. Psychodynamic insights are often not recognized by skilled behaviorally oriented therapists. Yet the importance of such insights can be found in their work using similar concepts couched in behavioral terms. Ylvisaker, McPherson, Kayes, and Pellett (2008), for example, used the term *metaphoric identity mapping* to help individuals identify personally relevant rehabilitation goals they were willing to work toward, given that they had deep personal meaning to the individuals. The authors noted that this is sometimes achieved by exploring heroic figures with whom the patients identify and using this knowledge to guide their behavioral management. This is a distinct Jungian concept, even though it was not recognized as such by these investigators (Prigatano, 2012).

Several of the studies mentioned previously are summarized in Table 21.8.

SUMMARY

The literature on providing psychological care for adolescents and young adults who have suffered moderate to severe TBI is perhaps the most extensive scientific literature to be found. Yet it is a very incomplete literature. This is in part due to the great variability in premorbid features of these individuals and the myriad of physical, cognitive, behavioral, and personality changes associated with this devastating condition. Detailed case studies are needed to provide clinicians a better understanding of how to best approach individual patients, and some efforts have been undertaken in this regard (Ben-Yishay & Diller, 2016). Of course, randomized control group studies are potentially valuable, but unless the generalized group findings can be applied to individual patients, the value of these studies for sustained psychological care for these patients remains unclear. What is clear, however, is that the quality of the therapeutic alliance and the patients' realistic appraisal (i.e., subjective awareness) of their clinical condition appear important in the long-term psychological care of individuals with a known brain disorder.

REFERENCES

Arciniegas, D. B., Anderson, C. A., & Rojas, D. C. (2011). Electrophysiological assessment. In J. M. Silver, S. C. Yudofsky, & T. W. McAllister (Eds.), *Textbook of traumatic brain injury* (2nd ed., pp. 115–126). Washington, DC: American Psychiatric Publishing.

Arciniegas, D. B., & Silver, J. M. (2011). Psychopharmacology. In J. M. Silver, T. W. McAllister, & S. C. Yudofsky (Eds.), *Textbook of traumatic brain injury* (2nd ed., pp. 553–569). Washington, DC: American Psychiatric Publishing.

Bédard, M., Felteau, M., Marshall, S., Cullen, N., Gibbons, C., Dubois, S., . . . Rees, L. (2014). Mindfulness-based cognitive therapy reduces symptoms of depression in people with a traumatic brain injury: Results from a randomized controlled trial. *Journal of Head Trauma Rehabilitation, 29*(4), E13–E22.

Ben-Yishay, Y., & Diller, L. (2011). *Handbook of holistic neuropsychological rehabilitation: Outpatient rehabilitation of traumatic brain injury.* New York, NY: Oxford University Press.

Ben-Yishay, Y., & Diller, L. (2016). *Turning points.* Youngsville, NC: Lash & Associates.

Ben-Yishay, Y., Rattok, J., Ross, B., Lakin, P., Silver, S., Thomas, L., & Diller, L. (1982). A rehabilitation-relevant system for cognitive, interpersonal and vocational rehabilitation of traumatically head injured persons. In Y. Ben-Yishay (Ed.), *Rehabilitation monograph No. 64: Working approaches to remediation of cognitive deficits in brain damaged persons* (pp. 1–15). New York, NY: New York University Medical Center Institute of Rehabilitation Medicine.

Bigler, E. D. (2011). Structural imaging. In J. M. Silver, T. W. McAllister, & S. C. Yudofsky (Eds.), *Textbook of traumatic brain injury* (2nd ed., pp. 73–90). Washington, DC: American Psychiatric Publishing.

Carhart-Harris, R. L., & Friston, K. J. (2010). The default-mode, ego-functions and free-energy: A neurobiological account of Freudian ideas. *Brain, 133*(4), 1265–1283.

Goldstein, K. (1942). *Aftereffects of brain injuries in war: Their evaluation and treatment. The application of psychologic methods in the clinic.* New York, NY: Grune & Stratton.

Goldstein, K. (1952). The effect of brain damage on the personality. *Psychiatry, 15*(3), 245–260.

Goldstein, K. (1954). The concept of transference in treatment of organic and functional nervous disease. *Psychotherapy and Psychosomatics, 2*(3–4), 334–353.

Hawley, C. A. (2003). Reported problems and their resolution following mild, moderate and severe traumatic brain injury amongst children and adolescents in the UK. *Brain Injury, 17*(2), 105–129.

Hoofien, D., Gilboa, A., Vakil, E., & Donovick, P. J. (2001). Traumatic brain injury (TBI) 10–20 years later: A comprehensive outcome study of psychiatric symptomatology, cognitive abilities and psychosocial functioning. *Brain Injury, 15*(3), 189–209.

Hsieh, M.-Y., Ponsford, J., Wong, D., & McKay, A. (2012). Exploring variables associated with change in cognitive behaviour therapy (CBT) for anxiety following traumatic brain injury. *Disability and Rehabilitation, 34*(5), 408–415.

Jennett, B., & Teasdale, G. (1981). *Management of head injuries*. Philadelphia, PA: Davis.

Kalff, D. (1980). *Sandplay*. Boston, MA: Beacon.

Klonoff, P. S. (2010). *Psychotherapy after brain injury: Principles and techniques*. New York, NY: Guilford.

Kristofersson, G. K., Beckers, T., & Krueger, R. (2016). Perceptions of an adapted mindfulness program for persons experiencing substance use disorders and traumatic brain injury. *Journal of Addictions Nursing, 27*(4), 247–253.

Malec, J. F. (2014). Comprehensive brain injury rehabilitation in post-hospital treatment settings. In M. Sherer & A. M. Sander (Eds.), *Handbook on the neuropsychology of traumatic brain injury* (pp. 283–307). New York, NY: Springer.

McCullagh, S., & Feinstein, A. (2011). Cognitive changes. In J. M. Silver, T. W. McAllister, & S. C. Yudofsky (Eds.), *Textbook of traumatic brain injury* (2nd ed., pp. 279–294). Washington, DC: American Psychiatric Publishing.

Mcintosh, T. K., Juhler, M., Raghupathi, R., Saatman, K., & Smith, D. (1999). Secondary brain injury: Neurochemical and cellular mediators. In D. Marion (Ed.), *Traumatic brain injury* (pp. 39–54). New York, NY: Thieme.

McMillan, T. M., & Wood, R. L. (Eds.). (2017). *Neurobehavioural disability and social handicap following traumatic brain injury* (2nd ed.). New York, NY: Routledge.

Meyer, A. (1904). The anatomical facts and clinical varieties of traumatic insanity. *American Journal of Psychiatry, 60*(3), 373–441.

Oddy, M., Coughlan, T., Tyerman, A., & Jenkins, D. (1985). Social adjustment after closed head injury: A further follow-up seven years after injury. *Journal of Neurology, Neurosurgery, and Psychiatry, 48*(6), 564–568.

Ponsford, J. L., Downing, M. G., Olver, J., Ponsford, M., Acher, R., Carty, M., & Spitz, G. (2014). Longitudinal follow-up of patients with traumatic brain injury: Outcome at two, five, and ten years post-injury. *Journal of Neurotrauma, 31*(1), 64–77.

Prigatano, G. P. (Ed.). (1986). *Neuropsychological rehabilitation after brain injury*. Baltimore, MD: Johns Hopkins University Press.

Prigatano, G. P. (1991). Disturbances of self-awareness of deficit after traumatic brain injury. In G. Prigatano & D. L. Schacter (Eds.), *Awareness of deficit after brain injury: Clinical and theoretical issues* (pp. 111–126). New York, NY: Oxford University Press.

Prigatano, G. P. (1999). *Principles of neuropsychological rehabilitation*. New York, NY: Oxford University Press.

Prigatano, G. P. (2012). Jungian contributions to successful neuropsychological rehabilitation. *Neuropsychoanalysis, 14*(2), 175–185.

Prigatano, G. P. (2018). Psychological adjustment to the effects of a moderate to severe traumatic brain injury. In J. M. Silver, T. W. McAllister, & D. B. Arciniegas (Eds.), *Textbook of traumatic brain injury* (3rd ed., pp. 817–839). Washington, DC: American Psychiatric Association Publishing.

Prigatano, G. P., Fordyce, D. J., Zeiner, H. K., Roueche, J. R., Pepping, M., & Wood, B. C. (1984). Neuropsychological rehabilitation after closed head injury in young adults. *Journal of Neurology, Neurosurgery, and Psychiatry, 47*(5), 505–513.

Prigatano, G. P., Klonoff, P. S., O'Brien, K. P., Altman, I. M., Amin, K., Chiapello, D., . . . Mora, M. (1994). Productivity after neuropsychologically oriented milieu rehabilitation. *Journal of Head Trauma Rehabilitation, 9*(1), 91–102.

Prigatano, G. P., & Salas, C. (2017). Psychodynamic psychotherapy after severe traumatic brain injury. In R. Wood, T. McMillan, & A. Worthington (Eds.), *Neurobehavioral disability and social handicap following traumatic brain injury* (pp. 188–201). Philadelphia, PA: Taylor & Francis.

Russell, W. R. (1971). *The traumatic amnesias*. Oxford, UK: Oxford University Press.

Schilder, P. (1934). Psychic disturbances after head injuries. *American Journal of Psychiatry, 91*(1), 155–188.

Schönberger, M., Humle, F., & Teasdale, T. W. (2006). Subjective outcome of brain injury rehabilitation in relation to the therapeutic working alliance, client compliance and awareness. *Brain Injury, 20*(12), 1271–1282.

Schönberger, M., Humle, F., Zeeman, P., & Teasdale, T. W. (2006). Working alliance and patient compliance in brain injury rehabilitation and their relation to psychosocial outcome. *Neuropsychological Rehabilitation, 16*(3), 298–314.

Sela-Kaufman, M., Rassovsky, Y., Agranov, E., Levi, Y., & Vakil, E. (2013). Premorbid personality characteristics and attachment style moderate the effect of injury severity on occupational outcome in traumatic brain injury: Another aspect of reserve. *Journal of Clinical and Experimental Neuropsychology, 35*(6), 584–595.

Sherer, M., & Sander, A. M. (Eds.). (2014). *Handbook on the neuropsychology of traumatic brain injury*. New York, NY: Springer.

Siegel, J. S., Ramsey, L. E., Snyder, A. Z., Metcalf, N. V., Chacko, R. V., Weinberger, K., . . . Corbetta, M. (2016). Disruptions of network connectivity predict impairment in multiple behavioral domains after stroke. *Proceedings of the National Academy of Sciences of the USA, 113*(30), E4367–E4376.

Siegel, R. L., Miller, K. D., & Jemal, A. (2016). Cancer statistics. *CA: A Cancer Journal for Clinicians, 66*(1), 7–30.

Silver, J. M., McAllister, T. W., & Yudofsky, S. C. (2011). *Textbook of traumatic brain injury*. Washington, DC: American Psychiatric Publishing.

Simpson, G. K., Tate, R. L., Whiting, D. L., & Cotter, R. E. (2011). Suicide prevention after traumatic brain injury: A randomized controlled trial of a program for the psychological treatment of hopelessness. *Journal of Head Trauma Rehabilitation, 26*(4), 290–300.

Smeets, S. M., Vink, M., Ponds, R. W., Winkens, I., & van Heugten, C. M. (2017). Changes in impaired self-awareness after acquired brain injury in patients following intensive neuropsychological rehabilitation. *Neuropsychological Rehabilitation, 27*(1), 116–132.

van Zomeren, A. H. (1981). *Reaction time and attention after closed head injury*. Amsterdam, the Netherlands: Swets & Zeitlinger.

Walker, A. J., Nott, M. T., Doyle, M., Onus, M., McCarthy, K., & Baguley, I. J. (2010). Effectiveness of a group anger management programme after severe traumatic brain injury. *Brain Injury, 24*(3), 517–524.

Warren, D. E., Power, J. D., Bruss, J., Denburg, N. L., Waldron, E. J., Sun, H., . . . Tranel, D. (2014). Network measures predict neuropsychological outcome after brain injury. *Proceedings of the National Academy of Sciences of the USA, 111*(39), 14247–14252.

Williams, C., & Wood, R. L. (2017). Disorders of emotion recognition and expression. In T. M. McMillan & R. L. Wood (Eds.), *Neurobehavioural disability and social handicap following traumatic brain injury* (pp. 30–42). New York, NY: Routledge.

Wilson, B. A. (2002). Towards a comprehensive model of cognitive rehabilitation. *Neuropsychological Rehabilitation, 12*(2), 97–110.

Ylvisaker, M., McPherson, K., Kayes, N., & Pellett, E. (2008). Metaphoric identity mapping: Facilitating goal setting and engagement in rehabilitation after traumatic brain injury. *Neuropsychological Rehabilitation, 18*(5–6), 713–741.

22

PSYCHOLOGICAL CARE OF CHILDREN WITH KNOWN OR SUSPECTED ACQUIRED BRAIN DISORDERS

BACKGROUND INFORMATION

The psychological care of children with known or suspected acquired brain disorders has not received adequate attention in the scientific or clinical literature. Three factors contribute to this situation. First, this is a heterogeneous group of children with potentially multiple problems. Although the concept of neural plasticity suggests that the brain is capable of reorganizational changes that may lead to a better recovery in children, often this is not the case. For example, Beauchamp, Dooley, and Anderson (2010) summarized the substantial problems that children with a history of traumatic brain injury (TBI) are likely to face in adulthood. Persistent cognitive difficulties not only influence academic achievements but also ultimately affect the level of gainful employment. These children also have high rates of depression and adjustment disorders that can negatively affect group or social activities. Table 22.1 summarizes these important observations.

A second contributing factor is that holistic neuropsychological rehabilitation programs have not been established for children despite some initial efforts to do so (Marcantuono & Prigatano, 2008; Prigatano & Naar-King, 2007). As noted in Chapter 21, such programs for adults have allowed for a clarification of psychological interventions that help build resiliency and aid the long-term adjustment process. There is no similar database for children.

Third, the psychological needs of these children are changing as they go through different stages of development (see Chapters 4 and 6, this volume). Separating improved cognitive functioning secondary to normally (and abnormally) occurring developmental changes versus actual recovery remains a very difficult

Table 22.1 Functional Characteristics of Adults with Childhood Traumatic Brain Injury

Cognitive difficulties
    Attention
    Processing speed
    Executive deficits
Psychiatric disorders
    ADHD
    Depression
    Adjustment disorder
Adaptive disorders
    Academic failure
    Unemployment
Social problems
    Isolation
    Low rates of participation

ADHD, attention-deficit/hyperactivity disorder.
Source: Reprinted from Beauchamp, M., Dooley, J., & Anderson, V., Adult outcomes of pediatric traumatic brain injury, in J. Donders & S. J. Hunter (Eds.), *Principles and Practice of Lifespan Developmental Neuropsychology*, 2010, p. 315–328, by permission of Cambridge University Press.

task (Jonsson, Catroppa, Godfrey, Smedler, & Anderson, 2013). Without this knowledge base, it is very challenging to systematically assess the effectiveness of various psychological intervention programs to help these children.

There are multiple reasons why neuropsychological rehabilitation programs for children have not developed. Perhaps the most obvious is financial. No one immediately benefits economically from the long-term psychological care of these children. This is not true for adults. If an adult patient with a brain dysfunction can return to work or be home for long periods of time without supervision, insurance companies clearly benefit. The family of the patient also benefits economically because less time needs to be devoted to the patient's care. Government agencies benefit because the person is not receiving social security benefits and becomes a taxpayer once again.

Another social factor further complicates the development of appropriate psychological care models for these children. Most knowledgeable clinicians would never send an adult with a brain disorder back to work without documenting that the person's neuropsychological status would justify a return to work and whether certain accommodations would be necessary. Children with known or suspected brain disorders, however, are routinely returned home and back to the school environment with either minimal understanding of their neuropsychological difficulties or minimal or no adequate accommodations to aid their psychological adjustment. As a result of this failure, many children can develop a series of behavioral and emotional disorders that could have been averted with proper psychological and educational interventions. Some of these children might even show improved neuropsychological functioning above and beyond developmentally based changes.

This chapter provides a brief historical overview of important insights relevant to fostering a positive long-term psychological adjustment for school-age children with known or suspected acquired brain disorders (including TBI). This is followed by a selected review of contemporary approaches to the psychological care of these children. Finally, three case vignettes are described that highlight a few important features of the psychological care of children with known or suspected disorders. I hope to demonstrate that currently the psychological care needs of such children are only partially understood and only being partially addressed by health care clinicians.

HISTORICAL PERSPECTIVE ON THE PSYCHOLOGICAL CARE OF CHILDREN WITH KNOWN OR SUSPECTED ACQUIRED BRAIN DISORDERS

Eduardo Sequin (1812–1888) was a French physician interested in helping improve the cognitive and behavioral functioning of children with developmentally based cognitive disabilities. In his 1866 book, *Idiocy and Its Treatment by the Physiological Method*, a series of physically oriented activities aimed at improving sensorimotor functioning and developing these children's "moral sense" were described. Quite interestingly, he stated the following (as cited in Caplan & Caplan, 1973, p. 263):

> We must teach every day the nearest thing to that which the child knows or can know. We must not forget to create gaiety and mirth several times a day: Happiness is our object as much, nay more, than progress, and children will not be sick if they laugh.

The words convey a very modern sentiment. Recent computerized cognitive retraining approaches to improve working memory do so by first presenting cognitive problems that the child has a reasonable chance of solving. If the problem is too difficult, the computer program allows for an automatic downward adjustment of the level of the cognitive problem so that the child has a greater chance of succeeding on the next learning trial (Klingberg, 2010). The second part of Sequin's statement can be applied to various forms of psychotherapy, in which the goal is to reduce the anxiety level, depression, and angry outbursts of the child by structuring activities (and the home and school environment) that produce a positive sense of well-being.

Marie Montessori (1870–1952) was very much influenced by Sequin's ideas. She believed that educational activities were the best means by which to treat children with "nervous disorders." She emphasized the importance of the educational environment, the teacher, and the need to use teaching materials that engage the child's natural desire to learn. The following is her famous dictum: "Development of the child's initiative through freedom of action, but not abandonment." That is, the teacher was physically present to carefully observe what the child was doing at all times. The teacher watched as the child manipulated objects or verbalized ideas or observations. The teacher would then provide the child, in a nonintrusive manner, with materials or an idea that allowed the child to continue the self-initiated learning process. Many teachers, including psychotherapists, recognize the wisdom of this basic approach to working with and teaching children with cognitive and behavioral problems. In both Sequin's and Montessori's approaches, there is a natural, "built-in" effort to help teach children to be more independent and therefore resilient when encountering problems. The importance and scientific evidence favoring this educational approach have been documented by Lillard (2005).

The impact of Goldstein's (1942) observations regarding the "loss of the abstract attitude" in adults with brain injury and the importance of separating "direct" versus "indirect" symptoms in brain dysfunctional adults also resonated with clinicians treating children. Psychiatrist Lauretta Bender (1938) noted that the psychological treatment of the brain-damaged child always required evaluating the "total problem." That is, the clinician must attempt to separate the secondary disturbances (Goldstein referred to these as the indirect symptoms) from the primary disturbances caused by the brain damage. Bender emphasized the need to understand the child's psychological needs (not just the neuropsychological disturbances). She emphasized that therapy should always include a warm, mothering relationship, with an extended period of dependency. Families should be involved in the treatment as early as possible. Finally, drives toward normality should be utilized. These early and insightful comments are echoed in the psychoanalytic work of Erik Erikson (discussed in previous chapters) and the more recent developmentally oriented work of Braga and Campos da Paz (2006).

Strauss and Lehtinen (1947) were early proponents of a purely cognitive retraining or educational approach to helping children with cognitive and behavioral disorders. Influenced by the neuroscience of their times (especially the writings of Lashley [1929]), they emphasized that the magnitude or volume of brain loss or damage was the most important variable in predicting the degree of cognitive impairment in brain dysfunctional children. Their emphasis was on retraining and educating the children in light of their cognitive and perceptual disturbances. Their emphasis was also on teaching psychologists to diagnosis and manage (when possible) the behavioral disturbance of these children. The subjective experiences of the children did not receive much attention.

With time, there was a re-emergence of interest in understanding the social problems of children with brain dysfunction (Birch, 1964). Attempts were made to clarify how these children should be psychologically examined (Diller & Birch, 1964). Traditional clinical psychological tests (e.g., the Rorschach test) and more experimental, neuropsychological tests (e.g., perception of embedded figures and motor tasks) were both considered to be potentially useful. The discussion included reviewing the varied human functions affected by a brain injury in children (Richardson, 1964) and the need to develop social environments to address those functions. Included activities emphasized, for example, stimulating intellectual functions, fostering social relationships, and internalizing norms and values, as well as play and fun (back to Sequin). Today, we would identify such programs as being "holistic" in nature. The need for such programs was recognized several years ago, but unfortunately they have not been adequately developed (Marcantuono & Prigatano, 2008).

CONTEMPORARY APPROACHES TO THE PSYCHOLOGICAL CARE OF SCHOOL-AGE CHILDREN AND YOUNGER ADOLESCENTS WITH A BRAIN DISORDER

The most frequent form of an acquired brain disorder in school-age children is TBI. The neuropsychological and psychiatric disturbances of children were reviewed in Chapter 6. These children, by and large, do not develop normally (Prigatano, 2008). Their cognitive and behavioral problems often result in low tolerance for frustration, with mood swings, a loss of friendships, and poor academic performance, as noted in Chapter 6. They are frequently socially isolated within their own school environment. Their parents are understandably concerned about these problems and often want help from a clinical neuropsychologist to guide these children's rehabilitation, educational experiences, and long-term psychological adjustment (Prigatano, 2008).

Clinical studies and follow-up observations of these children provide some general guidelines for psychological care. Although not all children present with behavioral problems, many do. For these children, psychological care is often first directed at getting their disruptive behaviors under control. Cohen, Heaton, Ginn, and Eyberg (2011) provided a useful case report of how disruptive behaviors were greatly reduced in an 11-year-old boy who suffered severe frontal lobe injury at age 10 years. Their approach was to implement a parent–child interaction therapy (PCIT) program in which the parent was first coached on how to establish "parental warmth and strengthening of the parent–child relationship" (p. 253). This was followed by coaching the parent on how to effectively respond to disruptive behaviors of the child. The authors suggested that "the child's compliant behaviors are reinforced through positive attention and praise, and noncompliant behaviors discouraged by contingent application of a time-out procedure" (p. 253). In younger children, this procedure certainly seems to be effective. However, as children grow older, they ultimately need to experience the practical and symbolic value of controlling impulsive and disruptive behaviors (Ylvisaker, McPherson, Kayes, & Pellett, 2008).

Cognitive–behavioral approaches for reducing maladaptive behaviors in children and adolescents after TBI have expanded to include several activities. For example, Pastore et al. (2011) include activities such as offering positive and negative reinforcement, shaping techniques, modeling desired behaviors, and identifying "dysfunctional thoughts" that reinforce maladaptive behaviors. The authors' broad approach further emphasizes the need to educate and work with parents to achieve desired behavioral outcomes. In assessing the effectiveness of cognitive–behavioral approaches, researchers in this field often focus on measurable changes in children's behavior or reports of parents on standardized questionnaires. They do not discuss in any detail how these children experience these therapeutic interventions and the long-term consequences of such treatments.

In addition to maladaptive and noncompliant behaviors in some children with an acquired brain disorder, some of these children "are too compliant." These children often lack initiative and have significant impairments in cognitive functioning. As they grow older, they have a high need for acceptance by others, and yet they lack the cognitive capacity to "think for themselves." They are at risk for being exploited by others and for not knowing how to deal with more complex interpersonal relationships during adolescence and adulthood. No publications have emerged that specifically focus on how to address these complex issues.

For both compliant and noncompliant school-age children with an acquired brain disorder, however, the need to engage them in the learning process is obvious and is often the next step in their care. This is a difficult task for many of these children because they often have cognitive deficits that make the learning process extremely challenging. This can be discouraging to them and their teachers. Frequently, teachers are ill prepared for educating such children, and many school environments are not structured for the necessary "one-on-one training" these children often require. This inevitably leads to "escapism"—from school, doing homework, and avoiding painful interactions with peers at school. Parents become equally distraught as they see their child doing poorly in school (Prigatano & Gray, 2007).

Some children clinically followed 10–15 years after moderate to severe TBI have reported how angry they were with their teachers. They often experienced their education as not being helpful to them. Rather, they experienced their education as simply trying to force them to learn academic material that they did not understand at the time (Prigatano & Naar-King, 2007). Their critiques need to be taken seriously because both educational and rehabilitation activities in which they were placed did not seriously attend to their subjective individual needs. They often remain socially isolated, with few friends in the past and in the present.

As noted previously, Beauchamp et al.'s (2010) review of the literature on the long-term outcome of children with moderate to severe TBI emphasizes these children's social isolation. The authors note that these children have considerable difficulty in school and consequently have low rates of employment in adulthood. It has been my clinical experience that not only do these children have problems with sustaining attention and speed of new learning but also many of them have a limited understanding of what happened to them (knowledge of how they were injured and awareness of their residual deficits). Moreover, they have major difficulties knowing what specific words mean. Their vocabulary level is consistently below age-matched peers as they proceed in school. Not knowing how words are used (both the denotation and the connotation of the words), they are ridiculed and unable to understand written and spoken lessons presented to them in school. Furthermore, they cannot "defend" themselves with words when attacked by other children who see that they are different (and therefore the other children want to exclude them from the group—a basic animal behavior or response). Building their vocabulary and reducing their anxiety and depression are crucial steps for sustaining them in school. This becomes, from the perspective of this book, the third guiding principle in the long-term psychological care of children with acquired brain disorders.

Understanding the phenomenological experiences of a child with an acquired brain disorder is often crucial to successful psychological care interventions, as illustrated in a report by Kiiski-Maki (2013). While working with a 12-year-old child with a brain hemorrhage (not a TBI), Kiiski-Maki first described the multitude of problems these children face when returning to school after a brain disorder. Given that they are easily fatigued, emotionally labile, and lacking understanding of what happened to them, they need guidance in knowing what to say to other children upon returning to school. They need guidance in how to approach their homework and school assignments. They need a safe place to express their fears and anger—but this does not always come out immediately. It requires the patience of a true Montessori approach. It requires patience on the part of the teacher and therapist to listen carefully to the child's concerns and address them at the level the child can understand and is comfortable talking about. It takes time and commitment to the therapeutic process. It is not the simple application of behavioral management techniques that helps many of these children truly cope in a meaningful way with the immediate and long-term effects of their brain injury.

Given the long-term adjustment issues these children face, the psychological care of these children requires the establishment of a long-term consultation relationship with the child and the parents. This ongoing relationship with the clinical neuropsychologist allows for two other services to be provided for the child. The clinical neuropsychologist needs to help reduce the social isolation for the child outside of the school environment. This should include a means by which to teach the child (and parent) methods to establish and maintain friendships. The work of Frankel and Myatt (2003) is especially useful for teaching parents how to foster the development of friendships in children who experience this as a difficult task. Their approach, however, has not been adequately applied to children with moderate to severe TBI or other acquired brain injuries.

Next, the clinical neuropsychologist should attempt to establish an ongoing dialogue with the child's parents about how to help the child function within the home environment in a manner that fosters resiliency. Depending on the psychological needs of the parents, this can be a relatively easy task or an exceptionally difficult one. Working with the parents is a delicate matter. The quality of the marital relationship often influences the parent–child relationship. The clinical neuropsychologist is not doing "marital therapy" or even "family therapy." Instead, the clinician attempts to work with the parents (and at times siblings) in a manner that allows the parents to explore activities and responsibilities that the child can engage in to help the child be more self-reliant.

A related aspect of psychological care for school-age children with neuropsychological impairments is to develop in the child and the parents a realistic understanding of the child's present and future adjustment difficulties without overwhelming either the child or the parents (Prigatano & Gray, 2010). This requires periodic dialogue at different stages of development and when a family crisis or major change occurs. This type of consultation requires the clinical neuropsychologist to draw from many sources of knowledge, as repeatedly emphasized in this book. When the child (and at least one parent) can count on the availability of the guidance of the treating clinical neuropsychologist during such times, the emotional distress is reduced and the new "crisis" or difficult situation can be dealt with more effectively.

Box 22.1 summarizes some of the more important features of the psychological care of school-age children with known or suspected acquired brain injuries. Table 22.2 briefly summarizes contemporary clinical approaches to psychological care of these children.

> **Box 22.1. Common Clinical Features Encountered in the Psychological Care of Children with Acquired Brain Injuries**
>
> 1. Get the disruptive behavior under control first.
> 2. Engage the child in the learning process and help them avoid escapism.
> 3. Build the child's cognitive abilities (with special attention to language functions) to improve academic and social skills.
> 4. Simultaneously work with the child on their cognitive and emotional changes. Be prepared to deal with "strong emotions" and have the time to address multiple needs of the child.
> 5. Establish a long-term consultation relationship with both the child and the parent(s).
>   a. Help the child reduce social isolation outside of the school environment.
>   b. Help the parent(s) foster resilient behaviors at home.
>   c. Guide the child at times of developmental or family crisis.

PSYCHOLOGICAL CARE OF THREE CHILDREN WITH KNOWN OR SUSPECTED BRAIN DISORDERS

The clinical cases discussed in this section highlight some of the psychological care issues common in school-age children and young adolescents with known or suspected brain disorders. The first case is of a child who suffered a moderate to severe TBI at age 4 years. She was followed for several years before psychological care efforts were attempted. Angry feelings, questions regarding sexuality in her adolescent years, and the desire for escapism highlight her particular psychological care issues. The second case is that of a 10-year-old child with cognitive difficulties associated with a right frontal cortical dysplasia and seizures. Self-doubts about her competencies were the focus of her psychological care. The third case is that of a 13-year-old boy thought to have an attention deficit disorder with associated learning difficulties. Efforts at cognitive and behavioral training to improve attention resulted in the unexpected finding of an intense anxiety reaction that had been misdiagnosed as an attention deficit disorder. Addressing unspoken fears became the focus of his psychological care.

Case Vignette 22.1

At age 4½ years, this female child suffered a TBI while a passenger in a minivan. Her injuries included facial fractures and an occipital facture, as well as a traumatic subarachnoid hemorrhage. Her admitting Glasgow Coma Score was 11. A later magnetic resonance imaging (MRI) scan of the brain revealed encephalomalacia in the right basal ganglia. Initially, she presented with left side weakness and hemiplegia, but her motor functioning substantially improved over time. Repeated electroencephalograms (EEGs) were read as normal, but she frequently complained of headaches. In time, she began to report stomachaches. Her attending pediatric neurologist believed that they might be related to anxiety. Her mother often had to pick her up from school because of the stomachaches. Periodic problems with anger were also noted at home. Consequently, she was referred for a neuropsychological examination at age 7½ years.

Selected neuropsychological findings obtained from testing this child are listed in summary form in Table 22.3. Approximately 3 years after the TBI, her speed of finger tapping was substantially below average for her age. However, with time, her speed of motor

Table 22.2 Contemporary Approaches to the Psychological Care of Children with Acquired Brain Injuries

INTERVENTION	STUDY SAMPLE	MAJOR FINDINGS	CONCLUSIONS
Parent–child interaction therapy in behavioral management following pediatric TBI (Cohn et al., 2011)	Case study of an 11-year-old boy with a right frontal–parietal brain injury secondary to an accidental gunshot wound. Since the accident, the child was described as verbally and physically aggressive, as well as emotional volatile, oppositional, and defiant.	The patient and his mother underwent a nine-session program of parent–child interaction therapy that fostered (1) a warm and supportive parent–child relationship and (2) the consistent application of reinforcement to control disruptive behavior. A clinically meaningful reduction of problematic behaviors was observed during this time. Parent distress also decreased during this time period.	Establishing a warm and supportive relationship even with an oppositional and defiant child is important in children's psychological care. Consistent use of behavioral modification techniques can greatly diminish disruptive behaviors in such children.
CBT for children and adolescents with TBI (Pastore et al., 2011)	28 patients received the psychological interventions and 12 patients did not receive the interventions. The interventions were quite diverse, but the study summarizes the various CBT techniques and therefore is useful to review. Children were treated at different time periods depending on the nature of their behavioral difficulty. Time of treatment was approximately 2½ years post onset of the brain insult.	Many behavioral findings are reported, with generalized improvement observed on the Child Behavior Check List for the treated group of children. Also, greater improvement was reported in the treated children as measured by the Socialization scale on the Vineland Adaptive Behavior Scales.	A variety of behavioral techniques are clearly usefully in improving the behavioral functioning of children and adolescents with TBI. This approach is clearly effective in providing Level 1 psychological care for these children.

(continued)

Table 22.2 Continued

INTERVENTION	STUDY SAMPLE	MAJOR FINDINGS	CONCLUSIONS
Individualized psychotherapeutic approach that incorporates an understanding of the child's neuropsychological impairments with an acquired brain injury (Kiiski-Maki, 2013)	Detailed case description of individualized psychotherapeutic efforts with a 12-year-old child following a brain hemorrhage. Detailed description of how physical and neuropsychological impairments impacted the child's ability to attend school, interact with peers, and tell others what she was experiencing. Psychotherapeutic interventions were aimed at guiding the child to make a good adjustment when faced with these difficult issues.	Specific approaches to helping the child improve academic performance are clearly described. This is done in conjunction with an equally clear description of how the child's emotional reactions could be expressed in a manner that helped the child improve her resiliency. A major finding of this case report was that the child and others like her often have many more feelings about their brain injury than they typically describe to parents or teachers. Helping the child deal with these strong (and often unspoken) emotions fostered the child's positive psychological development.	The major conclusion of this case study is that much can be done to help these children stay in school, improve school performance, and manage strong emotions about their clinical situation if the clinical neuropsychologist is adequately trained in psychotherapy as well as neuropsychology.

CBT, cognitive–behavioral therapy; TBI, traumatic brain injury.

Table 22.3 Serial Neuropsychological Test Findings of a Child Who Suffered a Moderate to Severe Traumatic Brain Injury at Age 4½ Years

TEST	FIRST TESTING (7 YEARS, 10 MONTHS)	SECOND TESTING (9 YEARS, 3 MONTHS)	THIRD TESTING (10 YEARS, 2 MONTHS)
Verbal IQ	82	71	71
Performance IQ	81	81	81
Vocabulary	8	6	4
Block Design	4	2	5
Trail Making Test Part A (Intermediate form)	39 seconds	27 seconds	25 seconds
Trail Making Test Part B (Intermediate Form)	122 seconds (1 error)	185 seconds (2 errors)	48 seconds
Finger Tapping (raw scores)			
Right hand	34.2	40.0	48.0
Left hand	12.6	32.8	27.3

movement improved bilaterally. Relative difficulties with the left-hand speeds continued to be observed. As would be expected given her MRI findings, she demonstrated substantial difficulties with visual–spatial problem-solving, as depicted in her low Block Design scale scores. Somewhat unexpectedly, however, her vocabulary scale scores showed a progressive decline with time. She seemed to have more difficulty keeping up with her peers with regard to knowing the definition of words.

At age 14 years, she was referred for psychotherapy because of growing "anger issues." At that time, she openly expressed her anger at having to go to school. Her academic achievements were clearly below average, but she said she "didn't care." She was angry with many of the girls at school who ridiculed her and called her names. One of the names she was called, beginning at approximately age 10 years, was "fat." In fact, she was not. However, she often refused to eat because she could not cope with the teasing. She did not have adequate language skills to "fight back" and therefore began to voice threats of violence toward those who teased her. She complained of continued stomach pain and often wanted to leave school early.

During neuropsychological testing sessions, she often was quiet and did not say much. However, when seen in psychotherapy sessions, she often was anything but quiet. She openly expressed her anger at the teachers, other children, and her father. Although she did not care about school, she had many questions she wanted answered regarding boys. The questions were the common questions teenage girls typically ask their mothers. How should boys treat you? How do you know if they love you? What should you do if they want "sex"? These and related questions were only briefly discussed with her mother because she was afraid her mother would tell her father that she was inquiring about such topics. She was angry at her father (for reasons not discussed here) and did not want her father to know anything about what she was struggling with.

For the next 2½ years, the child was seen periodically to discuss her concerns. Although weekly sessions were repeatedly suggested by the psychologist, the child would request an appointment only when she was seeking answers to her questions within the confidentiality confines of treating an adolescent. She would frequently voice her anger and frustrations, but she did not attempt to introspect about her feelings or to work with the psychotherapist toward some achievable goal. She would complain about behavioral contingencies her mother placed on her when she behaved in a manner that her mother did not deem acceptable. She wanted the psychotherapist to "fix things" in regard to these and related issues with her parents.

Eventually, she refused to go to school and demanded that she take online classes at home. This was her form of escapism. Despite multiple efforts, she refused to return to school. She seemed to appreciate the times the psychologist attempted to help build her vocabulary and help her remember information necessary to pass a driving examination. However, she resisted any attempt to improve her self-control or explore her underlying anxiety and depression. The efforts at psychological care were marginally helpful.

This type of scenario has been reported by others, particularly early clinical investigators who noted that the lack of intellectual development and associated personality development made these children unresponsive to traditional forms of psychotherapy (see Taylor, 1959). In hindsight, the PCIT program described by Cohen et al. (2011) may have been a better way of providing psychological care for this child. It would have focused on building the bond between mother and child and systematically coaching the parent to get disruptive behaviors under control first. Then meaningful engagement in the learning process may have proceeded more effectively.

Case Vignette 22.2

At 6 years of age, a female child was noted to periodically rub her hands together, an event associated with grunting sounds that lasted between 5 and 30 seconds. These events were described as occurring a few times each day. She underwent video EEG monitoring, and it was discovered that these behaviors were associated with spike wave activity arising from the right frontotemporal region of the brain. She was diagnosed with simple partial seizures. An MRI of the brain later revealed right frontal focal cortical dysplasia. She was referred for a neuropsychological examination before undergoing surgical resection of her dysplasia.

The clinical neuropsychological examination revealed a very pleasant child who was superior in her overall intelligence (Wechsler Intelligence Scale for Children Full Scale IQ of 127). There were no differences in verbal versus nonverbal problem-solving skills. Her performance on measures of verbal memory varied from average to above average. Her performance on a measure of visual–spatial memory task was in the average range. Speed for finger tapping was bilaterally slow in both hands (i.e., right-hand score of 29 taps, $T = 36$; left-hand score of 28.8 taps, $T = 37$). The patient underwent surgery and was subsequently seizure-free.

Approximately 3 years later, the child was again referred for a neuropsychological examination. She continued to be very pleasant and cooperative. However, before she was seen, it was noted that her academic performance in school had declined somewhat. The patient's mother noted that her daughter was now getting A's and B's, whereas in the past she was getting all A's. She said that her daughter seemed somewhat "lazy" and appeared less organized in her approach to schoolwork. She also noted that her daughter showed less interest in establishing friendships than she had in the past. Repeat testing revealed a Full

Scale IQ of 114 and increased difficulties on tasks involving verbal fluency and higher level planning and organizational skills. The findings suggested a possible decline in frontal lobe functioning. Noteworthy at the time was the mother's comment that her daughter seemed to "lack passion" about things she used to care a great deal about.

Specific suggestions to increase structure in the child's life and to engage her in problem-solving tasks were made. Perhaps more important, the clinical neuropsychologist showed an interest in the child's functioning and agreed to work with the child and parents to monitor her course and address whatever questions might arise in regard to improving her functioning.

A year later, the child and her mother returned. The child brought in brownies and a hand-written thank-you note acknowledging the help that had previously been provided to her. She was now doing much better in school. Her Full Scale IQ score was 122. Memory scores were also above average, and she was performing above average on tasks aimed at assessing problem-solving abilities. Although the child still described subtle problems in organization and planning, she was more attentive to how she approached problems. She was doing better in school, but she struggled with feeling less competent than she was in the past. She cautiously revealed this concern when privately talking with the clinical neuropsychologist.

To help build her confidence, she was enrolled in a summer friendship training program (as described by Frankel & Myatt, 2003). She blossomed during this time and recognized her superior abilities compared to those of other children enrolled in the program who had substantial cognitive and behavioral problems. Perhaps of equal importance, she and her mother developed a very positive therapeutic alliance during the 5 years when she was helped periodically. It was therefore natural for the patient and her mother to return when another problem arose during early adolescence. The child was now reported to not be telling the truth about completing homework assignments. She was also having difficulty falling asleep at night without a light. She was not expressing any emotional difficulties, but her behavior suggested otherwise.

The topics of depression and anxiety were discussed with the child, who was in her early adolescent years. Changes within the home were clearly stressful for her, but she was reluctant to discuss the details, which she knew—given her age—would ultimately also have to be discussed with her mother. Eventually, these problems resolved with the help of an outside counselor. Years later, the mother and child again contacted the clinical neuropsychologist because of recurring depression. This problem was addressed as before. As a result, this young woman was doing better from an emotional standpoint and began college training ahead of schedule. She and her mother continue to have periodic contact with the treating clinical neuropsychologist to discuss both positive and stressful events as they occur.

This case vignette highlights the importance of understanding a child's neuropsychological status, his or her phenomenological concerns, and monitoring and providing direction for the child over time. Such prolonged follow-up conveys an interest in helping the child deal with any problems encountered. This experience fostered a long-term positive neuropsychological consultation relationship with the child and her mother. It appeared helpful as the child faced different adjustment issues over time. This is often an important feature of successful psychological care of children with an acquired brain disorder.

Case Vignette 22.3

A 13-year-old boy was referred for a clinical neuropsychological examination because of a probable attention deficit disorder. The goal was to document his higher integrative brain functions and make further recommendations in his care. His medical history was notable for chronic migraines and an ongoing motor tic disorder. At times, he would involuntarily blink his eyes. This only occurred periodically. His mother and his teacher both noted that he was somewhat impulsive and inattentive in school.

The child's developmental history was normal, but it was suggested that perhaps he was a little slow in the development of speech. His mother reported that he could say only single words until he was approximately 18 months old. It was also noted that he was approximately 3 years of age before he was able to separate from his mother without showing signs of severe anxiety.

On formal neuropsychological examination, the boy's intelligence was normal (Full Scale IQ of 96). He did have relative difficulties in attention and working memory (Digit Span scale score = 7) as well as visual–spatial problem-solving skills (Block Design = 6). However, his verbal reasoning skills were within the normal range (Similarities = 10; Vocabulary = 11). His processing speed scores were above average (e.g., Coding = 12; Symbol Search = 12). He was mildly impulsive on some tasks. For example, on the Conners' Continuous Performance Test-II, he was judged to be both impulsive and inattentive. His profile was indicative of an attention deficit disorder.

This child was subsequently enrolled in a behavioral program called Stop & Think to improve his inattention and to inhibit his impulsive behavior. The program exercises were outlined in a manual. The training activities appeared to be helpful, and the patient and his mother were reporting improved attention with schoolwork. Then, after four treatment sessions, the child asked the treating clinical neuropsychologist an interesting question: "What if we run out of [training] materials?" The treating clinician replied that more materials would be developed, and the work together would continue. The child then asked if he could talk to the clinical neuropsychologist. The answer, of course, was that he could. He then asked the clinical neuropsychologist's opinion about gun control laws. This led into a discussion of his father, who owned a gun. He then stated that when his father drink alcohol, he physically abused him and his mother. He then noted that his parents were divorced and living apart, but his father would periodically return and visit both him and his mother.

The child then asked about the difference between anxiety and fear. After a somewhat academic discussion of the distinction, he then asked the treating clinical neuropsychologist whether he was ever afraid of anything. The question was answered in the affirmative, and a specific example was given when the treating neuropsychologist came face-to-face with a lion in Africa. The child then revealed what scared him the most: the computer game "Slenderman."

This game is based on a German fairy tale that can be especially frightening to children. The child brought the game to several psychotherapy sessions and played it with the treating clinical neuropsychologist. In the game, Slenderman follows the player in the dark while the player walks in the forest. If he catches the player and makes eye contact, he can steal the player's "soul." Several sessions were spent discussing why confronting Slenderman was so dangerous. The notion that persons can confront what is scaring them was discussed on multiple occasions, and finally the boy told the clinical neuropsychologist that he could tell his mother that his father scared him because he drank and had a gun. This was first discussed with the mother and then with the son and the mother conjointly. The mother acted to keep the father from coming to the house, and the child's fears lessened substantially. His grades continued to improve in school, and the diagnosis of an attention deficit disorder did not seem to apply. His attention and impulsive difficulties appeared to be related to anxiety, and when the source of that anxiety was properly treated, the problematic behaviors in school disappeared.

This case vignette has two important teaching points. First, a behavioral approach may be initiated to deal with an apparent neuropsychological problem. Yet the openness of the treating clinical neuropsychologist to discuss interpersonal concerns and unspoken sources of anxiety may ultimately prove most helpful to the child. Second, children, like adults, do not always (and most of the time do not) begin psychological treatments by clearly stating what is really bothering them. It is the building of a therapeutic relationship that allows for the dialogue to unfold so that the child begins to speak increasingly more about what is of concern. One discussion or idea leads to the next. This is directly in line with Erikson's comments (see Chapter 10, this volume) about what constitutes adequate evidence that a psychological treatment is effective. It is not gratitude per se. It is the demonstrated ability of the child (or the adult) to begin to talk more openly and directly about what is of concern. This, then, can lead to practical steps to face what is upsetting to the person and to enlist the services of the treating clinician to help the individual face those concerns. Practical steps are then taken to improve the psychological well-being of the child (and the adult).

SUMMARY

This chapter highlighted some of the diverse features involved in the psychological care of children with known or suspected brain disorders. It was noted that the care of these children has remained less developed than that for adults with known brain disorders. Understanding the neuropsychological difficulties of these children is the initial step in their psychological care. However, providing practical suggestions for managing the direct and indirect effects of their brain disorder often becomes the next step. When this is done in way that leads to a strong working alliance or therapeutic relationship with the child and at least one of the parents, other forms of psychological care can be provided. This often includes establishing a long-term professional consultation relationship (as noted in Chapter 1, this volume). Parents and child will return at different times in their developmental course to seek out further guidance and help as different developmental and family crises are encountered. Having a broad perspective of how to approach these varying problems and an openness to discussing whatever is concerning these children is at the heart of effective psychological care following a known or suspected brain disorder.

REFERENCES

Beauchamp, M., Dooley, J., & Anderson, V. (2010). Adult outcomes of pediatric traumatic brain injury. In J. Donders & S. J. Hunter (Eds.), *Principles and practice of lifespan developmental neuropsychology* (pp. 315–328). New York, NY: Cambridge University Press.

Bender, L. (1938). *A visual motor Gestalt test and its clinical use*. New York, NY: American Orthopsychiatric Association.

Birch, H. G. (Ed.). (1964). *Brain damage in children: The biological and social aspects*. Baltimore, MD: Williams & Wilkins.

Braga, L. W., & Campos da Paz, A. (2006). *The child with traumatic brain injury or cerebral palsy: A context-sensitive, family-based approach to development*. Boca Raton, FL: Taylor & Francis.

Caplan, F., & Caplan, T. (1973). *The power of play*. New York, NY: Anchor Press/Doubleday.

Cohen, M. L., Heaton, S. C., Ginn, N., & Eyberg, S. M. (2011). Parent–child interaction therapy as a family-oriented approach to behavioral management following pediatric traumatic brain injury: A case report. *Journal of Pediatric Psychology, 37*(3), 251–261.

Diller, L., & Birch, H. G. (1964). Psychological evaluation of children with cerebral damage. In H. G. Birch (Ed.), *Brain damage in children: The biological and social aspects* (pp. 27–43). Baltimore, MD: Williams & Wilkins.

Frankel, F. H., & Myatt, R. (2003). *Children's friendship training*. New York, NY: Taylor & Francis.

Goldstein, K. (1942). *Aftereffects of brain injuries in war: Their evaluation and treatment. The application of psychologic methods in the clinic*. New York, NY: Grune & Stratton.

Jonsson, C. A., Catroppa, C., Godfrey, C., Smedler, A.-C., & Anderson, V. (2013). Cognitive recovery and development after traumatic brain injury in childhood: A person-oriented, longitudinal study. *Journal of Neurotrauma, 30*(2), 76–83.

Kiiski-Maki, H. (2013). Brain injury to engage in a neuropsychotherapeutic process. In R. Laaksonen & M. Ranta (Eds.), *Introduction to neuropsychotherapy: Guidelines for rehabilitation of neurological and neuropsychiatric patients throughout the lifespan* (pp. 143–170). New York, NY: Psychology Press.

Klingberg, T. (2010). Training and plasticity of working memory. *Trends in Cognitive Sciences, 14*(7), 317–324.

Lashley, K. S. (1929). *Brain mechanisms and intelligence*. Chicago, IL: University of Chicago Press.

Lillard, A. (2005). *Montessori: The science behind the genius*. New York, NY: Oxford University Press.

Marcantuono, J. T., & Prigatano, G. P. (2008). A holistic brain injury rehabilitation program for school-age children. *NeuroRehabilitation, 23*(6), 457–466.

Pastore, V., Colombo, K., Liscio, M., Galbiati, S., Adduci, A., Villa, F., & Strazzer, S. (2011). Efficacy of cognitive behavioural therapy for children and adolescents with traumatic brain injury. *Disability and Rehabilitation, 33*(8), 675–683.

Prigatano, G. P. (2008). The problem of not developing normally and pediatric neuropsychological rehabilitation: The Mitchell Rosenthal Lecture. *Journal of Head Trauma Rehabilitation, 23*(6), 414–422.

Prigatano, G. P., & Gray, J. A. (2007). Parental concerns and distress after paediatric traumatic brain injury: A qualitative study. *Brain Injury, 21*(7), 721–729.

Prigatano, G. P., & Gray, J. A. (2010). Conducting feedback for pediatric neuropsychological assessment. In A. S. Davis (Ed.), *Handbook of pediatric neuropsychology* (pp. 495–500). New York, NY: Springer.

Prigatano, G. P., & Naar-King, S. (2007). Neuropsychological rehabilitation of school-age children: An integrated team approach to individualized interventions. In S. J. Hunter & J. Donders (Eds.), *Paediatric neuropsychological intervention* (pp. 465–475). New York, NY: Cambridge University Press.

Richardson, S. A. (1964). The social environment and individual functioning. In H. G. Birch (Ed.), *Brain damage in children: The biological and social aspects* (pp. 100–115). Baltimore, MD: Williams & Wilkins.

Sequin, E. (1866). *Idiocy and its treatment by the physiological method*. New York, NY: Wood.

Strauss, A. A., & Lehtinen, L. E. (1947). *Psychopathology and education of the brain-injured child*. New York, NY: Grune & Stratton.

Taylor, E. M. (1959). *Psychological appraisal of children with cerebral defects*. Cambridge, MA: Harvard University Press.

Ylvisaker, M., McPherson, K., Kayes, N., & Pellett, E. (2008). Metaphoric identity mapping: Facilitating goal setting and engagement in rehabilitation after traumatic brain injury. *Neuropsychological Rehabilitation, 18*(5–6), 713–741.

23

PSYCHOLOGICAL CARE OF PERSONS WITH BOTH EPILEPTIC AND NONEPILEPTIC (PSYCHOGENIC) SEIZURES

BACKGROUND INFORMATION

In Chapters 13–21, persons with unequivocal brain disorders were described, and efforts at their psychological care were discussed. Their symptoms often reflect the direct effects of a brain disorder (e.g., a seizure, aphasia, hemiplegia, memory impairments, and altered conscious perceptions of how their abilities have been adversely affected). However, these patients can also demonstrate what K. Goldstein (1942) referred to as "indirect effects" of their clinical condition. The indirect effects or symptoms typically reflect the "struggles to adapt" or the tendency to "avoid the struggles." Depression, anxiety, and social withdrawal are common indirect symptoms frequently observed in patients with a history of a brain disorder. These behavioral changes are often considered reactionary in nature and do not constitute a psychiatric disorder. There are, however, patients who have both a neurological disorder and a comorbid psychiatric disorder. When this occurs, the symptom presentation can be quite complicated. Patients who have epilepsy and also present with a psychogenic seizure disorder typify this clinical situation (Diprose, Sundram, & Menkes, 2016). This chapter focuses on the psychological care of these individuals and evaluates how the approaches to their psychological care are similar to, but in some ways different from, the treatment of patients with primarily underlying brain disorders.

EPILEPTIC SEIZURES AND NONEPILEPTIC EVENTS

An epileptic seizure (ES) is defined as "an abnormal paroxysmal cerebral neuronal discharge that results in alteration of sensation, motor function, behavior or consciousness. Seizures may be classified by type, etiology, and by epileptic syndromes" (Greenberg, 2010, p. 394). The traditional typologies of ES have been summarized for neuropsychologists by Lee (2010) and Barr (2015). Complex partial seizures (CPS), associated with focal neurological signs, are perhaps the most common form of ES. Recently, the term *focal* has been suggested to replace the term *partial* when describing this form of seizure activity (Fisher et al., 2017). Behaviorally, this type of seizure is characterized by a focal motor, sensory, autonomic, or psychic disturbance (i.e., disturbance of higher integrative brain functions) in which the person experiences some alteration of consciousness during the event. The presence of this type of seizure is confirmed when behavioral events suggestive of CPS are captured via video recordings and found to be correlated with the onset of an abnormal paroxysmal cerebral neuronal discharge as measured by electroencephalographic (EEG) recordings, typically on epilepsy monitoring units (EMUs). CPS or focal-onset seizures are often attributed to a disturbance of the temporal lobe of the brain (particularly the hippocampus). They can, however, originate from various sites within the brain, including the frontal lobes (Greenberg, 2010; Lee & Clason, 2008).

Nonepileptic seizure events are defined as "behavioral events that mimic epileptic seizures but do not have an epileptic mechanism" (King, Gallagher, Murro, & Campbell, 1993, p. 31). Rowan and Gates (1993) originally noted that these nonepileptic events could be physiological or psychological in nature. Physiological nonepileptic events can have many causes, including syncope, endocrine disturbance, and ischemic cerebral vascular events (Gates & Erdahl, 1993). Psychogenic nonepileptic seizures (NES) can also be associated with various psychiatric disorders, but dissociative reactions observed in conversion disorders and in some somatization disorders are most common (Hara et al., 2015; LaFrance & Zimmerman, 2010; Pick, Mellers, & Goldstein, 2015). In dissociative states, there appears to be an automatic "reflexive" or unconscious response to block from consciousness emotionally charged thoughts/feelings that appear overwhelming to the patient. It has been estimated that 50% of patients evaluated for epilepsy on EMUs are eventually diagnosed as having psychogenic NES or events (Barry & Reuber, 2010). It has also been reported that psychogenic NES-like events occur as comorbid conditions in at least 10% of patients with "true" epilepsy (Widdess-Walsh, Nadkarni, & Devinsky, 2010). A study from Japan estimated the co-occurrence of these conditions at 13.8% (Hara et al., 2015).

NEUROPSYCHOLOGICAL CONSEQUENCES OF EPILEPSY AND PSYCHOGENIC SEIZURES

Lee (2010) has provided a thorough review of the neuropsychological consequences of epileptic seizures and the medicines used to suppress seizure activity. Depending on seizure frequency, seizure type, seizure location, and the developmental state at the time of seizure onset, a wide variety of neuropsychological disturbances can be observed. Virtually any higher integrative brain function can be affected. Repeated grand mal seizures that occur early in life often are associated with a general failure to develop cognitively. Patients who experience these seizures often have below average IQ scores. Repeated focal abnormal discharges in the temporal lobes of the brain are often associated with memory impairments with or without associated below average performance on standardized tests of intelligence (Helmstaedter, Kurthen, Lux, Reuber, & Elger, 2003; Hermann et al., 2002). The medications to control epilepsy also are known to adversely affect concentration, processing speed, and at times memory (Lee, 2010, p. 103).

The effects of repeated nonepileptic or psychogenic seizures on neuropsychological functioning are not as clearly understood.

These patients, however, often have cognitive complaints (Prigatano & Kirlin, 2009). Their complaints are in multiple areas, including reports of word-finding difficulties in free speech as well as memory and concentration difficulties (Prigatano & Kirlin, 2009). Their cognitive complaints often correlate highly with self-ratings of anxiety and depression. In patients with epileptic seizures, there tends to be less of a correlation between the cognitive complaints and the affective status of the individual. This is not to say, for example, that depression is correlated only with cognitive complaints in persons with NES and not ES. It is only to say that the relationship is stronger in the former group compared to the latter group (Prigatano & Kirlin, 2009).

Patients with epileptic and nonepileptic seizures can perform below average on standardized neuropsychological tests (Martin, Bell, Hermann, & Mennemeyer, 2003). Neuropsychological test findings per se do not generally separate these two groups of individuals (Dodrill, 2010). In fact, C. Dodrill (personal communication, 1998) suggested that approximately 50% of patients with NES evaluated on an EMU demonstrate abnormal neuropsychological test findings. Some investigators have suggested that qualitative features of performance on memory tests may have some value in identifying patients with NES versus ES (Bortz, Prigatano, Blum, & Fisher, 1995). NES patients were noted, for example, to show a negative response bias on a verbal word recognition test. ES patients are less likely to show this pattern. The negative response bias was thought to possibly reflect the defense mechanism of denial which is a common feature of dissociative reactions.

Working memory (WM) difficulties are at times reported in this patient group (Bakvis, Spinhoven, Putman, Zitman, & Roelofs, 2010). Reportedly, patients with psychologically based NES have more difficulty successfully performing a WM task in which a picture of an angry face is used as a distractor after patients have been placed in a stressful situation. Other studies have especially suggested that such patients experience significant levels of anxiety and frustration over perceived abusive interpersonal experiences (Hendrickson, Popescu, Ghearing, & Bagic, 2015). The question thus arises as to whether the psychiatric features of NES patients can reliably separate them from ES patients.

PSYCHIATRIC FEATURES OF PATIENTS DIAGNOSED WITH EPILEPTIC VERSUS NONEPILEPTIC SEIZURES

Patients with epilepsy have been known to demonstrate a wide variety of psychiatric disorders. Reviewing earlier data, Lishman (1987) noted that patients with ongoing seizures were frequently unemployed and encountered significant social integration problems. However, patients with temporal lobe epilepsy were noted to be at especially high risk for psychiatric disability. In a more recent review, Mendez (2009) estimated that the prevalence of psychiatric disability in patients treated in epilepsy clinics is between 20% and 60%. Psychosis associated with recurring complex partial seizures was considered to be present in 10% of these epileptic individuals.

Depression, however, is the most commonly reported psychiatric disorder in patients with epilepsy. Lee's (2010) review suggested that depression is estimated to occur in 10–20% of patients with well-controlled seizures and in 20–60% of patients with intractable epilepsy (p. 135). Kanner (2013) noted the wide spectrum of depressive disorders in epileptic patients. He also brought attention to the fact that these depressed individuals frequently present with comorbid symptoms of anxiety (estimated to be as high as 45%). He argued that antidepressant drugs are the first line of defense in treating depression (and related disorders). The success rate for greatly reducing or eliminating depression in patients with persistent ES has been difficult to estimate, given the heterogeneity of this patient group.

However, Kanner (2013) suggested that up to a 50% decrease in symptoms can be observed, via pharmacological intervention, in many of these patients. When patients are not totally responsive to individualized drug treatments, psychotherapy is frequently attempted. Currently, cognitive–behavioral therapy (CBT) is often recommended as the treatment of choice.

Are the psychiatric disorders of patients with psychogenic NES in any way distinguishable from the disorders of those with ES? A considerable amount of work has gone into trying to answer this question (Schachter & LaFrance, 2010). Psychometric profiles of these two groups on standardized personality inventories such as the Minnesota Multiphasic Personality Inventory (MMPI) and the MMPI-2 notoriously do not separate the two groups (Dodrill, 2010). However, elevations on the Hypochondriasis (Hs) and Hysteria (Hy) scales have repeatedly been shown to be potentially useful in differential diagnosis. In some studies, patients with psychogenic NES tend to show the "conversion V" profile on the MMPI/MMPI-2. This profile is suggestive of an underlying conversion disorder or somatization disorder in which dissociative features are commonly observed (Bowman & Markand, 1996). It has also been noted that patients with psychogenic NES report more unusual somatic symptoms and higher levels of anxiety and depression compared to ES patients (Testa, Krauss, Lesser, & Brandt, 2012). Hendrickson et al. (2015) reported greater dissociative symptoms and higher levels of anxiety in psychogenic NES patients compared to ES patients. Depression may not be the most frequent psychiatric symptom in psychogenic NES patients, whereas it may be most prominent in ES patients. Also, psychogenic NES patients were observed to report a higher number of allergies compared to ES patients (Robbins, Larimer, Bourgeois, & Lowenstein, 2016). It was suggested that excessive reports of allergies by a patient may indicate an underlying somatization disorder.

Interestingly, patients with psychogenic NES have been noted to verbally describe their seizures using different terminology from that used by ES patients. In a very creative study, Plug, Sharrack, and Reuber (2009) noted that patients with epilepsy tended to "describe their seizures as an opponent acting under his own volition" (p. 999). The verbal imagery depicts "the patient as fighting against the seizure" (p. 999). In contrast, in psychogenic NES patients, the terminology used often involves metaphors regarding space and place. For example, psychogenic NES patients may use terminology suggesting that the "seizure" goes through them and they are now "out of a seizure." In the first case, there is an opponent force that one is fighting against; in the second case, the person is more of a passive agent allowing something to run its course (through the patient). It is important to note that patients with ES and psychogenic NES can use overlapping metaphoric language. The relative differences, however, have some intriguing features that may give a clue to the etiology of the disorder.

The underlying mechanism that actually produces an NES is still under debate. L. Goldstein, LaFrance, Chigwedere, Mellers, and Chalder (2010) described a "fear escape–avoidance model" originally proposed by Chalder (1996), who suggested the following:

> Within this model, temporally related environmental, cognitive, and sensory events can acquire through classical conditioning, the qualities of profoundly distressing or life-threatening experiences (e.g., trauma, abuse) to produce intolerable outcomes (e.g., fear and distress). Where the classically conditioned events/triggers are external (e.g., environmental), "active" behavioral avoidance measures are taken by the individual. When triggers are internal/subjective experiences (i.e., cognitive/emotional/physiological cues), inhibitory mechanisms expressed as dissociation may become "best option" ways of *in situ* nonbehavioral escape/avoidance of experiential (cognitive and sensory)

distress when the person is confronted with intolerable or fearful circumstances. (p. 283)

Although couched in behavioral terminology, this model is similar to the traditional psychodynamic model of Janet, Breuer, and Freud. Brown (2002) noted, for example, "By this view (the psychodynamic view), dissociation serves a defensive function, acting to protect the individual from the potentially overwhelming affect associated with the memory of traumatic events" (p. 223). In both cases, dissociation is viewed as an automatic, learned reaction to keep internally experienced intense anxiety from entering consciousness.

Some patients can actually trace back to when this learned response became automatic for them. For example, while a clinical neuropsychologist was conducting group psychotherapy with some of these patients (Prigatano, Stonnington, & Fisher, 2002), one patient reported in essence the following story: When her father was about to force sexual intercourse on her, she would consciously "move her mind to another place." She would actively not think about what was happening to her at the time—it was too overwhelming. She remembered thinking it was better that she was forced to have intercourse than her father forcing a younger sister to do so. These memories, when consciously reported in a group setting, were often followed by statements of intense anger and hatred. Some patients stated that they wished their own father would "rot in hell" or suffer terribly with cancer before he died for what he had done. In addition to anxiety, anger and rage are intense emotions that patients often keep out of consciousness via dissociation.

APPROACHES TO THE PSYCHOLOGICAL CARE OF PERSONS WITH NONEPILEPTIC SEIZURES

Several approaches to the psychological treatment of patients with NES have been described, including supportive psychotherapy, individual psychodynamically oriented psychotherapy, group psychotherapy, family therapy, and CBT (LaFrance, Reuber, & Goldstein, 2013). Table 23.1 briefly describes studies that highlight different approaches to the psychological care of persons with NES.

As suggested previously, the most commonly prescribed method of psychological treatment of patients with psychogenic NES is CBT. Treatment usually consists of approximately 12 sessions that focus on engaging patients in the therapeutic process and developing a model for them to better understand so that they can manage their psychogenic NES. The behavioral model has been summarized by L. Goldstein, Chalder, et al. (2010). The specific focus is on identifying "triggers" for psychogenic NES and developing cognitive–behavioral strategies to reduce these triggers in everyday life. LaFrance and Wincze (2015) provide a very readable and practical therapist guide to this treatment approach. It also includes a "Taking Control of Your Seizures" handbook for the patient to follow and to work on at home. LaFrance and Wincze aptly describe their approach as a "patient-led, therapist-guided approach" (p. 15). The influence of both behavioral therapy techniques and the patient-centered approach of Carl Rogers is clearly evident in this treatment manual.

A key feature of this treatment approach is that the patient conducts homework exercises to reduce the frequency of NES. Resistance to engaging in these exercises is often the focus of the therapeutic effort during the face-to-face interactions between the patient and the therapist. Several studies have shown that the frequency of NES declines when patients are actively engaged in taking practical steps to reduce psychogenic NES and to overcome resistance to doing so (L. Goldstein, LaFrance, et al., 2010). The permanency of these effects continues to be studied.

A major critique of CBT by psychodynamically oriented therapists is that CBT is

Table 23.1 Selected Studies Relevant to the Psychological Care of Persons with Psychogenic Nonepileptic Seizures

INTERVENTION	STUDY SAMPLE	MAJOR FINDINGS	CONCLUSIONS
Group psychotherapy for patients with psychogenic seizures (Prigatano et al., 2002)	15 patients diagnosed as having PNES were treated via two 6-month group psychotherapy (research) programs. 8 patients were treated in the first program and 7 in the second program. 9 patients (60%) completed at least 58% of the treatment sessions.	Of those completing the treatment protocols, 6 (66%) reported a decline in PNES events. One patient (11%) reported an increase. Dissociative phenomena were common, as was a history of sexual abuse. Each patient reported being in an adult situation that they found unacceptable or intolerable. None perceived a solution to their situation.	Persistent PNES appeared to be related to the recurrent experience of being in abusive or exploited relationships for which the person perceived no solution.
Individually tailored psychotherapy based on brief psychodynamic interpersonal approaches to functional neurological symptoms (Reuber et al., 2007)	Several patient groups with functional neurological symptoms were combined in this clinical report. The vast majority of the 63 patients treated had PNES (i.e., 68.3%). To be included in the data analysis, patients had to complete a median of six treatment sessions. Specific data on reduction of PNES were not reported.	At the end of therapy, an independent neurologist rated 54% of the primary symptoms unchanged, 23.8% improved (by at least 50%), and 22.2% resolved. "Economic inactivity correctly predicted failure to improve by at least 1 standard deviation on outcome measures" (p. 629).	Understanding how interpersonal conflicts contribute to functional neurological symptoms (via an interpersonal psychodynamic model) appeared helpful in reducing functional neurological symptoms. The percentage of improvement was impressive given the short duration of the psychotherapy. A key feature of this approach was to have the person recognize how early life experiences continue to influence maladaptive adult interpersonal behaviors and how they relate to symptoms.

CBT for PNES: a pilot RCT (Goldstein et al., 2010)	66 patients with PNES were randomized to two clinical treatment conditions: standard medical care SMC vs. CBT + SMC. Data analysis resulted in a comparison of 31 and 32 patients for the two treatment conditions noted. The study included 12 weekly sessions.	PNES showed a greater reduction in frequency at the end of treatment and at follow-up for the CBT group vs. the SMC group. There was a trend for the CBT group to be seizure free at 6-month follow-up. There was no difference between the two treatment groups regarding employment status at follow-up or the patients' self-reported levels of anxiety or depression.	CBT appears to be of substantial help in reducing the frequency of PNES. The treatment effects, however, were not paralleled by a significant difference in employment, anxiety, or depression in CBT-treated PNES patients.

CBT, cognitive–behavioral therapy; PNES, psychogenic nonepileptic seizures; RCT, randomized controlled trial; SMC, standard medical care.

focused solely on the reduction of symptoms (Level 1 form of care, as described in Chapter 12, this volume). CBT may not substantially address other factors in a person's life that greatly contribute to the comorbid problems of depression and anxiety. In fact, this was observed in the pilot randomized controlled trial conducted by L. Goldstein, Chalder, et al. (2010). Seizure frequency was reduced as a result of CBT, but self-reported levels of anxiety and depression did not substantially differ between the CBT group and the control group.

CBT for psychogenic NES may not facilitate a greater understanding of how interpersonal patterns of dysfunctional behavior, often emerging in childhood, are related to the development and persistence of psychogenic NES. More individualized psychodynamic approaches that target this dimension thus offer another treatment approach that appears useful (Reuber, Burness, Howlett, Brazier, & Grünewald, 2007). However, there is currently no data basis that convincingly argues for which type of psychological intervention is most successful in sustaining a positive long-term psychological adjustment for this complicated and somewhat heterogeneous patient group.

As noted previously, C. Dodrill (personal communication, 1998) suggested that 50% of NES patients have abnormal neuropsychological test findings. This observation is especially interesting when considering the historic observations of Charcot regarding what might produce "hysterical" seizures. Reportedly, Charcot suggested that in such patients the "nervous system was abnormal" (as cited in Trimble, 2010, p. 20). An impaired nervous system (i.e., brain) function coupled with psychologically traumatic events might combine to produce the clinical picture we now call psychogenic nonepileptic seizures. The case presented next is compatible with Charcot's observations.

PSYCHOLOGICAL CARE OF A PERSON WITH BOTH EPILEPTIC AND NONEPILEPTIC SEIZURES FOLLOWED FOR 10 YEARS

Medical History

At age 20 years, a left-handed young woman with 13 years of education began to have episodes characterized as a feeling of discomfort, with palpitations, dizziness, and generalized pallor with preserved consciousness. Within a year, these episodes changed and were followed by lip smacking, right-hand automatisms, and impaired consciousness. Occasionally, she also had episodes of urinary incontinence associated with these events, but she had no tongue trauma. After these episodes, she experienced fatigue and nausea and would often take 2- or 3-hour naps.

Her medical history was also significant for a history of a left temporal lobe meningioma, which was surgically resected a year prior to her first episode. The patient was medically followed and prescribed antiseizure medications, which partially controlled her seizures. Approximately 6 years later, an MRI of the brain revealed left mesial temporal sclerosis. She subsequently underwent a left amygdalohippocampectomy. She reported no major change in seizure frequency after the surgery. Continued medical evaluation of the patient revealed the complexity of her clinical condition. CPS were considered probable in light of left-onset temporal lobe spike wave activity during sleep and occasionally during the awake state. During such times, the patient had lip smacking and right-hand automatisms. Awareness was impaired.

She had, however, a second type of "seizure" not associated with abnormal EEG findings. During these times, she had a sensation that her heart was racing. She would begin to stiffen both arms and legs, with toes pointed forward and both arms flexed and extended. Her back would arch upward. It was unclear if she was aware of what was occurring. These events would last 1 or 2 minutes. When they ended, she would take a deep breath and appear to attempt to relax. She felt groggy and tired because of the stiffening of her arms and legs, but she did not need to nap. Occasionally, headache and/or nausea would follow these events. There was no tongue trauma or incontinence during these episodes. These episodes were diagnosed as being psychogenic in nature.

The patient's attending neurologists requested a neuropsychological consultation and testing. Her neuropsychological examination findings documented mild to moderate impairments in verbal learning and memory, as well as in verbal fluency and confrontational naming. Although she showed subtle improvement in her neuropsychological functions over time, her cognitive difficulties persisted. She also would have an occasional CPS as well as presumed psychogenic NES; therefore, she was not released to drive a vehicle. She was encouraged by her doctors to take medical disability, which she did.

Repeated Neuropsychological Consultations with Psychometric Testing

The patient had several neuropsychological consultations, which included psychometric testing on both an outpatient and an inpatient basis. When first seen on an EMU, the patient reported memory difficulties but no other cognitive impairments. She did not spontaneously report any affective disturbance. When performing a verbal learning and memory task that was difficult for her, she became tearful. Her Verbal IQ was initially measured at 87, with a Performance IQ of 81. She performed in the normal range on tests of executive functioning (e.g., the Wisconsin Card Sorting Test and the Trail Making Test Part B). She was slow in processing speed (Coding scale score of 4), but she was on several antiseizure medications. She could recall only 40% of the verbal information she learned on the Rey Auditory Verbal Learning Test but 100% of what she learned on the Brief Visuospatial Memory Test–Revised. Her performance on the Beck Depression Inventory and the Personality Assessment Inventory revealed no abnormal findings.

Approximately 9 months after her inpatient neuropsychological evaluation on an EMU, I saw her for her first neuropsychological examination. The psychometric findings regarding cognitive functioning were similar to those noted by the previous examiner. Although the patient did not report any difficulties with depression, during the interview she reported elevated anxiety. On a scale from 0 to 10 (0 = no anxiety, 10 = severe anxiety), she rated her anxiety level an 8. Her mother, who was also interviewed, agreed, estimating her daughter's anxiety level to be a 7 or 8 on the same scale. During this examination, the patient also had notable difficulties with naming (Boston Naming Test raw score was 39 out of 60, $T = <20$) and verbal fluency (on the Controlled Oral Word Association, she generated only 23 words, which was within the 12th to 22nd percentile for her age). During the next 2 years, three additional neuropsychological examinations were performed, with essentially the same findings. The patient did not report enhanced depression, but her mother reported that her daughter did have enhanced depression. She related the depression to her daughter's not working and being placed on medical disability. Anxiety was not specifically inquired about. The patient was placed on antidepressant medications in addition to her antiseizure medications. No further neuropsychological follow-up was deemed necessary at that time.

Approximately 18 months later, the patient was again hospitalized due to recurring seizure activity and again evaluated on an EMU. Her neuropsychological findings were fairly stable, but now the neurologist diagnosed her as having epileptic seizures and a predominance of nonepileptic events that had prompted her recent hospitalization. Because I had known this patient and examined her in the past, I was asked to speak with her in the EMU and discuss what might be done to help her with her psychogenic NES events.

The Beginning Efforts at Psychological Care

Much has been written about how to talk with patients who believe they have epilepsy but in fact have psychogenetic seizure activity (LaFrance et al., 2013). Most skilled examiners who have clinical sensitivity to these patients do not convey the message "It is all in your head." There is a tendency to relate it to "stress" and suggest the potential value of CBT to teach strategies that can eliminate if not reduce the NES (LaFrance et al., 2013).

I believe a more informed approach is to convey to the patient the following message: The present medical workup has not identified any abnormal electrical activity associated with the "spells" that were observed. Next, it is important to state that it is not known for sure what is causing the "spells" or "episodes" or "events." It is possible that they are being produced by some ill-defined psychological causes. If the patient is willing, the psychologist (or psychiatrist, nurse practitioner, or social worker) should take the time to explore with the patient whether psychological factors seem to be causing these events. It is very important to be honest with the patient that no one knows for sure what is causing these events—but it is reasonable to explore potential psychological causes. If the patient agrees, then before the patient leaves the EMU, the first psychotherapeutic consultation session should be scheduled. This conveys an interest and urgency in addressing the patient's symptoms. This was the approach I took with this patient.

During the first psychotherapeutic consultation session, an important point needs to be made if the patient is being approached from a psychodynamic perspective: The process of such psychotherapy can be lengthy and at times emotionally painful. The patient should seriously consider whether he or she wishes to pursue this form of treatment. If the patient does not, then the other option is to try a more behavioral or cognitive–behavioral approach to care. If the patient trusts the consulting clinical neuropsychologist (as this patient did based on her previous history), he or she will take time to consider this treatment. If the patient agrees to try this form of treatment, a positive psychotherapeutic bond is established and forms the basis of the honest dialogue that is to follow. This patient "did not rush" into psychotherapy and thought through whether she wanted to approach her NES in this manner.

The Psychotherapeutic Dialogue, the Reduction of Psychogenetic Seizures, and Psychological Care over an Extended Period of Time

As part of the initial dialogue, there was a discussion of the circumstances that surrounded having a probable psychogenic NES at work. A male supervisor was demeaning to her. He was not tolerant of her subtle word-finding difficulty and believed that it seriously interfered with her ability to successfully speak with customers. As a single mother, she feared losing her job. She had experienced this type of exchange with her supervisor in the past, but on that particular day it was overwhelming.

Rather early in the psychotherapy, she was able to describe being physically beaten by her father and her mother when she was a child. As a young adult, she now attributed this to the fact that they both abused drugs. But at the time (when she was approximately age 6 years), she was confused about why they were beating her. Apparently, she had done something wrong. She also described being pushed up against a wall at age 16 years and being repeatedly struck by her father after she told him that she was pregnant. During the first few psychotherapy sessions, she began having more dreams than she normally reported. The dreams often centered on her taking care of children. About the same time, she had an NES after arguing with her ex-husband about him being unduly firm and emotionally abusive to their son, for whom she took the major responsibility of raising. She was asked to keep a diary of her dreams, her reactions to her dreams, and a record of events leading up to any NES she might experience. She would often record her dreams, but she found it difficult to identify specific events leading up to an NES.

Approximately 2 months into the psychotherapy, she brought up something new. Had she told me that her current father was actually a stepfather? No, she had not. She was surprised she had not mentioned this before. Her real or biological father (who she repeatedly refused to refer to as her father—she preferred the term "sperm donor") had physically abused her as a young child. Her mother had separated from him when the patient was 3 years old. She had only vague memories of him.

The patient's dreams of children continued. Discussions of these dreams led her to state that caring for her son was the only really important thing in her life. As these topics were discussed, she was constantly concerned about my reaction to her. If I brought up a point that revealed a pattern of her behavior as it related to her mother and (now known) stepfather, she reacted sternly and would ask, "Are you saying it is *my fault* [that she experienced NESs]?" Eventually, she recognized a repeated pattern in her interaction with me (her psychotherapist). She would automatically assume I was blaming her for her NES rather than pointing out patterns of behavior that were associated with the emergence of an NES. Eventually, I would comment that her automatic reaction was that "I am guilty until proven innocent" rather than the other way around, which is a part of our culture and system of laws. Eventually, we both experienced some humor when this reaction automatically occurred. The patient could see or, better yet, directly experience how her emotional reactions were influenced by feelings in her rather than feelings in me. The therapeutic alliance was always strong, but it strengthened during this period of psychological care.

Approximately 4 months into the psychotherapy, we talked about how an NES would occur during the time she was combing her hair. She now had a memory of being beaten with a hard hairbrush on several occasions when her mother was using drugs. She became more aware of her present angry feelings toward her mother and at the same time felt guilty for having those feelings. In one psychotherapy session, I asked her to role play with me. She would role play her mother, and I would role play her. She (playing her mother) would not talk to me (role playing her) if I was angry. I pointed out that this put her into a box. There was no way of expressing her angry feelings about being treated unfairly by her mother.

This somehow led the patient to spontaneously discuss how she had started to exercise in order to lose weight. She indicated that her mother was not happy with this decision because she could injure her knee while exercising. Her mother was also concerned that exercising could trigger a seizure. I then asked her, for the first time, about her feelings about being overweight. She immediately went into what appeared to be a nonepileptic event. Her head dropped, and she became quiet. She then extended both arms to the back of her neck, saying that her neck was stiff. She then stretched out with both of her legs, with no tonic–clonic movements. Toes were extended and pointed forward. She was partially sitting in her chair and partially sliding to the floor. Her eyes began to close, and I specifically asked her to keep her eyes open and to maintain eye contact with me. I repeatedly stated that she needed to talk to me during this time and not shut off contact with me. With this, the seizure-like event ended.

This experience proved to be very important for both of us. I directly experienced how overwhelming feelings of anger, unfairness, and helplessness surrounded the development of this NES for the patient. She experienced, perhaps for the first time in her young adult years, how intense, unspoken emotions seemed to trigger her NES. She did not have to be convinced of this—she directly experienced that reality. She was also comforted by the experience of someone staying with her during this episode and keeping her from breaking contact with the outside world. She felt a sense of nurturance and care that she had not experienced before. The psychotherapeutic bond was now firmly established, and the frequency of NES began to noticeably decrease. As the NES became less frequent, discussions about her relationships with her child, mother, stepfather, sisters, and biological father became the repeated focus of attention. She continues to look forward to discussing her reactions and problems with each of them. These discussions seemed to help her understand the conflicts and to manage them more effectively.

During these times, psychotherapy has been repeatedly described as a process analogous to "turning the lights on in a dark room full of bear traps." All it allows one to do is to see where not to step in order not to hurt oneself any further. This analogy has been evoked several times in the course of her care, which has now extended into 5 years. She has experienced the reality that life is always filled with conflicts and disagreements. Understanding how past experiences and relationships influence her response to those conflicts continues to be "an eye opener" for her. She wants regular, predictable times to talk about relationships as she begins to navigate her present life circumstances. Her new tattoos reflect increasing emotional contact with her son. Her favorite songs reflect recurring issues with men who wish to date her. Her NES only occasionally appear, and when they do she is surprised by them. She was hoping "to get rid of them." When they occur, she now recognizes that she is more emotionally overwhelmed by these situations than she realized. This new understanding has armed her with a sense of wisdom about her situation and a growing appreciation that what she often experiences is anxiety, not a seizure. When seizures occur, she knows what is happening. She has had no emergency room visits during the time of her psychotherapy. This is in striking contrast to her several hospitalizations before this treatment. Table 23.2 describes some of the clinical features associated with her psychological care in comparison with other patients described in previous chapters.

SUMMARY

Although the patient described in this chapter had neuropsychological disturbances associated with her left temporal lobe meningioma, CPS, and medications, she also had psychogenic NES. This latter problem appeared to represent a true somatization disorder in which a dissociative reaction occurred when intense conflictual and unresolvable emotions could not be consciously experienced or managed. Childhood experiences of physical abuse appeared to be the cause of this reaction. In this woman's everyday adult life, arguments, angry feelings, feelings of unfairness, and feelings of not being protected could automatically and unexpectedly overwhelm her. This appeared to trigger or produce a psychogenic NES. The emotions underlying the experiences were complex, but anxiety was clearly a major feature. A slow but progressive understanding of her reoccurring patterns of behavior helped this patient. As of this writing, she has been free of psychogenic NES for several months. At times they will unexpectedly occur, but she is now in a much better position to manage what happens after these events. A sustained psychotherapeutic alliance based on understanding the patient's phenomenological experience in light of psychodynamic principles appeared most helpful.

When psychogenic NES brings a patient to the attention of a psychotherapist, the resolution of these events may be the goal of scientific studies aimed at assessing treatment effectiveness. However, for patients, the resolution of the NES can open new psychological vistas that allow them to see aspects of their behavior and life they had not previously recognized. This recognition can have a profound influence on their future behavior and can thereby substantially improve the

Table 23.2 Clinical Features Relevant to the Psychological Care of a Person with Both Epileptic Seizures and Nonepileptic (Psychogenic) Seizures

CLINICAL FEATURE	YES	NO	PARTIALLY
1. The dialogue between the patient and the clinical neuropsychologist was not rushed.	✓		
2. The patient was able to express her personal concerns.	✓		
3. The content of the concerns varied over time.	✓		
4. The patient experienced a sense of "realistic" hope in coping with her symptoms and her life situation.	✓		
5. The patient and the clinical neuropsychologist developed a positive therapeutic relationship that helped the patient sustain adaptive activities during difficult times.	✓		
6. Somatic symptoms (which appeared to be indirect effects of a brain disorder) were substantially reduced during periods of psychological care.	✓		
7. Anxiety/depression/anger and/or apathy were substantially reduced during periods of psychological care.	✓		
8. The patient was able to follow the guidance of the clinical neuropsychologist to improve functioning in everyday life activities.			✓
9. The patient was able to control impulses and delay gratification.			✓
10. The patient did not feel "alone" when dealing with her problems in life.	✓		
11. The patient attempted to "self-reflect" or "be more aware" of personal "strengths" and "limitations."			✓
12. The patient experienced enjoyment in the care or help of other living things (people, animals, the environment, etc.).	✓		
13. The patient experienced an understanding of the "problematic nature of their unique life" and was not overwhelmed or "defeated" by it or readily gave in to escapism to cope with life (Bettelheim, 1989).			✓
14. The patient could "live with" the restrictions produced by a brain injury "without resentment" or loss of hope (K. Goldstein, 1952).	✓		
15. The patient was able to obtain new insights into self by attending to why certain songs, stories, fairy tales, movies, tattoos, etc. had a special personal meaning that initially she did not understand.			✓

(*continued*)

Table 23.2 Continued

CLINICAL FEATURE	YES	NO	PARTIALLY
16. The patient's dreams or artwork often heralded changes in behavior that aided psychological adjustment before the consciously mediated changes occurred.	✓		
17. The psychological care interventions (including the dialogue) between the patient and the clinical neuropsychologist resulted in the patient talking more openly about problems and demonstrating self-directed efforts at improving psychological adjustment to the direct and indirect effects of the brain disorder.	✓		
18. The psychological care interventions were in harmony with the patient's cultural background and religious orientation.	✓		
19. The psychological care interventions resulted in a substantial decline in her NES.	✓		
20. The patient and family experienced two basic facts of life: (a) The individual's state of subjective sense of personal well-being fluctuates and (b) the psychological adjustment process is never static and therefore hope should never be abandoned.	✓		
Total	15	0	5

quality of their life. What distinguishes the psychological care of the patient discussed in this chapter from the care of patients with a brain disorder but no comorbid psychiatric disorder is the depth of the psychological dialogue. That dialogue was reflected in the patient's capacity to record dreams; associate to those dreams; experience conflicts within the therapeutic hour; and recognize, in part on her own, recurring patterns of behavior that substantially influenced relationships with people, including her psychotherapist. The dialogue allowed the patient to develop an adult view of the problematic nature of her life without giving in to escapism. Moreover, the dialogue enabled the patient to successfully manage problems that she once experienced as "unmanageable." This type of dialogue often takes more time, but it provides greater personal rewards for some patients.

Such dialogue may also result in greater medical rewards. Whitehead, O'Sullivan, and Walker (2015) published a very interesting article on the impact of psychogenic NES on surgical outcomes. The authors reported that patients identified as having both psychogenic NES and ES prior to surgery appeared to have poorer surgical outcomes. These physicians also suggested that successfully treating psychogenic NES in patients who also have ES might improve their surgical outcomes.

REFERENCES

Bakvis, P., Spinhoven, P., Putman, P., Zitman, F. G., & Roelofs, K. (2010). The effect of stress induction on working memory in patients with psychogenic nonepileptic seizures. *Epilepsy & Behavior, 19*(3), 448–454.

Barr, W. B. (2015). Neuropsychological assessment of patients with epilepsy. In W. B. Barr & C. Morrison

(Eds.), *Handbook on the neuropsychology of epilepsy* (pp. 1–36). New York, NY: Springer.

Barry, J., & Reuber, M. (2010). The use of hypnosis and linguistic analysis to discriminate between patients with psychogenic nonepileptic seizures and patients with epilepsy. In S. C. Schachter & W. C. LaFrance (Eds.), *Gates and Rowan's non-epileptic seizures* (pp. 82–90). New York, NY: Cambridge University Press.

Bortz, J. J., Prigatano, G. P., Blum, D., & Fisher, R. S. (1995). Differential response characteristics in nonepileptic and epileptic seizure patients on a test of verbal learning and memory. *Neurology, 45*(11), 2029–2034.

Bowman, E. S., & Markand, O. N. (1996). Psychodynamics and psychiatric diagnoses of pseudoseizure subjects. *American Journal of Psychiatry, 153*(1), 57–63.

Brown, R. J. (2002). The cognitive psychology of dissociative states. *Cognitive Neuropsychiatry, 7*(3), 221–235.

Chalder, T. (1996). Practitioner non-epileptic attacks: Report of a cognitive behavioural approach in a single case with a four-year follow-up. *Clinical Psychology and Psychotherapy, 3*(4), 291–297.

Diprose, W., Sundram, F., & Menkes, D. B. (2016). Psychiatric comorbidity in psychogenic nonepileptic seizures compared with epilepsy. *Epilepsy & Behavior, 56*, 123–130.

Dodrill, C. (2010). Use of neuropsychological and personality testing to identify adults with psychogenic nonepileptic seizures. In S. C. Schachter & W. C. LaFrance (Eds.), *Gates and Rowan's nonepileptic seizures* (pp. 136–141). New York, NY: Cambridge University Press.

Fisher, R. S., Cross, J. H., French, J. A., Higurashi, N., Hirsch, E., Jansen, F. E., . . . Roulet Perez, E. (2017). Operational classification of seizure types by the International League Against Epilepsy: Position paper of the ILAE Commission for Classification and Terminology. *Epilepsia, 58*(4), 522–530.

Gates, J. R., & Erdahl, P. (1993). Classification of non-epileptic events. In A. J. Rowan & J. R. Gates (Eds.), *Non-epileptic seizures* (Vol. 1, pp. 21–30). Boston, MA: Butterworth-Heinemann.

Goldstein, K. (1942). *Aftereffects of brain injuries in war: Their evaluation and treatment. The application of psychologic methods in the clinic.* New York, NY: Grune & Stratton.

Goldstein, K. (1952). The effect of brain damage on the personality. *Psychiatry, 15*(3), 245–260.

Goldstein, L., Chalder, T., Chigwedere, C., Khondoker, M., Moriarty, J., Toone, B., & Mellers, J. (2010). Cognitive–behavioral therapy for psychogenic nonepileptic seizures: A pilot RCT. *Neurology, 74*(24), 1986–1994.

Goldstein, L., LaFrance, W., Jr., Chigwedere, C., Mellers, J., & Chalder, T. (2010). Cognitive behavioral treatments. In S. C. Schachter & W. LaFrance, Jr. (Eds.), *Gates and Rowan's nonepileptic seizures* (3rd ed., pp. 281–288). New York, NY: Cambridge University Press.

Greenberg, M. (2010). *Handbook of neurosurgery.* Tampa, FL: Greenberg Graphics.

Hara, K., Adachi, N., Akanuma, N., Ito, M., Okazaki, M., Matsubara, R., . . . Matsuura, M. (2015). Dissociative experiences in epilepsy: Effects of epilepsy-related factors on pathological dissociation. *Epilepsy & Behavior, 44*, 185–191.

Helmstaedter, C., Kurthen, M., Lux, S., Reuber, M., & Elger, C. E. (2003). Chronic epilepsy and cognition: A longitudinal study in temporal lobe epilepsy. *Annals of Neurology, 54*(4), 425–432.

Hendrickson, R., Popescu, A., Ghearing, G., & Bagic, A. (2015). Thoughts, emotions, and dissociative features differentiate patients with epilepsy from patients with psychogenic nonepileptic spells (PNESs). *Epilepsy & Behavior, 51*, 158–162.

Hermann, B., Seidenberg, M., Bell, B., Rutecki, P., Sheth, R., Ruggles, K., . . . Magnotta, V. (2002). The neurodevelopmental impact of childhood-onset temporal lobe epilepsy on brain structure and function. *Epilepsia, 43*(9), 1062–1071.

Kanner, A. M. (2013). The treatment of depressive disorders in epilepsy: What all neurologists should know. *Epilepsia, 54*(Suppl. 1), 3–12.

King, D. W., Gallagher, B. B., Murro, A. M., & Campbell, L. R. (1993). Convulsive non-epileptic seizures. In A. J. Rowan & J. R. Gates (Eds.), *Non-epileptic seizures* (pp. 31–38). Boston, MA: Butterworth-Heinemann.

LaFrance, W. C., Jr., Reuber, M., & Goldstein, L. H. (2013). Management of psychogenic nonepileptic seizures. *Epilepsia, 54*(Suppl. 1), 53–67.

LaFrance, W. C., Jr., & Wincze, J. P. (2015). *Treating nonepileptic seizures: Therapist guide.* New York, NY: Oxford University Press.

LaFrance, W. C., Jr., & Zimmerman, M. (2010). Classification of nonepileptic seizures. In S. C. Schachter & W. C. LaFrance (Eds.), *Gates and Rowan's nonepileptic seizures* (pp. 199–212). New York, NY: Cambridge University Press.

Lee, G. P. (2010). *Neuropsychology of epilepsy and epilepsy surgery.* New York, NY: Oxford University Press.

Lee, G. P., & Clason, C. L. (2008). Classification of seizure disorders and syndromes, and neuropsychological impairment in adults with epilepsy. In J. E. Morgan & J. H. Ricker (Ed.),

Textbook of clinical neuropsychology (pp. 437–465). New York, NY: Taylor & Francis.

Lishman, W. A. (Ed.). (1987). *Organic psychiatry: The psychological consequences of cerebral disorder* (3rd ed.). Oxford, UK: Blackwell.

Martin, R., Bell, B., Hermann, B., & Mennemeyer, S. (2003). Nonepileptic Seizures and their Costs: The Role of Neuropsychology. In. G. P. Prigatano and N. Pliksin (Eds.). *Clnical Neuropsychology and Cost Outcome Research: A Beginning* (pp. 235–258). Psychology Press, N.Y.: New York.

Mendez, M. (2009). Neuropsychiatric aspects of epilepsy. In B. J. Sadock, V. A. Sadock, & P. Ruiz (Eds.), *Comprehensive textbook of psychiatry* (Vol. 1, pp. 198–206). Philadelphia, PA: Wolters Kluwer.

Pick, S., Mellers, J. D., & Goldstein, L. H. (2015). Misinterpretation of emotional facial expressions in patients diagnosed with dissociative seizures. *Journal of Neurology, Neurosurgery, and Psychiatry, 86*(9), e3.

Plug, L., Sharrack, B., & Reuber, M. (2009). Seizure metaphors differ in patients' accounts of epileptic and psychogenic nonepileptic seizures. *Epilepsia, 50*(5), 994–1000.

Prigatano, G. P., & Kirlin, K. A. (2009). Self-appraisal and objective assessment of cognitive and affective functioning in persons with epileptic and nonepileptic seizures. *Epilepsy & Behavior, 14*(2), 387–392.

Prigatano, G. P., Stonnington, C. M., & Fisher, R. S. (2002). Psychological factors in the genesis and management of nonepileptic seizures: Clinical observations. *Epilepsy & Behavior, 3*(4), 343–349.

Reuber, M., Burness, C., Howlett, S., Brazier, J., & Grünewald, R. (2007). Tailored psychotherapy for patients with functional neurological symptoms: A pilot study. *Journal of Psychosomatic Research, 63*(6), 625–632.

Robbins, N. M., Larimer, P., Bourgeois, J. A., & Lowenstein, D. H. (2016). Number of patient-reported allergies helps distinguish epilepsy from psychogenic nonepileptic seizures. *Epilepsy & Behavior, 55*, 174–177.

Rowan, A. J., & Gates, J. R. (1993). *Non-epileptic seizures*. Stoneham, MA: Butterworth-Heinemann.

Schachter, S. C., & LaFrance, W. C. (2010). Use of neuropsychological and personality testing to identify adults with psychogenic nonepileptic seizures. In S. C. Schachter & W. C. LaFrance (Eds.), *Gates and Rowan's nonepileptic seizures* (3rd ed., pp. 136–141). New York, NY: Cambridge University Press.

Testa, S. M., Krauss, G. L., Lesser, R. P., & Brandt, J. (2012). Stressful life event appraisal and coping in patients with psychogenic seizures and those with epilepsy. *Seizure, 21*(4), 282–287.

Trimble, M. (2010). Psychogenic non epileptic seizures: Historical overview. In S. C. Schachter & W. C. LaFrance (Eds.), *Gates and Rowan's nonepileptic seizures* (pp. 17–25). New York, NY: Cambridge University Press.

Whitehead, K., O'Sullivan, S., & Walker, M. (2015). Impact of psychogenic nonepileptic seizures on epilepsy presurgical investigation and surgical outcomes. *Epilepsy & Behavior, 46*, 246–248.

Widdess-Walsh, P., Nadkarni, S., & Devinsky, O. (2010). Comorbidity of epileptic and psychogenic nonepileptic seizures: Diagnostic considerations. In S. C. Schachter & W. C. LaFrance (Eds.), *Gates and Rowan's nonepileptic seizures* (pp. 51–61). New York, NY: Cambridge University Press.

24

PSYCHOLOGICAL CARE OF PERSONS WITH PSYCHIATRIC-BASED COGNITIVE COMPLAINTS

BACKGROUND INFORMATION

In the course of clinical practice of neuropsychology, adult patients are frequently referred because of subjective reports of decline in their memory. For many of these individuals, their cognitive complaints are not easily explained by any known physical cause. As noted in Chapters 1 and 10, a neuropsychological examination may help determine if there is evidence of an underlying brain disorder or if the memory complaints appear to be related to other causes, such as normal aging, medication effects (Papenberg et al., 2017), sleep disturbance (Gamaldo et al., 2019), and/or poor cardiorespiratory fitness (McAuley et al., 2011). Some patients with cognitive complaints also present with psychiatric symptoms. The relationship between psychiatric symptoms and cognitive complaints is often complicated. Nevertheless, a number of studies have reported mild to moderate correlations between certain psychiatric difficulties and subjective memory complaints (SMCs). In this chapter, selective studies on common correlates of SMCs in adults are first reviewed. The five essential questions that were posed to guide the psychological care of persons with brain disorders (see Box 12.4) are modified and adapted to individuals who appear to have psychiatrically based memory disturbances. How these patients are interviewed, examined, and given feedback concerning their neuropsychological test findings can clearly influence their psychological care. Clinical case vignettes are reviewed to highlight some important features relevant to this topic.

SUBJECTIVE MEMORY COMPLAINTS

Complaints of a poor or declining memory have been observed across the adult life span (Rowell, Green, Teachman, & Salthouse, 2016). Many factors appear to contribute to the subjective sense that one's memory is compromised and/or declining. Box 24.1 lists some of the well-known factors that contribute to subjective complaints of memory impairments. They include, of course, a possible underlying brain disorder; the normal adverse effects of aging on memory, especially in the older population; persistent negative affect in non-brain dysfunctional individuals; psychiatric disorders of various types; sleep disorders; medication side effects; and the overall health status of the individual, including dietary and exercise habits. The natural tendency of human beings to complain about a variety of difficulties also needs to be included in this list. These variables can interact with one another in complicated and at times unpredictable ways.

EFFECTS OF A BRAIN DISORDER ON MEMORY AND MEMORY COMPLAINTS

A description of the types of memory disturbances measured by standard neuropsychological tests in persons with various brain disorders can be found in Lezak, Howieson, Loring, Hannay, and Fischer (2004). Typically, a brain disorder will negatively affect the ability of the person to learn new information, even with practice, and then later retain that information after a distraction, particularly if that distraction exceeds 20–30 minutes. The "learning curve" as well as the amount of information recalled are clearly compromised in brain dysfunctional individuals compared to appropriately matched control groups. This occurs even when the person is putting forth adequate effort to recall the new information presented.

NORMAL ADVERSE AGING EFFECTS, PARTICULARLY IN THE ELDERLY POPULATION

As noted in Chapter 8, Davis et al. (2003) studied the learning and memory characteristics of normally functioning adult individuals who were classified into four age groups (30–45, 46–60, 61–75, and 76–90 years). The investigators employed a common verbal learning test used by clinical neuropsychologists—the Rey Auditory Verbal Learning Test (RAVLT). The authors demonstrated clear age differences in the number of words recalled on this serial verbal learning test over five trials as well as the number of words recalled after a 20-minute distraction. Older individuals indeed

---

Box 24.1. Common Correlates of Subjective Memory Complaints in Adults

1. A brain disorder
2. Normal adverse aging effects in the elderly population
3. Negative affects (e.g., depression, anxiety, and neuroticism)
4. Psychiatric disorders (e.g., bipolar disorders and somatization disorders)
5. Sleep disorders
6. Medication effects
7. Multiple health problems
8. Poor cardiorespiratory fitness and exercise
9. Poor nutrition
10. Natural tendency of humans to complain

had more difficulty learning and recalling this type of verbal information, especially in the 76- to 90-year-old group. Note, however, that the learning curve was normal across age groups. After each successful learning trial, there was a group tendency (irrespective of age) to recall more words. Also, both primacy and recency effects were observed on Trial 1 and on a 20-minute delayed recall trial in normally functioning adults. These findings characterize normal functioning, even in the elderly population. By understanding these relationships, clinical neuropsychologists can measure both the pattern and the level of verbal learning and memory and determine if they are normal for a person's age range and educational background. During the later years of life, the amount of information a person can learn and recall does decline. This can contribute to the subjective complaint of worse memory as one grows older.

NEGATIVE AFFECT AND MEMORY COMPLAINTS

Rowell et al. (2016) asked 3,798 healthy adults to complete questionnaires measuring various memory concerns. The authors administered two tests of verbal memory. In addition, subjects answered questions regarding their emotional state. Across all age groups, subjective complaints of memory were statistically related to objective memory performance, but the magnitude of the correlations was small (e.g., the r value was as low as .11 for persons aged 55–64 years and as high as .24 for persons aged 75–99 years). In contrast, measures of anxiety and depression correlated at a higher level with complaints of poor memory. Depression consistently correlated more strongly with self-reported frequency of forgetting at all age ranges (Table 24.1), but it was highest in the 75- to 99-year-old group ($r = .44$). Using structural equation modeling, they reported that "the relationship between memory complaints and negative affect was moderate in all age groups, and there was no evidence for moderation by objective memory" (p. 1255).

Similar findings were reported by Pearman and Storandt (2004). In a sample of 283 community-dwelling adults aged 45–94 years, the correlation between self-described poor memory and neuroticism scores was $r = -.42$. In contrast, a much smaller relationship was found in this older population between actual raw scores achieved when recalling information on the Logical Memory subtest of the Wechsler Memory Scale III and their memory complaints ($r = .23$).

In a recent study, Zlatar, Muniz, Galasko, and Salmon (2018) reported on the correlates of subjective cognitive decline (SCD) in 519 individuals aged 60–95 years. These individuals or their physicians were concerned about their cognitive functioning. More than 80% of these patients reported "persistent memory difficulties." Individuals were classified as having either no cognitive impairment (NCI) or significant cognitive impairment (SCI). SCD was not significantly correlated with scores using a composite measure of cognitive performance (which included their ability to recall short stories read to them from the Wechsler Memory Scale–Revised). However, there were significant correlations between SCD and self-reported levels of depression on the Beck Depression Inventory for both groups of individuals: $r = .32$ for the NCI group, and $r = .33$ for the SCI group. The magnitude of the correlation was almost identical for the two groups.

Williams et al. (2017) also asked a large sample of older, normally functioning adults ($N = 2,802$) to complete three memory tests, one of which was the RAVLT. In addition to measuring their depressive symptoms, the investigators also had these older individuals answer questions about their anxiety with regard to completing intellectual tasks. The authors did not specifically evaluate memory complaints. Their findings, however, are important. They reported that older adults with the highest level of anxiety (i.e., in the upper

Table 24.1 Commonly Reported Correlations with Subjective Memory Complaints

GROUP	CORRELATION (R)
Normal adults, aged 18–99 years (Rowell et al., 2016)	
Performance on verbal memory tests	.11–.24
Anxiety symptoms	–.34
Depressive symptoms	–.35
Neuroticism	–.29
Normal older adults, aged 45–99 years (Pearman & Storandt, 2004)	
Performance on a verbal memory test	.23
Neuroticism	–.42
Mix of normal and cognitively impaired older adults (Zlatar et al., 2018)	
Depressive symptoms in patients with no cognitive impairment	.32
Depressive symptoms in patients with significant cognitive impairment	.33
Patients with MDD vs. healthy controls (Beblo et al., 2017)	
Depressive symptoms, MDD group	.42
Depressive symptoms, healthy group	.28
Performance on a verbal memory test, MDD group	.30
Performance on a verbal memory test, healthy group	–.09
Patients with borderline personality disorder vs. healthy controls (Beblo et al., 2014)	
Borderline Symptom List	.54
Performance on a verbal memory test, BPD group	–.08
Performance on a verbal memory test, healthy group	.14

MDD, major depressive disorder.

quartile of the sample) performed worse on memory tests. As expected, demographic variables (i.e., age, race, sex, and educational level) correlated with performance on memory tests but in rather complicated ways. Most important, however, was the finding that self-reported anxiety levels overshadowed the effects of self-reported levels of depression on actual memory scores. The investigators noted that "depressive symptoms had only a small negative influence on memory functioning" (Williams et al., 2017, p. 988). Collectively, these findings suggest not only that the patients with psychiatric disorders might have memory complaints but also that, in some instances, their psychiatric disorder might influence their performance on memory tests.

PSYCHIATRIC DISORDERS, MEMORY COMPLAINTS, AND MEMORY FUNCTIONING

Given that self-reported levels of depression and anxiety correlate with memory complaints in relatively healthy adults, it appears that patients with psychiatrically diagnosed depression might also report memory difficulties. This, in fact, has been reported (Antikainen et al., 2001). Memory complaints were common in clinically depressed adults. As their depression decreased, reportedly so did their memory complaints. A relatively recent review of the literature suggests that various cognitive impairments can objectively exist in depressed patients, even when their clinically diagnosed depression is treated. Difficulties in thinking, concentrating, and making decisions have been specifically associated with the diagnosis of a major depressive disorder (MDD; Rock, Roiser, Riedel, & Blackwell, 2014). Subjective memory complaints in these depressed patients, however, often are not correlated with their actual test performance.

Quite relevant to the clinical neuropsychological examinations of depressed patients are the findings reported by Porter, Gallagher, Thompson, and Young (2003). They compared 44 adults with a confirmed diagnosis of an MDD (single episode or recurrent) who were free of psychotropic medications for at least 6 weeks prior to neuropsychological testing with 44 well-matched healthy controls. A series of neuropsychological measures were administered. One of the tests was the RAVLT, which is sensitive to aging effects and various brain disorders, as noted previously and throughout this text. The mean age of both groups was 32 years (but ages ranged from 19 to 61 years in the MDD group and 18 to 55 years in the control group). Regarding the RAVLT test findings, the authors reported that "a significant learning effect was observed across successive presentations . . . but no difference in learning curves between groups" (p. 216). This is an important finding. In the MDD group, the verbal learning curves on this measure were not different from those of normal controls, but the amount of verbal learning over trials was worse in the MDD patients. The difference in average total number of words recalled between the two groups, however, was small and nonsignificant (e.g., an average of 54 words for the control group and 50 words for the MDD group). Interestingly, the percentage of words recalled on the 20-minute delayed trial was 82.5% for controls and 75.7% for the MDD patients. The percentage of words recalled in the control group is in the range of what would be expected, given the wide range of ages of individuals in that group (Davis et al., 2003). The correlation between self-ratings of depression, using the Hamilton Rating Scale for Depression, and delayed recall of words after a 20-minute delay was significant but mild in terms of size effects ($r = .31$).

Children with disorders of depression have also been reported to show mild verbal learning and memory deficits using the RAVLT. Günther, Holtkamp, Jolles, Herpertz-Dahlmann, and Konrad (2004) compared 34 children with anxiety disorders (17 had a generalized anxiety disorder) to 31 children with depressive disorders (22 had a major depressive disorder) and 33 healthy controls. All children were medication-free at the time of testing. The mean age of the children was between 12.5 and 13.5 years across the three groups. Children with depressive disorders had mildly worse delayed free recall and recognition memory on the RAVLT compared to the other two groups, but the differences again were marginal. No correlations were reported between the level of anxiety or depression and test performance. Children with anxiety disorders performed as well as normal children on these two measures.

Using an experimental task of working memory, Sari, Koster, and Derakshan (2017) demonstrated that active worry in normal young adults reduces the efficiency of information processing and thereby compromises working memory. This may be one means by which anxiety and/or depression negatively affect verbal learning. Clinically, patients with anxiety and/or depression disorders often have relative difficulties learning information that is first presented to them on a single trial (a measure of working memory?). When given the opportunity to repeat the information over several trials (such as on the RAVLT), their performance often is within the normal range for their age and educational background. Two of the clinical case vignettes described later in this chapter demonstrate this finding.

It is also important to note that the emotional state of the patient can influence neuropsychological test performance, even in patients with a known brain disorder. Brown et al. (2014) demonstrated this reality when studying memory deficits in patients with temporal epilepsy. They reported that verbal memory, as measured by the California Verbal Learning Test, which is similar in format to the RAVLT, was substantially lower in patients with left temporal lobe epilepsy versus right temporal lobe epilepsy. This finding, however, was seen only in patients who had low anxiety scores. When anxiety levels were high, as measured by the Beck Anxiety Inventory, there were no significant differences in performance on this test of verbal memory between these two groups. The authors also noted that performance on the Rey Complex Figure Test was "significantly affected by anxiety and did not lateralize to either side" (p. 19).

Beblo et al. (2014) attempted to study memory complaints in 28 patients diagnosed with borderline personality disorder (BPD) compared to 32 healthy controls matched on age, educational background, and sex. However, the authors noted that several BPD patients had comorbid mental disorders, including anxiety disorders and disorders of depression. Patients also differed regarding their medications. Thus, the findings should be interpreted with considerable caution. Noteworthy about this report, however, is that this heterogeneous group of BPD patients reported considerably more memory difficulties than did the healthy controls. They did not differ from healthy controls on any of the memory tests administered, one of which was the RAVLT. Symptoms specifically associated with BPD showed the highest correlation with memory complaints ($r = .54$).

Beblo, Kater, Baetge, Driessen, and Piefke (2017) studied memory performance in everyday life (in addition to memory performance on psychometric tests) in 20 patients with MDD and 20 normally functioning control subjects. They again reported that MDD patients have many more memory complaints than matched controls, but their performance on memory tests was not different from that of the normal controls. In MDD patients, the correlation between memory complaints and verbal word list memory scores was $r = .30$ ($p = .22$) in their small sample; for the control subjects, the correlation was $r = -.09$ ($p = .69$). The point of these latter observations is that in depressed patients, there is often a small correlation with actual verbal learning and memory scores and level of depression. In larger sample sizes, this correlation is significant, but it accounts for a very small amount of test score variability.

SLEEP DISORDERS, MEMORY COMPLAINTS, AND MEMORY FUNCTIONING

It has been known for some time that reduced sleep time contributes to the experience of fatigue and increases errors in attention and vigilance (Banks & Dinges, 2011). Poor sleep quality has also been related to reports of poor memory for such tasks as recalling where an object was placed and recalling specific facts from reading materials. The magnitude of the relationships, however, is relatively small (Gamaldo et al., 2019). Specific sleep disorders, however, can clearly affect memory and related cognitive functions.

Untreated obstructive sleep apnea (OSA) has been related to substantial difficulties with vigilance. Variable findings have been reported as OSA relates to memory functioning (Beebe, Groesz, Wells, Nichols, & McGee, 2003). In a well-designed study, 60 adults with OSA were compared to 60 healthy volunteers on various neuropsychological measures (Twigg et al., 2010). Patients with OSA performed worse on the immediate and delayed free recall of short stories read to them from the Logical Memory subtests of the Wechsler Memory Scale. They did not differ, however, with regard to the percentage of information recalled. They also performed worse on tests of visual attention and visual working memory. However, there was no relationship between the severity of OSA and the degree of memory impairment. In a study using high-resolution magnetic resonance imaging (MRI) scans of the brain, 16 patients with newly diagnosed moderate to severe OSA were compared to 14 controls (Torelli et al., 2011). Several findings were reported, but the most interesting were reduced volume loss in the right hippocampus and worse memory performance in the OSA patients. In OSA patients, but not controls, there was a marked negative correlation between MRI findings and age. Total hippocampal volume was correlated with RAVLT delayed score when both groups of patients were combined ($r = 0.388$, $p = .03$).

In a very interesting study on treatment effectiveness for reversing memory impairments in patients with OSA, Zimmerman, Arnedt, Stanchina, Millman, and Aloia (2006) demonstrated that patients who used continuous positive airway pressure treatment an average of 6 hours per night for 3 months showed substantially improved memory performance as measured by the Hopkins Verbal Learning Test. Patients who used the treatment for fewer hours did not show significant improvement on this test of verbal memory.

As was the case with anxiety, the presence of OSA can interact with a known brain disorder to further negatively influence memory functioning. Wilde et al. (2007) compared a heterogeneous group of traumatic brain injured (TBI) patients with and without OSA. The TBI patients with OSA performed significantly worse on a number of neuropsychological tests. Percentage of information retained on the RAVT test was notable. Recall was 71.68% (±27.57%) in the TBI patients without OSA, whereas it was 49.98% (±25.42%) in the TBI patients with OSA. Collectively, these findings suggest that sleep disturbance can correlate with both memory complaints and memory performance in patients with and without a brain disorder.

MEDICATION EFFECTS

Medications are prescribed for a variety of health care problems, including those associated with sleep and mood disorders. It has long been recognized that drugs that have anticholinergic side effects can negatively affect memory, particularly in the elderly population (Mintzer & Burns, 2000). Prolonged use of strong anticholinergic medications has also been linked to the development of later dementia in some (but clearly not all) elderly individuals (Gray et al., 2015). When a patient is on medications that may produce anticholinergic effects and is either complaining of memory difficulties or demonstrating poor memory performance on neuropsychological tests, testing of the patient when off these medications may result in surprising effects. Also, the number of medications a person is taking often correlates with the number of health problems the person experiences. Subjective memory complaints have also been associated with a number of comorbid health conditions, which are described next.

HEALTH STATUS, CARDIORESPIRATORY FITNESS, AND EATING HABITS OF PATIENTS WITH SUBJECTIVE MEMORY COMPLAINTS

The relationship between multiple health problems and SMCs was studied in a very large sample (15,188 participants) of individuals in the Netherlands (Aarts et al., 2011). In this large sample, 26% considered themselves forgetful. Reports of memory difficulties were most prominent in older individuals with multiple health problems. It was further noted that patients with apparent psychological distress worried most about their memory difficulties. Poor eating habits and lack of exercise were related in complicated ways with memory complaints. Multiple interactions between various demographic characteristics and SMCs were also noted (and expected) in this very large sample.

In a large telephone survey, reports of healthy eating were associated with fewer memory complaints in young, middle-aged, and older adults (Small et al., 2013). In the same study, reports of regular exercise were associated with fewer memory complaints in the middle-aged and older groups.

In a randomized controlled study, Iuliano et al. (2017) demonstrated that a systematic 12-week exercise program reduced SMCs in older adults (mean age, 66.96 ± 11.73 years) but did not improve memory performance on tests of memory that included the RAVLT. Some less systematic studies have suggested not only improved SMCs in the elderly but also perhaps subtle improvement in speed of information processing as measured by the Wechsler Digit Symbol subtest (Kamegaya et al., 2012). There is consistent evidence, however, that regular aerobic exercises lead to improved cardiorespiratory functioning in all age ranges (McAuley et al., 2011). Improved cardiorespiratory fitness modestly, but positively, correlates with processing speed ($r = -.34$, $p = .05$; McAuley et al., 2011). Memory complaints are also related to cardiorespiratory fitness at a similar level (McAuley et al., 2011).

Finally, patients with chronic pain frequently report cognitive difficulties, especially problems with memory (McCracken & Iverson, 2001). Measures of depression consistently correlated with subjective reported cognitive complaints in these patients. Some reported correlations were as high as $r = .63$ (Roth, Geisser, Theisen-Goodvich, & Dixon, 2005) and accounted for nearly 30% of the variance of cognitive complaints in other studies (McCracken & Iverson, 2001).

THE HUMAN TENDENCY TO COMPLAIN

In our current society, aging is often at the top of the list of complaints. Closely associated are concerns with physical functioning, including sleep disturbances and muscular–skeletal pain. Equally common are complaints about the quality of service in multiple domains, complaints regarding making purchases, complaints about working conditions, and complaints about the government. Complaints do not always represent "pathology." They can reflect the human condition. McGraw, Warren, and Kan (2014) note, for example, that "humorous complaining" is helpful when one wants to amuse or obtain approval from others. This commonly occurs when the person is dissatisfied and has no control over the situation. Complaining can certainly serve many functions, but it is clearly a natural part of human behavior (Watzlawick, 1993). In clinical practice, it is especially important to understand the nature of the complaint from the patient's perspective and then provide interventions that may reduce that complaint if possible. This is especially true for psychiatrically based cognitive complaints.

Case Vignette 24.1: Memory Complaints and Depression in a Young Adult

A 39-year-old woman reported to her neurologist that she had difficulty following directions at work and remembering names of people. She also reported that she could forget entire conversations and had difficulty finding words in the middle of conversations. In addition, she noted a history of depression, anxiety, sleep disturbance, and headaches. Her history was significant for Graves' disease, for which she received radiation therapy. Two sisters had been diagnosed with possible multiple sclerosis. The patient's neurological examination and neuroimaging studies of the brain were repeatedly within the normal range.

Although she was of young age, she was concerned about the possibility of an undiagnosed brain disorder or, worse, a dementing condition. When asked to make subjective ratings about level of difficulty in cognitive and affective domains on a scale from 0 to 10 (0 = no problem, 10 = severe problem), she rated memory difficulties a 5, concentration difficulties a 10, word-finding difficulties an 8, irritability a 10, anxiety a 6, and depression a 4. Her self-reported level of depression was her lowest rating. No family member or significant other was able to provide a perception of her functioning in each of these domains.

On formal psychometric testing, her Wechsler Adult Intelligence Scale–Third Edition (WAIS-III) Full Scale IQ was 100, without notable disparity between any of the scale scores contributing to this measure (for details, see Prigatano & Caples, 2003). Her performance on the RAVLT was very informative. On Trial 1, she recalled 6 words, followed by 8, 10, 12, and 13 words on each of the remaining trials. On each trial, she improved on the number of words she could recall. After a 20-minute delay, she recalled 10 words. All scores were within the normal range. Other neuropsychological test findings were within the normal range. She was asked to complete the Minnesota Multiphasic Personality Inventory-2 (MMPI-2). Validity scales were within the normal range. She showed elevated scores (in the following degree of relative magnitude) of 2-3-7-8-4. The profile suggested a dysthymic disorder.

When the findings were reviewed with the woman, she was surprised that she could recall as much as she did on the verbal learning test. She said that she felt comfortable being examined by the neuropsychologist. She was appreciative of the time taken to listen to her concerns and the explanations of why her neuropsychological test performance did not suggest the presence of a brain disorder. She then talked a little more about stresses at work and in her current marriage. She noted how difficult it was for her to handle arguments and accept any criticism from others. She reported long-standing feelings of inadequacy and said that maybe she was more depressed than she had previously recognized. She agreed that her emotional state might be negatively influencing her cognitive abilities in everyday life. She asked for help in better managing her emotional state, and she was referred to a clinical psychologist in the community.

When first seen, she experienced cognitive difficulties that raised her concern about an underlying brain disorder. She wanted help in understanding the probable causes of her cognitive difficulties. The initial focus of the discussion between her and the clinical neuropsychologist was about her normal level and pattern of cognitive functioning. At first, nothing was said about how affective disturbances might be contributing to her cognitive complaints. Once a reasonable explanation was given to her regarding her neuropsychological performance, she asked what might cause her difficulties in everyday life. At that time, emotional difficulties were considered a possibility. The MMPI-2 profile was reviewed, and the elevation on the Depression Scale (Scale 2) was especially noted. She then shifted the focus of the discussion to long-standing difficulties she had controlling negative self-thoughts throughout her life. She noted often feeling "put down" by others. She was now "open" to seeking help for her depression. When she left the consultation room, she spontaneously thanked the clinical neuropsychologist for the consultation. It had helped her better understand her symptoms. She felt relieved in some ways and empowered to seek out psychological treatment. Although such consultations do not always end in positive results, this one did.

Case Vignette 24.2: Memory Complaints and Anxiety in a Middle-Aged Adult

A 51-year-old woman reported to her neurologist that she would frequently lose objects and had difficulty finding words when speaking with others. She noted that she frequently forgot her phone number, zip code, and even her husband's last name. She noted that this problem had occurred during the past 3 or 4 years, but it had become worse during the past 6 months.

She reported a family history of Alzheimer's disease in her grandfather and mother. She also reported a remote history of depression in herself, but she indicated that with medication and counseling, she greatly improved. She noted that for 30 years she smoked half a pack of cigarettes each day, but during the past year she had not smoked. She also reported ongoing hip pain, which responded positively to medication. She noted a "busy life" and a "heavy workload." She noted that as her memory difficulties were becoming worse, she was thinking of either changing jobs or possibly retiring.

In the clinical interview, she was asked to make subjective ratings of her cognitive and affective functioning in several domains (Table 24.2). Initially, concentration and word-finding difficulties were rated quite high, with very low ratings of anxiety or depression. Her performance on measures of intelligence was above average. On the WAIS-III, her Full Scale IQ was 112 and compatible with her educational background. Again, her performances on the various subtests were all in the expected range, with very little inter-subtest variability (Prigatano & Gagliardi, 2005). Her scores on additional neuropsychological tests were within the normal range. On the RAVLT, she recalled 8, 11, 11, 14, and 13 words on Trials 1–5, respectively. Her learning curve revealed some inefficiency in the learning process, but generally the total number of words she recalled improved with practice. The total number of words she recalled was normal for her age. She could also recall 14 out of 15 words after a 20-minute distraction.

In light of these and other findings, it was explained to the patient that her level and pattern of performance appeared to be within the normal range for her age, educational background, and level of above average intelligence. She had also been given the MMPI-2, and her profile was valid, with a clinical profile of 3-1. The potential relevance of these findings was then discussed. It was pointed out that such a profile at times suggests an underlying difficulty with anxiety and associated concerns about one's health.

The patient reported that currently she was not feeling anxious (which is common for such an MMPI-2 profile), but she agreed to talk to her physician about the need for medication to help improve her sleep. She responded well to the medication and then sought out counseling for anxiety and learned muscle relaxation exercises to help her relax at the end of the day. She changed jobs and was more satisfied working for her new employer compared to her previous employer. She was scheduled for a 9-month follow-up neuropsychological examination.

The patient arrived for her appointment, but she spontaneously noted that she did not think she needed to return for a repeat examination because she was doing so well. She said that she was very pleased with the initial consultation. She noted that when she was first seen, she did not feel anxious, but as she underwent various psychological treatments, she began to actually identify anxiety feelings for the first time. She stated that as strange as it seemed, she did not know she was so anxious when first seen. Her ratings of cognitive and emotional functioning during her follow-up examination revealed that she now identified mild anxiety in her life but far fewer cognitive subjective complaints (Table 24.2). With this knowledge, she seemed to be coping much better. During her second neuropsychological examination, her verbal learning curve was normal, and she could recall 15 out of 15 words after a 20-minute distraction.

In Chapter 12, it was suggested that certain guidelines could aid in the psychological care of persons with a brain disorder. These guidelines were applied to this patient's consultation; that is, her concerns of memory were listened to and taken seriously. She wanted an explanation of why she was having these difficulties. After the examination was completed, an explanation of her neuropsychological test findings was presented in an informative and empathic manner. She understood that her test scores were normal and in some cases above average, but she was initially cautious about accepting the possibility that her anxiety might influence her subjectively experienced cognitive difficulties. She sought out psychological treatment on her own and became aware that she was more anxious than she subjectively experienced. She was grateful for the initial neuropsychological consultation and returned for a follow-up examination to thank the clinical neuropsychologist for the initial insights provided. She made positive changes in her life and was functioning in a much more satisfying way. Improved resiliency was obvious.

Table 24.2 Subjective Ratings of Cognitive and Affective Functioning in a Middle-Aged Adult Before and After Psychiatric and Psychological Care: Case Vignette 24.2

DOMAIN	PRETREATMENT	POST-TREATMENT
Memory	5	1
Concentration	6	2
Word finding	7	2
Irritability	3	2
Anxiety	1	4–5
Depression	0	2
Getting lost in space	8	4
Fatigability	5	4

Source: Reprinted from Prigatano, G. P., & Gagliardi, C. (2005). Memory and anxiety: Neuropsychological test findings and subjective complaints in a 51-year old woman. *BNI Quarterly, 21*(1), 9–12. Reprinted by permission of Barrow Neurological Institute.

Case Vignette 24.3: Memory Complaints, Migraine Headaches, and Nonepileptic Events in a Middle-Aged Adult

A 56-year-old woman reported progressive decline in her cognitive abilities, especially in her memory and speech. She had a long-standing history of migraine headaches and a more recent history of having some "spells" that appeared psychogenic in nature. Her neurologist reported that her neurological examination was normal. Neuroimaging studies of the brain were also normal. However, the patient was clearly in distress, and therefore a neuropsychological examination was requested.

The patient reported having two master's degrees and was working in a stressful work environment. She often felt overwhelmed with the problems she encountered at work, but she believed they had no bearing on her cognitive and speech difficulties. She did agree that they contributed to her fatigue. Her husband spontaneously noted, however, that her "spells" appeared to come on when she was especially stressed. The patient did not appear to agree with this appraisal. The patient reported long-standing sleep difficulties in which she had trouble falling asleep and staying asleep. She was overweight and said that she was a "comfort eater."

When she talked, her speech was initially slow and at times she halted between comments. As she became more comfortable and appeared less distressed, however, her speech was of normal cadence and fluency. She and her husband were also asked to make subjective ratings regarding her cognitive and affective functioning. On the same scale used with the two patients previously described in this chapter, she rated memory difficulties a 5. Concentration difficulties were rated 8, word-finding difficulties were rated a 6, irritability was rated a 5, anxiety was rated a 9, depression was rated a 9, fatigue was rated a 10, and problems with directionality in space were rated a 7. Her husband rated her memory difficulties a 4, concentration difficulties a 5, word-finding difficulties as variable (between 2 and 8 depending on the situation), irritability 6–7, anxiety 8–9, depression a 10, fatigue a 10, and problems with directionality 3–4. Both she and her husband believed that fatigue, depression, and anxiety were more severe than her memory difficulties. It is also notable that they both rated problems with concentration higher than memory problems.

On examination, all neuropsychological test findings (including language and memory tests) were within the normal range, and some scores were above average. For example, on the RAVLT, the patient recalled 7 words on Trial 1, followed by 10, 11, 14, and 13 on the remaining trials. Again, some inefficiency in the learning process was observed, but the total number of words recalled was within the normal range. Perhaps more important, she could recall 15 out of 15 words after a 20-minute distraction.

When inquiries were made about her history, the question of whether she had ever been abused was asked. At that time, she stopped talking and began to close her eyes and become unresponsive to questions. The patient was asked to maintain eye contact with the clinical neuropsychologist, which, with effort, she was able to do. The "spell" passed. The patient was not tired or amnestic to what was being talked about.

When the examination was completed, it was explained to the patient that some of the inefficiency in learning appeared to be multifactorial in nature. Disturbed sleep, elevated anxiety and depression, and fatigue seemed to be contributing to her cognitive difficulties in everyday life. She cautiously listened to this feedback but said very little. She recognized that her speech improved when she was less distressed, but she still believed that cognitive difficulties were present despite the neuropsychological test findings. When referral to an experienced psychotherapist was suggested to address what appeared to be features of a dissociative disorder, she wanted time to think about whether she would follow up on this recommendation. Her husband seemed to agree with the conclusions and recommendations, but she was less enthusiastic about the findings.

Returning to the features that can guide the psychological care of an individual, it needs to be determined what the patient experienced. First, she experienced significant cognitive, physical, and emotional difficulties. She experienced these difficulties as being "physically caused." Second, she wanted a physical explanation and treatment for these difficulties. When the findings focused on her normal neuropsychological status and the probable multifactorial nature of her complaints (including psychiatric difficulties), she was cautious in her response. She did not openly challenge the findings, but clearly she was invested in her point of view despite the findings, which were obtained and explained in a supportive manner. Third, the focus of the discussion did not change with this feedback. She was invested in her point of view. She wanted relief, not insight or behavioral change. Fourth, given the patient's perceptions, no psychological treatment intervention was attempted. Fifth, there was no evidence of improved resiliency as a result of the neuropsychological consultation.

Unfortunately, the latter case scenario is common for many patients seen with psychiatrically based cognitive complaints. It is important that the consulting clinical neuropsychologist not become too discouraged when encountering this type of patient and dialogue. Patients are invested in their beliefs for good psychological and at times interpersonal and even financial reasons. It is the honest dialogue, coupled with careful empirical evaluation of a patient's neuropsychological examination findings, that can still point the way to further psychological care in the future. Some patients will return several months or years later if they realize that the dialogue was intended to help them and not to dispose of them with "a diagnosis." Some patients have returned to obtain further help and others have not. The key is to evaluate the multiple factors that can contribute to SMCs and to provide patients with a supportive, clinically relevant, and medically necessary neuropsychological examination (see Chapter 10, this volume) that has the possibility of helping them now or in the future.

Clinical features relevant to the neuropsychological examination and feedback sessions for patients described in Case Vignettes 24.2 and 24.3 are listed in Tables 24.3 and 24.4, respectively.

Table 24.3 Clinical Features Relevant to the Psychological Care of a Person with an Anxiety Disorder and Subjective Memory Complaints: Case Vignette 24.2

CLINICAL FEATURE	YES	NO	PARTIALLY
1. The patient experiences memory difficulties that significantly disrupt her life and wants an explanation of why she is having those difficulties.	✓		
2. The patient gives a fairly clear account of what she is experiencing.	✓		
3. The content of the patient's concerns was repeated out loud by the clinical neuropsychologist to ensure that the clinical neuropsychologist fully understood what the patient is experiencing and what she is worried about.	✓		

(*continued*)

Table 24.3 Continued

CLINICAL FEATURE	YES	NO	PARTIALLY
4. The patient appeared to put forth adequate effort when undergoing neuropsychological testing.	✓		
5. The patient felt that the basic neuropsychological test results were presented in an understandable and empathetic manner.	✓		
6. The patient was able to recognize and verbally state that anxiety and/or depression may be contributing to the SMCs.	✓		
7. The patient engaged the clinical neuropsychologist regarding the findings and began to explore whether psychological factors (vs. an underlying brain disorder) contributed to her SMCs.			✓
8. The feedback session with the patient led the patient to introduce previously unmentioned history that is compatible with the findings and clinical impressions of the clinical neuropsychologist.			✓
9. The patient's lifestyle is conducive to seeking out psychological/psychiatric treatments.	✓		
10. The patient acts on the treatment recommendations for psychological/psychiatric treatments.	✓		
11. The patient appears to experience greater resiliency in dealing with her memory difficulties after the clinical neuropsychological examination/consultation.			✓
Total	8	0	3

SMCs, subjective memory complaints.

Table 24.4 Clinical Features Relevant to the Psychological Care of a Person with Memory Complaints, Migraine Headaches, and Nonepileptic Events: Case Vignette 24.3

CLINICAL FEATURE	YES	NO	PARTIALLY
1. The patient experiences memory difficulties that significantly disrupt her life and wants an explanation of why she is having those difficulties.	✓		
2. The patient gives a clear account of what she is experiencing.			✓
3. The content of the concerns was repeated out loud by the clinical neuropsychologist to ensure that the clinical neuropsychologist fully understood what the patient is experiencing and what she is worried about.	✓		

Table 24.4 Continued

CLINICAL FEATURE	YES	NO	PARTIALLY
4. The patient appears to put forth adequate effort when undergoing neuropsychological testing.	✓		
5. The patient felt that the basic neuropsychological test results were presented in an understandable and empathetic manner.	✓		
6. The patient was able to recognize and verbally state that anxiety and/or depression may be contributing to the SMCs.		✓	
7. The patient engaged the clinical neuropsychologist regarding the findings and began to explore whether psychological factors (vs. an underlying brain disorder) contributed to her SMCs.		✓	
8. The feedback session with the patient led the patient to introduce previously unmentioned history that is compatible with the findings and the clinical impressions of the clinical neuropsychologist.		✓	
9. The patient's lifestyle is conducive to seeking out psychological/psychiatric help.			✓
10. The patient acts on the treatment recommendations for psychological/psychiatric treatments.		✓	
11. The patient appears to experience greater resiliency in dealing with her memory difficulties after the clinical neuropsychological examination/consultation.		✓	
Total	4	5	2

SMCs, subjective memory complaints.

SUMMARY

Subjective memory complaints correlate with several factors. The strength of the correlations appears to vary with the sample population being studied. In normally functioning adults, there is often a small (and at times significant) correlation with one's actual performance on tests of verbal learning and memory with SMCs. This is especially the case in older individuals. Repeatedly, however, ratings of depression and anxiety correlate at a higher magnitude with SMCs in normally functioning adults. The size of these correlations appears to increase in patients with psychiatric disorders (e.g., chronic pain disorder, major depressive disorders, and borderline personality disorder). Moreover, sleep disturbances, medication side effects, multiple health problems, poor diet, and poor cardiorespiratory fitness can also be influences contributing to SMCs.

The clinical neuropsychological evaluation of patients with psychiatric cognitively based complaints is a delicate task, but it offers an important opportunity to aid in patients' psychological care. Many of these patients can be helped by putting them at ease in the interview; taking seriously their cognitive complaints; examining them thoroughly; and providing feedback that is clear, concise, and empathetic. As they begin to experience how depression and anxiety may be contributing to the SMCs, many can be helped to seek appropriate psychiatric and psychological care. Others may not find the consultation immediately helpful, but with time they may return and acknowledge the importance of the clinical neuropsychological examination/consultation in providing further insights into their clinical condition, for which they later obtain appropriate care. Still others may not accept the findings or the recommendations for further psychological care. Clinical neuropsychologists should not be discouraged when this happens because even the most distressed psychiatric patients can often sense whether they received a thoughtful and caring consultation. Human nature is such that we are all prone to a variety of complaints. Thus, sometimes the consultation of health care providers (including clinical neuropsychologists invested in psychological care) is helpful, whereas in other instances it may not be. The goal, however, is to attempt to provide such care.

REFERENCES

Aarts, S., van den Akker, M., Hajema, K., Van Ingen, A., Metsemakers, J., Verhey, F., & van Boxtel, M. (2011). Multimorbidity and its relation to subjective memory complaints in a large general population of older adults. *International Psychogeriatrics, 23*(4), 616–624.

Antikainen, R., Hänninen, T., Honkalampi, K., Hintikka, J., Koivumaa-Honkanen, H., Tanskanen, A., & Viinamäki, H. (2001). Mood improvement reduces memory complaints in depressed patients. *European Archives of Psychiatry and Clinical Neuroscience, 251*(1), 6–11.

Banks, S., & Dinges, D. F. (2011). Chronic sleep deprivation. In M. H. Kryger, T. Roth, & W. Dement (Eds.), *Principles and practice of sleep medicine* (5th ed., pp. 67–75). St. Louis, MO: Elsevier.

Beblo, T., Kater, L., Baetge, S., Driessen, M., & Piefke, M. (2017). Memory performance of patients with major depression in an everyday life situation. *Psychiatry Research, 248,* 28–34.

Beblo, T., Mensebach, C., Wingenfeld, K., Rullkoetter, N., Schlosser, N., & Driessen, M. (2014). Subjective memory complaints and memory performance in patients with borderline personality disorder. *BMC Psychiatry, 14,* 255.

Beebe, D. W., Groesz, L., Wells, C., Nichols, A., & McGee, K. (2003). The neuropsychological effects of obstructive sleep apnea: A meta-analysis of norm-referenced and case–controlled data. *Sleep, 26*(3), 298–307.

Brown, F. C., Westerveld, M., Langfitt, J. T., Hamberger, M., Hamid, H., Shinnar, S., . . . Tracy, J. (2014). Influence of anxiety on memory performance in temporal lobe epilepsy. *Epilepsy & Behavior, 31,* 19–24.

Davis, H. P., Small, S. A., Stern, Y., Mayeux, R., Feldstein, S. N., & Keller, F. R. (2003). Acquisition, recall, and forgetting of verbal information in long-term memory by young, middle-aged, and elderly individuals. *Cortex, 39*(4), 1063–1091.

Gamaldo, A. A., Wright, R. S., Aiken-Morgan, A. T., Allaire, J. C., Thorpe, R. J., & Whitfield, K. E. (2019). The association between subjective memory complaints and sleep within older African American adults. *Journals of Gerontology: Series B, Psychological Sciences and Social Sciences, 74*(2), 202–211.

Gray, S. L., Anderson, M. L., Dublin, S., Hanlon, J. T., Hubbard, R., Walker, R., . . . Larson, E. B. (2015). Cumulative use of strong anticholinergics and incident dementia: A prospective cohort study. *JAMA Internal Medicine, 175*(3), 401–407.

Günther, T., Holtkamp, K., Jolles, J., Herpertz-Dahlmann, B., & Konrad, K. (2004). Verbal memory and aspects of attentional control in children and adolescents with anxiety disorders or depressive disorders. *Journal of Affective Disorders, 82*(2), 265–269.

Iuliano, E., Fiorilli, G., Aquino, G., Di Costanzo, A., Calcagno, G., & di Cagno, A. (2017). Twelve-week exercise influences memory complaint but not memory performance in older adults: A randomized controlled study. *Journal of Aging and Physical Activity, 25*(4), 612–620.

Kamegaya, T., Maki, Y., Yamagami, T., Yamaguchi, T., Murai, T., & Yamaguchi, H. (2012). Pleasant physical exercise program for prevention of cognitive decline in community-dwelling elderly with subjective memory complaints. *Geriatrics & Gerontology International, 12*(4), 673–679.

Lezak, M., Howieson, D., Loring, D., Hannay, H., & Fischer, J. (2004). *Neuropsychological assessment* (4th ed.). New York, NY: Oxford University Press.

McAuley, E., Szabo, A. N., Mailey, E. L., Erickson, K. I., Voss, M., White, S. M., . . . Mullen, S. P.

(2011). Non-exercise estimated cardiorespiratory fitness: Associations with brain structure, cognition, and memory complaints in older adults. *Mental Health and Physical Activity, 4*(1), 5–11.

McCracken, L. M., & Iverson, G. L. (2001). Predicting complaints of impaired cognitive functioning in patients with chronic pain. *Journal of Pain and Symptom Management, 21*(5), 392–396.

McGraw, A. P., Warren, C., & Kan, C. (2014). Humorous complaining. *Journal of Consumer Research, 41*(5), 1153–1171.

Mintzer, J., & Burns, A. (2000). Anticholinergic side-effects of drugs in elderly people. *Journal of the Royal Society of Medicine, 93*(9), 457–462.

Papenberg, G., Bäckman, L., Fratiglioni, L., Laukka, E. J., Fastbom, J., & Johnell, K. (2017). Anticholinergic drug use is associated with episodic memory decline in older adults without dementia. *Neurobiology of Aging, 55*, 27–32.

Pearman, A., & Storandt, M. (2004). Predictors of subjective memory in older adults. *Journals of Gerontology: Series B, Psychological Sciences and Social Sciences, 59*(1), P4–P6.

Porter, R. J., Gallagher, P., Thompson, J. M., & Young, A. H. (2003). Neurocognitive impairment in drug-free patients with major depressive disorder. *British Journal of Psychiatry, 182*(3), 214–220.

Prigatano, G. P., & Caples, H. (2003). Memory complaints and depression in a young adult: Case report. *Barrow Quarterly, 19*(4), 28–31.

Prigatano, G. P., & Gagliardi, C. (2005). *The BNI screen for higher cerebral functions in school age children: A manual for administration and scoring.* Phoenix, AZ: Barrow Neurological Institute.

Rock, P., Roiser, J., Riedel, W., & Blackwell, A. (2014). Cognitive impairment in depression: A systematic review and meta-analysis. *Psychological Medicine, 44*(10), 2029–2040.

Roth, R. S., Geisser, M. E., Theisen-Goodvich, M., & Dixon, P. J. (2005). Cognitive complaints are associated with depression, fatigue, female sex, and pain catastrophizing in patients with chronic pain. *Archives of Physical Medicine and Rehabilitation, 86*(6), 1147–1154.

Rowell, S. F., Green, J. S., Teachman, B. A., & Salthouse, T. A. (2016). Age does not matter: Memory complaints are related to negative affect throughout adulthood. *Aging & Mental Health, 20*(12), 1255–1263.

Sari, B. A., Koster, E. H., & Derakshan, N. (2017). The effects of active worrying on working memory capacity. *Cognition and Emotion, 31*(5), 995–1003.

Small, G. W., Siddarth, P., Ercoli, L. M., Chen, S. T., Merrill, D. A., & Torres-Gil, F. (2013). Healthy behavior and memory self-reports in young, middle-aged, and older adults. *International Psychogeriatrics, 25*(6), 981–989.

Torelli, F., Moscufo, N., Garreffa, G., Placidi, F., Romigi, A., Zannino, S., . . . Djonlagic, I. (2011). Cognitive profile and brain morphological changes in obstructive sleep apnea. *Neuroimage, 54*(2), 787–793.

Twigg, G. L., Papaioannou, I., Jackson, M., Ghiassi, R., Shaikh, Z., Jaye, J., . . . Morrell, M. J. (2010). Obstructive sleep apnea syndrome is associated with deficits in verbal but not visual memory. *American Journal of Respiratory and Critical Care Medicine, 182*(1), 98–103.

Watzlawick, P. (1993). *The situation is hopeless, but not serious: The pursuit of unhappiness.* New York, NY: Norton.

Wilde, M. C., Castriotta, R. J., Lai, J. M., Atanasov, S., Masel, B. E., & Kuna, S. T. (2007). Cognitive impairment in patients with traumatic brain injury and obstructive sleep apnea. *Archives of Physical Medicine and Rehabilitation, 88*(10), 1284–1288.

Williams, M., Kueider, A., Dmitrieva, N., Manly, J., Pieper, C., Verney, S., & Gibbons, L. (2017). Anxiety symptoms bias memory assessment in older adults. *International Journal of Geriatric Psychiatry, 32*(9), 983–990.

Zimmerman, M. E., Arnedt, J. T., Stanchina, M., Millman, R. P., & Aloia, M. S. (2006). Normalization of memory performance and positive airway pressure adherence in memory-impaired patients with obstructive sleep apnea. *Chest Journal, 130*(6), 1772–1778.

Zlatar, Z. Z., Muniz, M., Galasko, D., & Salmon, D. P. (2018). Subjective cognitive decline correlates with depression symptoms and not with concurrent objective cognition in a clinic-based sample of older adults. *Journals of Gerontology Series B: Psychological Sciences and Social Sciences, 73*(7), 1198–1202.

PART V

POSTSCRIPT

25

SYNTHESIS AND POSTSCRIPT

INTRODUCTION

As I finished the preceding 24 chapters, it was clear that the scope of the discussion of each topic covered was necessarily brief. This was dictated by the intention to integrate many sources of information and knowledge that were deemed relevant in the psychological care of persons with a brain disorder. As the book neared completion, further comments seemed to be in order to finish the task. Hence, in this chapter, I synthesize some of the observations made throughout the text as well as provide a few postscript comments. The motivation to write this book was based on the experience that clinical neuropsychologists have much more to offer their patients than psychometric evaluations of their higher integrative brain functions. The overarching goal has been to illustrate how this process might proceed for different patients with different brain disorders. Factors that repeatedly appear to either influence or correlate with the outcome of psychological care and treatment of patients with a brain disorder have been emphasized. It should now be clear that psychological care interventions can be quite diverse, depending on patients' clinical conditions, their perceived needs, and the skills and professional resources of the treating clinical neuropsychologist. Psychological care often includes various forms of psychotherapy, but it is not limited to these activities. Effective psychological care is predicated on an informed understanding of human nature, knowledge of the different patterns of normal and abnormal brain function observed over the life span, and the collective wisdom of many insightful people who have been invested not only in restoring patients' higher integrative brain functions when these functions have been compromised by a brain insult but also in providing psychological care of their fellow human beings.

REFLECTIONS ON HUMAN NATURE

This text began with a discussion of human nature as revealed by the developing (and declining) plan of the central nervous system. Although this approach reveals several important biological and neuropsychological characteristics of human beings relevant to their psychological care, the diverse manifestations of human nature that influence psychological care are not fully captured by this analysis. It is perhaps further revealed by describing (and, when possible, understanding) the behavior of individuals who have been recognized in history for how they have changed and shaped the world we inhabit. They have influenced our culture and how we think about and approach problems we face in life. Recall from Chapter 2 Vygotsky's comment that "man is not only a product of his environment; he is also an active agent in creating that environment" (as cited in Cole & Cole, 1979, p. 43).

Many lists have been constructed regarding the most important or influential people who have ever lived (e.g., "100 People Who Changed the World" [Sullivan & Daspin, 2015]). By and large, these individuals personified some of the defining aspects of human nature that reflect the "best and the worst" in all of us. Intellectual resolve and commitment to understanding the physical nature of the universe are seen in the influential work of people such as Galileo Galilei, Sir Isaac Newton, and Albert Einstein. Intellectual resolve in understanding the structure of the human body is reflected in the early work of Leonardo da Vinci. Likewise, Charles Darwin provided penetrating insights into the evolution of the human species and its similarities with other life forms. The important development of human compassion and empathy for others' suffering is seen in the work of many spiritual leaders, including Mother Teresa and Mohandas Gandhi. Total disregard for human suffering and the desire for power at any cost (a common but often not discussed human characteristic) are seen in the actions of people such as Adolf Hitler and Genghis Khan. A willingness to make great personal sacrifices to improve the living conditions of other people is seen in the efforts of Gandhi, Martin Luther King, Jr., and Nelson Mandela. The need to have a sense of humor and laugh in the face of disappointments and suffering in order to better cope with life's problems is personified in the work of such artists as Charlie Chaplin and Peter Sellers. The need for music and dance to express feelings not easily put into words, but that need to be expressed, is reflected in the musical compositions of many people from Mozart to John Lennon of the Beatles. The need to take courageous action is reflected in the acts of many political leaders who have improved the quality of our lives and sustained the right of humans to be free of slavery and tyranny in their many forms (e.g., Abraham Lincoln, Winston Churchill, and Franklin Delano Roosevelt).

Other influential people have personified the human striving to "control nature" in the service of mankind or for their own economic gain (e.g., Nikola Tesla and Thomas Edison), whereas others have used it to reduce illness (e.g., Louis Pasteur, Jonas Salk, and Christiaan Barnard). Still other important individuals have focused on understanding what motivates our behavior (e.g., Sigmund Freud, Carl Jung, and B. F. Skinner) and how to find meaning in life in the face of human suffering (e.g., Aristotle, Buddha, Muhammad, and Jesus Christ). Several religious leaders and doctrines have emphasized the importance of codes of conduct (e.g., the Bible, the Koran, and the Torah) to facilitate behavioral self-control as a means of living as harmoniously as possible with one another.

With all of these efforts, human nature continues to reflect often opposite and contradictory tendencies in thinking, feeling, and behaving. This is a reality that has to be constantly kept in mind when attempting to provide psychological care for a person with (and without) a brain disorder. The effectiveness of the psychological care is never stationary and requires ongoing efforts.

REFLECTIONS ON NORMAL AND ABNORMAL FUNCTIONING OVER THE LIFE SPAN

Underlying brain changes from conception to death (which are still not completely understood) reveal a complex array of activities that allow for human movement, learning, speech and language, problem-solving, and consciousness of the self and the outside world. Most fascinating is that the environmental demands experienced by human beings at different stages of life and in different psychosocial environments are interacting in a dynamic way with evolving and declining brain functions. Thus, the higher integrative brain functions are not "purely biological" or "purely environmentally based." They are a dynamic mixture of both. Whereas language development is a universal feature of human brain activity, the sounds and the written symbols that constitute a language system are quite diverse across cultures. This suggests both an innate flexibility of human brain development and, at the same time, a "fixed" pattern of brain changes that are required at different stages of life within a given culture.

During the time of Genghis Khan (De Hartog, 1989), fast and controlled riding of a horse and at the same time shooting an arrow in an accurate manner might well have been considered an important higher integrative brain function. In today's society, both the ability to clearly express scientific ideas mathematically and the ability to verbally present arguments that determine laws are important for modern problem-solving. Therefore, these activities would seem to reflect important features of higher integrative brain functions at this time in history. Throughout recorded history, human judgment in determining patterns of activity that signal probable future events and the ability to control emotions, but to act at the "right time," have been hallmarks of human nature, and they remain so today. The human brain, which determines human nature, truly appears to be an "inference machine," as suggested by Carhart-Harris and Friston (2010; see also Chapter 5, this volume).

Psychological care of another human being requires of the caregiver a capacity to draw inferences that lead to behavioral interventions (which potentially include a wide range of activities) to help facilitate the patient's psychological adjustment and to reduce human suffering. When the brain is damaged, the inferences are more difficult to achieve and the "when and how to act" are altered. The pattern of alteration is quite variable, depending on the nature of the brain lesion, its location, and the stage of brain development at the time of initial and delayed disruption. Interestingly, however, disturbance of language functioning has repeatedly been related to poor personal adjustment after a brain disorder based on traditional methods of observation and more modern neuroimaging techniques (Warren et al., 2014).

Another key observation about the development of the central nervous system is that human beings learn from and rely on others throughout their life. The bonding relationship or the attachment styles they form early in life seem to set a template for how they bond or attach themselves to others. Humans may or may not be consciously aware of this reality. It is a reality, however, that the psychological caregiver must constantly be aware of when attempting to guide the patient's behavior in a manner that reduces psychological distress and aids in a positive psychological adjustment to a brain disorder. The role of premorbid bonding styles in rehabilitation outcome has been clinically observed for many years (Prigatano, 1986). More recent empirical findings are now supporting this clinical observation (Sela-Kaufman, Rassovsky, Agranov, Levi, & Vakil, 2013).

Finally, human consciousness is an emergent brain function that can be altered in complex ways following a brain insult (e.g., brain tumor, stroke, and traumatic brain injury). It can also be altered by the emotional/motivational state of the person. This point emphasizes that the higher integrative brain functions, throughout the life span, reflect a complex integration of thinking and feeling that makes inferences possible or impossible. The need to attend to both the conscious and the unconscious characteristics of a person with a brain disorder is vital to the person's overall psychological care.

REFLECTIONS ON HOPE AND RESILIENCY

A repeated observation in scientific studies on the efficacy of various forms of medical and psychological treatments is the phenomenon of "placebo effects." Placebo effects tell us much about human nature and what is involved in psychological care. Placebo effects, when present, often reflect patients' belief that a treatment will help them. That belief is based on a trusting relationship with their doctor and a reasonable explanation of why a treatment may be effective. It is important to remember (from Chapter 12, this volume) that placebo effects positively affect symptoms but not necessarily the underlying disease process. However, hope and faith clearly guide our behavior and our choices in life. If we are hopeful that certain choices will lead to a healthier life (and help us avoid suffering), we often engage in those activities. The more we engage in activities that improve physical health and associated (momentary) psychological well-being, the better we do in life. This is true before and after any brain injury.

Erik Erikson's insightful observations about the role of trust and faith in psychological care and psychological adjustment to crises of various types need to constantly be kept in mind (see Chapter 4, this volume). Trust allows us to face what we fear without undue anxiety. Faith helps sustain meaning in life. Sometimes that faith is based on religious convictions. Sometimes faith is based on a reflective attitude toward one's own life and the lives of others. Faith simply means we have hope that a desired reality will occur in the future without a guarantee that it will in fact take place. Faith and hope are crucial for sustaining the human will to deal with adversity and not give in to escapism, which at times includes suicide (see Chapters 8 and 12, this volume).

In the context of this discussion, it is important to revisit what resiliency is all about. Recall that a conclusive definition has been difficult to achieve (see Chapter 12, this volume). Clearly, multiple factors contribute to resiliency. My preferred definition is that resiliency is the capacity within a person that helps the individual deal with adversity in life in an adaptive manner that, in turn, leads to greater functional achievements and an increased sense of self-efficacy with associated joy. The key to this definition is the ability to adapt to problems, challenges, losses, and disappointments in a manner that leads to increased self-efficacy relative to a person's stage in life. The experience of renewed self-efficacy should bring with it a sense of joy, not despair or negativity. This capacity is based on a history of secure relationships that have fostered hope, trust, and faith. The capacity, however, has to be sustained via environmental supports. This often means having attachment to a person, idea, or belief that sustains meaning in life in the face of suffering and a sense of self-doubt. Psychological care providers should be one of the environmental (interpersonal) supports that help sustain resiliency in the individual.

This book has focused on encouraging the clinical neuropsychologist to provide psychological care to patients with a brain disorder. It has emphasized the knowledge base and skills the clinical neuropsychologist needs to do this work. It is also helpful to reflect on what patients need to "bring to the table" in order for them to benefit from such care activities. First, patients have to be able to establish a trusting relationship with the treating clinician. Both brain injury and premorbid personality features can interfere with this ability. Next, patients must have the courage to honestly discuss or describe what is bothering them. This may not occur overnight, but patients will not be adequately helped until an honest dialogue is established. Third, patients need pre-brain injury experiences that foster hope in the future and a desire to help others as well as themselves. They need to spontaneously experience joy even in the smallest accomplishments, which leads to great self-efficacy. Finally, patients have to work hard at sustaining self-control as required by the social and moral demands of life. From the literary writings of Gandhi to the scientific studies of Mischel, Shoda, and Rodriguez (1989) and later work of Casey et al. (2011), it is clear that the ability to delay gratification is a key feature of adaptive living and of achievements later in life (see Chapter 4, this volume). At times, the first efforts at psychological care of children and some adults must focus on this dimension before later achievements can be attained.

It is important to realize that the ability to sustain trust and to work at delayed gratification is not always under conscious control. Unconscious conflicts or patterns of behavior can put into motion a series of behavioral responses that are self-defeating (see Chapters 1 and 5, this volume). This has been a recurring observation about human behavior (Watzlawick, 1993). It is precisely here that the insights of people such as Freud, Jung, and Erikson are so crucial to effective psychological care interventions. Being aware of potential unconscious influences on behavior helps the clinician draw inferences about what psychological interventions may be most helpful to a patient at a given time.

REFLECTIONS ON THE CLINICALLY RELEVANT FEATURES OF PSYCHOLOGICAL CARE

Starting with Chapter 13, 20 clinical features that appeared relevant to the psychological care of a person with a brain disorder were identified. The presence or absence of these features was recorded for different patients with different brain disorders occurring at different times in the life cycle. Not all of the features of these patients' psychological care were discussed in this book. However, it is interesting to note that those patients who generally achieved a positive psychological adjustment were judged to have at least 10 of the 20 features present during the course of their treatment. It is recognized that this is a highly subjective analysis, and future work is necessary to determine what features may be most important for different patients.

REFLECTIONS ON PARADOXES

In the Preface of this book, the importance of resolving paradoxes in science was noted. This insight was clearly expressed by Karl Pribram. He noted that in science, we often simply collect "facts" but, to use his words, true knowledge comes when we can successfully resolve paradoxes. A paradox is encountered, of course, when two opposing "facts" appear to be true. What are some of the paradoxes we face in providing psychological care of persons with a brain disorder that came to light while writing this book?

Paradox 1: Scientific understanding of human behavior and mental functioning is crucial to providing psychological care of a person with a brain disorder. The scientific understanding of human behavior is not crucial for psychologically helping people with a brain disorder.

This paradox has been perhaps most clearly articulated in the work of Carl Rogers (1965) on the process and outcome of successful psychotherapy. Although to be helpful to the patient, the treating clinician must have a good understanding of what is motivating and reinforcing a patient's thoughts and behaviors, psychological change is often dependent on how the patient perceives what is said or done in the course of psychotherapy. Thus, the patient's subjective experience is of maximum importance to the process of psychological care that attempts to improve the patient's subjective sense of well-being and achieve positive psychological adjustment to the effects of a brain disorder.

What seems most important is how the patient experiences the interpersonal relationship with the treating clinician. What the treating clinician does, however, should be dictated by the scientific understanding of the patient's neuropsychological strengths and weaknesses as well as by the understanding of the patient's personal history, psychodynamic features, cultural and religious backgrounds, and human nature.

An indirect expression of this same paradox is found in the experimental work cited by Posner and Rothbart (2007). Recall that in Chapter 3, an important finding was described regarding an infant's ability to detect and discriminate phonemic sounds of a foreign language. During infancy, a child can effectively discriminate not only the speech sounds of the parents' language but also the sounds of a foreign language. This suggests an innate "plasticity" of neuronal connections in relation to brain–brain relationships underlying language development—an important neuroscience "fact." Yet Posner and Rothbart also note that this occurs only when the infant is exposed to an actual person saying the sounds versus listening to a video recording. So the paradox is that the infant brain has the capacity to discriminate and learn different sound patterns not just by hearing them but by hearing them from a live person. On the audiotape, it is a human voice; in the interpersonal situation, it is a human voice. Why the difference?

The paradox may be resolved by considering the psychological observations of Erikson (see Chapter 4, this volume). The human brain is "wired" for an extended period of dependency on live caretakers (most often the parents). If the infant does not sense that a live person is there and attending to the infant's personal needs, the learning does not take place. Certain types of human interaction appear to be a necessary condition for certain types of learning to occur. Why this is the case may never be adequately answered by a purely reductionist scientific approach.

Paradox 2: Randomized controlled studies provide the most reliable and valid scientific information and should guide the clinical care of the individual. Data obtained from randomized controlled studies have limited value in guiding the psychological care of an individual patient. How can both be true?

Group data tell us about important quantitative relationships between selected variables. Detailed case reports tell us about how group data might be applied to the complexities of a multitude of individual problems a person faces. Experienced clinicians have observed different medical and psychological scenarios emerge over time in various patients. Throughout their years of practice, these clinicians have observed the likelihood that certain interventions lead to either positive or negative outcomes for individual patients who have similar or overlapping problems. This is as true for surgeons as it is for clinical neuropsychologists who seriously attempt to care for their patients. It is the human observations of multiple types of clinical problems (and persons) that guide meaningful, therapeutic interactions.

Paradox 3: Human beings (like all animals) survive by competing for resources. Therefore, by their nature, humans sustain their lives by often hurting others. This is embodied in Darwin's dictum about evolution, which states that only the strongest survive. Yet human beings find life worth living only when they help sustain the life of others and do not hurt others (insights from Gandhi and many others). This is the ultimate paradox faced in the psychological care of a person with or without a brain disorder. It is the ultimate paradox that religious societies and broader governmental societies have to face.

On the one hand, many (if not all) human beings are aggressive and inflict pain on others to sustain their own goals in life. On the other hand, many human beings seem to enjoy life by helping to sustain (and improve) the life of others. Joseph Campbell made the penetrating observation that human life continues precisely by benefiting from the sacrifices of others. Dictators know the truth in this statement. Religious leaders (from all religious perspectives) know another truth. Only by caring for others do many human beings ultimately foster their own psychological development and sense of well-being. Reasonable self-sacrifice and self-control are repeatedly described as crucial for spiritual self-development. Recognizing this paradox helps adult individuals make adult decisions rather than childish decisions. Resolving this particular paradox comes only by integrating multiple sources of knowledge about human beings over a lifetime.

REFLECTIONS ON PROVIDING PSYCHOLOGICAL CARE FOR PERSONS WITH A BRAIN DISORDER

In Chapters 1 and 12, guidelines were suggested to help clinicians psychologically improve their patients' psychological adjustment to a brain disorder. The notion of building patients' resiliency has been emphasized several times in this book. Traditional psychoanalytic theory refers to the same concept by the term *ego strength*. Factors that help build and maintain resiliency appear to vary somewhat across individuals. It is for this reason that several different interventions may be necessary at different times in a person's life to help build and sustain resiliency. It is important to restate that a person's subjective sense of well-being and ability to adjust to losses are constantly fluctuating. The adjustment process is never static and can change for the positive as well as the negative over time. Establishing, as best one can, a positive long-term consultation relationship with the patient is therefore often very important in the person's psychological care. That relationship can allow the patient to return when further assistance is needed to cope with life in light of the particular effects of the brain disorder. A long-term relationship provides an opportunity for patients (and at times families) to never be totally alone with the problems they face. It is a trusting relationship that helps build and sustain resiliency.

Although the nature of the brain disorder clearly influences how a patient perceives, thinks, and acts, a few studies have shown that the patient's premorbid personality features can be quite predictive of who ultimately returns to work after a severe traumatic brain injury (see Chapter 21, this volume). Clinical examples provided in this book also help demonstrate how the cultural background, learning history, and psychodynamic features of the person had an important bearing on the effectiveness of the psychological efforts that were attempted. These realities force upon us the absolute need to recognize the importance of integrating clinical psychology into the practice of clinical neuropsychology if we wish to provide more than psychometric testing services.

REFLECTIONS ON THE CURRENT HEALTH CARE ENVIRONMENT

Several years ago, I edited with my colleague, Neil Pliskin, a book titled *Clinical Neuropsychology and Cost Outcome Research: A Beginning* (2003). That book was intended to bring together several different perspectives that could help clinical neuropsychologists provide evidence concerning the clinical and economic value of their work in the health care markets of the United States. Since that time, health care has become more preoccupied with saving money, often at the cost of the patient and the family. A few months ago, driving into work each morning, I noticed a large billboard with the following advertisement: Medicine + Business = Advantage. The question to answer is "Advantage to whom?"

Are patients receiving better medical and psychological services? Are clinical neuropsychologists (or clinical psychologists, psychiatrists, neurologists, etc.) being rewarded for providing more effective and empathetic care of patients they are entrusted to treat? Do departmental meetings emphasize the need to provide better care? Or are such meetings focused on being economically more and more productive and cutting costs? Lip service is often given to the need to provide better care when the real goal is to provide empirical evidence that one's services exceed some supposed objective marker of quality of care compared to others in the field. This results in greater economic rewards from the government to the hospital.

Gandhi's teaching and writings (see Chapter 12, this volume) are inspiring because he was willing to address the truth no matter how uncomfortable that might become for him or others. This seems to be a basic striving of human nature and reflects the greatest achievement of human evolution to date. Clinical neuropsychologists have a great deal to offer in the psychological care of persons for whom they provide traditional psychometrically based services. Their scientific knowledge base continues to expand, but it must be tempered with "humanity." That is, it must be applied to help reduce the suffering of others as its major goal. Adding to the scientific database and improving revenues for employers are important goals. They foster intellectual stimulation and greater insight into the psychological effects of a brain disorder and provide income necessary to sustain our physical and social life. However, these must remain secondary goals. The primary goal should continue to be to reduce human suffering via clinically and scientifically informed psychological care of persons with a brain disorder.

REFERENCES

Carhart-Harris, R. L., & Friston, K. J. (2010). The default-mode, ego-functions and free-energy: A neurobiological account of Freudian ideas. *Brain, 133*(4), 1265–1283.

Casey, B., Somerville, L. H., Gotlib, I. H., Ayduk, O., Franklin, N. T., Askren, M. K., . . . Teslovich, T. (2011). Behavioral and neural correlates of delay of gratification 40 years later. *Proceedings of the National Academy of Sciences of the USA, 108*(36), 14998–15003.

Cole, M., & Cole, S. (Eds.). (1979). *A. R. Luria: The making of mind. A personal account of Soviet psychology*. Cambridge, MA: Harvard University Press.

De Hartog, L. (1989). *Genghis Khan: Conqueror of the world*. London, UK: Tauris Parke.

Mischel, W., Shoda, Y., & Rodriguez, M. L. (1989). Delay of gratification in children. *Science, 244*(4907), 933.

Posner, M. I., & Rothbart, M. K. (2007). *Educating the human brain*. New York, NY: American Psychological Association.

Prigatano, G. P. (Ed.). (1986). *Neuropsychological rehabilitation after brain injury*. Baltimore, MD: Johns Hopkins University Press.

Prigatano, G. P., & Pliskin, N. H. (2003). *Clinical neuropsychology and cost outcome research: A beginning*. New York, NY: Psychology Press.

Rogers, C. R. (1965). *Client-centered therapy*. Boston, MA: Houghton Mifflin.

Sela-Kaufman, M., Rassovsky, Y., Agranov, E., Levi, Y., & Vakil, E. (2013). Premorbid personality characteristics and attachment style moderate the effect of injury severity on occupational outcome in traumatic brain injury: Another aspect of reserve. *Journal of Clinical and Experimental Neuropsychology, 35*(6), 584–595.

Sullivan, R., & Daspin, E. (Eds.). (2015, December 25). 100 people who changed the world. *Life, 15*(19).

Warren, D. E., Power, J. D., Bruss, J., Denburg, N. L., Waldron, E. J., Sun, H., . . . Tranel, D. (2014). Network measures predict neuropsychological outcome after brain injury. *Proceedings of the National Academy of Sciences of the USA, 111*(39), 14247–14252.

Watzlawick, P. (1993). *The situation is hopeless, but not serious: The pursuit of unhappiness*. New York, NY: Norton.

AUTHOR INDEX

Note: For the benefit of digital users, indexed terms that span two pages (e.g., 52–53) may, on occasion, appear on only one of those pages.

Aaron, S. E., 377–79
Aaronson, N. K., 307
Aarsland, D., 257, 258
Aarts, S., 474
Abbass, A. A., 217–18
Abo, M., 367
Abou-Setta, A., 292–93, 294t, 297–98
Acanfora, D., 249–50
Acher, R., 122–23, 416
Ackermann, H., 73
Adachi, N., 452
Adamo, M. A., 98
Adams, H. P., 359
Adams, K. M., 8–9, 232, 233–34
Adams, L. M., 142
Adams, R. L., 141, 184
Adduci, A., 439–40, 443t
Adler, A., xi, 24
Adolfsson, R., 369–70
Adolphs, R., 75–76
Agranov, E., 122, 415–16, 489
Ahmed, S., 366
Ahtiluoto, S., 387
Aiken-Morgan, A. T., 467, 472–73
Akanuma, N., 452
Akshoomoff, N. A., 99–100
Albanese, A., 200–1

Albert, M. L., 7, 387
Albert, M. S., 385–86
Albert, S., 387
Albouy, G., 84, 85
Aldape, K., 303
Alderson-Day, B., 347, 357
Alexander, M., 232, 233, 237–38
Alexander, M. P., 366
Algra, A., 139
Alici, Y., 307
Al-Khindi, T., 197, 198
Allaire, J. C., 467, 472–73
Allan, L., 138
Allen, D. N., 232, 233
Allen, J. S., 232, 369
Allen, L. A., 257, 329
Alling, J., x–xi
Allison, R., 371, 377
Almairac, F., 26
Almli, C. R., 60
Aloia, M. S., 473
Alonso, J., 216–17
Als, H., 56
Alterman, R. L., 201
Altman, I. M., 11, 129, 158, 417–18, 430, 431t
Altonen, T. K., 141
Alves, G., 258

Amador, X. F., 149, 156
Amaral, D., 232
Amatya, B., 318
Ames, D., 359
Amin, K., 42, 183–84, 185, 417–18, 430, 431t
Amtmann, D., 291
Amunts, K., 36
Anastasi, A., 5
Andermahr, I., 324–27
Anderson, B. M., 127
Anderson, C. A., 95, 231, 232, 233, 330, 414
Anderson, C. S., 335–38
Anderson, G., 136
Anderson, K. E., 257–58, 270–75
Anderson, M. C., 73, 77, 78–79, 164
Anderson, M. L., 473
Anderson, P., 95
Anderson, S. W., 95, 103–4
Anderson, V., 105–6, 109, 110–11, 436–37, 440
Andrade, A., 96
Andrews, M., 155
Andrews-Hanna, J. R., 40, 87, 138
Andrieu, S., 387
Angermeyer, M., 216–17
Angulo-Barroso, R. M., 36
Antikainen, R., 387, 471
Anton, G., 157
Aquino, G., 474
Arciniegas, D. B., 95, 231, 232, 233, 414, 429
Arenth, P. M., 142
Argenta, P. A., 328
Arndt, S., 196
Arnedt, J. T., 473
Arnett, J. J., 53
Arnett, P. A., 284
Arrighi, H. M., 385–86
Askalan, R., 95
Askren, M. K., 57–58, 211, 490–91
Asplund, K., 139, 359, 369–70
Assal, F., 164
Asser, T., 339
Aström, M., 369–70
Atanasov, S., 473
Atangana, E., 323–24
Atherton, K. E., 83, 103
Auff, E., 232–33, 236–37
Aula, A., 137
Avena-Koenigsberger, A., 86, 121–22
Ay, H., 97
Ayduk, O., 57–58, 211, 490–91
Ayoub, K. W., 109
Azizi, H., 294t
Azulay, J., 9–10

Babikian, T., 109
Babyak, M. A., 235
Bäckman, L., 467
Bae, G. Y., 196–97
Baetge, S., 472
Bagic, A., 453, 454
Baguley, I. J., 429
Baiano, C., 260
Baiardi, P., 154–55
Baier, B., 127–28
Baisch, S., 329
Baker, F. A., 359
Baker, G., 184–85
Bakshi, R., 283, 284

Bakvis, P., 453
Bakx, W. G., 237–38
Baldassarre, A., 123–25, 127–28
Baldo, J. V., 40
Balestroni, G., 154–55
Ballard, C., 138
Ballard, C. G., 257
Ballman, K. V., 307
Bammer, R., 40
Banich, M. T., 95
Banks, S., 472–73
Barch, D. M., 106–7
Bargh, J. A., 11–12, 77–78, 80
Barker, W. W., 385
Barkhof, F., 233, 282–83
Barnes, M. A., 105
Barr, W. B., 8–9, 451–52
Barry, J., 452
Basom, J., 249
Bastille, J. V., 367
Bateman, A., 359, 367
Bates, E., 100
Bates, J. E., 323–24
Bates, T. C., 60
Baumfalk, A. E., 306
Bawden, H. N., 104–5
Baxter, L. C., 128–29, 164
Bayley, M. T., 139–40, 245–49
Beard, P. R., xi–xii
Beauchamp, M., 109, 436, 440
Beblo, T., 472
Bech, P., 258
Bechara, A., 196
Becher, J. G., 233
Bechor, Y., 249
Bechtold, K. T., 211
Beck, A. T., 208–9, 218, 359–60
Beckers, F., 97
Beckers, T., 430
Beckmann, C. F., 120–21
Bédard, M., 429
Beebe, D. W., 473
Behne, T., 19, 23, 62
Beier, M., 291
Bekkers, S. C., 235, 237
Belchev, Z., 160
Bell, B., 452, 453
Bell, E. M., 291
Bell, K., 387
Bello-Espinosa, L., 103
Bender, L., 9, 438
Benedetti, F., 209–10, 275–76
Benedict, R. H., 283–84
Benito-León, J., 291
Bensalah, Y., 368–69, 377–79
Benson, D. F., 392
Benson, H., 218
Benson, K., 4, 220
Bentele, K., 198–99
Bentivoglio, A. R., 200–1
Benton, A. L., 9–10
Benton, D., 370–71
Ben-Yishay, Y., xi, 9–10, 130, 218–19, 249, 250–51, 318, 413, 415, 416, 430, 433
Berencsi, A., 36
Bergen, D., 56
Berger, J. S., 60, 63, 103–4
Berger, K., 259

Bergloff, P., 123, 318
Berglund, P., 235
Bergquist, T., 9–10
Berlin, L., 71
Berliner, Y., 392
Berman, I., 160
Bernardin, L., 283
Bernardini, G. L., 323–24
Bernstein, C., 292–93, 294t, 297–98
Bernstein, R. A., 97
Berthier, M. L., 392
Berti, A., 127–28, 370, 371
Bertolino-Kusnerik, L., 141
Bertolucci, P. H., 343
Besser, A., 213
Bethell, C. D., 212
Bettelheim, B., xi, 23, 52, 111–12, 143, 220–21
Beverly, B., 10
Bhatia, K. P., 233
Biessels, G. J., 386–87
Bigi, S., 96
Bigler, E. D., 9, 95, 97, 109, 120, 128, 282, 413–14, 468
Binder, L. M., 370
Bingham, C. R., 62
Birch, H. G., 439
Bird, C. M., 328
Bishop, N. A., 40–42
Bisiach, E., 127–28
Biswal, B. B., 60, 63, 103–4
Bjørnerud, A., 40, 138
Black, S. E., 359
Blackwell, A., 471
Blakemore, S.-J., 62
Blanton, S., 369
Blatter, D. D., 120
Blecharz, K., 323–24
Bliwise, D. L., 83
Blos, P., 62
Blum, D., 453
Blumenfeld, A., 292
Blumenfeld, H., 20–21, 231, 302, 343, 366–67
Blumenthal, J. A., 235
Bly, B. M., 60, 63, 103–4
Boele, F., 318–21
Boes, A. D., 196
Bogner, J. A., 142
Bogousslavsky, J., 139
Boiardi, A., 306–7
Bokura, H., 196
Boland, P., 291
Bonan, I., 139
Bondi, M. W., 385, 386
Bonnelle, V., 120–21, 164
Book, H. E., 86, 217, 260, 267–68
Booth, H. D., 304
Borgaro, S. R., 9, 118–20
Bortz, J. J., 453
Boschin, E. A., 78
Bostrom, A., 292, 294t
Botteron, K. N., 60
Bottini, G., 370, 371
Boudewyn, A. C., 292, 294t
Bougakov, D., 7
Bourgeois, J. A., 454
Bowlby, J., 23, 56, 211
Bowlby, R., 50–51
Bowman, E. S., 454
Bradai, N., 139

Bradbury, M., 138
Braden, C., 9–10
Braga, L. W., 42–43, 110, 185, 220, 438
Brainin, M., 97
Brandt, J., 454
Brandt, L., 331
Brass, M., 74, 78
Braver, T. S., 78–79
Brazier, J., 456t, 458
Breen, K., 405–6
Breitbart, W., 307
Brett, S. J., 237
Brex, P. A., 283
Briscoe, S., 371, 377
Brodal, A., 139
Brodaty, H., 384, 385–86
Bronstein, J. M., 201
Brooks, B., 99, 100, 103
Brown, A. W., 142
Brown, F. C., 472
Brown, M., 73
Brown, P. D., 307
Brown, R. J., 258, 455
Brown, T., 291, 294t, 297, 298
Bruffaerts, R., 216–17
Brugel, D., 98, 99, 100–3
Brugger, P., 369
Brumpton, B., 216–17
Bruner, J. S., 49, 55
Bruss, J., 196, 202–3, 232, 310, 414–15, 489
Buchanan, K. M., 197–98, 202, 330–31
Buchanan, M. V., 70–71
Buckley, E., 369, 377–79
Buckley, M. J., 78
Buckner, J. C., 307
Buckner, R. L., 40, 87, 138
Budson, A. E., 328
Bulbeck, H. J., 318–21
Burgmans, S., 40
Burn, D., 275
Burness, C., 456t, 458
Burns, A., 473
Burns, R. S., 129
Burr, R. B., 120
Busnello, F. M., 291
Butler, C. R., 83, 103
Butters, N. M., 385
Butts, A., 385
Buunk, A. M., 11, 158, 327, 330–31, 335
Byrne, G. J., 258

Cabeza, R., 40–42, 135, 138
Cadden, M., 284
Caine, D., 231–33, 234–35
Calcagno, G., 474
Caldwell, D., 208–9, 218
Call, J., 19, 23, 62
Callejas, A., 123–25, 127–28
Calne, D. B., 277
Caltagirone, C., 128, 138–39, 149
Camp, J., 330
Campbell, J., 492–93
Campbell, L. R., 452
Campbell Burton, C., 335–38
Campos, J. J., 55–56
Campos da Paz, A., 110, 438
Cantor, S., 11, 304–6
Caplan, F., 438

Caplan, T., 438
Caples, H., 475
Carhart-Harris, R. L., 73, 87, 120–21, 416, 489
Carl, B., ix–x
Carlson, H., 103
Carmichael, S. T., 366, 367
Carone, D. A., 399
Carp, J., 62
Carpenter, M., 19, 23, 62
Carpenter, T. A., 21–22, 120
Carron, G., 366
Carrozzino, D., 258
Carskadon, M. A., 80, 82, 135
Carter, G., 405–6
Carty, M., 122–23, 416
Cascio, C. N., 62
Case, R., 57, 107
Casey, B., 36, 38, 39, 40–42, 57–58, 86, 103, 104, 211, 490–91
Castaneda, C., 387
Castillo, C. C., 196
Castillo, M., 231
Castriotta, R. J., 473
Catani, M., 7, 21
Catroppa, C., 105–6, 110–11, 436–37
Catt, S., 315, 317–18, 321
Cavanna, A., 275–76
Cence, B., 377–79
Cerutti, P., 154–55
Chacko, R. V., 7, 96, 123, 139, 414–15
Chalder, T., 454–58, 456t
Chalmers, A., 315, 317–18, 321
Chan, S. S., 330, 335
Chaney, J. M., 275
Chang, D., 335
Chang, K., 377–79
Chang, S., 303
Chaplin, C., 3
Chapman, L., 71
Chapman, S. B., 62, 100, 107
Chapple, K., 180, 200
Charman, T., 62
Charney, D. S., 212, 213
Chase, G., 257–58
Chataway, J., 359
Chelune, G. J., 118–20, 283–84
Chen, C., 377–79
Chen, D., 359
Chen, J., 270
Chen, M., 78
Chen, S. T., 474
Chen, Y.-H., 216–17, 270
Chester, S. K., 10
Chevignard, M., 98, 99, 100–3
Chiapello, D., 417–18, 430, 431t
Chiaravalloti, N. D., 283–84
Chicherio, C., 164
Chigwedere, C., 454–58, 456t
Choi, D., 96, 117–18
Choudhury, S., 62
Christensen, A.-L., 7, 8–9
Christensen, B., 139–40
Christian, C. W., 98–99
Chung, S., 199
Chung, Y. G., 338–39
Church, J. A., 106–7
Churchill, R., 208–9, 218
Chwalisz, K., 160

Ciccarelli, O., 283
Ciceri, E. F., 324
Cicerone, K. D., 9–10
Cirelli, C., 83
Claasen, A., 95
Claassen, J., 323–24
Clare, L., 405–10
Clark, A. N., 141, 211
Clark, J. C., 21–22
Clarke, P., 359, 369
Clason, C. L., 451–52
Cloninger, C. R., 221–22
Clusmann, H., 138–39
Coalson, D. L., 39–40
Cobos, G., 202
Coens, C., 307
Coetzer, R., xi–xii, 338
Cohen, A. L., 106–7
Cohen, B., 291, 294t, 297, 298
Cohen, L. R., 216–17
Cohen, M. L., 439, 443t, 446
Cohen-Zimerman, S., 79
Colantonio, A., 359
Cole, M., 20, 21, 24, 93, 488
Cole, S., 20, 21, 24, 93, 488
Colella, B., 139–40
Colle, F., 139
Collerton, D., 275
Colloca, L., 209–10, 275–76
Colohan, A., 141
Colom, R., 60
Colombo, E., 306–7
Colombo, K., 439–40, 443t
Concato, J., 4, 220
Confavreux, C., 283
Confrey, J. E., 62, 107
Conneman, N., 56
Coomans, M. B., 318
Cooper, J., 73, 77, 78–79, 164
Copeland, D., 323–24
Corbetta, M., 7, 96, 123–25, 127–28, 139, 414–15
Correa, D. D., 304, 306
Corsonello, A., 249–50
Costa, A. S., 392
Costa, L. D., 366
Costello, K., 298
Côté, C., 210
Cotter, R. E., 429–30
Coughlan, T., 414–15
Coulthard, E., 328
Cousins, N., 213
Cowan, D., 387
Cox, C. S. Jr, 105
Crabtree, G. W., 70–71
Cramer, H., 294t
Cramer, S. C., 359, 377–79
Crawford, J. D., 293, 294t
Crawford, R. K., 143–44
Crescini, C., 245–49
Criqui, M. H., 58
Cristante, L., 198–99
Critchley, M., 149, 369, 371
Cross, J. H., 451–52
Crowe, S. F., 370–71
Crutch, S. J., 392
Csikszentmihalyi, M., 215–16, 222–23, 350
Cucuzza, G., 138–39

Cuddapah, V. A., 302–3, 304
Cullen, N. K., 245–49, 429
Cummings, J. L., 254, 255–56, 258, 284

Daams, M., 282–83
Dale, A. M., 40, 138
Damasio, A. R., 95, 103–4
Damasio, H., 95, 103–4, 232
Dammann, G., 236–37
Dammann, O., 198–99
Dang-Vu, T., 84, 85
Daniele, A., 200–1
Dannemiller, J. L., 36
Danner, R., 236–37
Da Paz, A. Jr, 220
Darwin, C., xi, 31, 33, 185, 488
Daselaar, S. M., 135
Daspin, E., 488
Daum, I., 73
Davey, L., 150–51
David, A. S., 149, 156, 157
Davidson, J. R., 292
Davidson, M. C., 39, 40–42, 86, 103
Davies, P., 208–9, 218
Davis, D. R., 55
Davis, E. E., 59
Davis, H. P., 141, 468–69, 471
Davis, J. E., 232
Davis, M. K., 208–9, 211
Davis, R. J., 392
Dawson, K. A., 141, 184
Day, J., 318–21
Deacon, T., 21–22
de al Cadena, C., 284
Dean, S., 371, 377
Deary, I. J., 43–44, 60
De Boissezon, X., 120–21
de Champfleur, N. M., 26
Dede, A. J., 74, 75, 76, 80
Deering, F., 392
DeFreitas, V. G., 283–84
De Graaf, R., 216–17
De Haan, E., 139
De Hartog, L., 489
Dehghani, S., 235–36
DeLuca, J., 283–84
De Maat, S., 217–18
Demakis, G., 10
Dement, W. C., 80, 82, 88–89
Demler, O., 235
De Moor, C., 60
Denburg, N. L., 202–3, 310, 414–15, 489
Denes, G., 370
Denney, D., 156–57, 180
Dennis, M., 109
Deppe, M., 399
Derakshan, N., 471–72
Desharnais, R., 210
De Simoni, S., 121
de Souto Barreto, P., 387
D'Esposito, M., 60, 63, 103–4
Dettmers, C., 338
Deutsch, J., 367
DeVeber, G., 95, 96, 97
Devinsky, O., 452
Dhawan, V., 83, 103
Diamond, A., 55, 57, 59

Diaz-Olavarrieta, C., 284
di Cagno, A., 474
Dickstein, R., 367
Di Costanzo, A., 474
Dieckmann, H., 23
Diederich, N. J., 208–9, 210
Diener, H.-C., 97
Dijkers, M. P., 142
Dikmen, S. S., 118–20, 122, 142
Di Lazzaro, V., 97
Diller, L. E., 9–10, 130, 218–19, 249, 250–51, 413, 415, 416, 430, 433, 439
Dimou, L., 302–3
Dinges, D. F., 472–73
D'Iorio, A., 260
Diprose, W., 451
Dirks, P., 96
Di Russo, F., 120
Dirven, L., 307
Dissanayaka, N. N., 258
Dixon, P. J., 474
Djabelkir, L., 404–5
Djonlagic, I., 473
Dmitrieva, N., 469–71
Dobas, G., 294t
Dobkin, B. H., 359, 367
Dobkin, R. D., 256–57
Dockree, S., 217–18
Dodrill, C., 453, 458
Donald, M., 31–32, 33, 55, 67, 207
Donkelaar, H. J., 231
Donovick, P. J., 416
Dooley, J., 109, 436, 440
Dosenbach, N. U., 106–7
Dostoyevsky, F., 25
Dougherty, M. R., 62, 107
Douglas, K., 142–43, 144, 211–12, 213
Downey, A., 385, 387
Downey, S. P., 21–22
Downing, M. G., 122–23, 416
Downing, P. E., 370
Doyle, M., 429
Doyle, R. E., 99–100
Doyon, J., 21–22
Draper, B., 385–86
Dreer, L. E., 142
Dresselhaus, M. S., 70–71
Driessen, E., 217–18
Driessen, M., 472
Dromerick, A. W., 359
Dronkers, N. F., 40, 100
Drummond, K., 318
D'Souza, M., 293–97, 294t
Dublin, S., 473
Dubois, S., 429
Due-Tønnessen, P., 40, 138
Duff, F. J., 57
Duff, K., 141, 184
Duff, M. C., 211
Duffau, H., 26
Duffy, F. H., 56
Duhaime, A.-C., 98–99
Duncan, G., 275
Duning, T., 399
Dunn, P., 95
Dunning, K., 359
Dunsky, A., 367

Durston, S., 38, 39, 40–42, 86, 103
Dutta, R., 282–83
Dye, C., 385–86

Economos, A., 399
Edelman, G. M., 36–37
Ediebah, D. E., 307
Edwards, S., 370–71
Efrati, S., 249
Ehde, D. M., 291, 298
Ehrenreich, J. H., 232
Ehrt, U., 257
Eisenberg, H. M., 95, 104, 141
Ekman, S.-L., 384
Elger, C. E., 138–39, 452
Elias, L. J., 197–98, 202, 330–31
Ellereit, A. L., 158
Elliott, V. J., 237
Ellis, A., 107–8
Ellmo, W. J., 9–10
Eloni, D., 82
Embry, A. E., 377–79
Engvig, A., 40, 138
Epstein, L., 292, 294t
Ercoli, L. M., 474
Erdahl, P., 452
Erickson, K. I., 467, 474
Erikson, E. H., 4, 48–49, 50, 52–54, 60, 62, 63, 64, 67, 74, 130, 135, 142–43, 220, 242, 279, 350, 404, 438, 490, 492
Erikson, J. M., 49, 50, 54, 130, 404
Evans, A. C., 21–22, 60
Eve, M., 95, 104–5
Everson, S. A., 216–17
Ewers, M., 385–86
Ewing-Cobbs, L., 95, 104, 105, 107
Eyberg, S. M., 439, 443t, 446

Fachner, J., 359, 367
Fair, D. A., 106–7
Fait, K., 236
Falk, E. B., 62
Fallowfield, L., 315, 317–18, 321
Faltl, M., 232–33, 236–37
Fandakova, Y., 40
Fanning, P., 208–9
Fantie, B. D., 36–37
Farace, E., 139–40
Farah, M. J., 58
Farfel, G. M., 292
Fasano, A., 200–1
Fastbom, J., 467
Faust, M. E., 10
Fay, G. C., 104–5
Feder, A., 212
Fee, L., 249
Feinstein, A., 284, 414–15
Feinstein, J. S., 75–76
Feldstein, S. N., 141, 468–69, 471
Felteau, M., 429
Felton, M., 107–8
Fenson, J., 100
Fernyhough, C., 347, 357
Feroleto, C. C., 99–100
Ferrario, S. R., 154–55
Fertl, E., 232–33, 236–37
ffytche, D. H., 7, 21
Fields, J. A., 201, 255

Fiest, K., 292–93, 294t, 297–98
Filley, C. M., 330
Fink, G. R., 158
Fiori, V., 138–39
Fiorilli, G., 474
Fisher, R. S., 451–52, 453, 455, 456t
Fishlev, G., 249
Fishman, I., 283, 284
Fishman, P., 270–75
Fjell, A. M., 40, 138
Flanigan, S., 150–51
Flechsig, P. E., 38–39
Fletcher, D., 211
Fletcher, J. M., 95, 104
Flöel, A., 399
Foa, E. B., 236
Follett, K., 200
Fonagy, P., 211–12, 213
Forbes, P. W., 60
Ford, E., 315, 317–18, 321
Fordyce, D. J., 318, 415, 430, 431t
Formisano, R., 120
Fornara, R., 154–55
Forsblom, A., 359
Förstl, H., 157
Fossataro, C., 371
Fossella, J. A., 39, 40–42, 86, 103
Fotopoulou, A., 153–54
Fox, N. C., 392
Fox, P., 292
Fox, P. T., 73
Fraas, M., 9–10
Frackowiak, R., 73
Frank, J. B., 216
Frank, J. D., 216
Frankel, F. H., 441, 447
Franklin, N. T., 57–58, 211, 490–91
Franz, S. I., xi
Franzen, E., 33
Frasca, D., 139–40
Frasure-Smith, N., 235
Fratiglioni, L., 467
Freeman, J., 371, 377
French, J. A., 451–52
Fresan, A., 216–17
Freud, S., xi, 23, 24, 38, 80, 85–86, 208–9, 221–22, 488
Friedman, H. S., 58
Friedman, J., 257
Friel, J. C., 9–10
Frisch, S., 231, 232, 233, 234–35
Friston, K. J., 73, 87, 120–21, 416, 489
Fugl-Meyer, A. R., 135
Fugl-Meyer, K., 360, 370
Fulcheri, M., 258
Fürst, E. L., 249, 250
Furukawa, T. A., 218
Fuster, J. M., 6, 33, 38, 55, 249, 254

Gabrieli, J. D., 40, 73, 77, 78–79, 164
Gabrieli, S. W., 73, 77, 78–79, 164
Gade, A., 324–27
Gagliardi, C., 42, 185, 476
Galasko, D., 469
Galbiati, S., 439–40, 443t
Gale, S. D., 232
Galea, M., 318
Gallagher, B. B., 452

Gallagher, P., 471
Galván, A., 36, 38, 39, 40–42, 86, 103, 104, 108
Galvin, N., xi
Gamaldo, A. A., 467, 472–73
Gamino, J. F., 107
Gandhi, M., 214, 216, 221–22, 488, 490–91, 492, 494
Gandola, M., 370, 371
Ganesan, V., 95, 104–5
Ganong, W., 96–97, 231–32
Gara, M. A., 257
Garbarini, F., 371
Garramone, F., 260
Garreffa, G., 473
Garrett, R., 255
Garske, J. P., 211
Garvin, N., 232
Gates, J. R., 452
Gauguin, P., 25
Gazzaniga, M. S., 8
Gehring, K., 318–21
Geisser, M. E., 474
Genain, C. P., 293, 294t
Gensicke, H., 293–97, 294t
Gerhardt, C. A., 95, 109
German, W. J., 150–51
Germine, L. T., 63, 64
Gerrard-Morris, A., 95, 103
Gervan, P., 36
Getz, S. J., 255, 260
Geurts, J. J., 282–83
Geyer, S., 36
Ghearing, G., 453, 454
Ghiassi, R., 473
Gibbons, C., 429
Gibbons, L., 469–71
Giedd, J. N., 36, 38, 39, 56
Giesser, B., 298
Gilboa, A., 160, 416
Gill, M. M., 5, 26–27, 222
Gill-Body, K. M., 367
Gillespie, D. C., 318–21, 335–38
Gilsbach, J. M., 324–27
Gindri, P., 371
Ginn, N., 439, 443t, 446
Ginzburg, K., 236
Giorgi, I., 154–55
Giovagnoli, A., 306–7
Gitlin, L. N., 405
Giuntoli, L., 154–55
Giza, C. C., 109
Glader, E.-L., 139
Glaser, J., 79
Gleason, J. B., 59
Glisky, E. L., 64
Godfrey, C., 105–6, 436–37
Godin, G., 210
Goetz, C. G., 208–9, 210
Goetz, K., 307
Gogtay, N., 36, 38, 56
Goins, R. T., 212–13
Golan, H., 249
Goldberg, A., 292
Goldberg, E., 7
Goldberger, L., 154
Goldman, J. G., 258–60
Goldman, W. P., 141
Goldstein, F. C., 95, 104, 141

Goldstein, G., 232, 233
Goldstein, K., xi, 9–10, 20, 72, 100–3, 125, 126, 151, 165, 238, 334, 338, 414–15, 416, 438, 451
Goldstein, L. H., 452, 454–58, 456t, 460
Goldstein, S. A., 257–58
González, J.-M. M., 218, 291
Gonzalez-Castro, T. B., 216–17
Goodkin, D. E., 292, 293, 294t
Goplen, G. B., 197–98, 202, 330–31
Gorman, S., 105
Gorzalka, B. B., 370
Gosses, A., 405–6
Gotlib, I. H., 57–58, 211, 490–91
Gracey, F., 339
Graff, L., 292–93, 294t, 297–98
Graham, J. R., 126
Grant, I., 8–9, 39–40, 232, 233–34
Grant, R., 318–21
Gray, J. A., 58, 109, 187–88, 199, 200, 213, 440, 441
Gray, J. R., 78–79
Gray, S. L., 473
Greebe, P., 328–29, 335
Green, A., 384
Green, J. S., 468, 469
Green, R. E., 139–40
Greenberg, M., 97, 303, 304, 324, 451–52
Greenspan, A., 369
Greenstein, D., 36, 38, 56
Greenwood, R. J., 120–21, 328–29
Gregory, C. M., 377–79
Greicius, M. D., 143–44
Greiffenstein, M. F., 1
Griffin, H. J., 259
Grill, S., 257–58
Grivas, A., 138–39
Grodd, W., 73
Groen, R. J., 11, 158, 327, 330–31, 335
Groesz, L., 473
Gronenschild, E. H., 40
Gross, J. J., 359–60
Grossman, P., 293–97, 294t
Grossman, R. G., 324
Grotta, J., 96, 117–18
Grover, P. J., 121
Grubb, D., x–xi
Grubb, L., x–xi
Gruber-Baldini, A., 270–75
Grünewald, R., 456t, 458
Guetin, S., 404–5
Guilleminault, C., 135
Gundy, C. M., 318–21
Günther, T., 471
Gupta, P., 55–56
Gupta, S., 109
Gurgel, L. G., 291
Gürtler, R., 236–37
Gusnard, D. A., 73, 81–82
Guthrie, T., 71
Guty, E., 284
Gutzmann, H., 404

Haacke, E., 138
Haaland, K. Y., 118–20, 232, 233
Habbema, J. D. F., 139–40
Habets, E. J., 307
Hacker, C. D., 123–25, 127–28
Hackett, M. L., 335–38

Hadanny, A., 249
Hadjimichael, O., 283
Haggard, P., 73–74
Häggström, T., 359
Haidt, J., 19, 24–25
Haier, R. J., 26, 60, 63
Hajema, K., 474
Hakim, H., 1
Halfon, N., 212
Hall, C. S., 49, 50
Hallberg, I. R., 387
Hallett, M., 277
Halstead, W. C., xi, 5, 7, 26, 71–72
Ham, T. E., 121, 164
Hamberger, M., 472
Hamid, H., 472
Hamilton, D. A., 56
Hanlon, J. T., 473
Hänninen, T., 471
Happe, S., 259
Hara, K., 452
Harciarek, M., 157
Hare, D., 235–36
Hare, T. A., 36, 38, 104
Harper, K. T., 291–92
Harrington, M., xi
Harris, C., 200
Hart, S. L., 291, 292
Hart, T., 60, 140
Hartoonian, N., 291
Hartshorne, J. K., 63, 64
Hartz, A. J., 4, 220
Harwood, D. G., 385
Hashimoto, H., 126–27
Hasselkus, B. R., 406
Hassevoort, L., 144
Hassin, R. R., 79
Hatakeyama, T., 197
Hatfield, R., 197
Hauser, S. L., 293, 294t
Hauser-Lindstrom, D., 58
Hawes, E., 212
Hawking, S., 31
Hawley, C. A., 96, 416
Hawryluk, G., 233–34
Hayashi, K. M., 36, 38, 56
Haynes, J.-D., 74, 78
Haynes, R. B., 220
Head, D., 40, 87, 138
Heaton, R. K., 39–40, 118–20, 232, 233–34
Heaton, S. C., 439, 443t, 446
Hebb, D. O., 6–7, 26–27, 221–22
Hebben, N., 9
Heber, I. A., 392
Hécaen, H., 7
Heffernan, M., 385–86
Heffner, R. S., 21–22
Heijenbrok-Kal, M. H., 318
Heilman, K. M., 7, 39, 72, 126, 157
Heilman, M. K. M., 117–18
Heinz, A., 404
Heinze, H.-J., 74, 78
Heiserman, J. E., 11, 128–29, 150, 158, 164, 284
Hellyer, P., 121, 164
Helmstaedter, C., 138–39, 452
Henderson, S. W., 9–10
Hendin, B. A., 11, 158, 284

Hendrick, S. S., 275
Hendrickson, R., 453, 454
Henry, R., 291, 294t, 297, 298
Herbet, G., 26
Herbst, K., 100
Herculano-Houzel, S., 36–37, 302
Heringa, S. M., 386–87
Hermann, B., 452, 453
Herpertz-Dahlmann, B., 471
Herrmann, H.-D., 198–99
Herrmann, R., 236–37
Herrod, N. J., 21–22
Heslin, J., 328–29
Hess, K. R., 305–6
Hesselmann, G., 79
Higgins, J., 366
Higgitt, A., 211–12, 213
High, W. M. Jr, 95, 104
Higurashi, N., 451–52
Hilari, K., 359
Hill, S. W., 128, 150, 156–57, 307
Hillis, A. E., 138, 196–97
Hintikka, J., 471
Hiott, D. W., 235
Hirsch, E., 451–52
Hirst, W. D., 304, 324–27
Hirtz, D. G., 96, 97
Hoare, Z., 406–10
Hodges, J. R., 405–6
Hof, P. R., 40
Hofman, M. A., 39
Holmes, J., 335–38
Holst, G., 387
Holt, R. R., 5
Holtkamp, K., 471
Homskaya, E., 7
Honeyfield, L., 121
Honkalampi, K., 471
Hoofien, D., 160, 416
Hopkins, R. O., 232, 233
Hornbein, T. F., 232
Horstmann, A., 231, 232, 233, 234–35
Horvath, J., 136
Horwitz, R. I., 4, 220
Hoskinson, K. R., 109
Houeto, J. L., 200, 201
House, A., 335–38
Hovris, A., 275
Howard, G., 97, 137–38
Howard, V. J., 97, 137–38
Howes, H., 370–71
Howieson, D. B., 9, 468
Howlett, S., 456t, 458
Hoyt, C., 98–99
Hsieh, M.-Y., 218–19, 429
Huang, B. Y., 231
Hubbard, R., 473
Hudson, S., 291
Huenges Wajer, I. M., 328–29, 335
Hughes, A. J., 291
Hukkelhoven, C. W., 139–40
Humle, F., 430, 431t
Humphrey, N., 210
Hunot, V., 208–9, 218
Hur, K., 200
Husain, M., 328
Huttenlocher, P., 95

Huttenlocher, P. R., 55
Hütter, B.-O., 324–27, 328, 329–30
Hwang, Y.-H., 196–97

Iaria, G., 99, 100, 103
Iasevoli, L., 138–39
Iliescu, B. F., 36
Ilvonen, T., 324
Incalzi, R. A., 249–50
Incoccia, C., 120
Invernizzi, P., 370, 371
Islar, J., 293, 294t
Ismaila, A., 387
Ito, M., 452
Iuliano, E., 474
Iverson, G. L., 474
Iyer, M., 277

Jack, C. R., 385–86
Jackson, J. H., xi, 123–24
Jackson, M., 473
Jacobs, D., 387
Jacobs, M. P., 106–7, 149
Jacus, J. P., 11, 405–6
Jaffe, K. M., 104–5
Jahanshahi, M., 259, 275
Jäkel, S., 302–3
Jansen, F. E., 451–52
Jaramillo, K., 184
Jaye, J., 473
Jelley, H., 406–10
Jemal, A., 416
Jenkins, D., 414–15
Jenkins, P. O., 121
Jennett, B., 97–98, 413–14
Jentzsch, R. T., 231, 232, 233, 234–35
Jilka, S., 121, 164
Jimenez, W., 277
Jin, R., 235
Jobin, J., 210
Johnell, K., 467
Johns, K., 139–40
Johnson, D. R., 11, 304–5, 310, 313
Johnson, R., 144
Johnson, S. C., 120, 128–29, 164
Johnson, W., 43–44, 60
Johnston, F., 275
Johnston, K., 405
Johnston, M. V., 369
Jolles, J., 471
Jonas, W. B., 210
Jones, B., 359
Jones, H., 208–9, 218
Jones, K., 385–86
Jones, T. A., 366–67
Jonkman, L. E., 282–83
Jonsson, C. A., 105–6, 436–37
Joo, H. M., 338–39
Jouvet, M., 79, 82, 83–84
Jovanovic, A., 235–36
Juarez-Castro, I., 216–17
Juengst, S. B., 142
Juhler, M., 414
Julian, L. J., 283
Jung, C. G., ix, 1–2, 24, 26–27, 64–65, 208–9, 221–22, 488
Jung, R. E., 26, 63
Juvela, S., 324

Kagan, J., 60, 75–76
Kahn, R. L., 136, 137, 152–53, 371
Kahneman, D., 81, 87
Kail, R., 38, 39–40, 104
Kajaste, S., 235
Kakuda, W., 367
Kalaria, R., 138
Kalff, D., 419
Kalish, C., 107–8
Kalmar, K., 9–10
Kan, C., 474
Kanchana, S., 277
Kane, P., 329
Kang, D.-H., 196–97
Kanner, A. M., 453–54
Kaplan, E., 9, 99
Kaplan, G. A., 216–17
Kappelle, A. C., 318–21
Kappelle, L., 139
Kappos, L., 293–97, 294t
Kaptchuk, T. J., 209–10
Karama, S., 60
Karnath, H.-O., 127–28
Kasahara, M., 120
Kaschel, R., 249
Kashuba, A., 385
Kaste, M., 235
Kater, L., 472
Katona, C., 405
Katz, D. I., 366
Katzman, R., 385
Kawahara, T. N., 128–29, 164
Kayes, N., 111–12, 431t, 433, 439
Kazantzakis, N., 216
Kazui, H., 330
Keegan, B., 328
Keller, F. R., 141, 468–69, 471
Kemp, S. L., 60
Kenny, R., 138
Keppel, C. C., 370–71
Kerrigan, J. F., 199, 200
Kertesz, A., 183, 343–46, 392
Kessels, R. P., 386–87
Kessler, R. C., 235
Khan, F., 318
Khondoker, M., 455–58
Khoo, T., 275
Kihlstrom, J. F., 79
Kiiski-Maki, H., 441, 443t
Kilbride, C., 371, 377
Kim, H., 95
Kim, J., 60, 140
Kim, Y.-S., 196–97
Kimberg, D. Y., 60, 63, 103–4
Kime, S., 249–50, 333
King, D. W., 452
King, J., 95, 104–5
King, P., 50–51
Kinnunen, K. M., 120–21
Kirk, U., 60
Kirkpatrick, P. J., 327
Kirlin, K. A., 156–57, 452–53
Kiropoulos, L. A., 290–91
Kirton, A., 99, 100, 103
Kisely, S. R., 217–18
Kitchen, N., 328–29
Kito, Y., 330

Kitzmüller, G., 359
Klein, D., 8
Klein, M., 306–7, 318–21
Klein, R. B., 366
Klein, S., 208–9, 217–18
Klingberg, T., 38–39, 438
Klonoff, P. S., 9–10, 152, 160, 249–50, 366, 417–18, 430, 431*t*
Klucznik, R. P., 324
Knapp, P., 335–38
Kneebone, I. I., 359–60
Knight, J. A., 99
Knights, R. M., 104–5
Knuth, E., 107–8
Koch, C., 24
Kochan, N. A., 385–86
Koek, H. L., 386–87
Koele, S. L., 196
Koivumaa-Honkanen, H., 471
Kolb, B., 36–37, 151, 254
Kolk, A., 95
Konrad, K., 471
Kopelman, M. A., 153–54
Koretz, D., 235
Korkman, M., 60
Korpelainen, J. T., 129, 370
Kortte, K. B., 160
Koschera, A., 384
Koslowski, B., 55
Koster, E. H., 471–72
Kovacs, I., 36
Krack, P., 200, 201
Krakauer, J. W., 366, 367
Kral, T., 138–39
Kraus, J. F., 97–98, 117–18, 139–40
Krauss, G. L., 454
Kreiman, G., 24
Kreiter, K. T., 323–24
Kreitschmann-Andermahr, I., 328, 329–30
Kristes, S., 324–27
Kristofersson, G. K., 430
Kritzinger, R., 339
Kronvall, E., 331
Kros, J. M., 303
Krueger, R., 430
Kryger, M., 82
Kubin, M., 135
Kubo, Y., 330
Kubu, C., 200, 201
Kueider, A., 469–71
Kuhl, B., 73, 77, 78–79, 164
Kulisevsky, J., 258–59
Kumar, R., 200
Kumon, Y., 197
Kuna, S. T., 473
Kuoppamäki, M., 233
Kürten, J., 399
Kurthen, M., 452
Kwakkel, G., 367

Laaksonen, R., 10
Laatikainen, T., 387
Labbate, L., 235
la Cruz-Cano, E., 216–17
Ladwig, K.-H., 236–37
LaFerla, F., 136, 385
LaFleche, G., 232, 233, 237–38
LaFrance, W. C. Jr, 452, 454–55, 456*t*, 460

la Fuente-Fernández, R., 277
Lai, J. M., 473
Lai, M., 330, 335
Laine, M., 359
Laitinen, S., 359
Lam, S. W., 330, 335
Lamb, D. G., 9–10
Landis, S., 385, 387
Landis, T., 164
Lang, A., 200
Lang, C. E., 123–25, 127–28
Lang, S., 191–92, 202–3
Lang, U. E., 404
Langbecker, D., 307, 318
Langenbahn, D. M., 9–10
Langfitt, J. T., 472
Langhammer, A., 216–17
Langhorst, J., 294*t*
Lanotte, M., 275–76
Lansberg, M. G., 359
Larimer, P., 454
LaRocca, N. G., 298
Larsen, G., 213
Larsen, J. P., 258
Larson, E. B., 473
Lashley, K. S., 6–7, 125, 438–39
Lauche, R., 294*t*
Laughlin, S. B., 96, 302
Laukka, E. J., 467
Laurent-Vannier, A., 98, 99, 100–3
Lawrence, M., 360
Lawson, R., 275
Lawton, M. T., 97, 323, 324
Lazar, A. S., 83, 103
Lazarus, A. A., 208–9, 218
Lecours, A., 38–39
Lee, G. P., 451–52, 453–54
Lee, N. R., 39
Lee, S. J., 196–97, 338–39, 359
Leech, R., 120–21, 164
Lees, A. J., 260
Lefcourt, H. M., 213
Lehman, R. A., 118–20
Lehmann, M., 392
Lehtinen, L. E., 438–39
Lehtisalo, J., 387
Leichsenring, F., 208–9, 217–18
Leiguarda, R., 392
Leman, M. G., 139
Lengenfelder, J., 283–84
Lenroot, R. K., 39
Leo, G. J., 283
Leonard, G., 60
Leshner, A. I., 385, 387
Lespérance, F., 235
Lesser, R. P., 454
Lett, H. S., 235
Levack, W. M., 291
Levälahti, E., 387
Lévesque, L., 210
Levi, Y., 122, 415–16, 489
Levin, B., 255, 260
Levin, D. C., 233–34
Levin, H. S., 95, 104, 107, 109, 120, 141
Levin, V. A., 305–6
Levine, M., 387
Levine, S. C., 95

Levinzon, H., 160
Levy, N., 160
Levy, S., 367
Lewis, G., 208–9
Lewis, S. R., 335–38
Lezak, M. D., 9, 468
Li, X., 109
Liao, S., 104–5
Libertus, K., 55–56
Libet, B., 73–74
Liégeois, F., 95, 104–5
Lightbody, C. E., 335–38
Lilienfeld, S. O., 7
Lillard, A., 438
Lim, C., 232, 233, 237–38
Limback, E., 59
Lin, H.-Z., 270
Lind, K., 98, 99, 100–3
Lindgren, S. D., 196
Lindzey, G., 49, 50
Lis, A., 370
Liscio, M., 439–40, 443t
Lishman, W. A., 196, 237, 347, 453
List, J., 399
Liston, C., 38
Liu, T.-W., 377–79
Liverpool, M., 39
Livingston, G., 405
Ljunggren, B., 331
Loetscher, T., 369
Loewenstein, D., 385
Lomarev, M. P., 277
Lomay, V. T., 58
López-Narváez, M. L., 216–17
Lopiano, L., 275–76
Lorenz, K., 25
Lovell, M., 307
Lovera, J., 291, 294t, 297, 298
Lowenstein, D. H., 454
Lozano, A. M., 200, 201
Lu, T., 40–42
Luis, C. A., 385
Luis, M., 385
Luria, A. R., 7, 8–9, 20–21, 24–25, 38, 65, 71, 72–73, 87–88, 93, 123–24, 184, 185
Lusk, L., 36, 38, 56
Lustig, C., 40, 87, 138
Lutton, S., 328
Lux, S., 452
Luyten, P., 213
Lyketsos, C. G., 405
Lynch, J. K., 96, 97
Lynch, J. W., 216–17
Lynch, S. G., 156–57
Lynn, D., 292

Ma, H., 260
Maas, A. I., 139–40
Macdonald, R. L., 197, 198
Mace, N. L., 387
MacGregor, D., 95, 96
Machamer, J. E., 118, 120, 122
Mack, J. L., 328
MacLean, P. D., 22–23
MacWhinney, B., 55–56
Maddula, M., 328
Maeda, R., 153–54

Maes, J. H., 386–87
Magee, W. L., 359, 367
Magnotta, V., 452
Magrini, S., 323–24
Mai, J. K., 21, 33
Mai, X., 216–17
Maier, F., 122, 129, 158, 259
Maier-Ring, D., 338
Mailey, E. L., 467, 474
Majić, T., 404
Malec, J. F., 9–10, 142, 415
Malhotra, P., 328
Malikovic, A., 36
Manly, J., 469–71
Maquet, P., 84, 85–86
Marangolo, P., 138–39
Marcantuono, J. T., 436, 439
Marchand, W. R., 338–39
Marchetti, E., 291
Marcovitz, E., 367
Marder, K., 387
Margolis, R. L., 257–58
Marin, S. M., 343
Mark, M. H., 257
Markand, O. N., 454
Marks, W. J., 200
Marra, C., 328
Marriott, J., 292–93, 294t, 297–98
Marsh, L., 256–57
Marsh, R., 258
Marshall, J., 359
Marshall, L. F., 139–40
Marshall, S., 429
Marshall, V., 359
Martin, D. J., 211
Martin, R. A., 213, 282–83, 453
Masel, B. E., 473
Maslow, A., 219
Masterton, R. B., 21–22
Mateer, C. A., 10
Matsubara, R., 452
Matsuura, M., 452
Matt, G. E., 216–17
Matthes, J., 128, 150
Matthews, B., 23
Matthews, C. G., 39–40
Matthey, S., 232, 249
Maty, S. C., 216–17
Maudoux, A., 84, 85
Maurer, M. J., 307
Maurice-Williams, R., 197
Mavaddat, N., 327
Mawad, M. E., 324
Max, J. E., 95, 100–3, 104–5, 109, 196
May, R., 208–9
Mayberg, H. S., 209–10
Mayer, K., 249
Mayer, S. A., 323–24
Mayes, L. C., 213
Mayeux, R., 141, 468–69, 471
Mayfield, J. W., 232, 233
Mayo, N., 366
McAdams, D. P., 19, 52
McAllister, T. W., 122, 413, 414, 417
McAnulty, G. B., 56
McAuley, E., 467, 474
McCarthy, K., 429

McCracken, L. M., 474
McCullagh, S., 414–15
Mcewen, S., 366
McGee, K., 473
McGhee, P. E., 213–14
McGraw, A. P., 474
Mcintosh, T. K., 414
McIvor, G. P., 293, 294*t*
McKay, A., 218–19, 429
McKay, M., 208–9
McKnight, C., 155
McMillan, T. M., 413, 429
McMonagle, P., 392
McPherson, K., 111–12, 431*t*, 433, 439
McPherson, S. E., 254, 255–56, 258
McSweeny, A. J., 232, 233–34
Meadows, E. A., 109
Meca, A., 7
Medalia, A. A., 232
Mee, E., 196
Mehta, M. A., 121
Meier, M. J., 6, 9–10, 11
Meier, T. B., 138
Meinzer, M., 399
Meldolesi, J., 304
Mellers, J., 454–58, 456*t*
Mellers, J. D., 452
Mendelow, A. D., 329
Mendelsohn, D., 107
Mendez, M., 453
Menkes, D. B., 451
Mennemeyer, S., 453
Menon, D. K., 21–22, 120
Menza, M., 257
Merikangas, K. R., 235
Merkley, T. L., 109
Merriam, A. E., 232
Merrill, D. A., 474
Messaoudi, M., 404–5
Meston, C. M., 370
Metcalf, N. V., 7, 96, 123, 139, 414–15
Metsemakers, J., 474
Metzemaekers, J. D., 330–31
Meyer, A., 123, 414–15
Meyer, P., 98, 99, 100–3
Meyers, C. A., 11, 123, 304–6, 310, 313, 318
Middelkamp, W., 237–38
Middleton, L. S., 156–57
Miezin, F. M., 106–7
Mikkonen, M., 359
Milberg, W. P., 9
Miljkovitch, R., 249
Miller, B. L., 143–44
Miller, D. H., 283
Miller, F. G., 209–10
Miller, K. D., 416
Miller, T., 97–98, 117–18, 139–40
Millman, R. P., 473
Milner, B., 8
Milofsky, E., 49, 54
Miner, M. E., 95, 104
Mineyko, A., 103
Minich, N., 95, 103
Mintun, M., 73
Mintzer, J., 473
Mischel, W., 57, 490–91
Misic, B., 86, 121–22

Mitchell, A. J., 291
Mitchell, L. K., 258
Mitchell, P., 49
Miyake, H., 330
Mizutani, S., 367
Moerman, D. E., 210
Moessner, A. M., 142
Moffitt, T. E., 62
Mohr, D. C., 218, 283, 291, 292, 293–97, 294*t*, 298
Mohr, J., 96, 117–18
Mohr, J. P., 97
Moilanen, D., 232
Mok, V., 330, 335
Moll, H., 19, 23, 62
Monette, G., 139–40
Monin, J. K., 275
Montreuil, M., 180, 249
Moore, J., 367–68
Moore, P. A., 217–18
Moore, T. H., 208–9, 218
Moors, P., 79
Mora, M., 417–18, 430, 431*t*
Morberg, B. M., 258
Morgan, J. E., 8–9
Morgan, M. A., 328
Moriarty, J., 455–58
Morillo, C. A., 97
Morin, C., 368–69, 377–79
Moritz-Gasser, S., 26
Morley, D., 275
Morrell, M. J., 473
Morrison, J. H., 40
Morrone-Strupinsky, J., 10–11, 173
Morsella, E., 11–12, 77–78, 80
Mosch, S. C., 95, 100–3
Moscufo, N., 473
Moskowitz, A., 95
Moss, E., 98
Moss, M. B., 385–86
Motl, R. W., 298
Mott, T., 9–10
Moulaert, V., 235, 237
Moulaert, V. R., 237–38
Mowry, E. M., 298
Moy, C. S., 200
Mudar, R. A., 107, 211
Mulkern, R. V., 56
Mullen, S. P., 467, 474
Müller, F., 36
Müller, K., 231, 232, 233, 234–35
Mullins, L. L., 275
Muniz, M., 469
Murata, W., 369
Murias, K., 99, 100, 103
Murley, A. G., 254
Murphy, T., 95, 104–5
Murray, J., 335–38
Murro, A. M., 452
Myatt, R., 441, 447
Myers, R., 33
Myllylä, V. V., 129, 370

Naar-King, S., 436, 440
Nadkarni, S., 452
Nagaraja, H., 292
Nagy, Z., 38–39

Naing, L., 138
Nair, V. A., 138
Nation, K., 57
Naydin, V., 7
Neal, D., 371, 377
Neer, H., x
Neils-Strunjas, J., 211
Nelson, K. B., 96, 97
Neppi-Modona, M., 371
Nestler, E. J., 212
Newacheck, P., 212
Newcombe, F., 20
Newman, M. F., 235
Neylan, T., 291, 294t, 297, 298
Ng, G. Y., 377–79
Ng, L., 318
Ng, S. S., 377–79
Ng, Y.-T., 199
Ngandu, T., 387
Nguyen, D., 198–99
Nichols, A., 473
Nichols-Larsen, D. S., 369
Nicholson, C., 231
Nieminen, P., 129, 370
Nieminen-Kelhä, M., 323–24
Nieuwenhuys, R., 231
Nilsson, M. I., 360, 370
Nilsson, O. G., 331
Nitsche, M., 138–39
Noble, A. J., 329
Noble, K. G., 58
Nobre, A. C., 83, 103
Norman, M. F., 58
Northcott, S., 359
Nott, M. T., 429
Nunn, A., 292
Nuyen, J., 306–7

O'Brien, K. P., 11, 417–18, 430, 431t
Ochsner, K. N., 73, 77, 78–79, 164
O'Connor, D. A., 359
Odden, M., 212–13
Oddy, M., 414–15
Odell, M., 335
Odell-Miller, H., 359, 367
O'Donnell, M. B., 62
Ogden, J. A., 196
Ohayon, M. M., 135
Ohnishi, T., 197
Ohta, S., 197
Ohue, S., 197
Oka, Y., 197
Okazaki, M., 452
O'Keeffe, F., 95, 104–5
Oldham, P., 339
Oliveira, F. F., 343
Olver, J., 122–23, 416
O'Neill, B. P., 11, 304–5, 310, 313
O'Neil-Pirozzi, T. M., 142
Onillon, M., 249
Onofrj, M., 258
Onus, M., 429
Oosterman, J. M., 386–87
Opie, M., 100
O'Rahilly, R., 36
Orasson, A., 339
Oremus, M., 387

Orfei, M. D., 128, 149
O'Riordan, J. I., 283
Orman, J. A. L., 97–98, 117–18, 139–40
Ormel, J., 216–17
O'Sullivan, J. D., 258
O'Sullivan, S., 464
Outtrim, J., 120
Owen, A. M., 21–22, 157

Pachana, N. A., 258
Pagonabarraga, J., 258–59
Påhlhagen, S., 257
Pals, J. L., 19, 52
Pan, J.-L., 270
Papagno, C., 127–28
Papaioannou, I., 473
Papenberg, G., 467
Paquet, C., 180
Paradise, S., 9–10
Paradiso, S., 127
Parker, M., 359, 367
Parmenter, B., 156–57
Parsons, O. A., 8, 233–34
Parthasarathy, S., 96
Parton, A., 328
Passman, R. S., 97
Pastore, V., 439–40, 443t
Patierno, C., 258
Paton, J., 405
Patterson, C., 387
Patterson, M. B., 328
Patton, D., 141, 184
Patty, P., 330, 335
Paul, A. R., 98
Paul, D., 211
Paulesu, E., 370, 371
Pavisian, B., 284
Paxinos, G., 21, 33
Pearman, A., 469
Pedersen, K. F., 258
Pedone, C., 249–50
Peelen, M. V., 370
Peery, S., 323–24
Peigneux, P., 84, 85
Pelletier, D., 291, 294t, 297, 298
Pellett, E., 111–12, 431t, 433, 439
Penner, I. K., 293–97, 294t
Pepping, M., 318, 415, 430, 431t
Perani, D., 127–28
Pereira, S., 126
Pernigo, S., 153–54
Perrigot, M., 368–69, 377–79
Perry, T. E., 144
Persson, H. C., 338
Petersen, R. C., 385–86
Petersen, S. E., 73, 86–87, 104–5, 126, 127
Peterson, B. S., 36–37
Petrides, M., 21–22
Physio, B., 318
Pia, L., 370, 371
Piaget, J., 49, 55
Piano, C., 200–1
Piasetsky, E., 318
Pick, S., 452
Picot, M., 404–5
Piefke, M., 472
Piekema, C., 78

Pieper, C., 469–71
Piliavska, K., 338
Piotrowski, Z. A., 184–85
Pipe, J. G., 128–29, 164
Pisani, A., 328
Piscopo, F., 260
Pistolesi, E., 213–14
Pitchford, N. J., 59
Placidi, F., 473
Pliskin, N. H., 220, 493
Pluck, G., 258
Plug, L., 454
Plum, F., 80
Plunkett, K., 57
Polissar, N. L., 104–5
Poll, E., 324–27
Pollak, C., 292
Pollak, R., 143
Pollo, A., 275–76
Pollock, B. E., 307
Poltawski, L., 371, 377
Pommié, C., 404–5
Ponce, F., 202
Ponds, R. W., 160, 165, 250, 416, 430, 431*t*
Ponsford, J. L., 122–23, 140, 218–19, 416, 429
Ponto, L. L. B., 127
Pontone, G. M., 257–58
Popescu, A., 453, 454
Porras, M., 324
Porter, R. J., 471
Portet, F., 404–5
Posner, J. B., 80
Posner, M. I., 38, 55, 73, 86–87, 95, 104–5, 126, 127, 492
Post, M. W., 328–29, 331, 335
Postma, T. J., 318–21
Pouwels, P. J., 282–83
Povinelli, D. J., 55
Powell, J., 328–29
Power, E., 359
Power, J. D., 202–3, 310, 414–15, 489
Prabhakaran, V., 60, 63, 103–4, 138
Pradat-Diehl, P., 368–69, 377–79
Prasad, M., 105
Premack, D., 25–26, 62
Presley, R., 141
Pribram, K. H., x, 7, 26–27, 222, 491
Price, T. R., 307, 369–70
Prigatano, G. P., 4, 9–11, 24, 26–27, 28, 33, 42–43, 58, 74, 87, 88, 95, 108–9, 117, 118–20, 121, 122, 123–24, 125, 127, 128–30, 139, 144, 148, 149, 150, 152–53, 155, 156–57, 158, 160, 164, 173, 180, 183–84, 185, 187–88, 192–93, 198–99, 200, 208, 213, 217–20, 222–23, 229, 232, 233–35, 239, 249–51, 259, 284, 292, 307, 318, 333, 335–38, 348, 353, 357, 360, 370, 371, 372, 413, 414–16, 417–18, 419–20, 429, 430, 431*t*, 433, 436, 439, 440, 441, 452–53, 455, 456*t*, 475, 476, 489, 493
Priore, R., 284
Puhlik-Doris, P., 213
Pulman, J., 369, 377–79
Pulver, A., 339
Pußwald, G., 232–33, 236–37
Putman, P., 453
Pye, D., 258

Querfurth, H., 136, 385
Quest, R. A., 121
Quinn, C., 406–10
Quinn, N. P., 233, 259, 275

Rabinovici, G. D., 392
Rabinowitz, A. R., 60, 120, 140
Rabins, P. V., 387
Rafal, R. D., 359–60
Raghupathi, R., 414
Rahman, S., 259
Raichle, M. E., 40, 73, 78–79, 81–82, 87, 138
Raiford, S. E., 39–40
Raimo, S., 260
Raina, P., 387
Rainero, I., 275–76
Ramachandran, V., 152
Ramana, C. V., ix
Rammohan, K. W., 292
Rampen, A. J., 139–40
Ramsey, L. E., 7, 96, 123–25, 127–28, 139, 414–15
Randahl, G., 118–20
Ranta, M., 10
Rao, S. M., 283
Rapaport, D., 5
Rapp, M. A., 404
Rapport, L. J., 291–92
Rassovsky, Y., 122, 415–16, 489
Ratner, N. B., 59
Rattok, J., 318
Rayner, R., 23
Raz, N., 40, 138
Reen, G., 57
Rees, G., 24
Rees, L., 429
Reetz, K., 392
Regard, M., 369
Reger, S. L., 232, 233
Regier, N. G., 405
Reich, A., 392
Reich, S., 270–75
Reijneveld, J. C., 306–7
Reilly, J., 100
Reineke, A., 324–27
Reitan, R., xi, 7, 66
Rekate, H. L., 200
Rengo, F., 249–50
Rentz, D. M., 328
Reppold, C. T., 291
Reuber, M., 452, 454, 455, 456*t*, 458, 460
Reyes-Ramos, E., 216–17
Reyna, V. F., 62, 107
Reynolds, F., 377–79
Rhebergen, M. L., 328–29, 331
Ribbers, G. M., 318
Richardson, G. E., 208–9
Richardson, S. A., 439
Richardson, W. S., 220
Richman, J., 406
Ricker, J. H., 8–9
Ricker, J. R., xi–xii
Riedel, W., 471
Ringdahl, E. N., 232, 233
Rinkel, G. J., 328–29, 331, 335
Rivera-Navarro, J., 291
Rivkin, M. J., 56
Rizzone, M., 275–76
Robain, G., 368–69, 377–79
Robbins, N. M., 454
Robbins, T. W., 21–22
Robe, P. A., 306
Robel, S., 302–3, 304

Roberts, J., 330
Robertson, E., 73, 77, 78–79, 164
Robertson, I. H., 121, 164
Robertson, M., 330
Robins, C., 235
Robinson, P., 384
Robinson, R. G., 126–27, 369–70
Robinson-Smith, G., 369
Robottom, B., 270–75
Rochat, P., 26
Rochhausen, L., 158
Rock, M. R., 184–85
Rock, P., 471
Rodgers, D. L., 237
Rodrigue, K. M., 138
Rodriguez, M. L., 57, 490–91
Roebuck-Spencer, T., 117–18
Roelofs, K., 453
Rogers, C. R., 208–9, 219, 221–22, 455, 491–92
Rogers, R. D., 327
Rohling, M. L., 10
Roine, R. O., 235
Roiser, J., 471
Rojas, D. C., 414
Roland, P., 36
Rolland, Y., 387
Roman, C., 284
Romano, D., 371
Romigi, A., 473
Romito, L. M., 200–1
Romundstad, P., 216–17
Ronthal, M., 328
Rooney, A. G., 318–21
Root, J. C., 304, 306
Ropper, A., 283
Rorke, L. B., 98–99
Rose, J. E., 324
Rosenberg, J., 292
Rosenberg, W., 220
Rosenstein, L., 42, 183–84, 185
Ross, E. D., 121, 184
Ross, G., 49
Ross, R. E., 377–79
Rossor, M. N., 392
Roth, G., 82
Roth, H. L., 328
Roth, I., 405–6
Roth, J., 95
Roth, R. S., 474
Rothbart, M. K., 38, 55, 95, 492
Rothbaum, B. O., 292
Rothweiler, B., 142
Roueche, J. R., 318, 415, 430, 431t
Roulet Perez, E., 451–52
Rowan, A. J., 452
Rowan, E., 138
Rowe, J. B., 254
Rowe, J. W., 136, 137
Rowell, S. F., 468, 469
Rowley, H. A., 128–29, 164
Roy, P., 359
Roy, S., 283–84
Rubin, K. H., 95, 109
Ruby, P., 84, 85
Rudd, A., 153–54
Ruff, R. M., xi–xii, 10
Ruggiano, N., 144

Ruggles, K., 452
Rummans, T. A., 307
Rumsey, J., 60
Rusalovska, S., 217–18
Rushworth, M. F., 328
Russell, C. K., 387
Russell, W. R., 97–98, 413–14
Rutecki, P., 452
Ruth, T. J., 277
Ryan, K. A., 291–92
Rypma, B., 60, 63, 103–4

Saatman, K., 414
Sabatini, U., 120
Sacco, R. L., 97
Sachdev, P. S., 385–86
Sackett, D. L., 220
Saeger, W., 198–99
Saeki, K., 369
Saelens, B. E., 216–17
Safren, S., 218
Sahakian, B., 327
Sailer, M., 283
Saint-Cyr, J. A., 200
Sakaki, S., 197
Salas, C. E., xi–xii, 74, 144, 213, 217–18, 229, 250, 347–48, 359–60, 416, 419, 429
Salbach, N., 366
Saller, B., 324–27
Salmon, D. P., 385, 469
Salmond, C., 120
Salthouse, T. A., 43–44, 468, 469
Samuels, M., 283
Sander, A. M., 11, 118, 413
Sanders, H., 292
Sanders-Dewey, N. E., 275
Sandifer, P., 149
Sandroff, B. M., 298
Sanna, T., 97
Sano, M., 387
Santaguida, P., 387
Santangelo, G., 260
Saper, C. B., 21, 80, 199
Sari, B. A., 471–72
Särkämö, T., 359
Sarkar, M., 211
Sarno, M. T., 346–47, 359
Sasaki, N., 367
Sato, Y., 196
Sauvigné, K. C., 7
Savage, R. C., 109
Säveland, H., 331
Sawyer, A. M., 11, 304–5, 310, 313
Schachter, S. C., 454
Schacter, D. L., 11, 75
Schafer, R., 5
Schall, C., 232
Schechter, M. D., ix
Scheltens, P., 385–86
Schenk, T., 329
Scherer, H., 302–3
Schiavon, C. C., 291
Schiff, N. D., 80
Schijns, J., 233
Schilder, P., 123, 414–15
Schirmacher, A., 399
Schlaggar, B. L., 106–7

Schleicher, A., 36
Schmand, B., 255, 256, 258
Schmidt, A. T., 109
Schmidt, R., 338
Schmitz, T. W., 128–29, 164
Schneider, U. C., 323–24
Schnitzler, A., 249
Schnyer, D., 232, 233, 237–38
Schoefinius, A., 236–37
Schoenberg, M. R., 141, 184
Schofield, W., 216
Schönberger, M., 140, 430, 431t
Schöne, U., 392
Schormann, T., 36
Schott, J. M., 392
Schrag, A., 275
Schramm, J., 138–39
Schroeder, D. H., 43–44
Schroeter, M. L., 231, 232, 233, 234–35
Schulz, J. B., 392
Schulz, R., 275
Schulzer, M., 277
Schure, M. B., 212–13
Schwartz, J. E., 58
Schwartz, S., 85–86, 164
Schwartz, S. J., 7
Schweizer, T. A., 197, 198
Scott, J. G., 141, 184
Scott, K., 216–17
Scoville, W. B., 8
Searcy, J., 141
Seeley, W. W., 143–44
Seibert, P. S., 249
Seidenberg, M., 452
Seidl, T., 98
Sejnowski, T. J., 302
Sela-Kaufman, M., 122, 415–16, 489
Seligman, M. E., 221–22
Semenza, C., 370
Senathi-Raja, D., 140
Sequin, E., 437–38, 439
Seshadri, S., 399
Sevlever, G., 392
Sevush, S., 385
Shah, N., 4, 220
Shaikh, Z., 473
Sharlow-Galella, M. A., 9–10
Sharma, J., 283
Sharp, D. J., 120–21, 164
Sharrack, B., 454
Shaw, L. M., 385–86
Shedler, J., 217–18
Sheese, B. E., 95
Sherer, M., 11, 117–18, 123, 318, 413
Sherwood, A., 235
Sheth, R., 452
Shiel, A., 249
Shin, I. Y., 338–39
Shing, Y. L., 40
Shinnar, S., 472
Shoda, Y., 57, 490–91
Shope, J. T., 62
Shrubsole, K., 359
Shtompel, N., 144
Shukla, D. P., 335
Shulman, G., 123
Shulman, L., 270–75
Siddarth, P., 474

Siegel, J. S., 7, 96, 123–25, 127–28, 139, 414–15
Siegel, R. L., 416
Siironen, J., 324
Sikes, C. R., 292
Sikkes, S. A., 318–21
Silvani, A., 306–7
Silver, J. M., 122, 413, 414, 417, 429
Silver, S. M., 318
Silveri, M., 328
Simon, H. A., 81
Simpson, G. K., 429–30
Sinanović, O., 126
Sinclair, A., 96
Singh, S., 198–99
Siniard, A., 95
Sira, C., 10
Sitskoorn, M. M., 306–7, 318–21
Skinner, B. F., xi, 208–9, 221–22, 488
Sloan, J. A., 307
Slosman, D., 164
Small, G. W., 474
Small, S. A., 141, 468–69, 471
Smedler, A.-C., 105–6, 436–37
Smeets, S. M., 160, 165, 250, 416, 430, 431t
Smith, C., 96, 97, 120–21
Smith, D., 414
Smith, G. E., 385, 386
Smith, K. E., 298
Snaedal, J., 404–5
Snidman, N., 75–76
Snijders, T. J., 306
Snow, W. G., 366
Snyder, A. Z., 7, 40, 87, 96, 123, 138, 139, 414–15
Snyder, B. D., 392
Sohlberg, M. M., 10
Soinila, S., 359
Solms, M., 76–77, 154, 221
Solomon, A., 387
Somerville, L. H., 57–58, 211, 490–91
Sonesson, B., 331
Song, J., 107
Sontheimer, H., 302–3, 304
Soon, C. S., 74, 78
Sorin-Peters, R., 360
Soroudi, N., 218
Sospedra, M., 282–83
Sossi, V., 277
Southwick, S. M., 212, 213
Souza, L., 42–43, 185
Spada, A., 249–50
Spalletta, G., 128, 149
Sperber, K., 335
Sperry, R. W., xi, 8, 24, 80–81, 86
Spetzler, R. F., xi–xii
Spicer, J., 39, 40–42, 86, 103
Spikman, J. M., 11, 158, 327, 330–31, 335
Spinath, F. M., 60
Spinhoven, P., 453
Spitz, G., 122–23, 416
Sporns, O., 73, 86, 121–22
Spurrell, E. B., 216–17
Squire, L. R., 74, 75, 76, 80, 232
Stamatakis, E., 120
Stamatelopoulos, S., 339
Stanchina, M., 473
Stancin, T., 95, 103, 109
Starkstein, S. E., 126–27, 392
Staub, F., 127–28, 139

Steele, H., 211–12, 213
Steele, M., 211–12, 213
Steenwijk, M. D., 282–83
Stefani, A., 201
Stegmayr, B., 139
Stein, J., 216
Stein, R. I., 216–17
Steiner, C., 293–97, 294t
Steinfelt, V., 58
Stephens, S., 138
Stern, M., 200, 335
Stern, Y., 141, 468–69, 471
Sternberg, R. J., 60
Sterpenich, V., 84, 85
Stewart, D. E., 212
Steyerberg, E. W., 139–40
Stiles, J., 99–100
Stimpson, K. H., 377–79
Stockman, M., 39
Stoessl, A. J., 277
Stohler, C. S., 209–10
Stonnington, C. M., 455, 456t
Stoppa, E., 370
Storandt, M., 469
Strauman, T., 235
Straus, S. E., 220
Strauss, A. A., 438–39
Strazzer, S., 439–40, 443t
Street, A. J., 359, 367
Striedter, G. F., 21–22, 25, 33
Stroppini, T., 127–28
Stroud, C., 385, 387
Strube, M., 123
Sullivan, R., 488
Summers, J. D., 348
Sun, H., 202–3, 310, 414–15, 489
Sundram, F., 451
Sunnerhagen, K. S., 338
Suominen, P. K., 232
Sutterer, M. J., 196
Suzin, G., 249
Svansdottir, H., 404–5
Svenningsson, P., 257
Swank, P. R., 105
Szabo, A. N., 467, 474
Szasz, T., 216
Szelinger, S., 95

Tagliati, M., 201
Tahmasian, M., 158
Takashima, R., 369
Takaya, M., 330
Talvik, T., 95
Tamargo, R. J., 196–97
Tamplin, J., 359
Tanaka, H., 126–27
Tan-Kristanto, S., 290–91
Tanskanen, A., 471
Tanzi, R., 385–86
Taphoorn, M. J., 306–7
Taratuto, A. L., 392
Tardiff, S., 385–86
Target, M., 211–12, 213
Tate, R. L., 429–30
Tau, G. Z., 36–37
Tavares, J. T., 120
Taylor, E. M., 446
Taylor, H. G., 95, 103, 109

Taylor, L., 8
Tazopoulou, E., 249
Teachman, B. A., 468, 469
Teasdale, G., 97–98, 413–14
Teasdale, T. W., 430, 431t
Teasell, R., 126
Telzer, E. H., 62–63, 86–87
Temkin, N. R., 118–20, 122, 142
Tervaniemi, M., 359
Teslovich, T., 57–58, 211, 490–91
Testa, J. A., 142
Testa, S. M., 454
Thaler, N. S., 232, 233
Theisen-Goodvich, M., 474
Thetford, W., 71
Thomas, A., 258
Thomas, L. E., 138
Thompson, A. J., 73, 283, 292
Thompson, J. M., 471
Thomsen, I. V., 118, 120, 121, 122–23
Thorington, J., 232
Thornton, A. E., 283–84
Thorpe, R. J., 467, 472–73
Tickle-Degnen, L., 260
Tiernan, C. W., 36
Tikk, A., 339
Tinney, F. J. Jr, 62
Tiu, J., 257
Tjoa, C. W., 283
Todes, C. J., 260
Toga, A. W., 36, 38, 56
Tomasello, M., 19, 23, 62
Tomberg, T., 339
Tomlinson-Keasey, C., 58
Toni, D., 97
Tonini, A., 180
Tononi, G., 26, 83, 86
Toomela, A., 339
Toone, B., 455–58
Torelli, F., 473
Törnbom, K., 338
Törnbom, M., 338
Toron, J., 180
Torre, E., 275–76
Torres-Gil, F., 474
Tottenham, N., 38, 39, 40–42, 86, 103
Touchon, J., 404–5
Toukhsati, S., 235–36
Toure, H., 98, 99, 100–3
Tovilla-Zarate, C. A., 216–17
Towgood, K., 196
Town, J. M., 217–18
Toyonaga, T., 126–27
Tracy, J., 472
Tran, A., 235–36
Tran, T., 235–36
Tranel, D., 9, 75–76, 95, 100–4, 127, 196, 202–3, 232, 310, 414–15, 468, 489
Trapnell, P. D., 370
Trapp, B. D., 282–83
Trépanier, L. L., 200
Trimble, M., 330, 458
Trojano, L., 249–50
Trojanowski, J. Q., 385–86
Trollor, J. N., 385–86
Tröster, A. I., 200, 201, 202, 255, 256, 258
Truelle, J.-L., 180, 249
Tsang, A., 216–17

Tsouna-Hadjis, E., 339
Tsvetkova, L., 7
Tucker, J. S., 58
Tuffiash, E., 196–97
Tulsky, D. S., 283–84
Tulving, E., 75
Turken, U., 40
Turnbull, O. H., 76–77, 154, 217–18, 221, 359–60
Turner, A. P., 291
Tversky, A., 81
Twigg, G. L., 473
Tyerman, A., 414–15

Unverzagt, F., 283

Vähätalo, R., 232
Vaillant, E., 49, 54
Vaituzis, A. C., 36, 38, 56
Vajapeyam, S., 56
Vajkoczy, P., 323–24
Vakil, E., 122, 415–16, 489
Valdueza, J. M., 198–99
Valenstein, E., 7, 39, 117–18, 126
Vallar, G., 127–28
van Boxtel, M. P., 40, 474
van den Akker, M., 474
van den Bent, M. J., 303, 318
van den Berg, E., 386–87
van der Kolk, B. A., 292
VanDerwerker, C. J., 377–79
van Dijk, J. M. C., 330–31
van Heugten, C., 235, 237
van Heugten, C. M., 160, 165, 237–38, 250, 416, 430, 431t
van Husen, D. K., 338
Van Ingen, A., 474
van Kessel, E., 306
van Laar, P. J., 330–31
van Loon, E. M., 318
Vannatta, K., 95, 109
van Schie, P. E., 233
van Wegen, E. E., 367
van Weissenbruch, M. M., 233
van Zandvoort, M. J., 139, 306, 328–29, 331, 335
van Zomeren, A. H., 122, 414–15
Varis, J., 324
Vates, G. E., 97, 323, 324
Veenstra, W. S., 11, 158, 327, 330–31, 335
Veerbeek, J. M., 367
Vega, A. Jr, 8
Velazquez, J., 284
Vella, L., 283, 291
Vellas, B., 387
Vemmos, K. N., 339
Verbunt, J. A., 235, 237–38
Verfaellie, M., 232, 233, 237–38
Verhey, F., 474
Verma, N. P., 1
Vermeulen, R. J., 233
Verney, S., 469–71
Vickery, J., 292
Vighetti, S., 275–76
Viinamäki, H., 471
Vilchinsky, N., 236
Vilkki, J. S., 324
Villa, F., 439–40, 443t
Villringer, A., 231, 232, 233, 234–35
Vinarskaya, E., 7

Viñas-Guasch, N., 359–60
Vincent, J. L., 40, 87, 138
Vink, M., 160, 165, 250, 416, 430, 431t
Violi, D. A., 55–56
Visser-Meily, J. A., 328–29, 331
Visser-Meily, J. M., 328–29, 335
Vissers, T., 307
Vitale, C., 260
Vitiello, M. V., 135
Vocat, R., 127–28
Voelker, P. M., 95
Volkmann, J., 201
Volkov, O., 249
Vollmer, T., 283
Volpe, B. T., 324–27
Volterra, A., 304
Volz, L. J., 8
von Koch, L., 360, 370
Von Lehe, M., 138–39
Voon, V., 200, 201
Vortmeyer, A., 198–99
Vos, M. J., 307, 467, 474
Voss, M. W., 196
Vrenken, H., 282–83
Vuilleumier, P., 127–28, 164
Vukusic, S., 283
Vuurman, E. F., 40
Vygotsky, L., 20, 21, 38, 49, 72–73, 93, 488

Waber, D. P., 5, 59, 60, 63
Wachelder, E. M., 235, 237
Wada, T., 330
Wade, D. T., 235, 237–38
Wade, S. L., 95, 103
Wade-Martins, R., 304
Wadsworth, B. J., 49
Wager, T. D., 209–10
Wagner, D. R., 232
Wagner, G., 135
Wagner, J., 323–24
Wahlund, L.-O., 384
Waldman, A. D., 121
Waldron, E. J., 202–3, 310, 414–15, 489
Waldron-Perrine, B., 211, 291–92
Walhovd, K. B., 40, 138
Walker, A. J., 429
Walker, J., 292–93, 294t, 297–98
Walker, M., 464
Walker, R., 473
Wallace, G. L., 39
Walle, E. A., 55–56
Walsh, C., 385–86
Walz, N. C., 95, 103
Wang, N., 199
Wang, P. S., 235
Wang, W.-C., 135
Wang, W.-W., 270
Wang, X.-D., 270
Ward, A., 385–86
Ward, N., 73
Warren, C., 474
Warren, D. E., 202–3, 310, 414–15, 489
Wassermann, E. M., 277
Watkins, K. E., 8
Watkins, S., 302–3, 304
Watson, J. B., 23
Watson, J. D., 231–33, 234–35

Watson, R. T., 126
Watzlawick, P., 24, 222–23, 474, 491
Way, A., 359
Weaver, F. M., 200
Wechsler, D., 5, 39–40
Weddle, C., 39
Wefel, J. S., 11, 304–5, 310, 313
Wegener, S. T., 160
Weinberger, K., 7, 96, 123, 139, 414–15
Weiner, W., 270–75
Weinstein, E. A., 152–53, 155, 371
Weinstock-Guttman, B., 283, 284
Weintraub, D., 258–60
Weir, K., 213
Weiskrantz, L., 65
Welch, R. R., 216–17
Weller, M., 303
Wells, C., 473
Wen, P. Y., 303
Werner, C. J., 392
Westerberg, H., 38–39
Westerveld, M., 472
Westlye, L. T., 40, 138
Westmacott, R., 95
Wethe, J. V., 199, 200
Whishaw, I. Q., 254
Whitaker, R., 406–10
White, S. M., 467, 474
Whitehead, K., 464
Whitfield, K. E., 467, 472–73
Whitfield-Gabrieli, S., 40
Whiting, D. L., 429–30
Whittaker, R. G., 83, 103
Whyte, J., 60, 140
Widdess-Walsh, P., 452
Wienecke, R., ix
Wiener, S. I., 56
Wiener-Vacher, S. R., 56
Wiggins, R. D., 359
Wilde, E. A., 109
Wilde, M. C., 473
Wilder, L. S., 128–29, 164
Wildgruber, D., 73
Wilfley, D. E., 216–17
Williams, C., 107–8, 417
Williams, G., 237–38
Williams, J. R., 257–58
Williams, M., 469–71
Williamson, K. L., 158
Willison, J., 197
Willmott, C., 237–38
Wilson, B. A., 405–10, 416
Wincze, J. P., 455
Wingard, D. L., 58
Winkens, I., 160, 165, 250, 416, 430, 431t
Winn, H. R., 118, 120, 122
Winogron, H. W., 104–5
Wolf, P., 96, 117–18
Wolf, P. A., 216–17
Wolf, S. L., 359, 367
Wolf, T. R., 128, 149, 150, 157
Wolff, H., 71
Wolpe, J., 208–9, 218
Wong, A., 330, 335
Wong, D., 218–19, 429
Wong, G. K. C., 330, 335

Wong, J. L., 118–20
Wood, B. C., 318, 415, 430, 431t
Wood, D., 49
Wood, R. L., 249, 413, 417, 429
Wood-Dauphinee, S., 366
Woodin, M., 56
Woods, B. T., 95
Woods, D., 110–11
Woods, R. T., 406–10
Worrall, L., 359
Wright, C., 399
Wright, D., 292
Wright, E. C., 232, 233–34
Wright, R. S., 467, 472–73
Wulfeck, B., 100
Wulff, K., 83, 103

Xia, J., 335–38
Xia, Y., 377–79
Xie, C.-L., 270

Yakovlev, P., 38–39
Yankner, B. A., 40–42
Yarnall, A., 275
Yates, P., 307, 318
Yeates, K. O., 95, 103, 109
Yelnik, A., 139
Ylvisaker, M., 111–12, 220, 431t, 433, 439
Yoshida, T., 330
Young, A. H., 471
Young, A. W., 1
Ytterberg, C., 360, 370
Yudofsky, S. C., 122, 413, 414, 417
Yuen, K. S., 74, 347–48
Yuen, T., 212
Yung, W. A., 305–6

Zaatreh, M., 198–99
Zaiser-Kaschel, H., 249
Zajicek, J., 292
Zakopoulos, N., 339
Zaloshnja, E., 97–98, 117–18, 139–40
Zannino, S., 473
Zapparoli, L., 371
Zarychanski, R., 292–93, 294t, 297–98
Zebrowitz, L. A., 260
Zeiner, H. K., 318, 415, 430, 431t
Zeringue, A., 369
Zhang, H., 377–79
Zhou, J., 143–44
Ziegler, F., 49
Zienius, K., 318–21
Zikos, E., 307
Zilles, K., 36
Zimmerman, C., 249
Zimmerman, M. E., 452, 473
Zimmerman, R. A., 98–99
Zinno, M., 200–1
Zitman, F. G., 453
Zlatar, Z. Z., 469
Zoccolotti, P., 120
Zola-Morgan, S., 232
Zubieta, J.-K., 209–10
Zucco, T., 249
Zwinkels, H., 307

SUBJECT INDEX

Note: Tables and figures are indicated by *t* and *f* following the page number

Note: For the benefit of digital users, indexed terms that span two pages (e.g., 52–53) may, on occasion, appear on only one of those pages.

abstract reasoning
   human brain's capacity for, 72
   neural basis of, 33, 49, 63, 65–66
   rehabilitation of, 196
acupuncture, 377–79
adaptive functions cognitive domain, 204*t*
adolescents
   bilateral frontal contusions effects, 108–9
   brain disorders, psychosocial consequences of, 109, 111*b*
   CNS disruption, neuropsychological consequences, 107*f*, 107
   creativity, 53
   dopaminergic reactivity, 62–63
   empathy development, 62
   fidelity, 52–53
   fMRI studies, 62
   hemiplegia/hemiparesis, 375, 375*t*
   intimacy/isolation, 53
   neuropsychological examination, 176*b*, 179*b*, 182*b*, 183*b*, 185
   neuropsychological/psychosocial competencies, 62
   ontological brain changes, 36, 37*f*
   psychosocial development of, 52–53
   response inhibition network, 62
   reward sensitivity, 62–63, 108
   risk-taking behavior in, 108
   self-awareness/awareness of others, 62
   social relationships, 62, 108–9
   TBI, 439–41, 442*b*, 443*t*
adults
   CVAs in, 126
   decline, coping with, 64–65
   ego integrity, 53–54, 64
   memory in, 63
   midlife crisis, 64
   neuropsychological/psychosocial competencies, 63–64
   ontological brain changes, 39
   psychosocial development of, 51*f*, 53–54
   symbolism, 64–65
   TBI in, 122–23, 124*f*, 125*f*, 131*b*
   wisdom, 51*f*, 54, 64–65
age/education interactions, 42, 43*f*, 44*f*, 45
alien limb syndrome, 371, 378*t*
Alzheimer's disease. *See also* dementia
   characterization, 385
   clinical type dementia, 385
   interventions, 387
   memory impairments in, 120, 386–87
   neuropsychological impairments, 386–87
   self-awareness, 386–87
   self-awareness alterations in, 158
   word recall studies, 141

• 515

amnestic syndromes, 324–27, 333
amygdala in emotional learning, 75f
AnBI. *See* cerebral anoxia/cardiac arrest
aneurysmal SAH
　amnestic disorder, 333
　amnestic syndromes, 324–27
　anatomy, 326–27f
　aneurysms, intracranial, 323
anterior cerebral artery 324–27
　anterior communicating artery, 324–27, 325f
　apathy, 330, 335
　background, 323
　brain blood supply, 324, 325f
　decision-making, 327
　depression/anxiety, 328, 335–39
　executive functions, 331
　family/caregiver support, 338–39
　fatigue, 331, 335
　medical history, 331
　memory, 324–27, 329, 331, 332–33
　neuropsychological consultation, 332
　neuropsychological examination findings, 332
　neuropsychological impairments, 324–28, 325f
　posterior communicating artery, 324, 325f, 328
　psychiatric disturbances, 328
　psychological care, 331–35, 336t, 337t
　psychological care approaches, 335
　psychotic symptoms, 330
　PTSD, 329
　quality of life/coping, 330, 338
　self-awareness, 327, 330
　sleep, 331
　social isolation, 327, 330, 335
　therapeutic alliance, 339
aneurysms, intracranial, 323, 325f, 326–27f
animal cognition, 25, 26–27, 32–33
anosognosia
　brain lesions underlying, 157
　defined, 157
　patients, under reporting of symptoms by, 11
　psychological care, 219–20
　self-awareness, 149–50
anosognosia for hemiplegia
　case study, 149–50
　implicit awareness in, 153
　post-stroke, 126, 127, 129–30
anoxic brain injury (ABI). *See* cerebral anoxia/cardiac arrest
anterior communicating artery, 324–27, 325f
Anton's syndrome, 157, 328
aphasia. *See also* language
　background, 342
　case studies, 348–58, 351t, 353t
　in children, 357–58
　classification of, 343, 344t, 346f
　CVA-induced, 126, 353–54, 355t, 356t
　hemiplegia/hemiparesis, 343
　inner speech/worry loop, 347–48
　medical/psychosocial history, 348, 353
　memory, 347
　middle cerebral arteries, 343
　neurological deficits, 343
　neuropsychological consultation, 348, 353, 354
　neuropsychological deficits, 343
　patients, phenomenological experiences of, 346
　psychological care, 349, 354, 355t, 356t, 361t
　rehabilitation, holistic approaches, 360
　relationships, psychodynamic issues, 360

　sexual relationships, 360
　social isolation, 359, 360
　TBI-induced, 129–30, 348–53
art therapy, 377–79
astrocytes, brain function impacts, 304
astrocytoma, 303, 306
attachment in resiliency, 211, 489
attachment style and return to work 414
attention impairments
　cognitive domains, 204t
　neuroimaging studies, 164
　in older adults, 138, 145
　Parkinson's disease, 255, 256
　post-CVA, 126–27
　rehabilitation of, 196
atypical parkinsonism, 259–60, 262t, 269t
awake, nonaware state, 85

Barrow Neurological Institute Screen for Higher Cerebral Functions (BNIS), 42, 183
basilar artery aneurysm, 330
behavioral modification programs
　approaches to, 218
　cerebral anoxia/cardiac arrest, 249
BNI Screen for Higher Cerebral Functions for School-Age Children (BNIS-C), 42
body scanning, 338–39
borderline personality disorder (BPD), 472
botulinum toxin type A injections, 377–79
bounded rationality, psychology of, 81
brain–behavior relationships. *See also* higher integrative brain functions (HIBFs)
　activation patterns in memory repression, 164
　axon myelination, 38–39
　behavioral guidance systems, 35
　brain/behavior changes, evolution of, 21
　cognitive ability declines, 40–42, 41f
　cortical activity shift, 39
　cortical folding, 39
　cross-modality associations, 21, 22f
　dreaming, 80, 83, 85f
　embryology, 36, 37f
　fatigue following stroke, in older adults, 139
　gray/white matter changes, 39, 40, 41f
　higher order association cortex, 35, 39
　illiteracy, 42–43
　intentional activity, neuroimaging studies, 73
　language development, 32–33, 34–35, 38
ontological development, 32
　operant conditioning, 33, 35
　parietal cortex development, 21, 22f, 26, 38
　prefrontal cortex development, 21–22, 26, 33, 35, 38
　psychological care, 1–2
　in resiliency, 211–12
　sensorimotor cortex development, 37f, 37
　symbolism, 35
　synaptic homeostasis, 83
　synaptic pruning, 37, 38, 45
　temporal cortex development, 37f, 37, 38
brain blood supply, 324, 325f
brain disorders. *See also* CVAs; stroke; TBI
　adjustment process following, 207, 208b, 209b
　adolescents, 107f, 107
　avoidant personalities, 122, 156, 160, 165–66
　cortical thickness/frontal lobe dysfunction, 109
　employment, 122–23, 129
　lost normality problem, 117–18

patient's subjective experience alterations, case studies, 149
psychological care, 110, 129, 131b, 223, 224b, 225b
psychosocial consequences of, 109, 111b
toddlers/preteens, 104
word recall studies, 141
young adulthood, 118
brain tumors. *See* malignant brain tumors
Broca's aphasia, 344t

CADASIL, 399–400, 402t, 404t
carbidopa–levodopa, 260, 261
case studies
   aneurysmal SAH, 331–33, 336t, 337t
   anosognosia for hemiplegia, 149–50
   aphasia, 348–58, 351t, 353t
   aphasia in children, 357–58
   cerebral aneurysm/subarachnoid hemorrhage, 193–95, 197–98, 199b
   cerebral anoxia/cardiac arrest, 238–40
   children/TBI, 442–48, 445t
   CVA-induced aphasia, 126, 353–54, 355t, 356t
   dementia, 387–88, 389t, 391t, 392–96, 393b, 397t, 399t, 400, 402t, 404t
   glioblastoma, 308–10, 309t
   hemiplegia/hemiparesis, 371–75, 373t, 374t, 375t
   memory, 475–78, 477t, 479t, 480t
   multiple sclerosis, 284–87, 285f, 289t
   neuropsychological consultations, 192, 194f
   oligodendroglia, 311–15, 312t
   Parkinson's disease, 260–68, 262t
   patient's subjective experience alterations, 149
   seizures, 458–60, 463t
   TBI, 417t, 420–26, 421t, 422t, 423t, 425t, 427t
   TBI-induced aphasia, 348–53, 351t, 353t
caudate activation in memory repression, 164
cavernous malformation, 191–92
CBF studies, 78
CCRT (Core Conflictual Relationship Theme), 268
cell assembly concept, 6
cerebellum lesion effects, 59
cerebral aneurysms, neuropsychological consultations, 193–95, 196, 199b
cerebral anoxia/cardiac arrest
   apathy, 234f, 237
   background, 231
   depression/anxiety, 235, 236f, 242–43
   identity issues, 243
   long-term adjustment, 242–43
   medical history, 238
   neuropsychological impairments, 232, 234f, 238
   psychiatric disturbances, 234
   psychological care, 238–45, 244t, 246t
   psychosomatic difficulties, 236
   psychotic reactions, 237
   PTSD, 236
   quality of life, 235, 237
   resiliency, 250
   self-awareness, 237
   social isolation, 237
   support group/artistic activities, 246t, 249
   symptoms over time, 239, 242
   therapeutic alliance, 241, 242, 250
cerebral vascular accidents. *See* CVAs
children
   anger, 440, 445–46
   aphasia in, 357–58
   background, 436, 437t
   behavioral approaches, 449
   case studies, 442–48, 445t
   cognitive impairments, 440
   depression/anxiety, 442, 447
   disruptive behaviors, 439–40
   escapism by, 440, 442, 446
   historical perspective, 437
   holistic NRPs, 436–37
   learning process engagement, 440
   memory performance studies, 58–59
   neuropsychological consultation, 441
   parent–child interaction therapy (PCIT), 439, 443t, 446
   phenomenological experiences, 441
   psychological care, 437–42, 443t
   resiliency, 441, 447
   social isolation, 440
   TBI in, 437t, 439–41, 442b, 443t
   therapeutic alliance, 415–16
client-centered psychotherapy, 219
cognitive–behavioral therapy
   aneurysmal SAH, 335, 338
   defined, 4
   hemiplegia/hemiparesis, 377–79
   multiple sclerosis, 292
   Parkinson's disease, 257, 267, 268–70, 271t
   psychological care, 218
   seizures, 455–58, 456t
   TBI, 429
   TBI, in children, 439–40, 443t
cognitive domains, 204t
cognitive training, cerebral anoxia, 233–34, 246t
cognitive unconscious, 79
collaborative relationship. *See* therapeutic alliance
comfort, state of, 215
commerce without morality, 214
concept formation/reasoning cognitive domain, 204t
conduction aphasia, 343, 344t
conscious awake state, 80
consciousness/self-reflection. *See also* higher integrative brain functions (HIBFs)
   awake, nonaware state, 85
   behavioral choices, 80, 81
   cognitive unconscious, 79
   conscious awake state, 80
   conscious-centric bias, 78
   conscious control, 70
   displacement, 71
   dreaming, 80, 83, 85f
   ego/superego, 74
   empirical evidence, 70–71
   as human nature, 23, 26, 27, 35
   integrative brain functioning states, 79
   intentional desire to forget, 77
   life span functioning, reflections on, 489
   memory processes, neurophysiological evidence of, 74, 75f
   neural networks in, 73
   psychometric *vs.* biological intelligence, 71–72
   sensory–motor/perceptual skills role, 72
   sleep, 79–80, 82, 83f, 85f
   subjective experiences, 71
   unconscious control as human nature, 24, 27, 491
   unconscious influences on neuropsychological test performance, 79
   unconscious processes, behavioral evidence of, 77
   unconscious processes, neurophysiological evidence of, 73
constraint-induced movement therapy, 377–79
construction/motor performance cognitive domain, 204t
consultations. *See* neuropsychological consultation

COPD studies, cerebral anoxia effects, 233–34, 246t
coping. *See* quality of life/coping
core conflictual relationships, 86
cultural interactions, 42, 43f, 44f, 45
CVAs
   in adults, 126
   classification of, 96, 98t, 107f
   cognitive impairments, 127
   CVA-induced aphasia, 126, 353–54, 355t, 356t
   DMN, effects on, 106f, 106–7
   drawing deficits, 99
   focal, impacts on connectivity, 123–25, 124f, 125f
   hemiplegia/hemiparesis (*see* hemiplegia/hemiparesis)
   language development, 99–100, 126
   lost normality problem, 117–18
   memory and, 138–39, 145
   neuroimaging studies, 100, 103
   neuropsychological functioning effects, 95–96, 98, 101t
   in older adults, 137
   psychological care, 110
   psychosocial consequences in older adults, 142
   quality of life/coping, 142–44
   racial differences in, 137–38
   social judgment errors, 127
   visual–spatial disturbances in, 99
Cymbalta, 261

decision-making
   aneurysmal SAH, 327
   neural basis of, 81
   in toddlers/preteens, 57–58
deep brain stimulation (DBS), Parkinson's disease, 199b, 200, 275, 276f
default mode network (DMN)
   aging effects on, 384–85
   fMRI studies, 40
   in HIBFs, 86–87
   in older adults, 138, 384–85
   in outcome prediction, 202, 203f, 204t, 205f
   stroke effects on, 106f, 106–7, 120–22
delusional behavior, 330
dementia. *See also* Alzheimer's disease
   anticholinergic medications, 473
   background, 384
   behavioral approaches, 405, 407t
   CADASIL, 399–400, 402t, 404t
   caregiver support, 407t
   case studies, 387–88, 389t, 391f, 392–96, 393b, 397t, 399t, 400, 402t, 404t
   clinical Alzheimer's-type, 385
   as clinical syndrome, 385
   cognitive decline, 385, 404
   cognitive rehabilitation, 405–6, 407t
   early stage, 387, 404
   mild cognitive impairment, 385–86
   neurological/neuropsychological findings, 387, 392, 400
   in older adults, 143
   organic unawareness, 405–6
   posterior cortical atrophy, 392
   pre-emptive/rational suicide, 406, 407t
   prevalence, 136
   psychological care, 5, 388, 396, 400
   psychological care approaches, 404
   psychosocial/environmental approaches, 407t
   self-awareness, 158, 406–10, 407t
   self-efficacy, 387, 405, 406
   therapeutic alliance, 404, 405
   vascular dementia, 399

denial/denial of disability, 151–53, 154, 160, 164, 165–66
depression/anxiety
   aneurysmal SAH, 328, 335–39
   cerebral anoxia/cardiac arrest, 235, 242–43
   children, 442, 447
   hemiplegia/hemiparesis, 369–70
   malignant brain tumors, 313–14
   memory, 469–71
   multiple sclerosis, 284–85, 287, 290–91, 293, 297–98
   Parkinson's disease, 256–57, 266, 271t
   resiliency and, 212–13
   seizures, 452–54, 455–58, 459, 462
   stroke, 359–60
   TBI, 348, 429–30
   therapeutic alliance in, 224
development, human. *See* neuropsychological/psychosocial competencies
Digit Symbol Coding, young adults, 63
disorders of the body schema, 370
doctor/patient relationship in placebo effects, 210–11
documentation, 189
dogma, research funding and, 88–89
dreams, dreaming
   brain–behavior relationships, 80, 83
   individuality, preservation of via, 83–84
   individuality preservation via, 83–84
   in psychological care, 221, 414–15
   seizures, 460–61
   as self-reflection, 80, 83, 85f
   in TBI, as indication of mental state, 417

eloquent cortex concept, 202–3
employment
   post-stroke, 122–23, 129
   post-TBI, 430, 440
entitlement mentality, 214
epileptic seizures. *See* seizures
escapism
   by children, 440, 442, 446
   psychotherapy and, 220–21
   TBI and, 429
examination. *See* neuropsychological examination
executive functions
   aneurysmal SAH, 331
   cerebral anoxia effects, 232, 234f
   cognitive domain, 204t
   multiple sclerosis, 283–84, 285
   Parkinson's disease, 256, 257, 265

faith, 490
fear escape–avoidance model, 454–55
fervent monism, 7
flexible battery approach, 9
food choices studies, 78
freedom, free will, 216
free will, 73–74

Gandhi's experiments with truth, 214, 494
generalized anxiety disorder (GAD), 235, 257–58
glial cells functions, 302–3, 303f
glioma/glioblastoma, 303, 304–10, 305f, 306f, 309t, 318, 319t
global aphasia, 343–46, 344t

hallucinations, 307
Halstead–Reitan Neuropsychological Test Battery, 8
Hatha yoga, 338–39
hatred of hemiplegia, 369. *See also* hemiplegia/hemiparesis

health care environment, 493
hemiplegia/hemiparesis
    aphasia, 343
    background, 366
    body schema/body image changes, 368–69, 370
    case studies, 371–75, 373t, 374t, 375t
    characterization, 366, 368f
    depression/anxiety, 369–70
    libido/sexual activity, 370, 372, 375
    psychological care, 371, 377, 378t, 380t
    psychological impacts, 367
    quality of life/coping, 368–69, 371–75, 373t, 374t, 377–79
    rehabilitation, 367
    resiliency, 372, 375–77
    social isolation, 370–71
    therapeutic alliance, 380t
HIBFs. *See* higher integrative brain functions (HIBFs)
higher integrative brain functions (HIBFs). *See also* brain–behavior relationships; consciousness/self-reflection
    age/education interactions, 42, 43f, 44f, 45
    animal cognition, 32–33
    assessment of (*see* neuropsychological examination)
    awake/nonawake states relationships, 85
    cerebral hemispheres functions, 8
    clinical neuropsychology background, 5
    conscious/unconscious manifestations of (*see* consciousness/self-reflection)
    consultations (*see* neuropsychological consultation)
    cultural interactions, 42, 43f, 44f, 45
    deficit localization, 7–8
    evolution of, 31, 34b, 44–45, 67
    Halstead's model, 71–72
    hierarchical brain systems in, 87–88
    historical/contemporary observations, 86
    integrative functioning states, 79
    life span functioning, reflections on, 489
    Luria's model, 72–73
    motor inhibition, 33, 39–40
    nature of, historical perspectives on, 71
    neuroimaging studies, 73, 77, 78
    neuropsychological assessment, 8–9
    neuropsychological rehabilitation, 9–10
    ontological brain changes, 36–39, 37f
    phylogenetic brain changes, 36
    psychological care in, 11–12
    social interactions in development of, 49
    unconscious manifestations of, 88b
hippocampus activation in memory repression, 164
holistic neuropsychological rehabilitation programs
    cerebral anoxia/cardiac arrest, 246t
    children, 436–37
    TBI, 415–16, 417–18, 419, 430, 431t
hope, 142–43, 490. *See also* resiliency
human development. *See also* neuropsychological/psychosocial competencies
    CNS disruption (*see* brain disorders)
    empirical/clinical observations, 54
    life span functioning, reflections on, 489
    psychosocial theory of, 48, 51f
humanistic psychotherapy, 219
human nature
    animal cognition, 25, 26–27
    behavioral paradox in, 24, 25, 28, 50
    bonding, 23, 27, 28, 50–51
    brain/behavior changes, evolution of, 21, 22f
    CNS, natural plan of, 20f, 20
    consciousness/self-reflection, 23, 26, 27, 35

descriptive definition of, 19
destructive aspects of, 24, 27
emergent brain function, 24
existential struggles, 24
hope as necessity, 50
human corticospinal tract, phylogenetic changes in, 21–22
intentional activities, 23
language development, 23–24, 25–27
meaning in life, 24–25, 27
memory and, 474
in older adults, 144
psychological care, 27b, 28
reflections on, 488
social interactions/social heights, 21, 24, 25–26
summary of, 26
symbolism, 26–27
theory of mind, 25–26
therapeutic alliance, 27, 28
triune brain layers, functions, 22–23
unconscious control as, 24, 27, 491
universal questions, 23, 27, 28
humor, resiliency and, 211–12, 213–14
hydrocephalus, 330
hyperbaric oxygen therapy, 246t, 249
hypothalamic hamartomas, neuropsychological consultations, 198
hypoxia/hypoxemia, 232
hypoxic ischemia, perinatal, 98–99

impaired self-awareness. *See under* self-awareness
individuality, preservation of via dreaming, 83–84
infants
    bonding, 50–51
    emotional experiences in brain development, 56
    language development, 55–56
    limbic structures, 56
    motor inhibition, 55
    neuropsychological/psychosocial competencies, 55, 65
    occipital cortex development, 55
    ontological brain changes, 36, 37f
    psychosocial development of, 50–51, 51f
    social interaction in, 55
    visual cortex development, 55
    working memory capacity in, 55
in-press countertransference, 267–68
intuitive judgments, neural basis of, 81

knowledge without character, 214

language. *See also* aphasia
    abstract reasoning in, 72–73
    behavior, conscious/unconscious influences on, 88
    brain–behavior relationships, 32–33, 34–35, 38
    cognitive domains, 204t
    CVAs, 99–100, 126
    development, memory and, 55–56
    focal stroke, impacts on connectivity, 123, 124f, 125f
    human nature, 23–24, 25–27
    infants, 55–56
    Luria's model, 72–73
    mental process mediation by, 87–88
    neuropsychological examination, 179b, 183b
    rehabilitation of, 196
    school-age children, 57, 58–59, 60
    seizures, 452–53
    stroke, 99–100
    TBI, 99–100

SUBJECT INDEX • 519

learning
    children, engagement of, 440
    neural basis of, 6, 33, 35, 75f, 87
    neuropsychological examination, 179b, 183b
    word recall studies, in older adults, 141
Lewy body dementia, 5, 255, 385
life span functioning, reflections on, 489
loving-kindness mediation, 338–39

major depressive disorder, 235, 237, 369–70, 471, 472
malignant brain tumors
    anger, 313, 314, 315
    astrocytes, brain function impacts, 304
    astrocytoma, 303, 306
    background, 302
    caregivers/family members, support of, 317–18
    clinical features relevant to care, 315, 316t
    depression/anxiety, 313–14
    fatigue, 314, 318
    glial cells functions, 302–3, 303f
    glioma/glioblastoma, 303, 304–10, 305f, 306f, 309t, 318, 319t
    medical history, 308, 311
    neuropsychological consultation, 310, 313
    neuropsychological disorders, 304, 305f, 306f
    neuropsychological examination findings, 308, 309t, 311, 312t
    oligodendroglia, 311–15, 312t, 316t
    psychiatric disturbances, 307
    psychological care approaches, 315
    psychological care/glioblastoma, 308–10, 309t
    psychological care/oligodendroglia, 311–15, 312t
    psychotherapy, 313–15, 316t
    quality of life/coping, 306, 310, 318
    rehabilitation, 318–21, 319t
    therapeutic alliance, 314
mania, post-CVA, 127
mathematical ability, rehabilitation of, 196
MCA. See middle cerebral arteries (MCAs)
meaning in life. See quality of life/coping
memory
    age/education relationships in, 42–43
    aging (normal), 468
    in Alzheimer's disease, 386–87
    amygdala in emotional learning, 75f, 75–76
    aneurysmal SAH, 324–27, 329, 331, 332–33
    aphasia, 347
    background, 225b, 467
    brain disorder effects, 468
    cardiorespiratory fitness effects, 474
    case studies, 475–78, 477t, 479t, 480t
    cerebral anoxia effects, 232, 234f, 238–40
    cognitive domains, 204t
    cortical networks in, 33
    CVAs and, 138–39, 145
    declarative knowledge, 74, 75f
    depression/anxiety, 469–71
    development of, 55, 57, 62, 63
    eating habits effects, 474
    emotional state in, 472
    emotion/motivations relationship, 65
    facts about the world, 74–75
    formation of, 75–76
    health status effects, 474
    historical research on, 5, 8, 9–10
    human nature and, 474
    information processing speed, 471–72
    intentional desire to forget, 77
    language development and, 55–56

long-term memory systems organization, 75f
medication effects, 473
multiple sclerosis, 283–85, 286, 288
negative affect and, 469, 470t
neural basis of, 33
neuropsychological examination, 179b, 183b, 184
neuroticism and, 469
nondeclarative, 74, 75f, 75
in older adults, 64, 135, 138–39, 141, 145
Parkinson's disease, 255–56, 261–65
patterns of behavior influences by, 76–77, 85
performance studies, in children, 58–59
prefrontal cortex functioning in, 21–22, 24, 33
priming effects, 75
processes, neurophysiological evidence of, 74, 75f
psychiatric disorders, 471
psychological care, 4, 28, 481–82
rehabilitation of, 196
repression of, 77, 164, 165–66
seizures, 452–53
semantic, 74–75
sleep, 472
stroke effects on, 104–5
subjective cognitive decline correlates, 469
subjective complaints, 468b, 468
TBI, impairments due to, 118, 120
temporal cortex functioning in, 37
word recall studies, 471–72
working, unconscious influences on, 79
in young adults, 63
metaphoric identity mapping, 431t, 433
metaphors, use of, 111–12
middle cerebral arteries (MCAs)
    aphasia, 343
    aSAH, 324
    stroke, 96, 104, 127, 359–60
midlife crisis, 64
mild cognitive impairment, 385–86
mind defined, 6–7
mindfulness-based training
    aneurysmal SAH, 338–39
    multiple sclerosis, 293–97
    Parkinson's disease, 271t
    TBI, 429, 430
Minnesota Multiphasic Personality Inventory, 5
misoplegia, 369. See also hemiplegia/hemiparesis
MIT Young Adult Development Project, 39
modafinil (Provigil), 261, 292
multiple sclerosis
    background, 282
    caregiver support, 285–86, 290, 298–99
    case studies, 284–87, 285f, 289t
    clinical manifestations, 283
    cognitive–behavioral therapy, 292
    depression/anxiety, 284–85, 287, 290–91, 293, 297–98
    executive functions, 283–84, 285
    information processing speed, 283–84
    memory, 283–85, 286, 288
    mindfulness-based training, 293–97
    MRI studies, 283
    neuropsychological consultation, 285–86, 298
    neuropsychological impairments, 283
    placebo effects, 292
    psychiatric disturbances, 284
    psychological care, 5, 288–89, 289t, 293–98, 294t, 297f
    resiliency, 290
    self-awareness alterations in, 158

self-efficacy, 291
social isolation, 285–86
stress/mood management, 297
supportive–expressive group psychotherapy, 293
therapeutic alliance, 288, 294t, 297, 298
wellness and, 298
music therapy
aphasia, 359–60
cerebral anoxia/cardiac arrest, 246t, 249
dementia, 404–5
Parkinson's disease, 271t
myelination, 282

neural Darwinism, 36–37
neuronal group selection theory, 36–37
neuronal plasticity, 492
neuropsychological consultation
aneurysmal SAH, 332
aphasia, 348, 353, 354
background, 191–92
case studies, 192, 194f
cerebral aneurysms, 193–95, 196, 199b
children, 441
cognitive domains, 204t
hypothalamic hamartomas, 198
lesion location/functional connectivity, 124f, 125f, 196
malignant brain tumors, 310
multiple sclerosis, 285–86, 298
oligodendroglia, 313
outcome prediction, 202, 203f, 204t, 205f
Parkinson's disease, 199b, 200
patient/family education, 195
seizures, 459
therapeutic alliance in, 286
neuropsychological examination
adolescents/school-age children, 176b, 179b, 182b, 183b, 185
clinical exam, 180–87, 182b, 183b
differential diagnosis, 183–84
elements/principles of, 171–74, 182b, 183b
emotional expression/perceptual skills, 184–85
feedback session, 187, 188t
histories, from records, 174, 175b, 176b, 187
interview, 175, 179b, 187
office environment, 175–77
patient/family members, greeting, 175
report writing, 189
time/place orientation, 183–84
validity tests, 181–83
neuropsychological/psychosocial competencies
adolescence, 62
adulthood, 63–64
developmental overview, 65, 66b
infancy, 55, 65
older adults 50
school-age, 59
toddlers/preteens, 56–59, 57f, 65
young adulthood, 63
neurotransmitters, 254
non-accidental trauma (NAT), 98–99

obstructive sleep apnea studies, 473
older adults
attention in, 138, 145
chronic health care problems in, 136
CNS aging in, 135, 136f, 136, 137f
cognitive/physical declines, 137, 139, 145
CVAs in, 137
dementia in, 143
economic challenges, 137
human nature in, 144
information processing speed, 138, 139–40
memory in, 64, 135, 138–39, 141, 145, 468
neuroconnectivity in, 138–39
neuropsychological impairments, 137, 139, 145b
psychological care, 144, 145b
psychosocial consequences, 142, 145b
quality of life/coping, 142–44
self-efficacy, 137
sleep in, 135
stroke, fatigue following, 139
suicidal ideation, 143
TBI in, 137f, 139–41
word recall studies, 141
oligodendroglia, 311–15, 312t, 316t
organic unawareness, 242–43, 405–6
Organization of Behavior, The (Hebb), 6

paradoxes, 491
paranoid ideation, 307, 347
parent–child interaction therapy, 439, 443t, 446
parietal cortex development, 21, 22f, 26, 38
Parkinson's disease
apathy, 258
attention impairments, 255, 256
atypical parkinsonism, 259–60, 262t, 269t
background, 254
caregiver struggles, 256, 259, 261
cognitive–behavioral therapy, 271t
DBS, 199b, 200, 275, 276f
depression/anxiety, 256–57, 266, 271t
executive functions, 256, 257, 265
facial masking, 260
impulse control problems, 259–60
in-press countertransference, 267–68
medical history, 260
memory, 255–56, 261–65
music therapy, 271t
neuropsychological consultations, 199b, 200
neuropsychological examination findings, 261, 262t
neuropsychological impairments, 255, 278
patient struggles, 256
placebo effects, 275, 276f
problem-solving, 255, 256
psychiatric disturbances, 256
psychological care, 256, 260–68, 262t, 269t, 271t, 277b, 277
psychosomatic difficulties, 258
psychotic reactions, 258
quality of life/coping, 259, 271t
resiliency, 270, 278–79
self-awareness alterations in, 158, 258
social isolation, 259
subjective experiences, 256, 267
patient/family education. *See* neuropsychological consultation
pediatrics. *See* children
perception cognitive domain, 204t
personal adjustment/emotional function cognitive domain, 204t
placebo effects
multiple sclerosis, 292
Parkinson's disease, 275, 276f
in psychological care, 209, 490
posterior cerebral artery 323
posterior cingulate cortex self-reflective task studies, 128–29
posterior communicating artery, 324, 325f, 328
posterior cortical atrophy, 392

post-trauma amnesia (PTA), 121
pre-emptive/rational suicide, 406, 407t
prefrontal cortex
    activation in memory repression, 164
    development, 21–22, 26, 33, 35, 38
    lesion effects, 59, 103–4
    memory, functioning in, 21–22, 33
    self-reflective task studies, 128–29
problem-solving
    central integrative field factor (C), 72
    neural basis of, 33, 49, 63
    neuropsychological examination, 179b, 183b, 184
    Parkinson's disease, 255, 256
    rehabilitation of, 196
    school-age children, 60, 65–66
    TBI, 118, 119f
    unconscious influences on, 79
process approach (Kaplan), 8–9
Provigil (modafinil), 261, 292
psychodynamic psychotherapy
    Parkinson's disease, 268–70, 271t
    role playing, 461
    seizures, 456t, 460
psychogenic seizures. *See* seizures
psychogenic movement disorder, 149
psychological care
    aneurysmal SAH, 331–35, 336t, 337t
    aphasia, 349, 354, 355t, 356t, 361t
    background, 1–3, 207
    behavioral approaches to, 218
    behaviors, basic, 222–23
    brain disorders, 110, 129, 131b, 207, 208b, 209b, 223, 224b, 225b
    cerebral anoxia/cardiac arrest, 238–45, 244t, 246t
    children, 437–42, 443t
    client-centered psychotherapy, 219
    clinical neuropsychology background, 5
    cognitive–behavioral therapy, 218
    comfort, state of, 215
    definition of, 4
    dementia, 388, 396, 400
    dreams in, 221
    effectiveness of, 220
    evidence-based therapies, 4
    foundations of, 3, 12b
    freedom, free will, 216
    funding of, 4
    Gandhi's experiments with truth, 214
    glioblastoma, 308–10, 309t
    Hebb, observations from, 6
    hemiplegia/hemiparesis, 371, 377, 378t, 380t
    history of, 7
    humanistic psychotherapy, 219
    human nature, 27b, 28
    interventions, 4
    meaningfulness, 215–16, 221
    memory, 4, 28, 481–82
    memory, patterns of behavior influences by, 76–77, 85
    metaphors, use of, 111–12
    multiple sclerosis, 293–98, 294t, 297f
    neuropsychological consultation, 12
    neuropsychological test findings, 5, 8–9, 12
    older adults, 144, 145b
    Parkinson's disease, 256, 260–68, 262t, 269t, 271t, 277b, 277
    patients, psychological needs of, 10
    philosophical patience, necessity of, 4
    placebo effects, 209, 490
    practical questions in, 5–6
    psychodynamic approaches to, 216 (*see also* psychodynamic psychotherapy)
    reflections on, 491–93
    resilience, facilitation of, 4
    resiliency and, 211, 212f
    seizures, 460
    self-awareness, 165, 219–20
    self-efficacy and, 211–12, 213
    spirituality/religion and, 211–12, 214–15, 221
    TBI, approaches to, 428, 431t
    TBI, long term, 416, 417t
    TBI, observations relevant to, 413
    template, 229–230
    therapeutic alliance in (*see* therapeutic alliance)
    well-being/happiness, 215, 221–22
psychological coping, Eriksonian model, 210
psychological denial described, 157–58
psychometric tests background, 5, 8–9
psychoses, 307
psychosocial development model, 51f *See also* neuropsychological/psychosocial competencies
psychotherapy
    approaches to, 216
    client-centered, 219
    dementia, 400
    escapism and, 220–21
    humanistic, 219
    malignant brain tumors, 313–15, 316t
    memory, patterns of behavior influences by, 76–77, 85
    multiple sclerosis, 288–89
    Parkinson's disease, 265
    supportive–expressive group, 293
PTSD, 236, 329
putamen activation in memory repression, 164

quality of life/coping
    aneurysmal SAH, 330, 338
    cerebral anoxia/cardiac arrest, 235, 237
    CVAs, 142–44
    hemiplegia/hemiparesis, 368–69, 371–75, 373t, 374t, 377–79
    malignant brain tumors, 306, 310, 318
    multiple sclerosis, 298
    older adults, 142–44
    Parkinson's disease, 259, 271t
    TBI, 142–44, 237–38, 416, 417t, 430
    well-being/happiness, 215

rational awareness, 81
reaction times studies, 78
readiness potential (RP) in unconscious processes, 73–74
reduplicative paramnesia, 328
reports, written, 189
resiliency
    attachment in, 211, 489
    brain–behavior relationships in, 211–12
    cerebral anoxia/cardiac arrest, 250
    children, 441, 447
    depression/anxiety and, 212–13
    hemiplegia/hemiparesis, 372, 375–77
    humor and, 211–12
    multiple sclerosis, 290
    Parkinson's disease, 270, 278–79
    psychological care and, 211, 212f
    reflections on, 490
    self-efficacy in, 490
    TBI, 419, 426–27, 430

Rey–Osterrieth Complex Figure Test, 99, 104–5
robotic-assisted therapy, 377–79

saccular aneurysms, 324
scaffolding, 49
school-age children
    brain disorders, psychosocial consequences of, 109, 111b
    CNS disruption, neuropsychological consequences, 104
    cognitive development, 60
    cortical thickness/frontal lobe dysfunction, 109
    decision-making, 57–58
    delayed gratification, 57, 66
    education effects, 58
    emotional regulation, 57, 66
    fMRI studies, 60, 61f
    friend-making, 59–60
    industry/inferiority, 60
    information processing speed, 60
    language development, 57, 58–59, 60
    learning disability identification, 52
    natural response inhibition studies, 57f, 57–59
    neuropsychological examination, 176b, 179b, 182b, 183b, 185
    neuropsychological/psychosocial competencies, 56–59, 57f, 65
    ontological brain changes, 36, 37f
    play behaviors, 59–60
    problem-solving, 60, 65–66
    psychosocial development of, 51–52
    social interactions development, 52, 59
    socioeconomic status (SES) effects, 58
    tasks of development, 54–55
    TBI, 439–41, 442b, 443t
    toilet training, 52, 56
    turn-taking, 58
science without humanity, 214
Seashore Rhythm Test, 72
seizures
    allergies, 454
    background, 451
    case studies, 458–60, 463t
    CBT, 455–58, 456t
    characterization, 451–52
    depression/anxiety, 452–54, 455–58, 459, 462
    dissociative features, 452, 454, 461–62
    dreams, 460–61
    epileptic, 451
    fear escape–avoidance model, 454–55
    group psychotherapy, 456t
    hysterical, 458
    language, 452–53
    medical history, 458
    memory, 452–53
    neuropsychological consequences, 452
    neuropsychological consultation, 459
    neuropsychological test findings, 453
    patient terminology, 454
    psychiatric disorders, 453
    psychodynamic model, 455
    psychodynamic psychotherapy, 460
    psychogenic, 451
    psychological care, 460
    psychological care approaches, 455, 456t
    psychometric testing, 459
    recurring conflicts, 461–62
    somatization disorder, 454
    therapeutic alliance, 461, 462–64
self-awareness
    in adolescents, 62
    alterations, neuroimaging correlates, 164
    alterations, neuropsychological/behavioral correlates, 158, 161t
    alterations vs. psychological distress, clinical features, 157, 159t
    Alzheimer's disease, 386–87
    aneurysmal SAH, 327, 330
    anosognosia, 149–50
    assessment of, 149
    building, in TBI, 430, 431t
    cerebral anoxia/cardiac arrest, 237
    dementia, 406–10, 407t
    denial/denial of disability, 151–53, 154, 160, 164, 165–66
    impaired self-awareness, 148, 157, 165
    Parkinson's disease, 258
    patient's subjective experience alterations, 149, 161t, 166
    post-TBI, 121, 128, 129–30, 152, 164
    psychological care, 165, 219–20
    psychological distress, 157, 159t
self-efficacy
    dementia, 387, 405, 406
    multiple sclerosis, 291
    older adults, 137
    psychological care and, 211–12, 213
    in resiliency, 490
semantic aphasia, 344t
sensory neglect, 126
sertraline (Zoloft), 292
Severity of Brain Injury Stratification, 98t
shaken baby syndrome, 98–99
sleep
    aneurysmal SAH, 331
    behavioral definition of, 82
    brain changes during, 84, 85f
    disorders, memory effects, 472
    functions of, 83, 85
    NREM, 82
    in older adults, 135
    PET studies, 84
    REM, 82, 83–84, 85f, 85
    sleep spindles/K-complexes, 82
    slow-wave sleep (SWS), 82, 83, 85, 103
    stages of, 82, 83f
social isolation
    adolescents, 53
    aneurysmal SAH, 327, 330, 335
    aphasia, 359, 360
    cerebral anoxia/cardiac arrest, 237
    children, 440
    hemiplegia/hemiparesis, 370–71
    multiple sclerosis, 285–86
    Parkinson's disease, 259
somatoparaphrenia, 371
Speech Perception Test, 72
spirituality/religion, 211–12, 214–15, 221
stage theory models, 49, 54
stress/mood management in multiple sclerosis, 297
stroke. See also CVAs
    aphasia in children, 357–58
    arterial ischemic, 103, 104
    AVMs/aneurysms, 97
    classification of, 96, 98t, 107f
    cryptogenic, 97
    depression/anxiety, 359–60
    DMN, effects on, 106f, 106–7
    drawing deficits, 99
    fatigue following, in older adults, 139
    hemiplegia/hemiparesis (see hemiplegia/hemiparesis)
    hemorrhagic, 96–97

stroke (*cont.*)
  ischemic, 96–97, 347
  language development, 99–100
  MCA, 96, 104, 127, 359–60
  neuroimaging studies, 103
  neuropsychological functioning effects, 101*t*
  in older adults, 137
  perinatal, 97
  subjective experience alterations following, 151
  visual–spatial disturbances in, 99
  word recall studies, 141
subarachnoid hemorrhage. *See* aneurysmal SAH
subcortical (nonthalamic) aphasia, 344*t*
subdural hematoma, subjective experience alterations
    following, 150–51
subjective awareness, 80–81
subjective memory complaints. *See* memory
subthalamic nucleus, DBS/Parkinson's disease, 199*b*, 200
suicidal ideation, 143
suicide, pre-emptive/rational, 406, 407*t*
support group/artistic activities, 246*t*, 249
synaptic homeostasis, 83
systematic desensitization, 218

Tactual Performance Test, 72
TBI
  academic performance effects, 105–6
  in adolescents, 107, 439–41, 442*b*, 443*t*
  in adults, 122–23, 124*f*, 125*f*, 131*b*
  artwork, 417
  background, 413
  behavioral problems, 417
  brain atrophy studies, 120
  case studies, 417*t*, 420–26, 421*t*, 422*t*, 423*t*, 425*t*, 427*t*
  CBT in, 218–19
  in children, 437*t*, 439–41, 442*b*, 443*t*
  classification of, 96, 98*t*, 107*f*
  cognitive problems, 119*f*, 203*f*, 414–15
  cortical thickness/frontal lobe dysfunction, 109
  depression/anxiety, 348, 429–30
  DMN, effects on, 106*f*, 106–7, 120–22
  drawing deficits, 99
  dreams, 417
  employment, 430
  escapism and, 429
  fairy tales, 417, 448–49
  hemiplegia/hemiparesis (*see* hemiplegia/hemiparesis)
  holistic NRPs, 415–16, 417–18, 419, 430, 431*t*
  information processing speed, 104–6
  language development, 99–100
  longitudinal studies, 118, 119*f*
  lost normality problem, 117–18
  memory, patterns of behavior influences by, 76–77, 85
  memory impairments, 104–5, 118, 120, 165–66
  metaphoric identity mapping, 431*t*, 433
  motor inhibition, 33
  motor-related dysfunctions, 118–20, 119*f*
  music, insights provided by, 417, 426–27
  neuroimaging studies, 103, 120–21, 123, 413–14
  neuropsychological functioning effects, 95–96, 98, 101*t*
  neuropsychological rehabilitation, 431*t*
  neurotransmitter storm, 414
  obstructive sleep apnea studies, 473
  occupation outcome prediction, 415–16
  in older adults, 137*f*, 139–41
  patients, psychological needs of, 11
  personality/behavioral changes, 122

  post-trauma amnesia (PTA), 121
  problem-solving, 119*f*
  psychological care, long term, 416, 417*t*
  psychological care, observations relevant to, 5, 110, 413
  psychological care approaches, 428, 431*t*
  psychosocial consequences in older adults, 142
  quality of life/coping, 142–44, 237–38, 416, 417*t*, 430
  resiliency, 419, 426–27, 430
  salience network, effects on, 121
  self-awareness, building, 430, 431*t*
  self-awareness, prolonged impaired, 128, 129–30
  self-awareness alterations, neuroimaging correlates, 121, 164
  self-awareness alterations, neuropsychological/behavioral
      correlates, 158, 161*t*
  TBI-induced aphasia, 348–53, 351*t*, 353*t*
  therapeutic alliance, with children, 415–16
  visual–spatial disturbances in, 99
  word recall studies, 141
  young adulthood, 118–22, 119*f*, 413
temporal epilepsy, 472
temporal lobes, stroke effects on, 104–5
thalamic aphasia, 344*t*
thalamus activation in memory repression, 164
therapeutic alliance
  aneurysmal SAH, 339
  building, 241, 288, 298, 314
  cerebral anoxia/cardiac arrest, 241, 242, 250
  children, 415–16
  in children with TBI, 415–16
  dementia, 404, 405
  in depression/anxiety, 224
  hemiplegia/hemiparesis, 380*t*
  human nature, 27, 28
  malignant brain tumors, 314
  multiple sclerosis, 288, 294*t*, 297, 298
  in neuropsychological consultation, 286
  in placebo effects, 210–11
  in psychological care, 2, 211, 492
  seizures, 461, 462–64
toddlers/preteens. *See* school-age children
transcortical motor aphasia, 343, 344*t*
transcortical sensory aphasia, 344*t*
traumatic brain injury. *See* TBI
trust, 490. *See also* therapeutic alliance
truth, Gandhi's experiments with, 214, 494
tumors. *See* malignant brain tumors

unconscious mental activities, 88
unconscious processes
  behavioral evidence of, 77
  control as human nature, 24
  HIBFs manifestations, 88*b*
  influences on neuropsychological test performance, 79
  neurophysiological evidence of, 73

vascular dementia, 399
ventral striatum, reward sensitivity, 62–63
verbal deafness, 344*t*
verbal functions cognitive domain, 204*t*
violence, sources of in human nature, 214

well-being/happiness, 215. *See also* quality of life/coping
Wernicke's aphasia, 343, 344*t*
working memory. *See* memory
written reports, 189

Zoloft (sertraline), 292